Society in Question

Society in Question

Sociological Readings for the 21st Century

Fourth Edition

Robert J. Brym
University of Toronto

THOMSON

NELSON

Australia   Canada   Mexico   Singapore   Spain   United Kingdom   United States

THOMSON

NELSON

Society in Question: Sociological Readings for the 21st Century Fourth Edition

Robert J. Brym

Editorial Director and Publisher:
Evelyn Veitch

Executive Editor:
Joanna Cotton

Acquisitions Editor:
Cara Yarzab

Marketing Manager:
Lenore Taylor

Developmental Editor:
Glen Herbert

Production Editor:
Tammy Scherer

Senior Production Coordinator:
Hedy Sellers

Copy Editor:
Valerie Adams

Proofreader:
Karen Rolfe

Indexer:
Maura Brown

Permissions Coordinator:
Cindy Howard

Creative Director:
Angela Cluer

Interior Design Modifications:
Erich Falkenberg

Cover Design:
Andrew Adams

Cover Image:
Grant Faint/The Image Bank/ Getty Images

Compositor:
Carol Magee

Printer:
Webcom

National Library of Canada Cataloguing in Publication

Society in question : sociological readings for the 21st century / [edited by] Robert J. Brym. — 4th ed.

Includes index.
ISBN 0-17-622538-2

1. Sociology—Textbooks.
2. Canada—Social conditions.
I. Brym, Robert J., 1951-

HM586.S654 2003   301   C2003-906512-X

In memory of Jim Richardson, 1941–2003

— RJB

Preface

Society in Question is designed to supplement the main textbook in an introductory sociology course. I have therefore aimed for balanced coverage of major topics, approaches, and methods in current sociology. However, as the title and subtitle suggest, this book also tries to convey more than just a sense of what sociologists do for a living. The readings, and my introductions to them, are intended to speak plainly and vividly to contemporary Canadians about how sociology can help them make sense of their lives in a rapidly changing and often confusing world. The book's title is thus an intentional pun: as the nature of social life is called into question by vast and sometimes frightening forces over which we appear to have little control, sociological questioning offers the prospect of helping us understand those forces and make informed choices about how we can best deal with them.

This is a non-parochial collection of articles. I have not felt obliged to select only the works of authors who are Canadian citizens and hold PhDs in sociology (although the large majority are and do). The sociological imagination has influenced other disciplines. I have chosen some works by non-sociologists because they are good examples of how cognate disciplines have repaid the favour by enriching sociological thought. Moreover, I strongly believe that, especially in this era of globalization, Canadian sociologists have as much to learn from non-Canadians as from non-sociologists. That is why several non-Canadians are among the authors represented here.

I consider some of the pieces reprinted here to be modern classics, but I have tried wherever possible to select items that speak to key issues of social life today. More than three-quarters of the articles in this book were written after 1995 and more than 40 percent were written in the first years of the twenty-first century.

Finally, although I selected a few articles just because they cover important topics concisely and clearly, more rigorous criteria guided most of my choices. As I reviewed material for this collection, I tried to place myself in the shoes of a contemporary Canadian undergraduate who, entirely sensibly, takes the time to read only material that says something significant and non-obvious. Most of the articles in this book surprised me when I first read them and they continue to affect the way I see the world. Accordingly, the best indicator of the usefulness of this book will be the number of students who complete it and say that it helped ensure that they can no longer pick up a newspaper without thinking about the broader sociological significance of what they've read. That is just about the highest praise an introductory sociology instructor can receive.

ACKNOWLEDGEMENTS

I thank Myrna Dawson (University of Guelph), Bonnie Fox (University of Toronto), Kelly Hannah-Moffat (University of Toronto), and Adie Nelson (University of Waterloo) for useful advice in the selection of articles for this collection. I am also indebted to Brad Lambertus and the Nelson team of Cara Yarzab (Sociology Acquisitions Editor), Glen Herbert (Developmental Editor), Tammy Scherer (Production Editor), Valerie Adams (copy editor), and Karen Rolfe (proofreader) for their assistance in shaping this collection.

ROBERT J. BRYM
University of Toronto

PART 1 | THE FIELD OF SOCIOLOGY

I have been writing my autobiography since I entered graduate school. As autobiographies go, it is pretty unconventional. It records no personal events or dates, nor does it sketch interesting characters. My friends, enemies, colleagues, parents, wife, and children are not mentioned in it. It is not written as a personal narrative. Yet, indirectly, it is the story of my life.

My life story is embedded in my sociological writings. The pressing issues that trouble me have somehow been transformed into a research agenda. But I alone can plainly see the connection between my life and my writings. To the degree that my writings have any value to others, it lies in their contribution, however slight, to conversations and debates that people who call themselves sociologists have engaged in for more than a century. Those sociologists couldn't care less about whether I have found my research and writing useful in answering the political, ethnic, and economic issues that have weighed on me over the years.

Nor should they. Sociology is a science—a science that is not as precise as physics, which doesn't have to contend with human caprice, but a science nonetheless. That is, sociologists try to observe their chosen corner of reality in a systematic and controlled manner and to evaluate the validity of their ideas on the basis of whether their observations confirm or disconfirm them. The origins of those ideas are irrelevant, scientifically speaking. That is, I think, what the American writer Kurt Vonnegut meant when he wrote that the most beautiful marigold he ever saw was growing in a bucket of cat manure.

Here we have the great irony of much scholarship, sociology included. Scholars try to be dispassionate and objective, yet much scholarly activity is animated by real-life experiences and individual passions. For example, Albert Einstein believed on philosophical grounds that the universe is a deterministic system operating according to iron laws and that it is the physicist's job to discover those laws. When he was confronted by evidence that certain subatomic processes can be described only in terms of probable rather than certain outcomes, he objected: "God does not play dice with the universe." In this case, the evidence did not sway Einstein; his personal bent of mind, even his religious outlook, affected his evaluation of the evidence.

In their laudable efforts to be objective, some scholars lose sight of the fact that personal experiences and individual passions help them define certain problems as urgent and certain solutions to those problems as preferable. But few thoughtful and honest scholars can fool themselves for long with pious statements about being purely objective in their research. The plain fact is that objectivity and subjectivity each have an important role to play in science, including sociology. Objectivity is a reality check. Subjectivity leads us to define which aspect of reality is worth checking on in the first place.

In contrast to those who believe that objectivity is everything, many people are under the equally misguided impression that subjectivity tells all, that their own experience is the sole reliable guide to action, that their personal troubles are theirs and theirs alone. In his 1959 classic, *The Sociological Imagination*, part of which is reprinted here as Chapter 1, the late C. Wright Mills shows how wrong this commonsense view is.

When one person in a community is unemployed, says Mills, that is a personal trouble and perhaps a personal failing. When 30 percent of a country's work force is unemployed, as was the case in North

America during the Great Depression of 1929–39, that is a massive social issue. The best sociologists try to show how personal troubles are tied to social issues and how social issues, in turn, have developed historically. From Mills's point of view, good sociology is liberating. It promises to broaden your sense of what you can do with your life by showing how your subjective feelings and actions are a product of broad social and historical forces, and how you can act to alter those social and historical forces and thus improve the quality of your life. Although in some respects dated — Mills's tone was influenced by the fact that he wrote at the height of the Cold War; his language is sexist — his main argument is as true and inspiring today as it was 40 years ago.

Some students may consider sociology's promise too abstract, theoretical, or impractical. They may immediately see how the health professions, teaching, or engineering can help improve the world. Yet sociology's contribution may remain murky. Chapter 2, by Joel Charon, is good medicine for skeptics.

Charon says sociology's main practical contribution is that it can improve the workings of democracy. By his definition, a **democracy** is a society in which people think and act as they wish, control and limit the power of government, respect and protect minority rights, and enjoy equal opportunity for a decent life. Sociology lays bare the social conditions that promote freedom, limit state power, encourage respect for diversity, and undermine privilege. Can there be any more practical tasks for humanity than achieving these goals?

You have seen that the motivation for much sociological research is rooted in people's real-life experiences. It should therefore come as no surprise that sociology has unique characteristics in every national context in which it is practised. In other words, the collective experiences (or "histories") that characterize each society are reflected in its sociological traditions. Consider sociology in Canada. Chapter 3, by Robert Brym and Céline Saint-Pierre, shows that the feat of survival in the face of formidable geographical, economic, and political obstacles is a core theme in Canadian sociology. For instance, many of Quebec's sociologists have been preoccupied with the nature of *Québécois* identity and the emergence of a distinct Quebec society and nation despite English domination. This focus has led many Quebec sociologists to become deeply involved in the political and policy-making processes of their society. For reasons mentioned in the article, sociologists in the rest of Canada have been less involved in politics and policy-making than their *Québécois* counterparts. Yet a high level of interest in the country's ability to survive American domination is apparent in much sociological research outside Quebec. We thus see plenty of evidence in this country of the way sociology combines the analysis of individual experience, historical change, and social structure.

GLOSSARY

A **democracy** is a society in which people (1) think and act as they wish, (2) control and limit the power of government, (3) respect and protect minority rights, and (4) enjoy equal opportunity for a decent life.

CRITICAL THINKING QUESTIONS

1. What are the key aspects of the sociological perspective? What are the benefits of using this perspective?
2. In what ways can sociology show us how to make society more democratic?

3. What are the roles of objectivity and subjectivity in social science research?
4. How is sociology different from psychology?
5. What are the main features of sociology in English Canada and Quebec?

ANNOTATED BIBLIOGRAPHY

Robert J. Brym with Bonnie J. Fox, *From Culture to Power: The Sociology of English Canada* (Toronto: Oxford University Press, 1989). An overview of theoretical controversies and empirical findings in several of the main fields of sociological research in Canada outside Quebec.

Harry Hiller, ed. *Canadian Journal of Sociology* 26, 3 (2001). "Legacy for a New Millennium." This special issue of *The Canadian Journal of Sociology* reviews the major themes in Canadian sociology and the history of the discipline in this country.

Immanuel Wallerstein, ed., *Current Sociology* 46, 2 (1998). "The Heritage of Sociology and the Future of the Social Sciences in the 21st Century." This special issue of the journal of the International Sociological Association contains programmatic statements about the future of the discipline by leading scholars, including Canada's Margrit Eichler.

Irving Zeitlin, *Ideology and the Development of Sociological Theory*, 7th ed. (Upper Saddle River NJ: Prentice-Hall, 2001). A thorough introduction to classical sociological theory.

Chapter 1

The Sociological Imagination

C. WRIGHT MILLS

Nowadays men often feel that their private lives are a series of traps. They sense that within their everyday worlds, they cannot overcome their troubles, and in this feeling, they are often quite correct: What ordinary men are directly aware of and what they try to do are bounded by the private orbits in which they live; their visions and their powers are limited to the close-up scenes of job, family, neighbourhood; in other milieux, they move vicariously and remain spectators. And the more aware they become, however vaguely, of ambitions and of threats which transcend their immediate locales, the more trapped they seem to feel.

Underlying this sense of being trapped are seemingly impersonal changes in the very structure of continent-wide societies. The facts of contemporary history are also facts about the success and the failure of individual men and women. When a society is industrialized, a peasant becomes a worker; a feudal lord is liquidated or becomes a businessman. When classes rise or fall, a man is employed or unemployed; when the rate of investment goes up or down, a man takes new heart or goes broke. When wars happen, an insurance salesman becomes a rocket launcher; a store clerk, a radar man; a wife lives alone; a child grows up without a father. Neither the life of an individual nor the history of a society can be understood without understanding both.

Yet men do not usually define the troubles they endure in terms of historical change and institutional contradiction. The well-being they enjoy, they do not usually impute to the big ups and downs of the societies in which they live. Seldom aware of the intricate connection between the patterns of their own lives and the course of world history, ordinary men do not usually know what this connection means for the kinds of men they are becoming and for the kinds of history-making in which they might take part. They do not possess the quality of mind essential to grasp the interplay of man and society, of biography and history, of self and world. They cannot cope with their personal troubles in such ways as to control the structural transformations that usually lie behind them.

Surely it is no wonder. In what period have so many men been so totally exposed at so fast a pace to such earthquakes of change? That Americans have not known such catastrophic changes as have the men and women of other societies is due to historical facts that are now quickly becoming "merely history." The history that now affects every man is world history. Within this scene and this period, in the course of a single generation, one-sixth of mankind is transformed from all that is feudal and backward into all that is modern, advanced, and fearful. Political colonies are freed; new and less visible forms of imperialism installed. Revolutions occur; men feel the intimate grip of new kinds of authority. Totalitarian societies rise, and are smashed to bits — or succeed fabulously. After two centuries of ascendancy, capitalism is shown up as only one way to make society into an industrial apparatus. After two centuries of hope, even formal democracy is restricted to a quite small portion of mankind.

Everywhere in the underdeveloped world, ancient ways of life are broken up and vague expectations become urgent demands. Everywhere in the overdeveloped world, the means of authority and of violence become total in scope and bureaucratic in form. Humanity itself now lies before us, the super-nation at either pole concentrating its most coordinated and massive efforts upon the preparation of World War Three.

The very shaping of history now outpaces the ability of men to orient themselves in accordance with cherished values. And which values? Even when they do not panic, men often sense that older ways of feeling and thinking have collapsed and that newer beginnings are ambiguous to the point of moral stasis. Is it any wonder that ordinary men feel they cannot cope with the larger worlds with which they are so suddenly confronted? That they cannot understand the meaning of their epoch for their own lives? That — in defence of selfhood — they become morally insensible, trying to remain altogether private men? Is it any wonder that they come to be possessed by a sense of the trap?

It is not only information that they need — in this Age of Fact, information often dominates their attention and overwhelms their capacities to assimilate it. It is not only the skills of reason that they need — although their struggles to acquire these often exhaust their limited moral energy.

What they need, and what they feel they need, is a quality of mind that will help them to use information and to develop reason in order to achieve lucid summations of what is going on in the world and of what may be happening within themselves. It is this quality, I am going to contend, that journalists and scholars, artists and publics, scientists and editors are coming to expect of what may be called the sociological imagination.

1

The sociological imagination enables its possessor to understand the larger historical scene in terms of its meaning for the inner life and the external career of a variety of individuals. It enables him to take into account how individuals, in the welter of their daily experience, often become falsely conscious of their social positions. Within that welter, the framework of modern society is sought, and within that framework the psychologies of a variety of men and women are formulated. By such means the personal uneasiness of individuals is focused upon explicit troubles, and the indifference of publics is transformed into involvement with public issues.

The first fruit of this imagination — and the first lesson of the social science that embodies it — is the idea that the individual can understand his own experience and gauge his own fate only by locating himself within his period, that he can know his own chances in life only by becoming aware of those of all individuals in his circumstances. In many ways it is a tenable lesson; in many ways a magnificent one. We do not know the limits of man's capacities for supreme effort or willing degradation, for agony or glee, for pleasurable brutality or the sweetness of reason. But in our time we have come to know that the limits of "human nature" are frighteningly broad. We have come to know that every individual lives, from one generation to the next, in some society; that he lives out a biography, and that he lives it out within some historical sequence. By the fact of his living he contributes, however minutely, to the shaping of this society and to the course of its history, even as he is made by society and by its historical push and shove.

The sociological imagination enables us to grasp history and biography and the relations between the two within society. That is its task and its promise. To recognize this task and this promise is the mark of the classic social analyst. It is characteristic of Herbert Spencer — turgid, polysyllabic, comprehensive; of E.A. Ross — graceful, muckraking, upright; of Auguste Comte and Émile Durkheim; of the intricate and subtle Karl Mannheim. It is the quality of all that is intellectually excellent in Karl Marx; it is the clue to Thorstein Veblen's brilliant and ironic insight, to Joseph Schumpeter's many-sided constructions of reality; it is the basis of the psychological sweep of W.E.H. Lecky no less than of the profundity and clarity of Max Weber. And it is the signal of what is best in contemporary studies of man and society.

No social study that does not come back to the problems of biography, of history, and of their intersections within a society has completed its intellectual journey. Whatever the specific problems of the classic social analysts, however limited or however broad the features of social reality they have examined, those who have been imaginatively aware of the promise of their work have consistently asked three sorts of questions:

1. What is the structure of this particular society as a whole? What are its essential components, and how are they related to one another? How does it differ from other varieties of social order? Within it, what is the meaning of any particular feature for its continuance and for its change?

2. Where does this society stand in human history? What are the mechanics by which it is changing? What is its place within and its meaning for the development of humanity as a whole? How does any particular feature we are examining affect, and how is it affected by, the historical period in which it moves? And this period — what are its essential features? How does it differ from other periods? What are its characteristic ways of history-making?

3. What varieties of men and women now prevail in this society and in this period? And what varieties are coming to prevail? In what ways are they selected and formed, liberated and repressed, made sensitive and blunted? What kinds of "human nature" are revealed in the conduct and character we observe in this society in this period? And what is the meaning for "human nature" of each and every feature of the society we are examining?

Whether the point of interest is a great power state or a minor literary mood, a family, a prison, a creed — these are the kinds of questions the best social analysts have asked. They are the intellectual pivots of classic studies of man in society — and they are the questions inevitably raised by any mind possessing the sociological imagination. For that imagination is the capacity to shift from one perspective to another — from the political to the psychological; from examination of a single family to comparative assessment of the national budgets of the world; from the theological school to the military establishment; from considerations of an oil industry to studies of contemporary poetry. It is the capacity to range from the most impersonal and remote transformations to the most intimate features of the human self — and to see the relations between the two. Back of its use there is always the urge to know the social and historical meaning of the individual in the society and in the period in which he has his quality and his being.

That, in brief, is why it is by means of the sociological imagination that men now hope to grasp what is going on in the world, and to understand what is happening in themselves as minute points of the intersections of biography and history within society. In large part, contemporary man's self-conscious view of himself as at least an outsider, if not a permanent stranger, rests upon an absorbed realization of social relativity and of the transformative power of history. The sociological imagination is the most fruitful form of this self-consciousness. By its use men whose mentalities have swept only a series of limited orbits often come to feel as if suddenly awakened in a house with which they had only supposed themselves to be familiar. Correctly or incorrectly, they often come to feel that they can now provide themselves with adequate summations, cohesive assessments, comprehensive orientations. Older decisions that once appeared sound now seem to them products of a mind unaccountably dense. Their capacity for astonishment is made lively again. They acquire a new way of thinking, they experience a transvaluation of values: in a word, by their reflection and by their sensibility, they realize the cultural meaning of the social sciences.

2

Perhaps the most fruitful distinction with which the sociological imagination works is between "the personal troubles of milieu" and "the public issues of social structure." This distinction is an essential tool of the sociological imagination and a feature of all classic work in social science.

Troubles occur within the character of the individual and within the range of his immediate relations with others; they have to do with his self and with those limited areas of social life of which he is directly and personally aware. Accordingly, the statement and the resolution of troubles properly lie within the individual as a biographical entity and within the scope of his immediate milieu — the social setting that is directly open to his personal experience and to some extent his willful activity. A trouble is a private matter: values cherished by an individual are felt by him to be threatened.

Issues have to do with matters that transcend these local environments of the individual and the range of his inner life. They have to do with the organization of many such milieux into the institutions of an historical society as a whole, with the ways in which various milieux overlap and interpenetrate to form the larger structure of social and historical life. An issue is a public matter: some value cherished by publics is felt to be threatened. Often there is a debate about what that value really is and about what it is that really threatens it. This debate is often without focus if only because it is the very nature of an issue, unlike even widespread trouble, that it cannot very well be defined in terms of the immediate and everyday environments of ordinary men. An issue, in fact, often involves a crisis in institutional arrangements, and often too it involves what Marxists call "contradictions" or "antagonisms."

In these terms, consider unemployment. When, in a city of 100 000, only one man is unemployed, that is his personal trouble, and for its relief we properly look to the character of the man, his skills, and his immediate opportunities. But when in a nation of 50 million employees, 15 million men are unemployed, that is an issue, and we may not hope to find its solution within the range of opportunities open to any one individual. The very structure of opportunities has collapsed. Both the correct statement of the problem and the range of possible solutions require us to consider the economic and political institutions of the society, and not merely the personal situation and character of a scatter of individuals.

Consider war. The personal problem of war, when it occurs, may be how to survive it or how to die in it with honour; how to make money out of it; how to climb into the higher safety of the military apparatus; or how to contribute to the war's termination. In short, according to one's values, to find a set of milieux and within it to survive the war or make one's death in it meaningful. But the structural issues of war have to do with its causes; with what types of men it throws up into command; with its effects upon economic and political, family and religious institutions; with the unorganized irresponsibility of a world of nation-states.

Consider marriage. Inside a marriage a man and a woman may experience personal troubles, but when the divorce rate during the first four years of marriage is 250 out of every 1000 attempts, this is an indication of a structural issue having to do with the institutions of marriage and the family and other institutions that bear upon them.

Or consider the metropolis — the horrible, beautiful, ugly, magnificent sprawl of the great city. For many upper-class people, the personal solution to "the problem of the city" is to have an apartment with private garage under it in the heart of the city, and forty miles out, a house by Henry Hill, garden by Garrett Eckbo, on a hundred acres of private land. In these two controlled environments — with a small staff at each end and a private helicopter connection — most people could solve many of the problems of personal milieux caused by the facts of the city. But all this, however splendid, does not solve the public issues that the structural fact of the city poses. What should be done with this wonderful monstrosity? Break it all up into scattered units, combining residence and work? Refurbish it as it stands? Or, after evacuation, dynamite it and build new cities according to new plans in new places? What should those plans be? And who is to decide and to accomplish whatever choice is made? These are structural issues; to confront them and to solve them requires us to consider political and economic issues that affect innumerable milieux.

In so far as an economy is so arranged that slumps occur, the problem of unemployment becomes incapable of personal solution. In so far as war is inherent in the nation-state system and in the uneven industrialization of the world, the ordinary individual in his restricted milieu will be powerless — with or without psychiatric aid — to solve the troubles this system or lack of system imposes upon him. In so far as the family as an institution turns women into darling little slaves and men into their chief providers and unweaned dependants, the problem of a satisfactory marriage remains incapable of purely private solution. In so far as the overdeveloped megalopolis and the overdeveloped automobile are built-in features of the overdeveloped society, the issues of urban living will not be solved by personal ingenuity and private wealth.

What we experience in various and specific milieux, I have noted, is often caused by structural changes. Accordingly, to understand the changes of many personal milieux we are required to look beyond them. And the number and variety of such structural changes increase as the institutions within which we live become more embracing and more intricately connected with one another. To be aware of the idea of social structure and to use it with sensibility is to be capable of tracing such linkages among a great variety of milieux. To be able to do that is to possess the sociological imagination.

3

What are the major issues for publics and the key troubles of private individuals in our time? To formulate issues and troubles, we must ask what values are cherished yet threatened, and what values are cherished and supported, by the characterizing trends of our period. In the case both of threat and of support we must ask what salient contradictions of structure may be involved.

When people cherish some set of values and do not feel any threat to them, they experience well-being. When they cherish values but do feel them to be threatened, they experience a crisis — either as a personal trouble or as a public issue. And if all their values seem involved, they feel the total threat of panic.

But suppose people are neither aware of any cherished values nor experience any threat. That is the experience of indifference, which, if it seems to involve all their values, becomes apathy. Suppose, finally, they are unaware of any cherished values, but still are very much aware of a threat? That is the experience of uneasiness, of anxiety, which, if it is total enough, becomes a deadly unspecified malaise.

Ours is a time of uneasiness and indifference — not yet formulated in such ways as to permit the work of reason and the play of sensibility. Instead of troubles — defined in terms of values and threats — there is often the misery of vague uneasiness; instead of explicit issues there is often merely the weak feeling that all is somehow not right. Neither the values threatened nor whatever threatens them has been stated; in short, they have not been carved to the point of decision. Much less have they been formulated as problems of social science.

In the thirties there was little doubt — except among certain deluded business circles — that there was an economic issue which was also a pack of personal troubles. In these arguments about "the crisis of capitalism," the formulations of Marx and the many unacknowledged reformulations of his work probably set the leading terms of the issue, and some men came to understand their personal troubles in these terms. The values threatened were plain to see and cherished by all; the structural contradictions that threatened them also seemed plain. Both were widely and deeply experienced. It was a political age.

But the values threatened in the era after World War Two are often neither widely acknowledged as values nor widely felt to be threatened. Much private uneasiness goes unformulated; much public malaise and many decisions of enormous structural relevance never become public issues. For those who accept such inherited values as reason and freedom, it is the uneasiness itself that is the trouble; it is the indifference itself that is the issue. And it is this condition, of uneasiness and indifference, that is the signal feature of our period.

All this is so striking that it is often interpreted by observers as a shift in the very kinds of problems that need now to be formulated. We are frequently told that the problems of our decade, or even the crises of our period, have shifted from the external realm of economics and now have to do with the quality of individual life — in fact with the question of whether there is soon going to be anything that can properly be called individual life. Not child labour but comic books, not poverty but mass leisure, are at the centre of concern. Many great public issues as well as many private troubles are described in terms of "the psychiatric" — often, it seems, in a pathetic attempt to avoid the large issues and problems of modern society. Often this statement seems to rest upon a provincial narrowing of interest to the Western societies, or even to the United States — thus ignoring two-thirds of mankind; often, too, it arbitrarily divorces the individual life from the larger institutions within which that life is enacted, and which on occasion bear upon it more grievously than do the intimate environments of childhood.

Problems of leisure, for example, cannot even be stated without considering problems of work. Family troubles over comic books cannot be formulated as problems without considering the plight of the contemporary family in its new relations with the newer institutions of the social structure. Neither leisure nor its debilitating uses can be understood as problems without recognition of the extent to which malaise and indifference now form the social and personal climate of contemporary American society. In this climate, no problems of "the private life" can be stated and solved without recognition of the crisis of ambition that is part of the very career of men at work in the incorporated economy.

It is true, as psychoanalysts continually point out, that people do often have "the increasing sense of being moved by obscure forces within themselves which they are unable to define." But it is *not* true, as Ernest Jones asserted, that "man's chief enemy and danger is his own unruly nature and the dark forces pent up within him." On the contrary: "Man's chief danger" today lies in the unruly forces of contemporary society itself, with its alienating methods of production, its enveloping techniques of political domination, its international anarchy — in a word, its pervasive transformations of the very "nature" of man and the conditions and aims of his life.

It is now the social scientist's foremost political and intellectual task — for here the two coincide — to make clear the elements of contemporary uneasiness and indifference. It is the central demand made upon him by other cultural workmen — by physical scientists and artists, by the intellectual community in general. It is because of this task and these demands, I believe, that the social sciences are becoming the common denominator of our cultural period, and the sociological imagination our most needed quality of mind.

Chapter 2

Is Sociology Important? The Need for a Critical Understanding of Society

JOEL CHARON

In the final analysis, it may be true that ignorance is bliss. It may be true that people should be left alone with the myths they happen to pick up in interaction with one another. It may be true that a liberal arts education that does not have immediate practical value is worthless.

SOCIOLOGY AND A LIBERAL ARTS EDUCATION

I do not believe any of the ideas above, but I wonder about them a lot. One can more easily make a case for mathematics, foreign languages, writing, speech, psychology, and economics on the level of practical use. "The student needs to know these if he or she is to get along in life," the argument goes. It is far more difficult to make a case for sociology on the basis of practical use — unless, of course, by practical use one means thinking about and understanding the world. If a college education is ultimately an attempt to encourage people to wonder, investigate, and carefully examine their lives, then sociology is one of the most important disciplines.

Note its purpose: to get students to examine an aspect of life carefully and systematically that most people only casually and occasionally think about. It is to get people to understand what culture is

and to recognize that what they believe is largely a result of their culture. It is to get them to see that they are born into a society that has a long history, that they are ranked and given roles in that society, and that ultimately they are told who they are, what to think, and how to act. It is to get them to see that the institutions they follow and normally accept are not the only ways in which society can function — that there are always alternatives. It is to get them to realize that those whom they regard as sick, evil, or criminal are often simply different. It is to get them to see that those they hate are often a product of social circumstances that should be understood more carefully and objectively.

In short, the purpose of sociology is to get people to examine objectively their lives and their society. This process is uncomfortable and sometimes unpleasant. I keep asking myself, as I teach the insights of sociology, "Why not just leave those students alone?" And, quite frankly, I do not usually know how to answer this question. We are socialized into society. Shouldn't we simply accept that which we are socialized to believe? Isn't it better for society if people believe myth? Isn't it better for people's happiness to let them be?

I usually come back to what many people profess to be one primary purpose of a university

Source: Excerpted from "Is Sociology Important? The Necessity for a Critical Understanding of Society," in Joel M. Charon, *Ten Questions: A Sociological Perspective*, 3rd ed. © 1998. Reprinted with permission of Wadsworth, a division of Thomson Learning: www.thomsonrights.com. Fax: 800-730-2215.

education: "liberal arts." To me, the liberal arts should be "liberating." A university education should be liberating; it should help the individual escape the bonds of his or her imprisonment through bringing an understanding of that prison. We should read literature, understand art, and study biology and sociology in order to break through what those who defend society want us to know to reach a plane where we are able to see reality in a more careful and unbiased way. In the end, sociology probably has the greatest potential for liberation in the academic world: At its best, it causes individuals to confront their ideas, actions, and being. We are never the same once we bring sociology into our lives. Life is scrutinized. Truth becomes far more tentative.

SOCIOLOGY AND DEMOCRACY

THE MEANING OF DEMOCRACY

Liberation, as you probably realize, has something to do with democracy. Although democracy is clearly an ideal that North Americans claim for themselves, it is not usually clearly defined or deeply explored.

Sociology, however, explores democracy, and it asks rarely examined questions about the possibility for democracy in this — or any — society. To many people democracy simply means "majority rule," and we too often superficially claim that if people go to a voting booth, then democracy has been established and the majority does, in fact, rule. Democracy, however, is far more than majority rule, and majority rule is far more than the existence of voting booths.

Democracy is very difficult to achieve. No society can become perfectly democratic; few societies really make much progress in that direction. Democracy is also difficult to define. When I try, I usually end up listing four qualities. These describe a whole society, not just the government in that society. Although everyone will not agree that these are the basic qualities of a democracy, I think they offer a good place to begin.

1. *A democratic society is one in which the individual is free in both thinking and action.* People are in control of their own lives. To the extent that a society encourages freedom, we can call it a democratic society.

2. *A democratic society is one where the government is effectively limited.* Those who control government do not do what they choose to do. Voting, law, organization of people, and constitutions effectively limit their power. To the extent that government is effectively limited, we call it a democratic society.

3. *A democratic society is one where human differences are respected and protected.* There is a general agreement that no matter what the majority favours, certain rights are reserved for the individual and for minorities who are different from the majority. Diversity is respected and even encouraged. To the extent that diversity and individuality are respected and protected, we call it a democratic society.

4. *A democratic society is one in which all people have an equal opportunity to live a decent life.* That is, privilege is not inherited, people have equality before the law, in educational opportunity, in opportunity for material success, and in whatever is deemed to be important in society. To the extent that real equality of opportunity exists, we call it a democratic society.

These four qualities that make up the definition of democracy described here must be tentative descriptions, and people should debate their relative significance. Some will regard others to be more important, and some will regard only one or two of these qualities as necessary. I am only trying here to list four qualities that make sense to me and that guide my own estimate of whether societies are democratic.

If these qualities do capture what democracy means, however, it should be obvious that the questions and thinking that are basic to the sociological perspective are relevant to both the understanding of and working toward a democratic society. Because sociology focuses on social organization, structure, culture, institutions, social order, social class, social power, social conflict, socialization, and social change, *sociology must continually examine issues that are relevant to understanding a democratic society*. And, on top of this, because *sociology critically examines people and their society, it encourages the kind of thinking that is necessary for people living in and working for a democratic society*. One might, in truth, argue that *the study of sociology is the study of issues relevant to understanding democratic society*.

SOCIOLOGY: AN APPROACH TO UNDERSTANDING DEMOCRATIC SOCIETY

One of sociology's main concerns is the nature of the human being and the role of socialization and culture in what we all become. To ask questions about human nature is to ask simultaneous questions about the possibility for democratic society, a society built on qualities that are not often widespread in society: respect for individual differences, compromise, and concern over inequality and lack of freedom. The sociological approach to the human being makes no assumption of fixed qualities, but it has a strong tendency to see human beings as living within social conditions that are responsible for forming many of their most important qualities. A society tends to produce certain types of people and certain social conditions, encouraging one value or another, one set of morals or another, one way of doing things or another. Conformity, control of the human being, tyranny, and pursuit of purely selfish interests can be encouraged; but so, too, can freedom, respect for people's rights, limited government, and equality. *The possibilities for and the limits to a human being who can live democratically are part of what sociology investigates through its questions concerning culture, socialization, and human nature.*

Those who think about society must inevitably consider the central problem of social order: How much freedom and how much individuality can we allow and still maintain society?

Those who favour greater freedom will occasionally wonder: How can there really be meaningful freedom in any society? As long as society exists, how much freedom can we encourage without destroying the underlying order? Are there limits? If so, how can we discover them? What are the costs, if any, of having a democratic society? Those who fear disorder and the collapse of society might ask: How much does the individual owe to society? Such questions are extremely difficult to answer, but they are investigated throughout the discipline of sociology, and they push the serious student to search for a delicate balance between order and freedom. Too often people are willing to sell out freedom in the name of order; too often people claim so much freedom that they do not seem to care about the continuation of society. The sociologist studies these problems and causes the student to reflect again and again on this dilemma inherent in all societies, especially those that claim to be part of the democratic tradition. There can be no freedom without society, Émile Durkheim reminds us, for a basic agreement over rules must precede the exercise of freedom. *But the problem is: How many rules? How much freedom? There is no more basic question for those who favour democracy, and there is no question more central to the discipline of sociology.*

The question of social order also leads us to the questions of what constitutes a nation and what constitutes a society. These issues may not seem at first to have much relevance to democracy, but they surely do. It is easy for those who profess democracy to favour majority rule. It is much more difficult for any nation to develop institutions that respect the rights of all societies within its borders. A nation is a political state that rules over one or more societies. If it is democratic, then the nation does not simply rule these societies but responds to their needs and rights, from true political representation to a decent standard of living. If it is democratic, the question the nation faces is not "How can we mould that society to be like the dominant society?" but "How can we create an order in which many societies can exist?" If it is democratic, then the nation must balance the needs of each society's push for independence with the need for maintaining social order. *The whole meaning of what it is to be a society, as well as the associated problems of order and independence, are central sociological — and democratic — concerns.*

It is the question of control by social forces over the human being that places sociology squarely within the concerns of democracy. Much of sociology questions the possibility for substantial freedom. Democracy teaches that human beings should and can think for themselves. Much of the purpose of sociology, however, is to show us that our thinking is created by our social life, that, although we may claim that our ideas are our own, they really result from our cultures, from our positions in social structure, and from powerful and wealthy people. Even to claim that "we are a democracy!" can simply be part of an ideology, an exaggeration we accept because we are victims of various social forces. Our actions, too, result from a host of social forces that few of us understand or appreciate: institutions, opportunities, class, roles, social controls — to name only some — that quietly work on the individual, pushing him or her in directions not freely chosen. Sociology seems to make democracy an almost impossible dream, and to some extent the more sociology one knows, the more difficult democracy seems. *Indeed, sociology tends to simply uncover more and more ways in which human beings are shaped and controlled. This, in itself, makes sociology very relevant for understanding the limits of democracy. It causes one to seriously wonder if human beings can be free in any sense.*

As I said earlier in this chapter, however, *sociology as a part of a liberal education is an attempt to liberate the individual from many of these controls.* The first step in liberation is understanding: It is really impossible to think for oneself or to act according to free choice unless one understands the various ways in which we are controlled. For example, it is only when I begin to see that my ideas of what it means to be a "man" have been formed through a careful and calculated process

throughout society that I can begin to act in the way I choose. Only when I begin to understand how powerful advertising has become in developing my personal tastes as well as my personal values can I begin to step back and direct my own life. And even then, an important sociological question continuously teases the thoughtful person: Can society exist if people are truly liberated? If people question everything, can there still be the unity necessary for order?

The study of social inequality — probably the central concern within all sociology — is, of course, an issue of primary importance to understanding the possibility for a democratic society. It seems that it is the nature of society to be unequal. Many forces create and perpetuate inequality. Indeed, even in our groups and our formal organizations great inequalities are the rule. Why? Why does it happen? And what are its implications for democracy? If society is characterized by great inequalities of wealth and power, then how can free thought and free action prevail among the population? If a society — in name, a democracy — has a small elite that dominates the decision making, then what difference does going to the polls make? If large numbers of people must expend all of their energy to barely survive because of their poverty, where is their freedom, their opportunity to influence the direction of society, their right to improve their lives? If society is characterized by racist and sexist institutions, then how is democracy possible for those who are victims? *More than any other perspective, sociology makes us aware of many problems standing in the way of a democratic society, not the least of which are social, economic, and political inequality.*

This focus on social inequality will cause many individuals to look beyond the political arena to understand democracy. A democratic society requires not only limited government but also a limited military, a limited upper class, limited corporations, and limited interest groups. Limited government may bring freedom to the individual, but it also may simply create more unlimited power for economic elites in society, which is often an even more ruthless tyranny over individual freedom. *Sociology, because its subject is society, broadens our concerns, investigates the individual not only in relation to political institutions but also in relation to many other sources of power that can and do limit real democracy and control much of what we think and do.*

The democratic spirit cares about the welfare of all people. It respects life, values individual rights, encourages quality of life, and seeks justice for all. Sociology studies social problems. It tackles many problems, including those associated with human misery. Many people live lives of misery, characterized by poverty, crime, bad jobs, exploitation, lack of self-worth, stress, repressive institutions, violent conflict, inadequate socialization, and alienation of various kinds. These are more than problems caused by human biology or human genes; these are more than problems caused by the free choices of individual actors. Something social has generally caused misery to occur. *Although it is impossible for sociology — or a democratic society — to rid the world of such problems, it is part of the spirit of both to understand them, to suggest and to carry out ways to deal with them.* Democracy is shallow and cold if large numbers of people continue to live lives of misery.

What does ethnocentrism have to do with democracy? Is this central concern in sociology relevant to understanding and living in a democratic society? We return to the issue of respect for minorities mentioned earlier. Ethnocentrism, although perhaps inevitable and even necessary to some extent, is a way of looking at one's own culture and others in a manner antagonistic to a basic principle of democracy: respect for human diversity and individuality. To claim that our culture is superior to others is to treat other cultures without respect, to reject them for what they are, to believe that everyone must be like us. Such ideas encourage violent conflict and war and justify discrimination, segregation, and exploitation. Sociology challenges us to be careful with ethnocentrism. We must under-

stand what it is, what its causes are, and how it functions. An understanding of ethnocentrism will challenge us to ask: "When are my judgements of others simply cultural and when are they based on some more defensible standards (such as democratic standards)?" "When are my judgements narrow and intolerant; when are they more careful and thought out?" Even then, an understanding of ethnocentrism will not allow us to judge people who are different without seriously questioning our judgements. *Sociology and democracy are perspectives that push us to understand human differences and to be careful in condemning those differences.*

The sociologist's faith in the individual as an agent of social change is not great. Democracy is truly an illusion if it means that the individual has an important say in the direction of society. But if sociology teaches us anything about change that has relevance for democracy, it is that intentionally created change is possible only through a power base. If a democracy is going to be more than a description in a book, people who desire change in society — ideally, toward more freedom, limited government, equality of opportunity, and respect for individual rights — must work together and act from a power base, recognizing that the existing political institutions are usually fixed against them. And before we go off armed with certainty, we should remember that our certainty was probably also socially produced and that through our efforts we may bring change we never intended and may even lose whatever democracy we now have. Social change is complex, depends on social power, and is difficult to bring about in a way we would like. *The sociologist will examine the possibility for intentional social change in a democratic society and will be motivated to isolate the many barriers each society establishes to real social change.*

SUMMARY AND CONCLUSION

Democracy exists at different levels. For some, it is a simplistic, shallow idea. For others, however, it is a complex and challenging idea to investigate and a reality worthwhile to create. If it is going to be more than a shallow idea, however, then people should understand the nature of all society, the nature of power, ethnocentrism, inequality, change, and all the other concepts discussed and investigated in sociology. Whereas other disciplines may study issues relevant to understanding democracy and encourage people to think democratically, in a very basic sense this study is the heart of sociology.

It is important to understand society without bias — that is, even about something so personal as society, human beings should try to be objective, to set aside the cultural reality they have learned, and to understand the world as it actually is. This critical evaluation of what we believe has a lot to do with freedom, because without it we are left with a cultural bias we are barely aware of and one that will influence all that we think. Democracy means that one must understand reality not through accepting authority but through careful, thoughtful investigation. It is through evidence, not bias, that one should understand. It is through open debate, not a closed belief system, that one should try to understand. *The principles of science and democracy are similar. There is no greater test of those principles than the discipline of sociology: an attempt to apply scientific principles to that for which we are all taught to feel a special reverence.*

Because it is a critical perspective that attempts to question what people have internalized from their cultures, sociology is a threat to those people who claim to know the truth. It punctures myth and asks questions that many of use would rather not hear. To see the world sociologically is to wonder about all things human. To see the world sociologically is to see events in a much larger context than the immediate situation, to think of individual events in relation to the larger present, to the past, and to the future. To see the world sociologically is to be suspicious of what those in power do (in our society and in our groups), and it is constantly to ask questions about what is and what can be.

The sociologist wonders about society and asks questions that get at the heart of many of our most sacred ideas. Perhaps this is why it seems so threatening to "those who know"; and perhaps this is why it is so exciting to those who take it seriously.

Chapter 3

Sociology in Canada

ROBERT J. BRYM

CÉLINE SAINT-PIERRE

IS THERE A CANADIAN SOCIOLOGY?

Nearly 3000 Canadian citizens hold sociology PhDs and most of them are actively engaged in research and writing. Nonetheless, a case can be made for the view that there is no Canadian sociology. Canada is, after all, the most politically decentralized country in the world, a place where regional and neo-nationalist cultures flourish and the pull of the United States — economic, cultural, and political — is pervasive and growing. It may not seem an environment conducive to the development of a distinctive identity and clearly distinguishable national research traditions. For reasons mentioned below, Quebec is an exception. But for the more than 75 percent of Canada's population that lives outside Quebec — the nebulously defined "rest of Canada," sometimes referred to as the ROC — it arguably makes sense to consider sociology an appendage of the American discipline. Only 25 years ago, the great majority of sociologists in Canada were US citizens and even today there are many Canadian sociologists with US PhDs. Moreover, the flow is bidirectional. Although Canada's influence on American sociology is considerably less than its influence on Hollywood, both Canadian expatriates and sociologists residing in Canada have made important contributions to American sociology for decades. Is it reasonable, therefore, to speak of Canadian sociology at all?

We believe it is — and for three reasons:

1. The Quebec fact makes Canadian sociology unique. In Quebec, sociological problems have been defined to a considerable degree by the struggle to develop a unique Québécois identity and a Quebec nation. This makes Canadian sociology very different from its US counterpart.

2. A second aspect of Canadian sociology's distinctiveness is its survivalism. Twenty-five years ago, in a landmark survey of Canadian literature, Margaret Atwood noted that, just as America has its myth of the Frontier, and Britain its myth of the Island, Canada has its myth of Survival (*la survivance*) (Atwood, 1972: 32). Following Atwood, we may say that a core theme of Canadian sociology is the creation and survival of community in the face of hostile elements and outside forces. Much of what is distinctive about Canadian sociology concerns persistence in the face of formidable geography and Empire.

3. A third aspect of Canadian sociology's distinctiveness — and this applies only to the situation outside Quebec — is its tendency towards intellectual radicalism without a concrete policy orientation. In Quebec, sociologists have played a major role in formulating public policy. Although there are of course exceptions, few sociologists in the ROC have been able to serve in a capacity of

Source: This is a revised version of Robert J. Brym and Céline Saint-Pierre, "Canadian Sociology," *Contemporary Sociology* (26, 5: 1997) pp. 543–46. The authors thank the editors of *The Canadian Review of Sociology and Anthropology, The Canadian Journal of Sociology*, and *Sociologie et sociétés, 1988–97*, for their suggestions regarding important works and trends in English-Canadian and Quebec sociology.

intellectual leadership, either inside or outside the public bureaucracy.

Let us examine each of these features of Canadian sociology in turn.

QUEBEC SOCIOLOGY

The teaching of francophone sociology in Quebec dates from 1943, when the Faculty of Social Sciences was founded at Laval University in Quebec City. However, it was not until the period 1965–1980 that the discipline experienced a rapid increase in the number of sociology students, research grants, and publications by Quebec francophone sociologists (Fournier and Houle, 1980; Breton, 1989). From the beginning, the American and French sociological traditions strongly influenced sociological practice in Quebec. At the same time, however, Quebec francophone sociology clearly reflected the political, economic, demographic, and cultural concerns of the community in which it was rooted.

In the 1950s and 1960s, for example, teaching programs and research topics were structured mainly around themes and problems concerned with the identity and modernization of Quebec society (Dumont, 1993; Rocher, 1972). The 1960s was the period of Quebec's "Quiet Revolution," when the provincial government became heavily involved in managing the economy, control of the educational system was substantially wrested from the Catholic church, and the provincial bureaucracy was greatly expanded (Simard, 1979). Not surprisingly, therefore, sociological concerns focused on the question of how the Quebec francophone community could survive and adapt to the conditions of a rapidly modernizing society.

The Quiet Revolution failed to transform the Québécois into "masters in their own house." Immigrants still tended to assimilate into English culture, the francophone birth rate declined, and anglophones continued to dominate the private sector of the economy. This situation encouraged the emergence of neo-

nationalism as a significant political and intellectual force in the 1970s. In this atmosphere, sociological attention shifted to the problem of national and cultural emancipation from English-Canadian domination. Sociology became more critical and concerned with social classes (including the labour movement and the structure of the capitalist class), class struggles, and the nation-state (Bourque and Legaré, 1979). In the late 1970s and early 1980s, the analysis of social movements (Maheu and Sales, 1991) and the sociology of culture became increasingly popular. So did the sociology of gender relations, influenced by a strong feminist movement (Vandelac, 1985).

In a sense, developments in the 1970s and 1980s were a continuation of historical trends. Sociological research in Quebec has never rested above or beyond Quebec society. Its practitioners have been intimately involved in the province's political and social institutions and their analyses have been heeded. For example, sociologists have served as senior advisers and senior civil servants in the ministries of education, health and social services, culture, and labour. Leading sociologists — including Fernand Dumont, Guy Rocher, Yves Martin, and Marcel Rioux — have played an important intellectual leadership role and an important role in the transformation of Quebec society itself. At the same time, many sociologists have been involved in grass-roots movements such as the labour movement and urban citizens' groups.

The 1990s were a period of crisis in sociology worldwide and Quebec sociology was of course affected by global trends. The discipline fragmented intellectually as competition increased among different ways of doing sociology. Perhaps in the Quebec case there was also a connection between the intellectual fragmentation of the discipline and the fact that the neo-nationalist project had not been fully realized. Two referenda (1980 and 1995) failed to result in Quebec's political independence, and the popularity of the independentist *Parti québécois* declined (Daigle with Rocher, 1992). Many sociologists abandoned macro-sociological analysis for field research and empirical studies of new subjects in the 1990s. Qualitative research became dominant in several subfields, including the sociology of science and technology, migration and ethnic groups, health (Renaud, Doré, and White, 1989), education, work, family and youth, and clinical sociology (Enriquez, 1993). At the same time, there was renewed interest in theoretical and philosophical issues, particularly concerning the nature of modernity and postmodernity (Freitag, 1995).

Thus, since 1990, much of francophone sociology in Quebec has been transformed from a sociology of institutions based on macro-sociological paradigms to a sociology of actors based on micro-sociological approaches (Godbout, 1992). The practice of sociology has also become more interdisciplinary and comparative. Moreover, most Quebec sociologists now belong to international scholarly networks. They are linked by the agendas of their subfields more than the agenda of Quebec society as such. The specificity and uniqueness of Quebec sociology remains evident in the work of its practitioners, but Quebec sociology is now bound up with global sociology (Saint-Pierre and Lazure, 1990).

The globalization of Quebec sociology became even more evident by the end of the 1990s, when most Quebec sociologists turned their research efforts to such hot topics as the globalization of the economy, the impact of information technology, and the advent of a "knowledge society." Again, however, we notice the strong local flavouring. The impact of globalization on the cultural, political, and economic development of small societies such as Quebec; the development of health and care services in response to the increasing needs of the elderly; the growth of cultural diversity and the process of cultural transmission in small societies; the increasing role of science and technology in shaping the contours of Quebec society and in posing ethical dilemmas at the individual and societal levels; the new ways in which young people are integrated into the labour market; new expressions of citizenship and social identity — these are among the chief topics that show how global concerns now express themselves in the specificity of Quebec sociology (Bernard, Fournier, and Saint-Pierre, 1998; *Sociologie et Sociétés*, 1999).

SOCIOLOGY IN THE ROC

As in Quebec, much of what is unique about English-Canadian sociology is evident in its emphasis on the theme of survival. Before modern methods of communication and transportation compressed time and space, the most arresting thing about Canada was its sheer physicality — its intimidating size, topography, and climate. The manner in which distant powers forged a human community in this setting so fascinated political economist Harold Innis, the first giant of Canadian social science, that he devoted much of his influential career to examining how the interaction of geography, technology, and imperial demand made survival possible and structured Canadian society. In his later work on the relationship between various communications media and the rise of empires, Innis's historical and institutional approach took on a strong comparative flavour. His most famous student, Marshall McLuhan, carried on the tradition by analyzing how communications media structure human society and human sensibilities, eventually turning the world into a "global village" (Kroker, 1984).

Canadian social science's comparative and global emphases were soon eclipsed. They had little impact on English-Canadian sociology in the 1960s, when the rapid expansion of the discipline led to an influx of American-trained PhDs. They resonated more with the first large cadre of domestically trained sociologists in the 1970s. The generation of the 1970s discovered Innis — and Marx, particularly as he had been interpreted by Latin American students of economic dependency. During this period the Innisian problem was translated into the question of how survival was possible in the face of American might. Characteristic works explored how American control of Canadian manufacturing and resource industries distorted the country's economic growth, class structure, and political development. Canada was nearly as wealthy as the core countries of the global economy but in some respects its social structure resembled that of countries in the economic periphery. This situation made Canada seem to many sociologists an anomaly with few parallels.

However, by emphasizing the alleged uniqueness of Canadian social development, many English-Canadian sociologists in the 1970s ignored the impact of *global* forces on Canadian social structure. They also failed to see how the Canadian case could help explain variations in a wide range of social, political, and economic phenomena by means of comparative analysis (Brym, 1989; Brym with Fox, 1989). It was only in the late 1980s and early 1990s that these shortcomings were overcome. The return of English-Canadian sociology to local traditions of comparative and global analysis was demonstrated by the publication of such important works as Laxer's (1989) comparative study of the causes and effects of foreign economic ownership, Marchak's (1991) survey of the impact of globalization on the Canadian economy, and Clement and Myles's comparative work on class, gender, and postindustrialism (1994), the last of which could well become the worthy successor to John Porter's 1965 classic, *The Vertical Mosaic*, in terms of its impact on Canadian sociology. Significantly, works such as these are of interest not just because they teach us something about Canada but because they speak to larger issues in comparative and global sociology that concern a broad international audience.

The 1980s also witnessed the rapid rise of feminist sociology, which was more influential in English Canada than in most other parts of the world. Internationally recognized scholarly contributions were made to the analysis of domestic labour (Fox, 1980) and family policy (Eichler, 1988a), feminist methodology (Eichler, 1988b) and theory (Smith, 1987). Although gender equality in the administration and staffing of sociology departments was still atypical by the early 1990s, women had achieved equality with men in running English-Canada's sociology journals and its professional association, something that can be said about few other countries or regions.

Given this context, it is small wonder that the introduction of new schools of thought and the relative decline of old orthodoxies in the late 1980s and early 1990s were often mediated by feminism. For example, with a few noteworthy exceptions (e.g., Cheal, 1996), most of the postmodern analysis coming out of English Canada has been postmodernist feminism. Similarly, growing interest in interpretive and qualitative methods — and skepticism about the value of quantitative sociology — has often been associated with the adoption of a feminist methodology. Thus, perhaps more than elsewhere, the worldwide crisis of sociology has a distinct feminist flavour in English Canada.

Finally, let us turn to the third distinctive feature of Canadian sociology noted above. It is unremarkable that some sociologists in English Canada are more interested in abstract ideas than policy issues and would rather address like-minded intellectuals than the broader educated public. What is remarkable is that so many English-Canadian sociologists (in proportionate terms) have so little impact on the members of society, their ultimate constituency. In Quebec, as we have seen, many sociologists have acted as intellectual leaders and contributed in a major way to public life. The same is true, albeit to a lesser degree in proportionate terms, in the United States, where many sociologists help to set the terms of public debate on a wide range of policy issues. English-Canadian sociology is more radical than its American counterpart — political-economy and feminist approaches have been dominant forces in the ROC for 25 years — but, paradoxically, it is also less relevant to the lives of most citizens. To be sure, some leading English-Canadian sociologists are mindful of the policy implications of their research. But an outsider might justifiably be shocked to browse the major English-language sociology journals and see that sociologists have largely failed to contribute to public debate on the most pressing issues that face the country. Many Canadians are concerned about chronically high levels of structural unemployment, Quebec separatism, the implications of the North American Free Trade Agreement for the Canadian economy, and the threat to the health-care system posed by the forces of privatization. Yet the overwhelming majority of English-Canadian sociologists are mute on these issues. What John Porter wrote a third of a century ago is still true today: "It would probably be difficult to find another modern political system with such a paucity of participation from its scholars" (Porter, 1965: 503).

The degree to which sociologists play the role of public intellectual is related to the strength of social movements in their society. In Quebec, the nationalist movement has created abundant employment opportunities and a wide audience for public intellectuals. English Canada has no equivalent.

A factor of secondary importance in determining the prominence of public intellectuals is the relationship between branches of government. The American president and Congress are separated in a way that the Canadian prime minister and the Parliament are not. In Canada, if Parliament rejects an important bill supported by the prime minister, the government falls and a new election must be held. In contrast, in the US, even if Congress defeats a bill supported by the president, the president remains in office. As a result, every American congressperson is able to become a political entrepreneur in search of intellectuals who can shore up his or her policy positions. Not so in Canada, where the real experts tend to be employed not by the repre-

sentative structures of the state but by its administrative side (i.e., by the federal and provincial bureaucracies). The technocratic character of the bureaucratic audience virtually precludes the possibility that the resulting product will be written in a form accessible to the larger public, or even to the educated public (Brym and Myles, 1989).

Thus, its radicalism notwithstanding, the political environment of English-Canadian sociology prevents it from producing as many public intellectuals in proportionate terms as Quebec and the United States. The irony is that a community of scholars traditionally so concerned with the survival of the country has little to say about the many threats to its existence.

REFERENCES

Atwood, Margaret. (1972). *Survival: A Thematic Guide to Canadian Literature*. Toronto: Anansi.

Bernard, Paul, Marcel Fournier, and Céline Saint-Pierre. (1998). "Présentation: Au-delà_ de la crise, un second souffle pour la sociologie." *Sociologie et Sociétés*, 30, 1. On the World Wide Web at http://www.erudit.org/revue/socsoc/1998/v30/n1/001045ar.html (15 December 2002).

Bourque, Gilles, and Anne Legaré. (1979). *Le Québec, la question nationale*. Paris: Maspero.

Breton, Raymond. (1989). "Quebec Sociology: Agendas from Society or from Sociologists?" *Canadian Review of Sociology and Anthropology*, 26: 557–70.

Brym, Robert J. (1989). "The Great Canadian Identity Trap: Implications for the Comparative Study of Class and Power." *Canadian Journal of Sociology*, 14, 4: 495–501.

Brym, Robert J., with Bonnie J. Fox. (1989). *From Culture to Power: The Sociology of English Canada*. Toronto: Oxford University Press Canada.

Brym, Robert J., and John Myles. (1989). "Social Science Intellectuals and Public Issues in English Canada." *University of Toronto Quarterly*, 58, 4: 442–51.

Cheal, David. (1996). *New Poverty: Families in Postmodern Society*. Westport CT: Greenwood.

Clement, Wallace, and John Myles. (1994). *Relations of Ruling: Class and Gender in Postindustrial Society*. Montreal: McGill-Queen's University Press.

Daigle, Gérard, with the collaboration of Guy Rocher, eds. (1992). *Le Québec en jeu: comprendre les grands défis*. Montreal: Presses Universitaires de Montréal.

Dumont, Fernand. (1993). *Genèse de la société québécoise*. Montreal: Boréal.

Eichler, Margrit. (1988a). *Families in Canada Today: Recent Changes and Their Policy Consequences*, 2nd ed. Toronto: Gage.

Eichler, Margrit. (1988b). *Nonsexist Research Methods: A Practical Guide*. Boston: Allen and Unwin.

Enriquez, Eugéne. (1993). *L'analyse clinique dans les sciences humaines*. Montreal: Éditions Saint-Martin.

Fournier, Marcel, and Gilles Houle. (1980). "Le sociologie québécoise et son object: problématiques et débats." *Sociologie et sociétés*, 12, 2: 21–43.

Freitag, Michel. (1995). *Le naufrage de l'université et autres essais d'epistémologie politique*. Montreal: Nuit blanche éditeur and Paris: Éditions de la Découverte.

Godbout, Jacques. (1992). *L'esprit du don*. Paris: Éditions de la Découverte.

Kroker, Arthur. (1984). *Technology and the Canadian Mind: Innis/McCluhan/Grant*. Montreal: New World Perspectives.

Laxer, Gordon. (1989). *Open for Business: The Roots of Foreign Ownership in Canada*. Toronto: Oxford University Press Canada.

Maheu, Louis, and Arnaud Sales, eds. (1991). *Recomposition du politique*. Montreal: Presses Universitaires de Montréal and Paris: l'Harmattan.

Marchak, M. Patricia. (1991). *The Integrated Circus: The New Right and the Restructuring of Global Markets*. Montreal: McGill-Queen's University Press.

Porter, John. (1965). *The Vertical Mosaic: An Analysis of Social Class and Power in Canada*. Toronto: University of Toronto Press.

Renaud, Marc, Suzanne Doré, and Deena White. (1989). "Sociology and Social Policy: From a Love-Hate Relationship with the State to Cynicism and Pragmatism." *Canadian Review of Sociology and Anthropology*, 26: 426–56.

Rocher, Guy. (1972). *Talcott Parsons et la sociologie américaine*. Paris: Presses Universitaires de France.

Saint-Pierre, Céline, and Jacques Lazure, eds. (1990). "Savoir sociologique et transformation sociale." *Cahiers de recherche sociologique* (14).

Simard, Jean-Jacques. (1979). *La longue marche des technocrates*. Montreal: Éditions Saint-Martin.

Smith, Dorothy. (1987). *The Everyday World as Problematic: A Feminist Sociology*. Boston: Northeastern University Press.

Sociologie et Sociétés. (1999). 31, 2. Issue on "Citizenship and Social Identity." On the World Wide Web at http://www.erudit.org/revue/socsoc/1999/v31/n2/index.html (15 December 2002).

Vandelac, Louise. (1985). *Du travail et de l'amour*. Montreal: Éditions Saint-Martin.

PART 2 | FOUNDATIONS OF SOCIETY

Imagine standing at the end of a road 30 kilometres long. Allow each metre of the road to represent 100 000 years. The entire road will then signify the amount of time that has passed since life first appeared on the planet: about 3 billion years. From this long view, human beings are very recent arrivals, first assuming their present form only about 100 000 years ago, or just a metre down the road.

Recorded human history spans a much shorter distance. The development of agriculture, undoubtedly the single most important event in human history, took place approximately 10 000 years ago (only 10 centimetres down the road). The beginning of modern industry, arguably the second most important event in human history, dates from just over 200 years ago (a mere 2 millimetres down the road).

The evolution of agriculture and modern industry hint at what makes humans different from other animals: our advanced ability to create complex symbols (**abstraction**), make and use tools that improve our ability to take what we want from nature (**production**), and develop a complex social life (**cooperation**). These are the characteristics that enabled humans to survive and multiply despite a harsh natural environment and relatively poor physical endowments.

The first section of this book focuses on the building blocks of social life, the basic social mechanisms and processes involved in human abstraction, production, and cooperation. You will explore how symbolic communication between people, or **social interaction**, enables us to engage in social learning, or **socialization**. By means of socialization people acquire the languages, laws, science, values, customs, and beliefs — in short, the **culture** — of the groups to which they belong. When social interaction assumes a regular or patterned form, the relations among people form a **social structure**. Social structures may be, for example, hierarchical or egalitarian, tightly integrated or loosely organized; and different social-structural forms influence human thoughts and actions in different ways. The patterned behaviour of people embedded in a social structure is called a **role**. For instance, in some types of hierarchy, some people perform the role of slave, others the role of master. You will see that social structures and cultures are paradoxical features of social life. On the one hand, they are constructed anew, and often modified, at least a little, by each person in society. On the other hand, because social structures and cultures exist before any particular individual does, they help define and limit what the individual can think and what he or she can do. Hence the answer of many sociologists to the philosophers' debate about whether people are free or determined: They are both.

GLOSSARY

Abstraction is the human ability to create symbols in order to classify experience and generalize from it.

Cooperation is the human ability to give and receive aid from other humans. Social structures are typically created in order to facilitate cooperation.

Culture consists of the symbols that people use to communicate and organize their social life.

Production is a distinctively human mode of interacting with nature. It involves inventing tools and using them to make and improve the means of survival.

Roles are the behaviour patterns of people embedded in a social structure.

Social interaction is symbolic communication between people.

Socialization is the social process by which culture is learned.

Social structures are the patterns of social relations in which people are embedded and that provide opportunities for, and constrain, action.

PART 2A | SOCIAL INTERACTION AND SOCIALIZATION

Women working full-time in Canada's paid labour force earn about 73 cents for every dollar earned by men. Although that is up from 64 cents in 1985, there are still nearly five times more men than women in high-paying jobs (those in which people earn $51 000 or more per year). Meet the **glass ceiling**, a sociological barrier that makes it difficult for most women to rise to the top rungs of the job ladder.

What is the glass ceiling made of? Over 100 male chief executives and 400 female senior managers were asked in a 1998 survey sponsored by the Conference Board of Canada to indicate the top three barriers to women's advancement to senior levels. The barrier most frequently mentioned by the women: male stereotyping and preconceptions of women's roles and abilities. The barrier most frequently mentioned by the men: lack of job experience. These responses are not necessarily contradictory. In corporations and the public bureaucracy, male managers may slot talented women into communications and human resource jobs because of their preconceptions of what women are good at. Because of this bias, women may fail to get the kind of operational experience in the field or on the production line that could lead them to top managerial positions. In any case, the men and women who participated in the survey certainly agreed on one thing. The second most frequently chosen response by both groups was "commitment to family responsibilities." Married women still do most of the housework and child-care, while governments and corporations provide little in the way of parental support. The resulting career disruption, absenteeism, use of the part-time job option, and sheer physical and emotional exhaustion are major impediments to the advancement of women in the job hierarchy. Not surprisingly, therefore, among full-time workers in the paid labour force, *never-married* women earn about 90 percent as much as never-married men, but *married* women earn only about 65 percent as much as married men. Clearly, given current domestic, state, and corporate arrangements, women are penalized economically to the degree that their families are important to them.

In Chapter 4, Deborah Tannen explores another fascinating aspect of the glass ceiling: gender-specific conversational styles. Because the **primary socialization** (or early childhood upbringing) of women usually differs from that of men, they typically communicate in different ways at work. These differences matter in terms of career advancement. According to Tannen, "women's and men's conversational styles affect who gets heard, who gets credit, and what gets done at work." In other words, much miscommunication between men and women takes place on the job. Due to the distribution of power in the workplace and the nature of this miscommunication, the important contributions made by women often go unnoticed or even get mistaken for incompetence by male managers. Tannen's revealing case studies drive home the point that women's careers will benefit if women become more assertive at work and if male managers improve their ability to understand everyday, gendered, face-to-face interaction. Indeed, by assessing the impact of typical male and female conversational styles, Tannen's research contributes to this role change.

Social interaction no longer needs to be face-to-face, thanks to the development of the telephone and, more recently, the Internet. In the 1980s and early 1990s, most social scientists believed that social interaction by means of computer would involve only the exchange of information, not the formation of communities. Some science-fiction writers saw things differently. In his 1984 novel, *Neuromancer*, Vancouver-based author William Gibson coined the term "cyberspace." He envisioned a set of virtual communities where interaction takes place through computers, "a consensual hallucination experienced daily by billions of legitimate operators, in every nation. ... A graphic representation of data abstracted from the banks of every computer in the human system." In his 1992 novel, *Snow Crash*, American science-fiction writer Neal Stephenson popularized the idea of "avatars," or fictional representations of individuals in cyberspace. Stephenson believed that individuals in virtual communities could not only engage in a wide range of social interactions, but also present themselves differently from their real selves. In Stephenson's vision of cyberspace, people assume any persona they like through their avatars.

MIT sociologist Sherry Turkle has shown in her research that the future envisaged by Gibson and Stephenson has arrived. The Internet, she writes, has changed fundamentally the way the self is formed during social interaction. This is not just because the Internet creates many new opportunities to interact with people in distant locations. In addition, the Internet has spawned online role-playing games, discussion groups, "chat rooms," "weblogs" (or "blogs"), and "instant messaging" that allow users to interact anonymously. Anonymity encourages people to adopt new identities and explore parts of their selves they may have formerly concealed or suppressed. Moreover, the Internet allows people to play many roles simultaneously, rather than sequentially. In real life, you might play the role of son in the morning, student in the afternoon, and boyfriend in the evening. But on the Internet you can play different roles in different windows at the same time. Thus, according to Turkle, the Internet not only renders the self more plastic, but also divides it and distributes it over new psychic territory.

"Love at First Byte: Internet Dating in Canada" (online at www.societyinquestion4e.nelson.com) reports on an aspect of computer-assisted interaction that first emerged in the mid-1990s and is now commonplace: online dating. It is based on the world's first large-scale survey of online daters, conducted in Canada by Robert Brym and Rhonda Lenton. In 2000, 13 percent of adult Canadian Internet users — over 1.1 million people — had "read personal or dating ads" online or "checked out online dating services." The article outlines the social forces that are making online dating more popular. It also discusses the similarities and differences among online daters, Internet users in general, and the Canadian population as a whole. Some of its findings are perhaps surprising. For example, it turns out that most online daters are fairly ordinary, sociable individuals. Online dating has become mainstream. While over a quarter of online daters reported that they had misrepresented themselves online to stimulate interest, 60 percent said they formed at least one long-term relationship as a result of using online dating services, 37 percent met at least one person they regarded as a "partner," and 3 percent met someone they eventually married. Finally, people who meet online seem to have fewer negative experiences with their dates than people who meet their dates in more traditional ways.

In face-to-face and computer-mediated interaction, communication is two-way. There may be power differences between sender and receiver but everyone who is party to the interaction is by turns receiver *and* sender of messages. Not so when we interact with the mass media. When we watch television, for example, the television alone sends out messages and we alone receive them. Socialization occurs through a much more one-sided interaction process than is the case when we interact face-to-face or via computer.

Chapter 5 examines an important aspect of the mass media's one-sided communication with us. Eric Schlosser describes the explosion in children's advertising that began in the 1980s and the effects of this onslaught on children. We learn how advertisers, particularly those who use television, sell products by playing on children's deeply felt need to belong and their love of novelty and fun. Schlosser notes that many North American children can recognize some brands before they can speak. By the time they start school, most North American children are brand loyalists. Sociologists often refer to

secondary socialization as social learning that takes place after early childhood and outside the family. Here, however, we see that the entry of television into the nurseries of the nation blurs the distinction between primary and secondary socialization. Television is not a surrogate parent but it is a demanding big brother.

GLOSSARY

The **glass ceiling** is a sociological barrier that makes it difficult for most women to rise to the top rungs of the job ladder.

Primary socialization is social learning that takes place during early childhood, usually in the family.

Secondary socialization is conventionally defined as social learning that takes place after early childhood, usually outside the family. However, television blurs the distinction between primary and secondary socialization.

CRITICAL THINKING QUESTIONS

The www icons below indicate a question pertaining to an online article.

1. According to Deborah Tannen, what factors prevent women from advancing in the work force? Why do men get more recognition and rewards for the work they perform?

2. What is meant by the term "the glass ceiling?" Do you agree with Deborah Tannen that conversational style differences between men and women play a significant role in establishing the glass ceiling? What are some conversational rituals common among women? What are some other examples of language differences in the workplace that make women's experience different from men's experience?

3. How would you change gender socialization to reduce gender inequality in the workplace?

4. To what degree do Deborah Tannen's findings reflect gender inequality and socialization in the workplace? What are some other explanations for gender inequality in the workplace? How could Tannen make her argument more convincing and generalizable?

5. What are the similarities and differences among adult online daters, adult Internet users in general, and the Canadian adult population as whole?

6. Would you characterize online dating as less safe or safer than meeting dates in traditional ways? Why? How could you make online dating safer?

7. Why has online dating grown in popularity in recent years?

8. Does the traditional distinction between primary and secondary socialization still make sense? If so, why? If not, why not?

9. Has the mass media become as important as the family in early socialization? If so, why? If not, why not?

Chapter 4

The Glass Ceiling

DEBORAH TANNEN

A man who heads up a large division of a multinational corporation was presiding at a meeting devoted to assessing performance and deciding who would be promoted into the ranks of management. One after another, each senior manager got up, went down the list of individuals in his group and evaluated them, explaining whether or not they were promotable, and why. Though there were significant numbers of women in every group, not a single person singled out for advancement was female. One after another, every senior manager pronounced every woman in his group not ready for promotion because she lacked the necessary confidence. The division head began to doubt his ears. How could it be that all the talented women in the division suffered from a lack of confidence?

The situation described by this manager seemed to me to hold a clue to one described by a top executive at another multinational corporation who contacted me for help: "We started full of hope but we've reached an impasse. We are very successful at recruiting top women — they're creative, motivated, with fabulous credentials. They look just as good as the men when we hire them, if not better. But they don't get promoted. Years into our affirmative-action program, we still don't have any women in top management." The women who had been hired either were stuck at the level of middle management or had left the company or the field. He was describing what is sometimes referred to as the glass ceiling: an invisible barrier that seems to keep women from rising to the top. The problem is considered so widespread and serious that a Glass Ceiling Commission was created as part of the U.S. Civil Rights Act of 1991, chaired by the secretary of labor.

Many earnest executives sincerely believe that there is no glass ceiling but only a pipeline problem: When women have been in the pipeline long enough to work their way up, some will reach positions at the top. But the longer this situation prevails, the less tenable the pipeline theory becomes. According to a 1991 report by the United States Department of Labor, progress has been extremely slow. During the ten-year period from 1979 to 1989, the representation of women and minorities in the top executive positions of the one thousand largest American corporations rose from 3 percent to 5 percent. Another 1991 survey based on 94 randomly selected Fortune 1000–sized companies found women comprised 37 percent of employees, 17 percent of managers, but only $6\frac{1}{2}$ percent of executive-level managers.

The temptation is to see the cause of the glass ceiling as "sexism," and surely there is truth in this characterization. But "sexism" tells us where we are without telling us how we got there, and without providing help in getting out. I do not doubt there are men (as well as women) who do not wish to see women advance. It may be that the presence of women in their work lives is a complication that they did not bargain for when they chose their life's work. They may see every

Source: Excerpted from Deborah Tannen, *You Just Don't Understand* (New York: William Morrow and Company, 1994), pp. 132–59.

woman who fills a job in their field as taking that job from a man (rather than seeing half the men in their field as taking jobs that should have gone to qualified women). They may even feel that women do not belong in positions of authority, certainly not in authority over them. But not all men fit this description. There are many men who sincerely want to see women advance and are trying to do something about it.

In all the companies I visited, I observed what happened at lunchtime. I saw women who ate lunch in their offices and women who skipped lunch to run or exercise in the gym and women who ate in groups with other women or with men. I observed men who ate alone or with colleagues and a few who went home to have lunch with their wives. I observed young men who made a point of having lunch with their bosses, and men at high levels of management who ate lunch with the big boss. I rarely noticed women who sought out the highest-level person they could eat lunch with.

Early on, I became aware of an irony. On one hand, it was from men that I heard that if women weren't promoted, they simply weren't up to snuff, whereas women everywhere agreed that something outside themselves prevents women from advancing. But on the other hand, it was women, more often than men, who seemed to feel that all that was necessary for success was to do a great job, that superior performance would be recognized and rewarded. Yet looking around, I could see that much more seemed to go into getting recognized and rewarded, and I saw men more often than women behaving in these ways.

In addition to doing excellent work, you must make sure that your work is recognized. This may consist of making a point to tell your boss, or your boss's boss, what you have done — either orally, or by sending reports or copies of pertinent correspondence. If a group meets, the person who is the first to report the group's results may get the most credit for them, whether or not that person was the source of the ideas in the first place. When lunchtime comes, the one who eats lunch with the boss may be doing more

to get ahead than the one who stays in the office, eating a sandwich and working. Doing brilliantly at a project that no one knows about will do little good in terms of personal advancement; doing well in a high-profile project, or one that puts you into contact with someone in power who will thereby gain firsthand knowledge of your skill, may make the big difference when that person speaks up in a meeting at which promotions are decided. All of these dynamics could be derisively dismissed as "office politics," but they are simply a matter of human nature. How *are* the bosses to know who's done what? It is understandable (though not necessarily admirable) if they notice what happens before them and fail to notice what they would have to rout around to see. Put another way, influence flows along lines of affiliation and contact.

Here is a brief explanation of how conversational-style differences play a role in installing a glass ceiling. When decisions are made about promotion to management positions, the qualities sought are a high level of competence, decisiveness, and ability to lead. If it is men, or mostly men, who are making the decisions about promotions — as it usually is — they are likely to misinterpret women's ways of talking as showing indecisiveness, inability to assume authority, and even incompetence. A woman who feels it is crucial to preserve the appearance of consensus when making decisions because she feels anything else would appear bossy and arrogant begins by asking those around her for their opinions. This can be interpreted by her bosses as evidence that she doesn't know what she thinks should be done, that she is trying to get others to make decisions for her.

Again and again, I heard from women who knew they were doing a superior job and knew that their immediate co-workers knew it but the higher-ups did not. Either these women did not seem to be doing what was necessary to get recognition outside their immediate circle, or their superiors were not doing what was necessary to discern their achievements and communicate these upward. The kinds of things they were doing, like quietly coming up with the ideas that influence their groups and helping those around them to do their best, were not easily observed in the way that giving an impressive presentation is evident to all.

Even so small a linguistic strategy as the choice of pronouns can have the effect of making one's contributions more or less salient. It is not uncommon for many men to say "I" in situations where many women would say "we." One man told me, "I'm hiring a new manager; I'm going to put him in charge of my marketing division," as if he owned the corporation he worked for and was going to pay the manager's salary himself. Another talked about the work produced by all the members of his group in the same way: "This is what I've come up with on the Lakehill deal." In stark contrast, I heard a woman talking about what "we" had done, but on questioning discovered that it was really she alone who had done the work. By talking in ways that seemed to her appropriate to avoid sounding arrogant, she was inadvertently camouflaging her achievements and lessening the chances they would be recognized.

Sociolinguist Shari Kendall spent two days shadowing the technical director for a news/talk show at a local radio station. The woman, Carol, was responsible for making sure all the technical aspects of the show went smoothly, and she did her job very well. The following incident, presented and analyzed by Kendall, reveals both why Carol was so good at her job and why her excellence was likely to go unrecognized.

Carol knew she had a challenge on her hands: the "board op," the technician who sits at the soundboard (the radio show's control tower), was out sick, and Harold, the man filling in, was very, very nervous. He had to get all the right prerecorded bits of music and talk onto the air at the right time, make sure that callers got on just when the host wanted to talk to them, and generally throw switches in the right direction at the right moment — switches chosen from a dizzying array that made up the soundboard. Though Harold had a thorough technical knowledge of the equipment, he was unfamiliar with the routines of the show and inexperienced in this role. He was so nervous, he was shaking. For her part, Carol knew that if Harold fouled up, she would be blamed. She also knew that it is hard to throw a switch in the right direction with split-second timing when your hands are shaking. So, in addition to making sure he knew all the routines, she had to help Harold relax, which meant she had to make him feel competent and up to the job.

First Carol made sure that she gave Harold the information he needed to run the show and cautioned him about potential errors, all in a way that did not make him feel incompetent. Kendall points out that Carol gave Harold information phrased so as to imply it was not general technical knowledge (which he should have) but information particular to this show (which he could not be expected to have). For example, instead of saying, "Don't forget that tapes have a one-second lead-in," she said, "On this show everything has that one-second dead roll." Rather than saying, "Don't mix up the tapes; make sure you get them on in the right order," she said, "The only thing that people usually have trouble with is that they end up playing the promos and cassette tags and stuff in the wrong order." She avoided giving direct orders by saying, for example, "Probably we will want to re-cue the switch" when obviously it was he who had to re-cue the switch. In other words, Carol managed to apprise Harold of what he had to do without giving the impression she thought he was in danger of getting it wrong, and without framing him as potentially incompetent.

When she had done all she could to ensure that Harold knew what he had to do, Carol did not consider her job finished. She still wanted to make sure he felt calm and in control. She could have done this directly, by assuring him: "Now, look, you're a techie — you know a lot about this equipment; you'll do just fine," but when you think about it, that sounds condescending. Reassuring him would position her as superior and him as a novice needing reassurance. So she built up his confidence indirectly by framing him as an expert in an area in which he knew he was competent. She picked up his copy of *Mac Weekly* and engaged him in conversation about computers. He took this opportunity to give her information about purchasing used Macs. Kendall, who was in the room observing, noticed that Harold sat back, put his feet up, and visibly relaxed during this conversation. Right before her eyes, he was transformed from the nervous novice to the self-assured teacher. As I pictured this scene in my mind, it was as if someone had inserted a tube in his foot and blown him back up. Carol remained with Harold throughout the show, and when it proceeded without requiring anything of him, she again asked him questions about computers. She later told Kendall that she sometimes keeps technicians talking during periods when they're not working the sound-board to reduce tension and prevent errors.

Carol's efforts paid off. The self-confidence she inspired in Harold carried him through the show, which went without a hitch — a success that no one would know was due in part to Carol. Quite the contrary, imagine the impression their supervisor might have gotten had he come into the studio shortly before airtime and found Harold with his feet up, answering Carol's questions about computers. It is likely he would have thought, even if he didn't think it through, that Harold was very much in command of the situation, and Carol was a rather underqualified technical supervisor who needs technical advice from her pinch-hitting board op. How different this impression would have been had she been less competent — say, if she had rushed into the studio at the last moment, rather than early, and had been busily giving direct orders to the board op right up to airtime. Now that would have created an image of firm control, even as it would have rattled Harold and caused him to make errors.

In two other conversations Kendall analyzed, Carol was working with a colleague named Ron, the manager of another control room. It was Carol's job to see that all went smoothly with the technical aspects of her show; it was Ron's to see that everything went well with all shows. In this instance, Carol foresaw a potential problem with the telephone hookup to be used when her show went on the road the following week. Ron, however, had not foreseen any problem. Carol managed to call the potential problem to Ron's attention and to enlist his aid in heading it off. This show too went off without a hitch.

The proof of the pudding is in the eating. Carol had a low rate of technical errors on her watch. But the proof of her competence was invisible: the *absence* of errors. How do you get your bosses to see something that did not happen? Carol herself expressed concern that her excellent work and job skills might not be recognized when new appointments were made.

This example is hauntingly similar to one described by journalist Sharon Barnes, who tells of an office that had to switch from manual to computer operations. Barnes contrasts the way two managers, a man and a woman, handled the switch. The woman foresaw the need for computerization and gradually hired secretaries with computer experience, so the transfer to computerization took place without a ripple. The man did not prepare, so when the time came to switch to computers, his staff was in revolt. He mollified them by catering a lunch at which a consultant taught them what they needed to know. His troubleshooting was rewarded with a letter of commendation and a bonus. Barnes calls this "the white knight method" — letting problems happen and then ostentatiously solving them. This attracts attention, whereas making sure the problems don't arise in the first place is likely to go unnoticed — and unrewarded. According to Barnes, the white knight method is more common among men, the problem-preventing method more common among women.

Here is another example of a woman getting others to do their best at the risk of her own credibility. It comes from the curator of a private art collection. The young men who were responsible for constructing the art installations were generally competent with tools, but they were artists, not construction workers, so they did not always know how to execute what she wanted. Her job was complicated by the fact that they would not tell her when they didn't know how to do something. She noticed that one of the three had more knowledge and skill than the other two. He often set about doing a job while the others stood by — not asking, but not working either. She figured out that if *she* asked for an explanation, the other two, hearing the explanation they needed, would start working. In her own words, she got the information out by taking the stance "I'm just a girl who doesn't understand." Like Carol, she framed herself as ignorant in order to get the job done. In this situation, the curator was the boss. There was no one over her to observe the interaction, miss her intent, and conclude that she was underqualified. The knowledgeable man *did* once explode, "Every time we do something, you ask the same stupid questions!" She simply walked away and explained later — in private — what she was doing and why; he immediately understood and apologized.

This corrective was simple enough, but not likely to happen with a boss who might well say nothing but form his opinion and keep his counsel. Once again, there is no harm in assuming the ritual appearance of incompetence so long as everyone knows that it is ritual. When it is taken literally, and when only one person in an interaction is using that style, the strategic use of an appearance of incompetence can be mistaken for the real thing.

In these examples, women adjusted their ways of speaking to make sure the job got done. In a study I conducted, together with a colleague, of doctor–patient communication, I observed a pediatrician who spoke in a seemingly unsure way in order to buffer the emotional impact of what she was saying. Because her work involved not only examining her young patients and consulting with their parents but also reporting to other clinical staff, we had an unusual opportunity to hear her talking about the same information

under different circumstances, where she made a very different impression.

My colleague Cynthia Wallat and I analyzed the videotapes of the pediatrician talking in several different contexts about a child with cerebral palsy who had recently been diagnosed as having an arteriovenous malformation in her brain. In one of the videotapes, the doctor was examining the child in the presence of the mother. She pointed out that hemangiomas, visible as red marks on the child's face, were basically the same type of malady as the arteriovenous malformation in the brain. This gave the mother an opportunity to express a concern, and the doctor responded to the indirect question by providing an explanation:

> Mother: I've often wondered about how dangerous they — they are to her right now.
>
> Doctor: Well, um, the only danger would be from bleeding. *From* them. If there was any rupture, or anything like that. Which *can* happen. ... um, That would be the danger. *For* that. But they're ... mm ... *not* going to be something that will get worse as time goes on.
>
> Mother: Oh, I see.
>
> Doctor: But they're just *there*. Okay?

The doctor seemed rather insecure in this excerpt. Her talk was full of hesitations ("Well," "um," pauses). She uttered extra verbiage that didn't add meaning ("or anything like that," "which *can* happen"). She added phrases after her sentences were done ("the only danger would be from bleeding. *From* them." "That would be the danger. *For* that.") Emphasis seemed to fall in odd places.

But the doctor's hesitance and circumlocution in this setting contrasts sharply with her fluency and assurance when she talked about the same condition in a meeting with her peers. There she articulated part of the reason for her lack of fluency in speaking to the mother: She did not know how much information the parents already possessed about the danger of the child's condition, and she was not hesitant about the information she was imparting but about the effect it might have on the mother:

> uh, I'm not sure how much counselling has been *done*, *with* these parents, around the issue ... of the a-v malformation. Mother asked me questions, about the operability, inoperability of it, um, which I was not able to answer. She was told it was inoperable, and I had to say, "Well, yes, some of them are and some of them aren't." And I think that this is a — a — an important point. Because I don't know whether the possibility of sudden death, intracranial hemorrhage, if any of this has ever been dis*cuss*ed with these parents.

The physician, who showed so much hesitation and repetition in explaining the danger of the a-v malformation in the child's brain to the mother, expressed the same information in the staff meeting strongly and directly: There is a possibility of "sudden death, intracranial hemorrhage." When my colleague and I talked to the doctor, we were not surprised to learn that in speaking to the mother, she had been considering the emotional impact of telling a mother that her child might die suddenly because the a-v malformations could cause a hemorrhage in the brain at any time. When the mother asked this question, the doctor was in the midst of examining the child, so she could not take a half hour to discuss the danger and deal with the mother's reaction. Furthermore, the child was not her regular patient; she was examining her in connection with an educational placement. So she wanted to make sure that anything she said was coordinated with what the parents had been told by their own doctors.

The doctor's seeming lack of articulateness stemmed from her sensitivity to the potential impact of her diagnosis on the mother. And the mother appreciated this. She told us that of all the doctors she had taken her daughter to (and there had been many), she found this one to be the most considerate. In contrast, she said, she

had been given devastating diagnoses and prognoses by doctors with no regard to how the information might make her feel. For example, early in the child's life one doctor had told her in a matter-of-fact way, "Your child will be a vegetable," and then moved on to other topics.

Considering how the doctor spoke to the mother in comparison with how she spoke in a meeting with other medical staff makes it clear that her hesitance and other disfluencies did not reflect her level of competence but her awareness of the impact of what she was saying on the person she was talking to. But how often do we have a tape recording of the same person talking about the same topic in another setting? And how often, when women talk in tentative, even seemingly confused, ways in order to soften the impact of what they are saying, are they seen as lacking in competence or confidence?

We judge others not only by how they speak, but also by how they are spoken to. If we hear people asking lots of questions and being lectured to, an impression takes root that they don't know much and that those lecturing to them know a lot. This is why girls used to be told to make boys feel good on dates by asking them about subjects they're expert on and listening attentively to their answers. It is also what Japanese subordinates are supposed to do to make the boss feel important when they spend an evening with him, according to Japanese anthropologist Harumi Befu. Ellen Ryan and her colleagues have found that when a health care provider behaves in a patronizing way toward elderly patients, observers evaluate the patient as less competent.

If people are being spoken to as if they know nothing, we assume they know nothing. If people are addressed as if they are pretty smart, we assume they're pretty smart. This probably has some basis in most of the conversations we hear around us; it is a reasonable way to approach the world, trusting it to give us clues. But if women routinely take the position of novice or listener to make others feel smart, it is highly likely that those others, as well as observers, will underestimate their abilities.

Even worse, how a woman is addressed by others may have little to do with how she spoke in the first place. A consultant who worked fairly regularly with a small company commented to me that the new manager, a woman, was challenged and questioned by her subordinates more than her predecessor had been. He hadn't noticed any direct evidence that would lead him to question her competence, but he didn't really know the area they were working in. He added, "Maybe they know something about her abilities that I don't know." This seemed to me a double whammy. A woman who assumes a role that has previously been held by men will likely begin work with an aura of suspicion about whether she is up to the job, and this may well lead at least some of her co-workers to press her to justify her decisions. This very questioning then becomes evidence that she lacks competence — regardless of her real abilities.

Women may get more flak not only because their competence is in question but also because they are perceived as more vulnerable. A man who sails competitively commented that in a race, if he's looking for a hole, he picks a boat skippered by a woman or an older man; if you yell at them, he said, they are more likely to get out of the way. In the same spirit, Nancy Woodhull, a media and workplace consultant, points out that when corporate leadership changes and people jockey for position, they are especially likely to try to move in on turf held by women.

This insight helped me understand an experience that had puzzled and troubled me. I took part in a joint presentation together with a man whose style was different from mine. When I speak alone, as I generally do, I rarely get hostile comments from audience members because I always make sure to show the positive side of every style I mention and show the logic of *both* speakers when I give an example of a misunderstanding. I'm always careful not to make anyone look bad. My co-speaker, however, was more

provocative. Many of his anecdotes made either women or men look foolish.

When the question period came, this different tone had sparked a different response from the audience: some of the questions were hostile — especially from women. But most of the hostile questions were directed at me — including those that took issue with statements he alone had made. At the time, I was hurt and baffled, but in retrospect I could see what probably had happened. These women, riled by his tone and possibly put off by how he talked about women in some of his examples, looked at the stage and saw a large, gray-haired man with a caustic tone who did not hesitate to ruffle feathers, and a younger woman who was always conciliatory and eager not to offend. I was an easier target. My "open" manner left me open to attack.

Conversational rituals common among women involve each saving face for the other. One speaker is freed to take the one-down position (ritually, of course) because she can trust the other to, ritually again, bring her back up. Neither has to worry too much about casting herself in the best possible light because everyone is working together to save face for everyone else. I save your face, and you save mine.

Put another way, many of the conversational rituals common among women are designed to make others feel comfortable, and this often involves the speaker taking a one-down role herself, though as we have seen, this is usually a ritual the other person is expected to match. At the same time women who observe these rituals are not investing a lot of energy in making sure they themselves do not appear one-down, which means that's just where they may end up.

A couple of years ago, I arrived at a class I was teaching and found a newspaper journalist waiting outside the door. She told me she had been trying to get me on the phone, but because she had not succeeded in reaching me at my office, she had come ahead to the class because she wanted to sit in and write a short piece about me. Now the number of people who want to sit in on my classes, for various reasons, is considerable, so I have long had a firm policy that I do not permit auditors or visitors for any reason. Since I always conduct classes not as lectures but as discussions among students sitting in a circle, a stranger in our midst is a significant intrusion. There was no question in my mind that had the journalist gotten me on the phone beforehand, I would have told her this. But here I was faced with a poor woman who had made the trek all the way to my class, had waited for a long time, and was now looking at me directly and plaintively. I felt culpable for not having been in my office when she was trying to reach me, and I have a strong impulse to help everyone and inconvenience no one. I had to make a snap decision; I let her in.

At the end of the class, I collected assignments, and a few students had not followed my instructions. To save face for them, I said something like, "I'm sorry if my instructions weren't clear." I suspect some readers will be able to foresee what happened: Lo and behold, in the article she wrote, the journalist took this ritual apology as a literal admission of fault and used it to make me look bad: Imagine, she wrote, here's this expert on communication, and she can't even give comprehensible assignment instructions to her students.

I am sure that some people will think, "It serves her right. She opened herself up to this." And they are correct. The impulses that drove me to make others feel comfortable were driving me in a direction opposite from self-protection, which would have led me to deny the journalist entrance to my class (it was her problem, not mine, if she made the trip without getting permission to sit in), or, once she was there, would have led me to monitor my behaviour so as not to say anything that might appear as weakness — the kind of self-monitoring that leads others (including many men) not to apologize, take blame, admit ignorance, and so on.

It is interesting to consider, however, how well my impulse to accommodate the journalist worked for her. She risked rejection by showing up at the door of my class unannounced. In a way, she was counting on me to observe interactional rituals common among women, and in this case her hunch paid off.

All these examples dramatize how ways in which women are likely to talk may mask their true competence in the view of those who are required to judge their performance. When forced to evaluate people they do not work with day-to-day, executive and high-level managers will necessarily be influenced by what little exposure they have had to the people they are judging. In addition to the fleeting impressions of chance encounters, for many top executives this may mean the few times they have observed lower managers directly — when they are making presentations. And this is yet another situation in which knowing a lot doesn't automatically transfer into showing what you know. If most women's conversational rituals have prepared them for private speaking, the importance of formal presentations is yet another aspect of moving through "the pipeline" that puts many women at a disadvantage.

Public speaking is frightening for almost everyone. But standing up in front of a large group of people, commanding attention, and talking authoritatively are extensions of the socialization most boys have been forced to endure, as boys in groups tend to vie for centre stage, challenge the boys who get it, and deflect the challenges of others. Many of the ways women have learned to be likable and feminine are liabilities when it comes to public presentations. Most girls' groups penalize a girl who stands out or calls attention to herself in an obvious way.

A woman who works as a trainer for business people coming to the United States realized that a disproportionate amount of the criticism she and her colleagues delivered to the trainees was directed at women, especially in the nebulous category of "professional presence." They found themselves telling women, more often than men, that they did not speak loudly enough, did not project their voices, should stop cocking their heads to one side, should try to lower the pitch of their voices. A few women were told that their way of dressing was too sexy, their manner too flirtatious, if they wanted to be taken seriously in the American business environment. In a sense, they were appearing too "feminine." But there were also women who were told that they were too challenging and abrasive. They launched into questions without a lead-in or hedges; they asked too many insistent questions; they did not tilt their heads at all or seemed to be tilting them in challenging ways. Although the trainers did not think of it in these terms, you could say that these women were not "feminine" enough.

In at least one case, a particular trainee had to be told that she was coming across as both too flirtatious and too confrontational. In wondering why such a large percentage of women in her program (a small one to start with) had the basic skills down cold, yet seemed to be undermining their own effectiveness by their nonverbal behaviour, the trainer concluded that they had a very fine line to walk: The range of behaviours considered acceptable for them was extremely narrow. And, perhaps most important, the American professional business culture in which they were learning to fit was not only American but also American male.

All of the factors mentioned by the trainer indicate that making presentations is a prime example of an activity in which behaviour expected of women is at odds with what is expected of an effective professional. In fact, the very act of standing up in front of a group talking about ideas is something that was unthinkable for women not so long ago. The nineteenth-century abolitionist Abby Kelley was reviled as a "Jezebel" and "fornicator" because of her public speaking. Because she was physically attractive, men saw her as a dangerous seductress.

Once a woman (or man) does make public presentations, she (or he) is open to challenge or even attack. Many women have been told they cave in too quickly rather than stand their ground. Being able to deal effectively with public challenges is not something that comes easily to many women (or men). And there are regional and cultural differences in styles as well. One man, a sociologist from a small town, was invited to give a lecture at a major East Coast university where he was being considered for a faculty position. The questions from the floor were so authoritative that he became convinced he was talking to people who had obviously done research in his area, research that he had somehow missed in his review of the literature. After the talk, which he was sure he had bombed, he went to the library and scoured the sources for references to these men's work — references that did not exist. To his amazement (he had taken literally the tone of contempt in their questioning), he got the job. So he had occasion to discover that they had done no work in the field at all; they were simply challenging him to see how well he could defend his claims — and were satisfied and pleased with his rebuttals. Although he had successfully defended himself against this ritual assault, he had gotten the impression that they had more basis for their challenges than they actually had.

There are many women who are very successful public speakers. I once noted the different public-speaking styles of two presenters at a meeting — a man and a woman. Both were excellent speakers, but he filled the room with his expansive presence, whereas she brought the room in close. He told stories as if he were in church preaching to a crowd; she told them as if she were sitting in her living room with friends. (An audience member commented on how "natural" she sounded.) She did not tell jokes, as he did, but she was humorous. Whereas he remained straight-faced after saying something funny, she laughed along with her audience. The woman's public speaking was successful in a private-speaking sort of way, whereas his was successful in a more public-speaking, oratorical way.

This is not to say that there is only one way for a woman or a man to give successful presentations. Both women and men must learn to handle this special situation well in order to get recognition for the work they do, but women's socialization is usually more at odds with the requirements of presenting to a group.

If one of the reasons women are not promoted is that they are spending more time doing their jobs and less time promoting themselves, can the solution be for women to begin promoting themselves more? Veronica had an observant boss who noticed that many of the ideas coming out of the group were hers, but it was often someone else in the group who trumpeted the ideas around the office and got credit for them. The boss told Veronica she should take more credit for her ideas. But Veronica wasn't comfortable doing that. She tried and found she simply didn't enjoy work if she had to approach it as a grabbing game. She liked the atmosphere of shared goals and was comfortable in the knowledge that she was part of a group effort. Striving to get credit for herself felt like a lonely and not very admirable endeavour. Trying to follow her boss's advice made coming to work a lot less fun.

In a related pattern, I spoke to many women who claimed they simply were not comfortable standing out. And I spoke to men who had noticed women who seemed to feel that way. For example, a man who headed an educational film company called a woman into his office and told her the good news that one of the clients with whom she had dealt in the past had decided to make a large purchase for a new film library. Rather than saying, "Great! I'll give them a call right away," the woman said, "Maybe someone else should follow up this time, since I've already got the highest sales in the group for the month." Even though the sales staff did not work on commission, the manager was incredulous. "They *asked* for you," he said. "They liked working with you before, and you're the one they want. What kind of a company would I be running if I didn't give my clients the person they ask for?" This convinced her, and she accepted the assignment. But she had to think of it in terms of what was good for the company rather than what was good for her — or at least be *assigned* the job rather than appear to be *taking* it.

I saw this same force at work in a talented graduate student who had been working for me as a research assistant in addition to participating in a seminar I taught. One day I told her, in private, that I owed her two apologies. The first was because she had handed me a bill for her services as research assistant as we were leaving class, and I had misplaced it. The second was that I feared I had embarrassed her in class when I unthinkingly corrected a minor grammatical error she had made while speaking. She told me that, since I was bringing it up, there was something that had bothered her, but it wasn't either of the two things I mentioned. It was something else entirely. The students had gathered around me after the last class meeting of the term, discussing who would take the next course. She had expressed frustration that she could not afford to take the course, and everyone knew my policy against allowing auditors. But I had said, "Maybe I can make an exception for you." She had not been bothered by my publicly correcting her grammar or by my neglecting to pay her on time. What bothered her was my singling her out for special treatment.

Favouritism can wreak havoc in any group. But whereas anyone can see that those not in favour would resent those who are, it seems that many women are uncomfortable not only being out, but also being too obviously in. This has resounding implications for promotability. Unobtrusively doing excellent work does not threaten group belonging. But getting special recognition does. It may well spark resentment from co-workers. Resentment, in fact, can result from almost any action that ensures getting credit, especially from those above. In a large organization, everyone is really the servant of many masters. Whereas you are taking direction, or even orders, from an immediate supervisor, that supervisor is answerable to someone above, who is answerable to someone above that. And somewhere in the upper layers are those who determine your fate when it comes to ranking and promotion. Much depends, therefore, on your ability to make contact with the people above your boss. But if you do, you may well incur the rancour of your immediate boss and your peers. And this may be a burden that more women than men are hesitant to risk.

Besides the danger of provoking peer resentment (or related to it) is the different ways women and men are inclined to view self-aggrandizing talk. Letting others know about what you have done is almost always labelled boasting by women, and boasting is something most women have learned early on to avoid. In contrast, many men assume they have to let others know what they've done in order to get the recognition they deserve. Bragging about his exploits got Othello the hand of Desdemona; Kate had to learn to keep her mouth shut to marry Petruchio — the "shrew" who spoke up had to be "tamed."

The example of a professional couple illustrates the attitudes many women and men have toward displaying or downplaying their own accomplishments. Bridget and Sean were both successful real estate agents, but they had different habits of self-presentation. Sean made sure to let new acquaintances know what he had done; Bridget played down what she had done and assumed people would eventually learn of it from others and like her all the more for her modesty when they did. Bridget thought Sean was boastful; he thought she was foolishly and inappropriately self-deprecating. Neither thought of the other's way of talking as related to gender; they thought they were dealing with issues of personal character.

A widely publicized incident involving political consultant Ed Rollins is evidence that talking about one's accomplishments is a ritual common among men. Rollins managed the campaign of Republican candidate Christine Todd Whitman in her 1993 bid for the governorship of New Jersey. At a breakfast for journalists shortly after Whitman's victory, Rollins boasted that he had won the election for his candidate by his successful efforts to keep blacks from voting — for example, by making donations to African American churches in exchange for the ministers'

agreement not to preach get-out-the-vote sermons. When this boast hit the headlines, there was talk of knocking the candidate out of office and sending Rollins to jail. So he quickly explained that his boasts had been groundless, designed to embarrass his opponent James Carville, who was campaign manager for the Democratic candidate Jim Florio.

It is not clear whether Rollins was telling the truth when he first made the boast or when he later claimed it had been baseless. Whichever it was — and this may never be known — the case is a revealing example of the ritualized role of boasting. Rollins saw his role of campaign manager as a head-to-head fight with another man, Carville, and wanted to take ostentatious credit for his victory, so he boasted in a group about what he had done — or felt he could get away with claiming to have done. Another famous (or infamous) instance of boasting occurred when police located one of the men who allegedly had arranged an attack on figure-skater Nancy Kerrigan in part because he — rival skater Tonya Harding's "bodyguard" — had boasted openly to fellow students about what he had accomplished.

This incident, and the story of Ed Rollins's boasting, brought to mind an intriguing statement by Rupert Allason, a British member of Parliament who is an authority on the British intelligence services. He was explaining why he thinks women make better spies than men. On the occasion of the appointment of Stella Rimington as the first female director-general of the British Internal Security Service, Allason commented, "Women have always been good security operatives. While men tend to gossip about their job to impress friends, women gossip about trivia and keep their real secrets."

Linguist Penelope Eckert made similar observations of high school girls' and boys' secret-keeping habits. The high school girls Eckert studied told her that boys were better at keeping secrets than girls. Eckert hypothesized that this is not because boys are morally superior to girls but because, given the sex-separate social structure of the high schools, girls have something to gain by revealing other girls' secrets, whereas boys do not. Girls gain status by their social network — whom they are friends with. So showing that you know a girl's secrets is a good way to prove to others that you are friends with her. Boys, on the other hand, gain status by their own accomplishments. They gain nothing by demonstrating that they are close friends with girls, so they have no incentive to repeat their secrets. Instead, the boys are tempted to talk about what they've done or can claim to have done. This explains why, in the situation of a spy or a campaign manager, males' and females' abilities to hold their tongues are not-so-mysteriously reversed.

Whatever the motivation, women are less likely than men to have learned to blow their own horns — which means they may well not get credit for the work they have done, or, as Ed Rollins at least claimed, try to get credit for what they have not done. More women than men seem to have a sense that if they do this, they will not be liked. And the spectre of working in an environment where they are not liked may be more than they are willing to risk. The congeniality of the work environment is important to everyone, but the requirement that everyone like each other may be more central to women's notion of congeniality, whereas men may value other types of congeniality, such as easy banter. One man who heads a large division of a corporation commented that in recruiting for diversity, they usually get the minority men they want by offering them the most generous package of remuneration. In recruiting women, however, they are most successful by sending women to recruit other women. If the recruiter can convince a prospective woman that the company provides a positive work environment, it is successful in recruiting her even if she has competing offers that are more lucrative. In addition to providing evidence that a congenial work environment is very important to many women, this may also say something about why women are chronically paid less than men in comparable positions.

The most eloquent and amusing description I know of why someone fails to get credit for her work and how she changes her behaviour to rectify the situation is in a short story by the Irish writer Maeve Binchy entitled "King's Cross." As the story opens, Sara Gray, an overworked and underappreciated assistant manager in a travel office, is interviewing a prospective secretary named Eve, who turns out to be a mixture of the Lone Ranger and Mary Poppins. Eve swoops into Sara Gray's life and transforms it by showing her how to get recognition — and promotion.

The first thing Eve does is insist on addressing her boss as "Miss Gray," even though Sara protests that it sounds "snooty." Eve points out that the male managers and assistant managers all call Sara by her first name, though she addresses many of them as "Mr." When speaking of Miss Gray to others, she adopts a tone of respect bordering on awe that gradually creeps into the attitudes of others in the office. Eve tells Sara that "it is absolutely intolerable the way that people think they can come barging in here, taking advantage of your good nature and picking your brains, interrupting us and disturbing you from whatever you are doing." To put a stop to this, Eve sets herself up at the door to Sara's office and insists that anyone who wants to see Miss Gray must make an appointment.

Eve discovers that Sara has not been taking advantage of available perks such as an account at a taxi firm, a clothing allowance, and a small fund for redecorating her office. With the latter, Eve acquires a conference table and suggests how Sara might use it. She points out that when Sara last developed a wildly successful marketing idea, no one but her boss, Garry Edwards, knew that it had been hers, so he got the credit and the reward, since it came out of his division. Eve counsels:

> Next time, I suggest you invite Mr. Edwards and his boss and the marketing director and one or two others to drop in quite casually — don't dream of saying you are calling a meeting, just

suggest that they might all like to come to your office one afternoon. And then, at a nice table where there is plenty of room and plenty of style, put forward your plans. That way they'll remember you.

When Sara prepares work for Garry Edwards, Eve sends copies to others, so everyone knows it's her work. She encourages Sara to get an assistant who can cover her desk, so indispensability will not be an excuse for failing to send her to conferences or, eventually, promote her. She makes sure that Sara's name is on the list of guests to social events attended by executives. When Garry Edwards tries to undo Sara by blaming her for his own mistake, Eve's filing system yields a document proving that Sara had recommended the correct course of action. Garry Edwards is out, and Sara Gray gets his job, which she had, after all, been doing, without remuneration, all along.

This is, sadly for us all, just a fantasy, a work of fiction, though a delightful one to read. How nice it would be if Eve swept into each of our lives and ensured we got the credit we deserve. But the story, oversimplified (and entertaining) as it is, captures some of what individuals can do (and often fail to do) to achieve that felicitous result on their own.

I do not wish to imply that all inequities in recognition and promotion result from the behaviour — linguistic or otherwise — of individuals. Some forces are out of our hands, or at least extremely difficult to influence. A phenomenon having little to do with conversational style that may handicap women is mentoring.

An academic position was advertised at a major university. Everyone was welcome to apply. But one candidate was a favourite of someone on the faculty. The faculty member saw to it that his candidate was the last one scheduled for a presentation, and he let him know when the other candidates were giving their presentations. This enabled his candidate to attend the others' presentations and gauge the reaction of the audience — what went over well, what fell flat, what concerns were reflected in the questions asked. He took this information into account in planning his own talk, and he wowed the department enough to get the job. At least one woman who had applied for the job felt that she had been locked out by an "old-boy network."

Similar patterns can obtain in promotion, where one candidate has established a relationship with someone involved in the search. He may be informed of the opening earlier, told what is best to emphasize in his application or interview, and given an advantageous position in the queue. Is this illegal preferential treatment or just "mentoring," a system by which a younger person has a supporter and ally higher up who "brings him along"? If such supporter relationships are likely to spring up between someone established in the organization and someone new to it, it is likely that the older person will be male (since he probably entered the organization when there were few or no women in it) and also likely that the established person will be drawn to someone who reminds him of himself at that stage — who is therefore probably male too. It is not intentional "sexism," yet it is a pattern that favours men over women — not all men, of course, but it is a structure women are less likely to fit into.

At the same time that we seek to understand how ways of talking can work against women, we also must bear in mind that it may be harder for women to get promoted regardless of how they speak. Marjorie and Lawrence Nadler list a number of studies that show that stereotypes work against women. They cite, for example, Lea Stewart, who found that women are often given different task assignments than men with similar positions and qualifications, and the ones they are given are not those that lead to advancement. They also cite Cynthia Fink, who shows that there is a widespread belief that men are simply more suited to management. Finally, Garda Bowman, Beatrice Worthy, and Stephen Grayser show that managers believe women just don't have the decision-making skills or aggressiveness needed to succeed in managerial positions.

Not every woman, or every man, wants to be promoted, though the argument that women don't really want high-pressure jobs has been used to avoid giving them the chance. There are women and men who choose downward mobility, but I do not think there are many people who would choose not to have their work recognized. People whose contributions are appreciated become motivated to continue and increase their efforts, whereas those whose contributions are overlooked are more likely to leave, perhaps citing other reasons for their decision. So failing to recognize the achievements of those with styles that do not call attention to themselves is a loss not only to the individuals but also to the companies.

Talking, like walking, is something we do without stopping to question how we are doing it. Just as we cheerfully take a walk without thinking about which foot to move forward (unless a puddle blocks our path), we simply open our mouths and say what seems self-evidently appropriate, given the situation and person we are talking to. In other words, ordinary conversation has a ritual character, and the conversational rituals typical of women and men, though they obviously have a lot in common — otherwise we couldn't talk to each other — can also be different. And even subtle differences can lead to gross misinterpretation. In a situation in which one person is judging another and holds the key to a gate the other wants to pass through, the consequences of style differences can be dire indeed.

If more and more people understand the workings of conversational style, they will be able to adjust their own ways of talking and stand a better chance of understanding how others mean what they say. But at the same time, the more people gain an understanding of conversational style, the less necessary it will be for others to adjust their style. If supervisors learn to perceive outstanding performance regardless of the performer's style, it will be less necessary for individuals to learn to display their talents. On that happy day, the glass ceiling will become a looking glass through which a fair percentage of Alices will be able to step.

Chapter 5

Kids as Customers

ERIC SCHLOSSER

Twenty-five years ago, only a handful of American companies directed their marketing at children — Disney, McDonald's, candy makers, toy makers, manufacturers of breakfast cereal. Today children are being targeted by phone companies, oil companies, and automobile companies, as well as clothing stores and restaurant chains. The explosion in children's advertising occurred during the 1980s. Many working parents, feeling guilty about spending less time with their kids, started spending more money on them. One marketing expert has called the 1980s "the decade of the child consumer."[1] After largely ignoring children for years, Madison Avenue began to scrutinize and pursue them. Major ad agencies now have children's divisions, and a variety of marketing firms focus solely on kids. These groups tend to have sweet-sounding names: Small Talk, Kid Connection, Kid2Kid, the Gepetto Group, Just Kids, Inc. At least three industry publications — *Youth Market Alert*, *Selling to Kids*, and *Marketing to Kids Report* — cover the latest ad campaigns and market research. The growth in children's advertising has been driven by efforts to increase not just current, but also future, consumption. Hoping that nostalgic childhood memories of a brand will lead to a lifetime of purchases, companies now plan "cradle-to-grave" advertising strategies. They have come to believe what Ray Kroc and Walt Disney realized long ago — a person's "brand loyalty" may begin as early as the age of two.[2] Indeed, market research has found that

children often recognize a brand logo[3] before they can recognize their own name.

The discontinued Joe Camel ad campaign, which used a hip cartoon character to sell cigarettes, showed how easily children can be influenced by the right corporate mascot. A 1991 study published in the *Journal of the American Medical Association* found that nearly all of America's six-year-olds could identify Joe Camel,[4] who was just as familiar to them as Mickey Mouse. Another study found that one-third of the cigarettes illegally sold to minors were Camels.[5] More recently, a marketing firm conducted a survey in shopping malls across the country, asking children to describe their favorite TV ads. According to the CME KidCom Ad Traction Study II,[6] released at the 1999 Kids' Marketing Conference in San Antonio, Texas, the Taco Bell commercials featuring a talking chihuahua were the most popular fast food ads. The kids in the survey also liked Pepsi and Nike commercials, but their favorite television ad was for Budweiser.

The bulk of the advertising directed at children today has an immediate goal. "It's not just getting kids to whine,"[7] one marketer explained in *Selling to Kids*, "it's giving them a specific reason to ask for the product." Years ago sociologist Vance Packard described children as "surrogate salesmen"[8] who had to persuade other people, usually their parents, to buy what they wanted. Marketers now use different terms to explain the intended response to their ads —

such as "leverage," "the nudge factor," "pester power." The aim of most children's advertising is straightforward: get kids to nag their parents and nag them well.

James U. McNeal, a professor of marketing at Texas A&M University, is considered America's leading authority on marketing to children. In his book *Kids As Customers* (1992), McNeal provides marketers with a thorough analysis of "children's requesting styles and appeals."[9] He classifies juvenile nagging tactics into seven major categories. A *pleading* nag is one accompanied by repetitions of words like "please" or "mom, mom, mom." A *persistent* nag involves constant requests for the coveted product and may include the phrase "I'm gonna ask just one more time." *Forceful* nags are extremely pushy and may include subtle threats, like "Well, then, I'll go and ask Dad." *Demonstrative* nags are the most high-risk, often characterized by full-blown tantrums in public places, breath-holding, tears, a refusal to leave the store. *Sugar-coated* nags promise affection in return for a purchase and may rely on seemingly heartfelt declarations like "You're the best dad in the world." *Threatening* nags are youthful forms of blackmail, vows of eternal hatred and of running away if something isn't bought. *Pity* nags claim the child will be heartbroken, teased, or socially stunted if the parent refuses to buy a certain item. "All of these appeals and styles may be used in combination," McNeal's research has discovered, "but kids tend to stick to one or two of each that prove most effective … for their own parents."

McNeal never advocates turning children into screaming, breath-holding monsters. He has been studying "Kid Kustomers"[10] for more than thirty years and believes in a more traditional marketing approach. "The key is getting children to see a firm … in much the same was as [they see] mom or dad, grandma or grandpa,"[11] McNeal argues. "Likewise, if a company can ally itself with universal values such as patriotism, national defense, and good health, it is likely to nurture belief in it among children."

Before trying to affect children's behavior, advertisers have to learn about their tastes.[12] Today's market researchers not only conduct surveys of children in shopping malls, they also organize focus groups for kids as young as two or three. They analyze children's artwork, hire children to run focus groups, stage slumber parties and then question children into the night. They send cultural anthropologists into homes, stores, fast food restaurants, and other places where kids like to gather, quietly and surreptitiously observing the behavior of prospective customers. They study the academic literature on child development, seeking insights from the work of theorists such as Erik Erikson and Jean Piaget. They study the fantasy lives of young children, then apply the findings in advertisements and product designs.

Dan S. Acuff — the president of Youth Market System Consulting and the author of *What Kids Buy and Why* (1997) — stresses the importance of dream research. Studies suggest that until the age of six, roughly 80 percent of children's dreams are about animals.[13] Rounded, soft creatures like Barney, Disney's animated characters, and the Teletubbies therefore have an obvious appeal to young children. The Character Lab, a division of Youth Market System Consulting, uses a proprietary technique called Character Appeal Quadrant Analysis to help companies develop new mascots. The technique purports to create imaginary characters who perfectly fit the targeted age group's level of cognitive and neurological development.

Children's clubs have for years been considered an effective means of targeting ads and collecting demographic information; the clubs appeal to a child's fundamental need for status and belonging. Disney's Mickey Mouse Club, formed in 1930, was one of the trailblazers. During the 1980s and 1990s, children's clubs proliferated, as corporations used them to solicit the names, addresses, zip codes, and personal comments of young customers. "Marketing messages sent through a club not only can be personalized," James McNeal advises, "they can be tailored for a certain age or geographical group."[14] A well-designed and well-run children's club can be extremely good for business. According to one Burger King executive, the creation of a Burger King Kids Club in 1991 increased the sales of children's meals as much as 300 percent.[15]

The Internet has become another powerful tool for assembling data about children. In 1998 a federal investigation of Web sites aimed at children found that 89 percent requested personal information from kids; only 1 percent required that children obtain parental approval before supplying the information.[16] A character on the McDonald's Web site told children that Ronald McDonald was "the ultimate authority in everything."[17] The site encouraged kids to send Ronald an e-mail revealing their favorite menu item at McDonald's, their favorite book, their favorite sports team — and their name.[18] Fast food Web sites no longer ask children to provide personal information without first gaining parental approval; to do so is now a violation of federal law, thanks to the Children's Online Privacy Protection Act, which took effect in April of 2000.

Despite the growing importance of the Internet, television remains the primary medium for children's advertising. The effects of these TV ads have long been a subject of controversy. In 1978, the Federal Trade Commission (FTC) tried to ban all television ads directed at children seven years old or younger. Many studies had found that young children often could not tell the difference between television programming and television advertising. They also could not comprehend the real purpose of commercials and trusted that advertising claims were true. Michael Pertschuk, the head of the FTC, argued that children need to be shielded from advertising that preys upon their immaturity. "They cannot protect themselves," he said, "against adults who exploit their present-mindedness."[19]

The FTC's proposed ban was supported by the American Academy of Pediatrics, the National Congress of Parents and Teachers, the Consumers Union, and the Child Welfare League, among others. But it was attacked by the National Association of Broadcasters, the Toy Manufacturers of America, and the Association of National Advertisers. The industry groups lobbied Congress to prevent any restrictions on children's ads and sued in federal court to block Pertschuk from participating in future FTC meetings on the subject. In April of 1981, three months after the inauguration of President Ronald Reagan, an FTC staff report argued that a ban on ads aimed at children would be impractical, effectively killing the proposal. "We are delighted by the FTC's reasonable recommendation,"[20] said the head of the National Association of Broadcasters.

The Saturday-morning children's ads that caused angry debates twenty years ago now seem almost quaint. Far from being banned, TV advertising aimed at kids is now broadcast twenty-four hours a day, closed-captioned and in stereo. Nickelodeon, the Disney Channel, the Cartoon Network, and the other children's cable networks are now responsible for about 80 percent of all television viewing by kids.[21] None of these networks existed before 1979. The typical American child now spends about twenty-one hours a week watching television — roughly one and a half months of TV every year.[22] That does not include the time children spend in front of a screen watching videos, playing video games, or using the computer. Outside of school, the typical American child spends more time watching television than doing any other activity except sleeping. During the course of a year, he or she watches more than thirty thousand TV commercials.[23] Even the nation's youngest children are watching a great deal of television. About one-quarter of American children between the ages of two and five have a TV in their room.[24]

PERFECT SYNERGY

Although the fast food chains annually spend about $3 billion on television advertising, their marketing efforts directed at children extend far beyond such conventional ads.[25] The McDonald's Corporation now operates more than eight thousand playgrounds at its restaurants in the United States.[26] Burger King has more than two thousand. A manufacturer of "playlands" explains why fast food operators build these largely plastic structures: "Playlands bring in children, who bring in parents, who bring in money."[27] As American cities and towns spend less money on children's recreation, fast food restaurants have become gathering spaces for families with young children. Every month about 90 percent of American children between the ages of three and nine visit a McDonald's.[28] The seesaws, slides, and pits full of plastic balls have proven to be an effective lure. "But when it gets down to brass tacks," a *Brandweek* article on fast food notes, "the key to attracting kids is toys, toys, toys."[29]

The fast food industry has forged promotional links with the nation's leading toy manufacturers, giving away simple toys with children's meals and selling more elaborate ones at a discount. The major toy crazes of recent years — including Pokémon cards, Cabbage Patch Kids, and Tamogotchis — have been abetted by fast food promotions. A successful promotion easily doubles or triples the weekly sales volume of children's meals. The chains often distribute numerous versions of a toy, encouraging repeat visits by small children and adult collectors who hope to obtain complete sets. In 1999 McDonald's distributed eighty different types of Furby. According to a publication called *Tomart's Price Guide to McDonald's Happy Meal Collectibles*, some fast food giveaways are now worth hundreds of dollars.[30]

Rod Taylor, a *Brandweek* columnist, called McDonald's 1997 Teenie Beanie Baby giveaway one of the most successful promotions in the history of American advertising. At the time McDonald's sold about 10 million Happy Meals in a typical week. Over the course of ten days in April of 1997, by including a Teenie Beanie Baby with each purchase, McDonald's sold about 100 million Happy Meals. Rarely has a marketing effort achieved such an extraordinary rate of sales among its intended consumers. Happy Meals are marketed to children between the ages of three and nine; within ten days about four Teenie Beanie Baby Happy Meals were sold for every American child in that age group. Not all of those Happy Meals were purchased for children. Many adult collectors bought Teenie Beanie Baby Happy Meals, kept the dolls, and threw away the food.

The competition for young customers has led the fast food chains to form marketing alliances not just with toy companies, but with sports leagues and Hollywood studios. McDonald's has staged promotions with the National Basketball Association and the Olympics. Pizza Hut, Taco Bell, and KFC signed a three-year deal with the NCAA. Wendy's has linked with the National Hockey League. Burger King and Nickelodeon, Denny's and Major League Baseball, McDonald's and the Fox Kids Network have all formed partnerships that mix advertisements for fast food with children's entertainment. Burger King has sold chicken nuggets shaped like Teletubbies. McDonald's now has its own line of children's videos starring Ronald McDonald. *The Wacky Adventures of Ronald McDonald* is being produced by Klasky-Csupo, the company that makes *Rugrats* and *The Simpsons*. The videos feature the McDonaldland characters and sell for $3.49. "We see this as a great opportunity," a McDonald's executive said in a press release, "to create a more meaningful relationship between Ronald and kids."[31]

All of these cross-promotions have strengthened the ties between Hollywood and the fast food industry. In the past few years, the major studios have started to recruit fast food executives. Susan Frank, a former director of national marketing for McDonald's, later became a marketing executive at the Fox Kids Network. She now runs a new family-oriented cable network jointly owned by Hallmark Entertainment and the Jim Henson Company, creator of the Muppets. Ken Snelgrove, who for many years worked as a marketer for Burger King and

McDonald's, now works at MGM. Brad Ball, a former senior vice president of marketing at McDonald's, is now the head of marketing for Warner Brothers. Not long after being hired, Ball told the *Hollywood Reporter* that there was little difference between selling films and selling hamburgers.[32] John Cywinski, the former head of marketing at Burger King, became the head of marketing for Walt Disney's film division in 1996, then left the job to work for McDonald's. Forty years after Bozo's first promotional appearance at a McDonald's, amid all the marketing deals, giveaways, and executive swaps, America's fast food culture has become indistinguishable from the popular culture of its children.

In May of 1996, the Walt Disney Company signed a ten-year global marketing agreement with the McDonald's Corporation. By linking with a fast food company, a Hollywood studio typically gains anywhere from $25 million to $45 million in additional advertising for a film, often doubling its ad budget. These licensing deals are usually negotiated on a per-film basis; the 1996 agreement with Disney gave McDonald's exclusive rights to that studio's output of films and videos. Some industry observers thought Disney benefited more from the deal, gaining a steady source of marketing funds.[33] According to the terms of the agreement, Disney characters could never be depicted sitting in a McDonald's restaurant or eating any of the chain's food. In the early 1980s, the McDonald's Corporation had turned away offers to buy Disney; a decade later, McDonald's executives sounded a bit defensive about having given Disney greater control over how their joint promotions would be run. "A lot of people can't get used to the fact that two big global brands with this kind of credibility can forge this kind of working relationship," a McDonald's executive told a reporter. "It's about their theme parks, their next movie, their characters, their videos ... It's bigger than a hamburger. It's about the integration of our two brands, long-term."[34]

The life's work of Walt Disney and Ray Kroc had come full-circle, uniting in perfect synergy. McDonald's began to sell its hamburgers and french fries at Disney's theme parks. The ethos of McDonaldland and of Disneyland, never far apart, have finally become one. Now you can buy a Happy Meal at the Happiest Place on Earth.

NOTES

1. McNeal, James U. *Kids as Customers: A Handbook of Marketing to Children*. New York: Lexington Books, 1992, p. 6.
2. Cited in "Brand Aware," *Children's Business*, June 2000.
3. See "Brand Consciousness," *IFF on Kids: Kid Focus*, no. 3
4. Paul Fischer et al., "Brand Logo Recognition by Children Aged 3 to 6 Years: Mickey Mouse and Old Joe the Camel," *Journal of the American Medical Association*, December 11, 1991.
5. See Judan Dagnoli, "JAMA Lights New Fire Under Camel's Ads," *Advertising Age*, December 16, 1991.
6. Cited in "Market Research Ages 6–17: Talking Chihuahua Strikes Chord with Kids," *Selling to Kids*, February 3, 1999.
7. Quoted in "Market Research: The Old Nagging Game Can Pay Off for Marketers," *Selling to Kids*, April 15, 1998.
8. See Boas, Max, and Steve Chain. *Big Mac: The Unauthorized Story of McDonald's*. New York: E. P. Dutton, 1976. p. 127; Vance Packard, *The Hidden Persuaders* (New York: D. McKay, 1957), pp. 158–61.
9. McNeal, *Kids as Customers*, pp. 72–75.
10. Ibid., p. 4.
11. Ibid., p. 98.
12. For a sense of the techniques now being used by marketers, see Tom McGee, "Getting Inside Kids' Heads," *American Demographics*, January 1997.

13. Cited in Acuff, Dan S., with Robert H. Reiher. *What Kids Buy and Why: The Psychology of Marketing to Kids*. New York: Free Press, 1997. pp. 45–46.

14. McNeal, *Kids as Customers*, p. 175.

15. Cited in Karen Benezra, "Keeping Burger King on a Roll," *Brandweek*, January 15, 1996.

16. Cited in "Children's Online Privacy Proposed Rule Issued by FTC," press release, Federal Trade Commission, April 20, 1999.

17. Quoted in "Is Your Kid Caught Up in the Web?" *Consumer Reports*, May 1997.

18. See Matthew McAllester, "Life in Cyberspace: What's McDonald's Doing with Kids' E-mail Responses?" *Newsday*, July 20, 1997.

19. Quoted in Linda E. Demkovich, "Pulling the Sweet Tooth of Children's TV Advertising," *National Journal*, January 7, 1978.

20. Quoted in A. O. Sulzberger, Jr., "FTC Staff Urges End to Child-TV Ad Study," *New York Times*, April 3, 1981.

21. Cited in Steve McClellan and Richard Tedesco, "Children's TV Market May Be Played Out," *Broadcasting & Cable*, March 1, 1999.

22. Cited in "Policy Statement: Children, Adolescents, and Television," American Academy of Pediatrics, October 1995.

23. Cited in Mary C. Martin, "Children's Understanding of the Intent of Advertising: A Meta-Analysis," *Journal of Public Policy & Marketing*, Fall 1997.

24. Cited in Lisa Jennings, "Baby, Hand Me the Remote," *Scripps Howard News Service*, October 13, 1999.

25. Interview with Lynn Fava, Competitive Media Reporting.

26. Cited in "Fast Food and Playgrounds: A Natural Combination," promotional material, Playlandservices, Inc.

27. Ibid.

28. Cited in Rod Taylor, "The Beanie Factor," *Brandweek*, June 16, 1997.

29. Sam Bradley and Betsy Spethmann, "Subway's Kid Pack: The Ties That Sell," *Brandweek*, October 10, 1994.

30. Meredith Williams, *Tomart's Price Guide to McDonald's Happy Meal Collectibles* (Dayton, Ohio: Tomart Publications, 1995).

31. Quoted in "McDonald's Launches Second Animated Video in a Series Starring Ronald McDonald," press release, McDonald's Corporation, January 21, 1999.

32. See T. L. Stanley, *Hollywood Reporter*, May 26, 1998.

33. See Thomas R. King, "Mickey May Be the Big Winner in Disney-McDonald's Alliance," *Wall Street Journal*, May 24, 1996.

34. Quoted in James Bates, "You Want First-Run Features with Those Fries?" *Newsday*, May 11, 1997.

PART 2B

CULTURE

Michael Adams is a sociologist and president of Environics, one of Canada's leading public opinion firms. For more than 25 years he has been conducting surveys of Canadian and, in recent years, American culture. He is thus in an ideal position to know how Canadian and American beliefs, values, attitudes, and practices differ. In Chapter 6 he tells us, and his findings may surprise you.

Many observers characterize Canadians as a deferential people, quietly respectful of institutional authority. In contrast, it is often held that the Wild West never really died in the United States. In this view, anti-authoritarian beliefs and practices still pervade American culture. Adams shows this characterization is now dated. Over the past 40 years, respect for institutional authority has declined in all Western countries, but nowhere as much as in Canada. In our religious, political, and even sexual practices, we are now *less* deferential toward institutional authority and *more* tolerant of diversity than the Americans are. Our relatively low level of respect for institutional authority makes Canadian culture seem indistinct to some analysts. We are less inclined than the Americans are to rally around the flag. Adams, however, argues that our detachment from central authority and our high level of respect for diversity are precisely what make Canada's culture distinct.

An **ideology** is a system of ideas that justifies the existing social order. Ideologies are an important element of all cultures. Until the eighteenth century, *religious* ideas legitimized the social order. Especially in Western societies in the nineteenth and early twentieth centuries, *liberal* ideas largely took their place. In the second half of the twentieth century, *biological* arguments supplemented the liberal worldview.

Until the seventeenth- and eighteenth-century democratic revolutions in England, France, and the United States, it was widely believed that kings and queens ruled by "divine right." That is, royal authority was justified with reference to God's apparent will. By 1800, however, the foundation of this ideology had been undermined by the revolutionary notion that all men are created equal.[1] Yet a big problem remained. Although political and legal equality was beginning to spread, anyone could plainly see that enormous inequalities of wealth persisted. A new ideology justifying the social order was needed.

That new ideology was liberalism, which became entrenched in the nineteenth century. According to liberalism, the modern social order is unique in that it creates equality of opportunity. That is, in liberal social systems, everyone supposedly enjoys the same chance of achieving material success. To be sure, some people wind up more successful than others. Social inequality persists. From the liberal point of view, however, the only reason for continuing social stratification is that "natural" talents are not evenly distributed. Some people are simply smarter and more energetic than others, and they therefore benefit more from equality of opportunity.

From liberalism it was only a short step to **biological determinism**, an ideology that became popular in the twentieth century. Biological determinism holds that our innate biological characteristics deter-

---

[1] "White men" would be more accurate. The US Constitution defined Blacks as only 60 percent human, and it was not until 18 October 1929 that the Judicial Committee of the Privy Council in London overruled the Supreme Court of Canada and declared that women are indeed "qualified persons" for purposes of appointment to the Canadian Senate.

mine, among other things, how intelligent and industrious we are. Since, in turn, our intelligence and industry determine our success in life, it follows that the system of social inequality is ultimately a product of nature, not of human design.

In this section's second article, R.C. Lewontin, a leading American geneticist, takes issue with biological determinism. After arguing that biological determinism is an important part of our culture and, indeed, one of the dominant ideologies of our era, Lewontin dissects its logical and empirical fallacies. He shows that variations in intelligence are only partly genetically determined. Equally important in determining intelligence are the environment (family, school, etc.), which constantly interacts with our genes, and purely chance factors. If intelligence is not a product just of nature, it follows that neither is social inequality. Thus, without in any way diminishing the importance of biology in helping to make us who we are, Lewontin returns the analysis of social inequality to its rightful owners: the members of the sociological community.

This section's third article discusses another aspect of contemporary culture: consumerism. **Consumerism** is the practice of defining oneself in terms of the commodities one buys. It is not exactly news that most people buy particular styles of clothes, cars, and other commodities partly to project an image of themselves as powerful, sexy, cool, athletic, learned, or sophisticated. The use of jewellery and clothing to establish rank is as old as human society (see Chapter 12). Nor will it shock anyone to learn that advertising seeks to sell image more than substance. In the immortal words of one advertising executive in the 1940s, "It's not the steak we sell. It's the sizzle." Less obvious, however, is the way consumer culture turns *dissent* into a commodity, markets it to mass audiences, and thereby tames it. That is, consumer culture often turns expressions of radical protest into harmless commodities.

In "Hip-Hop From Dissent to Commodity: A Note on Consumer Culture" (online at www.societyinquestion4e.nelson.com) Robert Brym illustrates this process by examining the evolution of hip-hop music.

GLOSSARY

Biological determinism holds that innate physiological characteristics (genetic makeup, for example) determine intelligence, industry, and therefore the allocation of people to different positions in the social hierarchy.

Consumerism is the practice of defining oneself in terms of the commodities one buys.

An **ideology** is a system of ideas that justifies the existing social order.

CRITICAL THINKING QUESTIONS

The www icons on the next page indicate questions pertaining to an online article.

1. What are the main differences between Canadian and American culture today? What are the main similarities? Do the similarities outweigh the differences? Why or why not?
2. "Canada lacks a distinct culture." Discuss.
3. In explaining human behaviour, is it possible to separate nature form nurture, biology from culture? Explain your argument.
4. According to R.C. Lewontin, what is the ideology of biological determinism?
5. How can we explain inequality in society? Why do we not give the same material and physical rewards to farmers as we do to physicians?

w(w)w   6. On the Web, read the Angus Reid Group's "Why Is It Important to Track Pop Culture?" at http://www.angusreid.com/pdf/publicat/pop.pdf. Do you think the kind of research described in this article is valuable? Why or why not?

w(w)w   7. Can you think of elements of contemporary culture other than hip-hop that began as forms of radical protest and then developed mass appeal? Was the main force underlying the transformation commercial, or did other forces also come into play?

ANNOTATED BIBLIOGRAPHY

Richard Gruneau and David Whitson, *Hockey Night in Canada: Sport, Identities and Cultural Politics* (Toronto: Garamond, 1993). Canada's national sport is placed under the microscope in this engaging account, which shows how the global marketplace for commercial spectacle has altered the game and, along with it, Canadians' sense of themselves.

James Gleick, *Faster: The Acceleration of Just About Everything* (New York: Vintage, 2000). A breathless tour of one of the most pervasive features of Western culture.

Lyn Spillman, ed., *Cultural Sociology* (Oxford UK: Blackwell, 2002). A useful, up-to-date compendium of leading articles in the field.

Chapter 6

Canadian and American Culture: The Garden and the Jungle

MICHAEL ADAMS

If some countries have too much history, Canada has too much geography.
— William Lyon Mackenzie King

As countless commentators — most prominently the eminent sociologist Seymour Martin Lipset — have pointed out, historically, Canadians have been much more deferential to institutional authority than was the case among Americans. However, in the space of a single generation, Canadians have, for better or worse, by necessity and by choice, become much less deferential. On many registers we are now even more critical of institutional authority and of our élites than Americans are of theirs. Canadians can be likened to children on the last day of school, running and squealing in the schoolyard, free at last from the rules and discipline imposed by tradition. A nation of "repressed hedonists" — an apt description of our longest serving prime minister, quoted above — has decided that "peace, order, and good government" is not enough, and, like citizens around the world, we want some of the "life, liberty, and happiness" promised in America's founding declaration. For a very long time, Canadians lived under the not-always-benign rule of the church, the state and the large institutions of the industrial era — corporations, state monopolies and labour unions. Now we are freer to call the shots.

Since the 1960s, the widespread questioning of authority has become a fact of civic life in much of the Western world. However, Canada's evolution in this respect has been particularly rapid, to the point of being characterized as a "revolution" by Canada's pre-eminent journalist Peter C. Newman in his book *The Canadian Revolution: From Deference to Defiance*. Perhaps one reason for this is the Canadian surfeit of geography and dearth of history, as Mackenzie King observed half a century ago. As a result, no historical ideology has the sort of grip on our souls that the myth of the American Dream has south of the border. Even the Conquest (of Quebec by General Wolfe in 1759) has lost much of its resonance for Quebec francophones, thirty-five years after the Quiet Revolution. Instead, Canadians have a sort of flexible "geophilosophy," more pragmatic and rooted less in history and more in the multicultural, multimedia reality of their everyday existence. In today's wired world, both history and geography have lost most of their relevance for Canadians, in spite of the valiant efforts of the Charles R. Bronfman Foundation's Heritage Moments series of mini-docudramas. Today we have too much of neither, but perhaps instead have too little imagination to see ourselves as the world does — as the best place on earth.

Arguably, the relative lack of historical and ideological baggage has allowed Canadians to adapt rapidly to changing conditions both within our borders and around the world. It has also resulted in pronounced sociocultural differences between Canadians and Americans in the roles they ascribe to the fundamental institutions of religion, state, family, and the marketplace.

Despite their mythological adherence to the ideal of personal freedom, Americans, in fact, harbour a far greater confidence in many institutions than do Canadians. In general, Americans have a greater faith in the family, the state (that is, "America"), religion, and the market.

For example, Americans express far greater confidence in big business. Part of this difference can be attributed to the fact that "big business" in the United States usually means *American* big business. In Canada, "big business" is often a foreign-owned corporation, typically an American branch plant. In America, anti-trust laws force fierce competition. In Canada, public-sector monopolies and private-sector oligopolies have dominated many markets; the result was a culture of *ressentiment* — resentful dependence — which began to unravel in the late 1980s.

But now, Canadians have become "masters of suspicion," with both the positive and negative aspects that come with such a posture. In spite of our historical reputation for deference to elites, Canadians, who were once more religious than Americans, are now less so. Although mere church attendance figures fail to do justice to the phenomenally greater religiosity in the United States, they do illustrate important differences between the two countries. In the 1950s, 60 per cent of Canadians attended church every Sunday; today, that number is 30 per cent. In the United States, attendance continues to hover around 40 per cent, little changed from the level in the 1930s and '40s.

Even Quebecers, whose motto is *Je me souviens* (or "I remember"), have come to forget or reject a great deal of their sociocultural inheritance. With the exception, of course, of the French language itself, almost every other institution in that centuries-old society has been turned upside down. In the space of a single generation, people who came from families of ten children are today having only one child, or sometimes none. The decline in weekly church attendance among Quebec Catholics has been even more precipitous than in the rest of the country.

One factor that initially contributed to greater *Canadian* religiosity and deference to authority was the historical role played by the major Christian denominations. Historically, in Canada, the Catholic and Anglican churches, both very hierarchical organizations, played a dominant role. And they did so with explicit or tacit government sanction, in part through the constitutional provisions that protected Catholic and Protestant denominational schools. In contrast, the American constitution separated church and state. Evangelical or populist sects had to compete for the attention and adherence of their American flocks, thereby giving religion a less institutional focus.

Historically, this difference favoured greater religiosity in Canada. However, with faith in institutions declining in both countries, the more heterarchical orientation of religion in the United States has proven the more resilient and "market sensitive." In Canada, most mainstream Judeo-Christian denominations are losing their grip on the population. Moreover, many of the values traditionally associated with them have come under critical scrutiny, if they have not been largely discarded. These include deference to state authorities ("render unto Caesar"), patriarchal definitions of family, guilt, duty, and fear of divine retribution.

Not only does our research show that Canadians are far weaker than Americans on the dimension of religiosity, but that the secularization of our country shows no signs of abating. If anything, this trend is accelerating. Despite a nominal separation of church and state in the

United States, religion continues to play a major role in American politics, but virtually no role here. In this respect, the 49th parallel is a veritable "de-mystification zone." American politicians wear their religion on their sleeves; here, even the most devout politicians, including Reform Party leader Preston Manning, seldom mention their religious affiliation and Christian values.

Even Canadians who say they believe in God — still a majority — tend not to let this belief influence their lifestyle on a day-to-day basis. When it comes to their religious practices, they are more likely to apologize than proselytize. Reginald Bibby, the foremost sociologist of religion in this country, comments that "The vast majority of Canadians still call themselves Christian, but they're grasping bits and pieces of the traditional creed — 'the fragmented god.' We now see a high level of belief in almost anything imaginable, but there's no rhyme or reason to it. And when we try to measure the sort of guidance these private beliefs play in people's lives, there's really nothing there. There's no ultimate moral authority. So it really doesn't hold up to anything."[1]

On the other hand, four out of five Americans believe in life after death, a virgin birth and miracles. Almost all Americans (95%) believe in God, and a World Values survey conducted in 1992–93 found that more than four in five Americans consider themselves to be "a religious person."

In the United States, social or values issues can still play an important role in elections, inspiring US author Ben Wattenberg to recently write the influential *Values Matter Most*.[2] In Canada, it is unemployment and the deficit that are top public priorities in the late 1990s — both pragmatic economic issues. With tongue planted firmly in cheek, some Canadians have said the ultimate Canadian destiny is to redeem America. If this were ever to happen, it would be a secular redemption, a redemption from Redemption.

Just as Canadian religious institutions have suffered a greater decline in public confidence than have their American counterparts, so, too,

has there been a greater decline in confidence in government here. Traditionally, Canadians had far greater faith in the state than did their American cousins. Much of this phenomenon can be traced to the very different origins of the two countries. In several books, most recently *American Exceptionalism*, Lipset examines the historical and cultural differences between Canada and the United States in the founding myths of each country: the revolutionary and individualistic tradition of the United States, contrasted with the counter-revolutionary and communal tradition of Canada; the American rags-to-riches myth of Horatio Alger versus the Canadian theme of surviving adversity; the American promise of life, liberty, and the pursuit of happiness in contrast to the Canadian bargain of peace, order, and good government. In terms of political ideology, Canada inherited strong strains of Toryism, liberalism, and socialism. The United States has known only various trains of liberalism qualified by religious moralism.

Traditionally, Canada was very much a communitarian, or group-oriented society. According to Lipset, Canada's "organizing principle," our decision not to join the American Revolution in 1776 and break with England, left us with the values and priorities of the Old World, and an essentially Tory and conservative world-view. To restate the old joke: America was founded on the principle of the people against the government; Canada, on the other hand, was founded on the principle of the government against the people.

Old World Tory conservatism, which takes an organic, "Hegelian" view of society, sees the whole as greater than the sum of its parts and, as such, values group rights over individual rights. This particular world-view, along with the nation's climate, geography, and smaller population, has made Canadians generally accepting of state intervention in many aspects of their daily lives. Many observers have remarked that Canada was traditionally a very "Hegelian" society, a label that applies to the country's pre-eminent political philosopher, Charles Taylor.

This organic view was reflected in Canadians' constantly trying to accommodate competing interests within the framework of existing social institutions, a profoundly reformist (rather than revolutionary) ambition. However, it has now become apparent to Canadians that traditional institutions can no longer deliver the goods: the church can no longer deliver ever-lasting life, the state can no longer provide security from the cradle to the grave, and employers can no longer guarantee life-long employment.

As these formerly unassailable institutions crumble, Canadians are forced to forge new links and networks with communities of choice and of mutual interest, rather than looking to government or other élites to lead them through life. With the growth of social-values tribalism and the underground economy, Canadians have moved from an organic model of society to a rhizomatic one, where personal networking replaces a reliance on representatives, institutions or an idealized notion of the country.

Our research shows that Americans, in addition to a greater religiosity, are characterized by a strong belief in the importance of national superiority, a romantic need to demonstrate to the world the exceptionalism of their country and culture. American Republicans have distilled these values into their purified essence.

The summer blockbuster of 1996, *Independence Day*, starts out as just such a paean to American exceptionalism. However, by the end of the film it has become an exhortation to global unity in a common cause, with everyone included, from the First Lady to a stripper with a heart of gold, from a black soldier to a Jewish intellectual, with a sympathetic portrayal of a gay character tossed in for good measure. In the end, the entire world unites, under American leadership, to defeat the aliens from outer space. It's appealing, because this sort of ecumenism is so obviously absent from the US body politic these days.

Unfortunately, the tendency of Americans to identify themselves as simply "Americans" rather than "hyphenated" Americans appears to have done little to strengthen the social fabric in the United States. Indeed, as we can see from our synthesis map of values, the attitudinal differences between Canada's "distinct society" Quebec and the rest of the country pale in comparison to those that exist among the major regions of the United States. It may be argued that Canadians' institutional recognition of social pluralism, including state-sponsored bilingualism and multiculturalism, has provided a vehicle for the expression of *some* aspirations of ethnic communities. This has not made them any less Canadian: in fact, it has helped to make them *quintessentially* Canadian. It is not an exclusive disjunction, in which one is *either* ethnic or Canadian: one can comfortably be both, and the very Canadian trend toward more flexible personalities and a diffused sense of identity suggests that the recognition of a multicultural, fluid, and flexible reality need not encourage an ossified ethnic tribalism. Twenty-five years of public-opinion polling in Canada has taught me a seemingly paradoxical truth: Canadians feel *strongly* about their *weak* attachments to Canada, its political institutions and their fellow citizens. In other words, they feel strongly about the right to live in a society that allows its citizens to be detached from ideology and critical of organizations, and not to feel obliged to be jingoistic or sentimentally patriotic. Canadians' *lack* of nationalism is, in many ways, a distinguishing feature of the country. In the 1950s we said, "better dead than red." If you believe in an afterlife, maybe it's better to be dead, but Canadians are now too pragmatic to jeopardize their lives for any ideology.

Until recently more deferential to politicians, Canadians have been rejecting the authority of political office in much more dramatic ways than have Americans. Witness the near annihilation of the federal Conservatives in the 1993 election, and the introduction of the parvenu Bloc Québecois and the Reform Party as the second and third parties in the House of Commons. Canada has maintained a turnout rate of around 75 per cent in elections. The United States, on the other hand, is becoming increasingly plutocratic, with the rich and vested interests presiding over a nation where fewer than half the citizens exercise their franchise in presidential elections. In the Congressional elections of 1994, fewer than one in five Americans actually voted for the Republicans, who nevertheless took this "victory" as a mandate for sweeping change.

Despite their sometimes brutal individualism, Americans revere institutions as anchors for their values; Canadians are coming to see many of their institutions as ineffective or irrelevant. For example, Americans revere the office of President and consider it a "crisis of confidence" when the incumbent's approval rating falls below 40 per cent. For an extended period of time, former prime minister Brian Mulroney had an approval rating hovering around 10 per cent, a situation unheard of in the United States.

As I mentioned earlier, a frequently cited characteristic distinguishing Canada from other countries is our institutionalized tolerance of diversity. However, this policy, along with other sacred cows of government, has come under increasing scrutiny. In an attack on Canada's policy of multiculturalism, Neil Bissoondath writes, "It may be that one of the unstated desires behind the institution of multiculturalism was a wish to mark ourselves as different from the United States: if they have a melting pot, then we'll have a mosaic. If they ask immigrants to shrug off their past and assume a new identity, we'll ask immigrants to conserve their past and make it their only identity."[3] Mr. Bissoondath goes on to charge that a failure to accept each other "as simply Canadian" weakens the social fabric.

However, I believe that Canada's more receptive attitude to ethnic diversity is *not* a case of an individual pretending to be what he/she was in the past, but rather, the simple recognition of differences that exist in the present. This hypothesis is supported by the fact that, in Canada, there is a correlation between support for multiculturalism and modern trends (such as equality of the sexes) rather than traditional

trends (such as religiosity). Multiculturalism is a "modern" trend, located in the lower half of the map, rather than a "traditional" one that would be found near the top of the map. And perhaps the most modern of Canadians, the New Aquarians, are also the most supportive of ethnic diversity.

As in so many other areas, multiculturalism in Canada will likely evolve from a government program to some sort of "market multiculturalism" that's more voluntaristic and pragmatic than the current approach. For example, schools might emphasize their racial and ethnic diversity to attract students. Companies might promote multiculturalism in order to retain and attract both employees and customers. The average Canadian can savour the gastronomic and cultural diversity of Canada's global village.

Clearly, when compared to our hot-blooded cousins to the south, we conform to the shy and deferential stereotype: except when playing hockey, we are non-violent and courteous. We raise the tone at the end of sentences, transforming assertions into hypotheses so as not to give offence, often adding "eh" to emphasize our politeness. We will stop at Stop signs, even if no cars are in sight, and even if the sign says *Arrêt*.

Given these differences, is it any surprise that an international survey by a major condom manufacturer found that Americans have sex more often than any other people in the world, but that Canadians were most likely to say that the pleasure of their partner was very important? If Americans are hot Dionysians having sex in the sun, Canadians are cool Apollonians having sex in the snow, with the need for pragmatism that entails: blankets, mukluks and a realization that we are in this together.

Many Canadians believe that the 1990s have witnessed a steadily increasing income gap between the "haves" and the "have-nots"; in fact, this is only true for *earned* income. When transfers to lower-income individuals in the form of unemployment insurance, welfare, and old-age security are factored in, the overall income gap has remained fairly constant, but at a growing and unsustainable cost to government and the taxpayer. Therefore, as the *Globe and Mail's* Bruce Little observes, even though the market will probably continue to produce an inequitable distribution of earned income, governments will be increasingly unwilling and unable to offset this chilling trend.[4] However, in spite of the general retreat of governments, most Canadians continue to cling, however tenuously, to the principle of a kinder, gentler society. This stands in stark contrast to the social Darwinistic ideology that is dominant in the United States. Theirs is a world in which the fittest flourish while others languish. It is government by *triage*, in which resources are allocated to those deemed most worthy of being saved, or, more likely, those who have enough political clout to make their voices heard — older, well-off Americans being at the top of the list.

Despite these fundamental differences, there are indications that Canadian politics are replicating some American — or rather, some international — trends. The Ontario election of 1995, which saw a massive legislative majority accorded Mike Harris's Conservatives, witnessed a revolt by largely white, middle-class voters against an NDP government that they saw as "squandering" their tax dollars on policies of "overly generous" state welfare and employment equity (affirmative action). They voted in favour of a tax cut for the wealthy and middle class, with little concern for the plight of the poor. As columnist Allan Fotheringham put it, "Score one for the angry white guys." Canadians may still believe that the quality of our social programs distinguishes us from the United States, but a significant proportion of the population has come to question the price we pay for this benefit.

There are heated debates as to whether the cuts currently under way across the country are the solution to our economic problems, or an ideological reaction to market pressures. James Laxer, a political science professor at York University, argues that while the Harris government is *for the rich*, it is not a government *of the*

rich and was not elected by the rich.[5] While those in the highest income-tax brackets will benefit most from tax cuts, middle-class conservative supporters will benefit from "cultural benefits," i.e., hot button issues such as a hard line on punishing young offenders, and the scrapping of photo radar (the latter may have inspired David Cronenberg's latest film *Crash*).

Part of the cultural benefits accruing to people opposed to multiculturalism and alternative family structures is a feeling of ethnic and moral superiority. As *The Globe and Mail* put it in an article about the United States, but that could be equally applied to sentiments now evident in neo-conservative Ontario, "the big dogs are suddenly fed up with blacks, gays, immigrants and everyone else that isn't them. Throughout the land can be heard the creaking sound of drawbridge politics, as the no-longer-silent majority try to isolate themselves in the duchies of suburbia."[6] For his part, Laxer suggests that the Harris agenda reflects the theory wittily and ironically summed up by John Kenneth Galbraith that, "the problem with our society is that the poor have too much money, and the rich don't have enough."

In my opinion, analyzing the election of the Ontario Conservatives in terms of the Americanization of Canadian politics is only telling part of the story. I interpret this vote as an effort by Ontarians to reverse some of the excesses — however well-intended — of state intervention, and to restore fiscal responsibility to the public sector. The mid-1990s have seen governments of all political stripes — Liberal in Ottawa, New Democratic in Saskatchewan, Conservative in Alberta, and the PQ in Quebec — adopt many of the same fiscal and social policies. In 1996, in British Columbia, a slightly more interventionist New Democratic government was re-elected. Sure, there is some evidence of the Americanization of Canadian politics — after all, the plurality did vote in favour of free trade in 1988 — but there is just as much evidence that all Canadian governments are reducing services *reluctantly* and with little of the ideological fervour of the American right.

Canadians, I am convinced, are pragmatic, not ideological, people. They want a sustainable social-welfare state, perhaps not the social-democratic paradise envisioned by the Canadian left, but one that will still leave Canada a more egalitarian place than the republic to the south. It is no accident that other social-welfare states reacted to globalization in much the same manner as Canada: look at Germany or New Zealand or what was once socialist heaven on earth — Sweden. They all bit the fiscal bullet.

The sociocultural differences between Canada and the United States, like the differences between Quebec and the rest of Canada, or even between men and women, may be diminishing over time, but the differences that remain will, in my view, be significant and meaningful for many generations to come.

It is clear from the sociocultural data that, in spite of the many obvious similarities between the two countries, there are a number of significant differences in the values that guide and give meaning to the lives of people in each society. The first is in the flexibility we allow ourselves in terms of self-identity.

We Canadians are not without national pride. However, we question the assumption that national identity is the defining characteristic of community. This has afforded us a greater acceptance of diversity in each other's sense of self, and in the attachments people have with various communities. Here you are allowed, not only to be a hyphenated Canadian, but also to decide which side of the hyphen best describes and defines you from moment to moment. A sort of pragmatic tolerance is the rule, rather than a clearly defined identity dictated by tradition. America, on the other hand, has a firm tradition of rejecting, or ghettoizing, hyphenated identities, in favour of one strong national identity.

Is this because America was conceived, torn asunder, and then reunited within a crucible of violence? In Canada, we negotiated our independence from Mother England. After their

conquest in 1759, the British accommodated the French, starting with the Quebec Act in 1774. Allowing Quebecers to keep their language and customs, rather than pursue the course of assimilation, set a precedent for the non-violent accommodation of successive waves of immigrants. More recently, and thanks partly to the Charter of Rights and Freedoms, this same inclusiveness has opened up new possibilities for women, gays and lesbians, people with disabilities, and others wishing to "immigrate" into the mainstream of society.

Canadians' recent questioning and criticism of their institutions has also resulted in more flexible and open personal relationships than is the norm in the United States. In my opinion, our questioning of the family has not resulted in its devaluation, but rather in an assault on patriarchy, and a greater belief in the equality of women and young people. It has also resulted in a more flexible definition of family, including a greater acceptance of non-Scriptural relationships, such as sex outside of marriage, and gay and lesbian relationships. Now one-third of children in Canada are born to parents who are living together but not married, and less than half of Canadian families conform to the traditional model of married-parents-with-kids. Jean Dumas, an analyst at Statistics Canada remarked, "There is a real change, not only in the size of the family, but in the concept of the family. The flexibility with which the cell of society adapts to societal change is amazing. All the talk about the death of the family is nonsense."[7]

In America, common-law marriage and the birth of children out of wedlock is interpreted as a sign of moral decay and the disintegration of society. The religious and political right inveigh against such trends with routine moralizing. In Canada overall, the trend goes essentially unnoticed in politics and is as much a marketing challenge as a moral threat to mainstream churches. North of the border, unmarried couples are becoming the norm, with formerly Catholic Quebec in the vanguard. However, there is antagonism among some of Canada's older-values tribes on these questions.

In the United States, gender is now a major factor in Americans' political ideology and party choice. Women tend to support "kinder and gentler" policies that preserve the social-welfare state, and have thus become the backbone of the Democratic party. Men opt for a more competitive free-market economic model and Darwinistic social policies and are making the Republicans into a stag party. In America, it seems, "Men are from Mars and Women are from Venus."

In Canada, the ideological and partisan gap is far less pronounced. Yes, we see the tendency of women to be more on "the left" and men on "the right" of the political spectrum, but only a tendency. Canada's governing party, the Liberals, are slightly more popular among women than among men, but only slightly. Both the "left-wing" NDP, and the "right-wing" Progressive Conservatives draw similar levels of support from men and women. The further right-of-centre Reform Party is disproportionately male, but in Canada, unlike the United States, this positioning has served to limit Reform's appeal among mainstream male voters.

Further evidence of the advanced evolution of Canadian social values in the area of institutionalized gender stereotyping is the fate of the Miss Canada Beauty Pageant. Though nearly every US state, county, and town continues the ritual display of nubile female pulchritude, culminating in the annual Miss America and the redundant Miss Universe contests, Canada's CTV television network cancelled the Miss Canada contest in 1992 due to lack of interest on the part of sponsors and the general public. Meanwhile, in Texas, a related parody of Americana was played out when the mother of a would-be cheerleader, Wanda Webb Holloway, was convicted of plotting the death of the mother of her daughter's rival.

In addition to allowing for common-law and same-sex relationships, the Canadian redefinition of the family has resulted in a greater respect for the opinions of young people. One of the differences that distinguishes Canadian values from American is Canadians' greater adherence to the idea of an equal relationship with youth. Canadians are more egalitarian than Americans and more inclined to believe that young people are capable of making their own decisions, and should be accorded the same rights and responsibilities as any other member of society.

Americans, on the other hand, are more likely than Canadians to believe that young people do not really know what is in their best interest, and that they should let their elders tell them what to do. It is significant that in Canada, there is a positive correlation between rejection of authority and belief in an equal relationship with youth; in the United States these trends are independent of each other. Certainly it makes intuitive sense that a rejection of hierarchical relationships in general would include those based on age. So, why has this not happened in the US? Our data suggest that the answer may lie in the fact that in both countries people fear that permissive attitudes toward young people may facilitate criminal behaviour. The greater fear of crime in the US is reflected in a much harsher, more authoritarian attitude toward the young, one now realized in public curfews for youth and/or other exclusionary measures.

Another distinguishing characteristic of Canadians is our tendency toward non-violence. Canadians value peace and order and will likely continue to do so, even without a Mountie standing over their shoulder. Americans value freedom of the individual more than peace and order.

Despite public perceptions to the contrary, Canadian statistics show a decline in rates of violent crime that parallels a decline found in the United States. Statistics Canada reported that in 1995 the overall crime rate fell by 1 per cent, a decline for the fourth year in a row. Violent crime declined by 4.1 per cent in 1995, the largest drop since the agency started gathering such statistics in 1962.[8] In 1995, the homicide rate also hit a 26-year low. Despite this overall decline, Statistics Canada reported that there was an increase in the number and proportion of murders committed by youth.

The decline in overall crime rates in Canada and the US are due, at least partly, to the demographic reality of aging populations. This same demographic factor also helps explain why there is a higher hysteria over crime — older people tend to have a much greater fear of violence than do the young.

For their part, Americans express somewhat contradictory views on the topic of violence. On the one hand, they are more likely than Canadians to accept violence as normative, and even exciting, and are reluctant to institute the most modest of gun-control measures. At the same time, crime has long been one of the main issues of concern to the American public.

Violent-crime rates peaked in the United States in 1990, with the arrival of crack cocaine. In more recent years, there has been a decline in the rate of violent crime in the US. This can be attributed to a number of factors, including lower rates of crack use, the death or imprisonment of many of the worst offenders, and, as I just pointed out, an aging population. Nonetheless, the United States is far from being out of the woods, especially in view of recent social program cuts and an imminent "echo boom" of teenagers and young adults, the age groups most likely to commit crimes. In the United States (and, to a lesser extent, in Canada) it is expected that violent crime will increase in the years ahead, simply because of a significant rise in the 15-to-24-year-old population. Demography may not be destiny, but in this instance it is a wake-up call of sorts, especially in the United States.

In the United States, people who murder strangers have an 80 percent chance of getting away with it. It is a small step from recognition of this to a cost/benefit analysis on the part of those who, economically and socially, have little to lose by taking a chance on a life of crime.

And despite recent declines, the violent-crime rate in the United States remains many times higher than in Canada. Tom Pollock, head of Universal Pictures, pointed to Canada as evidence that there is not a correlation between on-screen violence and real-life violence. "We have a perfect control group," he said. "It's called Canada. They get all our records, movies and TV, yet their rate of violent crime is one-tenth that of the US. Toronto is on the other side of the lake from Buffalo but a world apart. What Canada has that we don't is strict gun control ... as well as less racial polarization and multi-generational poverty. Those are the real causes of violence."[9]

Both American and Canadian value systems are being shaped by the globalization of technology, trade, travel, finance, communications, and culture. Some people believe that these broad contextual trends are acting to homogenize our values and lifestyles, and it *is* true that Canadians consume massive amounts of American popular culture. But we are not alone in this: on the other side of the Atlantic, even the proud and ethnocentric French now watch more American movies than those made in their own country.

The similarities in the way we live are legion, from the food we eat to the cars we drive, and in our social-values research we see broad similarities in the evolution of our values from conformity to traditional codes (order, authority, Judeo-Christian morality, and attendant guilt) to more personalized, experiential values, with no theological pretensions or claims to universal validity. This pattern is particularly pronounced among the youth tribes.

In each country, baby boomers were in the vanguard of the new values: the quest for personal autonomy and self-fulfilment, the values most associated with the "Me Generation." Feminism, which was part of this search for autonomy and self-fulfilment, continues to be a strong trend in both countries, despite a backlash by those seeking to turn back the clock. So, too, is the trend away from asceticism and deferred gratification to hedonism and immediate gratification. On both sides of the border, people want to join the party, and have as much fun as possible on the roller coaster of life. They are less willing to wait for their ultimate reward in the next life (though Americans, much more than Canadians, continue to find comfort in the prospect of a more exalted world beyond death's door).

Individualism has been a growing trend in both the United States and Canada since the 1950s. However, our data indicate an important difference between the American and Canadian orientations to individualism: the American orientation can be characterized as "rugged individualism" and the Canadian version is more "responsible" than rugged. American individualism is more competitive. Our values research finds that Americans are much more likely than Canadians to embrace a sense of personal and national vitality and the stimulation of personal challenge; they are also more likely to admit to feelings of stress in the pursuit of success.

North of the 49th parallel, we treasure equality; south of it, they treasure freedom. Lipset points out that, historically, the United States also laid claim to being the land of equality of opportunity, with Canada being the land of élite accommodation of group interests. However, it appears to me that Canada is now more egalitarian than the United States, and that Americans continue to cling tenaciously to a myth of social mobility that, in reality, holds for only a small proportion of their population. For example, in Canada the richest 1 percent of the population holds about 25 percent of the nation's wealth; in the United States the richest 1 percent holds over 40 per cent of the wealth.[10]

Despite many signs that the United States is fast becoming a hereditary oligarchy, the ideal of social mobility — the belief that through education and hard work, anyone can rise to the top — remains a key component of the American Dream. There is insufficient recognition that growing proportions of Americans are born, not only into poverty, but also into hopelessness. To borrow Lord Durham's description of Canada in 1840, the United States is once again becoming two nations "warring within the bosom of a single state," only this time it is the rich versus the poor, with levels of violence approaching that of America's Civil War in the 1860s.

Even among the disadvantaged echelons of society, the American orientation to life is more judgmental and moralistic than is the Canadian. The American moral code is more firmly rooted in Judeo-Christian doctrine, a Manichean world of good and evil, right and wrong, good guys and bad guys, Eve created out of man's rib, and Adam created in the image of God and given dominion over the natural world. Canadian morality transcends traditional religious definitions; it can be characterized as a secular, pluralistic, and ecological morality, a greater responsibility for the other. The Canadian emphasis on egalitarian values goes beyond the equality of human beings — whatever their sex, age, race, ethnicity, or sexual orientation — to the consideration of non-human species and the natural environment. I expect this principle will be codified in the preamble the next time we amend the Canadian constitution. Canada's global village is a global garden.

It is my opinion that, although economic integration continues apace, there has been much less sociocultural assimilation of Canada by the United States than is often feared. In important ways, Canadians and Americans live different sorts of lives. Moreover, I predict such assimilation will not take place for many generations to come, if ever. Though our economic axis has become north-south, our cultural axis has become, like our population, cybernomadic. Whereas television was initially a force that helped create mass society and popular culture, the new technologies of VCRs, satellite TV, and the Internet all contribute to a sociocultural fragmentation of mass society in favour of personal choice and empowerment. Common ideals and even "common sense" are increasingly hard to maintain, and the American national motto — "*e pluribus unum*" — or "*out of many, one*" — has turned out to be a tragic joke. It is truly ironic that Canada, a country that historically accommodated and even celebrated differences, has actually ended up creating a culture where a broad range of values unites us, and differentiates us significantly from Americans. On the other hand, the United States, in its drive to create a melting pot that disparages cultural and linguistic diversity, has, in fact, developed into a country of mutually exclusive identities and many warring factions. They have become a nation of god-fearing Darwinists, we have become a collection of tolerant social democrats.

Many people see social fragmentation and tribalism on the rise around the world, and the United States reverting to the *ethnic* tribalism of the past. Others, like Francis Fukuyama and Gwynne Dyer see more sanguine, hopeful trends. If my reading of Canada is correct, this country may be the harbinger of a more utopian future, as we experience an evolution from traditional ethnic tribalism to a postmodern tribalism based on social values.

In fact, despite tribal differences, French and English Canadians have far more in common with each other in terms of values than either group has with the Americans (however offensive this observation might be to political ideologues of the "distinct society"). Notwithstanding the Quiet Revolution in Quebec and the Values Revolution in Canada as a whole, Canadians themselves are not revolutionaries: they are rebels and reformers. And in spite of our growing intimacy with American commerce and culture, Canada remains a distinct society on the northern half of the North American continent.

Even in the face of powerful international forces favouring integration, our roots, our history, our size, our degree of secularization, our institutions, and, yes, even our climate have created two very different sociocultural environments on this continent. If we are the kinder, gentler society of level playing fields, then America is the land of shining cities, each surrounded by a walled moat outside of which roams a marauding and dangerous underclass. In their own minds, most Canadians have decided which model they prefer: an overwhelming majority say they would choose to remain in Canada even if they had equal opportunities in the United States.

NOTES

1. Reginald Bibby, quoted in *Western Report,* June 10, 1996.
2. Ben Wattenberg, *Values Matter Most* (New York: The Free Press, 1995).
3. Neil Bissoondath, *Saturday Night*, October 1994, p. 20.
4. Bruce Little, *The Globe and Mail*, July 10, 1995.
5. James Laxer, *The Toronto Star*, July 16, 1995.
6. Graham Fraser, headline of *The Globe and Mail*, July 15, 1995.
7. Jean Dumas quoted by Fabrice Taylor, *The Globe and Mail*, July 8, 1995.
8. Elaine Carey, *The Toronto Star*, July 31, 1996.
9. *The Toronto Star*, July 11, 1995.
10. Carol Goar, *The Toronto Star*, May 14, 1995.

Chapter 7

Biology as Ideology

R.C. LEWONTIN

Our society was born, at least politically, in revolutions of the seventeenth century in Britain and the eighteenth century in France and America. Those revolutions swept out an old order characterized by aristocratic privilege and a relative fixity of persons in the society. The bourgeois revolutions in England, France, and America claimed that this old society and its ideology were illegitimate, and the ideologues of those revolutions produced and legitimized an ideology of liberty and equality. Diderot and the Encylopedists and Tom Paine were the theorists of a society of "liberté, égalité, fraternité," of all men created equal. The writers of the Declaration of Independence asserted that political truths were "self-evident; that all men are created equal; that they are endowed by their creator with certain unalienable rights; that among these are life, liberty, and the pursuit of happiness" (by which, of course, they meant the pursuit of money). They meant literally all *men*, because women were not given the right to vote in the United States until 1920; Canada enfranchised women a little sooner, in 1918 — but not in provincial elections in Quebec until 1940. And of course they didn't mean *all* men, because slavery continued in the French dominions and in the Caribbean until the middle of the nineteenth century. Blacks were defined by the United States Constitution as only three-fifths of a person, and for most of the history of English parliamentary democracy, a man had to have money to vote.

To make a revolution, you need slogans that appeal to the great mass of people, and you can hardly get people to shed blood under a banner that reads "Equality for some." So the ideology and the slogans outstrip the reality. For if we look at the society that has been created by those revolutions, we see a great deal of inequality of wealth and power among individuals, between sexes, between races, between nations. Yet we have heard over and over again in school and had it drummed into us by every organ of communication that we live in a society of free equals. The contradiction between the claimed equality of our society and the observation that great inequalities exist has been, for North Americans at least, the major social agony of the last 200 years. It has motivated an extraordinary amount of our political history. How are we to resolve the contradiction of immense inequalities in a society that claims to be founded on equality?

There are two possibilities. We might say that it was all a fake, a set of slogans meant to replace a regime of aristocrats with a regime of wealth and privilege of a different sort, that inequality in our society is structural and an integral aspect of the whole of our political and social life. To say that, however, would be deeply subversive, because it would call for yet another revolution if we wanted to make good on our hopes for liberty and equality for all. It is not a popular idea among teachers, newspaper editors, college professors, successful politicians, indeed anyone who has the power to help form public consciousness.

The alternative, which has been the one taken since the beginning of the nineteenth century, has been to put a new gloss on the notion of equality.

Source: *Biology as Ideology: The Doctrine of DNA* (Toronto: Anansi, 1991), pp. 19–37. Copyright © 1991 by R.C. Lewontin and the Canadian Broadcasting Corporation. Reprinted by permission of the House of Anansi Press.

Rather than equality of *result*, what has been meant is equality of *opportunity*. In this view of equality, life is a foot race. In the bad old days of the *ancien régime*, the aristocrats got to start at the finish line whereas all the rest of us had to start at the beginning, so the aristocrats won. In the new society, the race is fair: everyone is to begin at the starting line and everyone has an equal opportunity to finish first. Of course, some people are faster runners than others, and so some get the rewards and others don't. This is the view that the old society was characterized by *artificial* barriers to equality, whereas the new society allows a natural sorting process to decide who is to get the status, wealth, and power and who is not.

Such a view does not threaten the status quo, but on the contrary supports it by telling those who are without power that their position is the inevitable outcome of their own innate deficiencies and that, therefore, nothing can be done about it. A remarkably explicit recent statement of this assertion is the one by Richard Herrnstein, a psychologist from Harvard, who is one of the most outspoken modern ideologues of natural inequality. He wrote,

> the privileged classes of the past were probably not much superior biologically to the downtrodden which is why revolution had a fair chance of success. By removing artificial barriers between classes society has encouraged the creation of biological barriers. When people can take their natural level in society, the upper classes will, by definition, have greater capacity than the lower.[1]

We are not told precisely what principle of biology guarantees that biologically inferior persons cannot seize power from biologically superior ones, but it is not logic that is at issue here. Such statements as Herrnstein's are meant to convince us that although we may not live in the best of all conceivable worlds, we live in the best of all possible worlds. The social entropy has been maximized so that we have as much equality as possible because the structure is essentially one of equality, and whatever inequalities are left over are not structural but based on

innate differences between individuals. In the nineteenth century this was also the view, and education was seen as the lubricant that would guarantee that the race of life was run smoothly. Lester Frank Ward, a giant of nineteenth-century sociology, wrote, "Universal education is the power which is destined to overthrow every species of hierarchy. It is destined to remove all artificial inequality and leave the natural inequalities to find their true level. The true value of a newborn infant lies in its naked capacity for acquiring the ability to do."[2]

This was echoed 60 years later by Arthur Jensen at the University of California, who wrote about the inequality of intelligence of Blacks and whites: "We have to face it, the assortment of persons into occupational roles simply is not fair in any absolute sense. The best we can hope for is that true merit given equality of opportunity acts as a basis for the natural assorting process."[3]

Simply to assert that the race of life is fair and that different people have different intrinsic abilities to run it is not enough to explain the observations of inequality. Children seem, by and large, to acquire the social status of their parents. About 60 percent of the children of "blue collar" workers remain "blue collar," while about 70 percent of "white collar" workers' children are "white collar." But these figures vastly overestimate the amount of social mobility. Most people who have passed from "blue collar" to "white collar" jobs have passed from factory production-line jobs to office production-line jobs or have become sales clerks, less well paid, less secure, doing work just as numbing of the soul and body as the factory work done by their parents. The children of gas station attendants usually borrow money, and the children of oil magnates usually lend it. The chance that Nelson Rockefeller would have wound up pumping gas was pretty close to zero.

If we live in a meritocracy, in which each person can rise to the status allowed by his or her innate capacities, how do we explain this passage of social power from parent to offspring? Are we really just back in an old aristocratic situation?

The naturalistic explanation is to say that not only do we differ in our innate capacities but that these innate capacities are themselves transmitted from generation to generation biologically. That is to say, they are in our genes. The original social and economic notion of inheritance has been turned into biological inheritance.

But even the claim that the intrinsic ability to win success is inherited in the genes is not sufficient to justify an unequal society. After all, we might assert that there ought not to be any particular relationship between what one can accomplish and what social and psychic rewards are given. We might give the same material and psychic rewards to house painters and picture painters, to surgeons and to barbers, to professors who give lectures, and to the janitors who come in and clean up the classroom afterward. We might create a society on whose banners are inscribed, "From each according to his ability, to each according to his need."

To meet this objection to an unequal society there has been developed a biological theory of human nature that says that while the differences between us are in our genes, there are certain inborn similarities among us all. These similarities of human nature guarantee that differences in ability will be converted into differences in status, that society is naturally hierarchical, and that a society of equal reward and status is biologically impossible. We might pass laws requiring such equality, but the moment the vigilance of the state was relaxed we would return to "doing what comes naturally."

These three ideas — that we differ in fundamental abilities because of innate differences, that those innate differences are biologically inherited, and that human nature guarantees the formation of a hierarchical society — when taken together, form what we can call the *ideology of biological determinism*.

The idea that blood will tell was not invented by biologists. It is a dominant theme of nineteenth-century literature, and one can hardly appreciate the most praised and popular writers of the last century without seeing how a theory of innate difference informed their work. Think of Dickens's *Oliver Twist*. When Oliver first meets young Jack Dawkins, the Artful Dodger, on the road to London, a remarkable contrast in body and spirit is established. The Dodger is described as "a snub-nosed, flat-browed, common-faced boy ... with rather bow-legs, and little, sharp, ugly eyes," and his English was not the best. What can we expect from a 10-year-old street urchin with no family, no education, and only the lowest criminals of London for companions? Oliver's speech, however, is perfect (he knows when to use the subjunctive) and his manner is genteel. He is described as a pale, thin child, but with a good sturdy spirit in his breast. Yet Oliver was raised from birth in the most degrading of nineteenth-century British institutions, the parish workhouse, an orphan with no education and little to eat. He is described as having spent the first nine years of his life rolling about on the floor all day "without the inconvenience of too much food or too much clothing." Where amid the oakum-pickings did Oliver garner that sensitivity of soul and perfection of English grammer? *Oliver Twist* is a mystery novel, and that is its mystery. The answer is that although his food was gruel, his blood was upper-middle-class. His mother was the daughter of a naval officer. His father's family was well off and socially ambitious.

A similar theme is central to George Eliot's *Daniel Deronda*. We first meet Daniel, the young stepson of an English baronet, wasting his time in a fashionable gambling spa. When he becomes a bit older, he suddenly has mysterious longings for things Hebrew. He falls in love with a Jewish woman, studies the Talmud, and converts. The reader will not be surprised to learn that he is the son of a Jewish actress whom he has never seen but whose blood tells. Nor is this a madness only of the Anglo-Saxons. The Rougon-Macquart novels of Émile Zola were deliberately written as a kind of experimental literature to illustrate the discoveries of nineteenth-century anthropology. In the preface, Zola tells us that "heredity has its laws just like gravitation." The Rougon-Macquarts are a family descended from the two lovers of one woman, one of whom was a solid, industrious peasant, while the other was a wastrel and degenerate. From the dependable peasant descend solid, honest stock, while from the degenerate ancestor descend a long line of social misfits and criminals including the famous Nana, who was a nymphomaniac from early childhood, and her mother, Gervaise, the laundress, who despite beginning a solid entrepreneurial life, lapses into her natural indolence. When Gervaise's husband, Copeau, the father of Nana, was admitted to hospital with the DTs, the first question the physician asked him was, "Did your father drink?" The public consciousness of the period both in Europe and North America was permeated with the notion that intrinsic differences in temperament and merit will finally dominate any mere effect of education and environment.

The fictional Rougon-Macquarts are seen again in the equally fictional but supposedly real family of Kallikaks, who graced virtually every textbook of American psychology until the Second World War. The Kallikaks were supposed to be two halves of a family descended from two women of contrasting nature and a common father. This piece of academic fiction was meant to convince malleable young minds that criminality, laziness, alcoholism, and incest were inborn and inherited.

Nor were supposedly innate differences restricted to individual variation. Nations and races were said to be characterized by innate temperamental and intellectual differences. These claims were made not by racists, demagogues, and fascist know-nothings but by the leaders of the American academic, psychological, and sociological establishments. In 1923, Carl Brigham, who was later secretary of the College Entrance Examination Board, produced a study of intelligence under the direction of R.M. Yerkes, professor of psychology at Harvard and the president of the American Psychological Association. The study asserted: "We must assume that we are measuring inborn intelligence. We must face the possibility of racial admixture here in America that is infinitely worse than that faced by any European country for we are incorporating the Negro into our racial stock. The decline of the American intelligence will be more rapid ... owing to the presence here of the Negro."[4]

Yet another president of the American Psychological Association said that whenever there has been mixed breeding with the Negro, there has been deterioration of civilizations.[5] Louis Agassiz, one of the most famous zoologists of the nineteenth century, reported that the skull sutures of Negro babies closed earlier than the sutures of white babies, so their brains were entrapped, and it would be dangerous to teach them too much. Perhaps the most extraordinary of claims was that of Henry Fairfield Osborne, president of the American Museum of Natural History and one of America's most eminent and prestigious paleontologists, who worked out the sequence of evolution of the horse. He wrote,

> The northern races invaded the countries to the south, not only as conquerors but as contributors of strong moral and intellectual elements to a more or less decadent civilization. Through the Nordic tide which flowed into Italy came the ancestors of Raphael, Leonardo, Galileo, Titiano; also, according to Günther, of Giotto, Botticelli, Petrarca, and Tasso. Columbus, from his portraits and from busts, *whether authentic or not*, was clearly of Nordic ancestry.[6] [emphasis added]

Whether authentic or not, indeed! Over and over again, leading intellectuals have assured their audiences that modern science shows that there are inborn racial and individual differences in ability. Nor have modern biologists taken a different view. Except for a brief interruption around the time of the Second World War, when the crimes of Nazism made claims of innate inferiority extremely unpopular, biological determinism has been the mainstream commitment of biologists. Yet these claims are made without a shred of evidence and in contradiction to every principle of biology and genetics.

To realize the error of these claims, we need to understand what is involved in the development of an organism. First, we are not determined by our genes, although surely we are influenced by them. Development depends not only on the materials that have been inherited from parents — that is, the genes and other materials in the sperm and egg — but also on the particular temperature, humidity, nutrition, smells, sights, and sounds (including what we call education) that impinge on the developing organism. Even if I knew the complete molecular specification of every gene in an organism, I could not predict what that organism would be. Of course, the difference between lions and lambs is almost entirely a consequence of the differences in genes between them. But variations among individuals within species are a unique consequence of both genes and the developmental environment in a constant interaction. Moreover, curiously enough, even if I knew the genes of a developing organism and the complete sequence of its environments, I could not specify the organism.

There is yet another factor at work. If we count the number of bristles under the wing of a fruitfly, for example, we find that there is a different number on the left side than on the right. Some have more bristles on the left, some more on the right; there is no average difference. So, there is a kind of fluctuating asymmetry. An individual fruitfly, however, has the same genes on its left side as on its right. Moreover, the tiny size of a developing fruitfly and the place it develops guarantee that both left and right sides have had the same humidity, the same oxygen, the same temperature. The differences between left and right side are caused neither by genetic nor by environmental differences but by random variation in growth and division of cells during development: *developmental noise*.

This chance element in development is an important source of variation. Indeed, in the case of the fruitfly bristles, there is as much variation consequent on developmental noise as there is from genetic and environmental variation. We do not know in human beings, for example, how much of the difference between us is a consequence of the random differences in the growth of neurons during our embryonic life and early childhood. It is our common prejudice that even if one had practised the violin from a very early age, one would not be able to play as well as Menuhin, and we think of him as having special neuronal connections. But that is not the same as saying that those neuronal connections are coded in his genes. There may be large random differences in the growth of our central nervous systems. It is a fundamental principle of developmental genetics that every organism is the outcome of a unique interaction between genes and environmental sequences modulated by the random chances of cell growth and division, and that all these together finally produce an organism. Moreover, an organism changes throughout its entire life. Human beings change their size, not only growing larger as children, but as they grow old, growing smaller as their joints and bones shrink.

A more sophisticated version of genetic determinism agrees that organisms are a consequence of both environmental and genetic influences but describes differences between individuals as differences in *capacity*. This is the empty bucket metaphor. We each begin life as an empty bucket of a different size. If the environment provides only a little water, then all these buckets will have the same amount in them. But if an abundance is provided from the environment, then the small buckets will overflow and the large ones will hold more. In this view, if every person were allowed to develop to his or her genetic capacity, there would indeed be major differences in ability and performance, and these would be fair and natural.

But there is no more biology in the metaphor of innate capacity than there is in the notion of fixed genetic effects. The unique interaction between organism and environment cannot be described by differences in capacity. It is true that if two genetically different organisms developed in exactly the same environment, they would be different, but that difference cannot be described as different capacities because the genetical type that was superior in one environment may be inferior in a second developmental environment. For example, strains of rats can be selected for better or poorer ability to find their way through a maze, and these strains of rats pass on their differential ability to run the maze to their offspring, so they are certainly genetically different in this respect. But if exactly the same strains of rats are given a different task, or if the conditions of learning are changed, the bright rats turn out to be dull and the dull rats turn out to be bright. There is no general genetic superiority of one rat strain over another in finding its way through a problem.

A more subtle and mystifying approach to biological determinism rejects both the genetic fixity of the first view and the capacity metaphor of the second and is, instead, statistical. Essentially, it states the problem as one of partitioning the effects of environment and genes so that we can say that, perhaps, 80 percent of the difference among individuals is caused by their genes and 20 percent by their environment. Of course, these differences must be on a population level rather than an individual level. It would make no sense at all to say that of someone's height of five feet eleven and a half inches, five feet two were a result of her genes and the other nine and a half inches were put there by the food she ate. The statistical view considers the proportion of *variation* among individuals rather than partitioning a particular individual measurement. The statistical approach tries to assign some proportion of all the variation among individuals or groups to variation among their genes, and a second proportion that results from variation among their environments.

The implication is that if most of the variation in, say, intelligence among individuals is a consequence of variation among their genes, then manipulating the environment will not make much difference. It is often said, for example, that 80 percent of the variation among individual children in their IQ performance is caused by

variation in their genes and only 20 percent by variation in their environment. The result is that the greatest possible amelioration of environment could not eliminate more than 20 percent of differences among individuals, and the 80 percent would still be there because it is a consequence of genetic variation. This is a completely fallacious although plausible-sounding argument. There is no connection whatsoever between the variation that can be ascribed to genetic differences as opposed to environmental differences and whether a change in environment will affect performance and by how much. We should remember that any very ordinary arithmetic student in primary school in Canada can correctly add a column of figures vastly more quickly than the most intelligent Ancient Roman mathematician, who had to struggle with cumbersome X's, V's, and I's. That same ordinary student can multiply two five-digit numbers with a $10 hand-held calculator more quickly and accurately than a professor of mathematics could have a century ago.

A change in environment, in this case of cultural environment, can change abilities by many orders of magnitude. Moreover, the differences between individuals are abolished by cultural and mechanical inventions. Differences that can be ascribed to genetic differences and that appear in one environment may disappear completely in another. Although there may be biologically based average differences in physique and strength between a random group of men and random group of women (and these are less than usually supposed), these differences rapidly become irrelevant and disappear from practical view in a world of electrically driven hoists, power steering, and electronic controls. So the proportion of variation in a population as a consequence of variation in genes is not a fixed property but one that varies from environment to environment. That is, how much difference among us is a consequence of genetic differences between us depends, curiously enough, on environment.

Conversely, how much difference there is between us that is a consequence of environmental variation in our life histories depends on our genes. We know from experiments that organisms that have some particular genes are very sensitive to environmental variation while other individuals with different genes are insensitive to environmental variation. Environmen-tal variation and genetic variation are not independent causal pathways. Genes affect how sensitive one is to environment, and environment affects how relevant one's genetic differences may be. The interaction between them is indissoluble, and we can separate genetic and environmental effects statistically only in a particular population of organisms at a particular moment with a particular set of specified environments. When an environment changes, all bets are off.

The contrast between genetic and environmental, between nature and nurture, is not a contrast between fixed and changeable. It is a fallacy of biological determinism to say that if differences are in the genes, no change can occur. We know this to be true from medical evidence alone. There are many so-called inborn errors of metabolism in which a defective gene results, in normal circumstances, in a defective physiology. An example is Wilson's disease, a genetic defect that prevents its sufferers from detoxifying the copper that we all consume in minute quantities in our ordinary food. The copper builds up in the body and eventually causes nervous degeneration and finally death, some time in adolescence or early adulthood. Nothing could be more perfectly described as a genetic disorder. Yet people with this defective gene can lead a perfectly normal life and have a normal development by taking a pill that helps them get rid of the copper, and they are then indistinguishable from anyone else.

It is sometimes said that examples of changing the conditions of performance, such as the invention of Arabic numerals, or the calculator, or providing a pill, are beside the point because we are interested in some sort of basic unaided, naked ability. But there are no measures of "unaided" ability, nor are we really interested in them. There are some people who can remember long columns of figures and others

who are good at adding and multiplying large numbers in their heads. So why do we give written IQ tests, which, after all, are simply giving the crutch of paper and pencil to people who do not have the "unaided" ability to do mental arithmetic? Indeed, why do we allow people taking mental tests to wear eyeglasses, if we are interested in culturally unmodified "naked" abilities? The answer is that we have no interest in arbitrarily defined abilities, but are concerned with differences in the ability to carry out *socially constructed* tasks that are relevant to the structure of our actual social lives.

Aside from the conceptual difficulties of trying to ascribe separate effects to genes and environment, there are severe experimental difficulties in detecting the influence of genes, especially when we deal with human beings. How do we decide whether genes influence differences in some trait? In all organisms the process is the same. We compare individuals who are differently related to one another, and if more closely related individuals are more similar than are more distantly related ones, we ascribe some power to the genes. But herein lies the deep difficulty of human genetics. Unlike experimental animals, people who are more closely related to each other not only share more genes in common but they also share environment in common because of the family and class structure of human societies. The observation that children resemble their parents in some trait does not distinguish between similarity that comes from genetic similarity and similarity that arises from environmental resemblance. The resemblance of parents and children is the observation to be explained. It is not evidence for genes. For example, the two social traits that have the highest resemblance between parents and children in North America are religious sect and political party. Yet even the most ardent biological determinist would not seriously argue that there is a gene for Episcopalianism or voting Social Credit.

The problem is to distinguish genetic similarity from environmental similarity. It is for this reason that so much emphasis has been put on twin studies in human genetics. The idea is that if twins are more similar than ordinary sibs or if twins raised in completely isolated families are still similar, then this surely must be evidence for genes. In particular, there has been a fascination with a study of identical twins raised apart. If identical twins — that is, twins sharing all the same genes — are similar even though raised apart, then their trait must be strongly genetically influenced. Much of the claim for the high heritability of IQ, for example, comes from studies of identical twins raised apart.

Only three such studies have been published. The first and largest set of studies was reported by Sir Cyril Burt. This was the only study that claimed no similarity between the family circumstances of the families that raised separated twins. It also claimed a heritability of 80 percent for IQ performance. However, careful investigation by Oliver Gillie of the *Times* of London and Professor Leon Kamin at Princeton revealed that Burt had simply made up the numbers and made up the twins.[7] He even made up the collaborators whose names appeared with his in the publications. We need consider these claims no further. They represent one of the great scandals of modern psychology and biology.

When we look at the other studies, which actually give family details of the separated twins, we realize that we live in a real world and not in a Gilbert and Sullivan operetta. The reason that twins are separated at birth may be that their mother has died in childbirth, so that one twin is raised by an aunt and another by a best friend or grandmother. Sometimes the parents cannot afford to keep both children so they give one to a relative. In fact, the studied twins were not raised apart at all. They were raised by members of the same extended family, in the same small village. They went to school together. They played together. Other adoption studies of human IQ that are said to demonstrate the effect of genes have their own experimental difficulties, including the failure to match children by age, extremely small samples, and biased selection of

cases for study.[8] There is a strong effort on the part of parents of many twins to make them as similar as possible. They are given names beginning with the same letter and are dressed alike. International twin conventions give prizes for the most similar twins. One twin study advertised in the newspapers and offered a trip to Chicago for identical twins, thus attracting those who were the most similar.[9] As a consequence of such biases, there is at present simply no convincing measure of the role of genes in influencing human behavioural variation.

One of the major biological ideological weapons used to convince people that their position in society is fixed and unchangeable and, indeed, fair is the constant confusion between inherited and unchangeable. This confusion is nowhere more manifest than in the very studies of adoptions that are meant to measure biological similarities. In human populations, one carries out an adoption study like that of separation of identical twins to try to break the connection between resemblance that comes from genetic sources and resemblance that comes from the sources of family similarity. If adopted children resemble their biological parents more closely than they resemble their adopting parents, then the geneticists quite correctly regard this as evidence for the influence of genes. When one looks at all the studies of adoption in order to study the genetic influence on intelligence, there are two constant results.

First, adopted children do resemble their biological parents in the sense that the higher the IQ score of the biological parent, the higher the IQ score of the child who was adopted. So, biological parents are having some influence on the IQ of their children even though those children are adopted early, and putting aside the possibility of prenatal nutritional differences or ex-tremely early stimulation, it would be reasonable to say that genes have some influence on IQ scores. We can only speculate about the source of genetic influence. There is a premium on speed in IQ testing, and genes might have some influence on reaction times or general speed of central nervous processes.

The second feature of adoption studies is that the IQ test scores of the children are about 20 points higher than those of their biological parents. It is still the case that the biological parents with the higher IQ scores have children with higher scores, but the children as a group have moved well ahead of their biological parents. In fact, the average IQ scores of these adopted children are about equal to the average IQ of the adopting parents, who always do much better on IQ tests than the biological parents. What is at stake here is the difference between *correlation* and *identity*. Two variables are positively correlated if higher values of one are matched with higher values of the other. The ordered set of numbers 100, 101, 102, and 103 is perfectly correlated with the set of 120, 121, 122, and 123 because each increase in one set is perfectly matched by an increase in the other. Yet the two sets of numbers are clearly not identical, differing as they do by 20 units on the average. So the IQ of parents may be excellent predictors of the IQs of their children in the sense that higher values for parents are matched with higher values for offspring, but the *average* IQ value of their children may be much greater. For the geneticist, it is the *correlation* that indicates the role of genes; the heritability predicts nothing about changes in the group average from generation to generation. The adoption studies are a revelation of the meaning of IQ tests and of the social reality of adoption.

First, what do IQ tests actually measure? They are a combination of numerical, vocabulary, education, and attitudinal questions. They ask such things as "Who was Wilkins McCawber?" "What is the meaning of 'sudiferous'?" "What should a girl do if a boy hits her?" (Hitting him back is *not* the right answer!) And how do we know that someone who does well on such a test is *intelligent*? Because, in fact, the tests were originally standardized to pick out precisely those children in a class whom the teacher had already labelled intelligent. That is, IQ tests are instruments for giving an apparently objec-

tive and "scientific" gloss to the social prejudices of educational institutions.

Second, people who decide on an early adoption for their children are usually working-class or unemployed people who do not share in the education and culture of the middle class. People who adopt children, on the other hand, are usually middle-class and have an appropriate education and cultural experience for the content and intent of IQ tests. So adopting parents have, as a group, much higher IQ performances than the parents who have chosen adoption for their children. The educational and family environment in which these children are then raised has the expected result of raising all their IQs even though there is evidence for some genetic influence from their biological parents.

These results of adoption studies illustrate perfectly why we cannot answer a question about how much something can be changed by answering a different question, namely, are there genes influencing the trait? If we wanted seriously to ask the question posed by Arthur Jensen in his famous article "How much can we boost IQ and scholastic achievement?"[10] the only way we could answer would be to try to boost IQ and scholastic achievement. We do not answer it by asking, as Jensen did, whether there is a genetic influence on IQ, because to be genetic is not to be unchangeable.

Biological determinists claim that there are not only differences in ability among individuals but that these individual differences explain racial differences in social power and success. It is hard to know how one would get evidence about Black–white differences that did not totally confound genetic and environmental variation. Interracial adoptions, for example, are uncommon, especially of white children adopted by Black foster parents. Occasional evidence does appear, however.

In Dr Barnardo's homes in Britain, where children are taken as orphans soon after birth, a study was done of intelligence testing of children of Black and white ancestry.[11] Several tests were given at various ages, and small differences were found in the IQ performance between these groups, but these were not statistically significant. If nothing more was said about it, most of the readers would assume that the small differences showed whites were better than Blacks. But in fact the reverse was true. The differences were not statistically significant, but where there were any differences, they were in favour of Blacks. There is not an iota of evidence of any kind that the differences in status, wealth, and power between races in North America have anything to do with the genes, except, of course, for the socially mediated effects of the genes for skin colour. Indeed, there is in general a great deal less difference genetically between races than one might suppose from the superficial cues we all use in distinguishing races. Skin colour, hair form, and nose shape are certainly influenced by genes, but we do not know how many such genes there are, or how they work. On the other hand, when we look at genes we do know something about, genes that influence our blood type, for example, or genes for the various enzyme molecules essential to our physiology, we find that although there is a tremendous amount of variation from individual to individual, there is remarkably little variation on the average between major human groups. In fact, about 85 percent of all identified human genetic variation is between any two individuals from the same ethnic group. Another 8 percent of all the variation is between ethnic groups within a race — say, between Spaniards, Irish, Italians, and Britons — and only 7 percent of all human genetic variation lies on the average between major human races like those of Africa, Asia, Europe, and Oceania.[12]

So we have no reason *a priori* to think that there would be any genetic differentiation between racial groups in characteristics such as behaviour, temperament, and intelligence. Nor is there an iota of evidence that social classes differ in any way in their genes except insofar as ethnic origin or race may be used as a form of economic discrimination. The nonsense propagated by ideologues of biological determinism that the lower classes are biologically inferior to the upper classes, that all the good things in European culture come from the Nordic groups, is precisely nonsense. It is meant to legitimate the structures of inequality in our society by putting a biological gloss on them and by propagating the continual confusion between what may be influenced by genes and what may be changed by social and environmental alternations.

The vulgar error that confuses heritability and fixity has been, over the years, the most powerful single weapon that biological ideologues have had in legitimating a society of inequality. Since as biologists they must know better, one is entitled to at least a suspicion that the beneficiaries of a system of inequality are not to be regarded as objective experts.

NOTES

1. R.J. Herrnstein, *IQ in the Meritocracy* (Boston: Atlantic–Little, Brown, 1973), 221.
2. L.F. Ward, "Education" (manuscript, Special Collection Division, Brown University, Providence, RI, 1873).
3. A.R. Jensen, "How Much Can We Boost IQ and Scholastic Achievement?" *Harvard Educational Review* 39 (1969): 15.
4. C.C. Brigham, *A Study of American Intelligence* (Princeton, NJ: Princeton University Press, 1923), 209–10.
5. H.L. Garrett, *Breeding Down* (Richmond, VA: Patrick Henry Press, n.d.).
6. H.F. Osborne, letter, *New York Times*, 8 April 1924, 18.
7. R.C. Lewontin, S. Rose, and L.J. Kamin, *Not in Our Genes* (New York: Pantheon, 1984), 101–6.
8. L.J. Kamin, *The Science and Politics of IQ* (Potomac, MD: Erlbaum, 1974).
9. Ibid.
10. Jensen, "How Much Can We Boost IQ."
11. B. Tizard. "IQ and Race," *Nature* 247 (1974): 316.
12. R.C. Lewontin, *Human Diversity* (San Francisco: Scientific American Books, 1982).

PART 2C
SOCIAL STRUCTURE

Social structures are the patterns of social relations that bind people together and give shape to their lives. Consider hierarchy, one feature of social structure. Hierarchy refers to the degree to which power is unequally distributed in a social group. The more unequal the distribution of power, the greater the degree of hierarchy. In a family, for instance, the degree of hierarchy and the position of a child in the hierarchy profoundly influence the quality of his or her life. In a very hierarchical family the child may grow up to resent authority or cringe before it — or both. In a family without hierarchy, the child may be spoiled and remain selfish. As these examples illustrate, who you are is partly the result of the social structures through which you pass.

Despite its importance in shaping who we are, we seldom notice social structure in our everyday lives. In fact, we often deny its significance. That is because our culture places such strong emphasis on individual freedom and responsibility. Accordingly, we learn three rules about human behaviour from an early age:

- People are perfectly free to act as they wish.
- People can therefore choose right over wrong.
- If people choose wrong, we should judge them as moral inferiors.

Such thinking may be good for our egos, but it has little in common with sociology and is one of prejudice's most stubborn roots.

Chapter 8 offers a chilling illustration of the power of social structures. It reports an experiment in which middle-class American and Canadian university students were assigned the role of prisoner or guard in an artificial jail constructed by the experimenter. Almost immediately, the subjects were unable to distinguish between their roles and their former selves. Even though none of the subjects was instructed how to behave, the "guards" quickly learned to take pleasure in causing pain while the "prisoners" were wracked with hatred as they planned their escape. A lifetime of learning was suspended. The experiment had to be abandoned within a few days. Social structure had revealed its influence.

Émile Durkheim's *Suicide* is a forceful, classical exposition of the way one aspect of social structure — **social solidarity** — helps to shape us. A group's level of social solidarity is higher to the degree its members share the same values and interact frequently and intimately. In the section reprinted here as Chapter 9, Durkheim argues that social solidarity anchors people to the social world. It follows, he argues, that the lower the level of social solidarity in a group, the more a group member will be inclined to take his or her own life if he or she is in deep distress. Durkheim tests his argument by examining the level of social solidarity that characterizes the major religious groups in Europe. He demonstrates that the propensity of group members to take their own lives does indeed vary inversely with social solidarity. On the strength of Durkheim's argument one is obliged to conclude that social structure powerfully affects even an uncommon, antisocial action that is committed in private.

GLOSSARY

Social solidarity is higher in a group to the degree its members share the same values and interact frequently and intimately.

Social structures are the patterns of social relations that bind people together and give shape to their lives.

CRITICAL THINKING QUESTIONS

1. *Hitler's Willing Executioners* (New York: Alfred A. Knopf, 1996) is a controversial book by historian Daniel Goldhagen. He argues that that Germans during the Second World War for the most part participated enthusiastically in the systematic destruction of European Jewry. Read the book and decide whether Goldhagen's argument needs to be qualified in the light of Zimbardo's research.
2. Have you ever felt compelled to act against your will? What elements of social structure caused you to do so?
3. "The superiority of Protestantism with respect to suicide results from its being a less strongly integrated church than the Catholic Church." What does Émile Durkheim mean by this statement?
4. According to Durkheim, how is suicide associated with "the spirit of free inquiry" that animates Protestantism?
5. What are the social origins of egoistic suicide according to Durkheim?
6. "Suicide varies inversely with the degree of integration of the social groups of which the individual forms a part." Explain this statement and give examples to support your answer.

Chapter 8

Pathology of Imprisonment

PHILIP E. ZIMBARDO

In an attempt to understand just what it means psychologically to be a prisoner or prison guard, Craig Haney, Curt Banks, Dave Jaffe, and I created our own prison. We carefully screened over 70 volunteers who answered an ad in a Palo Alto city newspaper and ended up with about two dozen young men who were selected to be part of this study. They were mature, emotionally stable, normal, intelligent college students from middle-class homes throughout the United States and Canada. They appeared to represent the cream of the crop of this generation. None had any criminal record, and initially all were relatively homogeneous on many dimensions.

Half were arbitrarily designated as prisoners by a flip of a coin, the others as guards. These were the roles they were to play in our simulated prison. The guards were made aware of the potential seriousness and danger of the situation and their own vulnerability. They made up their own formal rules for maintaining law, order, and respect, and were generally free to improvise new ones during their eight-hour, three-man shifts. The prisoners were unexpectedly picked up at their homes by a city policeman in a squad car, searched, handcuffed, fingerprinted, booked at the Palo Alto station house, and taken blindfolded to our jail. There they were stripped, deloused, put into a uniform, given a number, and put into a cell with two other prisoners, where they expected to live for the next two weeks. The pay was good ($15 a day) and their motivation was to make money.

We observed and recorded on videotape the events that occurred in the prison, and we interviewed and tested the prisoners and guards at various points throughout the study. Some of the videotapes of the actual encounters between the prisoners and guards were seen on the NBC News feature "Chronolog" on November 26, 1971.

At the end of only six days, we had to close down our mock prison because what we saw was frightening. It was no longer apparent to most of the subjects (or to us) where reality ended and their roles began. The majority had indeed become prisoners or guards, no longer able to clearly differentiate between role playing and self. There were dramatic changes in virtually every aspect of their behaviour, thinking, and feeling. In less than a week, the experience of imprisonment undid (temporarily) a lifetime of learning; human values were suspended, self-concepts were challenged, and the ugliest, most base, pathological side of human nature surfaced. We were horrified because we saw some boys (guards) treat others as if they were despicable animals, taking pleasure in cruelty, while other boys (prisoners) became servile, dehumanized robots who thought only of escape, of their own individual survival, and of their mounting hatred for the guards.

We had to release three prisoners in the first four days because they had such acute situational traumatic reactions as hysterical crying, confusion in thinking, and severe depression. Others begged to be paroled, and all but three were willing to forfeit all the money they had earned if they could be paroled. By then (the fifth day), they had been so programmed to think of themselves as prisoners that when their request for parole was denied, they returned docilely to their cells. Now, had they been thinking as college students acting in an oppressive experiment, they would have quit once they no longer wanted the $15 a day we used as our only incentive. However, the reality was not quitting an experiment but "being paroled by the parole board from the Stanford County Jail." By the last days, the earlier solidarity among the prisoners (systematically broken by the guards) dissolved into "each man for himself." Finally, when one of their fellows was put in solitary confinement (a small closet) for refusing to eat, the prisoners were given a choice by one of the guards: give up their blankets and the incorrigible prisoner would be let out, or keep their blankets and he would be kept in all night. They voted to keep their blankets and to abandon their brother.

About a third of the guards became tyrannical in their arbitrary use of power, in enjoying their control over other people. They were corrupted by the power of their roles and became quite inventive in their techniques of breaking the spirit of the prisoners and making them feel they were worthless. Some of the guards merely did their jobs as tough but fair correctional officers, and several were good guards from the prisoners' point of view because they did them small favours and were friendly. However, no good guard ever interfered with a command by any of the bad guards; they never intervened on the side of the prisoners, they never told the others to ease off because it was only an experiment, and they never even came to me as prison superintendent or experimenter in charge to complain. In part, they were good because the others were bad; they needed the others to help establish their own egos in a positive light. In a sense, the good guards perpetuated the prison more than the other guards because their own needs to be liked prevented them from disobeying or violating the implicit guards' code. At the same time, the act of befriending the prisoners created a social reality that made the prisoners less likely to rebel.

By the end of the week, the experiment had become a reality, as if it were a Pirandello play directed by Kafka that just keeps going after the audience has left. The consultant for our prison, Carlo Prescot, an ex-convict with sixteen years of imprisonment in California's jails, would get so depressed and furious each time he visited our prison, because of its psychological similarity to his experiences, that he would have to leave. A Catholic priest, who was a former prison chaplain in Washington, DC, talked to our prisoners after four days and said they were just like the other first-timers he had seen.

But in the end, I called off the experiment, not because of the horror I saw out there in the prison yard, but because of the horror of realizing that I could have easily traded places with the most brutal guard or become the weakest prisoner full of hatred at being so powerless that I could not eat, sleep, or go to the toilet without permission of the authorities. I could have become Calley at My Lai, George Jackson at San Quentin, one of the men at Attica.

Individual behaviour is largely under the control of social forces and environmental contingencies rather than personality traits, character, will power, or other empirically unvalidated constructs. Thus we create an illusion of freedom by attributing more internal control to ourselves, to the individual, than actually exists. We thus underestimate the power and pervasiveness of situational controls over behaviour because (a) they are often non-obvious and subtle, (b) we can often avoid entering situations in which we might be so controlled, and (c) we label as "weak" or "deviant" people in those situations who do behave differently from how we believe we would.

Each of us carries around in our heads a favourable self-image in which we are essentially just, fair, humane, and understanding. For example, we could not imagine inflicting pain on others without much provocation or hurting people who had done nothing to us, who in fact were even liked by us. However, there is a growing body of social psychological research that underscores the conclusion derived from this prison study. Many people, perhaps the majority, can be made to do almost anything when put into psychologically compelling situations — regardless of their morals, ethics, values, attitudes, beliefs, or personal convictions. My colleague, Stanley Milgram, has shown that more than 60 percent of the population will deliver what they think is a series of painful electric shocks to another person even after the victim cries for mercy, begs them to stop, and then apparently passes out. The subjects complained that they did not want to inflict more pain but blindly obeyed the command of the authority figure (the experimenter) who said that they must go on. In my own research on violence, I have seen mild-mannered coeds repeatedly give shocks (which they thought were causing pain) to another girl, a stranger whom they had rated very favourably, simply by being made to feel anonymous and put in a situation in which they were expected to engage in this activity.

Observers of these and similar experimental situations never predict their outcomes and estimate that it is unlikely that they themselves would behave similarly. They can be so confident only when they are outside the situation. However, because the majority of people in these studies do act in non-rational, non-obvious ways, it follows that the majority of observers would also succumb to the social psychological forces in the situation.

With regard to prisons, we can state that the mere act of assigning labels to people and putting them into a situation in which those labels acquire validity and meaning is sufficient to elicit pathological behaviour. This pathology is not predictable from any available diagnostic indicators we have in the social sciences, and it is extreme enough to modify in very significant ways fundamental attitudes and behaviour. The prison situation, as presently arranged, is guaranteed to generate severe enough pathological reactions in both guards and prisoners as to debase their humanity, lower their feelings of self-worth, and make it difficult for them to be part of a society outside their prison.

Chapter 9

Egoistic Suicide

ÉMILE DURKHEIM

If one casts a glance at the map of European suicide, it is at once clear that in purely Catholic countries like Spain, Portugal, Italy, suicide is very little developed, while it is at its maximum in Protestant countries, in Prussia, Saxony, Denmark. The averages in Table 9.1 compiled by Morselli confirm this first conclusion.

The only essential difference between Catholicism and Protestantism is that the second permits free inquiry to a far greater degree than the first. The Catholic accepts his faith ready made, without scrutiny. He may not even submit it to historical examination since the original texts that serve as its basis are proscribed. A whole hierarchical system of authority is devised, with marvelous ingenuity, to render tradition invariable. All *variation* is abhorrent to Catholic thought. The Protestant is far more the author of his faith. The Bible is put in his hands and no interpretation is imposed upon him. The very structure of the reformed cult stresses this state of religious individualism. Nowhere but in England is the Protestant clergy a hierarchy; like the worshippers, the priest has no other source but himself and his conscience. He is a more instructed guide than the run of worshippers but with no special authority for fixing dogma. But what best proves that this freedom of inquiry proclaimed by the founders of the Reformation has not remained a Platonic affirmation is the increased multiplicity of all sorts of sects so strikingly in contrast with the indivisible unity of the Catholic Church.

We thus reach our first conclusion, that the proclivity of Protestantism for suicide must relate to the spirit of free inquiry that animates this religion. Let us understand this relationship correctly. Free inquiry itself is only the effect of another cause. When it appears, when men, after having long received their ready-made faith from tradition, claim the right to shape it for themselves, this is not because of the intrinsic desirability of free inquiry, for the latter involves as much sorrow as happiness. But it is because men henceforth need this liberty. This very need can have only one cause: the overthrow of traditional beliefs. If they still asserted themselves with equal energy, it would never occur to men to criticize them. If they still had the same authority, men would not demand the right to verify the source of this authority. Reflection develops only if its development becomes imperative, that is, if certain ideas and instinctive sentiments that have hitherto adequately guided conduct are found to have lost their efficacy. Then

TABLE 9.1 SUICIDE RATE BY RELIGIOUS COMPOSITION OF COUNTRY

RELIGIOUS COMPOSITION OF COUNTRY	SUICIDES PER MILLION INHABITANTS
Protestant	190
Mixed (Protestant and Catholic)	96
Catholic	58
Greek Catholic	40

reflection intervenes to fill the gap that has appeared, but which it has not created. Just as reflection disappears to the extent that thought and action take the form of automatic habits, it awakes only when accepted habits become disorganized. It asserts its rights against public opinion only when the latter loses strength, that is, when it is no longer prevalent to the same extent. If these assertions occur not merely occasionally and as passing crises, but become chronic; if individual consciences keep reaffirming their autonomy, it is because they are constantly subject to conflicting impulses, because a new opinion has not been formed to replace the one no longer existing. If a new system of beliefs were constituted that seemed as indisputable to everyone as the old, no one would think of discussing it any longer. Its discussion would no longer even be permitted; for ideas shared by an entire society draw from this consensus an authority that makes them sacrosanct and raises them above dispute. For them to have become more tolerant, they must first already have become the object of less general and complete assent and been weakened by preliminary controversy.

Thus, if it is correct to say that free inquiry, once proclaimed, multiplies schisms, it must be added that it presupposes them and derives from them, for it is claimed and instituted as a principle only in order to permit latent or half-declared schisms to develop more freely. So if Protestantism concedes a greater freedom to individual thought than does Catholicism, it is because it has fewer common beliefs and practices. Now, a religious society cannot exist without a collective *credo*, and the more extensive the *credo* the more unified and strong is the society. For it does not unite men by an exchange and reciprocity of services, a temporal bond of union that permits and even presupposes differences, but that a religious society cannot form. It socializes men only by attaching them completely to an identical body of doctrine and socializes them in proportion as this body of doctrine is extensive and firm. The more numerous the manners of action and thought of a religious character are, which are accordingly removed from free inquiry, the more the idea of God presents itself in all details of existence, and makes individual wills converge to one identical goal. Inversely, the greater concessions a confessional group makes to individual judgement, the less it dominates lives, the less its cohesion and vitality. We thus reach the conclusion that the superiority of Protestantism with respect to suicide results from its being a less strongly integrated church than the Catholic Church.

This also explains the situation of Judaism. Indeed, the reproach to which the Jews have for so long been exposed by Christianity has created feelings of unusual solidarity among them. Their need of resisting a general hostility, the very impossibility of free communication with the rest of the population, has forced them to strict union among themselves. Consequently, each community became a small, compact and coherent society with a strong feeling of self-consciousness and unity. Everyone thought and lived alike; individual divergences were made almost impossible by the community of existence and the close and constant surveillance of all over each. The Jewish church has thus been more strongly united than any other, from its dependence on itself because of being the object of intolerance. By analogy with what has just been observed apropos of Protestantism, the same cause must therefore be assumed for the slight tendency of the Jews to suicide in spite of all sorts of circumstances that might on the contrary incline them to it. Doubtless they owe this immunity in a sense to the hostility surrounding them. But if this is its influence, it is not because it imposes a higher morality but because it obliges them to live in greater union. They are immune to this degree because their religious society is of such solidarity. Besides, the ostracism to which they are subject is only one of the causes producing this result; the very nature of Jewish beliefs must contribute largely to it. Judaism, in fact, like all early religions, consists basically of a body of practices minutely governing all the details of life and leaving little free room to individual judgement.

The beneficent influence of religion is therefore not due to the special nature of religious conceptions. If religion protects man against the desire for self-destruction, it is not that it preaches the respect for his own person to him with arguments *sui generis;* but because it is a society. What constitutes this society is the existence of a certain number of beliefs and practices common to all the faithful, traditional and thus obligatory. The more numerous and strong these collective states of mind are, the stronger the integration of the religious community, and also the greater its preservative value. The details of dogmas and rites are secondary. The essential thing is that they be capable of supporting a sufficiently intense collective life.

So we reach the general conclusion: suicide varies inversely with the degree of integration of the social groups of which the individual forms a part.

But society cannot disintegrate without the individual simultaneously detaching himself from social life, without his own goals becoming preponderant over those of the community, in a word without his personality tending to surmount the collective personality. The more weakened the groups to which he belongs, the less he depends on them, the more he consequently depends only on himself and recognizes no other rules of conduct than what are founded on his private interests. If we agree to call this state egoism, in which the individual ego asserts itself to excess in the face of the social ego and at its expense, we may call egoistic the special type of suicide springing from excessive individualism.

But how can suicide have such an origin?

First of all, it can be said that, as collective force is one of the obstacles best calculated to restrain suicide, its weakening involves a development of suicide. When society is strongly integrated, it holds individuals under its control, considers them at its service, and thus forbids them to dispose willfully of themselves. Accordingly it opposes their evading their duties to it through death. But how could society

impose its supremacy upon them when they refuse to accept this subordination as legitimate? It no longer then possesses the requisite authority to retain them in their duty if they wish to desert; and conscious of its own weakness, it even recognizes their right to do freely what it can no longer prevent. So far as they are the admitted masters of their destinies, it is their privilege to end their lives. They, on their part, have no reason to endure life's sufferings patiently. For they cling to life more resolutely when belonging to a group they love, so as not to betray interests they put before their own. The bond that unites them with the common cause attaches them to life, and the lofty goal they envisage prevents their feeling personal troubles so deeply. There is, in short, in a cohesive and animated society a constant interchange of ideas and feelings from all to each and each to all, something like a mutual moral support, which instead of throwing the individual on his own resources, leads him to share in the collective energy and supports his own when exhausted.

But these reasons are purely secondary. Excessive individualism not only results in favouring the action of suicidogenic causes, but it is itself such a cause. It not only frees man's inclination to do away with himself from a protective obstacle, but creates this inclination out of whole cloth and thus gives birth to a special suicide that bears its mark. This must be clearly understood for this is what constitutes the special character of the type of suicide just distinguished and justifies the name we have given it. What is there then in individualism that explains this result?

A whole range of functions concerns only the individual; these are the ones indispensable for physical life. Since they are made for this purpose only, they are perfected by its attainment. In everything concerning them, therefore, man can act reasonably without thought of transcendental purposes. These functions serve by merely serving him. In so far as he has no other needs, he is therefore self-sufficient and can live happily with no other objective than living. This is not the case, however, with the civilized adult. He has many ideas, feelings, and practices unrelated to organic needs. The roles of art, morality, religion, political faith, science itself are not to repair organic exhaustion nor to provide sound functioning of the organs. All this supra-physical life is built and expanded not because of the demands of the cosmic environment but because of the demands of the social environment. The influence of society is what has aroused in us the sentiments of sympathy and solidarity drawing us toward others; it is society that, fashioning us in its image, fills us with religious, political, and moral beliefs that control our actions. To play our social role, we have striven to extend our intelligence, and it is still society that has supplied us with tools for this development by transmitting to us its trust fund of knowledge.

Through the very fact that these superior forms of human activity have a collective origin, they have a collective purpose. As they derive from society they have reference to it; rather they are society itself incarnated and individualized in each one of us. But for them to have a raison d'être in our eyes, the purpose they envisage must be one not indifferent to us. We can cling to these forms of human activity only to the degree that we cling to society itself. Contrari-wise, in the same measure as we feel detached from society we become detached from that life whose source and aim is society. For what purpose do these rules of morality, these precepts of law binding us to all sorts of sacrifices, these restrictive dogmas exist, if there is no being outside us whom they serve and in whom we participate? What is the purpose of science itself? If its only use is to increase our chances for survival, it does not deserve the trouble it entails. Instinct acquits itself better of this role; animals prove this. Why substitute for it a more hesitant and uncertain reflection? What is the end of suffering, above all? If the value of things can be estimated only by their relation to this positive evil for the individual, it is without reward and incomprehensible. This problem does not exist

for the believer firm in his faith or the man strongly bound by ties of domestic or political society. Instinctively and unreflectively they ascribe all that they are and do, the one to his Church or his God, the living symbol of the Church, the other to his family, the third to his country or party. Even in their sufferings they see only a means of glorifying the group to which they belong and thus do homage to it. So, the Christian ultimately desires and seeks suffering to testify more fully to his contempt for the flesh and more fully resemble his divine model. But the more the believer doubts, that is, the less he feels himself a real participant in the religious faith to which he belongs, and from which he is freeing himself; the more the family and community become foreign to the individual, so much the more does he become a mystery to himself, unable to escape the exasperating and agonizing question: to what purpose?

If, in other words, as has often been said, man is double, it is because social man superimposes himself upon physical man. Social man necessarily presupposes a society that he expresses and serves. If this dissolves, if we no longer feel it in existence and action about and above us, whatever is social in us is deprived of all objective foundation. All that remains is an artificial combination of illusory images, a phantasmagoria vanishing at the least reflection; that is, nothing that can be a goal for our action. Yet this social man is the essence of civilized man; he is the masterpiece of existence. Thus we are bereft of reasons for existence; for the only life to which we could cling no longer corresponds to anything actual; the only existence still based upon reality no longer meets our needs. Because we have been initiated into a higher existence, the one that satisfies an animal or a child can satisfy us no more and the other itself fades and leaves us helpless. So there is nothing more for our efforts to lay hold of, and we feel them lose themselves in emptiness. In this sense it is true to say that our activity needs an object transcending it. We do not need it to maintain ourselves in the illusion of an impossible immortality; it is implicit in our moral constitution and cannot be even partially lost without this losing its raison d'être in the same degree. No proof is needed that in such a state of confusion the least cause of discouragement may easily give birth to desperate resolutions. If life is not worth the trouble of being lived, everything becomes a pretext to rid ourselves of it.

But this is not all. This detachment occurs not only in single individuals. One of the constitutive elements of every national temperament consists of a certain way of estimating the value of existence. There is a collective as well as an individual humour inclining peoples to sadness or cheerfulness, making them see things in bright or sombre lights. In fact, only society can pass a collective opinion on the value of human life; for this the individual is incompetent. The latter knows nothing but himself and his own little horizon; thus his experience is too limited to serve as a basis for a general appraisal. He may indeed consider his own life to be aimless; he can say nothing applicable to others. On the contrary, without sophistry, society may generalize its own feeling as to itself, its state of health, or lack of health. For individuals share too deeply in the life of society for it to be diseased without their suffering infection. What it suffers they necessarily suffer. Because it is the whole, its ills are communicated to its parts. Hence it cannot disintegrate without awareness that the regular conditions of general existence are equally disturbed. Because society is the end on which our better selves depend, it cannot feel us escaping it without a simultaneous realization that our activity is purposeless. Since we are its handiwork, society cannot be conscious of its own decadence without the feeling that henceforth this work is of no value. Thence are formed currents of depression and disillusionment emanating from no particular individual but expressing society's state of disintegration. They reflect the relaxation of social bonds, a sort of

collective asthenia, or social malaise, just as individual sadness, when chronic, in its way reflects the poor organic state of the individual. Then metaphysical and religious systems spring up that, by reducing these obscure sentiments to formulae, attempt to prove to men the senselessness of life and that it is self-deception to believe that it has purpose. Then new moralities originate that, by elevating facts to ethics, commend suicide or at least tend in that direction by suggesting a minimal existence. On their appearance they seem to have been created out of whole cloth by their makers, who are sometimes blamed for the pessimism of their doctrines. In reality they are an effect rather than a cause; they merely symbolize in abstract language and systematic form the physiological distress of the body social. As these currents are collective, they have, by virtue of their origin, an authority that they impose upon the individual and they drive him more vigorously on the way to which he is already inclined by the state of moral distress directly aroused in him by the disintegration of society. Thus, at the very moment that, with excessive zeal, he frees himself from the social environment, he still submits to its influence. However individualized a man may be, there is always something collective remaining — the very depression and melancholy resulting from this same exaggerated individualism. He effects communion through sadness when he no longer has anything else with which to achieve it.

Hence this type of suicide well deserves the name we have given it. Egoism is not merely a contributing factor in it; it is its generating cause. In this case the bond attaching man to life relaxes because that attaching him to society is itself slack. The incidents of private life that seem the direct inspiration of suicide and are considered its determining causes are in reality only incidental causes. The individual yields to the slightest shock of circumstance because the state of society has made him a ready prey to suicide.

PART 3

SOCIAL INEQUALITY

Social inequality is a core — some would say the central — sociological problem. It has provoked and confounded analysts since the founding of the discipline. For example, the simplification of the capitalist class system forecast by Marx never took place. Instead of polarizing around a large class of impoverished workers and a tiny class of wealthy capitalists, the stratification system became more complex. Small business owners did not disappear. In recent years they have actually become more numerous as a proportion of the economically active population. What C. Wright Mills called an "occupational salad" of "white-collar" personnel — professionals, educated office holders, clerks, and so forth — became the largest component of the stratification system. Manual or "blue collar" workers experienced a rising standard of living (at least until the early 1970s) while their numbers as a proportion of the total labour force shrunk. The revolution that Marx expected never happened.

Poverty persists nonetheless. According to the government-funded National Council of Welfare, about one out of six Canadians are poor. Moreover, poverty has been feminized: a substantial majority of poor adults are women. True, most adult women now work for a wage in the paid labour force, a development unforeseen by Marx, Weber, Durkheim, and other classical sociological writers. On the other hand, women tend to be segregated in "pink-collar" jobs — occupations that pay relatively low wages and are analogous to women's traditional family roles as servers, teachers, and nurturers. Even today, it is uncommon for women to have authority over men in the workplace, and even intimate relations between women and men are strongly influenced by the distribution of authority between the sexes.

Another unanticipated development in the realm of social stratification concerns the tenacity of ethnic and racial inequality, which the founders of sociology expected to disappear under capitalism. They believed that large factories and bureaucracies would, in effect, homogenize people, forcing them to work together, treating them all the same, and making cultural differences between them less pronounced. Although ethnic and racial stratification has declined in Canada and elsewhere, different ethnic and racial groups still tend to occupy definite niches in the social hierarchy.

These are some of the key problems in stratification research and some of the chief issues examined in the chapters that follow.

PART 3A

CLASS AND GENDER INEQUALITY

Since the early 1970s, the average real income (or "purchasing power") of Canadians has risen little, substantially lowering the post–World War II trend toward higher real incomes. Also since the early 1970s, income inequality has increased: the richest 20 percent of Canadians earn a larger share of total national income than they did 20 years ago, the middle 60 percent earn less, and the poorest 20 percent earn about the same. The share of total after-tax national income earned by the richest 20 percent of Canadians is now about 42 percent. The middle 60 percent of Canadians earn about 50 percent of total after-tax national income. The share of total after-tax national income earned by the bottom 20 percent of Canadians is about 8 percent.

Little wonder, then, that poverty remains a serious and persistent problem, as Ann Duffy and Nancy Mandell show in Chapter 10. The **poverty rate** is usually defined as the proportion of Canadian families whose members spend more than 54.7 percent of their income on food, clothing, and shelter. Using that standard, the poverty rate fell between the end of World War II and the early 1970s, remained fairly steady at about one-eighth of the population up to the early 1990s, and then to rose to about one-sixth of the population by the end of the 1990s. Most poor people work for a living, but more of the poor are lone women and their small children than used to be the case. As Duffy and Mandell document, the social and personal costs of poverty remain staggering.

In Chapter 11, Wallace Clement and John Myles analyze the gendered nature of the working and professional/managerial classes in postindustrial societies. They derive their data from a large sociological survey conducted in Canada, the United States, Sweden, Norway, and Finland. Postindustrial society is characterized by a small and shrinking blue-collar or manual working class and a large and expanding service sector that employs white-collar workers. Clement and Myles argue that the decline of the manual working class is attributable to both an increasingly efficient manufacturing sector (which requires less manual labour) and the entry of most adult women of working age into the paid labour force (especially the service sector). This pattern of recruitment of women into the paid work force suggests that the capitalist labour market is not gender-blind. One reaches the same conclusion if one considers the consequence of women's labour force recruitment: once in the paid work force, women start to make gender-specific demands for labour market reform, such as expanded day-care facilities and pay equity with men.

It is in the category of clerical and related occupations that one finds the biggest gender discrepancy in employment patterns. In 1991, 31.6 percent of women in Canada's paid labour force worked in clerical and related occupations, compared with just 7.0 percent of men. This pattern repeats itself, although to a lesser degree, in all occupational categories. A gender division of labour is pervasive, and in general women get jobs with less income, less status, and less authority.

In all of the countries analyzed by Clement and Myles, women are much more likely to hold authority and decision-making positions in the service sector than in the manufacturing sector. However, even in the service sector, the proportion of women in authority and decision-making positions is less than the overall proportion of women in that sector. In fact, for most industries, the gender gap between men in authority and women in subordinate roles is bigger in services than in manufacturing. Thus, postindustrialism has so far consolidated, not eroded, the traditional sexual division of labour. True, women have been gaining ground in middle management positions, where they have authority mainly over other women. But they have been losing ground in upper management positions, where male authority is even more entrenched than it used to be a couple of decades ago.

Their disproportionately large share of domestic responsibilities hampers women's progress in the labour market. Without an affordable and accessible day-care system, for example, women continue to shoulder most of the responsibility for raising children. On average, therefore, they have less energy, time, and emotion to invest in paid work than do men. Nonetheless, Clement and Myles demonstrate that the greater the share of women's contribution to family income, the more decision-making power women have at home. In addition, they discuss national and class differences in the level of household equality.

Social inequality is not just about money and power. It is also about status. Alison Lurie wrote a fascinating social history of clothing, an excerpt from which is reprinted here as Chapter 12. With Lurie we move from the economic side of social inequality to its culture and symbols — in Weber's terms, Lurie focuses on how people use clothing to demonstrate their social status and thereby evoke esteem and gain prestige. By wearing clothes made of expensive materials, sporting many different outfits, keeping up with style changes dictated by expensive fashion houses, and conspicuously displaying labels, the better-off are able to demonstrate their perceived superiority (and the less-well-to-do are sometimes able to pass for something they are not). Lurie argues that many of the clothes we wear are uncomfortable, poorly designed for the activities that occupy us, wasteful of materials, and priced far above reasonable profit margins. But if they convey high status we put them on, put up with them, and even come to regard them as beautiful. That is because clothes are an important vehicle for the presentation of self in everyday social interaction, the conscious manipulation of how others see us, and how we see ourselves. Because clothing performs this function, personality shifts often accompany a change in costume; people dress to look and feel sexy, athletic, casual, formal, rich, and so forth.

GLOSSARY

The **poverty rate** is the proportion of Canadian families whose members spend more than 54.7 percent of their income on the necessities of food, clothing, and shelter.

CRITICAL THINKING QUESTIONS

1. What is meant by the "feminization of poverty?" Is the feminization of poverty an issue in Canadian society? Give examples from your reading to support your answer.
2. Why are Canadian women and children at greater risk of being poor than men are? What social factors are responsible for this?
3. What are the main cross-national differences in stratification discussed by Clement and Myles?
4. How has the working class changed in postindustrial societies according to Clement and Myles?
5. Outline the different ways in which clothing shows the social position of the wearer.
6. According to Alison Lurie, people use clothing to demonstrate social status and prestige. What other cultural symbols of social status do people commonly use?

ANNOTATED BIBLIOGRAPHY

Pat Armstrong and Hugh Armstrong, *The Double Ghetto: Canadian Women and Their Segregated Work*, 3rd ed. (Toronto: Oxford University Press, 1994). A classic account of gender inequality in Canada.

Richard Breen and David B. Rottman, *Class Stratification: A Comparative Perspective* (New York: Harvester Wheatsheaf, 1995). A concise and incisive overview of class stratification theories.

James Curtis, Edward Grabb, and Neil Guppy, eds., *Social Inequality in Canada: Patterns, Problems, Policies,* 4th ed. (Toronto: Prentice-Hall Canada, 2003). A definitive collection of up-to-date research on social stratification in Canada.

Chapter 10

Poverty in Canada

ANN DUFFY

NANCY MANDELL

POVERTY IN CANADA TODAY

Any discussion of poverty inevitably must confront the contentious issues of definition and measurement. It is easy to see that homeless, starving children in nineteenth-century Montreal (or modern Somalia) were poor; it is more difficult to identify those contemporary Canadians who have too little to get by and who are unable to participate in any meaningful fashion in the social, political, educational, or spiritual life of the nation.[1] While these individuals are not necessarily starving or homeless, they are "relatively deprived" in the nation and community in which they live. For years, government agencies, social researchers, and advocacy groups have struggled to arrive at meaningful standards of impoverishment — level of family income, costs of housing, food, clothing, fuel, etc. — that distinguish the poor. To date Canada has not arrived at an "official" definition of poverty and relies, uneasily, on Statistics Canada's low-income cut-offs (LICOs) to identify the poor. This resolution has been far from satisfactory and in recent years the definitional debate has greatly intensified, with, for example, some advocates weighing in with a much more restrictive conception of poverty (Sarlo, 1992; National Council of Welfare, 1999a; *Toronto Star*, 1999; Burman, 1996: 19–23).

In particular, "a market basket approach" is currently the centre of heated debate. In this approach, analysts determine the necessities the average Canadian family needs for economic and social existence — transportation, shelter, clothing, personal care, household needs, furniture, telephone, reading, recreation, school supplies, and so on. Families unable to afford the market basket are considered "poor." The net result has been a much more conservative approach to poverty. For example, the poverty line according to the market basket measure (1997) for a family of four in a large city is $25,647, in contrast to the low-income cut-off of $32,377 (pre-tax) (National Council of Welfare, 1999a: 5). Critics argue that the market basket approach is just as arbitrary and clumsy as the LICOs. For example, in some versions of the market basket approach, tea, coffee, eyeglasses, and dental care are not included on the grounds that the former two are optional and the later two can be obtained through private charities (Crane, 1998; National Council of Welfare, 1999a). Clearly, there are important political implications attached to definitions that produce either a more or less restrictive notion of the numbers of poor (National Council of Welfare, 1998a: 6).

Since any definition of poverty that goes beyond simple physical human survival is relative, defining poverty always involves drawing a somewhat arbitrary line below which the "poor" live. As a result, definitions of poverty are always subject to political pressures and agendas. A stricter definition may, at the stroke of a pen, dramatically reduce or increase the numbers of poor. For governments seeking to respond painlessly and inexpensively to pressures for social reform, reduction by redefinition is a tempting alternative.[2]

In the midst of these definitional debates, the best-known and most widely used measure continues to be the Statistics Canada definition (adopted in 1973; reset in 1992) that establishes income cut-offs below which people are considered to live in "straitened circumstances."[3] The cut-offs are based on the notion that poor families are those whose size of income requires them to spend more than 54.7 per cent of their gross income on food, clothing, and shelter, leaving few or no funds for transportation, health, personal care, education, household operation, recreation, or insurance. These income cut-offs vary in terms of the size of the household and the size of the area or residence (more than 500,000, 100,000–499,999, and so on), resulting in 35 separate low-income cut-offs. For example, a single person living in Regina in 1998 on less than $14,468 was considered "poor" by the Statistics Canada definition (1986 base), while a two-person family living on less than $15,202 in a rural area was deemed poor (National Council of Welfare, 1999a: 109).

While the Statistics Canada parameters provide us with a revealing portrayal of poverty in Canada, this portrait has serious limitations. It leaves out all Natives living on reserves, institutional inmates, residents of Yukon, the Northwest Territories, and Nunavut, and the homeless. It tells us nothing about the duration of poverty, that is, how long any one individual is poor. There is also considerable debate about the locational adjustments. According to Statistics Canada calculations, it is 31 per cent less expensive to live in rural areas. While research does suggest that shelter costs are lower than in the city, transportation costs are, in fact, higher. Further, access to subsidized public services such as child care, health services, and education, as well as to competitively priced goods, is likely restricted in many rural areas. The Canadian Council on Social Development, for example, calculates that rural costs are probably

about 88 per cent of those in large urban centres, but also points out that there are considerable differences between cities. In short, locational adjustments are likely both inaccurate and imprecise. Others argue that with the large tax bite, income cut-offs should be based on after-tax income.[4] In addition, the measures ignore differences in the actual level of need in the household. For example, severe disability and lack of access to subsidized services may significantly increase household economic needs (Ross et al., 1994: 26–31).

Finally, there are general problems attached to the Statistics Canada measures of poverty. Like many measures, they reinforce the notion that there are two kinds of people: the poor and the non-poor. This is a split that is too easily translated into "us" and "them" and sustains stereotypes of the poor as somehow different and, possibly, defective. In fact, poverty is a very porous identity.[5] In the course of a year or two, low-income Canadians may drift in and out of "official" poverty. Recent research examining low-income patterns between 1982 and 1993 found that most people had only one spell of low income within this time period lasting on average two years. Indeed, the chances of a period of low income ending after one year were better than 50 per cent and for most people (60 per cent) a period of low income was a temporary setback, not a persistent problem (Laroche, 1998). Unemployment, illness, accident, or disability may, even in the course of a month, tip the balance. Similarly, in the course of a lifetime, an interplay of key factors (notably, gender, age, marital status, and number of children) may trigger a slide into low income and poverty. Given these patterns, the problem of poverty needs to be understood as encompassing a broad continuum of individuals and families both below and above the designated "poverty line."[6]

Further, the poor are far from a homogeneous group. For example, the sources of income for the poor vary considerably. Many are "welfare poor" because the social assistance they receive is below the low-income cut-offs. In 1998, basic welfare assistance for a single parent with one child ranged from $11,300 in Saskatchewan to $13,695 in Ontario, but in each instance this benefit would place the individual well below the Statistics Canada low-income cut-offs (National Council of Welfare, 1999–2000: 40–1). In British Columbia (1998), for example, total welfare income provided only 38 per cent of the poverty-line income for a single employable individual and 61 per cent for a single parent with one child (ibid., 41). Being reliant on welfare for economic survival means living in poverty.

Many poor Canadians are termed "the working poor" because their earnings from work are below the low-income cut-offs. Of 1,108,000 poor heads of families under age 65 in 1997, 21 per cent were employed full-time and 35 per cent were employed part-time — leaving 36 per cent who did not work and 8 per cent who were unable to work (National Council of Welfare, 1991a: 86). Paid employment is no guarantee that poverty will be avoided. When the worker is a single parent, when only one parent in the family is employed, when the work is part-time, contract, short-term, irregular, low-wage, unskilled, and when there are dependent children in the home, employment frequently fails to provide an escape from poverty (Kazemipur and Halli, 2000; Ross et al., 1994: 76–9; Gunderson et al., 1990: 68–71).

Taken as a whole the portrait of poverty in Canada today is sobering. In 1997, 5.1 million Canadians — 17.2 per cent of children, women, and men in Canada — were poor. Among unattached individuals,[7] 36.3 per cent (1,496,000 Canadians) lived below the low-income cut-offs; among families, 14.3 per cent (1,203,000 families) did so (National Council of Welfare, 1999a). Predictably, these poverty rates are patterned by a variety of social factors. For example, there is a distinct regional dimension to Canadian poverty. In 1997, only 12.9 per cent of Alberta families were poor, while poverty was a fact of life for 18.9 per cent of Newfoundland families. Youth is also a critical determinant of poverty rates. Thirty-four per cent of families

(couples with children) headed by people under 25 years of age are poor. Families and individuals with low levels of education[8] are more likely to be poor, as are families with only one wage-earner. Not surprisingly, participation in the paid labour force is directly related to poverty rates, with "a good job [being] the best insurance against poverty for Canadians under the age of 65" (ibid.; Lawton, 1998). Finally, as discussed in more detail below, a complete intersection of factors such as gender, age, family structure and composition, race, ethnicity, and current social policies conditions poverty rates (Kazemipur and Halli, 2000; National Council of Welfare, 1999a; Ross et al., 1994).

THE FEMINIZATION OF POVERTY

Canadian women are particularly at risk of being poor. The "feminization of poverty" refers to the fact that women in many industrialized Western nations, as well as in developing countries, are more likely to be poor than men (Pearce, 1978; Goldberg, 1990). Though Canadian women continue to be better off than their American counterparts (as a result of lower rates of single parenthood and more generous social policies), the poverty rate for women in 1997 was 18.3 per cent and for men 14.3 per cent. As a result, women comprise 57 per cent of poor Canadian adults (National Council of Welfare, 1999a: 99). Further, at every age level adult women have higher poverty rates than men (National Council of Welfare, 1998a: 85, 36, 19). Nor is this a new problem. The ranks of the poor have long been populated by women who were deserted, widowed, or orphaned (Katz, 1975: 60; Simmons, 1986). Evidence suggests, too, that women figure among the poorest of the poor. For example, until recently the largest poverty gap for poor families (how far below the poverty line an individual or family lives) was found among female-headed single-parent families (under 65 with children under 18) (National Council of Welfare, 1998a: 53, 60; 1998b: 12).

Their situation improved marginally in 1997, when couples under 65 with children under 18 averaged $9,822 below the poverty line and headed the list of the poorest of the poor, followed closely by single-parent mothers at $9,377 below the poverty cut-off (National Council of Welfare, 1999a).

While the reasons behind women's impoverishment are complex they have much to do with traditional gender ideologies, inequities in the labour force, and flaws in our family law and responses to marriage breakdown. For generations, women have been expected to devote their lives to their unpaid duties in marriage and motherhood. Although many wives and mothers also worked for pay, this was generally seen as undesirable. Lower pay rates for women, rules against the employment of married women, and the peripheralization and stigmatization of "women's work" all reinforced the notion that women's place was in the home (Duffy and Pupo, 1992: 13–40).

Throughout the twentieth century, however, these notions came under increasing attack. The first and second waves of the women's movement, advanced education for women, and the reduction in family size, among other factors, undermined the traditional sexual division of labour. In particular, increasing numbers of Canadians have found that they simply cannot survive on the uncertain income of a single male (or female) breadwinner. The failure of wages to keep pace with inflation, increases in taxation, high rates of unemployment, and the loss of high-paying industrial and resource-extraction jobs have made the male-breadwinner family increasingly anachronistic. In 1997, 66 per cent of married women with children under age 16 and 59 per cent of women with children under age three were in the paid labour force (National Council of Welfare, 1999b: 12). Indeed, the poverty rate among husband-wife families would double (to 22.1 per cent of Canadian families) if these wives and mothers were not in the paid labour force (National Council of Welfare, 1999a: 100).

While much has changed, much remains the same. Women are still encouraged to focus their energies on marriage and motherhood; women's employment is still less well paid than men's, with full-time women workers earning about 73 per cent of male wages (Statistics Canada, 1999: 27). Women are still occupationally segregated into work with lower wages, less prestige, and less opportunity for advancement (Statistics Canada, 1998: 53). These employment inequities are likely to be further exacerbated if a woman is a recent immigrant or disabled or a member of a visible minority. For example, only 58 per cent of recent immigrant women aged 25–44 and holding a university degree were employed in 1996, in contrast to 86 per cent of comparable non-immigrant women (Badets and Howatson-Leo, 1999: 17). Similarly, the poverty rate for disabled women over 15 years of age is 29.5 per cent (Ross et al., 1994: 41). In short, a variety of factors intersect in a complex manner to compound some women's vulnerability to impoverishment.

Finally, almost all women, regardless of race, ethnicity, or disability, are still considered responsible for most child care, family caregiving, and housework. In the absence of adequate child-care and parental leave policies, juggling the conflicting demands of child care, housework, and paid work often means costly interruptions in labour force participation and/or peripheral employment as a part-time, casual, or contract employee (Marshall, 1993; Fast and Da Pont, 1997). Being employed in "women's work" or taking several years off to care for young children can translate into disaster when marriages end in divorce, when women face long years of widowhood, or when women become single parents.

Single parenthood, typically the result of divorce, can have devastating effects on women's economic well-being. An astounding 57.1 per cent of single-parent mothers are poor (1997), in contrast to a poverty rate of 11.9 per cent for couples with children (National Council of Welfare, 1999a). Without a male breadwinner in the family and with inadequate or non-existent support payments, many women cannot provide sufficient income for their families. For example, research on low-income patterns between 1982 and 1993 found that lone-parent women were particularly susceptible to long-term impoverishment, often spending between 5.1 and 6.9 years out of 10 in low income in contrast to the average of two years (Laroche, 1998). Further, as noted above, they are likely to sink deep into poverty.

Single parenting is a particularly potent combination when combined with youthfulness or young children. Single-parent mothers under age 25 have a staggering poverty rate of 93.3 per cent and single-parent mothers with children under age seven have an 80.2 per cent rate (National Council of Welfare, 1999a). However, contrary to powerful stereotypes, single mothers are not primarily teenagers having numerous babies so they can live off welfare payments. Teenage mothers comprise only 3 per cent of all single parents on welfare. Forty-nine per cent of single mothers have one child and another 31 per cent have two children (National Council of Welfare, 1998c: 33).

For many of these women, low income is a direct consequence of marriage breakup. The Economic Council of Canada's five-year survey of Canadian incomes found women's incomes (adjusted for family size) dropped by about 39 per cent when they separated or divorced and thereafter rose only slightly. Three years after the marriage breakup, women's incomes were still 27 per cent below their earlier level. Men's income (adjusted for family size), in contrast, increased by an average of 7 per cent. Along with the labour force inequalities discussed above, inadequate support payments produce the inequity. Only 68 per cent of divorces involving dependent children (1989) resulted in a child-support order, and those orders averaged a scant

$250 per child per month (Economic Council of Canada, 1992: 49). Further, as repeatedly explored in the media, problems persist in the successful collection of child-support payments from non-custodial parents.

Despite the clear neediness of single mothers, recent social policy initiatives have tended to make their situation worse. For example, in Ontario, single welfare mothers of school-age children are required to sign up for workfare,[9] and these mothers, along with other welfare recipients, are now required to get by on substantially lower rates of social assistance. This push to any form of paid employment is often coupled with inadequate child-care provisions. To further compound their plight, single mothers must also confront the persistent tendency to stigmatize mothers on welfare as somehow less worthy of social support than, for example, low-income two-parent families. Popular ideology suggests that single mothers who receive social assistance are simply being encouraged to have more children.[10]

Growing old provides little promise of relief to women. While policy initiatives between 1980 and 1996 have successfully eased much of the poverty burden for the elderly, it has by no means eliminated it. Unattached elderly women (65 and over) — typically, those who are widowed, divorced, or separated — face high rates of poverty. In 1997, 42 per cent of unattached women over age 65, compared to 27.2 per cent for unattached elderly men, lived below the low-income cut-offs.[11] Another 25 per cent of unattached older women are only slightly above the poverty line (earning 100 to 125 per cent of the poverty line) (National Council of Welfare, 1999a). Increasing age makes the problem worse. Unattached women aged 75–9 have a poverty rate of 48 per cent, rising to 53 per cent for unattached women 85 or older. Women are particularly at risk[12] because they are less likely to receive income from occupational pension plans, the Canada/Quebec Pension Plan, and investments. The traditional patterns of women's lives with work interruptions to take care of family responsibilities, work in low-paying jobs with poor benefits, and high rates of part-time and contractual work, contribute to high rates of female impoverishment whenever women find themselves without a spouse (McDonald, 1997).

Based on current trends in marriage, divorce, and life expectancy, an estimated 84 per cent of all Canadian women can expect to spend some portion of their adult lives without a male bread-winner in the home — as pregnant teens, single mothers, divorced middle-aged workers, and/or elderly widows (National Council of Welfare, 1990: 17). Today, as marriage is increasingly postponed, almost every woman will be self-sup-porting at some point. Yet few Canadian women live with these expectations and fewer still plan their work and marital lives to bring them finan-cial independence and solvency (Duffey et al., 1988). In a society that perpetuates unrealistic notions of romantic love, marital life, and par-enting, and in an economy premised on the peripheralized, low-wage, ghettoized work of women, many women continue to be set up for poverty.

Predictably, certain groups of women — immigrant women, the disabled, minority women, and Native Canadians — are at greater risk. Native women, for example, have lower than average labour force participation rates, lower than average earnings, and substantially higher rates of unemployment, partly because of the remote, rural areas in which many live (Federal, Provincial, and Territorial Advisory Committee, 1999: 47; Abella, 1984). Visible-minority and immigrant women frequently find that racial and ethnic discrimination, along with language difficulties and inadequate government policy, translate into long hours of low-wage work (Kazemipur and Halli, 2000; National Council of Welfare, 1990: 118–27). Foreign-born elderly women in all marital categories have lower average incomes than their Canadian-born counterparts. Elderly women who are recent immigrants and/or who come

from less-developed countries receive particu-larly low incomes (Boyd, 1989). Although the majority of disabled adults live on low incomes, disabled women are generally worse off than their male counterparts (Ross and Shillington, 1989: 28; Barile, 1992).

THE POVERTY OF CHILDREN

Interwoven with the impoverishment of women and families is the poverty of children. More than a million children[13] — 19.6 per cent of Canadian children in 1997 — are growing up poor (Crane, 1999). Young children (aged 0–11 years) have even higher poverty rates, with one-quarter (Ontario) to one-third (Newfoundland) living below the Statistics Canada low-income cut-offs (Cheal et al., 1997). Despite a unani-mous vote in the House of Commons in 1989 to eradicate child poverty by the year 2000 — the highly publicized Campaign 2000 — Canadian child poverty rates grew from 1989 to 1996 and remain high today (National Council of Welfare, 1999a). Indeed, although the number of Canadian children increased by just 6 per cent between 1989 and 1997, the number of poor children rose by 37 per cent, and since the mid-1980s Canadian children have had a consistently higher rate of poverty than adult Canadians under age 65 (Crane, 1999; National Council of Welfare, 1999a). Children constitute more than one-quarter of our poor and the child poverty rate in Canada is, with the exception of the United States, the United Kingdom, and Australia, the highest in the industrialized world (National Council of Welfare, 1999b: 7; Hurtig, 1999: 320).

Simple explanations for the expansion of child poverty, such as the dramatic increase in single-parent families, provide only part of the puzzle. While children in families headed by single mothers have extremely high poverty rates (60.4 per cent in 1997), most (56 per cent) poor chil-dren in Canada are growing up in two-parent families (National Council of Welfare, 1999a: 91). These children are poor because their parents are poor and their parents' poverty often stems from unemployment, underemployment, inadequate minimum-wage levels, and reduced social welfare supports (ibid.; Baxter, 1993).[14]

THE CHANGING FACE OF POVERTY

Poverty patterns are far from static or monochromatic. Over time there have been important changes in poverty and, depending on where you look in the population and in the country, there are significant variations in the nature of impoverishment.

In the 1960s and early 1970s, there were significant reductions in the rate and depth of poverty (Economic Council of Canada, 1992: 2). Progress slowed during the 1970s, and since 1973 the poverty rate had tended to fluctuate with the health of the economy (Ross and Shillington, 1989: 21; National Council of Welfare, 1988: 1). This is reflected, for example, in the marked decrease in the numbers of Canadians, from all types of families, living on low incomes during the 1970s. From the early 1980s to 1995, however, there was little evidence of decline in low-income rates and indications of increases of low income among some types of families (Zyblock and Lin, 1997). Most recently, poverty rates have been less inclined to mirror the ups and downs of the economy, suggesting that a more or less permanent underclass is emerging.

Among the general Canadian population, single parents are at a distinct disadvantage in terms of impoverishment, but this is also true for individuals living on their own. Among unattached (unmarried) individuals poverty rates have shown relatively little improvement. From 1980 to 1997, poverty rates for this population fluctuated from 41.4 per cent in 1980 to a low of 34.1 per cent in 1990 and back up to 36.3 per cent in 1997. Further, the depth of poverty experienced by unattached men and women under age 65 has remained alarmingly high from 1980 to the present. In 1997, unattached men and

women under age 65 were earning on average only slightly more than half (54 per cent and 55 per cent respectively) of the poverty line. In other words, these individuals were living almost $7,000 below the low-income cut-offs (National Council of Welfare, 1999a).

Similarly, there has been considerable regional variation in poverty rates. Although in the last several decades Ontario and Quebec have fairly consistently held their claims to having, respectively, among the lowest and highest provincial poverty rates, other provinces have been less consistent. Prince Edward Island has moved from above to below the national average in terms of poverty rates, while Alberta and British Columbia's poverty rates moved from below the national average to above or at the national level (ibid.). Amid these changes, poverty has also increasingly become an urban phenomenon.

THE LOST GENERATION: THE POVERTY OF YOUNG ADULTS

Among the alarming trends has been the growing vulnerability of young adults. Certainly the appearance of food banks on campuses signalled a dismal deterioration in the lives of many Canadian university and college students (McGrath, 1998). Young people who marry and have dependants are in a particularly difficult economic position. Although in 1997 young families (those headed by someone under age 25) comprised only 4 per cent of all Canadian families, they accounted for 11 per cent of poor families, and almost half (42.8 per cent) of young families were low income (Crane, 1999). As high rates of unemployment and underemployment continue to plague young workers, not surprisingly, the rates of poverty grow among families with young parents (under age 35).

From 1973 to 1986 there was also an increase in the number of poor families with two or more earners. This reflects, in part, the failure of real family wages to keep pace with rising costs, along with a failed commitment to maintain an adequate minimum wage. In 1973 minimum-wage legislation meant that someone who worked 40 hours a week over 52 weeks could earn a yearly income 20 per cent over the poverty line. By 1991 the same worker would have to work 50 hours a week for 52 weeks simply to reach the poverty line (Kitchen et al., 1991: 36). During this same period, education has become less of a barrier to impoverishment; by 1997, 7.7 per cent of heads of poor families and 23.4 per cent of poor unattached individuals held a university degree (National Council of Welfare, 1999a). Although these rates are the lowest among all educational categories and confirm the partial protection from poverty provided by higher education, the pattern also indicates that poverty may be "more a result of lack of job opportunities ... than a lack of education" (National Council of Welfare, 1997: 48; Hurtig, 1999: 133–4).

HOMELESSNESS

Another important shift in poverty patterns has been the dramatic emergence of urban homelessness in Canada and other industrialized countries. By the late 1990s, activists and analysts were pointing to homelessness as a "national disaster" and "national crisis" (James, 1999). Toronto), "a magnet for the homeless," provided shelter for an estimated 5,000 homeless people each night during the winter of 1998 (Gillespie, 1998). Research on shelter patterns suggests that one-fifth of those using shelter beds are children (under 18 years of age). Shelters and hostels, once considered stop-gap solutions, seemed increasingly entrenched as a long-term response to the homeless. Yet, even as the number of shelters and food banks grew, there were not enough available beds or services (Orwen, 1998). Toronto front-line workers estimated that two to four homeless people died each week and analysts suggested that, nationally, the number of Canadian homeless people was approaching 200,000 (Crowe, 1998).[15]

THE ELDERLY: THE SUCCESS STORY

Despite the unrelenting advance of homelessness in our urban centres, there is nothing inevitable about poverty. As dramatically evidenced by the fight against poverty among senior Canadians, it is possible to reverse established patterns of income inequality. Policy changes, including the creation of the federal Guaranteed Income Supplement in 1967 for low-income seniors, the creation of the Canada/Quebec Pension Plan in 1966, and the implementation of provincial supplements, have meant that instead of one-third (33.6 per cent) of all seniors being poor (as in 1980), a near-record low of less than one-fifth (17.0 per cent) are now living below low-income cut-offs (1997). Similarly, the poverty rate for poor senior couples went from 22.2 per cent in 1980 to 7.0 per cent in 1997 (National Council of Welfare, 1999a: 19, 20). Although the number of Canadians 65 and older has increased from 2.2 million in 1980 to 3.5 million in 1997 (a 59 per cent increase), the number of seniors living in poverty has decreased over this time period (ibid.).

The exception to these developments is the continuing plight of unattached (unmarried) seniors. As with other segments of the population, living on one's own leads to a higher poverty rate. This is particularly true of Canadians 65 and older. In 1980, more than two-thirds (68.7 per cent) of unattached women 65 and older and more than half (57.8 per cent) of comparable senior men were living below the low-income cut-offs. Since that time there has been marked improvement. However, much remains to be done — in 1997 42 per cent of senior unattached women and more than one in four senior unattached men were poor (ibid., 22).

STRUGGLING WITH POVERTY: THE PERSONAL EXPERIENCE

Being poor has always meant much more than getting by at some arbitrary level of income, and understanding poverty demands more than a statistical overview. Poverty often affects people's lives, their sense of self, and their most important relationships with others. Although the toll of poverty is most apparent in the lives of children, few adults survive impoverishment unscathed (Benner, 1998). For children and their families, poverty still generally translates into inadequate housing. In Calgary, Edmonton, Vancouver, and Toronto, poor children are likely to live with sub-standard heating, too little hot water, improper ventilation, generally unsafe conditions (exposed wiring and electrical outlets and so on), and too little space in which to play or study (Bragg, 1999). Even inadequate housing in large metropolitan areas may gobble up social assistance benefits, leaving little for other necessities, let alone for emergencies (Spears, 1999). Housing problems are frequently compounded by neighbourhoods plagued with high rates of crime and vandalism, inadequate play facilities, and hazardous traffic conditions (Marsden, 1991: 8; Kitchen et al., 1991: 6). Echoing nineteenth-century Montreal, recent research indicates that New Brunswick children were living in developing world conditions in dwellings with mud floors, leaking roofs, and no running water (Spears, 1991).

Housing problems combine with inadequate nutrition. Poor families often lack the income to maintain a nutritious diet. High housing costs and the spectre of homelessness mean that food budgets are stretched to the limit: "Juice wars we have at our place, 'You can't have that extra glass of juice.' They bring somebody in the house and the three of them are having a glass of juice and that's all the juice there is for the rest of the week. And there they are just drinking it down, and you're going. 'Oh my God, don't they understand anything?'" (Women for Economic Survival, 1984: 13). While Canada's food banks and soup kitchens provide a stop-gap solution for many families, many poor children clearly get by on too little food or food with high fat and sugar content (Kitchen et al., 1991: 7).

Predictably, poor housing and inadequate nutrition frequently combine to jeopardize the health of the poor (Hyndman, 1998). Repeatedly, research has demonstrated a relationship between poverty and poor physical health. For example, surveys report that low-income Canadians are four times more likely to report their health as only fair or poor and two times more likely to have a long-term activity limitation and one-third as likely to have dental insurance (Federal, Provincial, and Territorial Advisory Committee, 1999: 43). While national health care in Canada mitigates some of the worst health consequences, the poor often lack access to many important health services and certainly, contrary to a popular stereotype, do not "get it all free." Poor families in Alberta, whether on social assistance or working low-wage jobs, routinely lack access to dental and optical services as well as prescription medication (Williamson and Fast, 1998). Welfare recipients are particularly hard hit. For example, children in Ontario whose parents are on welfare are not covered for root canal procedures. If they need this kind of dental work, their teeth are simply pulled (Hudson, 1999: A1).

Not surprisingly, the poorest of the poor, the homeless, are frequently plagued with physical health problems, including malnourishment, chronic respiratory or ear infections, gastrointestinal disorders, sexually transmitted disease, and chronic infections. Indicative of the health concerns of the homeless, 38 per cent of homeless people in Toronto screened recently had been exposed to tuberculosis, in contrast to only 10 per cent of the general public.

The psychological health of the poor, in turn, reflects the painful social and emotional environment in which they live.[16] The pressure of poverty contributes to family breakdown and dislocation. Life often becomes unpredictable and insecure. Being poor means not knowing whether you will be able to continue living in your old home, whether you will retain custody of your children, whether your children will have to change schools and make new friends. In these and numerous other ways, the foundations of one's life may be shattered. Living with this profound uncertainty inevitably takes a toll on self-confidence and hopefulness.

Upheaval may permeate family life. Evidence suggests that poorer families are more subject to family violence, including child abuse and neglect (MacLeod, 1987: 20–1; Gelles and Cornell, 1990: 14–15). Growing up poor often means coping with a parent or parents who are themselves struggling with fear, anger, frustration, isolation, and despair. The emotional and psychological realities of poverty are complex, and reactions to poverty reflect the particular personal circumstances and history of each individual. Many poor adults and children cope with courage, resourcefulness, and a sense of humour, and many poor children grow up with positive adult role models and a strong sense of family loyalty. However, the adults in most poor children's lives are also often deeply troubled by their economic straits. Poverty typically means more than doing without; it means feeling cut off from the mainstream of our consumer society. With few exceptions, the lives and experiences of the poor are not reflected sympathetically on television or in the movies; the advertisements in magazines and on subway trains simply underscore the insufficiencies of their lifestyle. Life becomes an observer sport: watching other people get new jobs, buy new houses, or take their families to Disneyland. A 50-year-old woman, on her own, who had been looking for work for five months, voiced the alienation felt by so many: "I need a job. I want to work. I want to be able to pay my bills. I want to be solvent. I want to live!" (Burman, 1988: 54).

Each day small and large events underscore the poor person's marginalization in society. When the school organizes a bike hike, children without bikes have to sit in the classroom and do worksheets. Frustrated parents see their children left out and humiliated: "It visually stamps them as poor. You can hide many things, but when visually you're made poor, then something's bloody wrong" (Women for Economic Survival, 1984: 16). A woman buys food with a food voucher at her local grocery store and when change is owed, the cashiers engage in a loud conversation about whether "you're supposed to give them any money." Not surprisingly, the woman ends up feeling "like they were talking about somebody who wasn't a person. I just wanted to tell them to forget about it, keep the damn change" (Carniol, 1987: 90). Day by day and incident by incident, the chasm grows between poverty and "normal life," leaving poor adults and their children feeling more isolated, stereotyped, and rejected:

> I could read their mind, right, so that I know what they're saying. "Well he's unemployed, he's getting nowhere," right? Because that's what I'm doing right now, getting nowhere. (Burman, 1988: 204)

> People never really think of what it's like to be poor until they are poor themselves. It's a sad fact but it's true. They have to live it. My husband is not one of those "welfare bums." He tries; he tries really hard. (Baxter, 1988: 41)

When people become poor themselves, it comes as a shock that the negative stereotype now applies to them:

> When I went down there, I felt that I just stuck right out. I thought, "Oh my God, people think I'm on welfare." Typical stereotype I guess you're led to believe. You used to think, "It's those people who are on welfare," and now you discover you're one of those people. (Burman, 1988:86)

Being one of those people often means living with a stigma. Many poor are ashamed of their identity as poor, seek to hide it whenever possible, and feel there is something "wrong" with them:

> At the beginning [of being unemployed] I was feeling so good about myself that that was a lot easier.... Towards the end I was feeling like such a loser.... You portray this, it's written all over your face. (ibid., 196)

I need to move to a better place. There are so many losers living around me but being on welfare people think you're a loser anyway. (Baxter, 1988: 165)

Coping with stigmatization may mean being filled with anger at the injustices of a social system that seems to benefit so many other people:

I walked down the street one day. God, how do people buy their clothes, where are they getting their money, how come they have a job? ... Like, I just thought SHIT! (Burman, 1988: 203)

For some, when the impoverishment seems to grind on endlessly or when their personal situation deteriorates, anger and frustration give way to despair and depression. A recent national health survey of self-reported levels of self-esteem, sense of mastery, and sense of coherence predictably finds that larger percentages of those occupying the lowest income levels report low levels of all three measures of psychological well-being (Federal, Provincial, and Territorial Advisory Committee, 1999). Not surprisingly, poverty activists report that poor people often talk of periods of hopelessness and of suicidal depression.

Being poor and being on welfare can be a double whammy. Many of the poor, who must rely on social assistance for all or part of their income, report that dealing with the social work apparatus compounds feelings of stigmatization and vulnerability. Even when individual welfare workers are helpful and supportive, the relationship between worker and client is structured to erode the autonomy, power, and privacy of the poor. The negativity of some welfare workers merely exacerbates a bad situation: "Social assistance is based on the notion that women need help and can't make decisions. The system makes you feel like you failed at your role in life" (Blouin, 1992).

My worker is very strict. It's like being with my parents when I was younger. The worker controls my life. I hate it. (ibid.)

They have a real looking-down-on-you attitude, and my back just gets right up. I don't find them very pleasant people. I keep thinking how people less assertive than me deal with that. I bet there's a lot of people that cry. (Burman, 1988: 85)

Home visits by welfare workers, personal questions from workers, and the constant fear of being "reported to welfare" for having not followed all the rules tend to undermine clients' sense of personal power and self-confidence:

I never want to go back on welfare. Self-esteem while you are on welfare is really low. You end up being dependent on somebody you don't want to be dependent on. You don't have any say or any control over your own life. When I was a single parent on welfare and my kids were here, welfare was always checking up on me, social workers were pulling these short-notice visits, like five minutes notice, to see who was living at my house. (Baxter, 1988: 31)

Problems with the welfare apparatus are further complicated by the negative reactions of the general public to welfare recipients. Commonly, landlords will not rent to people on welfare, and women on welfare may find themselves labelled as desperate and available: "He wants to go to bed with me! I refuse and he says, 'You'll be sorry.' He figures I'm on welfare, I'm a single parent — I'm fair game" (Carniol, 1987: 86–7). Most commonly, the social assistance recipient has to confront the still popular belief, held by much of the general public as well as many social assistance workers, that people on welfare cheat (Blouin, 1992). Informed by the historical notions that many of the poor are not deserving and/or should be punished for their plight, attitudes towards the provision of adequate social assistance remain ambivalent at best.

As welfare cases soared in the recession of the early 1990s, public preoccupation with welfare fraud intensified. In 1991 the *Toronto Star* ran at least two major stories on welfare cheating, followed in 1992 by a front-page article on welfare abuse. Although a survey of welfare fraud by independent researchers indicated that less than 3 per cent of the welfare caseload involved cheating, prominent members of the community continue to protest that the welfare rules on eligibility are too lax and that penalties for welfare abusers are too lenient (Armstrong, 1992: A18; Sweet, 1991a: B1). The poor, who after all receive welfare benefits that leave them below the low-income cut-offs, must face the knowledge that numerous Canadians (some 20 per cent of whom admit to cheating on their income tax) (McCarthy, 1992) think of them as cheats. Even when the issue of cheating is set aside, many Canadians continue to hold harsh and unsympathetic attitudes towards welfare recipients (while overlooking government "handouts" to corporate interests) (Hurtig, 1999). Despite the proliferation of food banks and homeless people, fully one-third of the Canadian public think the government spends too much money on welfare, and one-quarter feel that most people on welfare could get along without it if they tried (Sweet, 1991b).

Being poor means living with the knowledge that in many ways one is despised or pitied by our consumer society, or, at best, considered to be irrelevant. Certainly, it typically means living on the far side of an ideological divide in which most non-poor Canadians do not understand or empathize with the day-to-day realities of living in poverty. Not surprisingly, this pattern of social alienation takes a heavy toll on personal and family life:

> There are times when I am so scared that I'm not going to find a job, I think, "What the hell is wrong with me?" I can get scared to death. I'll have periods of insomnia. I'll get very short-tempered with my husband and with the children. (Burman, 1988: 195)

> My husband and I are very close. In the past year with the pressure of his job when he suddenly turned 55, he's got very sharp with me. He yelled at me twice and he never yelled at me in his life. We're fighting for our relationship and we're fighting to survive. What's happening financially can destroy couples that are so close. (Women for Economic Survival, 1984: 14)

> If I say "no" to the children, they feel very depressed when they see other children taking things to school. The children feel very disappointed. They kind of lose love for you. They think that you don't love them. (ibid., 23)

The children, lacking the life experience and acquired coping skills of adults, are often most deeply wounded by poverty and its personal and familial consequences. Certainly, little is accomplished in terms of ensuring loyalty to social institutions and public values. When the adults in their lives are filled with confusion, frustration, anger, rage, humiliation, and fear, when their lives seem beyond their control and beyond hope, the children grow up truly impoverished.

The burdens placed on many poor children serve to perpetuate poverty and economic vulnerability. The fallout often begins before birth with inadequate prenatal nutrition or health care. Poor kids are twice as likely as other kids to suffer low birth weight, death in the first year, death from accidents, poor physical health, physical disabilities, and mental disorders (Reitsma-Street et al., 1993: 7). Predictably, poor children tend not to do as well in school. By age 11, one in three girls from families on social assistance performs poorly in school (for example, repeating a grade or being placed in a special class). Four of 10 children aged 12–16 living in subsidized housing perform poorly in school (Offord, 1991: 23).[17] Inevitably, children who do not do well in school are more likely to drop out, and dropouts are more likely to come from single-parent, minority group, and/or poorly educated families (Denton and Hunter, 1991: 133). Children from poor families are almost twice as likely to drop out of school as non-poor children. While children of average and low ability from well-to-do families are likely to stay in school, even children of high ability from poor families are likely to succumb to the pressures. Without a private place to study, with parents who are preoccupied with their economic plight, and with the ever-apparent need for more family income, students from poor families often see immediate employment as the best option (Kitchen et al., 1991: 10–11).[18] Unfortunately, in the long run their lack of education and skills may simply perpetuate their own and, later, their children's economic and social marginalization.

NOTES

1. This definitional problem is compounded by the pervasive ideology in Canadian society that we are a basically "classless society" (Allahar and Côté, 1998).

2. For example, P. Sainath, noted Indian journalist, recounts the struggles over such competing definitions of poverty. In the late 1980s, the government of India devised a very narrow definition of impoverishment that reduced the poverty rate to just over 19 per cent of the population. When a succeeding government dumped "this particular piece of dishonesty," the percentage of Indian people living in poverty soared to 39.9 per cent in 1997 (Sainath, 1996: 348–50).

3. Statistics Canada warns against the use of low-income cut-offs as a poverty line. The have also proposed an alternative, simpler measure — the low-income measure — which is 50 per cent of the median income in Canada.

4. Commencing in 1990, Statistics Canada published an appendix that included low-income cut-offs based on after-tax income. Estimating the number of people living in poverty using the after-tax method results in a reduction in the rate (for 1990) from 14.6 per cent to 11.5 per cent (Ross et al., 1994: 28).

5. A recent survey of labour and income dynamics in Canada found, for example, that between 1993 and 1994 over one million Canadians fell into poverty, almost as many climbed out, and slightly more remained poor in both years (National Council of Welfare, 1998a: 9).

6. In addition, historical trends increase or decrease vulnerability to official poverty. As evidenced most dramatically during the Great Depression, impoverishment may touch any individual or family.

7. "Unattached individuals" are those who are not married and who are not living with family members.

8. Level of education, however, does not dictate likelihood of poverty. Many Canadians who have relatively little education avoid impoverishment and, conversely, there are numerous families and individuals with post-secondary education who are still poor (National Council of Welfare, 1998a: 45).

9. Workfare refers to the increasingly popular policy of requiring able-bodied recipients of social welfare benefits to take some form of state-orchestrated employment. In Ontario, for example, some welfare recipients have been deployed into phone solicitation positions. Refusal to accept such positions may result in loss of welfare benefits. Needless to say, these initiatives have resulted in strong protests from poverty activists.

10. Research indicates that single-parent mothers have fewer children on average than two-parent families (National Council of Welfare, 1998a: 41).

11. However, the poverty gap (the amount of income needed to bring the population up to the poverty line) for unattached senior women (and men) is significantly *less* than that experienced by other parts of the poor population, notably unattached men under age 65 and single-parent mothers (National Council of Welfare, 1998a: 52).

12. Research suggests that the death of a wife actually decreases the risk of poverty for

her husband (as cited in McDonald, 1997: 557).

13. Not included in these figures are the 51 per cent of Native children who are poor (Kitchen et al., 1991: 15).

14. In 1999, the average Toronto single mother "on welfare" received $1,071.70 a month. She paid an average $680.53 in rent, which left $391.17 or $13.03 a day for food, clothing, transportation, a telephone, and other expenses (Hurtig, 1999: 292).

15. The Toronto Mayor's Task Force on Homelessness (headed by Anne Golden) found that 170,000 different individuals had used shelters for the homeless in Toronto between 1987 and 1996 (Golden, 1998).

16. The high rate of suicide among Aboriginal groups in Canada speaks, in part, to the effect of economic and social marginalization (Federal, Provincial, and Territorial Advisory Committee, 1999).

17. Research also indicates that parents' level of education influences the child's school readiness. Children whose parents are well-educated are more prepared for school at ages four and five than children whose parents are poorly educated. Clearly, this suggests a mechanism for the generational impact of poverty (Federal, Provincial, and Territorial Advisory Committee, 1999: 52).

18. Predictably, there is a clear relationship between living in low-income households and having a low level of prose literacy (Federal, Provincial, and Territorial Advisory Committee, 1999: 52).

REFERENCES

Abella, R.S. 1984. *Equality in Employment: A Royal Commission Report.* Ottawa: Ministry of Supply and Services.

Allahar, Anton L., and James E. Côté. 1998. *Richer and Poorer: The Structure of Inequality in Canada,* Toronto: James Lorimer.

Armstrong, Jane. 1992. "Is our welfare system being abused?" *Toronto Star,* 7 Mar., A7, A18.

Badets, Jane, and Linda Howatson-Leo. 1999. "Recent immigrants in the workforce," *Canadian Social Trends* 52 (Spring): 16–22.

Barile, Maria. 1992. "Dis-Abled Women: An Exploited Genderless Under-class," *Canadian Woman Studies* (Summer): 32–3.

Baxter, Sheila. 1988. *No Way to Live: Poor Women Speak Out.* Vancouver: New Star Books.

———. 1993. *A Child Is Not a Toy: Voices of Children in Poverty.* Vancouver: New Star Books.

Benner, Allan. 1998. "Report offers real portrait of poverty," *St. Catharines Standard,* 26 Nov., A7.

Blouin, Barbara. 1992. "Welfare Workers and Clients: Problems of Sexism and Paternalism," *Canadian Woman Studies* (Summer) 645.

Boyd, Monica. 1989. "Immigration and Income Security Policies in Canada: Implications for Elderly Immigrant Women," *Population Research and Policy Review,* 8: 5–24.

Bragg, Rebecca. 1999. "Housing top priority for Canada's poor," *Toronto Star,* 26 Mar., E4.

Burman, Patrick. 1988. *Killing Time, Losing Ground: Experiences of Unemployment.* Toronto: Wall & Thompson.

———. 1996. *Poverty's Bonds: Power and Agency in the Social Relations of Welfare.* Toronto: Thompson Educational Publishing.

Carniol, Ben. 1987. *Case Critical: The Dilemma of Social Work in Canada.* Toronto: Between the Lines.

Cheal, David, et al. 1997. "Canadian Children in the 1990s," *Canadian Social Trends* 4 (Spring): 1–9.

Crane, David. 1998. "Where do we draw the line on poverty?" *Toronto Star,* 4 Nov., E2.

———. 1999. "Children are the 'sound bite' in productivity," *Toronto Star*, 15 Apr., D2.

Crowe, Cathy. 1998. "In the calculation of real disasters homelessness has easily won its place," *Toronto Star*, 30 Oct., A21.

Denton, Margaret, and Alfred Hunter. 1991. "Education and the Child," in Richard Barnhorst and Laura C. Johnson, eds., *The State of the Child in Ontario.* Toronto: Oxford University Press.

Duffy, Ann, Nancy Mandell, and Norene Pupo. 1988. *Few Choices: Women, Work and Family.* Toronto: Garamond Press.

——— and Norene Pupo. 1992. *Part-Time Paradox: Connecting Gender, Work, and Family.* Toronto: McClelland & Stewart.

Economic Council of Canada. 1992. *The New Face of Poverty: Income Security Needs of Canadian Families*. Ottawa: Ministry of Supply and Services.

Fast, Janet, and Moreno Da Pont. 1997. "Changes in Women's Work Continuity," *Canadian Social Trends* (Autumn): 2–7.

Federal, Provincial, and Territorial Advisory Committee on Population Health for the Meeting of Ministers of Health, Charlottetown, PEI. 1999. *Toward a Healthy Future: Second Report on the Health of Canadians*. Ottawa: Minister of Public Works and Government Services.

Gelles, Richard J., and Claire P. Cornell. 1990. *Intimate Violence in Families*, 2nd edn. Newbury Park, Calif.: Sage.

Gillespie, Kerry. 1998. "Civilized society feared at risk," *Toronto Star,* 29 Sept., B1.

Goldberg, Gertrude Schaffner. 1990. "Canada: Bordering on the Feminization of Poverty," in Goldberg and Eleanor Kremen, eds., *The Feminization of Poverty: Only in America?* New York: Praeger.

Golden, Anne. 1998. "Breaking the cycle of homelessness," *Toronto Star*, 30 Sept., A18.

Gunderson, Morley, and Leon Muszynski, with Jennifer Keck. 1990. *Women and Labour Market Poverty.* Ottawa: Canadian Advisory Council on the Status of Women.

Hudson, Kellie. 1999. "Dentists root out 2nd-class care for welfare children," *Toronto Star*, 28 Mar., A1, A4.

Hurtig, Mel. 1999. *Pay the Rent or Feed the Kids: The Tragedy and Disgrace of Poverty in Canada.* Toronto: McClelland & Stewart.

Hyndman, Brian. 1998. "Being poor still means being sicker, dying younger than rich," *Toronto Star*, 8 Jan., A15.

James, Royson. 1999. "We can't turn backs on homeless," *Toronto Star*, 31 Mar., B2.

Katz, Michael B. 1975. *The People of Hamilton, Canada West: Family and Class in a Mid-Nineteenth-Century City*. Cambridge, Mass.: Harvard University Press.

Kazemipur, A., and S.S. Halli. 2000. *The New Poverty in Canada: Ethnic Groups and Ghetto Neighbourhoods*. Toronto: Thompson Educational Publishing.

Kitchen, Brigitte, Andrew Mitchell, Peter Clutterbuck, and Marvyn Novick. 1991. *Unequal Futures: The Legacies of Child Poverty in Canada.* Toronto: Child Poverty Action Group and the Social Planning council in Metropolitan Toronto.

Laroche, M. 1998. "In and Out of Low Income," *Canadian Social Trends* (Autumn): 20–4.

Lawton, Valerie. 1998. "Plight of the long-term jobless," *Toronto Star*, 7 Nov., B4.

McCarthy, Shawn. 1992. "Ottawa missing $90 billion a year as cheaters use cash to dodge taxes," *Toronto Star,* 30 Apr., A1, A32.

McDonald, Lynn. 1997. "The Invisible Poor: Canada's Retired Windows," *Canadian Journal of Aging* 16, 3: 553–83.

McGrath, Paul. 1998. "Food banks part of life on campus," *Toronto Star*, 23 Feb., F1, F2.

MacLeod, Linda. 1987. *Battered But Not Beaten: Preventing Wife Battering in Canada.* Ottawa: Canadian Advisory Council on the Status of Women.

Marsden, Lorna, chair. 1991. *Children in Poverty: Toward a Better Future.* Standing Senate Committee on Social Affairs, Science and Technology. Ottawa: Ministry of Supply and Services.

Marshall, Katherine. 1993. "Dual Earners: Who's Responsible for Housework?" *Canadian Social Trends* (Winter): 11–15.

Mulvany, C. Pelham. 1884. *Toronto: Past and Present.* Toronto: W.E. Caiger.

National Council of Welfare. 1988. *Poverty Profile 1988.* Ottawa: Ministry of Supply and Services.

———. 1990. *Women and Poverty Revisited.* Ottawa: Ministry of Supply and Services.

———. 1997. *Another Look at Welfare Reform.* Ottawa: Ministry of Supply and Services.

———. 1998a. *Poverty Profile 1996.* Ottawa: Minister of Public Works and Government Services Canada.

———. 1998b. *Child Benefits: Kids Are Still Hungry.* Ottawa: Minister of Public Works and Government Services Canada.

———. 1998c. *Profiles of Welfare: Myths and Realities.* Ottawa: Minister of Public Works and Government Services Canada.

———. 1999a. *Poverty Profile 1997.* Ottawa: Minister of Public Works and Government Services Canada.

———. 1999b. *Preschool Children: Promises to Keep.* Ottawa: Minister of Public Works and Government Services Canada.

———. 1999–2000. *Welfare Incomes: 1997 and 1998.* Ottawa: Minister of Public Works and Government Services Canada.

Offord, Dan. 1991. "Growing Up Poor in Ontario," *Transition* (Vanier Institute of the Family) (June): 10–11.

Orwen, Patricia. 1998. "Food bank use jumps 17% in GTA in just one year," *Toronto Star,* 11 Sept., A2.

Pearce, Diana. 1978. "The Feminization of Poverty: Women, Work and Welfare," *Urban and Social Change Review* 11 (Feb.): 28–36.

Reitsma-Street, Marge, Richard Carriere, Adje Van de Sande, and Carol Hein. 1993. "Three Perspectives on Child Poverty in Canada," *The Social Worker* 61, 1 (Spring): 6–13.

Ross, David, and Richard Shillington. 1989. *The Canadian Fact Book on Poverty.* Ottawa: Canadian Council on Social Development.

———, ———, and Clarence Lochhead. 1994. *The Canadian Fact Book on Poverty.* Ottawa: Canadian Council on Social Development.

Sainath, P. 1996. *Everybody Loves a Good Drought.* London: Review.

Sarlo, Christopher. 1992. *Poverty in Canada.* Vancouver: Fraser Institute.

Simmons, Christina. 1986. "'Helping the Poorer Sisters': The Women of the Jost Mission, Halifax, 1905–1945," in Veronica Strong-Boag and Anita Clair Fellman, eds., *Rethinking Canada: The Promise of Women's History.* Toronto: Copp Clark Pitman.

Spears, John. 1991. "NB seeks answer to childhood poverty," *Toronto Star,* 31 May, A21.

———. 1999. "Rent erodes tenants' income, study shows," *Toronto Star,* 23 Mar., A6.

Statistics Canada. 1998. "Sources of Income, Earnings and Total Income and Family Income," *The Daily,* Catalogue no. 11–001E, 9 June.

———. 1999. "Social Indicators," *Canadian Social Trends* (Spring): 27.

Sweet, Lois. 1991a. "Is welfare cheating running wild?" *Toronto Star,* 2 June, B1, B7.

———. 1991b. "Jobs offer hope as welfare cure," *Toronto Star,* 3 June, A15.

Toronto Star. 1999. "Poverty can't be measured away," 5 Apr., A16.

Williamson, Deanna L., and Janet E. Fast. 1998. "Poverty Status, Health Behaviours and Health: Implications for Social Assistance and Health Care Policy," *Canadian Public Policy* 24, 1: 1–22.

Women for Economic Survival. 1984. *Women and Economic Hard Times: A Record.* Victoria: Women for Economic Survival and the University of Victoria.

Zyblock, Myles and Zhengxi Lin. 1997. *Trickling Down or Fizzling Out?: Economic Performance, Transfers, Inequality and Low Income.* Ottawa: Statistics Canada.

Chapter 11

Gender, Class, and Postindustrialism in Canada, Scandinavia, and the United States

WALLACE CLEMENT

JOHN MYLES

There are two reasons why the male blue-collar worker is no longer symbolic of the class structure of the advanced capitalist economies. The first is the revolution in the forces of production that makes the direct producer of most goods increasingly redundant. The second, and equally important, reason has been the incorporation of women into the paid labour force. The massive entry of women into paid work in the latter part of the twentieth century has been as dramatic as the changes in industry composition and virtually inseparable from it. As Table 11.1 shows, from about the end of the Second World War until 1982 (about the time of our surveys), women increased their share of employment from approximately one-quarter to over two-fifths of the labour force. Finland is the exception to this pattern. By 1950 women already made up over two-fifths of the Finnish labour force, compared with a quarter or less of the labour force of the other countries.

As Table 11.2 on page 104 indicates, the labour-force participation of women tends to be rather higher in the Nordic countries than in North America. In the mid-1970s, the Norwegian level was closer to the North American pattern than to that of Sweden or Finland. By the early 1980s, however, Norway had drawn closer to the Swedish-Finnish levels.

Almost all of this growth in female employment occurred in services.[1] Indeed, if unpaid domestic labour were counted as an industry in the usual classifications, we might describe postindustrialism more in terms of the shift from unpaid to paid service work and put less emphasis on the "goods to services" metaphor. Most men (56 percent or more) continue to be employed in the traditional sectors associated with an "industrial" economy: goods and distribution. Most women — approximately two-thirds — are employed in the growing postindustrial sectors of the labour market, especially personal/retail, business, and social services.

TABLE 11.1 WOMEN'S SHARE OF THE LABOUR FORCE, 1950 AND 1982

	1950	1982
United States	28	42
Canada	21	40
Norway	27	42
Sweden	26	46
Finland	41	47

SOURCE: Compiled from data in Organisation for Economic Co-operation and Development (OECD), *The Integration of Women into the Economy* (Paris: OECD, 1985), p. 14.

Source: *Relations of Ruling: Class and Gender in the Postindustrial Societies* (Montreal: McGill-Queen's University Press, 1994), pp. 33–37, 135–40, and 201–10. Reprinted by permission of the publisher.

TABLE 11.2   LABOUR-FORCE PARTICIPATION BY SEX

	WOMEN		MEN	
	1975	1983	1975	1983
United States	53	62	85	85
Canada	50	60	86	85
Norway	53	67	86	86
Sweden	68	77	89	86
Finland	66	74	80	83

SOURCE: Compiled from data in Organisation for Economic Co-operation and Development (OECD), *The Integration of Women into the Economy* (Paris: OECD, 1985), p. 13.

As a result, the "new" — postindustrial — working class is predominantly female labour employed in clerical, sales, and service occupations in the service industries (see Table 11.3). And consequently the working class now has two prototypes rather than one: the traditional blue-collar male and the postindustrial female service worker. Moreover, variations in postindustrial employment patterns are experienced mainly by women. The large welfare states of Sweden and Norway, in particular, result in the fact that most women workers are employed by the state in those countries. Half of all employed Swedish women are in social services, compared with only a quarter of American women.

The significant fact about the postindustrial division of labour, then, is not so much that the working class of industrial capitalism has come to an end. Rather, a new working class employed in services has grown up alongside it. Superimposed on this material division of labour is a social division based on gender.

As we show in Figure 11.1, the working class in advanced capitalism has two sexes. In all five countries, women are more likely to be working class than men and less likely to be in any of the other three classes that exercise significant powers over production. In all five countries, women make up 50 percent or more of the working class and a minority of all other classes. But just what historical, social, or political significance should we attach to this fact?

Since the 1970s, it has been commonplace for feminist scholars to comment upon the "gender-blind" character of conventional class theory, but such a charge has had two rather different meanings. Sometimes the charge implies that the "male" preoccupation with class relations results in a disciplinary bias leading to the systematic neglect of gender relations — structured relations of domination and inequality between the sexes. To such a charge, class analysts can plead guilty without necessarily conceding that there are serious flaws in their theories or empirical claims *about* classes. There is no inherent reason why theories about classes must explain all forms of social domination and inequality.

The charge of being gender-blind, on the other hand, can also mean that analyses of classes and processes of class formation that overlook the gendered structure of class relations are both incomplete and incorrect. In short, class analyses that are gender-blind are incomplete on their own

TABLE 11.3   SELECTED CHARACTERISTICS OF WORKING-CLASS WOMEN

PERCENTAGE OF WORKING-CLASS WOMEN WHO ARE IN:	UNITED STATES	CANADA	NORWAY	SWEDEN	FINLAND
Clerical, sales, and service occupations	66	64	60	66	66
Goods and distributive industries	34	24	28	26	40
State employment	31	38	55	63	38
Unskilled jobs	86	79	81	77	83

FIGURE 11.1 CLASS DISTRIBUTIONS BY SEX AND NATION   ■ FEMALE   ■ MALE

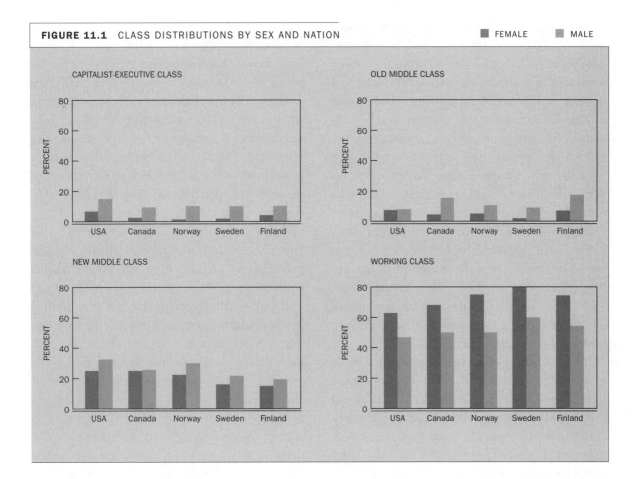

terms, not just when measured against the criteria of an alternative problematic. Capitalism and the labour market are not inherently gender-blind, as the conventional wisdom of both neoclassical and Marxian economic theory would have it.

The fact that a "worker" is female rather than male, that she comes to work in a skirt and blouse rather than in overalls, alters the relation between capital and labour in fundamental ways.[2] An example will suffice to illustrate.

The patriarchal organization of households means that most women sell their labour under very different conditions from those of most men. The burden of the "double day" of paid labour and unpaid domestic labour circumscribes both how much labour power women can sell in the market and the timing of its availability. One result is to transform the conditions under which the capital–labour wage relation is negotiated and the agenda of labour when it confronts capital at the bargaining table. The focus of "class struggle"

now expands to include new labour-force practices and state policies such as pay equity and daycare. In effect, the struggle over the price of labour and the conditions of its employment is transformed as a result of the conditions and extra-market social relations of the persons (women) who offer their labour for sale in the market. The upshot is irrevocably to alter the trajectory of class formation in *postindustrial* capitalism. Employers are faced with novel demands about the form of the pay packet, work schedules, and the fringe benefits they must negotiate. The state is faced with new demands for legislation and social programs to protect women against the market. As a result, labour unions and labour parties that fail to take up these demands, to incorporate the material interests of a working class that is predominantly female, become doomed to extinction. Likewise, a *class* analysis that does not take account of the changed conditions of the class struggle is doomed to failure.

Numerically, the labour force of traditional industrial labour markets was and is predominantly male (Table 11.4). In contrast, the labour force of the postindustrial sectors is dominated by women. Men are in the majority in both goods production (manufacturing, construction) and distribution (transport, utilities, communication, and wholesale trade), the sectors associated with both the first and the second "industrial revolutions." Here we would expect few women to achieve significant positions within capitalist relations of ruling. In contrast, women dominate in the more "modern" business, consumer, and public services. Female-dominated work sites are more numerous (schools, health care agencies), and there is less likelihood that women in authority will be required to exercise their authority over male subordinates.

There are reasons other than numbers to expect that gender differences in the distribution of positions of power and authority might abate in postindustrial labour markets. The first is the very "modernity" of the service industries. The growth of personal, business, and social services is a contemporary phenomenon, and, as Stinchcombe has shown, the organization of labour within firms, industries, and occupations tends to bear the imprint of the historical period of their foundation and growth.[3] Baron and Newman, for example, show that wage differentials between men and women are greater in "old" than in "new" job categories.[4] Second, state employment is more prevalent in the service sector, and studies of earnings differentials between men and women have shown that the gender gap narrows in the public sector, a result of both public policy and stronger labour unions.[5] Finally, postindustrial labour markets — and especially social and business services — tend to be not only "knowledge-intensive" but also "credential-intensive." Job-relevant skills in services tend to be acquired through the educational system rather than through on-going training and apprenticeship programs. This should benefit women, who are typically excluded from on-the-job training programs but who tend to have high levels of formal education.[6]

There is little question that postindustrialism has brought women into the exercise of economic power to a degree unprecedented in history (Table 11.5). In the United States, for example, women in postindustrial services fill almost half of all positions with power and authority, compared with less than 20 percent of such positions in goods and distribution. And as the pattern of consistently positive signs in Table 11.5 indicates, women in all countries have greater access to positions of power and authority in postindustrial services than in the traditional industrial core. But the question remains as to whether postindustrialism also means that the rules of the game have changed. Have postindustrial work sites been "degendered"? Does women's *representation* in positions

TABLE 11.4   PERCENT FEMALE BY INDUSTRY SECTOR, EMPLOYED LABOUR FORCE, FULL-TIME AND PART-TIME EMPLOYEES

SECTORS	UNITED STATES	CANADA	NORWAY	SWEDEN	FINLAND
Goods and Distribution	31	24	24	24	35
Goods	32	21	24	23	36
Distributive services	28	31	23	25	33
Postindustrial Services	61	61	57	67	68
Business, personal, and retail services	60	61	52	60	63
Social services and public administration	62	60	60	70	71

of power and authority more closely reflect their numbers? Has the law of anti-matriarchy been eroded?

The answer to the first of these questions is a clear no. In general, our results for all five countries do not support our postindustrial expectations. Women have not closed the gender gap in the more "modern" sectors of the economy. Of the twenty possible contrasts in Table 11.6 (page 108), only three indicate that women are better represented in postindustrial services, four indicate no difference between sectors, and thirteen indicate that women's underrepresentation is greater in the postindustrial, than in the industrial, sector of the economy. In Sweden and the United States, postindustrial services provide somewhat more scope for women to participate in decision making, but these gains are not reflected in greater access to the formal managerial hierarchy. Rather than eroding the traditional

sexual division of power, postindustrial labour markets appear to be the site of its consolidation (in the United States and Finland) and even growth (in Canada, Sweden, and Norway).

Some of the reasons for these results can be interpolated from closer inspection of differences among service industries. In those sectors of the service economy characterized by an unusual number of "good jobs," men have tended to appropriate an even larger share of power and authority, so that gender differences are augmented rather than diminished. Women's gains in postindustrial services are largely confined to the low-wage and unskilled sectors of the service economy.

To demonstrate the point, we divide the postindustrial sector into high-end (business and public) services, where wages and job skills are above average, and low-end (personal and retail) services, characterized by low wages and limited

TABLE 11.5   WOMEN'S SHARE OF DECISION MAKING AND AUTHORITY POSITIONS BY INDUSTRY, FULL-TIME EMPLOYEES ONLY (PERCENTAGES)

POSITIONS AND SECTORS	UNITED STATES	CANADA	NORWAY	SWEDEN	FINLAND
Middle and Upper Management					
Goods and distribution	18	19	5	5	15
Postindustrial services	46	44	20	35	52
Difference	+28	+25	+15	+20	+37
Decision Makers					
Goods and distribution	9	13	7	8	27
Postindustrial services	45	39	22	38	57
Difference	+36	+26	+15	+30	+30
Sanctioning Authority					
Goods and distribution	19	24	5	4	16
Postindustrial services	47	43	19	36	50
Difference	+28	+19	+14	+32	+24
Task Authority					
Goods and distribution	19	15	8	6	16
Postindustrial services	46	47	24	37	53
Difference	+27	+32	+16	+31	+37

TABLE 11.6   WOMEN'S REPRESENTATION IN DECISION MAKING AND AUTHORITY POSITIONS BY INDUSTRY, FULL-TIME EMPLOYEES ONLY*

POSITIONS AND SECTORS	UNITED STATES	CANADA	NORWAY	SWEDEN	FINLAND
Middle and Upper Management					
Goods and distribution	–12	–4	–16	–17	–27
Postindustrial services	–16	–20	–24	–27	–27
Decision Makers					
Goods and distribution	–17	–7	–10	–11	–10
Postindustrial services	–9	–15	–14	–6	–17
Sanctioning Authority					
Goods and distribution	–10	–7	–11	–13	–21
Postindustrial services	–10	–13	–19	–17	–22
Task Authority					
Goods and distribution	–11	–7	–8	–11	–22
Postindustrial services	–11	–9	–14	–16	–19

*Calculation of representation is simply percent female within a class subtracted from the female share of the total labour force. Calculated scores may show slight discrepancies; these are the result of rounding procedures.

job skills. As the results in Table 11.7 on page 109 show (Finland is excluded because of small sample size), women do comparatively well in the low end of the service economy but very poorly in high-end business and public services.

Here, however, our conclusions run into technical limitations imposed by the relatively small size of our national samples. Although our data *suggest* that gender differences are larger in postindustrial services than in goods and distribution, the number of cases involved is not sufficient to provide statistically robust evidence for this conclusion.[7] Quite simply, it may be that our conclusions are a result of sampling error. To test this assumption, Boyd, Mulvihill, and Myles examined Canadian census data to determine if similar results could be reproduced using census occupations.[8] The results were remarkably similar. For example, the "gender gap" — the percentage difference between men and women — in upper-management occupations in 1981 (the

time of our survey) was largest in business services (–6.6), followed by social services (–5.0), public services (–3.3), distributive services (–2.9), retail services (–1.8), manufacturing (–1.5), and personal services (–0.6).

None of this implies that women have not been gaining ground in the class hierarchy, but there have been two offsetting trends in the labour market: women have been improving their position relative to men in lower-level management and supervisory jobs but losing ground relative to men in upper-level management. As Boyd, Mulvihill, and Myles show, the gender gap has fallen among middle managers and supervisors in all industries except retail trade since 1971. In contrast, the gender gap in senior-management occupations has risen in all industries except social services.

Bringing these results together suggests the following. As women have entered the labour force in ever larger numbers, a rising share of

TABLE 11.7 WOMEN'S REPRESENTATION IN DECISION MAKING AND AUTHORITY POSITIONS BY POSTINDUSTRIAL SERVICE SECTOR, FULL-TIME EMPLOYEES ONLY

POSITIONS AND SECTORS	UNITED STATES	CANADA	NORWAY	SWEDEN
Middle and Upper Management				
Personal and retail services	–6	–2	(–7)	(–13)
Business and public services	–11	–16	–22	–20
Decision Makers				
Personal and retail services	–4	–11	(–2)	(+8)
Business and public services	–11	–16	–18	–9
Sanctioning Authority				
Personal and retail services	–6	–7	(–12)	(–5)
Business and public services	–11	–16	–22	(–22)
Task Authority				
Personal and retail services	–5	–5	(–7)	(+1)
Business and public services	–13	–11	–17	–21

( ) indicates estimates based on an underlying industry sample of less than 50. For Sweden, cell counts in personal and retail services are based on less than 20 cases. All other ( ) cells are based on 38 or more cases.

supervisory and middle-management positions have also opened to them. Women have acquired real economic powers in the public sphere to a degree unprecedented in Western history. Our Canadian results indicate that women encounter the "glass ceiling" to further advancement near the top of the class pyramid, where they begin to compete for positions that involve the exercise of significant authority over men, particularly over senior men. The result, as Mann suggests, is a form of neo-patriarchy, an economy ruled by senior males in which women may rule women but not men. Postindustrialism matters for women because the concentration of women in postindustrial services provides many more opportunities for the exercise of power over other women but not because the glass ceiling has been broken. Indeed, despite their small numbers in services, men have, if anything, been more effective at appropriating class powers in postindustrial, than in traditional industrial, work sites.

The division of domestic responsibilities is intimately associated with people's relationship to the labour force. For women, this has meant that these responsibilities have inhibited their paid working lives, while men have benefited both within the household by being relieved of an equitable responsibility for domestic work *and* within the paid labour force, where they have been advantaged over women burdened by their household duties. Employers have used women's weaker labour-market positions to keep wages down, thus further weakening women's economic power within the household. This entire system is reinforced by patriarchal ideologies and practices that privilege men over women.

Still, there are important gender differences within this broad pattern based upon nation, class, and status. The more economic clout a woman has within the household, as determined by her relative income contribution, the more say she has in making key financial and budgetary decisions. This economic clout is closely associated with her class position, especially for a few capitalist-executive women but more notably for a substantial number of new-middle-class women. There are some key national differences that transcend class and gender. Overall, the Nordic countries are much more equitable in their household decision making than is the United States, with Canada suspended in the middle. This pattern holds across classes and between sexes, whether in conventional or unconventional households, as indicated by spouse's income contribution.

In terms of actual practices, Swedish men stand out as the least progressive in sharing child-care responsibilities, while U.S. men resemble Canadian men. Norwegian men are the most equitable. For household tasks, however, Swedish men become more involved and U.S. men are the least likely to share responsibilities. Nevertheless, women in all these countries overwhelmingly carry the greatest load of domestic responsibilities.

Men in the propertied classes have made the least contribution to domestic work, while new-middle-class women were able to command greater sharing than those from other classes. Most sharing occurs when both partners are working class or a new-middle-class woman is living with a working-class man. The least occurs when women are housewives. These general patterns were upheld for all four countries, but again the overwhelming share of domestic work falls to women in every case.

Household responsibilities disrupt women's labour-force participation in Canada, especially for those currently other than full-time workers. A majority of women in all age groups had some disruption. Number of children affected the experience of disruptions, but even women without children were much more likely to be disrupted in their careers than all types of men by a margin of 43 percent to 17 percent. These disruptions affected women from all classes, although working-class women were most severely impacted. Progressive households where there is a more equal sharing of household tasks have the twin effects of decreasing women's labour-force disruptions rather substantially (by –13 percentage points) and increasing men's disruptions by a like amount (+11 percentage points).

Canadian men in unconventional households have attitudes toward traditional families very similar to the progressive attitudes of Nordic men and women; indeed, men in these unconventional income positions (where their wives earn as much or more than they do) are more progressive in some ways than Canadian women. Canadian women, while more progressive than U.S. women, are not as progressive as Nordic women on a variety of gender-related issues. Canadian men in unconventional income situations are therefore a key bridgehead for progressive gender issues.

The employment status of men matters little to their gender attitudes, but status matters a great deal for women, especially since many women are housewives (the least progressive women's status), while women employed full-time are the most progressive. Full-time working Canadian women more closely resemble Nordic women working full-time in terms of their gender attitudes than do their U.S. counterparts. The greater a woman's attachment to the labour force, the more her attraction to feminism.

Women are empowered *inside* the home when their class power exceeds men's (as in households with working-class men and new-middle-class women). When partners are of the same class, there are different effects: both working class is more liberating for women than both new middle class. When both have new-middle-class careers, it is the man's that takes priority.

Women with relatively more class power than men have a positive influence on their partner's attitudes toward gender issues, and, inversely, men with relatively more power have a reverse effect on women's attitudes. More powerful men tend to dampen women's feminist expectations.

Household-class combinations strongly influenced the attitudes of men toward traditional families, while men living with women working outside the home are much more progressive than those living with housewives. Housewives everywhere tend to be the least progressive women on gender issues. Again, men are more homogeneous in their views and women more diverse with respect to gender attitudes. The lack of unity on the part of women follows from their much more diverse statuses since some women obviously are housewives and others much more likely to be part-time workers, while men are concentrated in full-time status. At the foundation of the differences between men and women, however, is their radically distinct attachment to household responsibilities both on a day-to-day domestic level and at the broader level of careers. The basic gender difference in the intersection between domestic and paid work is fundamental to an understanding of work performed by both sexes.

So, how are families changing? We summarized the changes in income and domestic labour contributions into household types. For women we were able to examine three types: "traditional," where the woman does most of the domestic work and the man brings in most of the money; "transitional," where the woman contributes equally to the household income but there is no reciprocity in men's contribution to domestic labour; and "modern," where there is basic equality in both income and domestic work. It was more difficult to identify "modern" men because they are more reluctant than women to state that their wives contributed as much financially as they do. Still, it was possible to highlight some directions of change. The most modern relationships occur when a working-class man is with a new-middle-class woman, followed by homogeneous working-class families.

Men's gender attitudes are especially influenced by household types, with a major increase in support for feminist issues in all four countries in transitional situations. Women tend to be more strongly influenced by modern arrangements when they are most feminist.

Households are complex sites, where class and gender relations meet to mediate a variety of demands on an individual's behaviour and attitudes. These demands greatly influence the way Nordic and North American women experience the world since households tend to weaken their powers while enhancing men's. We have shown that the more women are attached to the labour force, the more progressive they are on feminist issues and the more influence they exert on their husbands' ideas and — however gradually — their practices in sharing domestic responsibilities. Age and, to some extent, education appear to work toward a more favourable approach to feminist issues, but the way remains contested by traditional men, who have the most power to lose. Before equality can be achieved in the paid labour force, much more attention to equality in the domestic sphere will be required. The point will be to change not only the attitudes of men but their domestic practices. The ongoing sites of struggle include the workplace and the household. In every case, it is the combination of class and gender factors that mediates the practice of inequality.

NOTES

1. For detailed analysis of the Canadian case see Monica Boyd, Mary Ann Mulvihill, and John Myles, "Gender, Power and Postindustrialism," *Canadian Review of Sociology and Anthropology* 28, 4 (1991): 407–36.

2. See Joan Acker, "Gender, Class and the Relations of Distribution," *Signs* 13, 3 (1988): 473–97.

3. A.L. Stinchcombe, "Social Structure and Organizations," in *Handbook of Organizations*, J.G. March, ed. (Chicago: McNally, 1965).

4. James Baron and Andrew Newman, "For What It's Worth: Organizations, Occupations and the Value of Work Done by Women and Nonwhites," *American Sociological Review* 55 (1990): 155–75.

5. See Monica Boyd and Elizabeth Humphreys, *Labour Markets and Sex Differences in Canadian Incomes,* Discussion Paper no. 143 (Ottawa: Economic Council of Canada, 1979); Margaret Denton and Alfred A. Hunter, *Equality in the Workplace Economic Sectors and Gender Discrimination in Canada*, Discussion Paper, Ser. A., no. 6 (Ottawa: Labour Canada, Women's Bureau, 1982).

6. See John Myles and Gail Fawcett, *Job Skills and the Service Economy*, Working Paper no. 4 (Ottawa: Economic Council of Canada, 1990).

7. In technical terms, tests for interactions across industrial sectors are not statistically significant.

8. Boyd, Mulvihill, and Myles, "Gender, Power and Postindustrialism."

Chapter 12

The Class Language of Clothes

ALISON LURIE

Clothing designed to show the social position of its wearer has a long history. Just as the oldest languages are full of elaborate titles and forms of address, so for thousands of years certain modes of dress have indicated high or royal rank. Many societies passed decrees known as *sumptuary laws* to prescribe or forbid the wearing of specific styles by specific classes of persons. In ancient Egypt only those in high positions could wear sandals; the Greeks and Romans controlled the type, colour, and number of garments worn and the sorts of embroidery with which they could be trimmed. During the Middle Ages almost every aspect of dress was regulated at some place or time — though not always with much success. The common features of all sumptuary laws — like those of edicts against the use of certain words — seem to be that they are difficult to enforce for very long.

Laws about what could be worn by whom continued to be passed in Europe until about 1700. But as class barriers weakened and wealth could be more easily and rapidly converted into gentility, the system by which colour and shape indicated social status began to break down. What came to designate high rank instead was the evident cost of a costume: rich materials, superfluous trimmings, and difficult-to-care-for styles; or, as Thorstein Veblen later put it, Conspicuous Consumption, Conspicuous Waste, and Conspicuous Leisure. As a result, it was assumed that the people you met would be dressed as lavishly as their income permitted. In

Fielding's *Tom Jones*, for instance, everyone judges strangers by their clothing and treats them accordingly; this is presented as natural. It is a world in which rank is very exactly indicated by costume, from the rags of Molly, the gamekeeper's daughter, to Sophia Western's riding habit, "which was so very richly laced" that "Partridge and the post-boy instantly started from their chairs, and my landlady fell to her curtsies, and her ladyships, with great eagerness." The elaborate wigs characteristic of this period conferred status partly because they were both expensive to buy and expensive to maintain.

By the early eighteenth century the social advantages of conspicuous dress were such that even those who could not afford it often spent their money on finery. This development was naturally deplored by supporters of the status quo. In colonial America the Massachusetts General Court declared its "utter detestation and dislike, that men or women of mean condition, should take upon them the garb of Gentlemen, by wearing Gold or Silver lace, or Buttons, or Points at their knees, or to walk in great Boots; or Women of the same rank to wear Silk or Tiffiny hoods, or Scarfes. ..."[1] What "men or women of mean condition" — farmers or artisans — were supposed to wear were coarse linen or wool, leather aprons, deerskin jackets, flannel petticoats, and the like.

To dress above one's station was considered not only foolishly extravagant, but deliberately

---

deceptive. In 1878 an American etiquette book complained,

> It is ... unfortunately the fact that, in the United States, but too much attention is paid to dress by those who have neither the excuse of ample means nor of social claims. ... We Americans are lavish, generous, and ostentatious. The wives of our wealthy men are glorious in garb as are princesses and queens. They have a right so to be. But when those who can ill afford to wear alpaca persist in arraying themselves in silk ... the matter is a sad one.[2]

CONTEMPORARY STATUS: FINE FEATHERS AND TATTERED SOULS

Today simple ostentation in dress, like gold or silver lace, is less common than it used to be; but clothes are as much a sign of status as ever. The wives of our wealthy men are no longer praised for being glorious in garb; indeed, they constantly declare in interviews that they choose their clothes for ease, comfort, convenience, and practicality. But, as Tom Wolfe has remarked, these comfortable, practical clothes always turn out to have been bought very recently from the most expensive shops; moreover, they always follow the current rules of Conspicuous Consumption, Waste, and Leisure.

At the same time, as high-status clothes have become superficially less gorgeous they have increasingly tended to take on an aura of moral virtue. A 1924 guide to good manners clearly suggests this:

> An honest heart may beat beneath the ragged coat, a brilliant intellect may rise above the bright checked suit and the yellow tie, the man in the shabby suit may be a famous writer, the girl in the untidy blouse may be an artist of great promise, but as a general rule, the chances are against it and such people are dull, flat, stale and unprofitable both to themselves and to other people.[3]

The implication is that an ill-dressed person is also probably dishonest, stupid, and without talent. Today this idea is so well established that one of our foremost historians of costume, Anne Hollander, has refused to admit that true virtue can shine through ugly or ragged clothes, as in the tale of Cinderella:

> In real life ... rags obviously cannot be "seen through" to something lovely underneath because they themselves express and also create a tattered condition of soul. The habit of fine clothes, however, can actually produce a true personal grace.[4]

In a society that believes this, it is no wonder that many of those who can ill afford to wear alpaca — or its modern equivalent, polyester — are doing their best to array themselves in silk. Popular writers no longer complain that those of modest means wear clothes above their rank; instead they explain how best to do so: how to, as the title of one such book puts it, *Dress for Success*. At the moment there are so many such guidebooks it may seem surprising that their advice is not followed by more people. However, as my friend the lady executive remarks, "wardrobe engineering won't do much for you if your work is lousy ... or if you're one of an army of aspirants in impeccable skirted suits all competing for the same spot. As with investment advice, once everyone agrees that it's the thing to do, it's time to look for value somewhere else."

There are other problems with dressing to advance your status professionally. First and most obviously, it is very expensive. The young executive who buys a high-priced suit instead of a stereo system or a week's vacation in Portugal or the Caribbean is giving up certain present pleasure for possible future success in a society that regards hedonistic self-fulfillment as a right. Second, there are one's colleagues to consider. For many people, agreeable working conditions and well-disposed birds are worth more than a possible promotion in the bush. The clerk who dresses like his boss is apt to be regarded by other clerks as a cold fish or an ass-kisser; the secretary in her severe skirted suit is seen as snotty and pretentious: Who does she think she is, in that getup? Moreover, somebody who is distrusted and disliked by his or her equals is very unlikely ever to become their superior. It is also a rare boss who wants to have employees who dress exactly as he or she does — especially since they are usually younger and may already have the edge in appearance. Fortunately for the manufacturers, however, there are more ways than one of advertising high status. Today, "simple," "easy-care," and "active" may be the bywords of fashion copy; but fashionable luxury, waste, and inconvenience continue to flourish in new forms.

CONSPICUOUS ADDITION: EATING AND LAYERING

The most primitive form of Conspicuous Consumption is simply to consume so much food that one becomes conspicuous by one's bulk, a walking proof of having dined often and well. Fatness, frequently a sign of high status in primitive tribes, has also been admired in more civilized societies. In late-nineteenth-century Europe and America it was common among well-to-do men, who often, as Robert Brain has remarked, "were as proud of their girth as a Bangwa chief, the big belly being a sign of imposing male power. It was a culture trait among German men, for whom fatness reflected wealth and status."[5] The late-Victorian woman, too, was often as handsomely solid and well-upholstered as her furniture.

In general, the fashionable size seems to vary according to real or imagined scarcity of food. When a large proportion of the population is known to be actually going hungry, it is chic to be well padded and to dine lavishly. When (as in England and America in the 1960s) there seems to be at least enough starchy food to go around, it becomes chic to be thin, thus demonstrating that one is existing on an expensive protein diet rather than on proletarian bread, potatoes, franks, and beans.

Another simple and time-honoured way of consuming conspicuously is to wear more clothes than other people do. "More" of course is relative: when most people went naked, the mere wearing of garments conferred prestige. In ancient Egypt, for instance, slaves and servants often wore nothing, or at most a brief loincloth; aristocrats put on clothes not out of modesty or for warmth, but to indicate rank. Even in colder climates and more puritanical societies it has generally been true that the more clothes someone has on, the higher his or her status. This principle can be observed in medieval and Renaissance art, where peasants wear relatively few garments, while kings and queens (including the King and Queen of Heaven) are burdened with layers of gowns and robes and mantles, even in indoor scenes. The recent fashion for "layered" clothes may be related, as is sometimes claimed, to the energy shortage; it is also a fine way of displaying a large wardrobe.

In any contemporary gathering, no matter what its occasion, the well-to-do can be observed to have on more clothes. The men are more likely to wear vests; the women are more apt to wear panty hose, superfluous scarves, and useless little wraps. Even in hot weather the difference is plain. At an outdoor restaurant on a summer day the customers who have more money and have had it longer will be the ones in jackets and/or long-sleeved shirts and dresses. If it gets frightfully hot they may roll up their sleeves, but in such a way that there is no doubt about their actual length. On the beach, though the rich may splash into the waves in suits as skimpy as anyone else's, the moment they emerge they will make a dash for the conspicuous raw-silk beach kimono, terry swim dress, or linen shirt that matches their bathing suit and restores the status quo.

CONSPICUOUS DIVISION

It is also possible to advertise one's rank by wearing more clothes consecutively rather than simultaneously. Traditionally, the more different outfits one can display, the higher one's status;

high society in the past has made this sort of display possible by the division of daily life into many different types of activity, each of which demands a special costume. As a 1924 book on etiquette puts it:

> In the world of good society, dress plays an important part in the expression of culture. There is proper dress for afternoon wear, and another for evening functions. There are certain costumes for the wedding, and others for the garden fête. The gentleman wears one suit to business, and another to dinner. Where civilization has reached its highest point, there has dress and fashion reached its finest and most exquisite development.[6]

The contemporary man does not need to have a morning coat, a frock coat, a dress coat, and a dinner jacket (and the appropriate trousers, shirts, and shoes) as he did in the early 1900s. Nor must the contemporary woman possess morning costumes, walking costumes, afternoon costumes, tea gowns, motoring outfits, and evening dresses — all of which it would have been considered extremely improper and embarrassing to wear at the wrong time or place. Today, the conspicuous multiplication of clothing continues to thrive, but now the emphasis is on sports rather than on social life. The truly fashionable person will have separate getups for tennis, jogging, hiking (winter and summer), bicycling, swimming, skiing, golf, and that anonymous and disagreeable sport known simply as "exercise." If he or she also goes in for team sports or dancing (ballet, modern, tap, folk, or disco) yet more costumes must be acquired, each one unique. From a utilitarian point of view there is no reason not to play golf in jogging clothes, or ride your bike in a bathing suit on a hot day — except of course that it would cause a drastic loss of prestige.

In order to maintain (or better yet to advance) status, it is not merely necessary to have separate costumes for each sporting activity; one must also have costumes — and where relevant, equipment — of properly high prestige. Just any jogging shoes, tennis racket, or leotards will not do; they must bear the currently correct brand and model names, which tend to change so fast that if I were to list them here they would be out of date by the time this book appears.

CONSPICUOUS MULTIPLICATION

Wearing a great many clothes at once is a burdensome and often unpleasantly hot form of Conspicuous Consumption; changing into different outfits for different activities is a nuisance. An alternative or supplementary way of demonstrating high status is to own many similar garments, so that you almost never wear exactly the same costume. The extreme case of this is the person who — like Marie Antoinette — never wears the same thing twice. Today such extravagance is rare and felt to be excessive, but the possession of a very large wardrobe is still considered charming by those who follow what Veblen called "pecuniary canons of taste."

F. Scott Fitzgerald, in a famous scene, describes the effect of Jay Gatsby's extensive collection of shirts on Daisy Buchanan:

> He took out a pile of shirts and began throwing them, one by one, before us, shirts of sheer linen and thick silk and fine flannel, which lost their folds as they fell and covered the table in many-colored disarray. While we admired, he brought more and the soft rich heap mounted higher — shirts with stripes and scrolls and plaids in coral and apple-green and lavender and faint orange, with monograms of Indian blue. Suddenly, with a strained sound, Daisy bent her head into the shirts and began to cry stormily. "They're such beautiful shirts," she sobbed, her voice muffled in the thick folds. "It makes me sad because I've never seen such — such beautiful shirts before."

The particular type of Conspicuous Consumption that consists in the multiplication of similar garments is most common among women. In men it is more rare, and usually associated either with dandyism or with great and rapidly acquired wealth, as in the case of the bootlegger Gatsby. A man who gets a raise or a windfall usually buys better clothes rather than more of them, and he has no need to wear a different outfit each day. Indeed, if he were seen to vary his costume as often as his female colleagues do he would be thought vain and capricious — perhaps even unstable. Monotony of dress is only a minor fault, though a man who wore the same tie to the office every day for a week would probably be considered a dull fellow.

For a woman, on the other hand, variety in dress is essential, and the demand for it starts very early. In America many girls in secondary school or even younger feel acute embarrassment about wearing the same outfit twice in the same week — let alone on consecutive days. Even if they own relatively few garments they will go to great lengths to combine them differently and to alter the total effect with accessories. So strong is this compulsion that quantity is usually preferred to quality, and shoddy new garments to well-made old ones. In terms of the struggle for status, this may be the right decision: young girls may not be able to recognize good clothes, but they can certainly count.

This female sense of the shamefulness of repetition persists into adult life. One of the most double-edged compliments one woman can give another is "Oh, you're wearing that pretty dress *again!* " (Men, who know no better, are forgiven such remarks.) Often the compulsion continues into old age: my mother, when nearly 90, still liked to appear in a different outfit each day "so as not to be boring." But it seems to be strongest among women in offices, for whom the fact that a colleague arrives at work on Tuesday in the same costume she was wearing on Monday is positive proof that she spent the intervening night unexpectedly at somebody else's apartment.

The constant wearing of new and different garments is most effective when those you wish to impress see you constantly — ideally, every day. It is also more effective if these people are relative strangers. If you live and work in an isolated country village, most of the people you meet will already have a pretty good idea of your rank and income, and they will not be much impressed if you keep changing your clothes. If you live in or near a city and work in a large organization, however, you will be seen often by the same people, but most of them will know little about you. Having a large and up-to-date sartorial vocabulary then becomes a matter of the first importance, especially if you have not yet established yourself socially or professionally. For this reason, it is not surprising that the most active supporters of the fashion industry today are young women in places like London and New York.

What is surprising, though, is the lengths to which this support can go. Many young working women now seem to take it for granted that they will spend most of their income on dress. "It's awfully important to look right," a secretary in a London advertising agency explained to me. "If a girl lives at home it'll be her main expense. If she's living in town, even sharing a flat, it's much harder. I'm always in debt for clothes; when I want something I just put it on my credit card. I know things cost more that way. But, well, take these boots. They were £89, but they were so beautiful, I just had to have them, and they make me feel fantastic, like a deb or a film star. All my friends are the same."

CONSPICUOUS MATERIALS: FUR AND LEATHER

Through the centuries, the most popular form of Conspicuous Consumption has been the use of expensive materials. For a long time this meant heavy damasked satins, patterned brocades, and velvets that were hand-woven at tremendous expense of time and labour. Today, when the machine-weaving of such fabrics is relatively simple, but hand labour and natural resources scarce, the desirable materials are wool, silk, leather, and hand-knits. When "artificial silk" (rayon) and nylon first appeared they were expensive and highly fashionable. But since the prestige of any fabric tends to vary in direct relation to its price per yard, the synthetic materials lost distinction as they became cheaper to produce; today "polyester" is a dirty word in many circles. "Natural" fabrics are chic now not only because of the current prestige of nature, but because they cost more than the synthetic alternatives.

The wearing of the skins and pelts of animals to indicate wealth has a varied history. In the past, when the world population of beasts was larger in proportion to that of people, only the furs of the least common animals conferred prestige. Those who had been enriched by their rapacity in war or trade might cover their floors or their beds with rugs made from the skins of the larger and more rapacious beasts, such as the tiger and the bear; or they might on formal occasions wear garments decorated or lined with the pelts of rare animals. Merchants wore robes trimmed with beaver, noblemen preferred sable, kings and queens (as they still do on ceremonial occasions) decked themselves in ermine. But common hides and furs were the dress of the common people. A leather jerkin meant a peasant, a sheepskin jacket a shepherd; the furs of common wild animals like the fox and the rabbit were associated with hunters and outlaws.

In the nineteenth century, however, as wildlife grew rarer, fur collars and cuffs began to appear on outdoor clothing, and fur muffs and tippets became popular. In the 1880s it suddenly became fashionable to decorate women's costumes and accessories with real or imitation dead animals, birds and even insects, and little capes of opossum, raccoon, and marten fur were worn. By the 1890s an entire coat made of or lined with fur had begun to suggest a large bank account rather than too great a familiarity with life in the backwoods.

The first fur coats were usually worn by men; it was not until the turn of the century that they were generally seen on women. For a while the fashion was unisexual; a stylish couple, for instance, might appear in public in identical raccoon coats. After the Depression, however — in spite of the efforts of manufacturers and fashion columnists — a fur coat on a man was a sign either of personal eccentricity or of sports or entertainment stardom — often of both. On a woman it was a conventional way of displaying wealth, with the rarer and more expensive furs such as mink and sable naturally ranking above the pelts of more common beasts.

Leather, particularly that of domestic animals like the cow and the sheep, took somewhat longer to become fashionable. Even today, garments made of hide have real status only if they come from rare and disagreeable animals like the llama and the alligator, or if they can be seen at a glance to have necessitated much tedious hand labour (dyeing, piecing, tooling, etc.).

In the sixties and seventies, when it became clear that many species of animals were threatened with extinction, fur coats became less popular. Many women refused to buy them, and hid any furs they already owned in the closet. Today, though coats made of the skins of rare wild beasts continue to be sold and worn, they have become associated with disregard for environmental values and a slightly murderous disposition. Wearing the fleece of sheep or the skins of cattle, on the other hand, is thought to be consistent with humanitarian views, and is still acceptable except to vegetarians.

CONSPICUOUS WEALTH: WEARING MONEY

Another primitive and simple way of displaying wealth is the wearing of actual money. In the past sharks' teeth, wampum, and coins, as well as many other forms of legal tender, have been made into jewellery or used to trim garments. Today, even in parts of the world where they cannot be used to buy lunch, such pieces retain some of their original prestige, and are often worn as accessories to high-fashion dress, to which they are believed to lend a barbaric glamour. Contemporary currency, which has no intrinsic value, is seldom or never made into jewelry, though the silver dimes and sixpences that have now been replaced by cheaper alloys are occasionally attached to bracelets and necklaces.

More common today, as well as in the past, is the decoration of the person with lumps of high-priced rock and metal. This method of announcing one's wealth also has the advantage of simplicity, since more people are aware of the approximate cost of such substances, especially when the local currency is based on them. The recent rise in the price of gold has made gold jewellery far more chic than it used to be, and diamonds, though their rise has not been so spectacular, retain their appeal. Materials such as rubies and emeralds, whose market price is less well-known, or which can more easily be imitated, are naturally less popular. Instant identification is desirable: platinum, though more costly than gold, never really caught on because most people couldn't tell it from silver or aluminum.

IN-GROUP SIGNALS

Sheer bulk and the wearing of many or obviously expensive garments and decorations are signs of status that can be read by almost anyone. More subtle sorts of Conspicuous Consumption are directed toward one's peers rather than toward the world in general; they are intended not to impress the multitude but to identify one as a member of some "in" group.

The costume of the upper-class British male, for example, is a mass of semiotic indicators. According to my informants,[7] he customarily wears striped shirts, sometimes with white collars, leaving plenty of cuff showing and always fastening at the wrist with cuff links. The shirt collars must be neither too long and pointed nor too round, and never button-down: "In fact, the

obsession of the gentleman is to avoid all extremes at all times." His suits, made by a "good" — i.e., superb — Savile Row tailor, are embellished in a number of small ways that will be noted by observant people: for instance, they may have extra buttons on the jacket cuff that can actually be buttoned, and a ticket pocket. The trousers will be cut fairly high in the waist and usually provided with buttons to which to attach braces or suspenders: "Wearing a belt is not done except with country suits, sometimes in the City called 'Friday suits,' since they are worn preparatory to going out of town. Older public-school men prefer to wear a tie around the waist rather than a belt." Ideally, the suit will be a dark pin stripe with a vest. The latter must never have lapels, which are "flashy" and "suggest the dandy or even the pouf." Recently, when one British politician became involved in a homosexual scandal, my informants remarked to one another that they were not really all that surprised: though his suit, hat, and watch chain were very reputable, "the lapels on his waistcoats were a nasty giveaway."

It is not only the clothes themselves that must be correct, but the haircut and the accessories. "A gentleman practically never wears sideburns or a hairstyle that covers his ears"; if he has a mustache it must be of moderate size. His eyeglasses must be of real tortoise shell or gold-rimmed, and he must carry the right umbrella. "Umbrellas are as talismanically magic as fairies' wands. They must be tightly rolled, and preferably never unrolled even in heavy rain." Old Etonians, however, always carry an unrolled umbrella.

Though the ordinary casual observer might miss or misinterpret these details, those in the know will recognize proper London tailoring — just as they will recognize the accent that means someone has gone to the right (i.e., sufficiently expensive) sort of school. Since they too have shopped abroad, they will also notice expensive foreign-made clothes, just as they would notice foreign words that happened to be dropped in conversation. To be acceptable, these must be the right sort of clothes, and from a currently fashionable country. Ideally, they should not be available at home; foreign fashions, like foreign words, are most prestigious when not too familiar. Once they have become naturalized they are no longer very chic — like the word chic itself. French T-shirts and Italian sandals, once high fashion, now cause no more thrill than the words boutique and espresso.

A similar law of diminishing returns affects foreign *types* of garment. The triangular head scarf tied under the chin, originally featured in *Vogue* as an exotic accessory, was so useful and soon became so familiar that it was a negative status indicator. The Oriental kimono, a glamorous import at the turn of the century, was by the 1930s associated with slatternly females of easy virtue, and today is one standard pattern for terry-cloth bathrobes. If such styles are to retain any of their initial prestige they must be made up in very costly materials: the head scarf must be of hand-woven wool and sprout hand-printed roses; the kimono must be of silk embroidered with golden dragons.

CONSPICUOUS LABELLING

Not long ago, expensive materials could be identified on sight, and fashionable men and women recognized Savile Row tailoring or a Paris designer dress at a glance. In the twentieth century, however, synthetics began to counterfeit wool, silk, linen, leather, fur, gold, and precious stones more and more successfully. At the same time, manufacturing processes became more efficient, so that a new and fashionable style could be copied in a few months and sold at a fraction of its original price. Meanwhile, the economic ability to consume conspicuously had been extended to millions of people who were ignorant of the subtleties of dress, who could not tell wool from Orlon or Schiaparelli from Sears Roebuck. As a result there was a world crisis in Conspicuous Consumption. For a while it seemed as if it might actually become impossible for most of us to distinguish the very rich from

the moderately rich or the merely well-off by looking at what they were wearing.

This awful possibility was averted by a bold and ingenious move. It was realized that a high-status garment need not be recognizably of better quality or more difficult to produce than other garments; it need only be recognizably more expensive. What was necessary was somehow to incorporate the price of each garment into the design. This was accomplished very simply: by moving the maker's name from its former modest inward retirement to a place of outward prominence. Ordinary shoes, shirts, dresses, pants, and scarves were clearly and indelibly marked with the names, monograms, or insignia of their manufacturers. The names or trademarks were then exhaustively publicized — a sort of saturation bombing technique was used — so that they might become household words and serve as an instant guide to the price of the clothes they adorned. These prices were very high, not because the clothes were made of superior materials or constructed more carefully, but because advertising budgets were so immense.

When this system was first tried, certain critics scoffed, averring that nobody in their right mind would pay $60 for a pair of jeans labelled Gloria Vanderbilt when a more or less identical pair labelled Montgomery Ward could be purchased for $12. Others claimed that consumers who wanted a monogram on their shirts and bags would want it to be their own monogram and not that of some industrialist they had never met. As everyone now knows, they were wrong. Indeed, it soon became apparent that even obviously inferior merchandise, if clearly labelled and known to be extravagantly priced, would be enthusiastically purchased. There was, for instance, a great boom in the sale of very ugly brown plastic handbags, which, because they were boldly stamped with the letters "LV," were known to cost far more than similar but less ugly brown leather handbags. Cotton T-shirts that faded or shrank out of shape after a few washings but had the word Dior printed on them were preferred to better-behaved but anonymous T-shirts. Those who wore them said (or were claimed in advertisements to say) that they felt "secure." After all, even if the shirt was blotchy and tight, everyone knew it had cost a lot of money, and if it got too bad you could always buy another of the same kind. Thus Conspicuous Consumption, as it so often does, merged into Veblen's second type of sartorial status.

CONSPICUOUS WASTE: SUPERFLUOUS DRAPERY

Historically speaking, Conspicuous Waste has most often involved the use of obviously unnecessary material and trimmings in the construction of clothing. The classical toga portrayed in Greek and Roman sculpture, for instance, used much more fabric than was really needed to cover the body, the excess being artistically if inconveniently draped over one arm.

Anne Hollander has written most perceptively about the use of superfluous draped cloth in medieval, Renaissance, and Baroque art. In preindustrial Europe, as she points out, cloth was the most important manufactured commodity, "the primary worldly good." Beautiful material was as admirable as gold or blown glass, and occupied far more space. The ownership of elaborate and expensive clothing was an important proof of social dominance. A single aristocrat sitting for his portrait, however, could wear only one luxurious outfit at a time. The display of many yards of velvet or satin behind him would suggest that he owned more such stuff and was able, in modern terms, to fling it around. Even after immensely full and trailing garments ceased to be worn, at least by men, excess drapery survived in art: it is notable, for example, in the paintings of Hals and Van Dyck and the sculptures of Bernini. The Frick Collection portrait of the Earl of Derby and his family "shows the family out of doors, standing on bare earth with shrubbery in the foreground and trees behind. But on the right side of the painting, behind the

earl, next to a column that might conceivably be part of a house, fifty yards of dark red stuff cascade to the ground from nowhere. So skillfully does Van Dyck fling down these folds that their ludicrous inconsequence is unnoticeable."[8]

Traditionally, as Ms. Hollander remarks, superfluous drapery has been a sign not only of wealth and high rank but of moral worth: angels, saints, martyrs, and Biblical characters in medieval and Renaissance art often wear yards and yards of extra silk and velvet. Drapery derived additional prestige from its association with classical art, and thus with nobility, dignity, and the ideal. Marble columns and togalike folds (occasionally, actual togas) were felt to transform the political hack into a national statesman and the grabby businessman into a Captain of Industry. As Ms. Hollander notes, Westminster Abbey and the Capitol in Washington, DC, are full of such attempted metamorphoses, frozen into soapy marble.

Excess drapery survives today in middlebrow portrait painting, causing over-the-hill industrialists, mayors, and society women to appear against stage backgrounds of draped velvet or brocade, the moral and economic prestige of which is somehow felt to transfer itself to them. Successful academics, I have noticed, are often painted in this manner: posed before velvet curtains, with their gowns and hoods and mortarboards treated in a way that recalls the idealized drapery and stiffened halos of Renaissance saints. (Appropriately, the halos of professors and college presidents are square rather than round.)

The use of superfluous fabric in costume never died out completely. During most of the period between 1600 and 1900, for instance, respectable middle-class and upper-class women wore a minimum of three petticoats; fewer than this was thought pathetic, and indicated negligence or poverty. Skirts were inflated with hoops or bustles to provide a framework on which to display great quantities of cloth, while overskirts, panniers, flounces, and trains demanded additional superfluous fabric. A fashionable dress might easily require twenty or thirty metres of material. Elaborate trimmings of bows, ribbons, lace, braid, and artificial flowers permitted yet more prestigious waste of goods. Men's clothing during the same period used relatively little excess fabric except in outerwear, where long, full coats and heavy capes employed yards of unnecessary cloth, adding greatly to their cost and to the apparent bulk of their wearers.

A glance through any current fashion magazine will show that the use of superfluous fabric today, though on a much more modest scale, is by no means outmoded. Expensive clothes are often cut more generously, and fashion photography tends to make the most of whatever extra material the designer provides, spreading it over prop sofas or blowing it about in the air. Even the most miserly excess of cloth may now be touted as a sign of prestige: a recent advertisement in *The New York Times* boasts of an extra inch in the back yoke of Hathaway shirts which, the manufacturer sobs, costs them $52 000 a year.

Wastage of material in the form of trimming, though less striking than it was in the past, still persists. Today, however, it is often thinly distinguished as practical. A prestigious shirt, for instance, has a breast pocket into which nothing must ever be put; the habit of filling it with pens and pencils is a lower-middle-class indicator, and also suggests a fussy personality. A related ploy, especially popular between the two World Wars, was the custom of embroidering everything with the owner's initials. This may in some cases have had a practical function, as in the separation of laundry, but — and more importantly — it also added conspicuously to the cost of the garment.

SUPERFLUOUS PERSONALITIES

Changing styles, of course, are another and very effective form of Conspicuous Waste. Although I do not believe that fashions alter at the whim of designers and manufacturers — otherwise they would do so far more often — it is certainly true that, when social and cultural changes prompt a shift in the way we look, the fashion industry is quick to take advantage of it, and to hint in advertising copy that last year's dress will do our reputation no good. When new styles do not catch on, other ploys are tried. A recent one is to announce with disingenuous enthusiasm that fashion is dead; that instead of the tyranny of "this year's look" we now have a range of "individual" looks — which are given such names as Classic, Feminine, Sporty, Sophisticate, and Ingenue. The task of the well-dressed liberated woman, the ads suggest, is to choose the look — or, much better and more liberated, *looks* — that suit her "lifestyle." She is encouraged, for instance, to be sleek and refined on the job, glowingly energetic on holiday, sweetly domestic at home with her children, and irresistibly sexy in the presence of what one department at my university has taken to calling her "spouse-equivalent." Thus, most ingeniously, life itself has been turned into a series of fashionable games, each of which, like jogging or scuba-diving or tennis, demands a different costume — or, in this case, a different set of costumes (winter/summer, day/night, formal/informal). The more different looks a woman can assume, the more fascinating she is supposed to be: personality itself has become an adjunct of Conspicuous Waste.

Men traditionally are not supposed to have more than one personality, one real self. Lately, however, they have been encouraged by self-styled "wardrobe engineers" to diversify their outward appearance for practical reasons. According to these experts, the successful businessman needs different sets of clothes in order to "inspire confidence in" (or deceive) other businessmen who inhabit different regions of the United States. This idea is not new, nor has it been limited to the mercantile professions. A former journalist has reported that as a young man he consciously varied his costume to suit his assignment. When sent to interview rich and powerful Easterners, he wore clothes to suggest that he was one of them: a dark-grey flannel Savile Row suit, a shirt from André Oliver or Turnbull & Asser, a Cartier watch of a sort never available at Bloomingdale's, and John Lobb shoes. "What you have to convey to rich people anywhere," he explained, "is that you don't have to try; so what you're wearing shouldn't ever be brand-new." New clothes, on the other hand, were appropriate when interviewing the *nouveau riche*; and since they might not recognize understated wealth, he (somewhat reluctantly, but a job is a job) would also put on a monogrammed shirt and Italian shoes with tassels.

When assigned to official Washington, this particular journalist took care to be three or four years behind current New York modes. "Washington hates fashion, especially New York fashion. The message should be, I am not attempting style; I am a man of the people, a regular fellow." He would therefore wear a somewhat rumpled pin-striped suit, a white shirt and a nondescript tie. Before leaving Manhattan he would get his hair cut shorter than usual. On the other hand, if he were sent to California, or were interviewing a writer, artist, or musician anywhere in the country, he would try to let his hair grow or rumple it up a bit. He would wear slacks and a good tweed jacket over a turtleneck shirt; if the interviewee were financially successful he would add an expensive watch or pair of shoes to this costume. Still other getups were appropriate and available — for the Midwest, Texas, the South, Continental Europe, and Britain.

When this system works it is no longer Waste; nor, since the clothes are deliberately chosen to blend into their surroundings, can they be called Conspicuous. But as the journalist himself remarked, clothes alone cannot disguise anyone, and the travelling salesman or saleswoman who engineers his or her wardrobe but not his or her voice, vocabulary, or manners may simply be practising Conspicuous Waste without its usual reward of enhanced status — let alone a rise in sales figures.

CONSPICUOUS LEISURE: DISCOMFORT AND HELPLESSNESS

Once upon a time leisure was far more conspicuous than it usually is today. The history of European costume is rich in styles in which it was literally impossible to perform any useful activity: sleeves that trailed on the floor; curled and powdered wigs the size, colour, and texture of a large white poodle; skirts two metres in diameter or with two-metre dragging trains; clanking ceremonial swords; starched wimples and cuffs and cravats that prevented their wearers from turning their heads or looking at anything below waist level; high-heeled pointed shoes that made walking agony; and corsets so tight that it was impossible to bend at the waist or take a normal breath. Such clothes proclaimed, indeed demanded, an unproductive life and the constant assistance of servants.

These conspicuously uncomfortable and leisurely styles reached an extreme in the late eighteenth century at the court of Versailles. The political and sartorial revolution that followed freed both sexes temporarily, and men permanently, from the need to advertise their aristocratic helplessness. Men's clothes became, and have remained ever since, at least moderately comfortable. Women's fashions, on the other hand, after barely ten years of ease and simplicity, rapidly became burdensome again and continued so for the next hundred years.

Urban middle-class clothing today, though it does not usually cause pain, makes anything more than limited activity awkward. It is hard to run or climb in a business suit and slick-soled shoes; and the easily soiled white or pale-coloured shirt that signifies freedom from manual labour is in constant danger of embarrassing its wearer with grimy cuffs or ring-around-the-collar. Urban women's dress is equally inconvenient. It should be pointed out, however, that inconvenience may be an advantage in some situations. A friend who often does historical research in libraries tells me that she always gets dressed up for it. If she is obviously handicapped by high heels, a pale, elegant suit, and a ruffled white blouse, the librarians will search the stacks for the heavy volumes of documents and old newspapers she needs and carry them to her, dusting them on the way. If she wears a sweater, casual slacks, and sensible shoes, they will let her do it herself. The same ploy would probably work for a man if he were middle-aged or older.

NOTES

1. Gerald Carson, *The Polite Americans: A Wide-Angle View of Our More or Less Good Manners over 300 Years* (Westport, CT: Greenwood Press, 1980), pp. 12–13.

2. Henrietta O. Ward, *Sensible Etiquette of the Best Society*, 18th ed. (Philadelphia: n.p., 1878), pp. 251–53.

3. Lillian Eichler, *Book of Etiquette*, vol. ii (Oyster Bay, NY: Nelson Doubleday, 1921), p. 147.

4. Anne Hollander, *Seeing through Clothes* (New York: Viking, 1978), p. 443.

5. Robert Brain, *The Decorated Body* (London: Hutchinson, 1979), p. 99.

6. Eichler, *Book of Etiquette*, p. 154.

7. The costume of the upper-class British male; I am indebted to Roland Gant and Nigel Hollis for this information.

8. Hollander, *Seeing through Clothes*, pp. 38–39.

PART 3B

ETHNIC AND RACIAL INEQUALITY

Ethnic groups are usually defined as social collectivities that are distinguished by ancestry and culture. **Races** have relatively unique ancestries and cultures too. In addition, races differ from ethnic groups and from each other in terms of visible physical characteristics, such as skin colour, that are socially defined as significant and that are significant in their social consequences.

Many people assume that cultural differences explain why some ethnic and racial groups are economically and politically more successful than others. In this view, only some groups are blessed with cultures that generate supportive families, respect for education, and an ethic of diligence and hard work. Other groups, culturally less well endowed, are condemned to broken families, low educational attainment, and limited occupational success. In Chapter 13, Stephen Steinberg questions these easy assumptions about the role of culture in determining ethnic and racial fortunes. He focuses on the successes of Asians and Jews in American society, the presumed successes of West Indian Blacks, and the failure of nearly 30 percent of American-born Blacks to escape poverty. Steinberg shows that, due to a selective immigration policy in the United States, the successful groups in American society arrived with a head start compared to relatively unsuccessful groups: they came with occupational experiences, educational backgrounds, and, in some cases, capital that enabled them to achieve rapid movement up the socioeconomic hierarchy. In contrast, American-born Blacks start their climb up the social hierarchy saddled with heavy historical and current liabilities: 200 years of slavery, 300 years of forced segregation, and continuing discrimination in employment, housing, and everyday life. Of course there are cultural differences between American-born Blacks and, say, Korean- and Japanese-Americans. But Steinberg's point is that these cultural differences are rooted in different historical and class experiences. In his judgment, culture is not an important *independent* cause of ethnic and racial success or failure.

In Chapter 14, Frances Henry and her colleagues provide an overview of how discrimination affects members of Canada's racial minorities. (While **prejudice** refers to negative *attitudes* towards members of an ethnic or racial group, **discrimination** refers to *behaviour* that has negative consequences for such groups.) They first sketch the changing racial composition of Canadian society; by 2001, nearly 18 percent of Canadians were members of racial minorities. The proportion is much higher in large cities, reaching 25 percent in Montreal, Edmonton, Calgary, and Winnipeg, 40 percent in Vancouver, and nearly 50 percent in Toronto. Chinese, Blacks, and South Asians each account for roughly a fifth of the racial-minority population. Henry and her colleagues summarize government-sponsored studies and public opinion polls that have found evidence of widespread racism in Canada, concluding that somewhere between 30 and 55 percent of Canadians hold racist views. They also describe the several white supremacist hate groups that have sprung up in Canada and they report on field experiments and statistical census studies that demonstrate significant racial discrimination in employment, particularly against Black Canadians.

Canada's Aboriginal peoples have fared worse than any other ethnic or racial group in the country. Their way of life was virtually destroyed by European colonization. They were robbed of land, culture, community, and even children. As a result, they now suffer more unemployment, poverty, alcoholism, infant mortality, and day-to-day violence than any other group in the country. Yet, ironically, some

Canadians fail entirely to recognize the historical and social context in which Aboriginal people became victims, instead blaming them for their plight. As J. Rick Ponting and Jerilynn Kiely note in Chapter 15, a 1994 survey showed that 31 percent of Canadians believe that "most of the problems of aboriginal peoples are brought on by themselves." Ponting and Kiely go on to review the results of the three main surveys on Aboriginal issues conducted in Canada between 1976 and 1994. They paint a picture full of irony and contradiction. Most Canadians are sympathetic to Aboriginals in the abstract, but they know little about them and give Aboriginal issues a low policy priority. On average, Canadians are opposed to "special status" for Aboriginal peoples yet on the whole they favour Aboriginal self-government. Most Canadians want action to solve Aboriginal problems — but only in the form of royal commissions to study the issues, not in the form of boycotts, demonstrations, and other assertive actions on the part of Aboriginal people themselves. Ponting and Kiely also note substantial regional variation in anti-Aboriginal feeling. Quebec stands out as the province most hostile to Aboriginal Canadians, especially their land claims. Ontario is most sympathetic. The overall pattern is that Aboriginal Canadians are viewed as especially problematic where they conflict with questions of ethno-national territorial control and least problematic in areas where they compose a small proportion of the population and make less threatening claims.

Given such widespread racial discrimination, most of Canada's other racial minorities have fared surprisingly well economically, especially after the immigrant generation. This is a tribute to their resourcefulness and industry and it is largely a consequence of their social background. Thus, according to the 1986 census, the median annual income of Black Canadians was 92.1 percent of the median annual income of Canadians of British origin. In contrast, the median annual income of Black Americans was only 67.3 percent of the median annual income of white Americans in 1990. Of the 12 ethnic and racial groups in Canada with a population over 250 000, East Indians had the third highest median income in 1986; the British ranked fourth. The economic achievement of most of Canada's racial minorities is due largely to the country's selective immigration policy, which favours immigrants with higher education and money. In brief, credentials and capital help to overcome the worst economic consequences of discrimination.

Economic differences persist among racial and ethnic groups in Canada. These are explored in depth in Chapter 16, by Hugh Lautard and Neil Guppy. Lautard and Guppy analyze Canadian census data from 1971 to 1996. They conclude that occupational differences between ethnic and racial groups have decreased substantially over the period they studied but that they are still considerable. Why do the differences persist? Mainly because some groups continue to be augmented by substantial numbers of immigrants, and immigrants suffer more disadvantages than native-born Canadians. For example, immigrants may lack English and French language skills and contacts in the wider community that could help them find better jobs. The Canadian-born children of immigrants are less disadvantaged in this regard, and their movement up the stratification system is therefore somewhat easier, even though discrimination persists, especially for members of some racial minority groups.

GLOSSARY

Discrimination is behaviour that has negative consequences for members of an ethnic or racial group.
Ethnic groups are social collectivities that are distinguished by relatively unique ancestry and culture.
Prejudice refers to negative attitudes towards members of an ethnic or racial group.

Races have relatively unique ancestries and cultures but they also differ from ethnic groups and from each other in terms of physical characteristics (e.g., skin colour) that are socially defined as important and that are important in their social consequences.

CRITICAL THINKING QUESTIONS

1. Do cultural differences explain why some ethnic and racial groups are more economically and politically successful than others? Give examples from the readings to support your answer.
2. What factors account for economic differences among racial and ethnic groups?
3. Identify the major racial minorities in Canada. How does discrimination affect them? How do you explain racial discrimination in Canada?
4. Is it still accurate to portray Canada as a vertical mosaic? Explain your answer using examples from the readings.
5. From a sociological perspective, how do you explain the problems of high alcohol and drug use and low education among Canada's Aboriginal peoples?
6. How do Canadians' attitudes toward Aboriginal peoples vary on different issues? Why do they vary in this way?

ANNOTATED BIBLIOGRAPHY

Augie Fleras and Jean Elliott, *Unequal Relations: An Introduction to Race, Ethnic and Aboriginal Dynamics in Canada*, 2nd ed. (Scarborough ON: Prentice-Hall, 1996). A comprehensive introduction to race and ethnicity in Canada.

Stephen Jay Gould, *The Mismeasure of Man* (New York: W. W. Norton, 1981). A brilliant, award-winning study of how the measurement of human intelligence has been closely connected to racist assumptions about human behaviour.

Peter S. Li, *Destination Canada: Immigration Debates and Issues* (Toronto: Oxford University Press, 2003). A thorough treatment of immigration in Canada.

Jeffrey Reitz and Raymond Breton, *The Illusion of Difference: Realities of Ethnicity in Canada and the United States* (Toronto: C. D. Howe Institute, 1994). Canadians often think Canada's "ethnic mosaic" differs from the American "melting pot." This book explodes the myth.

Chapter 13

Ethnic Heroes and Racial Villains

STEPHEN STEINBERG

Myths die hard, as the saying goes. To be sure, myths about race and ethnicity are deep-seated and often appear immune to change, but this is not because of some inherent potency or appeal. Myths are socially constructed. They arise in specific times and places, in response to identifiable circumstances and needs, and they are passed on through processes that can be readily observed. Whether a myth prospers or withers is always problematic; most, in fact, are relinquished or forgotten. To explain why some myths persist, we have to explore the relationship that these myths have to larger social institutions that promote and sustain them, and that in turn are served by them.

This chapter deals with myths that purport to explain why racial and ethnic groups occupy higher or lower places in the class system — why, in the popular idiom, "we have made it and they have not." The popular explanation, translated into respectable academic language by mainstream social scientists, is that "we" had the cultural virtues and moral fibre that "they" are lacking. If this theory were predicated on fact alone, it would be fairly easy to dispense with — for example, by showing that Jews, the archetype of ethnic success, arrived with occupational experiences and skills that gave them a headstart relative to other immigrants from eastern and southern Europe, that these latter groups were favourably positioned relative to Blacks, who were excluded from industrial employment altogether during the critical early phases of industrialization, and that racial minorities — Blacks in particular — have been encumbered across generations by discriminatory barriers that constitute the chief reason for their current economic plight. However compelling these facts might be, even when fully documented and analyzed, they are overpowered by other assumptions and beliefs that are almost universally shared in American society and that pervade American social science as well.

My point is that racial and ethnic myths about "making it" are embedded in a larger "success myth," one that is deeply rooted in American history and culture, and not easily countervailed. As Richard Weiss writes at the outset of his book on *The American Myth of Success*:

> the idea that ours is an open society, where birth, family, and class do not significantly circumscribe individual possibilities, has a strong hold on the popular imagination. The belief that all men, in accordance with certain rules, but exclusively by their own efforts, can make of their lives what they will has been widely popularized for well over a century. The cluster of ideas surrounding this conviction makes up the American myth of success.[1]

As Weiss goes on to say, the word "myth" does not imply something entirely false. The success myth was forged when the United States was a nation of yeomen and artisans, and it was sustained through two centuries of virtually uninterrupted territorial expansion and economic growth. There is much in our national experience to sustain notions of America as an open society where the individual can surmount impediments of "birth, family, and class." The problem arises when this simple schema glosses over major contradictions. To wit, colonial America was not just a nation of yeomen and artisans — one-fifth of its inhabitants were slaves, and the wealth that flowed from slavery had a great deal to do with the expanding opportunities for those early Americans who exemplified Puritan virtues of industry, frugality, and prudence. A problem also arises when success is equated with virtue, and failure with sin and personal inadequacy. Not only does this individualize success or failure, thus obscuring the whole issue of social justice, but it also treats virtue and its opposite as a matter of personal endowment, rather than as traits that need to be explained in terms of their historical and social sources.

It has never been easy to accommodate the success myth to the embarrassing realities of racial inequality. If the United States is an open society where the individual is not irreparably handicapped by "birth, family, and class," then how is racial hierarchy to be explained? When Gunnar Myrdal suggested in the 1950s that racism constituted an unhappy contradiction between American ideals and practices, this was heralded as a major advance. Indeed, the thrust of previous research had been to find in the cephalic index or in intelligence tests clear evidence of a biological inferiority that predestined Blacks to subordinate status. The discrediting of scientific racism is unquestionably one of the great triumphs of liberal social science. However, subsequent theorists developed a social-scientific variant of scientific racism that essentially substituted culture for genes. Now it was held that groups that occupy the lowest strata of society are saddled by cultural systems that prevent them from climbing the social ladder. As before, failure is explained not in terms of societal structures, but in terms of traits endemic to the groups themselves.

For the exponents of social-scientific racism, furthermore, culture is almost as immutable as the genes themselves. Thus, for example, Thomas Sowell writes:

Specific skills are a prerequisite in many kinds of work. But history shows new skills being rather readily acquired in a few years, as compared to the generations — or centuries — required for attitude changes. Groups today plagued by absenteeism, tardiness, and a need for constant supervision at work or in school are typically descendants of people with the same habits a century or more ago. *The cultural inheritance can be more important than biological inheritance*, although the latter stirs more controversy.[2]

As Sowell contends in this passage and his more extended disquisitions, a defective culture is the chief reason why Blacks have not followed in the footsteps of immigrants in their pursuit of the American Dream. Jews, on the other hand, are the perfect counter example — "the classic American success story — from rags to riches against all opposition."[3] Their formula for success amounts to having a certain cultural magic, called "human capital." To quote Sowell again:

Whether in an ethnic context or among peoples and nations in general, much depends on the whole constellation of values, attitudes, skills, and contacts that many call a culture and that economists call "human capital." ... The importance of human capital in an ethnic context is shown in many ways. Groups that arrived in America financially destitute have rapidly risen to affluence, when their cultures stressed the values and behavior required in an industrial and commercial economy. Even when color and racial prejudices confronted them — as in the case of the Chinese and Japanese — this proved to be an impediment but was ultimately unable to stop them.[4]

In the hands of Thomas Sowell, "human capital" is little more than an obfuscation for writing a morality tale whereby groups — notably Jews and Asians — who have "the right stuff" overcome every impediment of race and class to reach the economic pinnacle. Other groups — especially Blacks — suffer from historically conditioned cultural defects that condemn them to lag behind in the economic competition. Of course, Sowell's morality tale is not an original creation. His ethnic heroes and racial villains are merely an updated version of traditional folklore that pitted rugged cowboys against treacherous Indians (which also had racist overtones).

Nor is this racist folklore, masked as social science, politically innocent. Its covert ideological function is to legitimize existing racial inequalities. By placing cultural blame on the victims, the nation's vaunted ideals are reconciled with patently undemocratic divisions and inequities. By projecting collective Horatio Algers, in the unlikely forms of Jews and Asians, it is demonstrated that "success" is attainable by everyone, without regard to "birth, family, and class." Like all myths, the ethnic myth has an implicit moral: "we" are not responsible, morally or politically, for "their" misfortune.

NEW HEROES: ASIANS AND WEST INDIANS

Social science's enchantment with the success myth, replete with its cast of heroes and villains, has been renewed in recent years with the arrival of millions of immigrants, the majority of whom are Asians, West Indians, and Hispanics. That these new immigrants have generally settled in cities with large concentrations of poverty-stricken Blacks has only highlighted the contrast between upwardly mobile immigrants and inner-city Blacks. Invidious comparisons have been common in the popular press, and social scientists have churned out more spurious scholarship extolling cultural virtue and reciting the stock tale of triumph over adversity. That these new heroes — Asians and West Indians — belong to racial minorities has thickened the plot, since it demonstrates, according to these scholars, that "race" is not an insurmountable obstacle and cannot explain why so many Blacks are still mired in poverty.

Thomas Sowell is prominent among those who have advanced this point of view. In the passage quoted earlier, Sowell notes that Chinese and Japanese confronted "color and racial prejudices," but asserts that this "was ultimately unable to stop them." It is the West Indians, however, who provide Sowell with the clincher to his argument that it is culture, not race, that explains why Blacks languish in poverty:

> While not racially distinct from American Negroes, West Indians have had a different cultural background. ... These differences provide some clues as to how much of the situation of American Negroes in general can be attributed to color prejudice by whites and how much to cultural patterns among blacks.[5]

Several pages later Sowell is less equivocal:

> The contrast between the West Indians and American Negroes was not so much in their occupational backgrounds as in their behavioral patterns. West Indians were much more frugal, hard-working, and entrepreneurial. Their children worked harder and outperformed native black children in school.[6]

The passages above are examples of a unique logical fallacy, which might be called a "Sowellgism." It goes as follows:

> *Premise 1:* Blacks, Asians, and West Indians are all races.
> *Premise 2:* Asians and West Indians have succeeded.
> *Conclusion:* Race cannot explain why Blacks have not succeeded.

The trouble with this reasoning is that it uses an overgeneralized abstraction, "race," to gloss over crucial differences among the racial groups being compared with one another. Only in the most general sense can it be claimed that Asians, West Indians, and African Americans are all "races" that have been victims of racial stereotyping and discrimination. Although true, this proposition obscures the unique oppression that Blacks have endured throughout American history, beginning with two centuries of slavery and another century of official segregation, reinforced by the lynch mob and systematically unequal treatment in all major institutions. West Indians, of course, were also slaves, but living in island homelands that were predominantly Black, they have been insulated from the legalized and all-encompassing segregation that is unique to the African American experience.

Nor can this be dismissed as "history" that has no bearing on the present generation. If mobility is placed in correct sociological perspective, and regarded not as an individual event but as a process that occurs incrementally across generations, it becomes clear that America's legacy of racism has had a significant impact on the life chances even of today's Black youth. To say this is not to engage in "comparative suffering." It is merely to acknowledge the unique oppression that Blacks have experienced on American soil. Otherwise it is scarcely possible to explain why Blacks have been a perennial underclass in American society, and why they continue to lag behind other "racial" minorities.

THE MYTH OF ASIAN SUCCESS

In 1986 the five top recipients of the prestigious Westinghouse Science Talent Search were of Asian descent. This prompted a spate of articles in magazines and newspapers seeking to explain how a tiny minority, representing less than 2 percent of the national population, could achieve such bewildering success. The question, as framed by Malcolm Browne in an op-ed piece in *The New York Times*, is: "Do Asians have genetic advantages, or does their apparent edge in scientific skills stem from their special cultural tradition?"[7] Thus are we offered a choice between genes and culture as explanations for the academic excellence among Asians. Browne rejects genetic determinism, but has no such qualms with respect to cultural determinism. Paraphrasing an unnamed Westinghouse spokesman, he writes: "Tightly knit families and high respect for all forms of learning are traditional characteristics of Asian societies ... as they are for Jewish

societies; in the past a very high proportion of top Westinghouse winners were Jewish." Of course, as Browne himself remarks, "the odd thing is that until the twentieth century, real science scarcely existed in Asia." Undaunted by this apparent contradiction, he argues that Asian children are endowed with "an underlying devotion to scholarship — the kind of devotion imprinted on Asian children by a pantheon of ancestors" — that has made them receptive to Western scientific thought. Thus is a theory bent to accommodate inconvenient facts.

Two years later *The New York Times* ran another piece under the heading, "Why Do Asian Pupils Win Those Prizes?"[8] The author, Stephen Graubard, a professor of history at Brown University and editor of *Daedalus*, opines that Asians, who were eleven of the fourteen Westinghouse finalists from Cardozo High School in Queens, New York, have the advantage of stable families and Asian mothers who rear their children for success. With an air of resignation, he then turns the question onto Blacks and Puerto Ricans: "What is to be done for those hundreds of thousands of other New York children, many of illegitimate birth, who live with one parent, often in public housing, knowing little outside their dilapidated and decaying neighborhoods?" Since Graubard does not believe that the schools can do much to compensate for the defective culture of children from poverty backgrounds, these children are presumably condemned to languish in the cultural wasteland.

The same single-minded preoccupation with culture is found in yet another article in *The New York Times Magazine* on "Why Asians Succeed Here." The author, Robert Oxnam, president of the prestigious Asia Society, writes as follows:

The story of these new immigrants goes far beyond the high school valedictorians and Westinghouse Science scholars we read about in our newspapers. It is the story of a broader cultural interaction, a pairing of old Asian values with American individualism, Asian work ethics with American entrepreneurship. And, where those cultural elements have collided, it has also been a story of sharp disappointments and frustration.[9]

Once again, culture is the fulcrum of success. Like the other writers quoted earlier, Oxnam identifies "the strong family ties and powerful work ethics of Asian cultures" as "key factors in Asian-American achievement."

This theory of Asian success is a new spin on earlier theories about Jews, to whom Asians are explicitly compared. As with the theory of Jewish success, there are a number of conceptual and empirical problems that throw the theory into question:

1. The theory of "Asian" success lumps together some twenty-five nationalities that are very disparate in history and culture. It is only in the United States that they are assumed to share a common "Asian" heritage. Little or no evidence is put forward to substantiate claims that they share common values with respect to family and work, that these values are significantly different from those found among non-Asian groups, or that these values are the key factors in explaining which Asians get ahead or why more Asians do so than others. Here is a classic case of circular reasoning. Values are not measured independently, but inferred from success, and then posited as the cause of success.

2. Theories of Asian success gloss over the fact that large segments of the Asian populations in the United States are far from prosperous. Alongside dramatic and visible success, touted in the popular media, are deep pockets of poverty, exploitation, and despair. Moreover, if successful Asians are presumed to owe their success to distinctively Asian values with respect to family and work, then are we to assume that less affluent Asians are deficient in these values? Are they therefore less "Asian"?

3. As in the case of Jewish success, the prevailing theory of Asian success overlooks the operation of premigration class factors that go a long way toward explaining the destinies of these immigrants after their arrival. The issue here has to do with selective migration — that is, with who decides to emigrate and who is permitted entry. As Ezra Vogel, a scholar of China and Japan, has noted, Asian immigrants "are a very biased sample, the cream of their own societies."[10] They are drawn disproportionately from the intellectual and professional elites that, for one reason or another, have restricted opportunity in their home countries. Many of them have been admitted under the occupational preferences built into the new immigration law. In short, they are "successful" even before their arrival in America.

Data collected by the Immigration and Naturalization Service demonstrate the class character of Asian immigration. Table 13.1 reports the percentage of immigrant workers classified as professionals.[11] In the case of Indians, over three-quarters of immigrants with occupations are professionals; this reached a high point in 1969–71, when nine out of every ten Indians with occupations were professionals. Among Filipinos, Koreans, and Japanese the figures range between half and three-quarters; among Chinese, the figures are somewhat lower, but still much higher than for non-Asians. The influx of professionals of all nationalities reached a peak between 1969 and 1971, and declined thereafter. Nevertheless, the evidence is clear that a major segment of Asian immigration represents an educational and occupational elite.

Other data indicate that between 1965 and 1981 some 70 000 medical professionals — physicians, nurses, and pharmacists — came from the Philippines, South Korea, and India.[12] Another major source of immigrants has been students who enter the United States with student visas and then do not return to their home country. Of the 70 000 Chinese students from Taiwan between 1950 and 1983, it is estimated that 90 percent remained in the United States.

TABLE 13.1   PERCENTAGE OF PROFESSIONALS AMONG ASIAN IMMIGRANTS WITH OCCUPATIONS

	1961–65	1966–68	1969–71	1972–74	1975–77
China	31	35	47	37	31
India	68	67	89	84	73
Japan	44	50	45	37	28
Korea	71	75	70	51	38
Philippines	48	60	70	63	47
All Asians	40	52	62	54	44
All Immigrants	20	25	29	27	25

SOURCE: Adapted from Morrison G. Wong and Charles Hirschman, "The New Asian Immigrants," in *Culture, Ethnicity, and Identity*, William McCready, ed. (New York: Academic Press, 1983), pp. 395–97.

The same is true of tens of thousands of students from Hong Kong, Korea, and other Asian countries. What these figures indicate is not a dramatic success story, but merely the transfer of intellectual and professional elites from less developed nations.

These immigrants start out with the educational and occupational resources that are generally associated with educational achievement in the next generation. To put the cultural theory to a fair empirical test, one would have to compare the children of Asian professionals with the children of other professionals. Only in this way could we assess the significance of distinctive ethnic factors. It is hardly valid to compare the children of upper-middle-class Asian professionals with the children of unemployed Black workers, as is done when "Asians" are compared with "Blacks."[13]

Not all Asian immigrants, however, come from advantaged backgrounds. Indeed, in recent years the flow of immigrants has included large numbers of uneducated and unskilled workers. These are the "downtown Chinese," as Peter Kwong calls them in his book, *The New Chinatown*.[14] These immigrants have difficulty finding employment in the racially segmented labour market outside of Chinatown, and are forced to accept jobs, commonly in sweatshops and restaurants, that match their nineteenth-century counterparts in their debasing exploitation. It has yet to be demonstrated that the children of these super-exploited workers are part of an Asian success story. Indeed, the outbreak of gang violence among Chinatown youth has exploded another myth that had great currency in the 1950s; namely, that because of their close-knit families, delinquency is virtually nonexistent among the Chinese.[15]

In demystifying and explaining Asian success, we come again to a simple truth: that what is inherited is not genes, and not culture, but class advantage and disadvantage. If not for the extraordinary selectivity of the Asian immigrant population, there would be no commentaries in the popular press and the social science literature extolling Confucian values and "the pantheon of ancestors" who supposedly inspire the current generation of Asian youth. After all, no such claims are made about the Asian youth who inhabit the slums of Manila, Hong Kong, and Bombay, or, for that matter, San Francisco and New York.

THE MYTH OF WEST INDIAN SUCCESS

The mythical aspects of West Indian success, and the invidious comparisons between West

Indians and Blacks, predate the current wave of immigration. In *Beyond the Melting Pot*, published in 1963, Glazer and Moynihan wrote that "the ethos of the West Indians, in contrast to that of the Southern Negro, emphasized saving, hard work, investment and education."[16] Although Glazer and Moynihan offer no evidence to support their claims, their observations are consistent with those made by other observers over several decades.[17] The key issue, though, is not whether West Indians in New York had the exemplary cultural traits that were ascribed to them. The issue is whether these cultural traits *explain* West Indian success, or whether, on the contrary, West Indians were more middle-class to begin with, and this explains their different attitudes with respect to "saving, hard work, investment and education."

As with Asians, the factor of selective migration must be considered. To begin with, we need to distinguish between two waves of West Indian immigration: the first, during the 1920s; the second, after the 1965 Hart-Celler Act. The first wave of immigrants was a highly selective group. According to immigration records, almost all of the adults — 89 percent — were literate, a figure far higher than that for West Indians who did not emigrate, or for the southern Blacks to whom they are compared.[18] Over 40 percent of the West Indian immigrants were classified as skilled, and some of these were highly educated professionals. Thus, once again, in drawing overall comparisons between West Indians and African Americans, we are comparing groups that differ in their social class as well as their ethnicity. It has never been shown that West Indians are different in terms of "saving, hard work, investment and education" when compared with their social class equals who are not West Indian.[19]

In other words, before generalizing about "West Indian cultural values," we need to be clear about which West Indians we have in mind. This is sharply illustrated by Nancy Foner's study of West Indians in New York City and London.[20] Since both groups have the same cultural heritage, this factor cannot explain why West Indians in New York have been more successful than those in Britain. Foner shows that the two immigrant pools are different in occupational background. Those who flocked to Britain during the 1950s were responding to labour shortages and an open-door immigration policy for Commonwealth nations. Although many were skilled workers, only about 10 percent were classified as white-collar. In contrast, among West Indian legal emigrants to the United States between 1962 and 1971, 15 percent were professional workers and another 12 percent worked in other white-collar occupations. For this reason alone, it is not surprising that West Indians in New York have been conspicuously more successful than those in London.[21]

The selective character of West Indian immigration to the United States, as already suggested, "stacks the deck" in terms of any comparisons to African Americans. Especially at a time when there was virtually no indigenous Black middle class, the influx of a small West Indian elite of professionals, businessmen, and prominent individuals did in fact stand out, and seemed to support notions of West Indian cultural superiority. Two things have changed since the migration of the 1920s, however. In the first place, there is a sizable African American middle class. Second, West Indian migration has become more occupationally diverse than was previously the case. Therefore, we have to reconsider our assumptions regarding the social status of West Indians in relation to African Americans.

In a paper entitled "West Indian Success: Myth or Fact?" Reynolds Farley undertakes an extensive analysis of 1980 census data.[22] He concludes that there is more myth than fact in suppositions about West Indian success.

Farley divided his sample into five groups: native whites, native Blacks, Black immigrants pre-1970, Black immigrants post-1970, and Blacks of West Indian ancestry (born in the

United States but of West Indian parents or grandparents). On all relevant social and economic indicators, the four Black cohorts differ little among themselves, and where differences exist, they are small in comparison to the differences between Blacks and whites. For example, the figures below indicate the percentages of families that are female-headed:

Whites	11%
Native Blacks	37%
Black immigrants pre-1970	33%
Black immigrants post-1970	25%
West Indian ancestry	38%

Except for recent immigrants, female-headed households are as prevalent among West Indians as among native Blacks. Thus, the data do not support the widespread notion that West Indians have "strong families" in comparison to African Americans.

Nor do the data support the notion that West Indians are endowed with an entrepreneurial spirit that leads to business success. The following figures, adjusted for age, report the rate (per thousand) of self-employment among men:

Whites	87
Native Blacks	30
Black immigrants pre-1970	41
Black immigrants post-1970	22
West Indian ancestry	35

The rate of self-employment among recent West Indian immigrants is strikingly low (in contrast to what is found among recent Korean immigrants, for example). It is true that earlier West Indian immigrants and their descendants have a higher rate of self-employment than do native Blacks, but the levels are still much lower than that for whites. In short, self-employment is not so pronounced among West Indians as to support crude popular notions concerning "Jew-maicans," or, for that matter, more refined claims of "ethnic enterprise" and "entrepreneurial spirit" supposedly endemic to West Indian culture.

Similar patterns are found with respect to education, occupation, and income. West Indians are generally higher on these measures of social class than native Blacks, but the differences are not great and there is always the suspicion that they are an artifact of selective migration. For example, the figures below report the average earnings in 1979 of employed males between the ages of 25 and 64:

Whites	15 170
Native Blacks	9 380
Black immigrants pre-1970	7 460
Black immigrants post-1970	11 170
West Indian ancestry	10 720

Again, West Indians are much closer to native Blacks in their earnings than they are to whites, and recent West Indian immigrants have the lowest incomes of all five groups. On the basis of his analysis of these 1980 census data, Farley reached the following conclusion:

> We have shown that black immigrants and West Indians in 1980 were quite similar to native blacks on the most important indicators of social and economic status. There is no basis now — and apparently there was none in the past — for arguing that the success of West Indians in the United States "proves" that culture, rather than racial discrimination, determines the current status of blacks.[23]

The critical role that premigration factors play in a group's "adjustment" is even more vividly illustrated by the two waves of Cuban immigration. The first wave, occurring in the aftermath of the Cuban Revolution, consisted largely of Cuba's economic elites — professionals, businessmen, shopkeepers, and others disenchanted with Cuban socialism. The second wave, "the Mariel invasion," consisted of ordinary Cubans, including a small number of criminals and mental patients whom the Cuban government cynically placed aboard the boats. The first wave was welcomed, especially in southern Florida's depressed economy, and inspired exuberant articles, like the one in *Fortune* magazine on "Those Amazing Cuban Emigres."[24] The second wave received a far less hospitable reception, and were besmirched by sensational press reports suggesting that the Mariel Cubans were mostly criminals, lunatics, and degenerates.[25] The Cuban cultural magic seemed to have vanished.

In the final analysis, the attempt to use Asians and West Indians to prove that "race" cannot explain the plight of Black America is fallacious at best, and sinister at worst. It is based on an untenable juxtaposition of groups that look alike in terms of a simplistic racial classification (they are all "racial" minorities), but who are very different in terms of their social class origins, in terms of the structures of opportunity they encounter after their arrival, and even in terms of the depth of racism that limits access to these opportunities. This is not to deny that Asians and West Indian immigrants confront a difficult situation, one that calls forth all their cultural and personal resources. Nor is it to deny that both groups encounter racist barriers in their quest for a better life. It does not do them or ourselves any good, however, to use these struggling minorities to make specious comparisons to African Americans, and to minimize the significance of racism.

NOTES

1. Richard Weiss, *The American Myth of Success* (New York: Basic Books, 1969).
2. Thomas Sowell, *Ethnic America* (New York: Basic Books, 1981), p. 284. Emphasis added.
3. Ibid., p. 98.
4. Ibid., p. 282. For another view, see Stephen Steinberg, "Human Capital: A Critique," *Review of Black Political Economy* 14, 1 (Summer 1985), pp. 67–74.
5. Sowell, *Ethnic America,* p. 216.
6. Ibid., p. 219. For a similar popular account, see "America's Super Minority," *Fortune* 114 (November 24, 1986), p. 148.
7. Malcolm W. Browne, "A Look at Success of Young Asians," *The New York Times* (March 25, 1986), p. A31.
8. Stephen G. Graubard, "Why Do Asian Pupils Win Those Prizes?" *The New York Times* (January 29, 1988), p. A35.
9. Robert B. Oxnam, "Why Asians Succeed Here," *The New York Times Magazine* (November 30, 1986), p. 70.
10. Quoted in Fox Butterfield, "Why Asians Are Going to the Head of the Class," Education Supplement, *The New York Times* (August 3, 1986), section 12, p. 20.
11. These percentages are based on the number of immigrants who report having a job, thereby excluding nonworking women, as well as the old and young.
12. Illsoo Kim, "Ethnic Class Division among Asian Immigrants: Its Implications for Social Welfare Policies," unpublished paper presented at the Conference on Asian American Studies, Cornell University, October 24, 1986, p. 3.
13. If there is a distinctively ethnic factor in patterns of Asian mobility, it is that, like Jews of earlier generations, Asians realize that their channels of opportunity are restricted by prejudice. Closed off from the corporate fast lane, they are drawn to the professions. The sciences are particularly attractive to individuals who lack fluency in English. Data reporting SAT scores indicate that Asian American students score far above average on the math test, but far below average on the verbal test. *The New York Times*, section 12: "Education Life" (August 3, 1986), p. 3.
14. Peter Kwong, *The New Chinatown* (New York: Hill and Wang, 1987), pp. 5–6.
15. For example, see Henry Beckett, "How Parents Help Chinese Kids Stay Out of Trouble," series in the *New York Post* (July 11–13, 1955), and Betty Lee Sung, *The Story of the Chinese in America* (New York: Collier, 1971), p. 156.
16. Nathan Glazer and Daniel Patrick Moynihan, *Beyond the Melting Pot* (Cambridge: MIT Press, 1963), p. 35.

17. For example, Ira Reid, *The Negro Immigrant* (New York: Arno Press, 1969), originally published in 1939; James Weldon Johnson, *Black Manhattan* (New York: Knopf, 1930).

18. Nancy Foner, "West Indians in New York City and London: A Comparative Analysis," in Constance R. Sutton and Elsa M. Chaney, eds., *Caribbean Life in New York City* (New York: Center for Migration Studies, 1987), p. 123.

19. In their study of Jamaican and Black American migrant farm workers, Nancy Foner and Richard Napoli observed differences between the two groups that, at first glance, appear to support the cultural thesis. The Black American farm workers were frequently apathetic on the job, and squandered part of their wages on liquor and gambling. In contrast, the Jamaican workers "worked very hard, were extremely productive, and saved most of their earnings" (p. 492).

    To their credit, Foner and Napoli probe beneath surface behaviour, and show that the two groups have different origins and are recruited through different procedures. For Black Americans, migrant labour was a last resort and a dead end, whereas for Jamaicans the wages meant a higher living standard when they returned home, and the possibility of purchasing land or establishing a small business. Thus, the same work attracted a different calibre of worker, and the same pay provided different incentives.

    Second, as offshore workers, Jamaicans were recruited under a program that not only included a physical exam, but also considered their previous work record. They also had to meet a work quota to remain in the camp and to ensure that they would be hired again. In these ways the Jamaican recruiting system "seemed to weed out the kinds of workers who frequently travelled North in the Black American migrant stream" (p. 501). Nancy Foner and Richard Napoli, "Jamaican and Black-American Migrant Farm Workers: A Comparative Analysis," *Social Problems* 25 (June 1978), pp. 491–503.

20. Foner, "West Indians." Also, see Roy Simon Bryce-Laporte, "New York City and the New Caribbean Immigration: A Contextual Statement," *International Migration Review* 13, 2 (1979), pp. 214–34.

21. Foner, "West Indians," 123. In addition to differences in the occupational background of the two West Indian cohorts, Foner cites two other factors that help to explain why West Indians have fared better in the United States: (1) the migration spans a much longer period, and is already into the second generation, and (2) they benefited from having a pre-existing Black community that provided patronage for West Indian professionals and entrepreneurs, and that allowed West Indians to be cast into a privileged intermediary position between Black and white America (comparable in some ways to the position of the coloureds in South Africa).

22. Reynolds Farley, "West Indian Success: Myth or Fact?" unpublished manuscript (Ann Arbor: Population Studies Center, University of Michigan, 1987). Statistical data are taken from pp. 8, 11, and 13. Also see Reynolds Farley and Walter R. Allen, *The Color Line and the Quality of Life in America* (New York: Russel Sage, 1987), chapter 12.

23. Reynolds Farley, "West Indian Success: Myth or Fact?" p. 15.

24. Tom Alexander, "Those Amazing Cuban Emigres," *Fortune* 74 (October 1966), pp. 144–49.

25. Actually, less than 5 percent of the Mariel migrants were hardened criminals, mental patients, or other undesirables. See Robert L. Bach, Jennifer B. Bach, and Timothy Triplett, "The Flotilla 'Entrants': Latest and Most Controversial," *Cuban Studies* 11 (1981), pp. 29–48.

Chapter 14

The Victimization of Racial Minorities in Canada

FRANCES HENRY

CAROL TATOR

WINSTON MATTIS

TIM REES

Canada's population has become increasingly racially diverse. From what was a country inhabited largely by whites and Aboriginal peoples, the population has changed to include people from more than 70 countries. In addition, the source countries from which immigrants come have dramatically altered. In 1961, 90 percent of Canada's immigrants came from European countries; between 1981 and 1991, this figure declined to 25 percent. Almost half of all immigrants who came to Canada between 1981 and 1991 were Asian-born.

By 1986, 38 percent of Canadians had at least one ancestor who was neither French nor English. In the same year, racial minorities accounted for 6.3 percent, or 1.6 million, of Canada's population. Most members of racial-minority groups lived in Ontario (see Figure 14.1). In 1991, the figure had increased to 9.6 percent, or 2.6 million. Recent projections indicate that the racial minority population will rise to 17.7 percent — 5.7 million people — in the year 2001.

More than two-thirds of racial-minority immigrants to Canada come from Asia (see Figures 14.2, 14.3, and 14.4 on page 140).

Chinese constitute the most numerous group, with 1.3 million people, followed by South Asians (East Indians, Pakistanis, Sri Lankans, and Bangladeshis) and Blacks, with 1.1 million each. The next most numerous groups are West Asians and Arabs, Filipinos, Southeast Asians (Indochinese), and Latin Americans. The number of Latin American immigrants was expected to expand dramatically by the turn of the century.

By 2001, about half of the population of Toronto and two-fifths of the population of Vancouver are expected to be racial minorities. About one-quarter of the populations of Montreal, Edmonton, Calgary, and Winnipeg are expected to be racial minorities. In Ottawa–Hull and Windsor, one-sixth of the populations will consist of racial minorities. Halifax, Kitchener, Hamilton, Victoria, and Regina will have 10–14 percent (see Figure 14.5 on page 140).

These figures are taken from the Samuel projection of the numbers of racial minorities expected to live in Canada by the year 2001. Actual figures according to the most recent census (1996) show that about 10.7 percent of Canada's total population in 1996 was classified

Source: Excerpted from *The Colour of Democracy: Racism in Canadian Society*, 2nd ed. (Toronto: Harcourt Canada, 2000), pp. 86–91, 96–117. Reprinted by permission of Nelson, a division of Thomson Learning: www.thomsonrights.com. Fax: 800-730-2215.

FIGURE 14.1 RACIAL MINORITIES BY PROVINCE, 1986–2001 (PROJECTED)   ■ 1986   ■ 2001

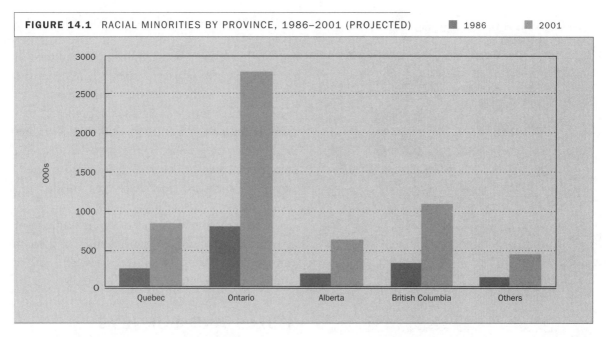

SOURCE: T.J. Samuel, *Visible Minorities in Canada: A Projection* (Toronto: Race Relations Advisory Council on Advertising, Canadian Advertising Foundation, 1992).

as "visible minority" by the census.[1] As in the earlier figures, Asians, including those from Southeast Asia and South Asia, predominate (see Table 14.1 on page 141). The provinces of

Ontario, British Columbia, and Quebec have the most racial-minority inhabitants (see Table 14.2 on page 142). There are also nearly 800 000 Aboriginal people in Canada. The largest cities

FIGURE 14.2 ETHNICITY OF RACIAL MINORITIES, 1986

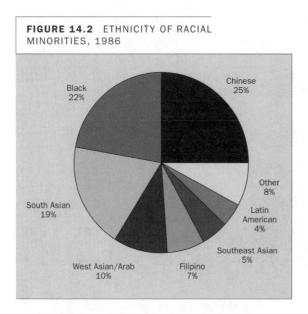

SOURCE: T.J. Samuel, *Visible Minorities in Canada: A Projection* (Toronto: Race Relations Advisory Council on Advertising, Canadian Advertising Foundation, 1992).

FIGURE 14.3 ETHNICITY OF RACIAL MINORITIES, 1991

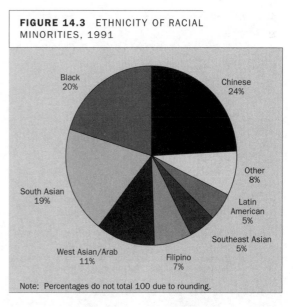

Note: Percentages do not total 100 due to rounding.

SOURCE: T.J. Samuel, *Visible Minorities in Canada: A Projection* (Toronto: Race Relations Advisory Council on Advertising, Canadian Advertising Foundation, 1992).

FIGURE 14.4 ETHNICITY OF RACIAL MINORITIES, 2001 (PROJECTED)

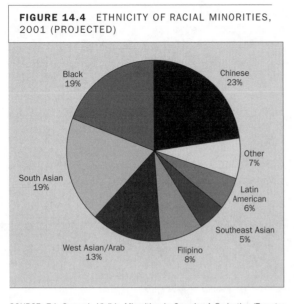

SOURCE: T.J. Samuel, *Visible Minorities in Canada: A Projection* (Toronto: Race Relations Advisory Council on Advertising, Canadian Advertising Foundation, 1992).

in Canada also contain the most racial-minority people. In 1996, Toronto led the list with 1 338 095, followed by Vancouver with 564 600

and Montreal with 401 425 (see Table 14.3 on page 143).

There are many kinds of data one can turn to in assessing the impact of these changes on the composition and complexion of immigrants to Canada. One source of data is the polls and surveys that seek to measure racist attitudes among individuals or groups. In the past two decades, many such surveys have been initiated by government agencies, politicians, the media, and academics.

A second source is the research findings of government commissions, academics, and commissioned studies by universities and other public-sector agencies.

POLLS AND SURVEYS

One of the first surveys of racist attitudes in Canada contained 57 attitudinal items pertaining to racial prejudice (Henry, 1978). The findings revealed that 16 percent of the white mainstream population was extremely intolerant

FIGURE 14.5 RACIAL MINORITIES IN SELECTED CENSUS METROPOLITAN AREAS, 1991 AND 2001 (PROJECTED)

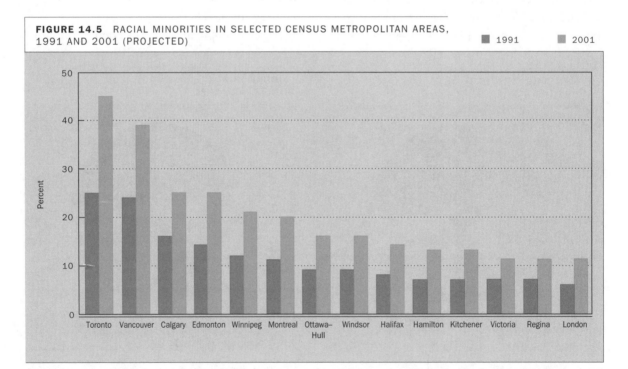

SOURCE: T.J. Samuel, *Visible Minorities in Canada: A Projection* (Toronto: Race Relations Advisory Council on Advertising, Canadian Advertising Foundation, 1992).

TABLE 14.1 VISIBLE MINORITIES IN CANADA BY ETHNIC GROUP, 1996

	NUMBER	PERCENTAGE
Total visible-minority population	3 197 480	99.9
Chinese	860 150	26.9
South Asian	670 585	21.0
Black	573 860	17.9
Arab/West Asian	244 665	7.7
Filipino	234 200	7.3
Latin American	176 975	5.5
Southeast Asian	172 765	5.4
Japanese	68 135	2.1
Korean	64 835	2.0
Visible minority, n.i.e.*	69 745	2.2
Multiple visible minority**	61 570	1.9

*Includes Pacific Islanders and other visible-minority groups; n.i.e. = not included elsewhere.

**Includes respondents who reported more than one visible-minority group.

Note: Percentages do not total 100 due to rounding.

SOURCE: Data from Statistics Canada, *The Daily*, Catalogue no. 11-001, February 17, 1998. Downloaded June 4, 1998, from http://www.statcan.ca/Daily/English/980217/d980217.htm.

and 35 percent somewhat racist. At least 18 percent had very liberal views about race, and a further 30 percent were somewhat liberal.[2]

The attitudinal survey literature has been remarkably consistent over the more than 20 years since that first survey was done. Most of the surveys show that between 10 and 20 percent of Canadians are extremely intolerant of racial minorities. Another 20–35 percent are somewhat racist. Combining these two findings suggests that a large segment of the population could be characterized as racist.

A decade after the Henry study, another survey found that between 7 and 20 percent of Canadians could be described as strongly racist in their views (Environics, 1988). Evidence of "hard core" racism included the following findings: 19 percent of Canadians agreed with "research findings" that Orientals were superior to whites, who were, in turn, superior to Blacks. Moreover, 13 percent of Canadians would exclude non-white groups from immigrating to Canada, 7 percent would not vote for a Black political candidate, and 9 percent would not vote for a Chinese candidate.

A 1989 survey conducted by researchers at the University of Toronto and York University was designed to determine whether there was a significant difference between the racial attitudes of decision makers — legislators, lawyers, administrators, and police officers — and those of the general population. The survey found that 23 percent of the "elite" Canadians thought minority groups needed to get rid of "harmful and irritating faults," compared with 39 percent of the general population who held the same view. Half of the decision makers and 70 percent of the general population felt that immigrants often bring discrimination upon themselves; 16 percent of the "elites" and almost one-third of the general citizenry believed that "races are naturally unequal" (Gould, 1990).

A 1989 poll in British Columbia, which receives most racial-minority immigrants settling in the West, indicated that many residents believed that immigration does not bring economic advantages to the province. These perceptions were held despite the fact that, shortly before, a highly publicized report by Employment and Immigration Canada found exactly the opposite to be the case. The report demonstrated that after ten years in Canada, Third World immigrants paid more taxes per capita than did western European immigrants. These perceptions were also not shaken by the well-reported findings of the province's central statistics bureau, which showed that Asian entrepreneurial immigrants contributed $122.9 million to the BC economy and $5.4 million to the Alberta economy in 1988. Although entrepreneurial immigrants from Asia created 15 000 jobs in Canada in 1988, nearly half of British Columbia's population thought there were too many immigrants of colour moving into the province.

TABLE 14.2   VISIBLE-MINORITY POPULATION OF CANADA BY PROVINCE, 1996

	TOTAL POPULATION	TOTAL VISIBLE-MINORITY POPULATION	VISIBLE MINORITIES AS % OF TOTAL POPULATION	GEOGRAPHIC DISTRIBUTION OF VISIBLE MINORITIES
Canada	28 528 125	3 197 480	11.2	100.0
Newfoundland	547 155	3 815	0.7	0.1
Prince Edward Island	132 855	1 520	1.1	0.0
Nova Scotia	899 970	31 320	3.5	1.0
New Brunswick	729 625	7 995	1.1	0.3
Quebec	7 045 085	433 985	6.2	13.6
Ontario	10 542 790	1 682 045	15.8	52.6
Manitoba	1 100 295	77 355	7.0	2.4
Saskatchewan	976 615	26 945	2.8	0.8
Alberta	2 669 195	269 280	10.1	8.4
British Columbia	3 589 760	660 545	17.9	20.7
Yukon Territory	30 650	1 000	3.3	0.0
Northwest Territories	64 125	1 670	2.6	0.1

SOURCE: Data from Statistics Canada, *The Daily*, Catalogue no. 11-001, February 17, 1998. Downloaded June 4, 1998, from http://www.statcan.ca/Daily/English/980217/d980217.htm.

In a Toronto survey in 1992, when asked how well their racial or cultural group was accepted, 80 percent of those surveyed in the Black Canadian community, 63 percent in the Chinese Canadian community, and 62 percent of the East Indian–Pakistani Canadian community felt there was some prejudice toward them in Toronto. Also, 73 percent of Blacks, 48 percent of Chinese, and 47 percent of East Indians–Pakistanis felt discriminated against in obtaining work, compared with 31 percent of Jews, 16 percent of Portuguese, and 15 percent of Italians. In terms of discrimination in the legal or court system, the survey found that 49 percent of Blacks felt they were discriminated against. Twenty-one percent of East Indians–Pakistanis felt this way, as did 9 percent of Chinese (*Toronto Star*, 1992).

A report by the Economic Council of Canada (1991) attempted to measure the changing attitudes toward prejudice over time by analyzing the results of 62 surveys taken from 1975 to 1990 by Gallup, Decima, Environics, and other polling organizations. The report found that respondents from communities with greater proportions of visible-minority immigrants were "likely to be more tolerant of racial and ethnic differences." The report also concluded that over time there were "diminishing levels of prejudice." However, the results should be approached with some caution, considering the unreliability and validity of the many data sources as well as the kind of statistical analysis performed, which tends to obscure important variables, such as the unit of analysis, the nature of the questions, the age distribution of the sample, and the socioeconomic status, educational background, and gender of the respondents.

A survey by the federal immigration department of 1800 adults and fourteen focus groups showed a "growing acceptance" of attitudes and practices that show a dislike for "foreigners." One-third of the respondents agreed it was important to "keep out people who are different

TABLE 14.3 VISIBLE-MINORITY POPULATION* OF CANADA, BY CENSUS METROPOLITAN AREAS, 1996

	TORONTO	VANCOUVER	MONTREAL
Total population	4 232 905	1 813 935	3 287 645
Total visible-minority population**	1 338 985	564 600	401 425
Black	274 935	16 400	122 320
South Asian	329 840	120 140	46 165
Chinese	335 185	279 040	46 115
Korean	28 555	17 085	3 505
Japanese	17 055	21 880	2 310
Southeast Asian	46 510	20 370	37 600
Filipino	99 115	40 715	14 385
Arab/West Asian	72 160	18 155	73 950
Latin American	61 655	13 830	46 705
Visible minority, n.i.e.†	45 655	6 775	3 485
Multiple visible minority‡	27 435	10 215	1 885

*The Employment Equity Act define the visible-minority population as persons, other than Aboriginal people, who are non-Caucasian in race or non-white in colour.
**The visible-minority groups are based on categories used to define the visible-minority population under the Regulations to the Employment Equity act.
†Not included elsewhere. Includes Pacific Islander groups or another write-in response likely to be a visible minority (e.g., West Indian, South American).
‡Includes respondents who reported more than one visible-minority group.

SOURCE: Data from Statistics Canada, *1996 Census of Canada*. Downloaded June 4, 1998, from http://www.statcan.ca:80/english/Pgdb/People/Population/demo40e.htm.

from most Canadians," while more than half were "really worried that they may become a minority if immigration is unchecked." Almost half admitted there were too many immigrants, even though most underestimated how many people were admitted (*Globe and Mail*, 1992).

Given the extent of ethnocentrism in Canadian society, it is not surprising that these concerns are expressed. However, the number of people who hold these negative attitudes but are not expressing them far exceed those who do, for "fear of being stamped racists" (Samuel, 1988; Wellman, 1978).

In a national survey undertaken by Decima Research in October 1993 for the Canadian Council of Christians and Jews, many myths were reflected in the responses of 1200 respondents. Nearly three-quarters of respondents rejected the concept of Canada as a multicultural mosaic, and 72 percent believed that different racial and ethnic groups should try to adapt to Canadian society rather than preserve their original cultures. The survey found that 41 percent of respondents thought that Canada's immigration policy "allows too many people of different cultures and races to come to Canada," and 53 percent agreed with the statement that "some racial and ethnic groups don't make enough of an effort to fit into Canada." Half agreed with the statement: "I am sick and tired of some groups complaining about racism being directed at them," and 41 percent agreed they are "tired of ethnic minorities being given special treatment."

Ekos Research Associates conducted a number of surveys on immigration and used their results to advise the federal government on immigration policy. Their results in 1992 showed that 43 percent of Canadians believed that too many immigrants took advantage of social programs. By 1994, their polls revealed a steady increase (from 30 percent in 1988 to 53 percent in 1994) in Canadians who believed that there were "too many immigrants." More than one-quarter of the sample also thought that too many "visible minorities" were being accepted. A 1996 poll indicated that 44 percent of respondents found immigration levels too high, and the same number said the levels were about right (*Globe and Mail*, 1996). The population appears to be evenly split on this issue, which has resulted in government policy to maintain the status quo.

A more sophisticated series of surveys have been undertaken by Berry and Kalin, who conducted two national surveys on attitudes toward multiculturalism. Although many more respondents were tolerant than intolerant, the latter group gave less positive ratings to visible-minority groups. This provides evidence of "differential evaluations of ethnic groups along racial lines, but predominately among those who are the most generally prejudiced" (Berry and Kalin, 1997: 9). Aboriginal people and those of Chinese origin were rated nearly as positively as those of European origin. Berry and Kalin's explanation is that while racism may be a factor in explaining why European groups are rated more positively than non-European groups, "it is clear that Canadians are not generally racist in the sense that they rate all non-European origin Canadians in the same way" (1997: 10). Their general conclusions are in keeping with the less sophisticated polls reported above: that 5–20 percent of Canadians "respond negatively to attitude statements about inclusion and acceptance of racial others" (Berry and Kalin, 1997: 11).

The findings of many of the polls and surveys undertaken on this subject demonstrate some of the paradoxes of racism in Canadian society.

HATE GROUPS

An ideology of white supremacy has long been considered within the bounds of respectable, defensible opinion in Canada. In the colonial era, Aboriginal peoples were portrayed by church and state as "heathens" and "savages" and somehow less than human. These images provided justification for the extermination, segregation, and subjugation of Aboriginal peoples. The dehumanizing impact of such blatant propaganda is clearly evident today in the conditions of many Aboriginal communities (Frideres, 1983).

The 1920s and the 1930s saw the development of racist organizations such as the Ku Klux Klan (KKK), which openly promoted hatred against Catholics, Jews, Blacks, and other minorities. The original Klan was founded in Tennessee in 1866. It established bases in Alberta, Manitoba, Saskatchewan, British Columbia, and Ontario, feeding on Canadian anti-Semitism and the fear of Blacks and southern Europeans. While the KKK in Canada today appears to have only a handful of members, a network of other groups peddle hate propaganda, including the Heritage Front, the Liberty Lobby, the Church of the Creator, the Church of Jesus Christ–Aryan Nation, the Aryan Resistance Movement, and the Western Guard. All these groups share an ideology that supports the view that the Aryan, or white, race is superior to all others morally, intellectually, and culturally and that it is whites' manifest destiny to dominate society.

Barrett (1987) has made a significant contribution to understanding the recent activities of the extreme right in Canada. He found 130 organizations but under 600 members, many of whom belonged to more than one organization. Hate groups are usually coteries centred on a leader with a mailing list. Aside from holding meetings, they promote their ideology through distributing their literature widely. They hold rallies and parades, distribute buttons, paint slogans, establish dial-a-message telephone lines, demonstrate, and hold counter-demonstrations at the rallies of others. They may engage in paramilitary training, hold church services, or engage in political canvassing.

Another strategy used by these groups is to defend their activities by presenting themselves as defenders of free expression. Since they consider themselves to be promoting the principles of civil libertarianism, any attempts to curb their activities are portrayed as censorship and therefore anti-democratic.

Barrett (1987) suggests that the main elements of white supremacist ideology are anti-communism, anti-liberalism, racism, and anti-Semitism. White supremacists perceive themselves as the "saviours of the white race and Western Christian civilization" (Barrett, 1987: 90). They believe that the survival of white society in Canada is in jeopardy because of the practice of allowing "non-Aryans" into the country. The Ku Klux Klan suggests that one alternative to the problem of too many racial minorities in Canada is for the government to give "$35 000 to each coloured family as inducement to return to Pakistan, Africa, and elsewhere in the Third World" (Barrett, 1987). It suggests that Jews, too, should be included in this form of "ethnic cleansing," and that the expansion of the white race should be encouraged by providing financial incentives for white parents to have more children.

Barrett concludes that the ideology of the radical right does, to some extent, reflect "what the majority of people think and feel privately, albeit often unconsciously." While hate groups and hate propaganda may be regarded as marginal phenomena, the impact of such extremists is, according to Barrett, disproportionate to their numbers. They gain notoriety and apparent influence by combining strong stances on sensitive policies (such as immigration), which are controversial and have a substantial popular base, with continuous racist appeals couched in emotional, inflammatory rhetoric and threats of violence.

Since the publication of Barrett's pioneering work, the numbers of right-wing groups have proliferated in Canada. KKK branches are active in all of Canada's major cities. Offshoot groups such as the Heritage Front, the Church of the Creator, the Knights for White Rights, and the Aryan Nation are flourishing. Their presence is felt in the many telephone "hot lines" established throughout the country that spew forth hate messages, many of which are directed at Aboriginal peoples and racial minorities. Multiculturalism and immigration policies are also frequently criticized. The messages hammer home the theme "Keep Canada White."

In the past decade, the League for Human Rights of B'nai B'rith (1992) has monitored the number and types of anti-Semitic incidents that have occurred in all regions of Canada. The data file includes a large variety of incidents, ranging from non-violent ones such as anti-Semitic graffiti to more violent incidents that involve damage to persons or property and the desecration of synagogues. A recent analysis of this file showed a "significant increase ... in the numbers of incidents of all kinds." The report noted that this may reflect a "growing tendency of intolerance." But, since longitudinal studies of intolerance are non-existent in Canada, it is not possible to determine whether intolerance or racist behaviour has increased (Economic Council of Canada, 1991).

These racist incidents target not only the Jewish community. Hate-group activity and hate propaganda are directed at members of the Black, Chinese, and South Asian communities. Reports from various multicultural and anti-racist organizations and networks, as well as the cases before the human-rights commissions and courts, support the findings of the League for Human Rights of B'nai B'rith (British Columbia Organization to Fight Racism, 1992; Mock, 1992).

In the early 1990s, the Canadian Human Rights Commission began launching actions to prohibit telephone hate lines. In Vancouver, its action resulted in a tribunal ordering a telephone hate line off the air. Similarly, in Toronto, the Heritage Front was issued with an injunction to stop producing hate messages. In Winnipeg, a human-rights tribunal ordered the Manitoba Knights of the KKK to cease airing its messages. The tribunal found "overwhelming uncontradicted evidence that the messages were likely to expose the persons involved to hatred and contempt by reason of their race, religion, national or ethnic origin, colour or sexual orientation."

This decision included not only the Manitoba chapter of the KKK, but also "any other individuals who are members of or act in the name of the Knights of the Ku Klux Klan." In recent years, the Internet has been used as a primary vehicle for the dissemination of hate propaganda (Anti-Defamation League, 1997). One prominent Web site was controlled by Canadian Ernst Zundel, using a base in California. The Canadian Human Rights Commission had, at the time of this writing, launched a tribunal hearing challenging the legitimacy of this method of distributing hate materials.

By 1992, racist violence was seen to be increasing in many Canadian urban centres. For example, over a period of a few weeks in 1993, three Tamil refugees were beaten in Toronto. One died as the result of the injuries inflicted by his white assailants, and one was paralyzed. These incidents must be considered in the context of a long history of racist attitudes toward immigrants and refugees (or those perceived to be "foreigners" by virtue of the colour of their skin). In 1987, Canadians reacted vehemently to the arrival of a few boatloads of Tamil and Sikh refugees who entered Canada without following the normal procedures, while at the same time expressing little concern about the equally unorthodox arrival of significant numbers of Polish refugees.

RECENT RESEARCH

The research on hate crimes and hate or bias incidents has increased in the last few years. Data from the United States, as well as the more limited data available in Canada, indicate that the majority of perpetrators of hate crimes or hate or bias incidents constitute a relatively homogeneous group. They are young, male, and tend to be involved in gangs (Gilmour, 1994). There is also some evidence that skinheads have been involved in anti-Semitic hate crimes. Further evidence was found in a study that documented that most right-wing violence was committed by skinheads, "and members of other neo-fascist groups such as the Western Guard

and anti-communist nationalists." The majority of attacks were motivated by racism, anti-communism, and anti-Semitism (Ross, 1992).

Research also indicates that actual acts of violence or hate crimes committed against racial and other minorities have increased. A study commissioned to determine the nature and extent of hate activity in Metro Toronto (Mock, 1996) offered the following definitions of hate activity:

- hate/bias crime: "criminal offense against a person or property that is based solely on the victim's race, religion, nationality, ethnic origin or sexual orientation"; and
- hate/bias incidents: "incidents of harassment and other biased activity that is not criminal, including name calling, taunting, slurs, graffiti, derogatory or offensive material, vandalism, and threatening or offensive behaviour based on the victim's race, creed, ethnicity or sexual orientation." (Mock, 1996: 14)

The study examined a wide variety of statistical indicators. These included the data from the only three agencies that keep such records, including the Metro Toronto Police Hate Crimes Unit. Qualitative measures such as interviews, focus-group discussions, and reviews of other available literature were also used. The findings reveal that

as the population of Metropolitan Toronto continues to become more diverse, and as difficult economic times continue to fuel the backlash against immigrants and minority groups, the reported incidents of hate motivated activity have steadily increased. While these findings could be the result of increased awareness of reporting mechanisms ... it is unlikely, since the anecdotal evidence of the perceptions of community workers and caseworkers corroborates the statistical findings. (Mock, 1996: 57)

Moreover, the groups most singled out were Jews, Blacks, and homosexuals.

Reported anti-Semitic incidents are at an all time high, in 14 years of documentation by the

League for Human Rights of B'nai B'rith Canada; and according to statistics gathered by the Metro Police, racially motivated incidents against Blacks and other people of colour, and hate motivated attacks on Gays and Lesbians have increased steadily over the last few years. (Mock, 1996: 49)

In a comprehensive statistical analysis of hate crimes in Canada, Roberts (1995) estimated that the total number of hate crimes committed in 1994 in nine major urban centres in Canada was approximately 60 000, including crimes motivated by race hatred as well as ethnicity and religion.

In sum, although the research evidence does not generally support an increase in negative attitudes, there has apparently been an increase in actual behaviour as measured by the escalation of hate-related criminal activity.

It also appears that media reports may generate more hate crimes and incidents. This is known as "the copy-cat effect." For example, an increase in anti-Semitic vandalism was reported after the airing of a program on racism, *Hearts of Hate*, on CTV. Members of the Jewish community and Jewish organizations also report an increase in hate activity whenever a "hate monger such as Zundel, Droege, or Burdi was featured prominently in the media without any counterbalance." Other minority groups report similar events (Mock, 1996).

Thus, racist behaviour stretches along a wide continuum. At one end are the overt and covert daily acts of discrimination involving a significant proportion of the mainstream community. At the other end of the continuum, one finds far more explicit and extreme racist activity in the form of hate propaganda and racial violence perpetrated by a small minority of the population.

DISCRIMINATION IN THE WORKPLACE

Concern over employment discrimination against people of colour, women, persons with disabilities, and Aboriginal peoples led the federal government to establish a royal commission on equality in employment (Abella, 1984). Its task was to inquire into the employment practices of eleven designated Crown and government-owned corporations and to explore the most effective means of promoting equality in employment for four groups: women, Native peoples, disabled persons, and racial minorities. Its findings echoed the conclusions of the report of the Task Force on the Participation of Visible Minorities in Canada (*Equality Now*, 1984) that racial bias and discrimination were a pervasive reality in the employment system. The commissioner, Judge Rosalie Abella, observed that "strong measures were needed to remedy the impact of discriminatory attitudes and behaviour." The remedy she recommended was employment equity legislation (Abella, 1984).

Federal employment equity legislation for the four target groups identified by the Abella Commission was first introduced in 1986 and strengthened in 1995. In that year, the annual report of the president of the Treasury Board revealed that small progress had been made with respect to the hiring of members of employment equity targeted groups. For example, the percentage of women in the public service increased from 42.9 percent in 1988 to 47.4 percent in 1995. The percentage of Aboriginal representation increased from 1.7 to 2.2 percent, while visible-minority representation increased from 2.9 to 4.1 percent. In all of these categories, the available labour pool is much higher.

Although the federal government has attempted to increase the representation of minorities in the public service, downsizing as well as residual racist attitudes have not led to significant gains. In addition, minority-group employees complained in a survey that employment practices were unfair and racially biased. A number of complaints to the Canadian Human Rights Commission, including a class action representing more than 100 employees of Health Canada, were made in the 1990s. Most involved professional employees who believed that they had not had equal access to promotional opportunities in the public service, particularly with respect to managerial positions. A tribunal of the commission found in favour of the complainants in the class action against Health Canada. In sum, there has been little real progress for minorities in the federal public service, largely due to the inability and unwillingness of this institution to respond to social and demographic imperatives.

At the level of the federally regulated private sector, more hiring has taken place. For example, in the banking sector, which has the best record of minority hiring, visible-minority representation has increased from 12.1 percent in 1989 to 13.7 percent in 1994. Communications rose from 5.3 to 7.2 percent, transportation from 3.8 to 4.3 percent, and all other areas from 3.7 to 6.2 percent (Samuel and Karam, 1996). Despite improvements in the overall position of racial minorities in employment regulated by the federal legislation, these groups are still concentrated in the lower sectors of the industries. For example, in banking, visible minorities are overrepresented in lower-level positions, such as tellers, and underrepresented in the managerial ranks.

In the late 1990s, responding to an aging and short-staffed bureaucracy, the Public Service Commission announced that it was hiring more than 2000 new employees. Since a report showed that the availability rate of visible minorities in the labour force was 12 percent but only 4.1 percent were represented in the public service, it might be thought that such minorities were likely to be especially recruited (Samuel, 1998).

Members of racial-minority groups have higher levels of education than do other Canadians. For example, in the late 1990s, 23 percent had university degrees, compared with 14 percent of other Canadians. Moreover, racial minorities had consistently higher levels of education than did other workers in the lower-paying occupations. In the category of "semi-professionals and technicians," for instance, 32.3 percent of racial-minority employees had university degrees, compared with 18.3 percent of others.

Despite higher levels of education, members of racial-minority groups were paid lower salaries than were other Canadians. Reitz, Calzavara, and Dasko (1981) demonstrated that considerable income disparities existed among various ethno-racial groups. People of colour, such as West Indians, and more recently arrived groups such as Portuguese, ranked lowest in incomes.

A decade later, the average salary for all levels of education for a member of a racial minority in both the upper and middle levels and other management occupations was approximately 18 percent lower than that of the total population (Employment and Immigration Canada, 1992: 57). Even in the "other manual workers" category, including all levels of education, members of racial minorities earned nearly 10 percent less than all other manual workers. Another study, issued in 1995 and provocatively entitled The Colour of Money, found that Aboriginal and visible-minority men earned significantly less income than did native-born and immigrant white men in Canada. The earnings differentials were not explained by socioeconomic variables such as education, place of schooling, occupation, and others, which were controlled for in this study. Even visible-minority men born in Canada suffered about a 10 percent earnings penalty. These differences were, however, not found among visible-minority women as compared with Canadian-born or immigrant white women. The researchers also noted that while there were clear-cut earning differentials between whites and visible minorities, there was also a considerable degree of heterogeneity within each of these categories (Pendakur and Pendakur, 1995).

One of the key barriers preventing immigrants of colour from access and equity in the labour market is credentialism. Studies in Ontario (Ontario Ministry of Citizenship, 1989) and British Columbia (Fernando and Prasad, 1986) showed that there is little recognition in Canada of the professional qualifications, credentials, and experience of immigrants.

Thousands of immigrants find their university degrees and trade diplomas of little value in Canada. These barriers affect doctors, teachers, social workers, nurses, engineers, and others.

Public-sector agencies also show a lack of representation of racial minorities. An audit done for the Ontario public service in 1986 showed that 77 percent of civil servants were white and only 11.9 percent were racial minorities, most of whom were clustered in lower-level positions. In 1989, racial minorities formed only 4 percent of the Metropolitan Toronto Police Force. Almost all of them were cadets, constables, or in training; only three had the rank of inspector (Small, 1992). In 1998, the representation of racial minorities had shown insignificant gains: three staff inspectors, three senior police officers, and only 7.4 percent of the total uniformed employees were racial minorities (Metro Toronto Police Services, 1998). In the late 1980s at the Toronto Board of Education, only 5 percent of the teaching staff were from racial minorities, but this figure increased to 8.5 percent with the inclusion of non-teaching staff. Only 6 percent were classified as managers. The Ontario Human Rights Commission has only one racial-minority director. The Metropolitan Toronto Housing Authority, which deals with large numbers of minority clients, has a minority contingent of only 16.7 percent, of whom 11 percent are at a middle- or senior-management level.

A survey of 672 corporate recruiters ("Canada's Employment Discriminators," 1989), hiring managers, and agency recruiters across Canada conducted by the Canadian Recruiters Guild concluded that there were gross deficiencies in Canada's recruitment and selection practices. It revealed that the moral, legal, and economic impact of recruitment was either not understood or simply ignored by recruiters.

A study undertaken by the Maritime School of Social Work at Dalhousie University in Halifax (Bambrough, Bowden, and Wien, 1992) tracked its racial-minority and Aboriginal graduates and found that minorities experienced con-

siderable difficulty in obtaining employment after graduation. Acadian and Black graduates took several more weeks than non-minority students to find their first job, and Blacks had to apply to many more employers and undertake many more interviews to get a job offer.

The study also found that upon graduation, Blacks found less desirable jobs than others, including limited or term positions and more part-time jobs. Of particular interest was the fact that Blacks were more often in jobs in which the chances for advancement were relatively low, as were salaries. The report concluded that "Black graduates have been less successful than the majority group in accessing the more prestigious social work jobs, such as those to be found in family counselling, hospital social work and in administrative/supervisory positions" (Bambrough et al., 1992).

Harish Jain, who has done extensive research (Jain, 1988; Jain and Hackett, 1989) on employment discrimination in Canada, suggested that racial minorities, as well as women, Aboriginal peoples, and people with disabilities, encounter both entry-level and postemployment discrimination in the workplace. Jain (1985) argued that human-rights statutes across Canada were ineffective in ensuring equality of opportunity in the workplace. Jain identified numerous job barriers in the employment system, including narrow recruitment channels and procedures (such as word-of-mouth recruitment, inflated educational qualifications, biased testing, prejudice and stereotyping in the job interview process, poor performance evaluation, lack of promotions, transfers, and/or salary increases). Unions are another potential source of both racism and sexism (Leah, 1989).

Non-English-speaking and racial-minority immigrant women are part of a segregated and marginalized work force and are employed mainly in three areas: private domestic service, service industries, and light manufacturing. Many immigrant racial-minority women working in the public sector are employed as cleaners, cafeteria workers, nurses' aides, and lower-level clerical workers (Vorst et al., 1989). Brand (1987) observed that most Black women work at low-status jobs in homes and institutions and do "Black women's work."

Research on the Caribbean communities in Toronto (Henry, 1994) has yielded some interesting information on the continuing impact of racial discrimination on employment. More than 100 in-depth interviews and many hundreds of hours of participant observation among persons of Caribbean origin in Toronto indicated that the community shows a fairly high level of institutional completeness, considering the recentness of Caribbean migration to Canada. Although there are no Caribbean-owned financial institutions within the community, most service and retail sectors have developed to the extent that goods and services of many kinds can be obtained from Caribbean-owned and -managed businesses.

One of the main reasons for private entrepreneurship among the community was the racial discrimination experienced by job seekers and workers employed in mainstream-owned and -managed firms. Difficulty in obtaining employment was often cited as a major reason for dissatisfaction with living in Canada. In addition, racial harassment on the job and the inability to advance in the company were cited as contributory factors in private entrepreneurship. Restaurateurs, clothiers, and variety-shop owners said they were "fed up" with racial harassment.

A research project focusing on diversity, mobility, and change among Black communities in Canada used primarily census data and made similar findings. It found that although Black people in Canada had levels of education similar to those of the total population, they had substantially lower incomes, were less likely to be self-employed, and were less likely to occupy senior-management positions. Many more Blacks than whites lived in poverty, and Black women had greater poverty rates than men (Torczyner, 1997).

A report on socioeconomic indicators of equality conducted among ethno-racial communities in Toronto in the early 1990s found that while the overall rate of unemployment in Metro Toronto was 9.6 percent, the unemployment rate of non-Europeans far exceeded this (Ornstein, 1997). For example, Africans had a 25.8 percent unemployment rate, followed by Mexicans and Central Americans at 24 percent and Tamils at 23.9 percent. Other groups with a higher than average unemployment rate included Arabs and West Asians, Sri Lankans, Vietnamese, and Aboriginal people. Jamaicans, especially youth between the ages of 15 and 24, had high rates of unemployment as compared with other youth in the same age category. The study also found a weak link between employment and education and concluded that groups with the most unemployment were not those with the least education; many non-European groups found it difficult to convert their educational qualifications into jobs.

Income is closely related to employment, and in the early 1990s Tamils, Sri Lankans, and Africans in Toronto had the lowest earnings (about $19 000), followed closely by East and Southeast Asians, Jamaicans, and South Americans. This figure is in sharp contrast to the average annual employment income of $31 300 and a mean annual income of $50 000. With respect to general indicators of poverty, 19 percent of all families in Toronto were living at or below the poverty line. The highest levels of poverty (33–37 percent) existed among Arabs, West Asians, Latin Americans, Blacks, and Africans. Three in five Toronto children from African nations lived in poverty, as did more than half the children of Jamaican, Iranian, other Arab and West Asian, and Central American parents. More than two-fifths of Aboriginal children, as well as those of Tamil and Vietnamese origin, lived in poverty.

Ornstein (1997) concluded that many people in Toronto were affected by poverty and inequality. The report acknowledged that the groups most affected were those who found access to employment, housing, education, and other resources constrained due to a variety of economic and social factors.

EMPLOYMENT AGENCIES

Allegations of racial discrimination in the operations of employment agencies in accepting and referring certain clients have been a concern for almost two decades. In 1975, the Canadian Civil Liberties Association (CCLA) conducted a survey of randomly selected employment agencies. The CCLA told agency representatives that it represented an out-of-town firm planning to locate in their community and asked whether, among the services provided, the agencies would agree to refer only white people for the jobs that had to be filled. Of the fifteen employment agencies in Metro Toronto that received this request, eleven said they would screen out persons of colour.

The study was repeated in 1976, surveying employment agencies in Hamilton, Ottawa, and London. Again, eleven of the fifteen agencies indicated their willingness to fulfill discriminatory requests. In 1980, the CCLA surveyed ten agencies in Toronto, seven of whom expressed a willingness to abide by a "whites only" restriction. In 1991, the CCLA repeated the survey for the fourth time, and of the fifteen agencies surveyed in four cities in Ontario, only three declared their unwillingness to accept discriminatory job orders.

Following are some examples of the agencies' responses.

It is discrimination, but it can be done discreetly without anyone knowing. No problem with that.

That's no problem, it's between you and me. I don't tell anyone; you don't tell anyone.

You are paying to see the people you want to see.

Absolutely — definitely ... that request is pretty standard here.

That's not a problem. Appearance means a lot, whether it's colour or overweight people. (Rees, 1991)

Although the role of employment agencies in colluding with discriminatory employers had long been known to those who monitor race relations in Canada, the publicity surrounding a complaint laid with the Ontario Human Rights Commission against two employment agencies in Toronto brought this issue into the public arena. Although the commission found discriminatory information about job applicants in some files, it maintained that the agencies did not have a deliberate policy of discriminating against job applicants. Accordingly, a settlement was reached in which the agencies agreed to develop written policies against accepting discriminatory job requests from employers and to provide training for their employees in race relations and employment equity.

Both agencies also said they would establish three-year employment equity plans, with goals and timetables that provided for the elimination of barriers in recruiting, referral, and placement services. The chief commissioner of the human rights commission was quoted as saying that this settlement "will provide a blueprint for all employment agencies in the province." A number of critics, however, noted that the settlement was fairly limited and did not adequately encompass all the aspects of this complex issue.

NOTES

1. The term "visible minority" is used in the Census of Canada as well as in publications that use census or other government-generated data. It is used in this chapter when discussing such research.

2. Polling and survey data from other countries are similar to those of Canada. For example, a survey conducted in the European Union countries revealed that racism is rampant. The

data showed that one-third of respondents are racist; some admitted that they were "very" racist, and others reported being "quite racist" (*North Africa Journal*, 1998). Surveys on racism and attitudes toward immigrants in Australia revealed similar figures to those of Canada (see Adelman et al., 1994).

REFERENCES

Abella, R. (1984). *Report of the Commission on Equality in Employment.* Ottawa: Supply and Services Canada.

Adelman, H., A. Borowski, M. Burnstein, and L. Foster (eds.). (1994). *Immigration and Refugee Policy: Australia and Canada Compared.* Melbourne: Melbourne University Press.

Anti-Defamation League. (1997). *High Tech Hate: Extremist Use of the Internet.* New York: ADL.

Bambrough, J., W. Bowden, and F. Wein. (1992). *Preliminary Results from the Survey of Graduates from the Maritime School of Social Work.* Halifax: Maritime School of Social Work, Dalhousie University.

Barrett, S. (1987). *Is God a Racist? The Right Wing in Canada.* Toronto: University of Toronto Press.

Berry, J.W., and R. Kalin. (1997). "Racism in Canada: Evidence from National Surveys." In L. Driedger and S. Halli (eds.), *Visible Minorities: Race and Racism in Canada.* Ottawa: Carleton University Press.

Brand, D. (1987). "Black Women and Work: The Impact of Racially Constructed Gender Roles on the Sexual Division of Labour." *Fireweed* 25: 35.

British Columbia Organization to Fight Racism. (1992). *Canada 125.* Surrey, BC: BCOFR.

"Canada's Employment Discriminators." (1989). *Currents: Readings in Race Relations* 5(2): 18–21. Toronto: Urban Alliance on Race Relations.

Canadian Civil Liberties Association. (1991). *Survey of Employment Agencies.* Toronto: CCLA.

Canadian Council of Christian and Jews. (1993). *Survey of Canadian Attitudes towards Ethnic and Race Relations in Canada.* Toronto: Decima Research.

Economic Council of Canada. (1991). *Report.* Ottawa.

Employment and Immigration Canada. (1992). *Annual Report, Employment Equity.* Ottawa: Minister of Supply and Services.

Environics. (1988). *Focus Canada Survey.*

Equality Now: Report of the Parliamentary Task Force on the Participation of Visible Minorities in Canada. (1984). Ottawa: Queen's Printer.

Fernando, T., and K. Prasad. (1986). *Multiculturalism and Employment Equity: Problems Facing Foreign-Trained Professionals and Trades-people in British Columbia.* Vancouver: Affiliation of Multicultural Societies and Service Agencies of British Columbia.

Frideres, J. (1983). *Native Peoples in Conflict.* Scarborough, ON: Prentice-Hall.

Gilmour, G.A. (1994). *Hate-Motivated Violence: A Working Document.* Ottawa: Department of Justice (May).

Globe and Mail. (1992). (October 14).

Globe and Mail. (1996). "Immigrant Levels Reflect Backlash." (October 30): A1.

Gould, T. (1990). "Who Do You Hate?" *Toronto Life* (October).

Henry, F. (1978). *Dynamics of Racism.* Ottawa: Secretary of State.

———. (1994). *The Caribbean Diaspora in Toronto: Learning to Live with Racism.* Toronto: University of Toronto Press.

Jain, H. (1985). *Anti-Discrimination Staffing Policies: Implications of Human Rights*

Legislation for Employers and Trade Unions. Ottawa: Secretary of State.

———. (1988). "Affirmative Action/Employment Equity Programmes and Visible Minorities in Canada." *Currents: Readings in Race Relations* 5(1): 3–7.

Jain, H., and R. Hackett. (1989). "Measuring Effectiveness of Employment Equity Programmes in Canada: Public Policy and a Survey." *Canadian Public Policy* 15(2): 189–204.

League for Human Rights of B'nai B'rith. (1992). *Annual Audit of Anti-Semitic Incidents.* Toronto: B'nai B'rith.

Leah, R. (1989). "Linking the Struggles: Racism, Sexism and the Union Movement." In Vorst et al., (eds.), *Race, Class, Gender: Bonds and Barriers.* Toronto: Between the Lines.

Metro Toronto Police Services. (1998). *Reporting Data.* Toronto.

Mock, K. (1992). *Combatting Hate: Canadian Realities and Remedies.* Toronto: League for Human Rights, B'nai B'rith Canada.

———. (1996). *The Extent of Hate Activity and Racism in Metropolitan Toronto.* Toronto: Access and Equity Centre of the Municipality of Metropolitan Toronto.

North Africa Journal. (1998). 18 (February 21).

Ontario Ministry of Citizenship. (1989). *Access: Task Force on Access to Professions and Trades in Ontario.* Toronto.

Ornstein, M. (1997). *Report on Ethno-Racial Inequality in Metropolitan Toronto: Analysis of the 1991 Census.* Access and Equity Centre of the (former) Municipality of Metropolitan Toronto.

Pendakur, K., and R. Pendakur. (1995). *The Colour of Money: Earnings Differentials among Ethnic Groups in Canada.* Strategic Research and Analysis. Ottawa: Department of Canadian Heritage.

Rees, T. (1991). "Racial Discrimination and Employment Agencies." *Currents: Readings in Race Relations* (Toronto) 7(2): 16–19.

Reitz, J., L. Calzavara, and D. Dasko. (1981). *Ethnic Inequality and Segregation in Jobs.* Toronto: Centre for Urban and Community Studies, University of Toronto.

Roberts, J. (1995). "Disproportionate Harm: Hate Crime in Canada: An Analysis of Recent Statistics." Ottawa: Department of Justice, Research, Statistics and Evaluation Directorate.

Ross, J.L. (1992). "Research Note: Contemporary Radical Right Wing Violence in Canada: A Quantitative Analysis." *Terrorism and Political Violence* 72(3) (Autumn).

Samuel, T.J. (1988). *Immigration and Visible Minorities in the Year 2001: A Projection.* Ottawa: Centre for Immigration and Ethnocultural Studies.

———. (1998). "Debunking Myths of Immigrants." *The Toronto Star,* June 17.

Samuel, T.J., and A. Karam. (1996). "Employment Equity and Visible Minorities in the Federal Workforce." Paper presented to Symposium on Immigration and Integration. Winnipeg (October 25–27).

Small, P. (1992). "Promote Minorities, Report Tells Police." *The Toronto Star* (September 11): A6.

Torczyner, J.L. (1997). *Diversity, Mobility and Change: The Dynamics of Black Communities in Canada.* Montreal: McGill School of Social Work.

Toronto Star. (1992). "Minority Community Survey."

Vorst, J., et al. (eds.). (1989). *Race, Class, Gender: Bonds and Barriers.* Toronto: Between the Lines.

Wellman, D. (1978). *Portraits of White Racism.* Cambridge: Cambridge University Press.

Chapter 15

Public Opinion on Aboriginal Rights

J. RICK PONTING

JERILYNN KIELY

The first national survey on Aboriginal issues was conducted by Ponting and Gibbins in 1976. With few exceptions, such as significant deterioration of support for First Nations in Quebec and British Columbia, the findings from that comprehensive survey still hold true today, as evidenced by the findings from Ponting's detailed, ten-year follow-up national study and an even more detailed 1994 national survey kindly provided to the authors by the Angus Reid Group. We shall discuss the main themes that emerge from those studies. In order to retain focus on the "big picture" and to avoid getting bogged down in detail, we usually report percentages only parenthetically, if at all. Similarly, readers are referred elsewhere (Ponting and Gibbins, 1980: 71–72; Ponting, 1987a: A1–A7) for the methodological details of the surveys. Suffice it to say here that in all three surveys the samples were large (over 1800) and the 1976 and 1986 surveys were conducted using face-to-face interviews in respondents' homes in the official language of the respondent's choice, while the 1994 survey differed by using telephone interviews. All three surveys were conducted by reputable polling firms.[1]

LITTLE KNOWLEDGE, LOW PRIORITY

Canadians know very little about Aboriginal affairs. In part, that is because we tend to pay little attention to most Aboriginal matters in the mass media and attach a low priority to Aboriginal issues, except when they touch close to home by involving personal inconvenience or threat to our livelihood. The evidence of this widespread ignorance is overwhelming, as measured by such indicators as not knowing the meaning of the term "Aboriginal people," not being aware of the existence of the Indian Act, not being aware of the existence of Aboriginal rights in the Constitution, and over-estimating by a factor of at least two the proportion of Native people in the Canadian population. Around 15 percent of Canadians are almost totally oblivious to Aboriginal matters in this country.

OPPOSITION TO SPECIAL STATUS

With the exception of a select few situations, such as First Nations' special relationship with

Source: Excerpted from "Disempowerment: 'Justice,' Racism, and Public Opinion," in *First Nations in Canada: Perspectives on Opportunity, Empowerment, and Self-Determination*, J. Rick Ponting, ed. (Toronto: McGraw-Hill Ryerson, 1997), pp. 174–92. Reprinted by permission of McGraw-Hill Ryerson Ltd.

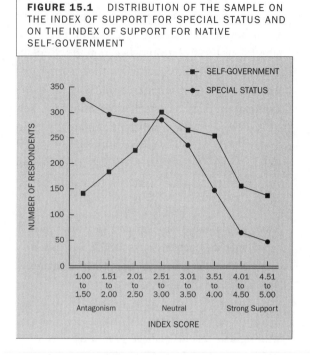

FIGURE 15.1 DISTRIBUTION OF THE SAMPLE ON THE INDEX OF SUPPORT FOR SPECIAL STATUS AND ON THE INDEX OF SUPPORT FOR NATIVE SELF-GOVERNMENT

the land, Canadians manifest a pronounced tendency to reject what they view as "special status" for Native people. This is shown in the curve in Figure 15.1, which plots the distribution of the sample on two indexes, one of which is the Index of Support for Special Status for Natives, in the 1986 survey. A respondent's score on this index is his or her average score on four items dealing with special institutional arrangements for Native people. As with most of the indexes reported in this chapter, this one comprises statements with which respondents are asked to indicate their degree of agreement or disagreement, on a scale ranging from "strongly agree" to "strongly disagree."[2]

In Figure 15.1 we shall observe that most respondents fall at the unsupportive end of the scale measuring support for special status for Native people. In 1986 even stronger opposition to special status was found in most questions that explicitly use the word "special." For instance, in 1986, when respondents were given two statements — one of which described special institutional arrangements for Native people and one of which did not — and were

asked to choose the one that came closer to their views, it was repeatedly found that almost two-thirds of respondents opted for the statement that denied special status to Native people. One concrete example of this involved the two statements: "For crimes committed by Indians on Indian reserves, there should be special courts with Indian judges" (only 27 percent chose this); and "Crimes committed by Indians on Indian reserves should be handled in the same way as crimes committed elsewhere" (65 percent chose this). By 1994, there was some softening of this antagonism to special status[3] and the issue had become less clear-cut. Some ambivalence had entered Canadians' minds. On some questions, Canadians were still more antagonistic than supportive.[4] On other questions, though, there was more support than antagonism.[5] Our interpretation of this discrepancy is that it is an indication of Canadians' opinions on Aboriginal issues being rather inchoate. Although opinions on Aboriginal issues are not exactly formless, because Aboriginal issues are so peripheral to most Canadians we should expect a less consistently structured set of opinions on these issues than on some other issues such as the environment or national unity.

Such opposition to "special status" as does exist is probably rooted both in the long-standing opposition of many Canadians outside Quebec to special status in Confederation for Quebec, and in a norm of equality that is widely held among Canadians.

Obviously, Canadians' orientation to "special status" for First Nations could have important implications for the degree of self-determination that is attainable under the federal government's "self-government" legislation. The division of public opinion on this is captured nicely by a 1994 question (L1) pertaining to "self-government for Canada's aboriginal peoples — that is, both status and non-status Indians, the Métis and the Inuit." The remainder of the question, and the equal division of respondents across the three response options, follows:

Which of the following three broad statements best describes how you feel about aboriginal self-government, or the right of aboriginals to govern themselves?

- Aboriginal peoples in Canada have an historic, existing, inherent right to self-government. (29%)
- The federal and provincial governments should allow aboriginal peoples to govern themselves. (27%)
- Aboriginal people have no more right to self-government than other ethnic groups in Canada. (28%)

We pursue these issues of rights and self-government in more detail below.

SUPPORT FOR SELF-GOVERNMENT AND ABORIGINAL RIGHTS

Paradoxically, antagonism toward special status coexists with a support for Native self-government and even for recognition of the inherent right to self-government as an existing Aboriginal or treaty right. For many Canadians, self-government is less a manifestation of special status than a basic democratic right of self-determination. This interpretation is suggested by the fact that in Figure 15.1 the curve representing the distribution of the sample on an Index of Support for Native Self-Government[6] exhibits a markedly different shape than the curve for the Index of Support for Special Status for Natives. The curve depicting support for Native self-government is akin to the famous bell-shaped curve, and the average score is slightly to the supportive side of the mid-point of the scale. The curve for support for special status is highly skewed.

Surprisingly, even when the notion of the inherent right to self-government was linked with the Charlottetown Accord, defeated in the 1992 nationwide referendum, a small majority of the 1994 sample favoured its recognition as an Aboriginal and treaty right.

The degree of autonomy of First Nations governments from provincial governments is of pivotal importance in defining the fundamental character of First Nations governments. Replacing non-Native bureaucrats with brown-faced bureaucrats who administer essentially the same provincial policies is not self-determination. Yet, that is precisely what a substantial majority (akin to the 1986 survey's two-thirds disapproving of special status) of the 1994 respondents preferred when given the option between two statements, as follows:

Aboriginals could develop and run their own programs in [such areas as health, education and child welfare] without the province having any authority. (19%)

versus

Aboriginals could manage the programs in these areas but they would still be subject to provincial laws and standards. (65%)

Canadians' views of the capability of Aboriginal governments are improving.[7] When Canadians were asked in 1994 "how much confidence you have ... in terms of the role they might play in working towards some solutions to aboriginal peoples' concerns," the chiefs of large bands garnered majority support, as did national Aboriginal organizations.[8] Also, there is plurality support for the eventual dismantling of the Department of Indian Affairs and Northern Development (DIAND) and strong majority support for the Manitoba approach of transferring DIAND responsibilities to Aboriginal control as "a model for moving towards aboriginal self-government across the country." However, indications are that on the matter of the representativeness of Aboriginal leaders, by 1994 the skeptics had closed the gap on the believers, such that the population had come to be evenly divided.[9]

GENERAL SYMPATHY

To some extent, support for Native self-government and Native rights is a reflection of a more general positive orientation toward, or attitudinal support for, Natives. This might be called "sympathy," if that word can be stripped of connotations of condescension. Overall, the Canadian population in both 1976 and 1986 tended to be more sympathetic than antagonistic toward Native people. This observation is based on respondents' scores on composite indexes of several questions in each survey.[10] In 1986 two separate indexes were used. Only 10–15 percent of Canadians were *consistently* antagonistic (strongly or mildly) toward Native people across both scales. Twice as many were *consistently* supportive. On both indexes, as on the 1976 index, the average score for the sample was well above the mid-point of the scale. Further evidence of a generalized sympathy comes from other questions not included in any of the indexes. For instance, in 1986 a majority (57 percent) disagreed with the statement "Indians are a bunch of complainers" (only 23 percent agreed), and a large majority (71 percent) disagreed with the statement "The more I hear and see about Indians in the news media, the less respect I have for them" (only 13 percent agreed).

However, there has been a deterioration in support for Native people over the almost two decades covered by the surveys. For instance, in 1976 an overwhelming majority (72 percent) agreed with the statement "Indians deserve to be a lot better off economically than they are now." By 1986, only a plurality agreed (48 percent versus 29 percent disagreeing). The question was not asked on the 1994 survey, but it was a smaller plurality that took the pro-Aboriginal stance in response to the following somewhat similar statement: "Most of the problems of aboriginal people are brought on by themselves" (40 percent disagreed; 31 percent agreed). Yet, on another question that might carry moral overtones to respondents who adhere to the Protestant work ethic, a solid majority of the 1994 sample agreed (57 percent versus 15 percent who disagreed) with the statement "Aboriginal people are hard-working and indus-

trious, and capable of earning their way if given a chance."

The deterioration in support for Native people can be seen in Table 15.1 on page 158. There we observe that in Canada as a whole, the victimization stereotype of Indians/Aboriginal people lost about half of its adherents (as a percentage of the total population) between 1976 and 1994, while the alcohol and drug-abuse stereotype almost doubled in prevalence during that period, to the point of reaching parity with the victimization view. Note that in 1976, British Columbia was right at the national average level of sympathy for Native people, but a decade later it was well below the national average. Whereas a majority of Quebeckers, perhaps expressing a shared sense of deprivation as an ethnic minority in Canada, viewed Indians as victims of racism or discrimination in 1976, by 1994 only one-fifth did. The view that alcohol or drugs was the main problem facing Indians was scarcely detectable in Quebec in 1976, but eighteen years later it was not only held by a large minority of Quebeckers, but was notably more prevalent in Quebec than the view of Aboriginal people as victims of racism and discrimination.

SENSITIVITY TO NATIVE PEOPLE'S SPECIAL RELATIONSHIP TO THE LAND

Respondents exhibited a generally supportive opinion for Native people on matters related to land and land-use conflict. Two examples, from among several available in the 1986 survey, are:

- a (slight) majority of Canadians agreed (versus one-third who disagreed) with the statement: "Where Natives' use of land conflicts with natural resource development, Native use should be given priority."

- a near majority disagreed (48 percent versus 37 percent agreeing) that giving Native people special hunting rights "just isn't fair."[11]

On a 1994 question a plurality agreed (44 percent versus 29 percent disagreeing) with the

TABLE 15.1   REGIONAL VARIATION IN PUBLIC OPINION ON ABORIGINAL ISSUES

ITEM OR STATEMENT	CANADA	ATL. CAN.	MTL.	REST OF QUE.	TOR.	REST OF ON	MB	SK	AB	VANC.	REST OF BC
Mean Score on Index of:											
Sympathy for Natives, 1976*	3.31	3.10	3.56		3.25		3.15	2.90	3.00	3.30	
Sympathy for Natives, 1986*	3.22	3.12	3.17	3.31	3.47	3.30	3.13	2.96	3.13	3.09	2.97
Sympathy for Indians, 1986*	3.29	3.09	3.42	3.45	3.48	3.38	3.39	2.91	3.08	3.04	3.04
Support for Special Status for Native People, 1986*	2.56	2.38	2.15	2.96	2.34	2.45	2.44	2.14	2.07	2.11	2.07
1994 Statement											
It just isn't right for Natives to have special rights that other Canadians don't have.											
% agreeing	41	47	57		24		53	55	47	41	
% disagreeing	34	36	32		30		37	34	36	46	
1994 Question											
Generally speaking, do you think Canada's aboriginal people are being reasonable or unreasonable in terms of their current land claims?											
Reasonable (%)	38	34	30		32		55	53	50	49	
Unreasonable (%)	41	45	66		21		41	43	38	46	
Main (1976)/Most Serious (1994) Problem Facing Indians (1976)/Canada's Aboriginal People (1994) Today?											
% citing racism or discrimination											
1976	39	27	51		36			31		44	
1994	21	20	20		18		23	28	22	24	
% citing alcohol or drugs											
1976	12	7	1		13			28		12	
1994	23	25	30		17		29	21	29	13	

*Denotes possible range is 1.0 to 5.0, where 5.0 is most sympathetic.

statement: "Aboriginals have a special relationship to the land and can be trusted as better caretakers of the environment."

OPPOSITION TO TACTICAL ASSERTIVENESS

Canadians tend not to be accepting of any escalation of First Nations' protest tactics beyond a rather tame level. Protest was a major focus of the 1976 survey (Ponting and Gibbins, 1981), and the 1994 survey also included several questions on the topic. The results are broadly similar over the two decades. In 1976, the use of the courts and of protest marches received majority approval, as did "requesting that a royal commission be formed to study Indians' problems."

The majority disapproved of the more assertive tactics of barricading roads or railroads crossing Indian reserves, and threatening violence. Even boycotting private businesses elicited strong disapproval ratings.

In 1994, among five tactics listed, the only one for which approvers outnumbered disapprovers was the blockading of natural resource extraction on land claimed by Aboriginal people.[12] A "peaceful blockade of a major highway to press for speedier action on land claims" met with resounding disapproval as did the strategy of unilaterally asserting sovereignty.[13] Even making a formal complaint to the United Nations was approved by only a little more than a third of the sample (37 percent versus 45 percent disapproving). Similarly, only one-third approved of delaying completion of a resource megaproject.

REGIONAL VARIATION

To this point, discussion of public opinion has been couched in terms of Canada as a whole. That, however, obscures important variations from one region of the country to another. Those regional variations take on considerable practical significance when one remembers that many of the reforms sought by First Nations require the approval of provincial governments.

In some provinces, notably Saskatchewan and now Quebec, support for Aboriginal people is clearly rather low, while in Ontario support is comparatively high. Table 15.1 provides examples from the three surveys. Note how Quebeckers stand out as thinking Aboriginal people are being unreasonable in their land claims and how a high proportion of people from that province, along with Manitobans and Albertans, view alcohol or drugs as the most serious problem or issue facing Aboriginal people in Canada. Conversely, alcohol and drugs rank as only the seventh most serious Aboriginal problem in British Columbians' view. All four western provinces also stand apart from the rest of Canada in thinking that Aboriginal people are being reasonable in their land claims.

Table 15.2 on page 160 depicts regional variation in answers to the open-ended question asking respondents to name the Aboriginal issue or problem that they think is most serious. In numerous ways, this table reveals that Canadians in different regions have a very different picture of Aboriginal matters. For instance, "Integration into society" is most commonly identified by Quebeckers as the most serious Aboriginal issue or problem, whereas, at the other extreme, it ranks ninth in importance in Saskatchewan. Ontarians and British Columbians rank education as the most serious Aboriginal issue or problem, whereas in Quebec it ranks seventh. Prairie residents stand apart as being more likely to see self-government as a more serious issue than do residents of other provinces. Regional subcultures are reflected in other ways, too. For instance, Alberta, with its frontier ideology's emphasis on self-reliance and "rugged individualism," has a notably higher proportion of respondents citing "lack of initiative or motivation" than do the Atlantic provinces and Quebec, where structural barriers to personal success are more widely recognized and acknowledged.

Regional variation is also pronounced on other measures not shown in Table 15.1 or 15.2. For instance, the proportion of the public that is oblivious to Native issues is much larger in Quebec than in the other provinces. In addition, familiarity with Native matters tends to be regionally specific. To the extent that Canadians are familiar with Native matters at all, that familiarity is usually confined to matters in their own region. The 1986 survey found that even on issues that are clearly of national applicability, such as Aboriginal rights in the Constitution or the 1985 amendments to the Indian Act to remove sex discrimination, regional variation emerges in respondents' degree of familiarity.

CAUSES OF HOSTILITY

The 1986 national survey offers some important insights into the causes of hostility toward government policies designed to help Aboriginal people. Using advanced statistical techniques, Langford and Ponting (1992) determined that ethnocentrism is a minor to negligible determinant of hostility. Instead, economic conservatism (the "free enterprise" belief that government should minimize its role in economic relations), prejudice, and perceptions of conflicting group interests[14] between Aboriginals and themselves are key determinants of respondents' policy preferences. Furthermore, there is an important *interaction effect* between prejudice and perceived group conflict. That is, to take a hypothetical example, if

TABLE 15.2 MOST SERIOUS ABORIGINAL ISSUE OR PROBLEM, BY PROVINCE, 1994

PROBLEM	CANADA		ATLANTIC CANADA		QUEBEC		ONTARIO		MANITOBA		SASKAT.		ALBERTA		BC	
	Rank	%	Rank	%	Rank	%	Rank	%	Rank	%	Rank	%	Rank	%	Rank	%
Alcohol/drugs	1	23.2	2	24.8	2	29.9	5	17.4	2	28.6	5	20.6	1	28.6	7	13.4
Integration in society	2	22.4	6	14.4	1	38.2	6	16.6	6	14.2	9	8.3	5	18.0	6	15.6
Racism/discrimination	3	20.8	3	20.4	3	19.6	3	18.4	3	23.3	2	27.7	2.5	21.8	1.5	24.0
Unemployment/jobs	4	20.2	1	31.2	5	13.7	2	20.4	1	29.4	1	30.5	4	21.3	4	19.8
Education	5	18.9	5	15.1	7	12.6	1	24.6	5	16.3	3	24.1	6	17.7	1.5	24.1
Land claims	6	16.3	10	10.0	4	16.9	4	17.6	8	10.5	8	8.8	7	13.4	3	23.1
Self-government	7	14.8	7	14.1	8.3	10.8	7	14.0	4	20.5	4	21.0	2.5	21.7	5	16.3
Culture/traditions	8	12.7	4	15.3	6	13.2	8	13.8	10.5	9.8	10	8.0	8	10.6	8	12.0
Poverty	9	10.1	8	11.6	8.3	10.8	9	8.4	10.5	9.9	6	12.6	9	9.3	9.5	11.1
Dependency on gov't/want everything for nothing/too much gov't funding/handouts	10	8.6	9	10.3	8.3	10.8	12	4.7	7	11.4	12	3.7	11	7.8	9.5	11.1
People don't understand them	11	5.5	11	8.9	11	4.9	10	7.5	13	4.2	13	2.8	13	2.6	12	4.3
Lack of initiative or motivation	12.5	4.3	—	0.0	12	2.3	11	5.4	12	7.1	7	11.1	10	8.9	13	2.6
Low self-esteem/self-worth/self-respect	12.5	4.3	12	3.7	13	1.2	13	3.3	9	10.2	11	7.2	12	7.4	11	8.2
Valid cases	**1493**		**139**		**451**		**395**		**66**		**66**		**160**		**209**	

SOURCE: Angus Reid Group Ltd.

a British Columbia logger has a low level of prejudice toward Natives, her perception that Native land claims threaten her livelihood from logging would have little impact on her support for Native self-government or on her support for special status for Natives. However, for another logger in whom the level of prejudice against Native people is high, that same perception that his livelihood is threatened by Native land claims will produce a dramatically lower level of support for both Native self-government and special status for Native people.

It is also possible to analyze these relationships from the opposite side. In doing so, we found that prejudice has very little impact on the dependent variables (support for Native self-government; support for special status for Native people) when the level of perceived group conflict is low. However, when perceived group conflict is high, prejudice again becomes an important determinant of Canadians' policy preferences toward Aboriginal people.

Our findings suggest the utility of distinguishing between two types of prejudice: dormant and activated. Prejudice against a group is dormant when it is unattached to any sense of conflict with that outgroup. Dormant prejudice has minimal effects on policy preferences vis-à-vis that outgroup. On the other hand, prejudice against a group is activated when it is linked to a perception of contemporary conflict with the outgroup. Such activated prejudice has important effects on policy preferences.

Regardless of whether prejudice is dormant, activated, or absent, economic conservatism was found statistically to produce antagonism toward Aboriginals and their preferred policies. Aboriginal people and their supporters might despair at that finding, in light of the contemporary influence of economic conservatism and the fact that substantial state financial participation will be necessary to overcome the effects of past and present racism, as the final report of the Royal Commission on Aboriginal Peoples asserted.

CONCLUSION

Although public opinion has softened slightly over the years on the issue of "special status" for First Nations, debilitating stereotypes remain alive in a significant minority of the non-Native population. In its broader contours, public opinion is no longer the ally that it was when social scientists first began monitoring it over two decades ago. Canadians have a low tolerance for precisely the kinds of protest strategies and tactics that create leverage for otherwise disempowered peoples. Aboriginal peoples have had to resort to those strategies and tactics and have paid the price in a deteriorating level of support from non-Native people. Furthermore, the very assertiveness that Aboriginal peoples are finding necessary to attain concrete results is likely to bring Aboriginal people into competition with private and commercial interests in the larger society. Non-Native people's perception of such competition as a threat is associated with opposition to government policies favoured by Aboriginal leaders.

Non-Native politicians might seek to discount non-Native public opinion on Aboriginal issues as uninformed, uninterested, and inconsistent. It is all three of those things. However, there are limits to how far politicians in office are willing to go when, as was the case in Canada in the mid-1990s, the courts are waivering, political opponents are seeking to reap political gain from government's policies toward Native people, financial costs increase relentlessly, and the recommended reforms veer off at a 180° angle from the increased level of accountability that the public seeks from the state.

Violence-prone right-wing extremist organizations do exist in Canada, but they have little influence and their main focus has not been on Aboriginal people. Of more concern should be the more influential right-wing ideologues. Their ethnocentric, anti-statist, pro–individual rights, radical egalitarian, fiscal retrenchment philosophy is profoundly antithetical to First Nations' needs. The probability is that they will inject partisan politics into Aboriginal issues such that Aboriginal people, lacking electoral clout, will again be buffeted by political forces that are largely beyond their ability to control. A real danger is that the political atmosphere created by right-wing ideologues will lead the state to offer either mere incremental, tokenistic change, which would exacerbate the problems of distrust of government, or conversely, to offer in desperation some drastic "solution" of radical equality. Neither approach offers true justice in the sense of arrangements that permit the survival and well-being of Indians as Indians (Boldt, 1993: 57).

NOTES

1. The 1986 national survey reported here was conducted with the aid of a Sabbatical Leave Fellowship from the Social Sciences and Humanities Research Council of Canada (SSHRCC) and with funding from SSHRCC (Research Grants Division), the Multiculturalism Directorate of the federal Department of the Secretary of State (Canadian Ethnic Studies Research Program), the University of Calgary, and the sale of reports issuing from the study. Data for the 1976 study reported here were collected under a generous grant from the Donner Canadian Foundation. The Angus Reid Group conducted the 1994 study reported here. The authors express their sincere appreciation to these supporters of the projects and to the respondents, research assistants, and other support staff members without whose assistance the projects would not have been possible. Data collection in 1976 and 1986 was done under contract by Complan Research Associates Ltd. and Decima Research Ltd., respectively. Percentages cited in this section do not sum to 100 percent because "Don't Know; No Response" is usually not reported here. In the 1994 survey, the "Don't Know; No Response" category was remarkably constant at about 15 percent of the sample.

2. The statements in the 1986 Index of Support for Special Status for Natives are shown below, and are followed by the percentage of the sample agreeing (strongly or moderately) and then the percentage disagreeing (strongly or moderately) with each one:

"If Parliament and the elected leaders of the Native people agreed that some Canadian laws would not apply in Native communities, it would be all right with me" (38 percent vs 44 percent);

"Native schools should not have to follow provincial guidelines on what is taught" (22 percent vs 67 percent);

"Native governments should have powers equivalent to those of provincial governments" (31 percent vs 51 percent); and

"Native governments should be responsible to elected Native politicians, rather than to Parliament, for the federal government money they receive" (28 percent vs 44 percent).

3. Given a choice of the RCMP having the "responsibility to enforce the law on aboriginal land reserves regardless of what the band leaders might want" and the RCMP "respect[ing] the wishes of the band leaders and leaving law enforcement up to the members of the reserve," a majority (56 percent of the 1994 sample) chose the former and only 25 percent chose the latter option.

4. For instance, given the statement "It just isn't right for natives to have special rights that other Canadians don't have," 41 percent of the 1994 sample agreed and 34 percent disagreed. Similarly, in that same survey 51 percent agreed with the statement "Aboriginal Canadians who eventually have self-government on their own land base should no longer have any special status or rights," while only half as many (26 percent) disagreed.

5. For instance, almost half (46 percent) of the 1994 sample agreed that "Aboriginals should have certain formally recognized rights such as these [exemption from certain taxes, special hunting and fishing rights]," while only 37 percent disagreed.

6. The Index of Support for Native Self-Government is made up of four items. A

respondent's index score is his or her average score across the four items. The items are listed below, and are followed by the percentage of the sample agreeing (strongly or moderately) and then the percentage disagreeing (strongly or moderately):

"It is important to the future well-being of Canadian society that the aspirations of Native people for self-government be met" (42 percent vs 33 percent);

"Those provincial premiers who oppose putting the right to Native self-government in the Constitution are harming Native people" (38 percent vs 34 percent);

"Most Native leaders who call for self-government for Native people are more interested in promoting their own personal career than in helping Native people" (30 percent vs 41 percent); and

"The Constitution of Canada should specifically recognize the right of Indians to self-government" (41 percent vs 40 percent).

7. In 1986, 30 percent of respondents thought that, if Native governments were adequately funded, they would be more capable than the federal government of meeting Native people's needs, while 18 percent thought the federal government would be more capable, and 37 percent thought that the two would be equally capable. In 1994, a large plurality (46 percent) was of the opinion that "if aboriginal self-government becomes a reality … the overall standard of living and living conditions of Canada's aboriginal peoples, let's say 10 years down the road," will improve, whereas 19 percent thought it would stay the same and 18 percent thought it would get worse. Eighteen percent did not express an opinion. The stability of the "anti-Aboriginal" opinion (at 18 percent) over the eight years is noteworthy.

8. The question also asked 1994 respondents how much confidence they have in each of several other players. The full results are as follows, with the numbers in parentheses representing "a lot of confidence," "a fair amount of confidence," "not much confidence," and "no confidence at all," respectively: Chiefs of large Indian bands (9 percent, 45 percent, 19 percent, and 9 percent); your provincial government (6 percent, 43 percent, 24 percent, and 10 percent); the federal government (8 percent, 45 percent, 23 percent, and 8 percent); Canada's justice system (10 percent, 43 percent, 23 percent, and 8 percent); the federal Department of Indian and Northern Affairs (5 percent, 42 percent, 26 percent, and 7 percent); Ovide Mercredi, leader of the Assembly of First Nations (15 percent, 40 percent, 14 percent, and 8 percent); Ron Irwin, the federal Minister of Indian and Northern Affairs (4 percent, 36 percent, 18 percent, and 7 percent); the Royal Commission on Aboriginal Peoples (7 percent, 40 percent, 19 percent, and 7 percent); and national Aboriginal organizations (9 percent, 50 percent, 15 percent, and 5 percent).

9. In 1986, in response to the statement "Most Native leaders who call for self-government for Native people are more interested in promoting their own personal career than in helping Native people," 30 percent agreed (anti-Native) and 41 percent disagreed (pro-Native). The 1994 survey asked: "Now, thinking about Canada's aboriginal leadership as a whole, based on your own impressions, do you think they represent the views and concerns of: all, most, some, or only a few of the aboriginal people in this country?" The responses were: 4 percent for "all"; 38 percent for "most"; 29 percent for "some"; and 13 percent for "only a few."

10. See Ponting and Gibbins (1980: 84–85) and Ponting (1987c: B11–B12) for the items constituting these indexes and for the distribution of the samples on those items.

11. In a 1988 national follow-up study, when the question was reworded to deal with special

fishing rights, rather than special hunting rights, the results were virtually identical.

12. The item was phrased as follows: "blocking resource companies from taking natural resources such as timber and minerals from lands claimed by aboriginals." Approval was given by 41.6 percent of the 1994 respondents, while 41.2 percent disapproved.

13. The item read: "Indian bands establishing gaming houses and other gambling facilities on their reserve lands without the approval of other government"; 70 percent disapproved; 15 percent approved.

14. Perceptions of conflicting group interests were measured in terms of such dimensions as the belief that Native people already receive excessive financial assistance from government, and the belief that Native people already exercise considerable power and influence with the federal or provincial government.

REFERENCES

Boldt, Menno. 1993. *Surviving as Indians. The Challenge of Self-Government.* Toronto: University of Toronto Press.

Decima Research Limited. 1987. *A Study of Canadian Attitudes toward Aboriginal Self-Government.* Toronto: Decima.

Langford, Tom, and J. Rick Ponting. 1992. "Canadians' Responses to Aboriginal Issues: The Role of Prejudice, Perceived Group Conflict, and Economic Conservatism," *Canadian Review of Sociology and Anthropology* 24, 2: 140–66.

Ponting, J. Rick. 1986. *Arduous Journey.* Toronto: McClelland and Stewart.

———. 1987a. *Profiles of Public Opinion on Canadian Natives and Native Issues.* Module 1. *Constitutional Issues.* Calgary: Research Report #87-01, Research Unit for Public Policy Studies, the University of Calgary.

———. 1987b. *Profiles of Public Opinion on Canadian Natives and Native Issues.* Module 2. *Special Status and Self-Government.* Calgary: Research Report #87-02, Research Unit for Public Policy Studies, the University of Calgary.

———. 1987c. *Profiles of Public Opinion on Canadian Natives and Native Issues.* Module 3. *Knowledge, Perceptions, and Sympathy.* Calgary: Research Report #87-03, Research Unit for Public Policy Studies, the University of Calgary.

———. 1988a. *Profiles of Public Opinion on Canadian Natives and Native Issues.* Module 4. *Native People, Finances, and Services.* Calgary: Research Report #88-01, Research Unit for Public Policy Studies, the University of Calgary.

———. 1988b. *Profiles of Public Opinion on Canadian Natives and Native Issues.* Module 5. *Land, Land Claims, and Treaties.* Calgary: Research Report #88-02, Research Unit for Public Policy Studies, the University of Calgary.

Ponting, J. Rick, and Roger Gibbins. 1980. *Out of Irrelevance: A Socio-Political Introduction to Indian Affairs in Canada.* Scarborough, ON: Butterworth.

———. 1981. "The Reactions of English Canadians and French Québécois to Native Indian Protest," *Canadian Review of Sociology and Anthropology* 18, 2: 222–38.

Chapter 16

Multiculturalism or Vertical Mosaic: Occupational Stratification among Canadian Ethnic Groups

HUGH LAUTARD

NEIL GUPPY

Words evoke powerful images. Portrayals of ethnicity in Canada — either as multiculturalism or vertical mosaic — present contrasting visions. Multiculturalism, the more current wording, implies equality among groups. In contrast, the phrase "vertical mosaic," first used almost 50 years ago, highlights inequality.

At face value multiculturalism means a multiplicity of equal cultures.[1] In practice the idea plays out in the many different ethnic institutions populating Canadian communities, from ethnic newspapers and radio stations to ethnic restaurants, churches, schools, and neighbourhoods. Multiculturalism also informs our educational traditions. In Canadian classrooms we find a growing emphasis on ethnically diverse social studies courses, greater recognition of different religious holidays, and more school celebrations of ethnic heritage. These, and many other examples, suggest a diversity of traditions. Different ethnic heritages provide separate identities within a common, egalitarian framework. At root, multiculturalism focuses on culture and equality.

The imagery of a vertical mosaic accepts only part of the multiculturalist vision. "Mosaic" stresses diverse ethnic identities. However, understanding the mosaic as vertical implies

evaluations of diverse traditions. Some traditions — and some cultures — are regarded as superior to others. Writing almost four decades ago, John Porter (1965) portrayed Canada as a "vertical mosaic." Porter saw Canada as an amalgam of social groups defined principally by class and ethnicity. Furthermore, he imagined these groups as vertically ranked on a series of inequality dimensions such as income, power, and prestige. At root, "vertical mosaic" focuses on social structure and inequality.

How useful are the contrasting images of the vertical mosaic and multiculturalism in understanding Canada in the 21st Century? Canada's population has grown and diversified both since 1965, when Porter published *The Vertical Mosaic*, and since 1971, when Canada adopted multiculturalism as official federal government policy. While no simple answer to the question is possible, more recent government legislation reveals that the contrasting images continue to inform contemporary policy debates.

For example, Section 15.1 of the Canadian Charter of Rights and Freedoms (1985) proclaims that "Every individual is equal before and under the law and has the right to the equal protection and equal benefit of the law without discrimination and, in particular, without discrimination based on race, national or ethnic origin, [and] colour...." However, despite the Charter's grounding in multicultural language, the legacy of the vertical mosaic has required additional legislation to help enhance the Charter's equality provisions. So, for example, the Employment Equity Act (1986) seeks to erase the subordinate positions of women, the disabled, Aboriginal peoples, and visible minorities. The act requires employers to hire according to equity targets. While proclaiming multiculturalism as official policy, the federal government has had to enact laws simultaneously to erode the vertical mosaic.

If the key proposition of *The Vertical Mosaic* still holds — that ethnicity shapes inequality — then legislation like the Employment Equity Act remains critical. This implies, though, that multiculturalism remains more ideology than fact, more rhetoric than reality. Is there a causal link between your ethnicity and your socioeconomic fortunes or misfortunes? We present new data that, when compared with trends published earlier, afford the longest historical perspective yet available on the association between ethnicity and occupation, based on 65 years of census data, from 1931 to 1996. As did Porter before us, we stress both social stratification (vertical) and social differences (mosaic).

IS THE SIGNIFICANCE OF ETHNICITY FOR INEQUALITY DECLINING?

In *The Vertical Mosaic* Porter described Canada as a nation fractured by ethnicity. Porter understood the French and the British as two "charter status" groups, commanding greater power and privilege than "entrance status" groups (i.e., other immigrants). He also understood the asymmetry of power favouring the British over the French. He claimed too that this asymmetry characterized non-charter immigrant groups as well, where ethnic inequality persisted. For him, "immigration and ethnic affiliation ... [were]

important factors in the formation of social classes" (Porter, 1965: 73).

Porter focused especially on the economic elite, in which he claimed "economic power belongs almost exclusively to those of British origin" (Porter, 1965: 286). Other groups were virtually absent. Power brokers were almost exclusively White Anglo-Saxon Protestants (WASPs). More recent analyses of modern-day power brokers, the wealthiest Canadians, or the economic elite show less British dominance. While the Thomson family, with its strong British roots, continues to be the wealthiest Canadian family, the corridors of power are now less WASP-ish (Clement, 1975; Ogmundson and McLaughlin, 1992; Nakhaie, 1997). At one time almost exclusively British, the Canadian elite, almost no matter how it is defined, now contains more people from other ethnic backgrounds.

Porter (1965) also used census data from 1931, 1951, and 1961 to make his case. By tabulating ethnic origin and occupation, he showed which ethnic groups dominated which job categories. For example, in the 1931 census he found British and Jewish groups were overrepresented in professional and financial occupations. Conversely, they were underrepresented in unskilled and primary jobs (e.g., fishing, logging). He wrote that the "French, German, and Dutch would probably rank next, followed by Scandinavian, Eastern European, Italian, Japanese, 'Other Central European,' Chinese, and Native Indian" (Porter, 1965: 81). His 1961 census data showed that, save for the French who had slid down a little, "the rough rank order persisted over time" (Porter, 1965: 90).

Why were different ethnic groups represented at higher and lower occupational levels? Porter proposed two complementary explanations. First, newcomers to Canada often brought with them different educational and occupational experiences. People of British heritage frequently came with professional qualifications that were officially recognized in Canada, whereas people from other ethnic backgrounds often arrived with little education and no professional skills. New entrants to Canada would thus reinforce the existing link between ethnic ancestry and social class (Porter, 1965: 86; 1985: 40–51).[2]

Second, Porter also argued that patterns of social mobility in Canada were correlated with ethnicity. Ethnic groups, he argued, either varied in how much they valued economic achievement and upward mobility, or felt that discrimination precluded their economic success in the wider labour market (Pineo and Porter, 1985: 360–61). Indeed Porter felt that multiculturalism would impede ethnic assimilation and perpetuate the link between social class and ethnicity.

Much social science research has assessed the adequacy of Porter's vertical mosaic imagery. No doubt insightful in his era, is it an accurate portrayal of ethnic inequality through the last half century? Since the end of World War II, the source of Canadian immigrants has shifted dramatically away from Europe and toward other continents, especially Asia. As well, Canada has changed its immigration policy. Now greater priority is given to the skills new entrants have, as opposed to their place of birth. For example, more emphasis is now placed on education and on fluency in at least one of the two official languages. Occupational experience is more valued than birthplace.

Some researchers have concluded that the vertical mosaic imagery simply needs revising to note its "colour coding." They argue that for people of visible minority background the association between ethnicity and social class has been retained. Now we have a "new ethnic mosaic, … redrafted along lines of race and colour" (Agocs and Boyd, 1993: 333; see also Lian and Matthews, 1998; Pendakur and Pendakur, 1998; Reitz, 2001). These scholars have typically used data from a single Canadian census to draw this conclusion.

Other research traditions have followed Porter's original lead and compared the patterns of association between ethnicity and social class

in successive census years. For example, Lautard and Loree (1984: 342) used detailed ethnicity and occupation data from 1931 to 1971 and concluded that "occupational inequality is still substantial enough to justify the use of the concept 'vertical mosaic' to characterize … ethnic relations in Canada" (see also Darroch, 1979; Pendakur, 2002). The census data used both by Porter and then Lautard and Loree combine both the foreign-born and the native-born. It therefore allows researchers to comment on trends over time, but it provides no test for the two explanations Porter offered about the association of ethnicity and class, which stress differences between foreign-born and native-born Canadians.

Boyd's (1985) research on the influence of birthplace on occupational attainment offers a test of the immigration interpretation. For foreign-born women and men, she demonstrated that ethnic ancestry was correlated with occupational attainment. Even when she compared immigrants with the same age, education, social origin, and place of residence, she found a correlation. For women who were foreign-born she found a "double negative" that reinforced the vertical mosaic. She concluded that birthplace and sex are important factors underlying the Canadian mosaic (Boyd, 1985: 441).

The exact nature of the link between ethnicity and inequality turns, at least in part, on issues of definition and methodology. Porter used the best data available to him but his approach had weaknesses despite his best efforts. The following are among the chief problems that any analyst must confront in trying to sort out whether "multiculturalism" or "vertical mosaic" best characterizes modern Canada.

ETHNICITY

How broadly or finely one chooses to define ethnicity is critical in these debates. Historically, male ancestral lineage was the defining feature of ethnicity, at least as used by Statistics Canada for measurement purposes. However, this definition is problematic. Inter-ethnic marriages occur across generations. National borders change. An increasing number of people consider themselves to be of "Canadian" ancestry since they are descendants of people who arrived in Canada generations ago.

Porter's view of the Charter status groups, the French and the British, drew no distinction between the English, the Irish, the Scottish, and the Welsh. Likewise, Statistics Canada for a long time was unable to publish distinct numbers for different Asian ethnic members. That is because the number of Koreans and Cambodians, for example, was simply too small. Typically, the following ethnic categories have been used in the census, with earlier censuses having even fewer distinct groups: British (English, Irish, Scottish, Welsh), French, German, Italian, Jewish, Dutch, Scandinavian, Eastern European (Polish, Ukrainian), Other European, Asian, and Native Indian.

OCCUPATIONS

Porter originally used five broad occupational categories (professional and financial, clerical, personal service, primary and unskilled, and agriculture). Lautard and Loree (1984) used a more detailed occupational categorization with hundreds of separate job categories for each census.

Occupations are, in important ways, just jobs. To show that members of different ethnic groups concentrate in some jobs and not others says nothing about inequality; it is only a comment about different jobs. Only if those jobs have different rewards attached to them does inequality become an issue. But what are the most salient rewards — income, working conditions, prestige, authority? The vertical mosaic clearly implies some hierarchy, but which hierarchy is not specified.

HISTORICAL COMPARABILITY

The number and kinds of occupations in Canada have changed over time. Should researchers use the most recent occupational listings and ignore older jobs? Likewise, the detail on ethnicity has changed historically, as has the way Statistics Canada collects this information.[3] Should only broad ethnic categories that are strictly comparable over time be used?

MEASURING OCCUPATIONAL STRATIFICATION BY ETHNICITY

We use census information for 1971, 1981, and either 1991 or 1996 and compare our results to earlier findings, beginning either in 1931 or 1951. Depending on the availability of data, we discuss trends over either a 40- or 65-year period. This provides enormous detail that we need to summarize. To do so, sociologists often measure occupational differentiation by calculating an index of dissimilarity, and stratification by an index of inequality.

Here first, by way of analogy, is how to understand the index of dissimilarity. In your college or university, think of the overall percentage of women and men enrolled (assume it is 55 percent and 45 percent respectively). Now think of the percentage of women and men in each of your classes. How well is the overall gender balance of 55/45 reflected in your individual courses? Extend this to think about all the courses available to students.

One way to summarize all this detail is to calculate for each course any difference in the percentage of women (or men) from the overall 55/45 average. This simple calculation summarizes how dissimilar each course is from the overall gender balance. Summing across all courses provides a convenient summary: the higher the index number, the greater the dissimilarity.

In our case we add the percentage differences between the occupational distribution of each ethnic group and that of the rest of the labour force. A separate calculation is done for women and men. The resulting indexes are the percentages of women and men in the ethnic groups who would have to be in a different occupation in order for there to be no occupational differences among ethnic groups.[4]

For example, say the index of dissimilarity for women of British origin is 8. This means that only 8 percent of the British women in the labour force would have to be in a different occupational category for there to be no difference between their occupational distribution and that of women of other ethnic origins. If the index of dissimilarity for men of Aboriginal origins is 33 percent, this indicates about four times as much differentiation, with one Aboriginal man in three having to be in a different occupational group in order for them to have the same occupational distribution as non-Aboriginal men. Averaging dissimilarity indexes for ethnic groups in each of a series of census years indicates trends in occupational differentiation among ethnic groups. We present such results for 1971, 1981, and 1996, and compare them with earlier findings for 1931, 1951, 1961, and 1971, for a combined time span of 65 years.

Dissimilarity, however, does not necessarily mean disadvantage or inequality. As a method of capturing stratification, as opposed to simply differentiation, sociologists have adopted another strategy. First, the occupations for each census year are ranked according to a socioeconomic scale based on prestige as indicated by the education and income associated with each job (e.g., Blishen and Carroll, 1978; Blishen, Carroll and Moore, 1987). Second, an index of relative occupational inequality is calculated for each ethnic group. To summarize occupational inequality, we use the index of net difference. This measure (unlike the index of dissimilarity, which is always positive) may be either negative or positive. An index of net difference with a minus sign indicates the group for which it was calculated is generally lower on the occupational "ladder" relative to the rest of the labour force, while a positive index indicates higher relative position. The greater the absolute size of the index,

whether positive or negative, the greater the degree of stratification, while a net difference of zero would indicate overall equality of occupational status.[5] While scales required for the calculation of indexes of net difference are available for 1971, 1981, and 1991, none has been developed for 1996. Similarly, the first socioeconomic index for occupations in Canada was prepared for 1951 (Blishen, 1958). We therefore analyze occupational inequality for 1971, 1981, and 1991 and compare our results with earlier findings for 1951, 1961, and 1971, for a combined time span of 40 years.

OCCUPATIONAL STRATIFICATION BY ETHNICITY, 1931 TO 1996

Table 16.1 contains indexes of occupational dissimilarity for sixteen ethnic groups in 1971 and seventeen groups in 1981 and 1996. Between 1971 and 1981 ethnic occupational differentiation generally declined. Exceptions include the indexes for men of Dutch and Scandinavian origin and women of Jewish origin, each of which are one point higher in 1981 than 1971, and the indexes for men of French and German origin and for Scandinavian women, which are the same for both years. Over the 1970s, average ethnic dissimilarity dropped 3 points among men, from 30 to 27 percent, while it declined 4 points among women, from 27 to 23 percent.

Between 1981 and 1996, ethnic occupational dissimilarity declined for ten of the 17 groups among both men and women. Exceptions to this trend include both men and women of German, Dutch, Scandinavian, Ukrainian, and Polish origin, as well as men of Hungarian origin. Women of Hungarian and Jewish origin have the same index of dissimilarity in 1996 as in 1981, as do men of British origin. Average ethnic dissimilarity, however, continued to decline: another 2 points for men and another 3 points for women, to 25 and 20 percent, respectively. Thus, in 1996, among the groups studied, an average of one man in four and one woman in five would have to be in a

TABLE 16.1 OCCUPATIONAL DISSIMILARITY* BETWEEN SELECTED ETHNIC GROUPS AND THE REST OF THE LABOUR FORCE, BY SEX: 1971, 1981, AND 1996

ETHNIC GROUP	MALE 1971	1981	1996	FEMALE 1971	1981	1996
British	15	10	10	16	9	8
French	14	14	11	18	14	12
German	15	15	18	11	9	12
Dutch	16	17	21	15	13	22
Scandinavian	17	18	21	12	12	15
Ukrainian	15	13	16	16	9	12
Polish	15	14	18	14	10	17
Hungarian	21	19	20	20	15	15
Italian	35	26	21	38	25	18
Portuguese	46	42	33	57	48	31
Greek	48	45	35	51	42	27
Yugoslav	33	31	26	35	29	22
Jewish	51	49	46	32	33	33
Chinese	52	44	36	34	30	25
South Asian	46	34	28	31	27	22
Indian and Metis**	41	37	33	32	29	28
Black	NI	32	28	NI	30	24
Mean ($\bar{X}$)	30	27	25	27	23	20
(Number of occupations)	(498)	(496)	(514)	(464)	(495)	(513)

* Each figure in the table indicates the percentage of the ethnic group that would have to have a different occupation in order for there to be no difference between the occupational distribution of the group and the rest of the labour force.
** Includes Inuit in 1996.
NI: Not included.

SOURCE: Special tabulations of census data.

different occupation for there to be no ethnic dissimilarity.

Table 16.1 also shows that for each of the census years studied there is a generally consistent pattern of ethnic occupational differentiation. Groups of North and East European origins exhibit below-average occupational dissimilarity, while — except for men of Italian origin in 1981 and men and women of Italian origin in 1996 — groups of South European, Jewish, Asian, Black, and Aboriginal origins show above-average dissimilarity. Moreover, if the next five largest visible minority groups (Arab/West Asian, Filipino, Southeast Asian, Latin American, and Japanese) are included in the averages for 1996, the latter would increase to 27 for men and 23 for women. Nevertheless, the declining levels of ethnic differentiation we have found for the 1971–96 period mark a continuation of the decreases reported by Lautard and Loree (1984) for 1931 to 1971. This 65-year decline, however, terminates in averages indicating considerable occupational dissimilarity among ethnic groups.[6]

As noted above, occupational dissimilarity does not necessarily involve inequality of occupational status. Table 16.2 on page 172 contains indexes of net difference for 1971, 1981, and 1991 for the ethnic groups discussed above. In 1971, with the exception of the indexes for men and women of British and Jewish origin, and men of South Asian origins, all indexes are negative, indicating the relatively low occupational status of the other groups. As well, in 1971, those of South European and Aboriginal origins have lower overall occupational status than the other groups. The latter pattern tends to hold through 1991, except for men of Yugoslav origin and, in 1991 only, men and women of Italian origin. Compared to 1971, in 1981 there are more positive indexes, including men of Scandinavian and East European origins. Women of Scandinavian origins have a positive index, while women of French and Ukrainian origin have an index of zero, for overall equality of occupational status. Between 1971 and 1981, ethnic occupational inequality generally declines, with virtually all indexes — whether positive or negative — becoming smaller. The only exceptions are the indexes for men of Chinese origin and women of Jewish origin, which increase in size by 4 and 3 points, respectively.

Between 1981 and 1991, average occupational inequality among ethnic groups continues to decline, but not as much as over the previous decade. Exceptions to the declining trend over the 1980s include men of Jewish origin and women of both Ukrainian and Jewish origin. The occupational disadvantage of both men and women of German origin and of women of Polish origin also increases, and that of women of South Asian and Aboriginal origins is up by 5 points. The index for men of Scandinavian origin drops slightly, while the indexes for men of Ukrainian, Polish, and Aboriginal origins and women of French origin show no change. Over the 1980s, too, the indexes for men of Chinese and South Asian origins become positive and negative, respectively. The greatest increase in relative occupational disadvantage is for Black men. Subject to differences in the data, the overall trend and pattern in ethnic occupational inequality are comparable to those reported by Lautard and Loree (1984) for census years studied by Porter (1965) (1951–1961) as well as 1971.

FROM VERTICAL MOSAIC TO MULTICULTURALISM: BETWEEN 1931 AND 1996

Has multiculturalism eclipsed the vertical mosaic? Is ethnic inequality, at least as measured by occupational stratification, a fact of Canadian history? Our results show that between 1931 and 1996 a decline in the significance of ethnicity, at least for occupational stratification, has occurred. However, ethnic origin continues to affect occupational stratification.

The trend in occupational dissimilarity indicates a reduction in the ethnic division of labour of 32 percent for men and 46 percent for women in 65 years. Slowly but surely social differentiation based on ethnicity is eroding. With respect to occupational stratification there has been a reduction of 50 percent for men and 44 percent for women, although over a shorter time span (1951 to 1991). While these historical comparisons are admittedly crude, we caution that precise calculations are impossible.

Do these results imply a "collapse" of the vertical mosaic? No. Between 1971 and 1996 both occupational differentiation and occupational stratification have eroded, but for both women and men, differences persist. There are certainly no firm grounds to conclude that multiculturalism has trumped the vertical mosaic.

Porter's "vertical mosaic" interpretation of Canadian society rested upon far more than ethnic occupational differentiation. As we noted above, the penetration of ethnic members into elite groups, a key element of the vertical

TABLE 16.2   NET DIFFERENCE IN OCCUPATIONAL STATUS* BETWEEN SELECTED ETHNIC GROUPS AND THE REST OF THE LABOUR FORCE, BY SEX: 1971, 1981, AND 1991

ETHNIC GROUP	MALE 1971	1981	1996	FEMALE 1971	1981	1996
British	0.13	0.06	0.04	0.14	0.06	0.04
French	−0.06	−0.04	−0.01	−0.02	0.00	0.00
German	−0.08	−0.02	−0.04	−0.09	−0.04	−0.06
Dutch	−0.09	−0.06	−0.04	−0.10	−0.06	−0.04
Scandinavian	−0.08	0.01	−0.01	−0.01	0.03	0.01
Ukrainian	−0.09	0.01	0.01	−0.13	0.00	0.02
Polish	−0.08	0.03	0.01	−0.12	−0.01	−0.03
Hungarian	−0.06	0.03	0.03	−0.13	−0.03	0.00
Italian	−0.22	−0.12	−0.04	−0.35	−0.19	−0.05
Portuguese	−0.38	−0.33	−0.27	−0.62	−0.40	−0.29
Greek	−0.27	−0.31	−0.20	−0.48	−0.36	−0.22
Yugoslav	−0.12	−0.05	−0.04	−0.29	−0.18	−0.10
Jewish	0.36	0.30	0.34	0.24	0.27	0.29
Chinese	−0.04	−0.08	0.02	−0.20	−0.14	−0.07
South Asian	0.26	0.09	−0.03	0.19	−0.09	−0.14
Indian and Metis**	−0.35	−0.25	−0.25	−0.23	−0.18	−0.15
Black	NI	−0.02	−0.12	NI	−0.02	−0.07
Mean ($\bar{X}$)	0.17	0.11	0.09	0.21	0.12	0.09
(Number of occupational ranks)	(498)	(468)	(485)	(464)	(467)	(485)

• A negative figure indicates relatively lower occupational status, a positive figure relatively higher status. Zero indicates overall equality of occupational status. The greater the absolute size of the index, the greater the inequality..

** May not equal the number of occupations in Table 16.1 because of tied ranks.

NI: Not included.

SOURCE: Special tabulations of census data.

mosaic, has remained limited. Nevertheless, some progress has been made here too, as the new "entrepreneurial" immigration category suggests, and certainly visible minorities have done well in selected occupational niches — among professionals, for example (Lambert, Ledoux, and Pendakur, 1989).

The research design that we have employed prevents us from investigating which of Porter's two dynamics best explains the continuing level of ethnic inequality: differential immigration or blocked mobility. Our reading of the research literature suggests that immigration continues to be the more important factor, especially in terms of visible minorities (McDade, 1988; Sorensen, 1995). That is, ethnicity has less of an effect on inequality for native-born Canadians than it does for immigrants. However, immigration patterns cannot be the sole explanation because our results are also consistent with research showing that some visible minorities, for example men of black and South Asian heritage, face earning penalties in the labour market, penalties that are consistent with the blocked mobility thesis (e.g., see Geschwender and Guppy, 1995; Li, 1990; Lian and Matthews, 1998; Pendakur and Pendakur, 1998).

Finally, whatever the actual extent and sources of the vertical mosaic, it coexists with other aspects of ethnic and racial inequality beyond the scope of our analysis, including prejudice, hate and violence, as well as systematic and systemic discrimination in recruitment, interviewing, hiring, promotion, training and termination practices. Similarly, among the "paradoxes of racism in Canadian society" is the "invisibility" of visible minorities "excluded from ... political, social, and economic institutions.... [as well as from] the official history of Canada" (Henry et al., 1995).

NOTES

The authors gratefully acknowledge the assistance of Kaitlin MacDonald and Robin Hawkshaw in preparing this paper. The research reported here was supported by an SSHRCC Research Grant awarded to Hugh Lautard and a Killam Research Fellowship awarded to Neil Guppy.

1. The Canadian Heritage Web site provides the government's answer to the question, What is multiculturalism? "Canadian multiculturalism is fundamental to our belief that all citizens are equal." Retrieved November 20, 2002, from http://www.pch.gc.ca/progs/multi/what-multi_e.cfm.

2. For much of Canada's history, foreign-born workers have had a higher level of education than have native-born Canadians (see Légacé, 1968; Boyd, 1985). What this average hides, however, is the tendency for immigrants to be either relatively well or relatively poorly educated.

3. Prior to the 1981 census, the question to determine ethnic origin was: "To which ethnic or cultural group did you or your ancestor (on the male side) belong on coming to this continent?" In 1981 the question was: "To which ethnic or cultural group did you or your ancestors belong on first coming to this continent?" Notice, especially, how difficult it is for Aboriginal people to answer such a question accurately. Beginning in 1981, multiple ethnic origins were accepted, and the 1996 question read: "To which ethnic or cultural group(s) did this person's ancestors belong?" Our ethnic categories for 1981 and 1996 are based on single responses and exclude those reporting multiple ethnic or cultural origins, except for multiple origins involving only constituent groups of certain categories. For example, British includes persons who report their origin(s) to be British or any one or more of English, Irish, Scottish, Welsh, etc., but no non-British origin(s). Scandinavian includes persons who report their origin(s) as Scandinavian or any one or more of Danish, Icelandic, Norwegian, Swedish, etc., but no non-Scandinavian origin(s). Although the 1996 *Census Guide* still made it clear that ethnic origin did not refer to citizenship, "Canadian" was for the first time among the examples listed with the question itself. Our data, however, corroborate Li's (2003:128) observation that "the growth of people reporting Canadian origin ... did not have a measurable impact on the reporting of ethnic minorities."

4. The index of dissimilarity may also be obtained by adding either the positive or the negative differences between two percentage distributions (cf., Darroch, 1979:8).

5. Specifically, a negative index of net difference indicates the extent to which the probability that a member of the ethnic group in question will have a lower occupational rank than a member of the rest of the labour force

exceeds the opposite probability, assuming random pairing. A positive value indicates the opposite relation, while zero would indicate that the two probabilities are the same (Lieberson, 1975: 279–80).

6. Just as Lautard and Loree's (1984) average dissimilarity for men in 1961 (29) was about double that reported by Darroch (1979), our 1971 averages for men (30) and women (27) are roughly double Darroch's 1971 average for men and women combined. This shows why trend comparisons are so important; the dissimilarity measure is sensitive to the number of occupations used (Lautard and Loree, 1984: 336). The level of dissimilarity reported by other authors is important as a statement about ethnic differences (i.e., how big or small they might be), but it is comparison over time, using a consistent methodology, that answers questions about how ethnic divisions are changing in Canada.

REFERENCES

Agocs, Carol, and Monica Boyd. (1993). "The Canadian Ethnic Mosaic Recast: Theory, Research and Policy Frameworks for the 1990s" in J. Curtis *et al.* eds., *Social Inequality in Canada: Patterns, Problems, Policies* (pp. 330–52). Toronto: Prentice-Hall.

Blishen, Bernard R. (1958). "The Construction and Use of an Occupational Class Scale." *Canadian Journal of Economics and Political Science, 24* (4): 519–31.

Blishen, Bernard R., and William K. Carroll. (1978). "Sex Differences in a Socio-economic Index for Occupations in Canada." *Canadian Review of Sociology and Anthropology, 15* (3): 352–71.

Blishen, Bernard R., William K. Carroll, and Catherine Moore. (1987). "The 1981 Socio-economic Index for Occupations in Canada." *Canadian Review of Sociology and Anthropology, 24* (4): 465–88.

Boyd, Monica. (1985). "Immigration and Occupational Attainment." In M. Boyd, *et al.*, eds., *Ascription and Attainment: Studies in Mobility and Status Attainment in Canada* (pp. 393–446). Ottawa: Carleton University Press.

Clement, Wallace. (1975). *The Canadian Corporate Elite*. Toronto: McClelland and Stewart.

Darroch, Gordon. (1979). "Another Look at Ethnicity, Stratification and Social Mobility in Canada." *Canadian Journal of Sociology, 4* (1): 1–25.

Geschwender, Jim, and Neil Guppy. (1995). "Ethnicity, Educational Attainment, and Earned Income among Canadian-Born Men and Women." *Canadian Ethnic Studies, 27* (1): 67–83.

Henry, Frances, Carol Tator, Winston Mattis, and Tim Rees. (1995). *The Colour of Democracy in Canadian Society*. Toronto: Harcourt Brace.

Lambert, M., M. Ledoux, and R. Pendakur. (1989). "Visible Minorities in Canada 1986: A Graphic Overview." Ottawa: Policy and Research Unit, Multiculturalism and Citizenship.

Lautard, Hugh, and Donald Loree. (1984). "Ethnic Stratification in Canada, 1931–1971." *Canadian Journal of Sociology, 9* (3): 333–44.

Légacé, Michael D. (1968). "Educational Attainment in Canada." Dominion Bureau of Statistics, Special Labour Force Survey No. 7. Ottawa: Queen's Printer.

Li, Peter. (1990). *Ethnic Inequality in a Class Society*. Toronto: Thompson.

Li, Peter. (2003). *Destination Canada: Immigration Debates and Issues*. Don Mills: Oxford University Press.

Lian, Jason, and David Ralph Matthews. (1998). "Does the Vertical Mosaic still Exist? Ethnicity and Income in Canada, 1991." *Canadian Review of Sociology and Anthropology, 35* (4): 461–81.

Lieberson, Stanley. (1975). "Rank-sum Comparisons between Groups." In David R. Heise, ed., *Sociological Methodology 1976* (pp. 276–91). San Francisco: Jossey-Bass.

McDade, Kathryn. (1988). "Barriers to Recognition of the Credentials of Immigrants in Canada." Discussion Paper 88.B.1. Ottawa: Institute for Research on Public Policy.

Nakhaie, M. Reza. (1995). "Vertical Mosaic among the Elites: The New Imagery Revisited." *Canadian Review of Sociology and Anthropology, 34* (1): 1–24.

Ogmundson, Richard, and J. McLaughlin. (1992). "Trends in the Ethnic Origins of Canadian Elites: The decline of the BRITS." *Canadian Review of Sociology and Anthropology, 29* (2): 227–42.

Pendakur, Ravi. (2002). *Immigrants and the Labour Force: Policy, Regulation, and Impact.* Montreal: McGill-Queen's University Press.

Pendakur, K., and Pendakur, R. (1998). "The Colour of Money: Earnings Differentials among Ethnic Groups in Canada." *Canadian Journal of Economics, 31* (3): 518–48.

Pineo, Peter, and John Porter. (1985). "Ethnic Origin and Occupational Attainment." In M. Boyd, et al., eds., *Ascription and Achievement: Studies and Status Attainment in Canada* (pp. 357–92). Ottawa: Carleton University Press.

Porter, John. (1965). *The Vertical Mosaic: An Analysis of Social Class and Power in Canada.* Toronto: University of Toronto Press.

Porter, John. (1985). "Canada: The Social Context of Occupational Allocation." In M. Boyd, et al., eds, *Ascription and Achievement: Studies in Mobility and Status Attainment in Canada* (pp. 29–65). Ottawa: Carleton University Press.

Reitz, Jeffrey G. (2000). "Immigrant Skill Utilization in the Canadian Labour Market: Implications of Human Capital Research." *Journal of International Migration and Integration, 2* (3): 347–78.

Sorensen, Marianne. (1995). "The Match Between Education and Occupation for Immigrant Women in Canada." *Canadian Ethnic Studies, 27* (1): 48–66.

PART 4

SOCIAL INSTITUTIONS

The social structures that comprise human societies are nested like Russian dolls or Chinese boxes. There are structures within structures within structures. The smallest are known as **microstructures**. Microstructures are small, localized sites of face-to-face interaction, such as families. Social relations in microstructures tend to be emotionally deep and enduring, which is why people value them for their own sake. **Macrostructures**, in contrast, are larger, less localized, and more impersonal. People participate in macrostructures for specific, instrumental reasons — to earn money, get an education, and so on. **Global structures** are even larger, more remote, and more impersonal. They involve relations between whole societies and between nations.

Institutions are found at both the micro- and macrostructural levels of society. Institutions are social structures that, to varying degrees, fulfill basic human needs. These needs include:

- the reproduction of the species and the nurturance and primary socialization of small children, a set of functions that is usually performed by the family (see Part 4A);
- the maintenance and renewal of legitimate authority, a set of functions which is performed by the political system (see Part 4B); and
- the production and distribution of material resources, a set of functions that is performed by the economy (see Part 4C).

In keeping with the overall theme of this book, the articles in this unit focus on how powerful social forces, such as globalization, consumerism, and rationalization, are reshaping major social institutions. Some of the articles highlight not just the fact that social institutions fulfill basic human needs, but that basic human needs are flexible and may therefore be fulfilled by a wide variety of institutional forms. The articles also show that the adaptation of families, political systems, and economies to new conditions is often disorienting for the people who live and work in them. Some people react by organizing resistance to change and attempting to return to the old state of affairs. The very term "institution" may suggest a solid and stable establishment, but in reality social conflict is never far below the surface of any modern institution.

GLOSSARY

Global structures are the largest and most impersonal patterns of social relations, sometimes spanning the entire globe, including relations within and between societies and nations.

Institutions are micro- and macro-level social structures that address basic human needs, such as reproduction, nurturance, and primary socialization (the family; the maintenance and renewal of legitimate authority (the political system); and the production and distribution of material resources (the economy).

Macrostructures are large, non-localized, impersonal sets of social relations. People participate in them for specific, instrumental reasons.

Microstructures are small, localized, emotionally intense patterns of social relations. People value such relations for their own sake.

PART 4A

FAMILIES

The **nuclear family** consists of a husband and wife living in the same household with at least one child. In the **traditional nuclear family**, only the husband is employed in the paid work force. In the **nontraditional nuclear family**, both the husband and the wife are employed in the paid work force. **Non-nuclear families** include childless couples, lone parents living with at least one child, and husbands and wives with no children living at home. Finally, some Canadian households are not recognized as families by the Canadian census. These **nonfamily households** include people living alone and people who are living together but who are neither married nor bound by common law (e.g., gay couples). Preliminary (late 2002) returns from the most recent Canadian census do not include this breakdown of household types. However, they indicate that in 2001, 51.0 percent of Canadian households were married families, 10.0 percent were common-law families, 11.3 percent were lone-parent families, and 27.6 percent were nonfamily households.[1]

As one moves from traditional nuclear families to nontraditional nuclear families to non-nuclear families to nonfamily households one also moves from shrinking to expanding categories. The traditional nuclear family is no longer the predominant family form because so many women have entered the paid work force, especially since the 1960s. Today, both spouses work in the paid work force in about two-thirds of Canadian husband–wife families. Non-nuclear families are increasingly common for several reasons. More women are deciding not to have children so they can pursue higher education and careers. Infertility affects some couples. Non-nuclear families are also more common because the proportion of Canadians who marry is down, the divorce rate is up, and the rate of remarriage after divorce is down. Finally, nonfamily households are more common since more single people, including the elderly, can afford to live on their own and since gay lifestyles are more widely accepted than they used to be, at least in large urban areas.

The facts listed above should not lead one to conclude that the family is in a state of collapse. Several surveys show that more than three-quarters of Canadians regard the family as the most important thing in their lives, more important than career and religion. In one poll, more than 90 percent of respondents with children at home said that the family is becoming *more* important to them. The overwhelming majority of adults still want to marry and have children. The family is not a crumbling institution. What is happening, however, is that people are freer than they once were to establish the kinds of family arrangements that best suit them. For instance, because most adult women are now employed in the paid work force, and because changes in divorce laws have made the division of property after divorce more equitable, women now have a measure of economic independence that gives them greater freedom to end unsatisfying marriages and seek more gratifying relationships. This does not spell the end of the family but the possibility that more suitable family forms can take shape.

One alternative family form that is becoming increasingly prevalent is the homosexual union, which Adie Nelson analyzes in Chapter 17. In Canada and other countries, laws are being changed to give the partners in homosexual unions the same rights and obligations as the partners in a marriage. It is highly

---

[1] The percentages do not add up to 100.0 percent due to rounding. As of this writing (September 2003) the Canadian government seems to be on the verge of allowing gay couples to marry.

doubtful that any religious organization will ever be compelled by the state to bless homosexual unions. Moreover, in many countries due to political and religious opposition, homosexual unions are not likely to be defined as *legal* marriages any time soon; legally speaking, a marriage will be able to take place only if the partners include a single woman and a single man. But *sociologically* speaking, as Nelson shows, there can be little doubt that long-term homosexual unions are marriages, and the social units they form are families.

An important stage in the life cycle of most families involves the birth of a child. Yet childbirth today is very different than it was 150 years ago. Beginning in the nineteenth century, the medical profession came to control more and more of the birthing process. In the twentieth century, physicians, nurses, and pain-control medication became the norm, and surgical procedures became common. Midwives became a thing of the past. Today, we live in an era of thoroughly "medicalized" childbirth.

In the 1980s, some feminists began to criticize the medicalization of childbirth on the grounds that it decreased women's control of their own bodies, alienated women from what could be a deeply emotionally enriching experience, and in some respects *increased* health risks to both mother and child. For example, the critics argued that many unnecessary caesarean sections were being performed. They claimed, moreover, that the higher the degree of medical intervention during childbirth, the more likely the mother would suffer postpartum depression. In Chapter 18, Diana Worts and Bonnie Fox qualify this critique in an important way. Their study of women's childbirth experiences in Toronto shows that some women do indeed find the birthing process as alienating as the critics say. Others, however, consider medical intervention irrelevant to their satisfaction with the birthing process while still others are pleased with medical intervention. Worts and Fox show that the quality of social support women receive during and after giving birth partly determines how much medical intervention they require, their level of satisfaction with the birthing process, and their likelihood of experiencing postpartum depression. They conclude by emphasizing the need for more social support from women's partners, friendship networks, and state-supported social services.

Wife abuse was one aspect of many marriages that used to be hushed up, but it is now increasingly made public and often precipitates divorce. Nonetheless, much wife abuse still goes unreported and many marriages are still the site of abusive relationships. Moreover, much violence against women takes place outside families. In Chapter 19 Holly Johnson shows how much: 51 percent of the 12 300 women interviewed in a 1993 Statistics Canada survey reported that at least one man had physically or sexually assaulted them. True, several other surveys have shown that rates of female violence against men are about the same as rates of male violence against women. However, Canadian, American, and Scottish research shows that when women commit acts of violence against men they tend overwhelmingly to be acting in self-defence. Moreover, men's violent acts against women are much more likely to result in medical treatment and police intervention than women's violent acts against men.

GLOSSARY

Non-nuclear families include childless couples, lone parents living with at least one child, and husbands and wives with no children living at home.

A **nontraditional nuclear family** is a nuclear family in which both the husband and the wife are employed in the paid work force.

A **nuclear family** consists of a husband and wife living in the same household with at least one child.

Nonfamily households include people living alone and people who are living together but who are neither married nor bound by a common-law union (e.g., gay couples).

Traditional nuclear families are nuclear families in which only the husband is employed in the paid work force.

CRITICAL THINKING QUESTIONS

1. What is the difference between a marriage and a homosexual union? Is the distinction likely to become blurred or disappear entirely in the next decade or so? Why or why not?
2. How does Canada compare to other countries in the degree to which it has accorded homosexual unions the same rights and obligations as marriage?
3. How do rates of wife assault and sexual assault vary with the age, marital status, household income, and educational attainment of the victim? How do you explain these variations?
4. How do Worts and Fox qualify the traditional feminist critique of medicalized childbirth?
5. Worts and Fox recommend increasing the social support available to women giving birth. How could this be accomplished for women without partners?

ANNOTATED BIBLIOGRAPHY

Margrit Eichler, *Family Shifts: Families, Policies, and Gender Equality* (Toronto: Oxford University Press, 1997). A penetrating analysis of how Canadian families have changed and how public policies need to be reformed to take account of new realities.

Bonnie Fox, ed., *Family Patterns, Gender Relations*, 2nd ed. (Toronto: Oxford University Press, 2001). The definitive Canadian reader in sociology of the family.

Carol Stack, *All Our Kin: Strategies for Survival in a Black Community* (New York: Harper and Row, 1974). This highly regarded participant-observation study shows how kinship networks adapt to conditions of extreme poverty. The author convincingly demonstrates that there are functional alternatives to the nuclear family that are required by non-middle-class social settings.

Chapter 17

What Is a Family? The Homosexual Challenge

ADIE NELSON

On the surface, answering the question, "What is a family?" would not seem to pose a very formidable challenge. Regardless of what type of family we grew up in or what type of relationship we are currently involved in, the image of the prototypical "ideal family" comes to mind readily enough: the benevolent, but firm father who sits at the head of table and of the household, the emotionally expressive wife/homemaker/mother and, of course, their two or more children. The imagery is especially potent because it is sheathed in the "charm of hominess" (Gottlieb, 1993: 270), or a vision of Home Sweet Home in which the family is portrayed as offering a safe harbour from a sometimes heartless world. The scene suggested is reminiscent of a Norman Rockwell painting — the white picket fence, the gingham-clad daughter and denim-clad son playing happily with the frolicking puppy, mom's chocolate-chip cookies cooling on the window sill, dad cutting the festive turkey — and creates an enticing portrait of comfort, cosiness, and security.

The patriarchal heterosexual nuclear family is routinely praised by conservative political parties (Conway, 1990: xi). It is championed as universal, idyllic, and sacred. However, as Abbott and Wallace (1992: 73) observe, one of the subtle consequences of heralding this image of the family is that it constructs an evaluative framework by which all relational forms are to be judged. Thus, a particular type of family, characterized by a gendered division of labour (that is, the male "breadwinner" and the female "housewife") is depicted "as the normal, natural and inevitable family form." Implicitly, forms of relationships that depart from or challenge this imagery are viewed as "deviant" (Gavigan, 1997) — even though Canadian families are much more varied than this image of the family suggests. Moreover, inasmuch as "good people" enter into "good" (i.e., conventional) relationships, those involved in nontraditional family forms may be regarded as suspect or inferior.

Gottlieb (1993: 7) notes that, in its origins, the word "family" stems from *famulus*, the Latin word for "servant." The word *familia* was used originally in classical times to refer to the live-in staff of a household, and from there it came to mean the household itself or the members of it. The term *pater familias* was so commonly used to refer to a "householder" that it took on the connotation of "an ordinary citizen." *Mater familias* was also commonly used to refer to the "woman of the house" in the sense of the person who directed its domestic affairs. Already the gendered division of household responsibilities (man's realm was public, woman's was private) was evident in the common terminology.

Our ideas of what is and is not a family are products of our society, reflecting dominant ideologies about the social roles of men and women, about their sexuality and sexual behaviour, about fertility and procreation, and about the care and socialization of children. Given that these issues intersect within discussions of the family, any attempt to answer the question, "What is a family?" predictably evokes intense debate.

Source: © Adie Nelson 2002, Department of Sociology, University of Waterloo.

For example, the issue of whether homosexual relationships can constitute a family has considerably agitated people who categorize homosexuality as a "sexual perversion" and view homosexuals as a threat to the normative social order (Allen, 1993; Cossman, 1996). Thus, some analysts maintain that the family must include "adults of *both* sexes, at least two of whom maintain a socially approved sexual relationship, and one or more children of their own, or adopted, of the sexually cohabiting adults" (Murdock, 1949: 1, emphasis added).

Although the first gay "marriage" to be widely publicized in Canada took place in 1977, when two gay men were married by a Unitarian-Universalist minister in Winnipeg (Jackson and Persky, 1982), until relatively recently, Canada has not been guided by a concept of "different, but equal" when it comes to same-sex relationships (Kinsman, 1996). It was only in 1969, following Prime Minister Pierre Trudeau's famous comment that the "state has no place in the bedrooms of the nation," that homosexual acts committed in private, between two consenting adults of at least 21 years of age, were decriminalized. However, until 1995, the "age of consent" for engaging in homosexual acts remained higher than the age at which one could legally engage in heterosexual acts. It is also notable that in 1993, when Gallup Canada first attempted to gauge public attitudes towards same-sex marriages, 76 percent of Canadians expressed opposition. It was only in February 2000 that less than half (48 percent) opposed homosexual marriages. While subsequent polls suggested growing support for same-sex marriages, with up to two-thirds now expressing support of gay marriages, approval varies by age group. For example, among 18- to 29-year-olds, 67 percent express support and 29 percent express opposition. Among people 65 and over, however, the figures are 14 percent and 79 percent, respectively (Bricker and Greenspon, 2001: 267).

Similarly, while the vast majority (91 percent) of Canadians believe that homosexuals should enjoy equal rights in relation to job opportunities, there is less support (61 percent) on the question of whether gay couples should have access to the same benefits as heterosexual couples. Another polling milestone was reached in June 2001, when a Leger marketing poll found majority support for gay adoption. Yet as recently as 1988 only 25 percent of Canadians agreed that gays should be allowed to adopt children (Bricker and Greenspon, 2001: 267).

Further evidence of the shift in thinking towards the question of what is a family is evidenced by changes made to the Canadian census (EGALE, 2001a). While the 1981 Canadian census was the first to report on common-law marriages, the 2001 Canadian census included two questions that recognize same-sex, common-law unions. It also explicitly recognized that children are being raised in same-sex households — even in jurisdictions where provincial or territorial laws do not permit same-sex couples to formally adopt or share guardianship of their children. According to Statistics Canada, a "census family" is now defined as "a now married couple (with or without never-married sons and/or daughters of either or both spouses), a couple living common-law (again, with or without never-married sons and/or daughters of either or both partners), or a lone parent of any marital status, with at least one never-married son or daughter living in the same dwelling." In addition, many rights and obligations that were once exclusively associated with marriage (e.g., the right to spousal support) have now been extended to couples living in marriage-like relationships. In 2000, for example, the federal government of Canada enacted the Modernization of Benefits and Obligations Act "recognizing same-sex couples equally with opposite-sex couples in some 68 federal laws" (EGALE, 2001b). A year earlier, following a Supreme Court of Ontario ruling that an Ontario law excluding gays and lesbians from a definition of common-law couples was unconstitutional, the Ontario government passed an omnibus bill that amended 67 of its laws to include same-sex couples. In June 1999, when the Quebec National

Assembly unanimously passed Bill 32, the Quebec government became the first Canadian province to ensure that same-sex couples would receive all the benefits and responsibilities of opposite-sex couples. Omnibus provincial initiatives have also taken place in Nova Scotia, while some limited laws to extend equality to same-sex couples have been enacted in New Brunswick (addressing spousal support) and Alberta (in relation to step-parent adoption and joint adoption by same-sex partners). In June 1999, the British Columbia government introduced the "Definition of Spouse Amendment," which expanded the definition of a spouse in that province to ensure that "persons of the same gender" would be treated the same as opposite-sex couples in relation to such matters as, for example, wills, estates, and inheritance.

In introducing this change into law, BC Attorney General Ujjal Dosanjh announced that "the legislation is proof that this government is committed to supporting stable family relation-ships, whether they involve traditional families, common-law families, or same-sex relation-ships.... All British Columbians deserve the same rights and benefits in life and death" (EGALE, 1999). British Columbia was also the first province to open the door to same-sex adoption. Yet, in October 2001, the Supreme Court of British Columbia ruled that the rights of same-sex couples to marry under the equality provi-sions of the Canadian Charter of Rights and Freedoms were secondary to the "main purpose of marriage, which is to provide a structure within which to raise children" (quoted in Arnold, 2001). According to this ruling, "same-sex and opposite-sex relationships are, at their core, demonstrably different" and "[t]he objec-tive of limiting marriage to opposite-sex couples is sufficiently important to warrant infringing the rights ... [of same-sex couples]. The gain to society from the preservation of the deep-rooted and fundamental legal institution of opposite-sex marriage outweighs the detrimental effect of the law" (quoted in Arnold, 2001). Earlier, in 1995, the Supreme Court of Canada expressed a similar view and identified procreation as the "ultimate

purpose of marriage" in the case of *Egan vs. Canada*.

While opposite-sex partners are uniquely able to procreate, gays and lesbians can also become parents in a variety of ways. One study finds that about one in five gay men and a third of lesbians have been married and that some have children from those marriages (Harry, 1983). The new reproductive technologies have also influenced gay and lesbian parenting with artificial insemi-nation by donor sperm. This innovation is largely responsible for the "lesbian baby boom" since the mid-1970s (Taylor, 1997: 75). In an attempt to link the baby genetically to both female partners, one partner in a lesbian couple may be inseminated with the sperm of a male relative of the other partner (Salholz, 1990). The new reproductive technologies have not only resulted in increasing numbers of lesbian co-parents but also, albeit less commonly, children born to gay biological fathers and surrogate mothers. Science may also hold additional breakthroughs for gay couples. For example, in September 2000, newspaper headlines reported that gay male couples may, in the near future, be able to sire "motherless" children through cell nuclear replacement, a technique originally designed to treat infertility and metabolic disor-ders. This procedure allows scientists to "replace the nucleus from the egg of a female donor with the nucleus from a sperm cell. The resulting 'male egg,' which would contain only male DNA, would then be fertilized in vitro by sperm from another man and implanted in the womb of a surrogate mother who would carry the child to term" (Honore, 2000).

Noting that heterosexual couples who intend to remain childless are not legally barred from marrying and that many gays and lesbians are already parenting children, Martha Bailey (2000: 20) maintains that "extending marital rights and obligations, or even marital status, to same-sex couples will not derail the state objective of encouraging procreation." In general, those who favour the legalization of same-sex marriage maintain that granting gays and lesbians the right to marry is important both in practical and symbolic terms. Beyond the various economic and practical advantages that marriage confers, it is anticipated that the right to legally marry would promote social acceptance and function as an important source of social support for gays and lesbians as they pursue long-term relationships. As noted by Justice L'Heureux-Dubé in a dissenting opinion in *Egan vs. Canada*:

> Given the marginalized position of homosexuals in society, the metamessage that flows almost invariably from excluding same-sex couples from such an important social institution is essentially that society considers such relationships to be less worthy of respect, concern and consideration than relationships involving members of the opposite sex.

Allowing same-sex couples the right to marry, she maintained, could go a long way toward redressing this situation and "may be of greater value and importance to those affected than any pecuniary gain flowing from that recognition" (quoted in Bailey, 2000: 46).

However, and in marked contrast, for religious fundamentalists and other conservative groups, the case against gay marriage is unambiguous: marriage is a union of opposite-sexed persons and attempts to recognize gay families must be vigorously repelled. Consider, for example, that in June 1999, a Baptist preacher from Topeka, Kansas, announced that he and a group of his followers would be leading a demonstration on the steps of the Supreme Court of Canada to protest its decision to extend the definition of "spouse" to same-sex couples. According to the preacher, Canada had become the "sperm bank of Satan" (Anderssen, 1999). On other occasions, like-minded people have wielded posters proclaiming such sentiments as, "God made Adam and Eve, not Adam and Steve" (Salholz, 1993; Smolowe, 1996). In addition, not all gay activists support the legalization of same-sex marriage. Some oppose same-sex marriage on the grounds that it is too derivative of heterosexual unions and mimics a traditionally

repressive institution that is based on property rights and institutionalized husband–wife roles (Johnson, 1996). It is also argued that legalizing same-sex unions could further stigmatize homosexual relations that occur outside of committed, long-term relationships. Would legalizing same-sex marriages result in further stereotypes of homosexuals and define "good gays" as those who confine themselves to sexual relations with a spouse and who parent children, and "bad gays" as those who do not (Allen, 1997; Cossman, 1996, 1997)? As Michelle Owen (2001: 96) observes, "[W]hen same-sex couples present themselves as 'normal' in pursuit of formal recognition, the polarization of 'family' and 'not family' is effectively cemented." She rhetorically asks, "Are queers 'family'? Could queers be 'family'? Should queers be 'family?'"

In March 2001, the Netherlands became the first jurisdiction in the world to allow same-sex couples to legally marry. Prior to that time, registered partnership legislation (available to both same-sex and opposite-sex couples in that country) made partnership and marriage virtually identical in relation to rights and obligations. In 1989 Denmark was the first country in the world to enact registered partnership legislation for same-sex couples. Registered partnership legislation has also been enacted in Norway, Sweden, Iceland, France, Hungary, Finland, and Germany. In Spain, the 1998 Stable Couples Act extends partial marital rights and obligations to same-sex couples as well as to registered opposite-sex couples. In the United States, legislative reactions to the issue of same-sex marriage have been mixed. In 1996, the US Congress passed and President Clinton signed the Defense of Marriage Act, a federal statute declaring marriage to be a "legal union of one man and one woman," denying gay couples many of the civil advantages of marriage, and relieving states of the obligation to grant reciprocity, or "full faith and credit" to marriages performed in another state. As a result of the Defense of Marriage Act, 35 states had by 2003 passed laws to ban same-sex marriage and block out-of-state marriage licences obtained by gay or lesbian couples. Other states tried to pass such legislation but failed. In 1998, Hawaii and Alaska held constitutional referenda on whether or not to amend their state constitutions to continue the exclusion of same-sex couples from legal marriages. In both cases, voters elected to do so. However, in what seems an attempt to arrive at a compromise, Hawaii enacted a "reciprocal beneficiaries" law that grants same-sex couples, as well as others (excluding heterosexual couples) who are not legally allowed to marry (e.g., two sisters, a widowed mother, and her unmarried son) to register as a domestic partnership and entitles them to a limited range of marital rights and obligations.

As of the time of writing (September 2003), Canada seems poised to follow the path established by the Netherlands and Belgium and become the third country in the world to recognize same-sex marriages. In June 2002, in an historic first, the adoption of Bill 84 in Quebec extended full parental rights to homosexual couples. It also gave same-sex couples who entered into a "civil union" the same status and obligations as heterosexual married couples (Seguin, 2002). A year later, the Ontario Court of Appeals struck down the common-law definition of marriage as "the union of one man and one woman," reformulated it as "the voluntary union for life of two persons," and ordered that this new definition take effect immediately. In ruling in favour of the recognition of same-sex marriage, Ontario became the first Canadian province in which gay and lesbian couples could legally marry. Shortly thereafter, the federal government announced that it would not appeal the decision of this court nor other, similar rulings in British Columbia and Quebec that declared bans on same-sex marriage to be unconstitutional. In a statement released to the press on June 17, 2003, Prime Minister Jean Chrétien announced: "[W]e will be proposing legislation that will protect the right of churches and religious organizations to sanctify marriage as they define it. At the same time, we will ensure that our legislation includes

and legally recognizes the union of same-sex couples" (in Lunman, 2003). Justice Minister Martin Cauchon additionally declared that the federal government was committed to drafting this legislation, referring it to the Supreme Court and presenting it before the House of Commons for a free vote as expeditiously as possible. He said, "It's a great day for Canadians ... I'm very proud to be part of this country" (in Lunman, 2003).

As might be expected, however, not all Canadians have demonstrated equal levels of enthusiasm. The Alberta Tory government has already announced that it will challenge the proposed changes to the definition of marriage. This response is, perhaps, predictable enough, given that Canada has a divided jurisdiction in matters of family law and, that under the Constitution Act, the provinces and the federal government share the responsibility for marriage and marriage-like relationships. Thus, while marriage and divorce (including custody maintenance upon divorce) fall under federal jurisdiction, provincial laws govern such matters as adoption, matrimonial property disputes, guardianship, and — most importantly in the present context — the licensing and formation of a valid marriage ceremony. As Alberta's Justice Minister Dave Hancock has pointedly remarked, "Can we reredefine marriage? Probably not, that's in the federal jurisdiction.... Can we say that we will not recognize marriage in Alberta unless it adheres to the 'opposite-sex' definition that we have in our act? Yes, I believe that we can" (in Lunman, 2003). Alberta Premier Ralph Klein has also asserted that his government will invoke the "notwithstanding clause" (Section 33) of the Constitution to protect against any challenges to provincial responsibility to recognize marriages. Although rarely invoked since the Canadian Charter of Rights and Freedoms became law in 1982, the "notwithstanding clause" allows Parliament or a provincial legislature to expressly exempt a law for a five-year renewable term from the Charter guarantees of fundamental freedoms, legal rights, and equality rights. Opposition to extending marriage rights to same-sex couples has also been expressed by the Canadian Alliance, some Liberal backbenchers and Tory MPs, and an assortment of self-described "concerned citizens" on radio talk shows and in "Letters to the Editor" across Canada. For example, a lengthy "Comment" attacking the federal government's decision appeared in Canada's national newspaper, *The Globe and Mail*, on June 18, 2003. Its highly placed signatories included the archbishop of Halifax; the Anglican bishop of the diocese of Saskatchewan; the general counsel/public affairs of the Seventh Day Adventist Church in Canada; the president of Pauktuutit, Inuit Women's Association of Canada; the president of Focus on the Family Canada; the president of Nunavut Tunngavik Inc.; the director of the Islamic Society of North America; and academics from seven Canadian universities. The statement concluded, "This remedy is not in continuity with the history, tradition and values of Canadian society.... Canadians ... should resist any approach that would undermine an institution so essential to the well-being of Canadians past, present, and future ("Don't Kiss Off Marriage," 2003).

It is evident that same-sex unions challenge conventional thinking on the family. Reflective of this, until relatively recently, researchers studying families tended either to ignore gay families or to depict them as profoundly pathological. Although in recent years there has been a knowledge explosion in this area (e.g., Arnup, 1995, 1997; O'Brien and Weir, 1999; Weston, 1991), Karen Williams (1995: 98–99) observes a counter-tendency to "present fairy tale versions of our lives in which we are all happy individuals, partners and family members." Research on gay and lesbian families in Canada has largely tended to draw upon small, nonrepresentative samples of white, middle-class, well-educated respondents (e.g., Nelson, 1993). However, it seems that the families of gays and lesbians may be most remarkable for their utter ordinariness. For example, studies find no significant differences between the children of gay and lesbian parents and children of heterosexual parents (Patterson, 1997, 2001; Flaks et al., 1995; Allen and Demo, 1995). Similarly, despite research that proclaims lesbian couples the most egalitarian of all forms of intimate partnerships (Blumstein and Schwartz, 1983; Eldridge and Gilbert, 1990), it appears that these relationships are not immune to the violent and abusive behaviour that occurs among heterosexual and gay male couples (Coleman, 1994; Waterman et al.). Paralleling the patterns found in heterosexual relationships, violence in lesbian relationships also tends to increase in both frequency and severity over time, to be associated with the dynamics of power and dependency (Renzetti and Miley, 1996) and the use of alcohol or other drugs (Lockhart et al., 1994; Schilt, Lie, and Montagne, 1990).

There can be no doubt that same-sex families challenge many of our taken-for-granted assumptions. They challenge the commonsense assumption that human beings have a heterosexual destiny and that the ways in which most of us conduct our sexual affairs are both natural and morally right. They challenge classification systems surrounding the family and marriage, gender, love, and sexual experiences. Said differently, same-sex families remind us that human behaviour is not as simple as those who believe in a "natural order" suggest. It is evident that the term "family" has become a fluid concept.

REFERENCES

Abbott, Pamela, and Claire Wallace. (1992). *The Family and the New Right*. London: Pluto.

Allen, Carol. (1993). "Who Gets to Be Family? Some thoughts on the Lesbian and Gay Fight for Equality." In Linda Carty, ed., *And Still We Rise: Feminist Political Mobilizing in Contemporary Canada* (pp. 101–07). Toronto: Women's Press.

Allen, Katherine R. (1997). "Lesbian and Gay Families." In Terry Arendell, ed., *Contemporary*

Parenting: Challenges and Issues (pp. 196–218). Thousand Oaks, CA: Sage.

Allen, Katherine R., and David H. Demo. (1995). "The Families of Lesbians and Gay Men: A New Frontier in Family Research." *Journal of Marriage and the Family, 57* (1) (Feb.): 111–27.

Anderssen, Erin. (1999). "Gay-Bashing Preacher Calls Off Protest," *Globe and Mail* (June 29). On the World Wide Web at http://www.egale.ca/archives/press/9906299gm.htm.

Arnold, Tom. (2001). "B.C. Court Says No to Gay Marriage," *National Post* (October 4): A1, A15.

Arnup, Katherine, ed. (1995). *Lesbian Parenting: Living with Pride and Prejudice.* Charlottetown: Gynergy Books.

Arnup, Katherine. (1997). "In the Family Way: Lesbian Mothers in Canada." In Meg Luxton, ed., *Feminism and Families: Critical Policies and Changing Practices* (pp. 80–97). Halifax: Fernwood Publishing.

Bailey, Martha. (2000). *Marriage and Marriage-Like Relationships.* On the World Wide Web at http://www.lcc.gc.ca/cgi-bin/repere_en.c...y%2C+Martha&language=en&range=1&numdoc.

Blumstein, P. and P. Schwartz. (1983). *American Couples: Work, Money, Sex.* New York: William Morrow.

Bricker, Darrell, and Edward Greenspon. (2001). *Searching for Certainty: Inside the New Canadian Mindset.* Toronto: Doubleday Canada.

Coleman, V.E. (1994). "Lesbian Battering: The Relationship between Personality and the Perpetuation of Violence," *Violence and Victims, 9* (2): 139–52.

Conway, John F. (1990). *The Canadian Family in Crisis.* Toronto: James Lorimer and Company.

Cossman, Brenda. (1996). "Same-Sex Couples and the Politics of Family Status." In Janine Brodie, ed., *Women and Canadian Public Policy* (pp. 223–78). Toronto: Harcourt Brace and Company.

Cossman, Brenda. (1997). "Family Inside/Out." In Meg Luxton, ed., *Feminism and Families: Critical Policies and Changing Practices* (pp. 124–41). Halifax: Fernwood Publishing.

"Don't Kiss Off Marriage." (2003). *The Globe and Mail,* June 18: A19.

EGALE. (2001a). "Press Release: 2001 Census to Recognize Same-Sex Couples." May 10. On the World Wide Web at http://www.egale.ca/pressrel/010510-e.html.

EGALE. (2001b). "Census Kit." On the World Wide Web at http://www.egale.ca/documents/census-kit-e.htm.

EGALE. (1999). "BC Introduces New Same Sex Laws, Commits to Omnibus Legislation." (July 9). On the World Wide Web at http://www.egale.ca/pressrel/990709.htm.

Eldridge, N.S., and L.A. Gilbert. (1990). "Correlates of Relationship Satisfaction in Lesbian Couples." *Psychology of Women Quarterly, 14* (1) (March): 43–62.

Flaks, D.K., I. Ficher, F. Masterpasqua, and G. Joseph. (1993). "Lesbians Choosing Motherhood: A Comparative Study of Lesbians and Heterosexual Parents and Their Children," *Developmental Psychology, 31* (1): 105–14.

Gavigan, Shelly A.M. (1997). "Feminism, Familial Ideology and Family Law." In Meg Luxton, ed., *Feminism and Families: Critical Policies and Changing Practices* (pp. 98–123). Halifax: Fernwood Publishing.

Gottlieb, Beatrice. (1993). *The Family in the Western World from the Black Death to the Industrial Age.* New York: Oxford University Press.

Harry, Joseph. (1983). "Gay Male and Lesbian Relationships." In Eleanor D. Macklin and Roger H. Rubin, eds., *Contemporary Families and Alternative Lifestyles: Handbook on Research and Theory* (pp. 216–34). Newbury Park, CA: Sage.

Honore, Carl. (2000). "'Male Egg' Couple Enable Two Men to Conceive a Child," *National Post* (September 26): A1, A12.

Jackson, E., and S. Persky. (1982). *Flaunting It: A Decade of Gay Journalism from the Body Politic.* Toronto: Pink Triangle Press.

Johnson, Fenton. (1996). "Wedded to an Illusion: Do Gays and Lesbians Really Want the Right to Marry?" *Harper's* (November): 41–50.

Kinsman, Gary. (1996). *The Regulation of Desire: Homo and Hetero Sexualities,* 2nd edition. Montreal: Black Rose Books.

Lockhart, L.L., B.W. White, V. Causby, and A. Issac. (1994). "Letting Out The Secret: Violence in Lesbian Relationships," *Journal of Interpersonal Violence, 9* (4): 469–92.

Lunman, Kim. (2003). "Ottawa Backs Gay Marriage," *The Globe and Mail,* June 18: A1, A8.

Murdock, George. (1949). *Social Structure.* New York: Free Press.

Nelson, Fiona. (1993). *Lesbian Motherhood: An Exploration of Canadian Lesbian Families.* Toronto: University of Toronto Press.

O'Brien, Carol Anne, and Lorna Weir. (1999). "Lesbian and Gay Men Inside and Outside Families." In Nancy Mandell and Ann Duffy, eds., *Canadian Families: Diversity, Conflict and Change* (pp. 111–39). Toronto: Harcourt Brace.

Owen, Michelle K. (2001). "'Family' as a Site of Contestation: Queering the Normal or Normalizing the Queer?" In Terry Goldie, ed., *In a Queer Country: Gay & Lesbian Studies in the Canadian Context* (pp. 86–102). Vancouver: Arsenal Pulp Press.

Patterson, Charlotte. (1997). "Children of Lesbian and Gay Parents: Summary of Research Findings." In A. Sullivan, ed., *Same-Sex Marriage: Pro and Con* (pp. 146–54). New York: Vintage Books.

Patterson, Charlotte. (2001). "Family Relationships of Lesbian and Gay Men." In Robert M. Milardo, ed., *Understanding Families into the New Millennium: A Decade in Review* (pp. 271–68). Minneapolis, MN: National Council on Family Relations.

Renzetti, Claire M., and Charles H. Miley. (1996). *Violence in Gay and Lesbian Domestic Partnerships.* New York: Haworth Press.

Salholz, Eloise. (1992). "The Future of Gay America." In Ollie Pocs, ed., *Human Sexuality 92/93.* Guilford, CT: Duskin.

———. (1993). "For Better or For Worse," *Newsweek* (May 24): 69.

Schilit, R., G. Lie and M. Montagne (1990). "Substance Abuse as a Correlate of Violence in Intimate Lesbian Relationships," *Journal of Homosexuality, 9*: 5–65.

Seguin, Rheal. (2002). "Gay Couples in Quebec Get Full Parental Rights," *Globe and Mail,* June 8: A1, A7.

Smolowe, Jill. (1996). "The Unmarrying Kind," *Time,* April 29: 68–69.

Taylor, Ronald L. (1997). "Who's Parenting? Trends and Patterns." In Terry Arendell, ed., *Contemporary Parenting: Challenges and Issues* (pp. 68–91). Thousand Oaks, CA: Sage.

Waterman, C., L. Dawson, and M. Bologna. (1989). "Sexual Coercion in Gay and Lesbian Relationships: Predictors and Implications for Support Services." *Journal of Sex Research,* 26: 118–24.

Weston, Kath. (1991). *Families We Choose: Lesbians, Gays, Kinship.* New York: Columbia University Press.

Williams, Karen. (1995). "The Good Mother." In Katherine Arnup, ed., *Lesbian Parenting: Living with Pride and Prejudice* (pp. 98–110). Charlottetown, PEI: Gynergy Books.

Chapter 18

The Social Context of Medicalized Childbirth

DIANA WORTS

BONNIE FOX

GIVING BIRTH: TWO WOMEN'S STORIES

Meredith gripped the edges of her hospital bed, every muscle in her body tightened in defence. Another contraction. This was more than she could bear. For hours now, they had been coming one on top of another. And they hurt. They hurt more than she had ever imagined possible. She wanted an epidural to take away the pain.[1] But the nurse had told her to be patient; the anesthesiologist was tied up in surgery. Meredith was indignant. This was inhumane! Surely she should not have to endure more.

Hugh stood by the bed, uncertain how to help. "Try to slow down your breathing; look at me," he offered. The room was tiny and airless. There was barely space for the bed and intravenous pole, and even less room for the couple to maneuver. And now a resident had come in, wanting to take a medical history. It was all too much. Where *was* the anesthesiologist?

Meredith had been in labour for twelve hours. The first contractions had wakened her at 2 a.m. that morning. At 7 a.m. she and Hugh had left for the hospital. But shortly after their arrival things had taken a wrong turn. Tests had indicated the baby might be too large for Meredith's pelvis; and this raised concerns about its well-being. Although the hospital staff had not seemed overly concerned, Meredith's anxiety levels had

shot up. The doctor on call had broken the "bag of waters" surrounding the baby to assess the situation.[2] To everyone's relief, the fluid had been clear; the baby was not in serious trouble. However, the procedure had almost immediately accelerated the pace of the labour, producing very strong contractions with little space between them. Meredith had been unprepared for any of this. It had left her feeling drained, physically and emotionally. Now all she wanted was something to take away the pain.

After what seemed an eternity, the anesthesiologist arrived. The epidural was set up with some difficulty; but it was not all Meredith had hoped. Almost immediately she found she was numb — and immobilized — from her upper chest to her toes.[3] She felt cold, and began to shake uncontrollably. Although she knew that many women experience some trembling immediately after receiving epidural anesthesia, her reaction was more violent than most. The nurse brought her a warm blanket, but still the shaking wouldn't stop.

By 10 p.m. that evening Meredith had progressed little more than halfway through her labour.[4] She was suffering from heartburn and nausea.[5] Her legs were immobilized, one arm was completely numb, and the other was hampered by a blood pressure cuff. She felt helpless. By 3 a.m. Meredith and Hugh had seen three shifts of nurses. A couple from their prenatal classes had come and gone, baby in hand. And still, Meredith was not ready to deliver.

Finally, at 5 a.m. in the morning, Meredith was examined and told it was time to start pushing her baby out into the world. Still attached to a monitor and intravenous pole, and with an epidural catheter taped to her back, she found it extremely difficult to co-ordinate the massive effort needed. After an hour and a half with no progress she was exhausted and declared she could go no further. She was moved to a delivery room where, disoriented and panicky, she hauled herself awkwardly onto the table. The doctor informed her that the baby was still too high in her pelvis for a forceps delivery; the only option remaining was a cesarean section.[6] Meredith lost whatever shreds of composure remained. All that work, all that pain, all that worrying, and now the baby was to be born by surgery after all. What had it all been for?

The medical staff prepared Meredith for the cesarean, with Hugh standing by. Weighing 3.7 kg, Laura was born about half an hour later. The baby was in perfect health; Meredith, however, did not fare as well. She was left with pain in her neck and jaw from the uncontrollable shaking, an infection that required treatment with antibiotics, an incision that caused her pain for several weeks, and a legacy of anger over the way things had gone that took months to heal. In the postpartum ward she had difficulty holding Laura, and could not get the baby to nurse properly. From Meredith's perspective, this was, quite simply, a birth in which "everything that could possibly go wrong did go wrong."

In a nearby hospital, Celia stood in the shower adjoining her labour room, her husband Paul waiting patiently outside the door. For two hours she let the water run over her, breathing deeply, relaxing her muscles, and calming her fears. Celia wanted very much to give birth without medical intervention. She knew that where such procedures are concerned "one thing often leads to another," in a cascade of interventions that may ultimately compromise the well-being of mother and/or baby. She felt prepared

to work with her body, and to trust that her labour would follow its own course safely.

It was nearly two weeks past Celia's due date. The previous day her doctor had recommended the topical application of a hormonal preparation to "get things started."[7] But on examining her and finding that dilation was already underway, he had decided this was no longer appropriate. There had been some worrying signs, though. The baby was big and its head was high (meaning the labour might be long); and the length of time that had passed since Celia's due date meant the baby's health might be at risk.[8] A full-scale induction — the stimulation of labour using intravenous chemical hormones — had been scheduled for the following day.

Celia had not looked forward to the possibility of an induced labour. She wanted to be in control of her mental and physical capacities. She did not relish the thought of being confined to bed by monitoring equipment and/or an epidural, or of being held to a strict time line.[9] But all these interventions were likely to accompany an induced labour.

Much to her relief, Celia had gone into labour on her own at midnight the night before the scheduled induction. The contractions had been strong from the start, but walking and deep breathing had helped. After a few hours at home, Celia and Paul had headed to the hospital. The contractions, however, had stopped on their arrival. Celia had been disappointed, thinking her labour would be induced after all. But the attending physician had been sympathetic; knowing Celia's feelings about induction, he had suggested she take a long shower to "think it over."

Now at 8 a.m., Celia stepped out of the shower. As she did so, the "bag of waters" surrounding the baby ruptured spontaneously, and contractions began again. Over the next four hours, as the labour increased in intensity, Celia moved from pacing the floor of the labour room to sitting in a lazy-boy chair. All the while she did deep breathing through her contractions, and kept her eyes closed to help maintain her concentration. It took a great deal of energy to stay with the contractions, but she felt up to the task. Paul stayed in the room with her, waiting, watching, and comforting by his presence.

At midday, the labour moved into high gear. Celia began to use shallow breathing to get through the contractions. Paul massaged her hands and feet to help her relax. The contractions were extremely painful, but Celia maintained her focus and took each one as it came. The nursing staff entered the room from time to time. Seeing the couple working together, they left quietly. No doctors examined Celia internally. No one told her how far she had (or had not) progressed. As Celia worked with the contractions, she felt her labour was progressing just as it should.

By 3 p.m. in the afternoon the contractions were strong enough that Celia felt "about ready to jump off a bridge." The doctor arrived and found she was fully dilated. However, as the baby's head was still high, he suggested Celia have an epidural and get some rest, and that they reassess the situation in a couple of hours. Celia was reluctant, having come this far without medical assistance. So the doctor suggested, once again, that she take a shower and give it some thought. This time Celia stood not more than ten minutes under the running water before she began to feel an urge to push with each contraction. This, she knew, was a sign that the baby had moved down.

Celia got out of the shower and was examined. This time, her baby was indeed ready to be born. She moved to the labour bed and, squeezing Paul's hand hard, pushed with every ounce of strength she possessed. The baby inched its way down. The doctor applied warm compresses to avoid a tear or the need for a cut to enlarge the opening.[10] After forty-five minutes, Melissa — a healthy 4.1 kg — emerged with a wail. She was placed on Celia's belly for a few minutes, then wrapped and placed in her arms. Admiring her daughter, Celia felt both proud and fortunate. Three times she had faced the prospect of a medicalized birth and three times she had been able to work with her body to avoid it. She felt strong and ready to go forward into the future.

THE CRITIQUE OF MEDICALIZED CHILDBIRTH

Celia and Meredith are both participants in a study of first-time parents.[11] Their stories chronicle their passage into motherhood—an event that many have argued has major social implications for women (Oakley 1980a, 1980b; Martin 1987; Davis-Floyd 1992). But the implications of Meredith's and Celia's birth stories are very different. Meredith felt both physically injured and emotionally shattered by her experience. Celia felt energized and empowered. For Meredith, labour was simply impossibly hard work; for Celia it was much, much more. Labour "worked" for Celia, but not for Meredith.

Observers have drawn on just this kind of contrast to develop a critique of medicalized childbirth in Western societies. Writers from various academic disciplines — from medicine (Tew 1995; Chalmers, Enkin, and Keirse 1989) and public health (Brown et al. 1994), to psychology (Ball 1987; Collins et al. 1993), sociology (Oakley 1980a, 1980b; Graham and Oakley 1981; Katz Rothman 1982, 1989), and anthropology (Jordan 1978; Romalis 1981; Kay 1982; MacCormack 1981; Martin 1987; Michaelson 1988; Sargent and Stark 1989; Davis-Floyd 1990, 1992, 1994) — have contributed to the critique. They have been joined by childbirth educators (Kitzinger, 1972; Barclay, Andre, and Glover 1989; Chamberlain et al. 1991; Priya 1992), policy analysts (Eakins 1986), and the popular press (Arms 1981; Mitford 1992). Despite differing backgrounds and orientations, these authors unanimously criticize the extent to which, and the manner in which, medical professionals exercise control over the birth process — and not incidentally, over women — in Western society. Medicalized childbirth, they suggest, is both evidence of, and a contributing factor to, women's subordinate position in society.

In general, the critics argue that medicalization decreases the birthing woman's control over her own body and its functions, and alienates her from a potentially empowering experience. They suggest that medical professionals, acting on a definition of childbirth as hazardous, intervene in what is essentially a natural process. They argue, further, that childbirth in a hospital setting separates the physical from the emotional, social, psychological, and spiritual dimensions of the process, and hence addresses only one facet of what should be a holistic event. Finally, they point out that medicalization has led to a shift in the focus of concerns from the woman to the unborn baby: success is equated with the birth of a healthy baby, and the woman's well-being has come to be seen as relatively unimportant.

All this might be well and good if it clearly improved physical outcomes for mothers and babies. However, the critics also cite evidence that modern medicine often falls short of its claims in this regard: improvements in maternal and infant health, they argue, can be traced primarily to more general advances in public health and living standards, while medical interventions are often associated with unnecessary risks to the health and well-being of mother and child (Tew 1995).

Among sociologists, Ann Oakley's (1980a, 1980b, 1984) work has been especially important in developing the critique of medicalized birth. Using postpartum depression as a measure of women's well-being (or lack thereof), Oakley effectively criticizes standard physiological explanations, and relates the condition instead to the amount of medical intervention (i.e., drugs and technology) used during labour and delivery (Oakley 1980b). The problems associated with medically managed births are further elaborated in a more rigorous study by Entwisle and Doering (1981), who find that the most critical aspect of medical intervention, with respect to the woman's feelings about the birth, is whether or not she retains consciousness — and thus a sense of control — through the birthing process.

The issue of women's control over what happens to them during labour and delivery has been at the heart of the critique. Thus, for example, anthropologist Emily Martin (1987) argues that social relations in childbirth increasingly mimic the class relations of industrial production under capitalism: women's bodies are seen as more or less efficient machines, women as unskilled workers, and doctors as managers. The significance of the analogy between birthing women and waged workers lies in the fact that both or little have no control over the production process for which they labour.

THE HISTORY OF MEDICALIZATION, PART 1: MEDICAL CONTROL

Critical historians expand on this analysis by demonstrating that current practices have not always been the preferred way of managing childbirth. They chronicle how a formerly woman-centred event — occurring in the woman's home and attended by a midwife and female friends and relatives — was transformed into an occasion for hospitalization and medical management and control. These writers argue that male medical practitioners wrested control from women, and later secured their position by instituting near-universal hospitalization.

In the United States and Canada, the process by which male doctors displaced female midwives was part of a campaign to attract patients. Because they were unorganized in the early part of the nineteenth century, doctors had to compete in an unregulated marketplace populated by a variety of medical practitioners. Childbirth offered advantages in the struggle to build a clientele: it gave the doctor access to an entire family of potential patients, and entailed the management of a process whose outcome was usually positive regardless of the skills of the attendant (Wertz and Wertz 1979).

As the status of doctors as a group rose over the course of the nineteenth century, these "male midwives" increasingly drew their reputations from their medical training (Donegan 1978; Wertz and Wertz 1979). Their patients' heightened expectations pushed them to "do something" while attending a birth. Intervention typically involved the use of instruments aimed at speeding up the delivery and, later in the century, anesthesia for pain relief (Wertz and Wertz 1979). Unfortunately, strong Victorian norms about modesty prevented doctors from gaining clinical experience in medical school, so the range of their skills was tremendous, and their intervention during birth was often harmful to the woman, the baby, or both (Leavitt 1986).

In Canada, doctors also secured their position by lobbying persistently against the training and registration of midwives through the nineteenth and twentieth centuries (Biggs 1990; LaForce 1990; Arnup 1994: 76). Their campaign was an ideological one that played on prejudices about social class as well as gender: midwives were portrayed as dirty, ignorant, and dangerous, in contrast with the gentlemanly doctors and their "scientific" knowledge (Biggs 1990). In addition, childbirth was increasingly defined as "dangerous," thus requiring a doctor's presence (Biggs 1990; LaForce 1990).[12] Hospitalization followed from this redefinition of birth: in 1926 (the first year statistics were gathered on the subject), fewer than 20 per cent of births took place in hospital, but by 1960 nearly 95 per cent were occurring there (Arnup 1994: 74). Childbirth had become almost exclusively a medical matter, with midwives practising only on the fringes.

During the 1990s, however, pregnant women's options broadened somewhat. By the end of the decade, midwives were being licensed and funded by the provincial health-care systems in Ontario, B.C., and Quebec (Bourgeault 1999).[13]

CHILDBIRTH IN TORONTO TODAY

How typical of childbirth today, then, is Celia's non-medicalized birth? And how typical is Meredith's highly medicalized one? Our in-depth interviews with forty Toronto-area women suggest that medically managed births are the norm for first-time mothers. Births like Celia's, on the other hand, are rare.[14] Well over

half the women interviewed had their labour artificially stimulated with oral or intravenous medication, and/or by artificial rupture of the membranes. These techniques — however useful — bring with them constant monitoring, restricted mobility, and very strong contractions, usually requiring the use of epidural anesthesia.

For the vast majority of the women in the study, the baby's heart rate and their own contractions were monitored electronically as long as the woman laboured in the hospital. Most were monitored using belts around their abdomen. In a few cases, an internal clip was attached directly to the baby's scalp.[15] Either way, continuous electronic monitoring — in contrast to intermittent ultrasonic or manual techniques — restricted the woman's movements and often meant she was confined to bed.

The vast majority of these first-time mothers were also given epidural anesthesia — likewise associated with constant monitoring and restricted or complete loss of mobility. A few were given Demerol, a narcotic used to manage pain in early labour. And a couple were given sleeping pills to allow them to rest in early labour.

Most women in the study were happy with their decision to use pain medication. Some, however, suffered adverse reactions, particularly to epidural anesthesia (e.g., shaking, vomiting, difficulty breathing), and/or got more than they bargained for (e.g., immobility and numbness, and difficulty coordinating pushing during the actual birth). In a few cases women got less than they bargained for: the procedure gave them little pain relief. Some women — those who were discovered immediately *after* the administration of an epidural to be ready or nearly ready to deliver — felt in retrospect that if they had been assessed more carefully they would have refused the medication.

About a quarter of the women gave birth with the help of forceps or a vacuum extractor — both mechanical aids to delivery. Births by these methods were preceded by an episiotomy, or incision to enlarge the outlet of the birth canal. A couple of women with episiotomies also tore (in one case, a third-degree tear required forty stitches). Among those who did not require mechanical assistance delivering their babies, a similar number either sustained a small tear (usually requiring minimal repair and healing with little difficulty) or were given an episiotomy. At least one woman felt the episiotomy was "the worst part" of giving birth. In several cases the procedure was carried out without consulting the woman. For most, the episiotomy was a source of considerable pain — and occasionally infection, and/or subsequent restitching — for several weeks postpartum.

Fifteen per cent of the women in the study gave birth by cesarean section. In one case this was planned in advance because the baby was in a breech (head-up) position. In the remaining cases the decision was made after many hours of labour, either because the baby was in trouble (rare), or because the baby did not descend through the birth canal after an extended period of pushing.

"Natural" births — those not involving the use of pain medication, artificial stimulation, assisted delivery, or surgery — were rare among the women interviewed. Only four women gave birth in this way. In addition, one woman had a straightforward labour in which the only intervention was a low-level from of induction — the topical application of a hormonal preparation to initiate contractions. And for another woman the only form of medical management was electronic fetal monitoring — which she appreciated for the information it gave her on the strength of the contractions and the baby's condition. One woman had no intervention until the last moments, when a vacuum extractor was used to speed up the delivery. A couple of women had only epidural anesthesia administered very near the end of their labours.

The general picture, then, is one in which some form of medical intervention/assistance is the norm for first-time mothers. This picture contrasts with the stated hopes and expectations of the forty participants in the first-time parenting study, prior to giving birth. During pregnancy, ten of the women interviewed expressed a strong desire for a "natural" birth. Only two wanted medically managed births, in both cases to manage pain. The remainder of the women in the study anticipated being flexible in the face of the unknown — though most hoped for minimal intervention. The disjuncture between what is hoped for and what is delivered suggests that the contrast between stories like Meredith's and Celia's captures something real, and that the critics do indeed raise important questions about the medical management of childbirth today.

At the same time, though, the results of some empirical research suggest that the critique needs further development. For example, apparently only middle-class women desire a sense of control over what happens during the birth. For working-class women, control means a variety of things — control over pain according to one study (Nelson 1983) and control over their own behaviour according to another (McIntosh 1989). Other research shows that, although some women are alienated by their experience of medicalized birth, many women across social classes welcome medical intervention, if not management, and are quite satisfied with their hospital deliveries (Gordon 1988; McIntosh 1989; Sargent and Stark 1989; Davis-Floyd 1992; Lazarus 1994).

WOMEN'S RESPONSES TO MEDICALIZED BIRTH

How did the women in the first-time parenting study react to the medical management they encountered? Many were, in contrast to Meredith, quite satisfied with their medicalized births — even when they had hoped to give birth "naturally." One reason for a shift in attitude was that all these women identified very closely with their babies' interests. This was especially evident where monitoring procedures indicated that the baby might be at risk. Judy, who sought and received pain relief during labour, and who ultimately gave birth by cesarean section, reflected afterward on her experience, "There's nothing wrong with him, so it's perfect for me. That's all I wanted. I didn't care how he came out." Joanne also gave birth by cesarean section, after a lengthy struggle to avoid medical intervention. Her concern for the well-being of her baby — despite her own strong desires for a non-medicalized birth — prompted her to comment, "You just want to have your baby. And it's like, 'well, do what you have to do.'" Sue, who welcomed an epidural during labour, but wound up with a forceps delivery as a result, also understood her experience in terms of the baby's needs: "To be honest, I don't think at the time I really cared. I think it was just, 'make sure the baby's okay, and get her out.'"

Negative reactions to medicalized births tended to occur some days or weeks later, among women with healthy babies. Just over half of the women in the study were angry, upset, or had other negative feelings about their experience of labour and delivery. (Two-fifths of the women felt positive, and for two women feelings about the birth were overshadowed by subsequent medical emergencies involving the mother or child.) Some of the negative reactions centred around reasons that were consistent with the critique of medicalized childbirth: loss of control (even among women for whom staying in control had not been a high priority) or negative reactions to specific forms of medical intervention (e.g., epidurals that numbed all sensation, monitoring that restricted movement, or augmentation that made the contractions intolerable). Natalie, who had an epidural despite her desire to avoid intervention, said afterward that "I don't really feel like I had a vaginal birth because it was nothing…. I feel like I missed something." Zoe, who had no firm birth-related goals beforehand, reflected afterward that "I think being hooked up to all this equipment and not being able to walk or get up made me feel very vulnerable and very frustrated."

On the other hand, several women reacted negatively to events not necessarily caused by medical management (e.g., long labours or a poorly positioned baby). And more important, nearly a quarter complained that medical staff had *failed* to intervene soon enough (or at all) to help them manage their pain. Carla felt abandoned by hospital staff who "totally lose the fact that there's actually some pain involved here." She "didn't like the experience at all because I felt like I was at their mercy." Similarly, Esther felt that medical personnel were unresponsive during her long and painful labour: "My experience at the hospital has been that they do things which cause you pain, and then they wait a very long time to give you pain relief." Trish gave birth without medical intervention (having gone into the experience with a flexible attitude). However, in the weeks afterward she appeared to be suffering from depression, which she attributed to the pain she had endured in labour.

Women who reacted positively to their birth experience sometimes did so for reasons consistent with the critique of medicalization — for example, those who cited the absence of pharmaceutical or technological intervention, or the ability to stay in control. Nora, who had planned a home birth, found her hospital birth "great" because "I really felt a lot of control all the way through, and I think one of my biggest fears about hospitals was not being in control…. I felt like I was making the decisions."

Some, however, reacted positively for altogether different reasons. Among them were women who highlighted the absence of pain, and the tremendous support they received from those around them, even where there was medical intervention. Marie, whose primary goal during labour was to avoid pain, said afterward that because her birth was "pain-free," "it was wonderful; it was great." Karen had wanted to avoid intervention, but wound up with an epidural. She commented afterwards that, "I now pray to the epidural god." Nora, who had a positive experience despite hospitalization and medical intervention in what was to have been a home birth, attributed her response not only to the feeling that she had "done everything I could" to avoid intervention, but also to having been surrounded throughout her long labour by a "wonderful circle of friends."

Thus, the women in this study reacted in a variety of ways to the experience of giving birth. Moreover, many of their reactions suggest that the critical understanding of medicalized birth as alienated and alienating may be an oversimplification. Their stories suggest that the absence of medical intervention does not necessarily make for a positive and empowering experience; neither does medical intervention necessarily leave women feeling alienated and disempowered. The question we must ask, then, is what factors beyond the absence of medical control *per se* might make labour "work" for women.

THE HISTORY OF MEDICALIZATION, PART II: WOMEN'S AGENCY

While most histories of the medicalizaion of childbirth argue that current arrangements have been forced on women — that male doctors systematically took over control of the process from birthing women and their female attendants — the work of Judith Leavitt (1986) presents a somewhat different view. Leavitt argues that women's agency was central to the process of medicalization, and that in fact many of the changes addressed women's needs and desires at the time. Moreover, according to Leavitt, doctors gained control over childbirth only gradually, and not until it moved into the hospital setting. Prior to that time, there is evidence that many doctors were critical of unnecessary intervention, and that when they did intervene it was primarily out of concern for the woman they were attending, rather than for other reasons. In short, Leavitt suggests that the dynamics of medicalization are not reducible to a collective desire on the part of medical men to control access to birthing women.

Instead, a number of factors appear to have been at work in the transformation of childbirth. First, the nineteenth-century reality was that women approached the event with apprehension and fear because it was indeed hazardous. One in thirty women died from complications arising during the birth, and many others were left permanently disabled (Leavitt 1986: 25).[16] Women coped with the threat of childbearing by surrounding themselves with women friends and relatives, who provided support and assistance, and by engaging the services of an experienced female midwife for information and help. In the process, new mothers were "brought to bed" for three to four weeks — sometimes more — by women who assumed responsibility for the household throughout the period of confinement (Leavitt 1986). Wertz and Wertz (1979) use the term "social childbirth" to describe this way of handling the event.

During the nineteenth century, however, women's attitudes toward the risks associated with childbearing began changing. Instead of simply accepting "fate" with respect to life and death, they increasingly believed people could shape and even control their destinies (Wertz and Wertz 1979). Thus they searched for ways to improve outcomes in childbirth. According to Leavitt (1986: 38),

> Women garnered support from their networks of companions, but they continued to fear childbirth because of the possibilities of death or disability. It was precisely these fears that led women away from traditional birthing patterns to a long search for safer and less painful childbirths.

As a result, women invited male doctors to attend their births. They believed their training had taught them more about handling problems than the training of female midwives (Donegan 1978; Wertz and Wertz 1979; Leavitt, 1986). Nevertheless, when a male doctor attended a birth, the woman giving birth and the women surrounding her retained control over the doctor's actions: he could intervene only with their consent, and the procedures used (e.g., anesthesia or forceps) were subject to the women's approval (Wertz and Wertz 1979; Leavitt 1986). Doctors who did not accommodate women's wishes during childbirth "risked losing patients and damaging their reputations among a whole community of women" (Leavitt 1986: 59).[17]

Another key reason women chose medical attendants was that they offered the promise of pain relief. Physicians increasingly used chloroform and ether through the latter half of the nineteenth century and into the twentieth century. But women themselves were instrumental in defining their goal as a painless birth (Leavitt 1986). This is clearest in the struggle that took place early in this century around "twilight sleep" (the use of scopolamine to permit women to labour and deliver "asleep," and to wake with no memory of the pain). Upper- and middle-class women fought for this kind of birth, while doctors resisted. Advocates of twilight sleep were often feminists seeking some measure of control over their labours and deliveries (Leavitt 1986). Because doctors were dependent upon women's invitations to attend births, they could ignore women's wishes "only at great risk to their own practice" (Leavitt, 1986: 140).

A major consequence of the demand for physician assistance, however, was to change the definition of birth: once a normal physiological process, childbirth was now an illness requiring a doctor, hospitalization, and medical procedures. This change ultimately shifted control from the birthing woman to the doctor in attendance (Leavitt 1986).

Although women initially sought medical care during labour and delivery in an attempt to reduce the risks to their lives and health, those who gave birth in hospital during the latter part of the nineteenth century were in fact more likely to die or suffer injury as a result. Doctors understood the iatrogenic (i.e., doctor-caused) nature of the infections that often took women's lives (Wertz and Wertz, 1979). By the 1880s the campaign to prevent puerperal fever included recognition of the need for better sterilization methods and increased control over the whole process: "doctors had to regard each woman as diseased, because birth provided the occasion and medicine the cause for infection" (Wertz and Wertz 1979: 128).[18] Birthing women were

therefore subjected to a regimen of procedures that were ultimately controlling and dehumanizing. Thus, certain aspects of medical management arose primarily out of a desire to improve outcomes for childbearing women.

As well — and often overlooked in the literature — postpartum hospital stays early in the century involved "social care" as well as medical care. Women typically had two or three weeks of care and help with their babies while they were in the hospital (Wertz and Wertz 1979). It could be argued that with the demise of a world in which women and men lived segregated lives — in "separate spheres" — and the corresponding erosion of women's tight personal networks, "social childbirth" at home became less and less feasible (Rapp and Ross 1986; Strong-Boag 1988). The extended hospital stays that replaced care in the home remained common until recently.

GIVING BIRTH IN SOCIAL CONTEXT: ONE FINAL STORY

The risk that critics take in emphasizing the issue of control is that of implicitly condemning women who welcome medicalized birth as contributing to their own powerlessness and alienation. It may be more useful, instead, to direct attention to the *context* within which women's choices during childbirth are made. In her discussion of home birth, sociologist Barbara Katz Rothman (1982) argues that a *dignified transition to motherhood depends upon the receipt of adequate social support.* Perhaps, then, women who approach childbirth without much social support welcome the support of medical intervention instead, while those with strong support systems find themselves less in need of medical assistance. The story that follows — also that of a participant in the first-time parents study — shows how social support may be important on many levels during labour, delivery, and the early postpartum period.

Nora sat in her living room, along with her partner Glen and midwife Ellen, and contemplated the options now before her. She wanted very much to give birth at home — with Glen, Ellen, and friend Barb in attendance — and had made all her plans accordingly. She was well informed and in good health, and all signs during her pregnancy had indicated this would be a "low-risk" birth. But as events were now unfolding, it seemed her plans might have to be revised. The prospect of a hospital birth frightened Nora and filled her with a deep sense of loss. She needed Ellen's guidance. Through long discussions during her pregnancy, she knew the midwife's philosophical approach matched her own, and that her skills and knowledge would help keep medical intervention at bay. Nora needed to feel certain she was making the right decision.

It was sixteen days past Nora's due date, and there were signs the baby's health might be compromised if the birth did not take place soon. Nora had tried to initiate labour with vigorous daily walks, but to no avail. Her doctor advised an induction, and booked it for the following day, leaving the decision as to whether to follow through in the hands of Nora, Glen, and Ellen.

In the hours before the scheduled induction, Nora and Glen had tried more intensive means of inducing labour at home. Still there were no contractions. Now it was time for a decision. With Ellen's help they worked out a compromise. They would seek the lowest level of medical assistance — the topical application of a chemical hormone — to try to get contractions started. Afterwards they would return home in the hope that labour would proceed uneventfully.

But once more, they were disappointed. Three times that day they went in for the treatment. By midnight Nora was having mild contractions, only to have them stop when she fell asleep. The next morning Ellen advised Nora that a full-scale induction was probably necessary to sustain her labour. Nora knew that meant the birth would take place in hospital.

By 9:30 a.m. that morning Nora, Glen, Ellen, and Barb were settled in a labour room. Much to her surprise, Nora found the hospital setting less alienating than she had anticipated. Ellen's

presence was crucial in that regard. She provided trusted continuity of care, reassurance, advice, and help with comfort measures. She negotiated on Nora's behalf, kept her informed, and made her feel a part of each decision. And she handled all the necessary paper work, freeing Glen to devote his attention to his partner. For Nora, this kind of support turned an experience she had dreaded into one she later described as "just wonderful."

Labour progressed very slowly. At 2:30 p.m. in the afternoon the doctor advised rupturing the membranes to speed up progress. After consultation with Ellen, Nora agreed. However, within thirty seconds of the procedure, Nora went into what she later described as "hyperactive labour." The abruptness of the onset was overwhelming. Nora felt shocked and afraid. She doubted her ability to handle the contractions, and worried that something had gone terribly wrong with her labour. But once again her support team came through for her. Ellen reassured her that what she was experiencing was normal and helped her cope; Glen provided emotional support and grounding; and Barb offered practical help with comfort measures. The fear subsided and Nora was able to handle the contractions in spite of their strength.

After three hours of very high-intensity labour, dilation had progressed somewhat, but Nora was still nowhere near ready to deliver her baby. Feeling she could not continue for what promised to be several more hours, Nora requested an epidural. She later recalled the administration of the epidural as "the worst part of the whole labour." Having to stay motionless through contractions while the needle and catheter were inserted into her back felt to her like "torture." And in the end the medication proved effective for only about ten minutes.

But there was a good reason for the intensity of the labour at this point. Within twenty minutes Nora was ready to deliver her baby. She pushed for a little under an hour, with Ellen, Glen, and Barb acting as a "cheering team." This part of the labour was hard work and a bit overwhelming.

But as Nora later explained, the excitement of her support team took away her fear. Baby Luke was born at 7:20 p.m., into the hands of the midwife. Nora, exhausted but proud, was grateful to be surrounded by three people she trusted to hold and comfort her newborn.

Nora, Glen, and Luke left the hospital three hours later. They felt confident, knowing they had round-the-clock access to advice and follow-up care from Ellen. Glen's mother and Nora's sister would do the housework for the first two weeks. And a strong network of friends (one of whom was also a midwife) would be close at hand to offer emotional support and practical advice on parenting — and when the time came, to share childcare.

Glen, whose work allowed him some flexibility, and who planned to be as much a part of their son's care as Nora, would be at home for the first two months of their child's life. The family's departure from the hospital immediately after the birth meant that Glen was never separated from Luke in the early days of learning how to parent. The strong bond that developed between father and son continued at least into Luke's third year, when the study ended.

Glen's involvement affected Nora's experience of the postpartum period as well. In contrast to nearly all the other mothers interviewed for this study, Nora felt there was someone else in her child's life whom she could trust absolutely with his care. Two months after Luke's birth — a point at which most mothers were struggling with lack of sleep, isolation, and overwork — Nora responded without hesitation to a question about how her life had changed, with "I'm in *heaven* — just *heaven*."

THE SIGNIFICANCE OF THE IMMEDIATE SOCIAL CONTEXT

Nora's story highlights the importance of the immediate social context within which women give birth. This context can shape decisions made during labour and delivery, and the woman's subjective experience of childbirth and early parenting. Key to the social context are the quality of the support received during labour and delivery, and more importantly, the *degree to which the responsibility for childbearing is shared* rather than falling on the shoulders of the mother alone. Nora was fortunate. She felt surrounded by supportive individuals on all counts. Another participant in the study, Karen, was more representative of the new mothers interviewed. She was very much alone in her responsibility for her daughter — both during and after labour. She and her husband Jerry had struck a traditional-style "bargain" upon marriage: although Karen earned the higher income, enjoyed her work, and had the more stable employment history, she would care for their home and family while Jerry would take primary responsibility for their financial needs. In addition, Karen could not count on support from her family, who were busy with their own lives, or Jerry's family, with whom she was not close. Her close friends did not have children, and the activities she shared with them did not encompass her new role as a mother. Karen (quoted earlier as "now pray[ing] to the epidural god") was more than happy to accept medical assistance during the birth of her child.

LABOUR IN SOCIAL CONTEXT

Sensitivity to social context can shed light on women's responses to childbirth that appear anomalous from the perspective of the critique of medicalization. In general, the interviews with the forty first-time mothers and their partners indicate that women who could count on solid support from their partner and/or other relatives after they gave birth were more likely to resist medical management. Those whose support was weak or non-existent were more likely to find medical management acceptable, perhaps even desirable.

This was particularly evident where pain medication was concerned. Pain, or its avoidance, was clearly a major component of these women's experience; it was a central theme in two-thirds of their birth stories. Nearly all of the happiest, most empowered women reported having experienced very little pain — or very little that they could not handle — during labour. Nancy gave birth to twins with the help of an epidural. She recalled the experience as "really, really terrific 'cause I didn't have the pain." In contrast, the most distressed women often spoke at great length about the pain they experienced in labour. Jeanne recalled her labour as "gruesome," and involving "sheer and utter panic" because of the amount of pain she experienced.

Ironically, some women chose pain medication for reasons that appear consistent with the critique of medicalized childbirth — the desire to "stay in control," to think and make decisions, and to act in a "rational" manner, during labour and delivery. For these women, staying in control was premised on being able to manage pain. As Joanne described it,

> I didn't feel in control when I was feeling the contractions. But I could really concentrate with the epidural. That's what I liked about it. I could really *think about what I was doing....* [Otherwise], it was too much, I think, to comprehend.

Despite a long struggle to avoid medical intervention, Joanne felt that "the fact that the epidural takes the pain away makes such a big difference 'cause ... you use your head." Several others found that they became "human again" once they had obtained some measure of pain relief.

Indeed, staying in control meant different things to different women. Some defined it in a way that was consistent with the critique of medicalization: the ability to influence the course of their labours and deliveries through their input into decisions. But a few women defined control in a more limited way: simply remaining conscious, rational, and aware of what was happening. Both of these definitions suggest that women may experience labour as being "out of control" for reasons other than the use of medical intervention per se. In fact, more important

than control (in the sense of not being subjected to medical procedures) seems to be whether or not the woman's needs — as she defines them — are addressed during labour.

In addition, many of the women's comments suggest that pain management is connected to larger social factors. In a context where childcare is the personal responsibility of the parents, especially the mother, pain relief during labour can leave a woman feeling more able to assume the work of parenting immediately afterwards. Judy had these thoughts on the matter:

> Yeah, it was hard. I mean, being up for that many hours and then right away having to function again. Yeah it's hard, so ... I can't imagine. Next time I'm just going to ask for the epidural and cesarean. Forget the labour.

The promise of pain relief, then, is that it gets women through a physically taxing experience in better shape to take on the heavy responsibilities of parenting. Women may seek pharmaceutical pain relief in a social context where this kind of assistance is readily available and commonly accepted, and where ongoing support for new parents is weak.[19]

In fact, strong social support does not seem to reduce the need for pain medication in labour. Among the participants in the first-time parenting study, this kind of support was generally provided by the woman's partner. There was a strong relationship between whether or not the partner was generally supportive and whether or not (or how quickly) the woman sought pain medication in labour. Supportive partners were generally empathic to the woman, and as a result shared experiences and responsibilities related to the care of home and family (measured by their ongoing involvement in, and responsibility for, housework). Women whose partners were supportive in this way felt they could expect responsibility for the baby to be shared in the days, weeks, and years following the birth of their child.

Women whose partners offered little ongoing support generally requested pain relief early in their labours. Just over half of the women in the study fit this profile. On the other hand, women with solid support from their partners — a quarter of those in the study — most often went to great lengths to avoid medical intervention in labour. Two of these women gave birth without medical intervention, despite having very long and painful labours.[20]

Some women found that the support of those around them was fundamental to their ability to manage anxiety as well. Nearly all of the women in the study experienced anxiety during labour — in many cases directly connected to their anticipation of mounting pain. As Sally explained, "I wasn't frightened of what was happening. I was frightened of mounting pain. I didn't want to be left alone." She found that as long as her partner stayed with her she could manage her anxiety. Likewise, Nora (in the third story) found that during her delivery "They [her partner, friend, and midwife] were all screaming [with excitement].... and maybe that took away the fear. It was kind of their excitement." Thus, in the case of both pain and anxiety, social support had a significant impact on decision-making about intervention in labour.

THE IMMEDIATE POSTPARTUM PERIOD IN SOCIAL CONTEXT

In addition, women's support networks seemed to protect them from experiencing the brief periods of emotional volatility commonly known as "baby blues," which often occur a few days after giving birth. Women themselves made the connection between emotional volatility and lack of support. Those who experienced periods of tearfulness often hesitated to label their feelings baby blues, but saw them, instead, as responses to isolation and the overwhelming responsibilities they now faced. Erica referred to this condition as "the shock of everything coming on." Carla spoke more specifically about the enormity of the responsibilities and the lack of support systems encountered by new parents.

> It was so scary the first few days, you know. You don't know what you're supposed to do .... The

awesome amount of responsibility sort of just hits you, and it was like, "oh my God," you know, "we're responsible for this little person now; nobody is going to help us." Not that they helped us much in the hospital, but still you had that sort of fall-back position.

More than half of the women in the study had relatively little support beyond the first few days postpartum. All of these women experienced one or more episodes of baby blues. In several cases the episode occurred upon discharge from the hospital or upon the partner's return to work. In contrast, half of the women with substantial support had no baby blues — including two women with the most difficult births.[21]

In addition, social support seemed to offer some protection against the onset of more serious forms of emotional upset following the birth. Thus, for example, Margaret, who had a history of depression, insisted that the strong support of her mother-in-law kept her from suffering a relapse during this vulnerable time.

BEING A PATIENT IN SOCIAL CONTEXT

Personal responsibility for childrearing was not only a part of the broader social context within which these women gave birth. It was also actively produced by the medical institutions they attended. The postpartum hospital stays of many women in the study were affected by recently established "early release" policies. These policies stipulated that women giving birth vaginally were released after twenty-four hours, and those giving birth by cesarean section were released after three days. This meant that there was little opportunity to attend any classes in breastfeeding or babycare that may have been offered. In addition, the vast majority of women in the study were given little or no individual instruction in, or assistance with, babycare by the nurses on the floor — even when they specifically requested it. Instead, they were left to figure out how to feed, change, and bathe their babies on their own. Sara's and Leslie's comments were typical: "Once you're up there, you're on your own; you sink or swim"; "You feel like you're left on your own right away." Similarly, Robin was told, after repeated requests for instruction in bathing her baby, "Just do the best you can …. It's your baby." Worse still, when she asked the nurse on duty about the possibility of dehydration (her baby was admitted to the emergency ward two days after his release "as dehydrated as a baby can be and still be alive"), she was told, "What do you want me to do about it?" Occasionally advice was offered on breastfeeding; however, several women complained that the instructions they received were contradictory.[22]

Medicalized birth, then, "gives birth" to a mother who typically has just had her own vulnerability underlined, at a time when she is about to undertake what may be the most demanding task of her life. It offers support to the body and nothing more, and withdraws it abruptly following the delivery of a healthy baby. Because medicalized childbirth offers insufficient assistance, it communicates the message that the woman is alone (with perhaps the help of a partner) in her long-term responsibility for the care of the new child. That motherhood is a private responsibility may be the most important message conveyed.

A few women, however, had very different experiences on the maternity wards in these same hospitals. These women were very appreciative of the care they received during their postpartum stay. Judy commented that, "Everyone there [on the ward] was just *so* amazing. They were great." Irene felt that, "Everybody [on the ward] was just so wonderful and supportive." Both Judy and Irene were recovering from cesarean sections. In fact, all of the women who felt positive about their postpartum hospital stay had medical problems known to the hospital staff. These women were "patients" in a way that healthy new mothers were not. As such, they received both personal care and instruction in babycare — services not generally available to women without obvious medical need.

In addition, new mothers were more likely to elicit the support of partners when they were clearly suffering from a medical condition or recovering from surgery. Men whose wives were ill were far more likely than others to be doing the full range of housework and babycare. Their partners' medical problems seemed to facilitate their own involvement in babycare, making it both necessary and socially acceptable that they be active parents from the start. Although this was especially true for fathers who had expressed a strong desire to be involved in babycare beforehand, even men who had resisted their partners' earlier attempts to get them to share housework took on a much larger share when their wives were undeniably in need of recovery.

Ironically, then, becoming a patient — that is, having a highly medicalized birth — may enable new mothers to elicit various forms of help and support to which they would not otherwise have access. It may be, then, that the problem with medical management is not only that it alienates by supplanting a woman-centred process, but also that it substitutes for more general social support of women and their children, and offers instead only a limited kind of help. This suggests one possible reason for women's "accommodation" to the medical model during labour and delivery: a realistic assessment of available options. Where general social supports for childbearing and parenting are in short supply, women's apparent acquiescence to medical control may be understood, despite its obvious limitations, as one means of strengthening personal resources to meet the enormous challenges ahead — of making labour "work" for women.

CONCLUSION: MAKING LABOUR WORK

It appears, then, that one way to reconcile the disjuncture between the critique of medicalized birth and women's subjective experiences and personal choices is to pay more attention to the social context within which childbirth takes place. Although women have played, and continue to play, a major role in determining how birth is managed, the choices they make cannot be understood in isolation from the social context in which they gave birth. The circumstances shaping women's lives affect how they approach and experience childbirth.

Key to those circumstances is the extent to which responsibility for the work of childrearing falls to the mother. Our society offers few collectively organized social supports to new mothers. As a result, the support women receive — or do not receive — through personal networks can be critical to their experience of labour and the immediate postpartum period, and the actions they take to cope with that experience.

When we understand women's choices during birth in this light, we avoid the trap of blaming women for their "acquiescence" to medical control. No less importantly, though, we broaden the focus of our efforts to change the situation: it becomes clear that, for women to be strengthened by their experience of childbearing, a variety of resources may need to be channelled in support of parenting.

Giving birth has the potential to work for women by empowering them to meet new challenges. But, as we have seen, making labour work in this way means paying attention to the more concrete meaning of "work" — the labour involved in childrearing. By spreading this workload more evenly — that is, by providing ongoing social support for the tasks involved in raising a child — we may succeed in making labour work for women. Conversely, we should perhaps not be surprised, in the current era of cutbacks to social services, to see women making labour work for them by turning increasingly to the pharmaceutical and technical supports offered by modern obstetrics.

NOTES

The research reported here was supported by the Social Science and Humanities Research Council of Canada (grant no. 410-94-0453) and the University of Toronto. We wish to thank Sherry Bartram for excellent research assistance; Liz Walker, Ann Bernardo, and Rebecca Fulton for timely transcribing; Emily Worts for helpful comments on an earlier draft of the chapter, and the forty women who shared their stories with us.

1. This is a type of anesthesia used in labour.
2. This procedure is known as artificial rupture of the membranes, or ARM. It may be performed to speed up a long labour, but in Meredith's case the doctor was looking for meconium (the contents of the unborn baby's intestines), which is often released into the waters when the baby is under stress during labour.
3. Epidural anesthesia involves the administration of a drug, similar to dental anesthesia, into the space between the membranes surrounding the spinal cord. The drug is administered through a needle and catheter in the lower back. The catheter is then taped securely to the woman's back to hold it in place. Some women experience non-life-threatening side effects like Meredith's.
4. Progress during the first stage of labour is measured in terms of the dilation (i.e., the diameter of the opening of the cervix, or neck of the womb). The cervix is generally closed prior to labour. As the labour progresses it gradually opens to a diameter of 10 centimetres, or full dilation. At this point the woman begins to actively work with the contractions to push the baby down through the birth canal. This is known as the second stage of labour.
5. Some women experience these sensations near the end of the first stage of labour. Meredith had them longer than most.
6. Forceps resemble a large set of salad servers. They fit around the baby's head, and may be used to accomplish delivery when the baby has moved partway through the birth canal. An alternative method involves the use of a vacuum extractor — a device not unlike a large suction cup that attached to the baby's head to speed up the last stages

of the delivery. Assisted deliveries are fairly common — but by no means universal — with first babies.

A cesarean section is a surgical birth, in which the baby is delivered through an incision in the woman's lower abdomen. Except in dire emergencies (or at the women's request) it is generally performed using epidural anesthesia, so the woman remains conscious. A shield is placed between her head and abdomen to block her view of the surgery.

7. The treatment referred to here is the application of prostaglandin gel to the woman's cervix. Prostaglandin helps soften the cervix to prepare it for dilation, and may initiate contractions as well.

8. The reason for this is that the placenta (the temporary organ that supplies the baby with nutrients and oxygen during pregnancy) may function less effectively as it "ages."

9. The electronic fetal monitor is a device used to continuously monitor the baby's heart rate and the length, strength, and spacing of the woman's contractions. External monitoring uses two belts around the woman's abdomen to attach the monitoring devices. Internal monitoring replaces one of the belts with a clip attached to the baby's scalp.

10. This type of incision is known as an episiotomy. It is performed to speed up the delivery or avoid a tear (both controversial reasons), or to permit the use of forceps or a vacuum extractor to assist in the delivery.

11. All names used are pseudonyms. The interviews with these women were part of a larger study of first-time parents, involving both members of the couple making this transition. All the couples who participated in the study had taken childbirth education classes, and were, in fact, recruited through these courses. All gave birth in a hospital.

Interviews were conducted for a pilot study in 1991 and 1992, and for the main study in 1995 and 1996. Each member of the couple was interviewed separately, during pregnancy, when their child was two months old, around the child's first birthday, and around the child's second birthday. The man and woman were interviewed together when their child was six months old. Among other things, these interviews provided detailed information on the couple's division of household labour, and the support they received from friends and relatives. In addition, the woman was interviewed alone a few days after giving birth. Most of the material for this chapter is based on the latter set of interviews; however, background material is also drawn from the former set.

12. Because this latter shift occurred at a time when women were excluded from medical schools, medical management continued to mean management by men.

13. While midwives were being licensed and funded in Ontario by late 1993, only one of the women in the study of first-time parents had a midwife at her side.

14. This general observation is consistent with hundreds of stories gathered during Diana Worts's eight years as a childbirth educator and birth attendant.

15. This is a more accurate, but also more invasive, way to assess fetal well-being.

16. This was at a time when women had far more pregnancies than they do today.

17. Wealthy women were the first to invite doctors to attend their births, and their class status undoubtedly reinforced their power in the situation.

18. Puerperal fever is an "infection of the genital tract after delivery." It was eventually discovered to have been caused during the latter part of the nineteenth century by doctors who went directly from dissecting corpses to attending women in labour without washing their hands (Pritchard and MacDonald 1976: 757).

19. Interestingly, Leavitt (1986: 128) quotes turn-of-the-century discussion that links pain-

less birth to the move toward women assuming individual responsibility for their babies: "In scopolamine deliveries, the woman went to sleep, delivered her baby and woke up feeling vigorous: 'so free from fatigue that she could leave her bed at once and care for her own baby.'"

20. Some of these women also had daily help from their mother or mother-in-law. A small number of women in the study with very supportive partners faced unexpected circumstances, such as serious concerns about the baby's well-being, that necessitated the use of medical procedures despite the support they received.

21. All the remaining women with strong support experienced very disturbing events in the postpartum period, such as serious health problems or the presence of extremely disruptive in-laws, which complicated their reactions.

22. This general picture of dissatisfaction contrasts with most women's experience during labour and delivery. Many volunteered comments on how "wonderful" the care on the labour floor had been. Again, this distinction is consistent with that found in stories collected during Diana Worts's eight years as a childbirth educator and birth attendant.

REFERENCES

Arms, S. 1981. *Immaculate Deception: A New Look at Women and Childbirth in America* (Boston: Houghton Mifflin).

Arnup, K. 1994. *Education for Motherhood: Advice for Mothers in Twentieth-Century Canada* (Toronto: University of Toronto Press).

Ball, J. 1987. *Reactions to Motherhood: The Role of Postnatal Care* (Cambridge: Cambridge University Press).

Barclay, L., C. Andre, and P. Glover. 1989. "Women's Business: The Challenge of Childbirth," *Midwifery* 5: 122–33.

Biggs, C.L. 1990. "'The Case of the Missing Midwives': A History of Midwifery in Ontario from 1795–1900" in *Delivering Motherhood: Maternal Ideologies and Practices in the 19th and 20th Centuries*, eds. K. Arnup, A. Levesque, and R.R. Pierson (London: Routledge), 20–35.

Bourgeault, I. 1999. Personal communication.

Brown, S., J. Lumley, R. Small, and J. Astbury. 1994. *Missing Voices: The Experience of Motherhood* (Melbourne: Oxford University Press).

Chalmers, I., M. Enkin, and M. Keirse. 1989. *Effective Care in Pregnancy and Childbirth*, v. 1 and 2 (Toronto: Oxford University Press).

Chamberlain, M., B. Soderstrom, C. Kaitell, and P. Stewart. 1991. "Consumer Interest in Alternatives to Physician-Centred Hospital Birth in Ottawa," *Midwifery* 7: 74–81.

Collins, N., C. Dunkel-Schetter, M. Lobel, and S. Scrimshaw. 1993. "Social Support in Pregnancy: Psychosocial Correlates of Birth Outcomes and Postpartum Depression," *Journal of Personality and Social Psychology* 65 (6) 1243–58.

Davis-Floyd, R. 1990. "The Role of Obstetrical Rituals in the Resolution of Cultural Anomaly," *Social Science and Medicine* 31 (2): 175–89.

———. 1992. *Birth as an American Rite of Passage* (Berkeley: University of California Press).

———. 1994. "The Technocratic Body: American Childbirth as Cultural Expression," *Social Science and Medicine* 38 (8): 1125–40.

Donegan, J. 1978. *Women and Men Midwives* (Westport, CT: Greenwood).

Eakins, P. 1986. *The American Way of Birth* (Philadelphia: Temple University Press).

Entwisle, B., and S. Doering. 1981. *The First Birth: An American Turning Point* (Baltimore: Johns Hopkins University).

Gordon, J. 1988. "Childbirth: The Mother's Perspective" in *Feminist Research: Prospect and Retrospect*, ed. P. Tancred-Sheriff

(Kingston and Montreal: McGill-Queen's University Press).

Graham, H., and A. Oakley. 1981. "Competing Ideologies of Reproduction: Medical and Maternal Perspectives on Pregnancy" in *Women, Health and Reproduction*, ed. H. Roberts (London: Routledge & Kegan Paul).

Jordan, B. 1978. *Birth in Four Cultures: A Cross-Cultural Investigation of Childbirth in Yucatan, Holland, Sweden and the U.S.* (St. Albans, VT: Eden Press).

Katz, Rothman, B. 1982. *Giving Birth: Alternatives in Childbirth* (Harmondsworth: Penguin).

———. 1989. *Recreating Motherhood: Ideology and Technology in a Patriarchal Society* (New York: Norton).

Kay, M.A. 1982. *Anthropology of Human Birth* (Philadelphia: F.A. Davis).

Kitzinger, S. 1972. *The Experience of Childbirth* (Harmondsworth, UK: Penguin).

LaForce, H. 1990. 'The Different Stages of the Elimination of Midwives in Quebec' in *Delivering Motherhood: Maternal Ideologies and Practices in the 19th and 20th Centuries*, eds. K. Arnup, A. Levesque, and R. Roach Pierson (London: Routledge), 36–50.

Lazurus, E. 1994. "What Do Women Want?: Issues of Choice, Control and Class in Pregnancy and Childbirth," *Medical Anthropology Quarterly* 8 (1): 25–46.

Leavitt, J. W. 1986. *Brought to Bed: Childbearing in America. 1750 to 1950* (New York: Oxford).

MacCormack, C. 1982. *Ethnography of Fertility and Birth* (London: Academic Press).

Martin, E. 1987. *The Woman in the Body: A Cultural Analysis of Reproduction* (Boston: Beacon).

McIntosh, J. 1989. "Models of Childbirth and Social Class: A Study of Eighty Working-Class Primagravidae," *Midwives, Research and Childbirth* 1: 189–214.

Michaelson, K. ed. 1988. *Childbirth in America: Anthropological Perspectives* (Westport, CT: Bergin & Garvey).

Mitford, J. 1992. *The American Way of Birth* (London: Victoria Golancz).

Nelson, M. 1983. "Working-Class Women, Middle-Class Women and Models of Childbirth," *Social Problems* 30 (3): 284–97.

Oakley, A. 1980a. *Becoming a Mother* (New York: Schocken).

———. 1980b. *Women Confined: Towards a Sociology of Childbirth* (Oxford: Martin Robertson).

———. 1984. *The Captured Womb: A History of the Medical Care of Pregnant Women* (Oxford: Basil Blackwell).

Pritchard, J.A., and P.C. MacDonald. 1976. *Williams Obstetrics*, 15th edn. (New York: Appleton-Century-Crofts).

Priya, J. 1992. *Birth Traditions and Modern Pregnancy Care* (Shaftsebury, Dorset: Element Books).

Rapp, R., and E. Ross. 1986. "The 1920s: Feminism, Consumerism, and Political Backlash in the United States" in *Women in Culture and Politics: A Century of Change*, eds. J. Friedlander, B.W. Cook, A. Kessler-Harris, and C. Smith-Rosenberg (Bloomington: Indiana University Press), 52–61.

Romalis, S. 1981. *Childbirth: Alternatives to Medical Control* (Austin: University of Texas Press).

Sargent, C., and N. Stark. 1989. "Childbirth Education and Childbirth Models: Parental Perspectives on Control, Anesthesia, and Technological Intervention in the Birth Process," *Medical Anthropology Quarterly* 3 (1): 36–51.

Strong-Boag, V. 1988. *The New Day Recalled: Lives of Girls and Women in English Canada, 1919–1939* (Markham, ON: Penguin).

Tew, M. 1995. *Safer Childbirth?* (London: Chapman & Hall).

Wertz, R., and D. Wertz. 1979. *Lying In: A History of Childbirth in America* (New York: Schocken).

Chapter 19

Violence against Women

HOLLY JOHNSON

INTRODUCTION

Victimization surveys were designed initially to address the need for information about crimes not reported to the police and to provide a source of crime statistics that complement the long-standing Uniform Crime Reporting survey of police-reported data. Canada has a history of crime victimization surveys dating back to the late 1970s; however, it had become apparent that, while they are proficient at measuring property offences and perceptions of crime, these surveys were not designed to measure the more sensitive kinds of victimizations that primarily affect women, such as wife assault and sexual violence. In attempting to measure a wide variety of crimes, these omnibus surveys did not allow for detailed analysis of all types of violence and threats to women, the emotional and physical consequences, the decisions women make to use support services and their satisfaction with these services, and other detailed information that is necessary for the development of public policy around this issue. Thus, the federal Department of Health commissioned the Violence against Women survey in recognition of the lack of reliable statistical data on which to test theories and develop policies and programs to address violence against women. Canada's first national survey on male violence against women was conducted by Statistics Canada early in 1993.

The design of this survey evolved out of the tradition of victimization surveys, whereby a random sample of the population is interviewed about their perceptions of crime and their experiences of victimization, and their responses are weighted to represent the population at large. A total of 12 300 women 18 years of age and over across the ten provinces were interviewed for this survey. Random selection helps ensure that those who respond are statistically representative of everyone in the population and that the results can be generalized to the population at large. The Violence against Women survey differs, however, from traditional victimization surveys, such as Canada's General Social Survey (GSS), the National Crime Survey in the United States, and the British Crime Survey, in important ways. Drawing on his experience with two telephone surveys of women in Toronto, Smith (1994) articulates a number of strategies designed to improve the accuracy of survey data on sensitive subjects such as wife assault and sexual assault. "Violence" in crime surveys is typically defined in legalistic terms through a single question embedded among a series of other crimes. Non-traditional surveys, on the other hand, tend to use broader definitions that "take women's subjective experiences seriously." Smith advocates, for example, the use of multiple measures at different points in the survey to offer many opportunities for respondents to divulge a previously forgotten incident or one that may be painful to recall. He also recommends giving greater attention to building rapport between respondents and

Source: Adapted from "Violence against Women," in *Crime in Canadian Society*, 5th ed., Robert A. Silverman, James J. Teevan, and Vincent F. Sacco, eds. (Toronto: Harcourt Brace, 1996), pp. 210–21. Reprinted by permission of Nelson, a division of Thomson Learning: www.thomsonrights.com. Fax: 800-730-2215.

interviewers through open-ended questions that allow respondents to speak in their own words, and through the careful selection of interviewers.

Smith also criticizes traditional crime victimization surveys for a narrow emphasis on annual victimization rates. The GSS asks respondents about incidents that took place during the twelve months preceding the interview. While twelve-month rates avoid problems of memory recall and are useful for tracking trends over time, they can obscure the scope of the problem. Eighty percent of violent incidents reported to the Violence against Women survey occurred *before* the twelve months leading up to the survey. Arbitrarily assigning one year as the cutoff point for victim or non-victim status may skew the analysis of correlations and consequences of victimization. Many women designated non-victims may continue to suffer serious consequences of previous victimization, and the comparison of their responses with those of recent victims may produce misleading results.

Careful testing of survey questions, multiple measures, selection and training of interviewers, and lifetime victimization rates were all incorporated into the design of the survey. In addition, the approach that was developed was particularly sensitive to the constraints that apply to surveying women about their experiences of violence over the telephone in a household setting, including respondent burden, the sensitivity of the information being sought, and the difficulty of responding to questions while the abuser may be present in the home. In discussions with women who had been victims of violence, the survey designers felt strongly that the appropriate approach would take account of the many realities of the women responding, and should be flexible, sensitive, and offer options as to when and where the women would participate.

One unique aspect of the Violence against Women survey was the extensive consultation process undertaken during the design and development phases. Advice and recommendations on the methodology and content of the survey were sought through ongoing discussions with a wide variety of experts, academics, government representatives, the police community, shelter workers, counsellors and advocates for battered women, as well as victims of violence seeking support in shelters and sexual assault counselling groups. These groups were instrumental in helping to design question wording that is sensitive, and that respondents can understand as reflective of their experiences. This was accomplished through lengthy discussions over the content of the questionnaire and issues to be addressed, focus group testing of question wording, one-on-one interviews with drafts of the questionnaire, and two large field tests.

A common concern among survey researchers is one of biased results if a large proportion of respondents refuse to participate in the survey or refuse to answer specific questions. There are a number of reasons why a woman may not wish to reveal her experiences to an interviewer over the telephone: she may feel her experience is too personal or painful to discuss; she may be embarrassed or ashamed about it; she may fear further violence from her abuser should he find out; or, she may have forgotten about it if it was minor or happened a long time ago (Smith, 1994). A survey of this nature asks the women responding to disclose the most intimate and perhaps the most troubling details of their lives to a stranger over the telephone. Even more important, from an ethical point of view, researchers must never lose sight of the possibility that with every telephone call the respondent could be living with an abusive man and that her safety could be jeopardized should he learn of the content of the survey. The selection and training of interviewers are critical factors in enabling a relationship of trust to develop between interviewers and respondents, a climate in which respondents feel safe and comfortable enough to discuss their experiences. Another important aspect of the approach developed for this survey, from the point of view of respondents' safety, was to provide options as to when and where they would participate. At the outset of the interview, every woman was provided with a toll-free telephone number that she could use to call back to resume the interview in the event that she had to hang up suddenly. A great many women took advantage of this option. A total of 1000 calls were received on the toll-free line over the five-month period of interviewing, and 150 were women wanting to continue an uncompleted interview that they had had to interrupt or calling to add additional information to a completed interview. This kind of interest and commitment to the interview process indicates an exceptional level of emotional commitment that this line of questioning can provoke and to which survey researchers must respond. Over one-half of all calls were from women wanting to verify the legitimacy of the survey, many at the point of sensitive questions about violence in their lives. One-quarter wanted more information about the sponsorship of the survey and how they could obtain the results. Many women called to express their appreciation for the opportunity to be involved in the survey and commended the government for taking the issue seriously.

This chapter presents the results of the Violence against Women survey as they relate to the prevalence of violence and emotional abuse by marital partners and sexual violence by men other than spouses. But this survey goes beyond quantifying women's experiences of criminal violence. The importance of this survey lies in its ability to put women's experiences of violence into a context that recognizes the parallels among violence inside and outside the home, threats to women's feelings of security that they experience routinely through sexual harassment, women's fear of victimization, and how women manage threats to their safety in their everyday lives. It allows an elaboration of our understanding of violence against women and the impact it has on their lives. Much recent scholarship recognizes the links between women's experiences of all types of violence and threats to women's personal security in the public and private spheres (Kelly, 1988; Stanko, 1990; Dekeseredy and MacLean, 1990). Criminal violence is only one dimension of a much broader problem manifest in the day-to-day lives of all women. To address only one type of violence,

wife assault or specific forms of sexual assault, for example, is to deny the wider social context in which women routinely feel threatened by male violence. It is to disregard the very real connections between the violence in women's lives by intimates, men they know and trust, perhaps a work colleague, a doctor, or a relative, and men they fear as strangers. Frightening and potentially volatile situations, such as being followed or leered at, with the implied threat of sexual violence, are very threatening experiences that cause women to feel fearful and insecure. These factors play a central role in shaping women's perceptions of their safety, and yet most traditional crime victimization surveys or family violence surveys do not consider them an important component of women's victimization. Some writers have described this range of violent and intimidating behaviours as a "continuum" of violence in women's lives because of the similar effects of these experiences on the female victim (Kelly, 1988; Stanko, 1990). It is this continuum that this survey is attempting to address.

CONSTRUCTING DEFINITIONS OF VIOLENCE

The broad objectives of this survey were to provide reliable statistical information about the extent and the nature of violence against women and women's fear of violence. Definitions of violence against women used in statistical surveys vary widely. They include psychological and emotional abuse, financial abuse, and sexual coercion, as well as physical and sexual assault as legally defined (Dekeseredy and Kelly, 1993; Koss and Gidycz, 1985). The prevalence of "violence" was estimated by this survey using questions based on legal definitions of physical and sexual assault as contained in the Canadian Criminal Code. These strict definitions were necessary in view of the fact that respondents would be asked a series of questions about the actions they took to get help, including reporting to the police, whether the incident resulted in an offender appearing in court, and their satisfaction with the action taken by the police and the courts.

The range of behaviours considered sexual assault under Canadian law include unwanted sexual touching up to violent sexual attacks with severe injury to the victim. Physical assaults range from face-to-face threat of imminent attack up to and including attacks with serious injury. Sexual violence outside marriage was measured through responses to two questions:

Sexual Attack

Has a male stranger (date or boyfriend or other man known to you) ever forced you or attempted to force you into any sexual activity by threatening you, holding you down or hurting you in some way?

Unwanted Sexual Touching

Has a male stranger (other man known to you) ever touched you against your will in any sexual way, such as unwanted touching, grabbing, kissing or fondling?

Physical violence by men other than marital partners was measured through the following two questions:

Physical Attack

Now I'm going to ask you some questions about physical attacks you may have had since the age of 16. By this I mean any use of force such as being hit, slapped, kicked or grabbed to being beaten, knifed or shot. Has a male stranger (date or boyfriend or other man known to you) ever physically attacked you?

Threats of Attack

The next few questions are about face-to-face threats you may have experienced. By threats I mean any time you have been threatened with physical harm since you were 16. Has a male stranger (date or boyfriend or other man known to you) ever threatened to harm you? Did you believe he would do it?

Incidents that involved both sexual and physical attack were counted only once as a sexual assault.

Women were not asked about unwanted sexual touching in dating and marital relationships. While technically these behaviours are legally crime, in the testing of the questionnaire the majority of respondents found this concept to be ambiguous and confusing and there was a concern among the survey designers that the responses to these questions would be of questionable validity. Coercive sexuality is the norm in North American society, where young men are expected to initiate sexual activity and to apply a certain amount of pressure on women, and women are expected to resist and to agree to sex only reluctantly (Clark and Lewis, 1977). The lines around "unwanted sexual touching" in intimate or dating relationships thus become blurred. Still, the data are included below.

Ten questions were used to measure violence by a marital partner (including legally married and common-law partners), taking account of Smith's advice to offer many opportunities for disclosure in order to overcome hesitancy on the part of the woman responding. Development of these items began with the violence items listed in the Conflict Tactics Scale (CTS), which was developed by Murray Straus and his colleagues at the University of New Hampshire (Straus, 1990). These items were then tested in focus groups of abused women, and two pilot tests were undertaken with random samples of women. A number of modifications were made throughout the testing phase in response to ambiguity in the question wording. The original CTS item "threatened to hit or throw something at you" was altered to read "threatened to hit you with his fist or anything else that could hurt you." Similarly, the item "threw something at you" has been clarified to read "thrown anything at you that could hurt you." The item "hit you with something" now reads "hit you with something that could hurt you." These modifications were made following field testing in which some respondents were clearly confused about whether to include incidents in which they were threatened or hit in a playful way with harmless objects that could not possibly hurt them. The addition of an item on forced sexual activity recognizes the reality of sexual violence in marriage.[1] (The complete list of items is contained in Table 19.1.)

THE PREVALENCE OF VIOLENCE AGAINST WOMEN

According to the Violence against Women survey, 51 percent of Canadian women have experienced at least one incident of physical or sexual assault since the age of 18 (Table 19.2). Women are at greater risk of violence by men they know than by strangers. Almost one-half of all women (45 percent) have been victimized by men known to them (spouses, dates, boyfriends, family, acquaintances, etc.) while 23 percent have experienced violence by a stranger. These percentages add to more than 51 percent because of the very high number of women who reported violence by both strangers and known men.

TABLE 19.1   NUMBER AND PERCENTAGE OF EVER-MARRIED WOMEN 18 YEARS AND OVER WHO REPORTED VIOLENCE BY A MARITAL PARTNER,* BY TYPE OF ASSAULT

TYPE OF ASSAULT	NUMBER (000s)**	PERCENT**
Total	2652	29
1. Threatened to hit her with his fist or anything else that could hurt her	1688	19
2. Thrown anything at her that could hurt her	1018	11
3. Pushed, grabbed, or shoved her	2221	25
4. Slapped her	1359	15
5. Kicked, bit, or hit her with his fist	955	11
6. Hit her with something that could hurt her	508	6
7. Beat her up	794	9
8. Choked her	607	7
9. Threatened to use or used a gun or knife on her	417	5
10. Forced her into any sexual activity when she did not want to by threatening her, holding her down, or hurting her in some way	729	8

*Includes common-law partners.

**Figures do not add to totals because of multiple response.

TABLE 19.2   NUMBER AND PERCENTAGE OF WOMEN 18 YEARS OF AGE AND OVER WHO HAVE BEEN PHYSICALLY OR SEXUALLY ASSAULTED, BY RELATIONSHIP OF PERPETRATOR

RELATIONSHIP	NUMBER (000s)**	PERCENT**
Total	5377	51
Spouse or ex-spouse	2652	29*
Date-boyfriend	1724	16
Other known man	2461	23
Stranger	2456	23

*Based on the number of women who have ever been married or lived with a man in a common-law relationship.

**Figures do not add to totals because of multiple response.

Almost four women in ten (39 percent) have been victims of sexual assault. One in four women reported unwanted sexual touching, and the same proportion reported a violent sexual attack. A much smaller proportion, 17 percent, have been physically threatened or assaulted by men other than spouses.

The percentage of women who have been assaulted by a spouse or live-in partner is 29 percent. Overall, rates of violence in previous marriages were estimated to be 48 percent compared with 15 percent in marriages that were current at the time of the interview. There is a continued risk of violence to women from ex-partners despite a divorce or separation. In fact, 19 percent of women assaulted by a previous partner said the man was violent during a period of separation, and in one-third of these cases the violence became more severe during that time.

As Table 19.1 illustrates, the most common forms of violence inflicted on women by marital partners were pushing, grabbing, and shoving followed by threats of hitting, slapping, throwing something at them, kicking, biting, and hitting with fists. While the percentage of women who have been beaten up, choked, sexually assaulted, or had a gun or knife used against them are all less than 10 percent, in each of these categories, between 400 000 and 800 000 Canadian women have been affected.

Not only do Canadian women report significant levels of violence, a majority of those who have been physically or sexually assaulted have been victimized more than once. The greatest risk of repeat victimization is in the area of sexual violence. Sixty percent of women who have been sexually assaulted by someone other than a spouse reported more than one such incident, and 26 percent were assaulted *four times or more*. Four in ten women who have been violently sexually attacked, and six in ten who reported unwanted sexual touching, said it happened to them more than once.

Women are at risk of sexual violence in a variety of locations and situations. As Figure 19.1 illustrates, almost one-half of all sexual assaults (46 percent) occurred in a private place such as the woman's home, the man's home, someone else's home, or in a car. For some, sexual assault is an occupational hazard (10 per-

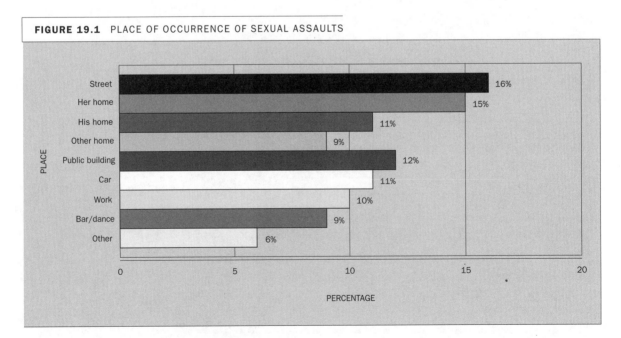

FIGURE 19.1   PLACE OF OCCURRENCE OF SEXUAL ASSAULTS

SOURCE: Based on material from Violence against Women survey, 1993.

cent occurred at the woman's place of work) and not an uncommon risk of being on the street, at a bar or dance, and using public buildings.

In the majority of cases, wife assault is characterized by this survey as ongoing or repeated acts of violence, in which incidents recur and increase in severity over time. Although pushing, grabbing, and shoving were the most commonly reported type of violence, only 5 percent of women said this was the only thing that happened to them, and only 4 percent said they were just threatened. As Table 19.3 shows, the majority of abused women said they were assaulted on more than one occasion, and one-third were assaulted more than ten times. This table also shows how much more violent men from previous marital relationships were. Ten percent of women reporting violence by a current partner said it happened more than ten times compared with 41 percent of women who were assaulted by a previous partner.

EMOTIONAL ABUSE BY MARITAL PARTNERS

Research shows that a great deal of violence against wives occurs in the context of the man's possessiveness, jealousy, and demands or criticisms over her domestic performance (Dobash and Dobash, 1984; Hart, 1988; Walker, 1979). The man's obsessiveness about his wife and his desire to control her have also been cited as pre-

cursors to wife killings (Daly and Wilson, 1988; Walker, 1984; Wilson and Daly, 1992, 1994). Emotionally abusive behaviour, therefore, is important contextual information about wife battering. Emotional abuse was measured in this survey through responses to statements about the partner's efforts to jealously guard the woman's contact with other men, to isolate her from outside support, to control her whereabouts, or to degrade her through name-calling and put-downs. As Table 19.4 on page 214 illustrates, the percentage of ever-married women reporting emotional abuse by a spouse is higher than the percentage reporting violence: 35 percent said their partner has done one or more of these things to them compared with 29 percent who experienced physical or sexual violence. Emotional abuse was used in conjunction with violence by the majority of violent men: three-quarters of women who were assaulted by a spouse were also emotionally abused. A much smaller proportion (18 percent) who reported no physical violence by a marital partner were nonetheless emotionally abused.

Obsessive and controlling behaviour feature prominently in serious battering relationships. Emotional abuse is present in the majority of violent relationships, but the frequency of emotionally abusive and controlling behaviours on the part of violent men increases dramatically as the seriousness of the battering increases (Wilson,

TABLE 19.3 PERCENTAGE OF WOMEN 18 YEARS AND OVER WHO HAVE EXPERIENCED VIOLENCE BY A SPOUSE, BY NUMBER OF OCCURRENCES

NUMBER OF OCCURRENCES	EVER-MARRIED WOMEN	CURRENT PARTNER	PREVIOUS PARTNER
Total	100	100	100
1	35	59	24
2–5	22	22	22
6–10	9	7	11
11 or more	32	10	41
Not stated	2	— *	2

* Not statistically reliable.

TABLE 19.4 PERCENTAGE OF EVER-MARRIED WOMEN REPORTING EMOTIONAL ABUSE, BY TYPE OF PHYSICAL VIOLENCE

TYPE OF EMOTIONAL ABUSE	ALL WOMEN	LESS SEVERE VIOLENCE*	MORE SEVERE VIOLENCE*
Total**	35	79	95
1. He is jealous and doesn't want her to talk to other men	19	48	72
2. He tries to limit her contact with family or friends	16	39	65
3. He insists on knowing who she is with and where she is at all times	22	44	70
4. He calls her names to put her down or make her feel bad	21	49	81
5. He prevents her from knowing about or having access to the family income, even if she asks	10	24	44

*Previous spouses only.
**Figures do not add to totals because of multiple response.

Johnson, and Daly, 1995). In cases of severe violence by an ex-spouse, emotionally abusive and controlling behaviours were used by 95 percent of abusers (Table 19.4). Severe violence was defined as being beaten up or worse or receiving injuries that required medical attention.

For a controlling and abusive man, his partner's pregnancy may represent to him a threat to his exclusive control over her and to her exclusive attention and affection toward him. Overall, 21 percent of women physically or sexually assaulted by a spouse were assaulted during pregnancy. Violence during pregnancy was four times more frequent among women who experienced the most severe forms of violence than among others victimized less severely (33 percent as compared with 8 percent). These findings add important empirical support to theories that explain wife assault as a function of gender relations, male dominance and power, and control in marital relationships.

CORRELATES OF VIOLENT VICTIMIZATION

Sample surveys like the Violence against Women survey lend themselves to an analysis of the distribution of violent victimization within the population. In other words, they allow us to describe who is at greatest risk of being victimized according to certain social characteristics of Canadian women. Table 19.5 outlines the percentage of women who have ever been physically or sexually assaulted by a spouse or sexually assaulted by someone other than a spouse according to their age, marital status, household income, and education. Since these characteristics are subject to change over time and may have changed significantly between the time of the assault and the time of the interview, these calculations are based on a snap-shot of experiences in the 12 months preceding the survey.

Women learn about sexual violence and threats to their safety at a young age. Young women 18 to 24 years of age experienced rates of sexual assault twice that of women in the next age group (25 to 34) and had rates of wife assault that were three times higher. Although characteristics of perpetrators are not shown in this table, the same distinct age effect is evident in men who are violent toward their wives. The rate of wife assault in newer marriages, that is, relationships of two years or less, was almost three times the national average.

Other personal characteristics that are associated with age also show up as strong predictors of risk of sexual assault. For example, single

TABLE 19.5 TWELVE-MONTH RATES OF WIFE ASSAULT AND SEXUAL ASSAULT, BY SOCIODEMOGRAPHIC CHARACTERISTICS OF WOMEN

SOCIODEMOGRAPHIC CHARACTERISTICS	WIFE ASSAULT*		SEXUAL ASSAULT
Twelve-month rate	3	*percentage*	5
Age Group			
18–24	12		18
25–34	4		8
35–44	3		5
45 and over	1		1
Marital Status			
Married	2		2
Common-law	9		7
Separated	n/a		10
Divorced	n/a		13
Single	n/a		15
Widowed	— **		—
Household Income			
Less than $15 000	6		7
$15 000–$29 999	3		6
$30 000–$59 999	3		5
$60 000 or more	3		5
Education			
Less than high school	3		4
High school diploma	3		5
Some postsecondary education	3		8
University degree	3		4

*Based on women who were married or living with a man in a common-law relationship in the twelve months preceding the survey.
** Not statistically reliable.

women and those with some postsecondary education (the largest proportion of whom are in the youngest age group) report the highest rates of sexual assault. In the case of wife assault, a woman's education has no bearing on her risk, although her partner's education does seem to have an effect: men without a high school education assaulted their wives at twice the rate of men with a university degree. Men who were out of work in the year prior to the survey committed assaults against their wives at twice the rate of employed men. Finally, women living in common-law relationships had rates of violence by a spouse that were four times as high as women legally married.

Contrary to common stereotypes of battered women, household income is not as strong a factor in wife assault as some others. Women living in households with incomes under $15 000 have rates of wife assault that are twice the national average; however, rates for women in high-income households ($60 000 and over) are the same as rates for women in the middle-income range. Rates of sexual assault also decline slightly as the woman's household income increases, but not markedly.

Rates of violent victimization vary depending on the geographic area in which a woman lives. Women living in urban areas have somewhat higher rates of wife assault and sexual violence; women living in British Columbia and Alberta report the highest provincial rates and New-foundland women the lowest (Table 19.6). It is not clear to what extent these provincial differences may be attributed to cultural differences and the willingness or reluctance of the women responding to report their experiences to an interviewer, or whether these are indicators of real differences in the levels of violence against women. The general east–west pattern with rising rates in the western provinces is consistent with police statistics and theories that the greater migration into British Columbia and Alberta results in fewer social controls in these provinces and subsequent increases in criminal activity. Newfoundland, on the other hand, is a province with much higher out-migration and lower in-migration than others, which may produce greater social cohesion and controls against behaving violently. These provincial patterns, together with the relatively weak relationship between wife assault and household income, must cause us to question certain assumptions about the links between poverty and abuse, since Newfoundland, one of the most economically depressed areas of the country, has the lowest rates of violence against women.

CONCLUSIONS

The Violence against Women survey provides empirical evidence of widespread violence against women in Canadian society. Three in ten women who have ever been married or

TABLE 19.6 LIFETIME RATES OF WIFE ASSAULT AND SEXUAL ASSAULT, BY PLACE OF RESIDENCE

PLACE OF RESIDENCE	WIFE ASSAULT*		SEXUAL ASSAULT
Total ever assaulted	29	*percentage*	27
Urban/Rural			
Urban	30		38
Rural	26		30
Province			
British Columbia	32		45
Alberta	30		42
Saskatchewan	25		32
Manitoba	26		35
Ontario	25		38
Quebec	22		31
New Brunswick	23		33
Nova Scotia	27		35
Prince Edward Island	22		39
Newfoundland	14		25

*Based on women who have never been married or living with a man in a common-law relationship.

lived with a man in a common-law relationship have experienced violence by a marital partner, and almost four in ten women have been sexually assaulted. A great many women have been victimized more than once.

Violence and the threat of violence are lessons learned early in life. Young women have the highest rates of sexual assault, and young women in new marriages are at greatest risk of violence from their equally young male partners. Common-law marital status elevates the risk of wife assault. The highest rates of wife assault are reported to have occurred in relationships that have ended, quite often from estranged spouses. Emotionally abusive and controlling behaviour is common in men who assault their wives, especially as the severity of the violence escalates.

Some writers would argue that "lifestyle" and "routine activities" are central to developing an explanation of how personal characteristics affect rates of violent victimization. Adherents of this position maintain that victimization rates reflect differences in exposure to risk that result from occupational and leisure activities. To the extent that lifestyle puts people in dangerous places, or out on the street late at night, their risk of victimization will increase. Crime victimization surveys have shown that young people have fewer family responsibilities and a more active lifestyle than older people, which allow them to engage in evening activities outside the home. In the context of the lifestyle/routine activities perspective, the higher victimization rates of young women would be explained by the greater likelihood that these women are unmarried, free from family responsibilities, and active in evening activities that put them in close proximity to offenders.

There are problems in attempting to apply the lifestyle/routine activities approach to violent victimization of women, however. As the Violence against Women survey indicates, women face a greater risk of violence in familiar places by men they know. While lifestyle and routine activities may play a role in stranger attacks, or in under-

standing sexual assault as an occupational hazard for some women, they cannot account for the very high rate of violence involving intimates. Clearly, a different perspective is necessary to explain the causes of wife assault and dating violence, since the greatest risk factor, according to lifestyle/routine activities, is to be married, dating, or living with a man. This is the "activity" that puts women in close proximity to an offender and at risk of violence. Similarly, in a significant proportion of cases of sexual assault, the risky activity is dating, or having a father, a colleague, or a neighbour. The victim-blaming focus of this perspective, when applied to situations of sexual violence and wife assault, helps perpetuate negative stereotypes about women who "ask for it" by their appearance or style of dress or who stay with a violent man because somehow they enjoy it, relieving men of the responsibility for their violence. What is needed for a clearer understanding of why so many men are violent toward women is a focus on the offender and on societal factors that legitimate male dominance over women in so many aspects of life. For example, what is the role of emotional abuse in battering relationships, and how does it keep women from leaving the men who abuse them? What assumptions do men make about the "availability" of young women in particular as acceptable targets for sexual violence? How have the criminal justice system and other helping systems reinforced cultural messages that violence against women will be tolerated? These are the questions and the orientation necessary to tackle the important research issues and policy decisions ahead in the area of violence against women.

NOTE

The author wishes to thank Karen Rodgers, Canadian Centre for Justice Statistics, and the editors for their comments and suggestions on an earlier draft.

1. The manner in which the Conflict Tactics Scale is typically introduced to respondents, as a list of ways of settling differences, is problematic:

it is potentially very confusing to respondents and not appropriate for orienting them toward thinking about violence they have suffered at the hands of their partners. While some respondents may think about experiences of violence as ways of settling differences, a great many may not, which must cause us to question the reliability and validity of a scale to measure violence that was, in fact, designed to address ways of resolving conflict. There is substantial evidence that many acts of aggression by men against their wives are not precipitated by an argument or disagreement between them, and it is questionable whether respondents would think them appropriate to include. The Violence against Women survey represents a significant departure from other surveys employing the CTS in that it has an extensive lead-up to questions about spousal violence through detailed questions about fear of violence in public places, precautionary behaviour, sexual harassment, and sexual and physical violence by strangers, dates and boyfriends, and other known men. This survey is concerned not with ways of settling disagreements but with violence against women, and this context will have been established at this point.

Traditional usage of the CTS asks respondents to quantify each violent act or blow, a seemingly impossible task for victims of repeated or ongoing violence. Emphasis throughout the Violence against Women survey is on the number of different occasions a marital partner has been violent, the types of violent acts, and the level of injury and emotional upset suffered by the victim, and not on counting each threat or blow.

REFERENCES

Clark, Lorenne, and Debra Lewis. 1977. *Rape: The Price of Coercive Sexuality*. Toronto: The Women's Press.

Daly, M., and M. Wilson. 1988. *Homicide*. New York: Aldine de Gruyter.

Dekeseredy, Walter, and Katharine Kelly. 1993. "The Incidence and Prevalence of Woman Abuse in Canadian University and College Dating Relationships." *Canadian Journal of Sociology* 18(2): 137–59.

Dekeseredy, Walter, and Brian MacLean. 1990. "Research Women Abuse in Canada: A Realist Critique of the Conflict Tactics Scale." *Canadian Review of Social Policy* 25: 19–27.

Dobash, R., and R. Dobash. 1984. "The Nature and Antecedents of Violent Events." *British Journal of Criminology* 24: 269–88.

Hart, B. 1988. "Beyond the 'Duty to Warn': A Therapist's 'Duty to Protect' Battered Women and Children." In K. Yllo and M. Bograd (eds.), *Feminist Perspectives on Wife Abuse*. Beverly Hills: Sage.

Kelly, Liz. 1988. *Surviving Sexual Violence*. Minneapolis: University of Minnesota Press.

Koss, Mary, and C. Gidycz. 1985. "Sexual Experiences Survey: Reliability and Validity." *Journal of Consulting and Clinical Psychology* 53: 422–23.

Smith, Michael. 1994. "Enhancing the Quality of Survey Data on Violence against Women: A Feminist Approach." *Gender and Society* 8(1): 109–27.

Stanko, Elizabeth. 1990. *Everyday Violence: How Men and Women Experience Sexual and Physical Danger*. London: Pandora.

Straus, Murray. 1990. "Measuring Intrafamily Conflict and Violence: The Conflict Tactics (CTS) Scales." In Murray Straus and Richard Gelles (eds.), *Physical Violence in American Families: Risk Factors and Adaptations to Violence in 8145 Families*. New Brunswick, NJ: Transaction.

Walker, L. 1979. *The Battered Woman*. New York: Harper Perennial.

———. 1984. *Battered Woman Syndrome*. New York: Springer.

Wilson, M., and M. Daly. 1992. "Who Kills Whom in Spouse Killings? On the Exceptional Sex Ratio of Spousal Homicides in the United States." *Criminology* 30(2): 189–215.

———. 1994. "Spousal Homicide." *Juristat* 14: 8.

Wilson, M., H. Johnson, and M. Daly. 1995. "Lethal and Nonlethal Violence against Wives." *Canadian Journal of Criminology* 37: 331–61.

PART 4B

POLITICS AND SOCIAL MOVEMENTS

Voters are unhappy, in Canada no less than in other democratic countries. Surveys repeatedly show that Canadians are growing increasingly cynical about politics and distrustful of politicians. As a result, fewer Canadians are voting; while three-quarters of eligible voters cast ballots in the 1984 federal election, only two-thirds did so in 1997. In addition, political loyalty is becoming antique. That is, voters are more willing than ever to switch their allegiance from one party to the next in succeeding elections. They are swayed less by ideologies, principles, and programs than by personalities and fleeting issues. Consequently, Canada's political landscape gyrates wildly from one election to the next. The fortunes of some parties rise as quickly as the fortunes of other parties decline.

Despite the widespread discontent that mars Canadian politics, voters are more highly educated than ever and they are just as interested in politics as past generations of voters. However, they are more likely than past generations to express their interest and sophistication by participating in non-conventional forms of politics. Thus, in a 1980 survey, 24 percent of Canadians said they had joined in a boycott, attended an unlawful demonstration, joined an unofficial strike or occupied a building or a factory at least once. In a 1990 survey, the comparable figure was nearly 33 percent and in 2000, 30 percent. Participation in non-conventional politics is most common among young, highly educated people. Therefore, if present trends continue, one may reasonably expect participation in non-conventional forms of politics to increase in coming years.

In Chapter 20, Harold Clarke and his associates document the growing cynicism of the Canadian electorate and blame it squarely on the growth of what they call "brokerage politics." Brokerage politics involves party leaders organizing focus groups, public opinion polls, and informal canvasses of voters to determine the hot issues of the day. With this information in hand, party leaders delineate the varied interests of the electorate. They then work out a strategy for organizing a coalition of diverse interests that, they hope, will support their party. They use advertising firms, public relations experts, and "spin doctors" to help them project an image of the party and its leaders that will appeal to the diverse interests in their desired coalition. In this way, party leaders "broker" a coalition of supporters.

The components of the brokered coalition change over time. That is because new political exigencies emerge, and they often require that parties strengthen their ties to some interest groups and weaken their ties to others. As a result, party policies are also in flux. The goal of parties in a system of brokerage politics is not to adhere to relatively fixed sets of principles but to manipulate the electorate in order to gain and maintain power. (That is why, for example, the Liberals did a quick flip-flop on the free trade issue in the early 1990s; they felt they had to switch from an anti–free trade to a pro–free trade position in order to win office.) The system of brokerage politics seems highly democratic because parties listen intently to the opinions of groups of voters. But the system is in fact unresponsive to voters' group interests, which are likely to be watered down or sacrificed entirely as parties seek to broker coalitions between diverse groups. This is a major source of voters' cynicism.

Because brokerage politics fails to bring together stable coalitions of interests, the party system lacks a mechanism that reliably identifies possible solutions for big new political problems. How then do Canadian citizens deal with big new political problems? One method was noted above: they engage in nonconventional politics. A second method involves forming new parties. In the 1930s, the CCF and

Social Credit parties emerged in the West when the Liberal and Conservative parties failed to accommodate Western interests. Similarly, in the 1990s, the Reform Party (now the Canadian Alliance) and the *Bloc Québécois* emerged to represent distinct regional interests that could not find a voice inside the existing parties.

The *Bloc Québécois* is not just the federal voice of Quebec. It is the *separatist* voice of Quebec at the federal level, a party for the large number of Quebeckers who want to opt out of Confederation. Quebec separatism is, of course, Canada's perennial and, according to many analysts, biggest political problem. Separatism is not, however, either the first or the most recent vision of the ideal future (or "utopia") that has animated Quebec politics since, say, 1950. In Chapter 21, Jean-Philippe Warren recaps the utopian visions that have animated Quebec politics over the past half-century. These utopias include the desire for (1) the creation of a true democracy, (2) the creation of a culture of openness, (3) the renewal of nationalism (in both federalist and separatist variants), and (4) the establishment of a social democracy in which social justice prevails. Warren boldly evaluates the extent to which it is worthwhile for Quebeckers to continue fighting the battles of their predecessors. He also assesses the extent to which old ideas could usefully give way to a new understanding of Quebec's present condition and ideal future.

Politics has been likened to a machine that determines "who gets what, when, and how." From this point of view, politics involves more than just elections and the passage of laws by legislatures. It also involves riots, petitions, sit-ins, occupations, boycotts, strikes, and other forms of collective action against people in positions of authority. This is politics "beyond the rules," as it were.

Chapter 22 examines one such form of collective action: the strike. Robert Brym shows how changing government and corporate policies have influenced patterns of strike activity in Canada. From the end of World War II until the mid-1980s, the frequency of strike activity in Canada was sensitive to the phase of the business cycle. During boom periods, unemployment was low and strikes were relatively numerous. That is because in boom times workers were in a good bargaining position. Union strike coffers were full, alternative jobs were available, and employers wanted to settle strikes quickly so they could continue earning high profits. In contrast, during economic slumps workers were in a poor bargaining position. Strike coffers were strapped for cash, alternative jobs were few, and employers had little interest in meeting workers' demands because business was slow. As a result, strikes were infrequent.

Beginning in 1973, however, governments and corporations began to take actions and pass laws that undermined union power and the effectiveness of strikes as a weapon in the struggle to improve workers' standard of living. They felt compelled to limit workers' demands due to rising competitiveness in the global economy. The full economic recovery of Germany and Japan from World War II, the rise of South Korea, Taiwan, and other "Asian Tigers" as major players in international commerce, and Canada's agreement to establish a free-trade zone with the United States and Mexico all pushed Canadian governments and corporations to keep wages and benefits down, even if that meant undermining unions and their ability to mount effective strikes. Sensing that they could achieve little by striking, workers tended not to strike even in boom periods after 1986. The association between the phase of the business cycle and the strike rate thus disappeared. In this manner, heightened international competition among businesses changed the nature of Canadian politics in general and the effectiveness and frequency of strike action in particular.

One would, however, be mistaken to think that protest against authority has died off in the era of globalization. New forms of collective action have crystallized. These include protest marches against globalization and campaigns against developing countries' "sweatshops."

In the last few decades, transnational corporations involved in apparel and sports shoe production have moved their factories to low-wage countries such as Malaysia, Indonesia, and Vietnam. There, workers are paid extremely low wages and toil very long hours in often-dangerous conditions. In the West, a movement has emerged among university students, labour unions, human rights organizations, religious groups, and other activists to protest the existence of these Third World sweatshops — and the athletes such as Tiger Woods and Michael Jordan who lend their support to Nike and make large sums of money by appearing in Nike ads.

Activists are especially adept at using the Internet to embarrass Nike into changing its labour practices. For example, in 2001, Jonah Peretti, a graduate student at the Massachusetts Institute of Technology (MIT), discovered that for US$50 Nike lets consumers personalize their shoes by submitting a word or phrase that can be stitched onto the shoes under the swoosh. Peretti filled out the form and sent them $50, asking them to stitch "SWEATSHOP" onto his shoes. Here is the e-mail correspondence that ensued:

From: "Personalize, NIKE iD" <nikeid_personalize@nike.com
To: "Jonah H. Peretti" <peretti@media.mit.edu
Subject: RE: Your NIKE iD order o16468000

Your NIKE iD order was cancelled for one or more of the following reasons: 1) Your Personal iD contains another party's trademark or other intellectual property 2) Your Personal iD contains the name of an athlete or team we do not have the legal right to use 3) Your Personal iD was left blank. Did you not want any personalization? 4) Your Personal iD contains profanity or inappropriate slang, and besides, your mother would slap us. If you wish to reorder your NIKE iD product with a new personalization please visit us again at www.nike.com

Thank you, NIKE iD

From: "Jonah H. Peretti" <peretti@media.mit.edu
To: "Personalize, NIKE iD" <nikeid_personalize@nike.com
Subject: RE: Your NIKE iD order o16468000

Greetings,

My order was canceled but my personal NIKE iD does not violate any of the criteria outlined in your message. The Personal iD on my custom ZOOM XC USA running shoes was the word "sweatshop." Sweatshop is not: 1) another's party's trademark, 2) the name of an athlete, 3) blank, or 4) profanity. I choose the iD because I wanted to remember the toil and labor of the children that made my shoes. Could you please ship them to me immediately.

Thanks and Happy New Year,

Jonah Peretti

From: "Personalize, NIKE iD" <nikeid_personalize@nike.com
To: "Jonah H. Peretti" <peretti@media.mit.edu
Subject: RE: Your NIKE iD order o16468000

Dear NIKE iD Customer,

Your NIKE iD order was cancelled because the iD you have chosen contains, as stated in the previous e-mail correspondence, "inappropriate slang". If you wish to reorder your NIKE iD product with a new personalization please visit us again at nike.com

Thank you, NIKE iD

From: "Jonah H. Peretti" <peretti@media.mit.edu
To: "Personalize, NIKE iD" <nikeid_personalize@nike.com
Subject: RE: Your NIKE iD order o16468000

Dear NIKE iD,

Thank you for your quick response to my inquiry about my custom ZOOM XC USA running shoes. Although I commend you for your prompt customer service, I disagree with the claim that my personal iD was inappropriate slang. After consulting Webster's Dictionary, I discovered that "sweatshop" is in fact part of standard English, and not slang. The word means: "a shop or factory in which workers are employed for long hours at low wages and under unhealthy conditions" and its origin dates from 1892. So my personal iD does meet the criteria detailed in your first email. Your web site advertises that the NIKE iD program is "about freedom to choose and freedom to express who you are." I share Nike's love of freedom and personal expression. The site also says that "If you want it done right ... build it yourself." I was thrilled to be able to build my own shoes, and my personal iD was offered as a small token of appreciation for the sweatshop workers poised to help me realize my vision. I hope that you will value my freedom of expression and reconsider your decision to reject my order.

Thank you, Jonah Peretti

From: "Personalize, NIKE iD" <nikeid_personalize@nike.com
To: "Jonah H. Peretti" <peretti@media.mit.edu
Subject: RE: Your NIKE iD order o16468000

Dear NIKE iD Customer,

Regarding the rules for personalization it also states on the NIKE iD web site that "Nike reserves the right to cancel any personal iD up to 24 hours after it has been submitted". In addition, it further explains: "While we honor most personal iDs, we cannot honor every one. Some may be (or contain) other's trademarks, or the names of certain professional sports teams, athletes or celebrities that Nike does not have the right to use. Others may contain material that we consider inappropriate or simply do not want to place on our products. Unfortunately, at times this obliges us to decline personal iDs that may otherwise seem unobjectionable. In any event, we will let you know if we decline your personal iD, and we will offer you the chance to submit another." With these rules in mind, we cannot accept your order as submitted. If you wish to reorder your NIKE iD product with a new personalization please visit us again at www.nike.com

Thank you, NIKE iD

From: "Jonah H. Peretti" <peretti@media.mit.edu
To: "Personalize, NIKE iD" <nikeid_personalize@nike.com
Subject: RE: Your NIKE iD order o16468000

Dear NIKE iD,

Thank you for the time and energy you have spent on my request. I have decided to order the shoes with a different iD, but I would like to make one small request. Could you please send me a color snapshot of the ten-year-old Vietnamese girl who makes my shoes?

Thanks,

Jonah Peretti[1]

---

1. "Making Nike Sweat," Jockbeat, *Village Voice*, February 14–20, 2001. Courtesy of Jonah Peretti.

Nike did not respond to Peretti's final e-mail but the correspondence was published on the Web and in *The Village Voice* (at http://www.villagevoice.com/issues/0107/jockbeat.php), causing a public relations fiasco for Nike.

The campaign against Nike forms the subject of Chapter 23, by Graham Knight and Josh Greenberg. Knight and Greenberg explain why Nike is the focus of persistent anti-sweatshop protests even though its production practices are no different from those of some other large transnational corporations. They show that it is precisely Nike's success economically and symbolically that makes it the main target of anti-sweatshop protest. They also argue that the kind of social activism typified by the anti-sweatshop campaign will pose an ongoing problem for some transnational corporations. That is because the movement is decentralized, ethically based, and uses tactics that are able to turn a corporation's promotional power against its interests and image.

CRITICAL THINKING QUESTIONS

1. What is more democratic — a system of brokerage politics or a system in which various group interests are firmly aligned with specific parties?
2. Can non-conventional politics and new parties adequately express the interests of dissenting Canadian citizens?
3. Outline the utopian visions that have animated Quebec politics over the past half-century.
4. According to Jean-Philippe Warren, how worthwhile is it for Quebeckers today to fight the battles of their predecessors? What alternative does he propose?
5. In Canada, how did strike frequency vary with the phase of the business cycle between 1945 and 1986? Between 1987 and 2000?
6. What changes in government and corporate policy altered the association between the phase of the business cycle and the frequency of strikes in Canada after the mid-1980s?
7. Why has Nike become the focus of the anti-sweatshop movement?
8. In what ways does the campaign against developing countries' sweatshops differ from the strike movement? What accounts for these differences?

ANNOTATED BIBLIOGRAPHY

Doug Baer, ed., *Political Sociology: Canadian Perspectives* (Toronto: Oxford University Press, 2002). Covers the major issues in the study of Canadian politics from a sociological perspective.

William K. Carroll, ed. *Organizing Dissent: Contemporary Social Movements in Theory and Practice*, 2nd ed. (Toronto: Garamond, 1997). A useful collection of articles on non-conventional politics in Canada.

Kenneth McRoberts, *Quebec: Social Change and Political Crisis*, 3rd ed. with a postscript (Toronto: Oxford University Press, 1999 [1976]). The definitive account in English of the political, economic, and social dimensions of the Quebec question.

Chapter 20

Canadian Elections and the Limits of Brokerage Politics

HAROLD D. CLARKE

JANE JENSON

LAWRENCE LEDUC

JON H. PAMMETT

AN ANGRY AND CYNICAL ELECTORATE

For a number of years politicians have been the target of a dissatisfied citizenry, which feels left out of the political process and unhappy about its outcomes. In 1992, an angry electorate rejected the Charlottetown Accord, a proposal to get Quebec to sign the constitution of Canada. Other population consultations, such as those carried out by the Spicer Commission after the defeat of the Meech Lake Accord, turned up high levels of public grumpiness, which fed into the whole subsequent discussion of constitutional politics. In addition, in the 1993 election campaign, much was made by the Reform Party of its promise to make politicians more responsive and more responsible. The populist agenda of the new party resonated for many voters who were dissatisfied with old-style politics.

Canadians do not believe that the problem is of their own making. They place the blame squarely on politicians and the political process. The public remains interested in elections, and

most citizens cast a ballot when given the opportunity to do so. Yet voters give the parties exceedingly low marks for their contribution to democratic debate and the presentation of alternative futures. Figure 20.1 shows that, despite the array of new issues and long-running controversies that crowd the agenda, citizens do not exhibit any growing tendency to feel that politics is too complicated for them to understand. Indeed there has been a slight increase in feelings of subjective political competence. If anything, voters feel more rather than less capable of understanding politics, despite the abandonment of the familiar discourse of postwar Keynesianism and the adoption of unfamiliar neoconservative frameworks.

Nor are Canadians turning away from politics. Many of them take an interest in elections. In 1993 a majority (52 percent) of the voters reported that they were "very interested" in that election, while an additional 32 percent said they were "fairly interested." Levels of interest in elections have remained high over the last decade, therefore providing no evidence that the years of

Source: Excerpted from Harold D. Clarke, Jane Jenson, Lawrence LeDuc, and Jon H. Pammett, "The Politics of Discontent," in *Absent Mandate: Canadian Electoral Politics in an Era of Restructuring*, 3rd ed. (Toronto: Gage Educational Publishing, 1996), pp. 176–87. Reprinted with permission.

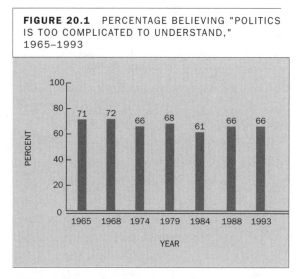

FIGURE 20.1 PERCENTAGE BELIEVING "POLITICS IS TOO COMPLICATED TO UNDERSTAND," 1965–1993

SOURCE: *Canadian National Election Studies* (1965–79), *Political Support in Canada Studies* (1984–93) Inter-University Consortium for Political and Social Research (Ann Arbor, MI).

political and economic turbulence have caused the voters to withdraw their attention or concern.

Election interest also translated into rates of participation in campaign-related activities, which were generally as high as in the previous election in 1988, which was itself an election that provoked a great deal of attention. In spite of the slightly lower voting turnout in 1993, Figure 20.2 shows that the various other dimensions of political participation remained at or near the same level. Many people continue to discuss politics with others, and the percentage of the population that reported attempting to influence their friends' vote jumped from 18 percent to 23 percent. Four-fifths of the electorate had watched a television program about the campaign, while similar numbers reported reading about the election in a newspaper or hearing about it on the radio. The portrait of the voters that emerges from these data is one of a reasonably interested, active group, not discouraged by the complexity of the issues or fearful of discussing the new economic schemas.

Yet, voters are not happy, and they place the blame for their distress squarely at the door of politicians, especially those practising brokerage politics. In brokerage politics, parties do not

have a fixed and predictable position on issues. Instead, before each election, parties canvass the electorate to learn how public opinion is distributed on a range of salient issues. Parties then try to negotiate or "broker" a coalition of supporters that will lead them to electoral victory.

If we examine additional measures of voters' sense of external efficacy as well as of their sense of trust, we see that all these indicators have moved in the direction of greater dissatisfaction. As Figure 20.3 on page 226 shows, the percentage of people feeling they had no say in government hovered in the range of 49 percent to 57 percent from 1965 to 1988, but in 1993 it shot up to 65 percent. Two-thirds of the electorate, rather than a half, now report strong feelings of being ignored. Over the same period the perception that the system itself was unresponsive showed a steady increase, reaching even greater heights in 1993 than the already elevated levels of 1988. In 1993 four-fifths of the voters said they believed that their elected representatives, the members of Parliament, quickly lose touch with their constituents. Two-thirds felt that the government did not care about people like them. In both cases, the reported levels of

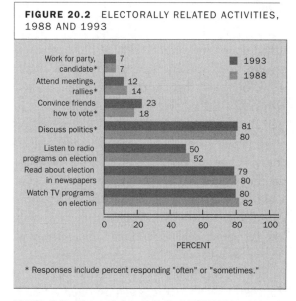

FIGURE 20.2 ELECTORALLY RELATED ACTIVITIES, 1988 AND 1993

* Responses include percent responding "often" or "sometimes."

SOURCE: *Political Support in Canada Studies* (1988, 1993) Inter-University Consortium for Political and Social Research (Ann Arbor, MI).

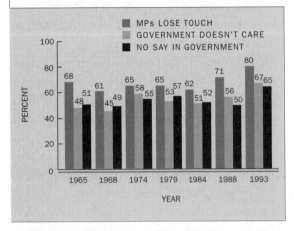

FIGURE 20.3 PERCENTAGES BELIEVING MPs LOSE TOUCH WITH CONSTITUENTS, GOVERNMENT DOESN'T CARE WHAT THEY THINK, AND PEOPLE LIKE THEM HAVE NO SAY, 1965–1993

SOURCE: *Canadian National Election Studies* (1965–79), *Political Support in Canada Studies* (1984–93) Inter-University Consortium for Political and Social Research (Ann Arbor, MI).

external political inefficacy in 1993 were the highest on record.

Many voters also believe that the political authorities are untrustworthy, and survey evidence suggests that these beliefs have become more widespread in recent years. Between 1988 and 1993, the size of the group considering authorities to be "smart" dropped by 9 percent, while that which thought them trustworthy declined by 17 percent (Figure 20.4). When asked about authorities' stewardship of the taxpayers' dollars, fully 93 percent of the voters in 1993 believed that money was being wasted, climbing to that level from an already high 80 percent in 1988.

In giving such evaluations the Canadian electorate is not expressing a generalized cynicism to all things political, however. Both post-election and inter-electoral public opinion surveys reveal a capacity and a willingness among voters to make choices about where to direct their criticisms. Voters do recognize that political parties make a significant contribution to democratic politics. As Table 20.1 shows, parties are most often valued as facilitators of representation and participation.[1] Levels of approval of activities such as repre-

senting "everybody," encouraging people to become politically active, and finding consensus are substantially higher than other characteristics of parties, even if they remain distressingly low in absolute terms (only about a third of the population, after all, gives parties high marks on these general democratic activities).

But voters are profoundly and almost universally dissatisfied with brokerage politics. Almost two-thirds of respondents consider that the parties do not offer real choices, while 69 percent think that the parties fail to tell the voters about the really important problems facing the country. Moreover, there is virtual consensus that political parties pay too much attention to winning elections and not enough to governing afterwards (81 percent) and to gaining partisan advantage rather than solving important problems (89 percent). The most dramatic result in Table 20.1, and the one that most clearly indicates that the practices of brokerage politics contribute to the public's cynicism, is the 91 percent of the respondents who report that they anticipate a "big difference" between "what a party says it will do, and what it actually does if it wins an election."

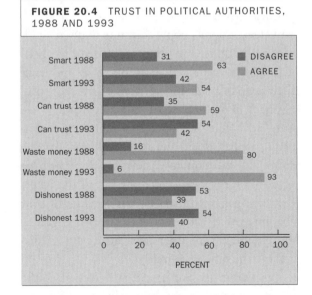

FIGURE 20.4 TRUST IN POLITICAL AUTHORITIES, 1988 AND 1993

SOURCE: *Political Support in Canada Studies* (1988, 1993) Inter-University Consortium for Political and Social Research (Ann Arbor, MI).

TABLE 20.1 EVALUATIONS OF POLITICAL PARTIES, 1991

	AGREE (%)	DISAGREE (%)	DON'T KNOW (%)
Parties spend too much time bickering and quarrelling rather than solving important problems facing the country	**89**	6	5
In elections political parties don't tell people about the really important problems facing the country	**69**	21	11
Political parties and democracy always go together — no parties, no democracy	50	**26**	24
Political parties generally try to look after the best interests of everybody and not just the interests of those who vote for them	33	**57**	10
Parties give people a say in politics that they couldn't have as individuals	44	**41**	15
There is often a big difference between what a party says it will do, and what it actually does if it wins an election	**91**	4	5
Parties usually are more interested in winning elections than in governing afterwards	**81**	12	7
Parties do a good job of encouraging people to become active in politics	31	**51**	18
Political parties do more to divide the country than to unite it	**56**	28	17
Parties don't offer voters real choices in elections because their policies are all pretty much the same	**63**	26	10
Parties generally do a good job in helping groups reach agreement about what government should be doing	29	**50**	21

Note: Boldface percentages indicate negative response.

SOURCE: *Political Support in Canada Studies* (1991) Inter-University Consortium for Political and Social Research (Ann Arbor, MI).

Other surveys confirm this finding. In a 1991 study, André Blais and Elisabeth Gidengil found that the highest level of political cynicism over twelve different measures were recorded in response to a statement that "most candidates in federal elections make campaign promises they have no intention of fulfilling.[2] They also found that the electorate reserved its harshest judgement for the parties' capacity to provoke meaningful consideration of the issues. Fully 87 percent of their respondents agreed with the statement that "the parties confuse the issues rather than provide a clear choice on them" while 81 percent thought the parties "squabbled" too much.[3]

In commenting on such findings, the Royal Commission on Electoral Reform and Party Financing indicted the parties and their behaviour, saying that "feelings about confusing issues and squabbling may ... partly reflect the limited efforts by parties to engage in political education and discussion of policy issues."[4] Indeed, the message is quite clear. Canadian citizens are not "turned off" electoral politics per se. They are interested and they want to be involved. Yet, they feel that they do not have access to the political process and that politicians and governments are neither sufficiently responsive nor reliable. Oftentimes, voters behave as if they feel they have no choice but to "throw the rascals out," even if the replacements are not likely to be very different. Thus, the electorate is not simply cynical. It is angry and exhibits high levels of dissatisfaction with brokerage politics.

THE LEGACY OF BROKERAGE POLITICS: PERMANENT DEALIGNMENT

Crucial to the story of Canadian voters is the longstanding legacy of a party system characterized, from the beginning of the twentieth century, by a style of politics that has minimized real debate about alternatives. It is a system that has frequently focused more on leaders and image politics, and in which parties have taken over each other's policies. Thus, the economic and social positions adopted by the two main parties have often been indistinguishable from each other. Moreover, when there were policy differences, it was often hard to predict on the basis of its past actions which position any party would adopt. That the Liberals carried on much of the neoconservatism of the Tories after 1993 is only the most recent example of policy flip-flops and convergence over the years.

Accompanying the pliability in programmatic stances and policy positions of parties has been a high level of flexibility in the responses of Canadian voters when elections invite them to make choices. As we might expect in a party system in which much of the public has not developed enduring ties to political parties rooted in ideology or group loyalties, Canadian voters exhibit few qualms about switching from one party to another as the winds of approval change. The electorate has been willing to abandon earlier decisions on short notice and it has become accustomed to shifting easily among alternative parties, candidates, leaders, and party policies once it decides that it is time to try something new. Few voters have been patient enough to wait out an extended stretch of time before abandoning a position, person, or party. This unwillingness to think long-term has been encouraged by parties that have promised quick-fix solutions. As such, it has now become a real constraint on any party's ability to experiment with proposing alternative projects for the future.

Moreover, in part because of the fluidity of issues, leaders and their ability to stitch together policy stances have become an important factor accounting for voting choice, especially among flexible partisans. When parties emphasize leadership and voters focus on the leaders, discussion is deflected toward general considerations of public confidence in these individuals. Popular evaluations of the leaders are, of course, based partly on their stance on issues and partly on their perceived personal characteristics. Nevertheless, the prominent role frequently accorded the leaders during election campaigns ensures that any policy discussion occurs around the public utterances and personal skills of these few persons, and that their character and public confidence in their ability to carry out policy become inextricably intertwined with the consideration of the electoral issues themselves. This emphasis on leaders and leadership may enable parties to avoid discussion of conflict-creating or unpopular policy alternatives that might damage their fortunes during the campaign. Yet, it also ensures that leaders bear the brunt of public displeasure when the quick-fix policies produced in this way do not work. Individual party leaders have become both the anchors of the brokerage system and its major casualties. The fate of former Conservative prime minister Kim Campbell in the 1993 election is only the most recent, and perhaps most dramatic, manifestation of this aspect of brokerage politics.

Whether the behaviour of the parties or the flexibility of partisan ties in the electorate is the ultimate source of brokerage politics is a question that can never be answered satisfactorily. Indeed, any question about ultimate cause is incorrectly posed. The process over time has been one of learning by both voters and politicians. Political parties have learned that their electoral coalitions are fragile creations, requiring constant and careful tending. For their part voters have learned that they will not be offered clear choices about the future in elections and therefore often seek only to bring about a "change."

The impact of this interactive learning process has been clearly visible in elections since the mid-1960s. Canadians have been fickle in their attachments to political parties, changing not only their votes but also their party identification. Such a situation can be characterized as one of dealignment. A dealigned party system is one in which volatility is paramount, where there are frequent changes in electoral outcomes as well as lots of individual flexibility. The 1993 election, which decimated the Conservatives' parliamentary delegation at the same time as it fractured the House of Commons into five parts, is an obvious result of such dealignment. It is, however, only the most recent manifestation of what has been a long-standing characteristic of federal electoral politics, revealed earlier in the big swings of 1958, 1968, and 1984.

An alternative kind of party system is one that is aligned. Where alignment exists, large numbers of people believe that their interests and those of others like them are best served, over the long haul, by a particular party that offers something different from its competitors. Voters in an aligned party system consider that a particular party advances the cause of specific social groups and espouse readily identifiable ideological positions. Moreover, parties can be differentiated by their ties to particular groups and commitments to specific alternatives. One result is that in an aligned party system voters settle into recurrent patterns of political thought and behaviour.

As these patterns begin to break down, a process of dealignment takes hold. A variety of factors may give rise to dealignment, including shifts in the parties' links to social groups, abandonment of ideological commitments, or changes in the composition of the electorate. Thus, the retreat from postwar Keynesian economics in many countries has been associated with a dealignment of party systems, as social classes and other social groups found themselves bereft of allies or abandoned by their previously favoured party. Other analyses have identified a dealignment following the "new politics" preferred by the baby-boom generations first voting in the 1970s and 1980s in Western Europe and North America.[5]

Configurations of support for Canadian parties have not been adequately explained by long-term forces such as social class, religion, or other group characteristics. Nor has ideology been a strong correlate of either partisanship or voting, and the party system has long defied a simple left/right depiction.[6] Moreover, if federal politics has always been characterized by strong regional patterns of party and electoral support, these have never been stable over time. For example, the Liberal "stronghold" of Quebec crumbled before the Tories led by their new leader from Quebec, Brian Mulroney, in 1984. Only two elections later, that party virtually disappeared from that province's electoral map following the overwhelming victory of the Bloc Québécois. The map of the West has been similarly reconfigured since the Reform Party came on the scene.

We have seen that parties are not able to call on loyal electorates and instead have attempted to harness a variety of less predictable short-term forces to achieve victory. It is the predominance of short-term forces that has led us to be skeptical about whether 1993 marks any realignment, despite the dramatic changes and the appearance of new parties. For a party system to be realigned, changes would have to be more than temporary and patterns would have to begin to jell into a stable shape. The specific circumstances of the 1993 events as well as the history of earlier elections suggest a cautious assessment.

First, the Bloc Québécois, despite its success in becoming the official opposition, has publicly proclaimed that it has little intention of being a contender in the next election.[7] Thus, federal politics in Quebec is destined to undergo another major shift. History gives us even more reason to expect continued instability. For example, before the Conservatives were returned to power in the turbulent election of 1988, three successive governing parties had gone down to defeat — the Liberals in 1979, the Tories in 1980, and the Liberals in 1984. Indeed, prior to 1988, the only post-1945 federal election to produce consecutive majority governments was that of 1953. Moreover, if the Tories' back-to-back victories in 1984 and 1988 led to speculation about a realignment in which the Conservatives would replace the Liberals as the "government party," their spectacular defeat in 1993 quickly undermined that proposition.

Another possible suggestion is that the Tories' electoral successes in the 1980s simply started a process of dealignment that became evident in 1993. It is difficult to sustain such a hypothesis. Over the last two decades, at least, there is abundant evidence of widespread flexibility in partisan attachments and volatility in electoral behaviour and results. Thus, unlike other party systems in which a convergence of specific events and changes in the electorate in the 1970s and 1980s triggered a dealignment, it is quite likely that the current dealignment of the Canadian party system is rooted in now distant events and conditions.

Election results over several decades reinforce the story told by the survey evidence; the Canadian situation is one of permanent dealignment. Whatever its sources, the consequences of this ongoing phenomenon are very visible in the contemporary volatility of electoral politics. Nonetheless, a situation of permanent dealignment does not imply that nothing has changed. Rather, it means that change itself is a key strand of the fabric of federal politics. In 1993, as in previous years, we have seen that levels of partisan identification remained high, at the same time that large numbers of voters shifted the direction of their allegiance. They moved to the new parties and thereby produced the 1993 successes of the Bloc Québécois and the Reform Party. It is far too early — and on the basis of past experience quite unlikely — that these voters will be any more than the "fair-weather friends" that they have already been for the Liberals, Conservatives, or NDP. Massive shifts from party to party from one election to another are not unusual, nor have they proved to be a reliable indicator that a realignment had occurred or was in the offing.

INTO THE FUTURE

Despite the change in government in 1993, the project for restructuring the Canadian economy and its place in the world continues. Continuity may be observed in both the Liberal government's willingness to pick up the neoconservative torch passed to it by the soundly defeated Tories and its decision to do so in ways that will contribute little if anything to lessening the electorate's dissatisfaction with brokerage politics. A number of policy reversals as well as dramatic initiatives hardly hinted at in the campaign took place. The Liberal government has acted in this way despite the exceedingly high levels of dissatisfaction with such party behaviour already evident in the various public opinion data.

The Liberals of course are not the only party that has been criticized for failing to live up to its campaign promises. In the aftermath of its 1993 success, some observes chastised the Reform Party, which had pledged a new approach to politics, for accepting the perks of office and softening some of its policy positions. Although Reform leaders insist that the essentials of their agenda will remain intact, the forces that encourage parties, new or old, to play the traditional brokerage game did not disappear in 1993. One of the most important of these forces is the flexibility of voters' partisan attachments. This flexibility will continue to generate a strong potential for electoral volatility in the years ahead, and parties ignore it at their peril. If the party system fragmented in 1993, past experience gives us little guide as to whether the patterns yielded by this fragmentation will endure. Rather it encourages a good deal of skepticism about their durability. All parties will continue to face the challenge of building winning coalitions in elections, and dramatic reversals of fortune for any party can readily occur.

Despite these continuities there have been changes. The most dramatic and consequential is the consolidation of the restructuring project. The postwar commitment to Keynesian economic policies and constitutional reform has given way to neoconservative economics and constitutional stalemate. These have produced their own responses among the electorate. High levels of dissatisfaction with traditional political forms have not led to alienation or demobilization. Rather, as the events of constitutional debate in the early 1980s first demonstrated and then as the conflicts over free trade and Meech Lake confirmed, Canadians have been seeking new routes to representation. Sometimes this has led to demands for forms of direct democracy, such as the constitutional referendum in 1992. Sometimes it has been expressed in support for a political party, such as the Reform Party, which promises to change the old ways of doing things. And sometimes it has generated new routes to representation, which by-pass the party system and channel energy in the direction of interest groups and social movements.

All of these are signs that there is a serious public thirst for maintaining and extending the spaces of democratic politics. Whether the party system and electoral politics will quench this thirst remains the great unknown as we face the next century. The challenge put to parties and elections, the traditional institutions of democratic governance, is to rise to the occasion and finally begin to fulfill their assigned task of organizing choice and mobilizing change.

NOTES

1. Harold D. Clarke and Allan Kornberg, "Evaluations and Evolution: Public Attitudes toward Canada's Federal Parties, 1965–1991," *Canadian Journal of Political Science* 26 (1993): 292.

2. André Blais and Elisabeth Gidengil, Making *Representative Democracy Work: The Views of Canadians,* vol. 17 of the Research Studies of the Royal Commission on Electoral Reform and Party Financing (Toronto: Dundurn Press, 1991), Table 3.1, p. 35.

3. Ibid., Table 3.5, p. 42.

4. Royal Commission on Electoral Reform and Party Financing (RCERPF), *Reforming Electoral Democracy* (Ottawa: Supply and Services, 1991), vol. 1, p. 226.

5. For a detailed overview of this literature, comparing Western Europe to Canada, see Maureen Covell, "Parties as Institutions of National Governance," in Herman Bakvis, ed., *Representation, Integration and Political Parties in Canada,* vol. 14 of the Research Studies of the RCERPF (Toronto: Dundurn Press, 1991).

6. See Harold D. Clark and Marianne Stewart, "Canada," in Mark Franklin et al., eds., *Electoral Change: Responses to Evolving Social and Attitudinal Structures in Western Countries* (Cambridge: Cambridge University Press, 1992), and Janine Brodie and Jane Jenson, "Piercing the Smokescreen: Brokerage Parties and Class Politics," in A.-G. Gagnon and A.B. Tanguay, eds., *Canadian Parties in Transition: Discourse, Organization, Representation* (Toronto: Nelson, 1988).

7. The BQ did run in the 1997 election.

Chapter 21

French Quebec, the Quiet Revolution, and After: Glories and Miseries of Four Utopias[1]

JEAN-PHILIPPE WARREN

This essay focuses on four visions of the ideal society ("utopias") formulated by the French population in Quebec in the past four decades. My starting point is the Quiet Revolution (1960–70). During the 1960s Quebec undertook massive reforms aimed at getting rid of what many observers judged to be its backward character. Blaming mostly the Catholic Church's domination of the province, French Canadian intellectuals and militants dreamed of establishing a society in which democracy, tolerance, justice, and openness would prevail. This is how, in the space of just a decade, a largely traditionalist and closed society was transformed by the dreams of a new generation of *Québécois*.[2] This essay relates the story of these dreams and their fate.

The four utopias of the 1960s and the 1970s were as follows:

1. the realization of a thoroughly democratic political system;
2. the achievement of Quebec independence or the construction of a completely bilingual Canada;
3. the establishment of a socialist society ("social democracy"); and
4. the translation of the old language of values into a new humanism adapted to the technological age in the making.

Analysis of these utopias can help us better understand the ideologies and commitments of Quebec social movements during the past four decades, reveal the main political and social tendencies of this period, and, consequently, underline the challenges facing Quebec society today. You will see that, following two decades of struggle and great expectations (the 1960s and 1970s), a period of disillusionment set in. In this respect, Quebec was no different from other countries in the Western world, where the radical 1960s and 1970s eventually gave way to a more conservative era. Reassessing the utopias of the 1960s and 1970s will also serve to emphasize the importance of not forgetting them, even if they must now be understood in a new light.

1. DEMOCRACY

It is easy to forget today, but one of the chief debates that helped Jean Lesage and his Liberal Party get elected in 1960 turned on the question of political morality. The Union Nationale Party, led by Maurice Duplessis, dominated Quebec politics since the 1930s. Duplessis was premier from 1936 to 1939 and from 1944 to 1959. He turned patronage (e.g., hiring and giving government contracts to political friends) and corruption (e.g., accepting bribes) into a

Source: © Jean-Philippe Warren 2002.

political system. Characteristically, Duplessis once started a speech by addressing his audience as "Électeurs, électrices, électricité" ("Male Electors, Female Electors, Electricity"), reminding voters in the small village he was speaking in that they had better vote for his party if they wanted to get connected to the province's electrical grid.

Duplessis organized politics into an efficient machine for reinforcing his personal domination. Companies had to pay a "commission" for every government contract they obtained, and the regime's friends had to contribute to Union Nationale coffers if they expected personal favours. Duplessis was also careful to discredit the provincial Liberal Party. He accused it of being a refuge for French Canada's enemies. Did the Liberal Party not support compulsory military service in 1942, forcing the *Québécois* to fight "England's" war against Germany, as if Quebec were still an English colony, he persistently asked the electorate? Was the Liberal Party not a nest of dangerous socialists, as evidenced by its support for more state intervention in economic life? Duplessis's propaganda tarnished the reputation of everybody who stood in his way. Nor did he stop at words. He took action — often brutal action — to rid himself of opponents. He crushed the prolonged and bitter Asbestos strike (1948) by sending in the police to beat up the strikers. He imposed restrictive new regulations at Laval University that compelled Father Georges-Henri Lévesque to resign as dean of the *Faculté des sciences sociales*. And so forth.

One of the most famous articles published in Quebec in the 1950s was Gérard Dion and Louis O'Neill's "L'Immoralité politique dans la province de Québec" (1956). The authors denounced the "flood of stupidity" that Quebec was witnessing and the complete "perversion of conscience." Their words were harsh for they feared the destruction of democracy in Quebec. This is why, for both of them, an urgent reform of political morals by means of general civic education seemed necessary. "The work has to speed up before demagogues and would-be fascists

render the masses so stupid that any effort to right the situation becomes impossible."[3] This was also what the intellectuals grouped around the *Rassemblement* (formed in 1956) and the *Unions des forces démocratiques* (formed in 1958) believed. These two political organizations did not seek to become political parties. Rather, they sought to purify Quebec's politics by educating ordinary *Québécois*. "In 1958, French Canadians must begin to learn democracy from scratch," wrote the young Pierre Elliott Trudeau.[4] If the masses were not ready to exercise their political rights, the solution was not to abolish democracy altogether but to elevate political consciousness.

The generation that came of age after World War II was dedicated to establishing liberal democracy in Quebec like no generation before. At last, for instance, Aboriginal peoples gained the right to vote at the federal and provincial level in the 1960s. To be sure, there were violent elements in provincial politics, including people who thought traditional liberal democracy was a sham and were willing to plant bombs in mailboxes to prove their point. In 1970 the Front de Libération du Quebec (FLQ) proclaimed: "We wash our hands of the British parliamentary system; the Front de Libération du Québec will never let itself be distracted by the electoral crumbs that the Anglo-Saxon capitalists toss into the Quebec barnyard every four years."[5]

Believing Quebec was on the eve of a popular uprising, the FLQ kidnapped and murdered Pierre Laporte, Quebec Vice-Premier and Minister of Labour, plunging the country into the 1970 "October crisis," during which martial law was declared, federal troops marched into the province, and arbitrary mass arrests were made. Yet this outburst of violence cannot make us forget the peaceful and democratic way in which most of Quebec's political disputes were dealt with. Many democratic struggles elsewhere — notably the civil rights movement in the United States, which sought to heal much deeper and more painful wounds — witnessed bitter violence. Most of the members of the postwar generation believed that the people were the sole repository of power and that transparency was the cardinal quality of a democratic regime. This meant an insistence on participatory democracy (universal, mass participation in politics) and the eradication of corruption from public affairs. Notwithstanding the absurdity of most of their claims, the radical groups of the 1970s (the FLQ, the Marxist-Leninists, the Maoists, extremists in labour unions, etc.) attacked liberal democracy for not being democratic enough and extended the critique of the parliamentary system as a system of corruption and favouritism.

In 1978 the ruling party, the *Parti Québécois*, adopted laws restraining companies and trade unions from contributing to the electoral funding of political parties and forcing the latter to state their incomes and expenses. Recently, the *Bloc Québécois* has been trying to adhere to these funding rules in Ottawa despite the fact that other federal parties do not follow similar principles and have no intention of doing so. Numerous other provincial laws confirm the commitment of *Québécois* to the health of their democracy.

In Canada, the Trudeau government did not have similar success in its attempt to change the electoral process and political organization in general. Of course, less needed to be done because most of Canada outside Quebec was already a vigorous, albeit imperfect, democracy in the 1970s. It is nevertheless obvious that Bay Street did not lose control over Parliament, that thousands of jobs for political friends were created in the 1970s, and that networks of political patronage remained strong. Characteristically, of the 25 cabinet ministers appointed to Trudeau's first government, 15 were given prestigious federal offices after they left politics.[6] Trudeau's commitment to establishing participatory democracy during his 1968 leadership campaign soon vanished, leaving Canadian politics in pretty much the same state as when he came to power.

This is not to say that Canada is not a democracy and should not, as such, be regarded with envy by the world community. It is to say that

democracy, here and abroad, is a work in progress, and that *Québécois*, having made considerable headway in their province, must continue to fight for greater openness of public institutions at the federal and provincial levels. Major changes await us if we want to live up to the dreams of our predecessors. At the provincial level, one of these might involve reassessing the constituency-based, simple majority ballot. In the 1998 Quebec election, fully one-third of the deputies were elected with less than 50 percent of the popular vote in their ridings because so many people voted for losing candidates. Many analysts are now talking about partly adopting a system of proportional representation, as in Western Europe. In addition to the traditional vote for local candidates, this would involve people voting for a province-wide list of candidates established by each political party. It might take, say, 40 000 votes from anywhere in the province to elect each person on a party's list. In that case, few votes would be wasted and representation in the Quebec legislature would much more closely reflect the political will of the people. The fact that the percentage of people exercising their right to vote is slowly but inexorably dropping election after election is one indication among others that democracy in Quebec (and Canada as a whole) is amenable to improvement. The concentration of ownership of the Canadian press in the hands of a few giant conglomerates is another big problem area for Quebec and Canadian democracy.

2. A NATION IN THE MAKING

Louis Tardivel, the religious owner of the newspaper *La Vérité*, and Henri Bourassa, the founder of the newspaper *Le Devoir*, knew each other well and respected each other's commitments. But while Louis Tardivel wrote a novel (*Pour la Patrie*, 1895) in which he predicted an independent Quebec by 1945, Henri Bourassa wrote and spoke to convince English Canadians to help him build a bilingual and bicultural Canada respectful of the two founding nations.

When Bourassa died in 1952, neither dream had become reality. The national question remained unresolved. The Quiet Revolutionaries split on this issue, most of the older half joining the federalist camp and most of the younger half joining the nationalist camp.

The historical context nurtured the dreams of both federalists and nationalists. On the one hand, nationalism had been discredited by the horrible atrocities of the fascist regimes during World War II. Furthermore, the Western European countries were trying to unite into a single political body, paving the way, according to optimists, to a world government. On the other hand, colonies around the globe (including, ironically, Canada, which adopted its flag in 1965, its national anthem in 1980, and repatriated its Constitution from London in 1982) were striving for independence from their metropolises while invoking the principle of self-determination recognized by the United Nations.

For French-Canadian federalists, Canada belonged to both francophones and anglophones even if the two founding peoples did not always act like equal partners. With this view in mind they helped to enact the Official Languages Bill (1969) in spite of strong resistance from conservative factions in English Canada, who feared so-called "French power." French-Canadian federalists believed that nearly every Canadian would eventually speak English and French fluently. Moreover, they felt that once Canada was a bilingual country, Quebec would not have the right to speak for all French Canadians.

In contrast, separatists did not believe Canada could ever be a true home for Francophones. English Canadians, they said, had never respected them. They argued, for example, that during World War II the federal government asked the provinces to temporarily hand over their control of income tax but never gave it back. Historically, the federal government even refused things as trivial as bilingual postage stamps, insisting instead on stamps extolling Canada's attachment to the British Empire.

French Quebec, said the separatists, shared nothing with the rest of Canada. Moreover, lost in what appeared to be a North American ocean, many *Québécois* felt in danger of being assimilated to the English majority. Securing the *Québécois* nation could only be achieved through the political autonomy of the province, they concluded.

Quebec's last 40 years of history has been summarized by some analysts as a political struggle between sovereigntists and federalists. But these analysts fail to underline how much both camps came to share as they evolved:

1. *Culture as a state policy.* Despite their continuous quarrelling, Quebec federalists and Quebec separatists were both convinced nationalists, proud of being a citizen either of Quebec or Canada. Jacques Parizeau, leader of the *Parti Québécois* during the 1995 referendum, once said that he and Trudeau agreed on everything except where to put the national capital. And in fact, while the Quebec government was adopting programs to promote local culture, the federal government, under the guidance of those who exercised "French power," was mounting a campaign to protect Canadian culture from American influence. Artists, magazines, television and radio broadcasting, as well as thousands of institutions, associations, groups, and organizations received government funding conditional on promoting "Canadian content." The federal government gave itself the mandate of building a Canadian nation out of British, French, Aboriginal, and other elements, while the Quebec government imagined having a mandate to forge a Quebec nation out of (for the most part) the *Québécois*. Yet despite heading in different directions, the principles at the crux of Canada's and Quebec's actions were similar. Opposed when they were addressing Canadian cultural issues, they stood shoulder to shoulder at international consultation tables for the protection

of local particularities. They tried to save Quebec and Canadian culture from the invasion of "McWorld" by creating state cultural institutions (Radio Canada, *Télé Québec*), distributing grants to artists and intellectuals (Canada Council for the Arts, Ministère de la culture), establishing quotas on "Canadian" and "Quebec" content, and controlling investment in cultural institutions (some companies engaged in cultural production must be two-thirds Canadian-owned by law).

2. *Language as the only legitimate criterion for defining a nation.* A second area of commonality between sovereigntists and federalists involves the criterion they employ for defining a nation. They did not always agree on this matter. In the 1960s, the federal Commission on Bilingualism and Biculturalism had legitimized the "two equal founding nations" idea. In 1972, however, the federal government passed a bill on multiculturalism. Many Quebec nationalists accused Trudeau of betrayal, of watering down the idea of two equal founding nations. To the sovereigntists it seemed that other immigrant groups were now being awarded almost the same status as the *Québécois*. Partly in reaction, the Quebec government passed Bill 101 in 1977. Its aim was to protect not just the French language, but also the values and traditions of the *Québécois*. Yet in the 1980s and 1990s more and more Quebec nationalists came to acknowledge that a state can promote only language and that cultural diversity is not a dilution but an enrichment of national traditions. The Quebec nation many *Québécois* have come to believe in is a "nation of cultures" — very much like Canada with its multiculturalist policies — and not a homogeneous nation composed exclusively of people of French descent. For example, historian Gérard Bouchard, a leading separatist thinker, asserts that the *Québécois* should be defined "strictly by a linguistic criterion."[7] As a result of the widespread acceptance of

this idea, promoting *Québécois* culture now involves little more than subsidizing the creation of cultural products in Quebec, regardless of their cultural content. This is similar to the situation in the rest of Canada, where cultural products created in Canada are equated with Canadian culture.

3. *Quebec as a people.* A third area of commonality between sovereigntists and separatists concerns the idea that French-Canadian Quebeckers form a *Québécois* people. The *Québécois* have come a long way since the nineteenth century, when they called themselves *Canadiens* to distinguish themselves from the British, and since the turn of the twentieth century, when they called themselves French Canadians to distinguish themselves from Canadians who spoke English. Today, the *Québécois* feel little or no attachment to their linguistic "brothers" and "sisters" in other provinces. For their part, the leaders of the provincial and federal Liberal parties speak of *Québécois* interests without even trying to convince the *Québécois* that they are members of the same family as Francophones outside Quebec. The same recognition was embodied in the ill-fated Meech Lake Accord, which was designed to entice Quebec to recognize Canada's constitution. The Accord recognized Quebec — not French Canada — as a "distinct society," that is, a society enjoying special status in Confederation.

Today the national question remains unresolved. The 1980 and 1995 Quebec referenda on sovereignty ended in bitter defeat for the sovereigntists. Trudeau's dream of a bilingual Canada is an almost complete failure, except in the Acadian part of New Brunswick and despite episodic vitality in other French-Canadian communities outside Quebec. Not only is French as a first language not progressing outside Quebec, its only chance of maintaining itself as a first language is to stay within Quebec's borders. The numbers are there to remind anyone of the fragility of the French fact in Canada. In 1971, the percentage of people speaking French at home outside Quebec was a mere 4.4 percent. In 1981, it was down to 3.8 percent. Ten years later, it fell to 3.2 percent. In 1996, it dropped to 2.9 percent. This picture is discouraging for anyone hoping to achieve Henri Bourassa's and Pierre Trudeau's dream of a Canada which would be not just officially bilingual but where French as a first language would flower from coast to coast.

3. SOCIAL JUSTICE

The generation that came of age after World War II committed itself to erecting a welfare state in Canada and Quebec. (A "welfare state" guards citizens from the ravages of the market by providing some level of protection against ill health, unemployment, poverty, etc.) The federal and Quebec bureaucracies were in their infancy in 1940. Twenty years later, things had changed dramatically. Governments were playing a large and growing role in public affairs. In 1950 Quebec was, according to some observers, a "priest-ridden province." In 1980, it was a state-controlled province.

Trudeau made speeches in the 1950s on behalf of establishing socialism in Canada and flirted with the New Democratic Party. He was not alone. In Quebec, many people advocated state intervention in domains previously reserved for the Roman Catholic Church. Soon, education, previously controlled by the Church, came under state jurisdiction and state social programs replaced private charities.

An interventionist state was thought to be necessary for many reasons. The state was a rational institution in an age when efficiency and functionality became watchwords. In an age of universalism, it was viewed as a neutral and inclusive institution in which people of different national origins and religions could be treated equally. The state was regarded, moreover, as a means of "domesticating capital," that is, avoiding recurrent financial and industrial crises.

Finally, an interventionist state was widely construed as a means of leading Canadians to the creation of a "just society" in which equality would prevail. Labour unions in particular were fighting for a more equitable distribution of wealth and power.

Many of Trudeau's articles in the 1950s constituted a defence of Keynesian economic theory. (John Maynard Keynes was the leading British economist who first advocated massive state intervention to end the Great Depression of 1929–39.) Thus, it is not surprising that under Trudeau's government state intervention reached new heights. The federal debt grew nine-fold under his administration. He fostered a national energy policy, restricted foreign investment in Canada, created regional development programs, and so forth. Quebec did not trail behind for long. In the US State Department Quebec came to be known as "Cuba North." In a little less than a decade, Quebec created thousands of municipal councils and regional boards, hundreds of health institutions, innumerable social services, programs for the protection of agricultural lands, giant Crown Corporations such as Hydro-Quebec, and so on. The state intervention movement even radicalized itself in the 1970s. Concluding that socialism could never be implemented in Canada, some revolutionaries turned their hopes towards an independent Quebec. Pierre Vallières, for example, the author of the famous *White Niggers of America*,[8] intertwined nationalist sentiments with socialist beliefs.

The deep and prolonged recession of 1981–82, by far Canada's worst economic crisis since World War II, rattled the foundations of the welfare state ideologically and practically. Practically, it meant that the Trudeau spending years were over. In Quebec, the return of Liberal Robert Bourassa to power (1985) brought an end to the liberal spending policies of the *Parti Québécois* years (1976–85). However, privatization of government-owned enterprises and cuts in social programs did not reduce the size of the state as much as is sometimes thought. In fact, in absolute numbers, the state apparatus continued to grow along with Quebec's population. Government transfers (welfare payments, unemployment insurance, etc.) as a percentage of personal income even increased, from 10 percent in 1970 to 17 percent in 1990 to approximately 20 percent in 2000. In comparison with the United States, Quebec and Canada maintained their social-democratic proclivity. The continuation of a national health-care system is testimony to the country's disputed but still strong commitment to social democracy.

Ideologically the change was more drastic. The state changed its role from arbiter and organizer of the economy to a merchandiser of labour and a servant of the market. The new ideology (known as neo-conservatism in the United States but more accurately called neo-liberalism), does not oppose the state as such. It only wants the state to eliminate all values from its vocabulary save the value of cost-efficiency and let nothing other than the market determine social priorities. The neo-liberal state defines people more as paying clients than citizens with rights. This ideology accompanied the signing of the Free Trade Agreement between Canada and the United States in 1989 (largely supported by Québécois, in contrast with the rest of Canada), its broadening to include Mexico in 1993, and subsequent discussions to eventually create a free trade zone encompassing all of North and South America. This process can only contribute to a further subordination of politics to financial and industrial priorities and interests.

4. A NEW HUMANISM

The first publishing success in Quebec in the second half of the twentieth century was Jean-Paul Desbiens's *Les Insolences du frère Untel*,[9] a book in which the author, a young friar, declared war on Quebec's traditional culture. That 50 000 copies were sold in less than three months reveals how popular and long-awaited Desbiens's criticisms were. Desbiens criticized French-Canadian culture in three ways. First, he said, it was an outmoded island in the midst of a progressive American continent. The French Canadians might use "an American clock" but they lived in "the Middle Ages." The inventions of science, new literary currents, new conceptions in the arts — all this was censored by a clerical authority that associated modernity with evil and erected ideological walls to "protect" French Canadians from the "perverse" influence of an English and Protestant continent. Second, according to Desbiens, French-Canadian culture imposed a cult of mediocrity on French Canada. "Joual" (the French dialect of the *Québécois*) was for him the self-evident syndrome of this cult. For Desbiens, Joual represented a defeat of the spirit and a laziness of the mind. It was evidence of the abysmal lack of education in the province. Not only did people speak Joual, he complained, they thought Joual. The language crisis was terrible and patent proof of the crisis of French-Canadian civilization, wrote Desbiens. Finally, he argued, French-Canadian culture advocated fear and obedience: "What we are practicing here is purity by sterilization, orthodoxy by silence, security by material repetition. We imagine there is only one way to walk straight, to go nowhere, only one way to never be mistaken, never search for anything, only one way to never get lost: sleep. We have invented a radical means of fighting the caterpillars: cut down the trees."[10] The Catholic Church's doctrine was one reason this situation came to prevail in Quebec, according to Desbiens. By insisting continuously on one's duties and not on one's freedom, by exercising its omnipresence and overwhelming authority over almost every field of activity, the clergy served as a sentinel against rebellious, dissident, and deviant attitudes and beliefs, ending up obliterating the very meaning of free will.

Contrary to what has often been stated, however, the Church was not inactive in the secularization of Quebec society. After all, Desbiens himself was a friar in the Mariste order. He was the expression of a new religious ethic that catalyzed the will for social reform and promoted the individual's triumph over authoritarian institutions. It is no coincidence that the Quiet Revolution took place during the Vatican II Council. Abbot Louis O'Neill, Father Lévesque, and committed Catholics like Fernand Dumont and Robert Lalonde drew from this new religious ethic the moral energy to confront the Catholic Church itself.

The search for a new culture took two directions, both closely connected to reform of the educational system. For a century, French-Canadian intellectuals had considered education the core of all reform. "Without school," said early-twentieth-century Quebec nationalist intellectual Lionel Groulx, "nothing is possible. With school, everything is possible." This is close to what many intellectuals of the 1960s believed.

Firstly, some intellectuals tried to adapt the classical colleges' humanism to the new conditions of a technological and modern society. Humanism, they argued, had to incorporate the developments of the human sciences, to be more open to other cultures and beliefs, and to be founded on the rights of the individual. A 1963 government report ratified this perspective: culture was not a catechism of questions and listed answers but a toolkit that enabled every citizen to prepare for the modern industrial world. The creation of the CEGEPS (two-year college) system in 1969 grew out of this report. Spending two years in CEGEPS between high school and university, each student would now have an opportunity to learn the basics of philosophy, humanities, and the social sciences, thus assimilating the lessons of a general but ever-changing humanism.

Secondly, some intellectuals, going further, insisted on a culture that would not only help individuals adapt to the new era, but would encourage them to question society as it was and strive for a better world. Sociologist Marcel Rioux, fearing a world in which all creativity would disappear under the steamrollers of machinery, technology, and computerization, associated education with the imaginative search for new possibilities: "To speak of culture in our modern society is to speak … of surpassing oneself through values, imagination, and creativity."[11] Rioux insisted among other subjects on the teaching of art in schools so as to introduce students to a world where they could be their own creation.

In the 1960s and 1970s Quebec's culture flourished like never before, at least quantitatively. The Quiet Revolution brought about the creation of the *Ministère des Affaires culturelles du Québec*, the founding of many publishing houses (the number of titles published annually rose from 260 to 4000 between 1962 and 1977), the establishment of the National Film Board, the popularity of *chansonniers* like Gilles Vigneault and Georges D'or, who were not just singers but cultural icons, and so on. Between 1960 and 1970, the number of university students doubled. The number of artists and art teachers grew from 683 to 3805 between 1951 and 1971.[12] Television transformed itself from a medium of information to an agent of socialization.

More generally, the decline of the traditional nuclear family, the erosion of religious practice, the liberalization of sexual behaviour, and the emancipation of women deeply affected Quebec society. Looking back at the 1950s through the films of the era can be a big shock to anyone who is unaware of the rapid and radical cultural transformations that originated in the 1960s and created a vastly more open and progressive culture in place of the earlier conservatism. Unique to Quebec was the almost complete secularization of social life that was brought about by restricting the Catholic Church to a very narrow role in private affairs. In the 1960s, the "priest-ridden province" rid itself of the widespread influence of the priesthood.

The quest for a new culture — specifically, for a new humanism — ended with the rise of a consumer society. The great celebration of "we-ness" in the 1960s raised hopes of a more fraternal and convivial society. But the 1970s and 1980s opened the way to an increasingly individualistic society in which people were increasingly concerned with their own destiny. The 1960s also raised hopes for an authentic human culture that would enable every person to discover his or her real self. But disillusionment swiftly replaced this optimism. The pervasive influence of American culture — Hollywood cinema, Walt Disney philosophy, a fast-food mentality — jeopardized the formulation of a new humanism. As Rioux put it: "The Americanization of Quebec is, to my eyes, a most important and anguishing question.... Humanity, which was once condemned to a thermonuclear death … is now more and more threatened by a cultural death...."[13]

Notwithstanding Rioux's condemnation, the consumer society made more and more inroads into Quebec culture. In 2000, 50 percent of Quebec households had two colour television sets, 46 percent owned a gas barbecue, and two-thirds were connected to cable TV. In 1990, 300 000 movie performances were shown on theater screens; in 2000, the number rose to about 650 000 — and 85 percent of all movies were American productions. Instead of turning their liberty into an existential or spiritual search, the *Québécois* soon preferred inquiring about the latest car models. Instead of taking advantage of the cultural opportunities offered to them, they became couch potatoes enslaved to their television sets. At least, this is what the generation that came of age in the aftermath of World War II tended to believe. What was missing among the younger generation and in Quebec society as a whole, they said, was what Fernand Dumont called "transcendence." He wrote: "A society is not an aggregate of people pursuing their individual roads according to their interests; nor is it a closed field where factions struggle for their privileges independently of any rules other than the power of numbers or money."[14] A society, continued Dumont, must be capable of judging its inner value by resorting to some abstract transcendence. Failing to

achieve such a judgment, a society condemns itself, according to Dumont, to disappearance as a distinct entity.

This cultural revolution had perhaps a deeper impact in Quebec than elsewhere in Canada, for the will to escape a closed and homogeneous religious universe resulted in calling into question all institutionalized authorities. But, in opposition to Rioux's and Dumont's harsh judgments, the general Americanization of French Canadian culture did not only mean the progressive establishment of an atomized and materialist society. It also meant the rise of pluralism, a greater tolerance toward different ways of living, and an attachment to simple and fundamental human values. "Beyond political rhetoric," concluded two sociologists on the basis of a national survey, "Quebec's uniqueness can readily be seen in the province's young people of the 1990s."[15] Among other unique features, Quebec's teenagers, they declared, are more open than teenagers elsewhere in Canada to premarital sex, homosexuality, and abortion, and they enjoy their family life more. Overall, their main characteristic seems to be a "lifestyle flexibility" that regards culture as a series of options and opportunities rather than a set of widely accepted values.

CONCLUSION

The reader has certainly noticed that the four great utopias of the Quiet Revolution did not materialize in contemporary Quebec, at least not completely. This observation allows me to reach three conclusions.

Conclusion 1: If one were obliged to summarize in a single sentence the development of Quebec after 1960, one would have to underline two radical social changes that are unique to Quebec history when compared to the rest of North America. First, with the Quiet Revolution, "French Canadians" began to call themselves "*Québécois.*" Second, clerical French Canada gave way to a state-controlled Quebec. But besides these two changes, the challenges Quebec faces today resemble pretty much those of every other

Western society. For example, the fact that Quebec is a minority nation struggling for the recognition of its rights is not unique. In Canada, Aboriginal peoples are also trying to achieve national recognition. Corsicans in France, Basques in Spain, and the Scottish in the United Kingdom are only some of the other small nations searching for a way to preserve their language and to promote local autonomy through new political arrangements. It is one of the great lessons of the twentieth century that modern states have to find a way to accommodate basic human rights with the collective ambition of nations. Canada has not yet found all the answers to the dilemma nor the secret to equilibrium. But it represents one of the greatest social laboratories of what that equilibrium could be like and leads the way for other countries that today confront the same problems.[16]

Conclusion 2: The Quiet Revolution failed to achieve some of its goals. Bare statistics show the failure of the attempt to create a bilingual Canada. A sovereign Quebec now seems a remote dream. Canadian and Quebec social democracy are on the decline. Democracy is experiencing a crisis. There seems to be little desire to renew humanism. On the other hand, the Quiet Revolution accomplished a complete and largely beneficial transformation of morals and attitudes. For example, in spite of persistent sexism in many quarters, women have gained a status they lacked in the 1950s. Lately, *Québécois* have been found in national surveys to be very tolerant toward immigrants and visible minorities — in spite of a certain level of persistent racism (anti-Semitism, for example, has a long history in Canada, particularly in Quebec). Multiculturalism has brought about a recognition of Canada as a nation of nations. The Charter of Rights and Freedoms is accepted by the vast majority of the provincial population, the only question being whether it should have precedence over the National Assembly in Quebec City. It is worth noting that Quebec passed a *Chartre des droits et libertés de la personne* in 1975 (the provisions of which were extended in 1981) that has quasi-constitutional status and covers not only public law, like its Canadian counterpart, but also private law. The Quebec government was also the first provincial government to sign treaties with First Nations' representatives and has encouraged a new policy of negotiation instead of sterile confrontation.

Conclusion 3: I am not one to believe that a utopia is something that can be fully realized here and now. A utopia is first and foremost a source of inspiration. Obviously, democracy, nationalism, social democracy, and humanism have made inroads in Quebec over the years. But much more must be done if we want Canada to be a place where justice, tolerance, openness, and transparency prevail. If this lesson in humility is remembered, the utopias of the 1960s and 1970s, with all their excesses and their self-evident weaknesses, will not have been dreamt in vain. In this sense, they constitute a useful reminder that if the Canada of 2004 cannot be changed, the Canada of 2054 is yet to be built. That Canada, inescapably, we will have to build together.

NOTES

1. I thank Robert Brym and Valérie de Courville Nicole for their useful comments on a draft of this essay.

2. In this chapter, "*Québécois*" refers to French Quebeckers and "Quebeckers" refers to the entire population of Quebec.

3. Gérard Dion and Louis O'Neill, "L'Immoralité politique dans la province de Québec," *Le Devoir* (14 August 1956).

4. Pierre Elliott Trudeau, "Some obstacles to democracy in Quebec," *Canadian Journal of Economics and Political Science* XXIV: 3 August 1958: 303.

5. "FLQ Manifesto," on the World Wide Web at http://www.ola.bc.ca/online/cf/documents/1970FLQManifesto.html#top (23 November 2002).

6. Stéphane Kelly, "Pierre Elliott Trudeau et son maître. Une éducation politique," *Argument* (I, 1: Fall 1998) 29–40.

7. Gérard Bouchard, *La Nation québécoise au futur et au passé* (Montreal: VLB, 1999) 69.

8. Pierre Vallières, *White Niggers of America: The Precocious Autobiography of a Quebec "Terrorist,"* Joan Pinkham, trans. (Toronto: McClelland and Stewart, 1971). [First French edition, 1969.]

9. Jean-Paul Desbiens, *Les Insolences du frère Untel* (Montreal: Les Éditions de l'homme, 1960).

10. Ibid., 55–56.

11. Marcel Rioux, *Rapport de la Commission d'enquête sur l'enseignement des arts au Québec* (Quebec: l'Éditeur officiel du Québec, 1968) quoted in Pierre W. Bélanger et Guy Rocher, dir., *École et société au Québec: Éléments d'une sociologie de l'éducation* (Montreal: HMH, 1970) 462.

12. Marcel Fournier, *Les Génération d'artistes* (Quebec: IQRC, 1986) 97.

13. Marcel Rioux, "Remarques sur les industries de l'âme," *Question de culture*, 7, "*La culture: une industrie?*" (Quebec: IQRC, 1984) 50 and 49.

14. Fernand Dumont, *Raisons communes* (Montreal: Boréal, 1995) 218.

15. Reginald W. Bibby and Donald C. Posterski, *Teen Trends. A Nation in Motion* (Toronto: Stoddart, 2000), 115–36. [First non-abridged edition, 1991].

16. Michael Ignatieff, *The Rights Revolution* (Toronto: Anansi, 2000).

Chapter 22

Affluence, Power, and Strikes in Canada, 1973–2000

ROBERT J. BRYM

Common sense suggests affluence breeds contentment. On this assumption, people with secure jobs, good working conditions, and high wages are happier than people who face the prospect of unemployment, poor working conditions, and low wages. Moreover, according to the common-sense view, happier workers are less likely to strike. After all, compared to unhappy workers, their needs and demands seem closer to having been met. They appear to lack the deprivations that would motivate them to strike.

It follows from the common-sense view that there ought to be an observable association between measures of strike activity and measures of economic well-being. Figure 22.1, covering the 1973–2000 period, seems to suggest there is such an association.[1] The graph's horizontal axis shows *GDPpc* (Gross Domestic Product per capita), or the total value of goods and services produced in Canada in a year divided by the number of people living in the country at year end. GDPpc is an indicator of the economic well-being of the average Canadian. It is measured in constant (1992) dollars to eliminate the influence of inflation. In effect, this indicator of economic well-being shows the purchasing power of the average Canadian in a given year. Meanwhile, the graph's vertical axis shows *weighted strike frequency*, or the number of strikes that took place in Canada each year divided by the number of non-agricultural workers in the country. The curve formed by

annual scores on these two variables slopes downward. This suggests that when well-being is low,

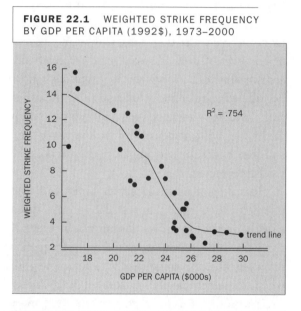

FIGURE 22.1 WEIGHTED STRIKE FREQUENCY BY GDP PER CAPITA (1992$), 1973–2000

Notes: (1) R^2 measures the degree to which the independent variable is associated with (or "explains") variation in the dependent variable. If the independent variable accounts for none of the variation in the dependent variable, the value of R^2 is 0. If it accounts for all of the variation, its value is 1. The R^2 given here is adjusted for the number of cases. (2) The "trend line" is a LOWESS curve. LOWESS stands for "locally weighted scatterplot smoothing." After dividing the values of the independent variable into a number of equal parts, the LOWESS curve computes least squares regression lines for each part and then smoothes the lines. This reveals patterns in the data that may be obscured by a single linear regression line computed over all values of the independent variable.

Source: Copyright © Robert J. Brym, 2003. Originally published in James Curtis, Edward Grabb, and Neil Guppy, ed., *Social Inequality in Canada: Patterns, Problems, Policies 4th ed.*, (Scarborough: Prentice-Hall Canada, 2003). I thank Jonah Butovsky, John Fox, Morley Gunderson, Alan Harrison, Reza Nakhaie, Gregg Olson, and Michael Shalev for helpful comments on a draft of this chapter.

propensity to strike is high; and when well-being is high, propensity to strike is low. Affluence, it seems at first glance, does breed contentment.

Case closed? Hardly. GDPpc is an average, and averages can mask more than they reveal. For instance, GDPpc could conceivably rise when the purchasing power of high-income earners (a minority of the population) rises a lot and the purchasing power of middle- and low-income earners (a majority of the population) falls a little. In that case, rising GDPpc would mask the fact that most people are worse off.

Because workers who strike are unlikely to be rich, we need a better measure of workers' well-being than GDPpc. One candidate is the *unemployment rate*. Unemployment is more likely to affect ordinary workers than the well-to-do. Doctors rarely lose their jobs, and business executives, even if they are fired, can live relatively comfortably off savings in the typically short period before they find work again. On the other hand, unemployment is likely to result in a sharp decline in living standards for ordinary workers, and sometimes the period before they find a new job is protracted.

How then does strike activity vary with the unemployment rate? Figures 22.2 and 22.3 provide the surprising answer. During the first half of the 1973–2000 period, weighted strike frequency fell when the unemployment rate rose, and rose when the unemployment rate fell (see Figure 22.2). In other words, when workers were most economically deprived, they were *least* inclined to strike, and when they were most secure in their jobs, they were *most* inclined to strike. This is just the opposite of the common-sense view, outlined above. Equally unexpected are the results for the second half of the 1973–2000 period (see Figure 22.3). After 1986, the relationship between the unemployment rate and weighted strike frequency virtually disappeared. Thus, the trend line summarizing the association between weighted strike frequency and the unemployment rate shows little trend. What accounts for the inverse association between the unemployment rate and weighted strike frequency in the 1973–86 period? What accounts for the near disappearance of this

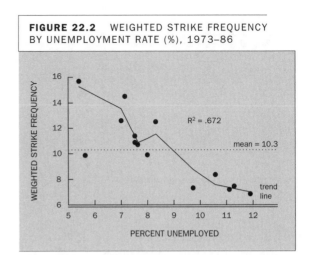

FIGURE 22.2   WEIGHTED STRIKE FREQUENCY BY UNEMPLOYMENT RATE (%), 1973–86

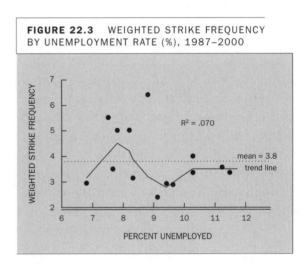

FIGURE 22.3   WEIGHTED STRIKE FREQUENCY BY UNEMPLOYMENT RATE (%), 1987–2000

inverse association after 1986? These are the intriguing questions I address in the remainder of this chapter.

STRIKE RESEARCH ON THE EFFECT OF THE BUSINESS CYCLE

The existing body of strike research goes a long way toward explaining the trend for the 1973–86 period, although not, as you will see, for the 1987–2000 period. Many strike researchers begin with the observation that capitalist economies undergo recurrent "boom and bust" cycles.

During bad times, unemployment is high and business profitability low. During good times, unemployment is low and business profitability high. They then go on to note the existence of an association between the business cycle and strike frequency (Rees, 1952). They argue that, as unemployment falls, strike incidence rises. That is because workers are in a better bargaining position during good economic times. Accordingly, at the peaks of business cycles workers are more likely to enjoy higher savings and alternative job opportunities. At the same time, workers know employers are eager to settle strikes quickly since business is so profitable. Strikes are therefore relatively low-risk. In contrast, during economic downturns, workers are less well off and have fewer job alternatives. They understand employers have little incentive to meet their demands because profitability is low and inventories high. Workers avoid strikes during troughs in the business cycle since they are riskier than in economic good times. From this point of view, workers' contentment, levels of felt deprivation, and other states of mind are unimportant as causes of strike activity. What matters is how *powerful* workers are. Their bargaining position or their ability to get their own way despite the resistance of employers is what counts. Said differently, strike research suggests we can arrive at superior explanations for variations in strike activity by thinking like sociologists, not psychologists.

The association between strike incidence and the business cycle (or its proxy, the unemployment rate) was first demonstrated empirically for the United States (Ashenfelter and Johnson, 1969) and shortly thereafter for Canada (Smith, 1972). Since then, researchers have shown that the association between strike incidence and the business cycle was a feature of most advanced capitalist countries in the twentieth century (Hibbs, 1976). However, later research also introduced three important qualifications to the argument.

First, before World War II, the North American system of collective bargaining between workers and employers was not well institutionalized. In Canada, for example, the legal right to organize unions, bargain collectively, and strike

with relatively little constraint dates only from 1944. Before then, strikes were often fights for union recognition. They were therefore less responsive to economic conditions (Cruikshank and Kealey, 1987; Jamieson, 1973 [1957]: 102; Palmer, 1987; Snyder, 1977). As a result, in Canada and the United States, the effect of the business cycle on strike incidence is stronger for the post–World War II period than for the pre–World War II period.

The second important qualification concerns the fact that, in much of Western Europe, the institutional environment mitigates the effect of economic conditions on strike frequency. One important aspect of the institutional environment is the degree of centralization of bargaining units. Strikes are negotiating tools. They are therefore more frequent during periodic contract renewals than between contracts. In much of Western Europe, however, centralized, nationwide bargaining among workers, employers, and governments means that entire sectors of the work force come up for contract renewal and negotiation at the same time. Thus, aggregate measures of strike frequency are affected not just by the phase of the business cycle but by the periodicity of contract renewal schedules. In contrast, the absence of a centralized bargaining structure in Canada and the United States makes aggregate measures of strike frequency more sensitive to the business cycle in North America (Harrison and Stewart, 1994; Snyder, 1977; Franzosi, 1989).

Union density, or the proportion of the non-agricultural labour force that is unionized, is another aspect of the institutional environment that influences strike activity. Unions educate workers and enable them to speak with one voice. Their organizational assets allow unions to mobilize workers. It follows that union density will influence strike action, although strike frequency is often less affected than are strike duration and the average size of strikes (Shorter and Tilly, 1971).

Finally, the third condition limiting the impact of the business cycle on strike frequency is political. In many Western European countries, left-wing or social democratic parties have formed governments or at least achieved representation in Cabinets. This has the effect of moving negotiations over the division of rewards in society from the labour market, where strikes are important bargaining tools, to the political sphere. Where labour is powerful enough to negotiate favourable income redistribution and welfare policies at the political level, industrial conflict tends to recede.[2] Agreeing to limit strike action has even been used as a bargaining chip in exchange for income redistribution and welfare concessions in Sweden, Germany, and other Western European countries. Thus, in the 1970s and 1980s, strike frequency in Sweden, for example, was relatively insensitive to the business cycle (Franzosi, 1989; Hibbs, 1978; Korpi and Shalev, 1980).

In sum, a substantial body of research demonstrates an association between the business cycle and strike frequency. Moreover, it shows that the association is strongest in North America in the post–World War II era because that is the setting least influenced by mitigating institutional and political variables (Paldam and Pedersen, 1982).

In the context of this research, Figure 22.2 is as ordinary as Figure 22.3 is puzzling. The strong inverse relationship between the unemployment rate and strike frequency for the 1973–86 period is wholly in line with expectations derived from the research literature. However, contrary to what we are led to expect by the research literature, there is little discernible trend for the 1987–2000 period. The unemployment rate is very *weakly* associated with strike frequency in the latter period. Said differently, cyclicality appears to have been largely wrung out of Canada's labour relations system in the last 14 years of the twentieth century, at least in terms of its influence on the incidence of industrial disputes. With respect to its impact on strike incidence, the business cycle was somehow repressed — and this in precisely the setting (post–World War II North America) where its impact was previously the greatest.

Why? What accounts for the repression of the business cycle as a determinant of the incidence of Canadian industrial disputes? That is the question on which the remainder of this

chapter turns. An intimation of my answer lies embedded in my decision to divide the recent history of Canadian industrial disputes into two 14-year periods, as in Figures 22.2 and 22.3. Inspection of scatterplots suggested that a shift in the direction of the relationship between the unemployment rate and weighted strike frequency took place after 1986. Since data were available for 14 years following 1986, I chose to examine the relationship for a period of equal duration before 1987. That period ends in 1973.

Using 1973 as the cut-off is also justifiable on historical grounds, for 1973 was the year of the first oil shock. In that year, due to war in the Middle East, the price of oil on world markets tripled, intensifying already high inflation and galloping wage demands. As a result, a strike wave that had been growing since the mid-1950s gained force and crested in 1974–75. In the entire history of Canadian labour, the only strike action that matched that crest was the Winnipeg General strike of 1919 and the ensuing sympathy strikes that stretched all the way from Amherst, Nova Scotia, to Victoria, British Columbia (see Figure 22.4). Understandably, therefore, the strikes of 1974–75 caused a strong reaction among government and corporate leaders. They soon took measures to make it substantially more costly for workers to strike. Thus, 1973 marks the beginning of an historical era, one aspect of which is the substantive focus of this chapter.

In the balance of this chapter, I outline how, from the mid-1970s to the 1990s, government and corporate leaders weakened unions and made it more difficult for workers to achieve their goals. These actions had the effect of making strikes less frequent and repressing the effect of the business cycle on the propensity to strike. As you will see, they explain the near-trendless trend line in Figure 22.3.

A NEW ECONOMIC AND POLITICAL CONTEXT

Government and business leaders reacted to the 1919–20 strike wave by sending in troops to

FIGURE 22.4 WEIGHTED STRIKE FREQUENCY, 1901–2000

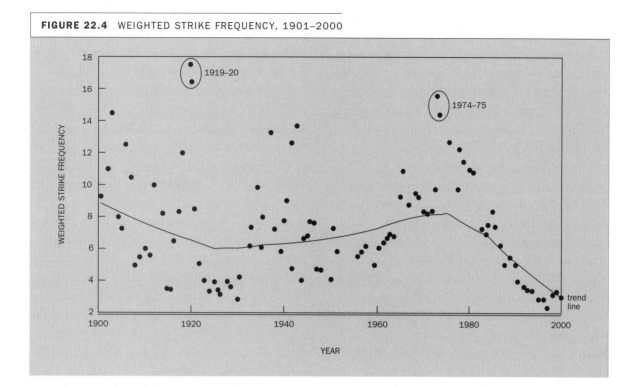

restore order, throwing union leaders in jail, legislating strikers back to work, and changing laws to allow the deportation of British-born immigrants, who were thought to dominate the strike leadership (Bercuson, 1990 [1974]). Faced with a strike wave of similar proportions in 1974–75, government and business leaders again felt drastic action was necessary. However, the political, institutional, and cultural environment had changed between these two extraordinary episodes of labour unrest. As a result, strategies for controlling labour were different. In 1944, Canadian workers had won the right to organize, bargain collectively, and strike with relatively little constraint. In the context of three decades of post-war prosperity, their new rights allowed them to win substantial gains in real earnings and a massive expansion of state supports and services. In the mid-1970s, business leaders and governments sympathetic to business felt they had to control labour unrest while fighting wage gains and the growth of the welfare state. To accomplish these tasks, they organized a neo-conservative "counter-revolution" that continues to this day.

The neo-conservative counter-revolution was, however, motivated by more than just the strike wave that crested in the mid-1970s. Rising government debt and global competition also contributed to the decision to go on the political offensive (Johnston, 2001).

Government borrowing rose quickly in the 1970s and 1980s. By the end of that period, interest payments were consuming a quarter of the federal government's annual budget. With indebtedness threatening to cripple government programs, the neo-conservative claim that debt reduction is sound public policy made sense to more and more people.

At the same time, global competition was becoming fiercer. By the early 1970s, Japanese and West German industry had fully recovered from the destruction of World War II. Manufacturers in these countries were exporting massive quantities of finished goods to North America and other markets. In the 1980s, South Korea, China, and other countries followed suit. With growing global competition threatening the welfare of Canadian industry, big business had to develop new strategies to survive and prosper. One such strategy involved restructuring: introducing computers and robots, eliminating middle management positions, outsourcing parts manufacturing, and so forth. Another strategy aimed at increasing business opportunities and ensuing job growth by creating a free trade zone encompassing Canada and the United States (MacDonald, 2000).

Controlling labour while cutting debt, restructuring, and promoting free trade required deep ideological change. Business leaders therefore set about the task of redefining in the public mind the desirable features of the market, the state, and the relationship between the two. From roughly the end of World War II until the mid-1970s, labour demands focused on improving wages and state benefits. Now, an imposing ideological machine sought to convince the public that high wages and generous state benefits decrease the ability of Canadians to compete against workers in other countries. Massive job losses will result (the neo-conservative argument continued) unless wages are held in check and state benefits slashed. That was the main message of Canada's two neo-conservative, corporate-funded think tanks and pressure groups, the Fraser Institute, founded in 1974, and the Business Council on National Issues (BCNI), founded in 1976. The creation of these bodies in the mid-1970s signalled that, like its counterpart in the United States, the Canadian business elite was becoming more ideologically and politically organized and unified (Akard, 1992; Langille, 1987).

One important sign of neo-conservative success was the outcome of the 1988 "free trade" federal election (Richardson, 1996). Just four days before the election, a Gallup poll showed the pro–free trade Progressive Conservatives with the support of only 31 percent of Canadians intending to vote. The anti–free trade Liberals enjoyed a commanding 43 percent of the popular vote while the anti–free trade New Democratic Party stood at 22 percent. At about the same time, an Angus Reid poll disclosed that most Canadians opposed free trade by a margin of 54 percent to 35 percent. A majority of Canadians apparently sensed that free trade might open the country to harmful competition with giant American companies, thus leading to job losses and deteriorating living standards.

Then, a mere 100 hours before the first votes were cast, a little-known organization, the Canadian Alliance for Trade and Job Opportunities (CATJO), swung into high gear. CATJO was funded exclusively by the BCNI. With a campaign budget larger than that of the two opposition parties combined, CATJO bankrolled a media blitz promoting the PCs and their free trade policies. A barrage of brochures, newspaper ads, and radio and television commercials supported the idea that Canadian prosperity depends on the removal of all taxes and impediments to trade between Canadian and the United States. CATJO argued that if goods and services could be bought and sold across the border without hindrance, and capital invested without restraint, good jobs would proliferate and Canada's economic future would be assured. The CATJO onslaught succeeded in overcoming some of the public's fears and drawing attention away from the opposition. On election day, the PCs won with 43 percent of the popular vote. The free trade agreement with the United States was signed just six weeks later.

The free trade agreement, later broadened to include Mexico, sharply increased competition for investment between jurisdictions, leading to a "downward harmonization" of labour policies (Gunderson, 1998). Just as water seeks its lowest level, capital that is allowed to flow freely between jurisdictions will seek the jurisdiction with the lowest costs and therefore the highest profit potential, all else the same. Increasingly, jurisdictions will compete for investment by offering outright tax concessions to investors and ensuring competitive labour costs in the form of lower state benefits, wages, and rates of labour disruption due to strikes. As Canadian workers learned, persistent demands for higher wages — indeed, failure to make wage and other concessions — increase the prospect of plant closings. Where capital mobility is unrestricted, it is only a short hop from southern Ontario to "right to work" states like Georgia or the Maquiladora free trade zone of northern Mexico. In this context, unions lose bargaining power and strikes become riskier actions with a lower probability of achieving their aims.[3]

The slew of government budget cutbacks that took place in the 1990s also had a negative influence on strike incidence. Since workers who go out on strike sometimes quit or lose their jobs, declining income-replacing state benefits make strikes riskier for them. In other words, many of the cutbacks of the 1990s increased the potential cost of job loss to workers and therefore ensured that strike incidence would drop. Restricting eligibility for employment insurance and welfare were two of the most important policy measures affecting the readiness of workers to strike.

High government debt, intense global competition, and neo-conservative publicity and lobbying continued to push the Canadian electorate to the right in the 1990s. The Reform Party became the official opposition, its popularity aided by the defection of members of the working class, most of them non-unionized, from the Liberals and the NDP (Butovsky, 2001). The ruling Liberals, meanwhile, adopted much of the neo-conservative agenda. To varying degrees, all major parties supported the new industrial relations regime that had begun to crystallize in the mid-1970s.

A NEW INDUSTRIAL RELATIONS REGIME

Beginning in the mid-1970s, governments adopted a series of measures aimed at better controlling labour (Panitch and Swartz, 1993 [1985]). Among them was the establishment of wage and price controls that limited only wages in practice yet claimed to require equal sacrifices from labour and business. That strategy was followed in 1975 by the Trudeau government, establishing the Anti-Inflation Board for a three-year period. Blessed by business and condemned

by the labour movement, the anti-inflation program suspended collective bargaining for all workers in Canada. By undermining the ability of strikes to achieve wage gains, it also dampened labour militancy. A similar approach was taken in 1982, when the federal government passed the Public Sector Compensation Restraint Act. The act imposed a two-year wage limit on federal employees, eliminating their right to bargain and strike. The provinces soon passed similar laws. In some cases, provincial cutbacks were even more draconian than those implemented at the federal level. Public employees in Quebec, for example, took a 20 percent pay cut. In 1991, the federal government announced a one-year wage freeze for federal employees, followed by a 3 percent limit on wage increases for the next two years. By 1993, even the Ontario NDP was backing wage restraint. In that year, the government of Bob Rae introduced a "Social Contract" that overruled the provisions of existing collective agreements and effectively reduced the wages of all 900 000 provincial employees for a three-year period.

A second method of labour control involved amending a variety of laws and regulations. For example, governments persistently broadened the definitions of "management" and "essential service," thereby denying many public sector workers the right to strike. Thus, in 1984 nearly 76 percent of public service workers negotiating contracts were designated as providing managerial or essential services. In the preceding set of negotiations, fewer than 47 percent of those workers were so designated. In addition, and to varying degrees, governments imposed restrictions on political strikes and secondary picketing (picketing beyond the plant or department affected by a strike). They increased employers' rights to fight organizing drives and employees' rights to attempt decertification. They banned strikes in designated work sites, weakened the ability of unions to discipline members who carried out anti-union activities, permitted unions to be sued, and, in most jurisdictions, allowed the use of replacement workers. One result of these actions was that, beginning in 1984, union density began to decline (see Figure 22.5).

Finally, throughout the 1980s, and particularly after Brian Mulroney's Progressive Conservative government was elected in 1984, federal and provincial governments increasingly adopted *ad hoc* back-to-work legislation to weaken workers' bargaining position and thereby limit strike action. Used on average only 0.2 times per year in the 1950–54 period, back-to-work laws were passed on average 5.0 times per year in the 1975–79 period and 5.4 times per year in the 1985–89 period.

At first, limiting the right to strike was widely viewed as a temporary measure necessitated by fear of a resurgence of the strike wave of 1974–75, the highest inflation rates Canada had ever seen, and the deep recessions of 1981–82 and 1991–92. However, limiting the right to strike became a matter of enduring if unstated public policy, largely because economic and political conditions required a less expensive and less militant work force. By the mid-1980s, a new labour relations regime had crystallized. One of its main purposes was to render labour's ultimate bargaining tool — the strike — increasingly superfluous as a means of bargaining for improved terms of employment.

CONCLUSION: THE WITHERING AWAY OF THE STRIKE?

About 1960, some influential social scientists predicted that the strike was "withering away." The working class, they wrote, had become "embourgeoisified" due to growing affluence. Class conflict was supposedly becoming "institutionalized" in stable systems of collective bargaining. These developments were viewed as a sort of natural evolutionary process, part of the peaceful unfolding of the "inner logic of industrialization" (Ross and Hartman, 1960; Dahrendorf, 1959).

In the 1960s and 1970s, an international strike wave caught these social scientists by surprise. It cast doubt on the validity of their generalizations. Now, however, amid an international "resurgence of labour quiescence" (Shalev, 1992) that has lasted more than two decades, some observers may be tempted to argue that affluence has at last caused the strike to wither away. For them, the generalizations of 1960 may appear valid after all.

My analysis suggests we should avoid this conclusion. I have shown that a measure of average affluence (GDPpc) is inversely associated with weighted strike frequency but is a poor measure of the economic conditions that shape the lives of Canadian workers. The unemployment rate is a much better indicator of workers' economic conditions; and for the 1973–86 period, the unemployment rate varied inversely with weighted strike frequency. This suggests that the relative power or bargaining position of workers — not their level of affluence — determined their propensity to strike. Complicating the story, however, is a fact most researchers have overlooked. In the 1987–2000 period, the inverse relationship between the unemployment rate and weighted strike frequency nearly disappeared.[4] The business cycle had little effect on workers' propensity to strike. The reason? Actions taken by employers and governments

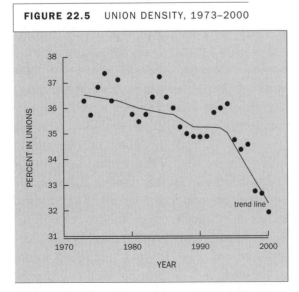

FIGURE 22.5   UNION DENSITY, 1973–2000

from the mid-1970s to the late 1990s — introducing free trade, cutting budgets for a wide range of government assistance programs, passing laws and regulations that undermined unions — disempowered workers and rendered the strike a less effective weapon.

In sum, the history of Canadian industrial relations since the mid-1970s suggests that the "inner logic" of industrial capitalism is driven by power, not alleged evolutionary imperatives such as the rising average level of affluence. Industrial relations systems *are* institutionalized forms of class conflict, that is, enduring legal resolutions of historically specific struggles between workers and employers. But "enduring" does not mean "permanent." Trends lasting a few decades should not be confused with the end of history. Industrial relations systems change when power is massively redistributed between classes. In Canada, for example, a massive redistribution of power in favour of workers took place from the mid-1940s onward, when workers won the legal right to unionize and strike and were in a position to extract increased disposable income and benefits from employers and governments. Another massive redistribution of power, this time in favour of employers, took place after the mid-1970s. The Canadian industrial relations regime was transformed on both occasions. The transition from the first regime to the second was marked by a change in the relationship between strike frequency and the business cycle. It follows that, however difficult it might be to imagine in the current industrial relations climate, another massive shift in the distribution of power in society could once again help the strike regain its former popularity.

NOTES

1. Data sources for this chapter are as follows:
   - *Population:* CANSIM (2002b).
   - *Gross Domestic Product per capita:* CANSIM (2002a).
   - *Strikes:* "Series E190-197 ..." (2001); "Chronological Perspective ..." (2001).
   - *Union membership:* "Series E175-177 ..." (2001); Human Resources Development Canada (2001); "Union membership..." (2000).
   - *Non-agricultural workers* (1902–10 and 1912–20 interpolated): *Fifth Census ...* (1915), Table 1, p. 13; *Labour Organizations ...* (1973) pp. xxii–xxiii; *1994–1995 Directory ...* (1995) p. xiii; "Union membership ..." (2000).
   - *Unemployment:* CANSIM (2001).

2. That is why the influence of union density on strike action peaks at intermediate levels of union density and then tapers off. In countries with the highest proportion of unionized workers, unions tend to exert considerable political influence.

3. As Morley Gunderson commented on a draft of this chapter, the argument developed here is also an argument about wage concessions. Moreover, for strike incidence to fall, the *joint* cost of strikes to both workers *and employers* must increase. In the present case, the cost of strikes to employers has increased, partly because strikes threaten the loss of global market share.

4. See, however, Cramton and Tracy (1994), who reach similar conclusions about the United States in the 1980s.

REFERENCES

Akard, Patrick J. (1992). "Corporate Mobilization and Political Power: The Transformation of U.S. Economic Policy in the 1970s." *American Sociological Review, 57:* 587–615.

Ashenfelter, Orley and George Johnson. (1969). "Bargaining Theory, Trade Unions, and Industrial Strike Activity." *American Economic Review,* 59: 35–49.

Bercuson, David Jay. (1990 [1974]). *Confrontation at Winnipeg: Labour, Industrial*

Relations, and the General Strike, rev. ed. Montreal: McGill-Queen's University Press.

Butovsky, Jonah. (2001). *The Decline of the New Democrats: The Politics of Postmaterialism or Neoliberalism?* Ph.D. dissertation, Department of Sociology, University of Toronto.

CANSIM. (2001). "Unemployment Rate Age 15+ SA CDA." On the World Wide Web at http://chass.utoronto.ca/cansim/ (4 April).

CANSIM. (2002a). "G.D.P., Expenditure-Based, 1992$/Gross Domestic Pr at Market Prices." On the World Wide Web at http://chass. utoronto.ca/cansim/ (7 January).

CANSIM. (2002b). "Population of Canada, by Province/Canada." On the World Wide Web at http://chass.utoronto.ca/cansim/ (7 January).

"Chronological Perspective on Work Stoppages in Canada (Work Stoppages Involving One or More Workers), 1976-2000." (2001). On the World Wide Web at http://labour-travail.hrdc-drhc.gc.ca/doc/wid-dimt/eng/wsat/table.cfm (27 March).

Cramton, Peter C. and Joseph S. Tracy. 1994. "The Determinants of U.S. Labour Disputes." *Journal of Labor Economics, 12*: 180–209.

Cruikshank, Douglas and Gregory S. Kealey. (1987). "Strikes in Canada, 1891–1950." *Labour/Le Travail, 20*: 85–145.

Dahrendorf, Ralf. (1959). *Class and Class Conflict in Industrial Society.* London: Routledge & Kegan Paul.

Fifth Census of Canada, 1911, Vol. VI. (1915). Ottawa: Census and Statistics Office, Department of Trade and Commerce.

Franzosi, Roberto. (1989). "One Hundred Years of Strike Statistics: Methodological and Theoretical Issues in Quantitative Strike Research." *Industrial and Labor Relations Review, 42*: 348–62.

Gunderson, Morley. (1998). "Harmonization of Labour Policies under Trade Liberalization." *Industrial Relations* 53. On the World Wide Web at http://www.erudit.org/erudit/ri/v53no1/gunder/gunder.html (9 April 2001).

Harrison, Alan and Mark Stewart. 1994. "Is Strike Behavior Cyclical?" *Journal of Labor Economics* 12: 524–53.

Hibbs, Douglas. (1976). "Industrial Conflict in Advanced Industrial Societies." *American Political Science Review, 70*: 1033–58.

_____. (1978). "On the Political Economy of Long-Run Trends in Strike Activity." *British Journal of Political Science, 8*: 153–75.

Human Resources Development Canada. (2001). Special tabulation on union membership, 1960–2000.

Jamieson, Stuart. (1973 [1957]). *Industrial Relations in Canada*, 2nd ed. Toronto: Macmillan.

Johnston, William A. (2001). "Class and Politics in the Era of the Global Economy." In Doug Baer, ed., *Political Sociology: Canadian Perspectives* (pp. 288–306). Don Mills ON: Oxford University Press.

Labour Organizations in Canada 1972. (1973). Ottawa: Economics and Research Branch, Canada Department of Labour.

Langille, David. (1987). "The Business Council on National Issues and the Canadian State." *Studies in Political Economy, 24*: 41–85.

MacDonald, L. Ian, ed. (2000). *Free Trade: Risks and Rewards.* Montreal and Kingston: McGill-Queen's University Press.

1994–1995 Directory of Labour Organizations in Canada. (1995). Ottawa: Minister of Supply and Services Canada.

Paldam, Martin, and Peder Pedersen. (1982). "The Macroeconomic Strike Model: A Study of Seventeen Countries, 1948–1975." *Industrial and Labor Relations Review*, 35: 504–21.

Palmer, Bryan D. (1987). "Labour Protest and Organization in Nineteenth Century Canada, 1820–1890." *Labour/Le Travail, 20*: 61–83.

Panitch, Leo, and Donald Swartz. (1993 [1988]). *The Assault on Trade Union Freedoms: From*

Wage Controls to Social Contract, 2nd ed. Toronto: Garamond Press.

Rees, Albert. (1952). "Industrial Conflict and Business Fluctuations." *Journal of Political Economy*, 60: 371–82.

Richardson, R. Jack. 1996. "Canada and Free Trade: Why Did It Happen?" In Robert J. Brym, ed. *Society in Question* (pp. 200–09). Toronto: Harcourt Brace Canada.

Ross, Arthur M. and Paul T. Hartman. (1960). *Changing Patterns of Industrial Conflict*. New York: Wiley.

"Series E175-177: Union Membership in Canada, in Total, as a Percentage of Non-agricultural Paid Workers, and Union Members with International Affiliation, 1911 to 1975 (thousands)." (2001). On the World Wide Web at http://www.statcan.ca/english/freepub/11-516-XIE/sectione/sectione.htm#Unions (29 March).

"Series E190-197: Number of Strikes and Lockouts, Employers and Workers Involved and Time Loss, Canada, 1901 to 1975." (2001). On the World Wide Web at http://www.statcan.ca/english/freepub/11-516-XIE/sectione/sectione.htm#Unions (29 March).

Shalev, Michael. (1992). "The Resurgence of Labour Quiescence." In Marino Regini, ed., *The Future of Labour Movements* (pp. 102–32). London: Sage.

Shorter, Edward, and Charles Tilly. (1971). "The Shape of Strikes in France, 1830–1960." *Comparative Studies in Society and History*, 13: 60–86.

Smith, Douglas A. (1972). "The Determinants of Strike Activity in Canada." *Industrial Relations*, 27: 663–77.

Snyder, David. (1977). "Early North American Strikes: A Reinterpretation." *Industrial and Labor Relations Review*, 30: 325–41.

"Union Membership in Canada — 2000." (2000). *Workplace Gazette: An Industrial Relations Quarterly*, 3 (3): 68–75.

Chapter 23

Promotionalism and Subpolitics: Nike and Its Labour Critics

GRAHAM KNIGHT

JOSH GREENBERG

INTRODUCTION

On May 12, 1998, Phil Knight, CEO of the sportswear giant Nike, appeared at the National Press Club in Washington to announce "new initiatives to further improve factory working conditions worldwide and provide increased opportunities for people who manufacture Nike products" (Nike, 1999). Knight admitted that Nike's products — and by implication its corporate identity — had become "synonymous with slave wages, forced overtime and arbitrary abuse" (Dionne, 1998). The context for Knight's speech was political as well as economic. Nike had recently suffered a significant drop in its share price in connection with the Asian financial crisis and projections about sales and profits had been revised downwards. But the speech also came on the heels of a series of public relations problems in regard to the campaign being waged by non-governmental organizations (NGOs), labour unions, student groups, and other activists in the U.S. and elsewhere against sweatshop labour practices in developing countries. These practices included below-subsistence wages, hazardous and stressful working conditions, forced overtime, long working hours, abusive management, and denial of worker rights to organize independent unions. While several western transnational corporations (TNCs) have

been targets of anti-sweatshop criticism, Nike in particular has become the principal object of anti-sweatshop activism and the growing media publicity of the issue (Greenberg and Knight, 2001), especially since the mid-1990s. In its coverage of Knight's speech *The New York Times* noted that Nike had recently been "pummelled in the public relations arena" over its handling of sweatshop allegations (Cushman, 1998).

In this chapter, we address two questions: firstly, why Nike has become the most prominent target of anti-sweatshop criticism, given that its production practices do not vary significantly from those of its major competitors, and secondly, why Nike has faced persistent public relations problems over the issue. We make two arguments. The first is that Nike is the principal target of anti-sweatshop activism because of its symbolic as well as economic prominence. Nike has become a celebrity corporation as a result of its high-profile advertising and promotional practices, which have made it into not only a commercial success but also a magnet for activist criticism. Secondly, we argue that social activism poses a challenge for corporate public relations because it is ethically motivated, has a decentred network form of organization, and relies on the use of "reflexive" tactics that turn the kind of promotional power corporations rely on against corporate interests and image.

Source: © Graham Knight and Josh Greenberg. Original version published in *Management Communication Quarterly*, (2002) 15 (4): 541–57.

PROMOTIONALISM: COMMUNICATING CORPORATE IDENTITY

Nike has become a principal target of anti-sweatshop activism not only because it is the largest company in the global sports shoe and apparel industry, but also because it has achieved public prominence as a celebrity corporation. Nike has successfully integrated the way it has constructed and communicated different aspects of its corporate identity into an effective promotional strategy that associates its brand name and image with positive social values ranging from athleticism and fitness to social and environmental responsibility to patriotism (Cole, 1996; Cole and Hribar, 1995). Nike has been adept at using promotionalism to craft a flexible, multifaceted identity that enables the company to represent itself simultaneously as serious and "cool," socially conscious and fashionable, earnest and ironic, image-conscious and technologically sophisticated (Goldman and Papson, 1998). Following Wernick's (1991) definition, promotionalism can be seen as a mode of corporate image-making that extends beyond conventional advertising and integrates different types of communication to the point where functional differences between them become blurred. So, for example, when Tiger Woods, Mia Hamm, and Lance Armstrong promote Nike, Nike also promotes Woods, Hamm, and Armstrong, and there is no clear or fixed distinction between who or what is doing the promoting and who or what is being promoted.

Promotionalism entails the management of a corporation's public presence with a view to translating it into an asset that serves the corporation's economic success. The construction and circulation of a corporate identity is the mechanism by which public presence is managed (Cheney and Christensen, 2001). Corporate identity, which is signified above all by the brand name, logo, and slogan, serves several functions. Externally, corporate identity aims to distinguish the corporation from market rivals. This operates economically, in terms of the range, appeal, and price of the company's products, but also socially, in terms of determining the corporation's place and reputation in the wider community. Corporate identity is used strategically to motivate consumer and investor identification with the organization and its products, and as a way to legitimate the corporation and its activities. Internally, corporate identity is designed to secure organizational unity as well as identification, loyalty, and motivation on the part of staff. In all respects, identity concerns the generation of trust.

Although it is widely recognized that corporate identity is becoming increasingly significant, that significance varies structurally. Identity and promotionalism play an especially critical role for brand name, consumer goods companies that operate in buyer-driven commodity chains. Buyer-driven commodity chains are typical of the apparel and athletic footwear industries where high rates of product turnover are the norm. In buyer-driven chains, economic success depends on control over and heavy investment in the initial and final stages of the production process — over product conception, design, and styling on the one hand, and marketing, advertising, product display, and consumer relations on the other — where symbolic values are paramount (Gereffi, 1994; Korzeniewicz, 1994). The intervening stages of production are contracted out to factories in developing countries where low skilled, cheap labour — especially young migrant women who are also considered to be more compliant and reliable — is relatively plentiful (Carty, 1995). These are also countries where local political elites often seek to attract investment from Western transnational corporations (TNCs) by ensuring environmental and labour standards are poorly enforced or non-existent, and where social stability often depends on authoritarian (and even violent) methods of social control.

Buyer-driven commodity chains entail a dissociation of production and consumption that is economic as well as geographical. Manufacturing labour costs are only a small fraction of the final price consumers will pay for the product. The total costs of promotion, including product styling and design, outweigh those of actual production as new styles, models, and lines are constantly required to ensure the growth of consumer demand. Constant product innovation and turnover mean that the brand name and logo become the principal means to stabilize corporate identity and public recognition.

NIKE'S PROMOTIONAL STRATEGY

Nike's promotional strategy has comprised two major aspects. The first is the use of endorsements and sponsorships to promote not only its products but also social causes, such as protection of the environment or support for the rights and aspirations of the socially disadvantaged or excluded (e.g., African Americans, women, and the disabled), by emphasizing self-empowerment and personal affirmation through sport, fitness, and physical activity (Cole, 1996; Cole and Hribar, 1995; Stabile, 2000). The use of endorsements and sponsorships as a way to promote social causes blurs the line that normally separates commercial and noncommercial activity. Nike's products and brand name, its corporate identity, its social activism on behalf of others (especially the disadvantaged or those at risk), the identity of celebrity endorsers, and the identity of the sports these endorsers play, all feed into the promotional mix. The integration of endorsements and sponsorships enables Nike to represent itself as a socially responsible corporate citizen promoting sport as a solution to social problems. However, the problems these causes address, such as environmental degradation or poverty, tend to be defined in a way that strips them of their material determinants. They are defined chiefly as problems of attitude and disposition for which Nike and the corporate economy should not be held responsible. Material inequalities and social divisions are at

once acknowledged and effaced through the fusion of ethical and commercial interests and the promotion of affirmative values (Cole and Hribar, 1995; Cole, 1996).

Nike's "If you let me play" advertising campaign vaunting the personal and social benefits of female participation in sport and its Participate in the Lives of American Youth (P.L.A.Y.) program, launched in 1994, are the most prominent examples of the integration of commercial and ethical promotionalism. Both were framed as the response to a problem of social exclusion and disadvantage. This was articulated more explicitly in the case of the P.L.A.Y. program. According to Phil Knight, P.L.A.Y. was the company's reaction to a "crisis in America," as children were denied access to sport and play due to cutbacks in school sport programs and the lack of safety in community playgrounds (Business Wire cited in Goldman and Papson, 1998: 109). The publicity campaign promoting the P.L.A.Y. program on television made use of Nike endorsers such as Michael Jordan and Olympic track star Jackie Joyner-Kersee to narrate visual images of the "social alienation of poverty and their transcendence via sports" (Goldman and Papson, 1998: 109; see also Cole, 1996). If the responsibility for providing youth access to sport and recreation was no longer being met by the state, Nike represented itself as willing to step in and fill the void.

The second aspect of Nike's promotional strategy has been the extensive use of information subsidies. In Gandy's formulation, "information is characterized as a subsidy because the source of that information causes it to be made available at something less than the cost a user would face" otherwise (1992: 61). Gandy distinguishes "direct" from "indirect" information subsidies. Nike provides direct information subsidies to the media inasmuch as it acts as a source of information about its business activities, sponsorships, community programs, and so forth. The reciprocal effect is that the media also provide indirect information subsidies to Nike inasmuch as media coverage, at least good news coverage, enhances the presence and value of Nike's identity in the public sphere, where consumers and investors acquire the information that determines how they act.

Nike's ability to make use of information subsidies has been expanded by the development of the Internet as a communications tool. As part of its "nikebiz" Web site Nike republishes selected press coverage in edited and unedited form. While much of this consists of favourable coverage, Nike has also included some coverage of its critics, by including its own FAQ page on labour issues, letters responding to activist groups such as the Clean Clothes Campaign, and, recently, a 12-minute virtual video tour of Nike factories in Asia. The Web site plays a role similar to that of the department store window. Several items are put on display, and the browser is positioned as a consumer who is free to pick and choose which elements strike his or her interest: products to buy, share price trends to contemplate, or ethical concerns to allay. In this way, the Web site enables Nike to unify its communication with different audiences and audience segments in a single virtual space. Answering its critics is a way to display openness and to reassure consumers concerned about the ethics of its products. It is also a way to speak to investors whose decisions are calculated in terms of prospective sales and revenue.

PROMOTIONALISM AS ITS OWN PROBLEM

The extent to which promotional culture has become dominant in the public sphere speaks not only to the importance of corporate identity in the marketplace, but also to the blurring of boundaries between the marketplace and the wider social, political and cultural environment. Promotionalism is directed ultimately at increasing consumption. For example, when Nike lost market share and leadership to Reebok in the mid-1980s, its response was to refocus its

promotionalism on female consumers by incorporating an appeal to and celebration of women's aspirations for autonomy and self-empowerment (Cole and Hribar, 1995). Similarly, Nike's use of African-American celebrity endorsers like Michael Jordan to promote both social causes and commodities makes use of racial imagery in a way that goes beyond and effaces specifically racial meanings (Cole, 1996). Jordan is represented in Nike's promotionalism as the personification of universal values rather than the values of a particular community whose interests have been shaped by social exclusion.

In addition to these strategies, which have been aimed primarily at expanding market share, Nike has also used a promotional logic to address problems that have arisen outside the marketplace. As Cole (1996) and Stabile (2000) note, Nike's integration of marketing and social responsibility has generally been a response to controversy and crisis originating in civil society. The P.L.A.Y. program, for example, came in the wake of bad publicity Nike suffered in the late 1980s and early 1990s from its association with a wave of "sneaker crimes" when media reports of youths being mugged and even killed for their sport shoes began to circulate. The finger was pointed at Nike precisely because of the powerful effect its promotionalism was thought to have on creating an obsession to own Nike products on the part of those unable to pay. The racialized coding of the sneaker crime wave put Nike in particular in the spotlight because of the company's association with African-American sports celebrities like Michael Jordan.

What the sneaker crime crisis represents is an example of promotionalism's *reflexive* character. Reflexivity denotes both reflection (or representation) and reflex (or reaction). In the former sense, promotionalism reflects the identity that corporations such as Nike try to convey (e.g., rebellious, progressive, cool, ironic) through their advertising, marketing, sponsorships, and so on. At the same time, promotionalism is also reflexive to the extent that it reacts back upon itself in ways that undermine its intended aims. In this sense promotionalism is not only a solution to corporate communication and identity, it is also a source of new problems that result precisely from the side effects of success (Beck, 1997). By making Nike into a celebrity corporation with a prominent public profile and presence, promotional success has also made Nike into a prominent public target of social criticism levelled in terms of the alleged breach between what the company claims to represent and what the effects of its practices are. In the case of the sneaker crime crisis, the reflexive effect of promotionalism was confined to the negative side effects of consumption. In the case of anti-sweatshop criticism, on the other hand, the effect of reflexivity has shifted to the sphere of production. Activists have criticized and protested the working conditions in Nike's factories in terms of a failure to respect and implement the values that Nike invokes in its claims of social responsibility and individual empowerment. Because corporate identity has to circulate in the public sphere where its meaning cannot be totally controlled, activists have been able to open up a space between Nike's preferred identity and its actual image, and counter-brand the company as a sweatshop employer.

COUNTER-BRANDING NIKE: ACTIVISM AND SUBPOLITICS

The counter-branding of Nike as a sweatshop employer should be understood in the context of social activism as a form of "subpolitics" (Beck, 1997). Subpolitics is the politics of interest groups, social movements, activism, and advocacy groups whose interests radiate out beyond the sphere of institutional politics, and whose targets include power centres other than the state. If politics represents the intervention of the state and market economy in the everyday life-world of social and cultural experience, then subpolitics represents the life-world's reciprocal feedback effect on the system (Habermas, 1987).

Subpolitics confronts the state and the market with their attempts to appropriate and exploit the norms and expectations of everyday life. Central to the motivation of the anti-sweatshop movement is a belief that Nike is hypocritical in the way it lays claim to social responsibility yet continues to exploit young female workers in the developing world. The logic of the anti-sweatshop critique is thus one of "communicative action" geared to mutual understanding and consensus rather than "strategic action," which is aimed at competitive success (Habermas, 1987). This is a general feature of new social movements (NSMs), which are oriented not towards the immediate, material self-interest of participants but to questions of shared meaning, social justice, and social solidarity (Carroll, 1997; Jasper, 1997). Many NSMs share an altruistic dimension as their actions entail an interest in the welfare of others (Melucci, 1996). In much the same way, the subpolitics represented by the anti-sweatshop movement is less about achieving material gains for the movement than it is about creating social understanding and support for others. Anti-sweatshop activism involves a desire to empathize with and care about the situation, interests, and aspirations of those at a distance (workers in developing countries) while assuming a critical stance towards something that is culturally and geographically more proximate (the corporation).

Subpolitics also differs from formal politics in that it is oriented more to questions of short-term tactics rather than long-term strategy. NSMs such as the anti-sweatshop movement assume a looser, more mobile and flexible form than more bureaucratically structured organizations. Whereas state and corporate organizations constitute definite centres of power where binding decision-making occurs, NSMs are typically organized in terms of network arrangements (Castells, 1996). This makes NSMs transient and reliant on a more pluralistic range of tactics that may also lack a strong sense of overall strategy. The anti-sweatshop movement consists of a network of different groups (unionists, students, religious groups, etc.) engaged in diverse activities such as culture jamming (mass media sabotage), conventional public protests, participation in shareholders' meetings, and regulatory initiatives such as the Worker Rights Consortium (Klein, 2000; Sage, 1999; Shaw, 1999). The communicational success of NSM groups such as the anti-sweatshop movement can also be attributed to the growing use of the Internet as a tool for information sharing. The Internet is seen by many to have levelled the playing field of corporate-activist relations by diminishing the corporation's gatekeeper role in the communication of critical information (Coombs, 1998; Heath, 1998). For example, according to Medea Benjamin of the international NGO, *Global Exchange*, "every time we do an action, we send an E-mail and a hundred people show up. It's like magic. We couldn't do it without E-mail" (Bullert, 1999: 4).

As we argued above, the anti-sweatshop movement differs from conventional social movements in that its organizational structure is decentred, mobile, and transient. In part, this is a result of the way in which new communication technologies such as the Internet bind the participants together in a virtual, rather than actual, geographical space. But at the same time, it is also because the movement consists of a coalition of groups that, under other circumstances, might find themselves on different sides of the political and ideological fence (e.g., environmental activists and labour unionists). What makes NSMs such as the anti-sweatshop movement so powerful is that traditional activist groups such as the labour movement, whose interests tend to be more particularistic (e.g., preserving jobs), can work cooperatively with other groups such as religious organizations and students, whose interests are based on considerations that are more ethical and normative than material. Indeed, it was not until the anti-sweatshop movement spread onto university campuses in the mid- to late 1990s that the issue demanded intense and ongoing attention in the mainstream media (Greenberg and Knight 2001).

The anti-sweatshop campus campaigns began in earnest in 1997, when a small but well-organized group of students at Duke University successfully pressured the administration there to adopt a "Code of Conduct" that would require the university to purchase and authorize the sale of clothing bearing the university's logo only from dealers that abided by standards pertaining to health and safety, wage, child-labour provisions, and factory location disclosures. In July 1998, a national coalition of student anti-sweatshop groups was formed under the umbrella name United Students Against Sweatshops (USAS). In a short time, thanks to the use of the Internet, close to 200 campus organizations had sprung up across North America (though less extensively in Canada, where university logo-wear is less popular and intercollegiate sports less commercially minded and funded). Newspaper reporting on the sweatshop problem increasingly referred to campus sit-ins and other student protests. At Georgetown University, students occupied the university president's office for four days to demand a meeting with the administration in order to establish a Code of Conduct there. Similarly, at the University of Wisconsin, student activists staged a 97-hour sit-in at the main administrative buildings before finally being granted a meeting with the administration. The UW protest was hugely successful, as nearly all of the students' demands were met (Hausman, 1999). In a more spectacular case, the University of North Carolina anti-sweatshop group, Students for Economic Justice, held a nude-optional party titled "I'd Rather Go Naked Than Wear Sweatshop Clothes." Shortly afterwards, in a show of solidarity, 12 student activists at Syracuse University in upstate New York cycled nude across their campus in late March to demonstrate their commitment to abolishing the sale of sweatshop garments there. Between February and April 2000, anti-sweatshop sit-ins had been held at universities in Pennsylvania, Michigan, Wisconsin, Oregon, Iowa, and Kentucky, as well as SUNY-Albany, Tulane,

Purdue, and Macalester (Featherstone, 2000). In Canada, anti-sweatshop campaigns were organized at Concordia University, George Brown College, the University of Guelph, McMaster University, Queen's University, Ryerson University, the University of Toronto, the University of Waterloo, the University of Western Ontario, and York University. An organization linking Canadian college and university groups — Students Against Sweatshops-Canada — was formed in February 1999 (Students Against Sweatshops-Canada, 2000). For the first time in nearly three decades, university students had become politically engaged and the power elite had taken notice.

By raising controversy over Nike's labour practices, the anti-sweatshop movement has not only questioned the reality of production conditions and workers' rights in developing countries. It has also thrown Nike's sincerity and credibility into question (Habermas, 1987). Nike has been presented with a problem whose resolution is not only practical, but also communicational. Its communication problem is particularly acute inasmuch as issues of sincerity and credibility penetrate to the heart of corporate identity. Nike's public relations response to the anti-sweatshop movement, however, has compounded this communication problem. Despite the view that corporate public relations have become increasingly proactive, Nike's response to its anti-sweatshop critics has been largely reactive and marked by a reluctance to take seriously its critics' arguments and claims. Nike has relied on a strategy of issues management aimed at deflecting and dispersing blame, making rhetorical commitments to social responsibility, and subduing controversy.

NIKE'S RESPONSE TO ITS CRITICS

Boje (1999; see also Harvard Business School, 2000) has identified four stages through which Nike's response to sweatshop criticisms has

developed. The first stage, up to the early 1990s, was one of avoidance: Nike disclaimed responsibility by displacing blame onto its contractors. In stage two, from 1993 to 1996, Nike's response switched to one of denial that the problem existed in a systematic and widespread way, and pointed to its own corporate code of conduct, first formulated in 1992, as evidence of this. This was followed in 1996 and 1997 (stage three) by a period of intensified media publicity after the 1995 discovery of the El Monte sweatshop in California and the 1996 exposé of the Kathy Lee Gifford line of Wal-Mart clothing being made under sweatshop conditions. Though not directly implicated in these events, Nike claimed its monitoring system was independent and commissioned a report by the global auditing firm GoodWorks International to testify to this. The GoodWorks report, which gave Nike a largely favourable review, was subsequently criticized by the media and academics as well as activists for its shoddy methodology and failure to acknowledge the key issue of wages (Boje, 1998). Knight's National Press Club appearance in May 1998 marked the beginning of the fourth stage and the prospect of some material improvement in working conditions.

Nike's reactive posture, its reluctance to address criticisms on major issues like wage levels, and its continued hostility towards some critics point to the limitations of promotionalism and the difficulty that promotionally oriented issues management has in coming to terms with anti-sweatshop subpolitics. The heart of issues management is a concern on the part of the corporation to manage the public policy process in a way that minimizes interference by outside actors, such as the state (Heath, 1988). In this respect, Nike's reluctance to address the issue of manufacturing wage levels, despite the relatively small proportion of total costs they comprise, represents a desire to preserve autonomy in the marketplace. When Nike translates social responsibility into philanthropic initiatives such as environmental projects, micro loans for local entrepreneurs, or education and fitness programs in developing countries, it also demonstrates a concern to maximize promotional returns. These are initiatives to which Nike can attach its name and corporate identity in a more visible and lasting way than wage increases.

The rise of issues management in the 1970s coincided with the neo-liberal turn in economic thinking, as governments began to redefine their role from one of legislative and regulatory intervention to one of facilitation and mediation in circumstances where corporate conduct became socially problematic. This was the model adopted by the American government in response to the growing controversy about sweatshops. In 1996 the Clinton administration brokered an agreement — the Apparel Industry Partnership (AIP) — between several apparel industry companies and other interested parties, including labour and human rights NGOs. The AIP, which gave rise to the Fair Labor Association (FLA), included Nike as a charter member. The formation of the AIP/FLA marked the institutionalization of sweatshops as a multilateral issue whose resolution was seen to lie in long-term consensus building around voluntary corporate codes of labour conduct, monitoring, and public accountability, rather than legislative or regulatory intervention.

The construction of an issue by means of this kind of multilateral process has two consequences for how the issue is framed and communicated publicly. Firstly, responsibility is generalized and dispersed among several parties so that no single organization bears the burden of accountability. Membership in the AIP/FLA enabled Nike to share its responsibility for the sweatshop issue with other corporate members and demonstrate publicly its willingness to resolve the problem in a voluntary and cooperative way. This means that Nike and other TNCs that are caught in the spotlight of bad publicity are able to point to one another as evidence that the problem is systemic rather than specific. Secondly, the generalization and dispersion of the issue implicates all the parties to institutional arrangements like the AIP/FLA in the responsibility for resolution. Resolution for the problem then becomes a matter of organizational politics, of negotiation and compromise. Because there are so many different actors to coordinate efforts with, Nike is unable to act on its own without disrupting the broader environment in which other participants must also act.

What has emerged from the interaction between Nike and anti-sweatshop activists is a dialectic of issues and crisis management. Nike's attempts to construct the issue in a systematic and institutionally manageable way are constantly punctured by activist claims about local crisis situations such as the recent controversy over the Kukdong factory in Atlixco, Mexico (Maquilla Solidarity Network, 2001; Nike, 2001; Verité, 2001). The effect of this is to reframe the issue of sweatshops as a problem of both Nike's factory conditions and its public credibility and sincerity. Nike's vulnerability to the publicity of sweatshop criticism stems from the fact that activists do not fit the mould of typical corporate stakeholders such as investors, consumers, or even employees. Stakeholders are assumed to have a direct, objective stake in the corporation's performance; they are assumed to have a vested interest of some kind that defines this stake and the issues or concerns that arise from it. Each stakeholder puts something at risk in his or her relationship with the corporation, and also stands to benefit directly from that relationship. It is the balance of benefits and risks that induces stakeholders to limit their claims and that allows for compromise solutions when stakeholder interests conflict. The interests of most anti-sweatshop activists, however, do not involve direct personal benefit and cost (with the possible exception of the labour movement). Their stake is really a mediated and mediating one, namely the interests of other stakeholders, Nike's workers in developing countries, who are already disregarded or marginalized. This means that activists' actions and claims are less likely to be constrained by considerations of material self-interest than those of other stakeholders.

CONCLUSION

Nike is faced with two problems. It must address in a substantive way criticisms of the conditions of production in its contract factories. It must also convince its critics that it is sincere in its claims and efforts to make acceptable improvements, while taking account of the way expectations and standards can be constantly revised. Because Nike has attempted so extensively to turn its claim to social responsibility into promotional capital, its sincerity problem in particular can be addressed successfully only in ways that reduce the appearance of direct promotional benefit. Regardless of the practical steps it can take to improve working conditions, wages, and worker rights, activist criticism, public suspicion, and the uncertainty these imply will doubtless persist as long as Nike continues to treat social responsibility as simply part of a promotional strategy.

For the anti-sweatshop movement the challenge of communicating its views is one of both access and content. Although the Internet has something of a democratizing effect on the capacity to communicate, it functions primarily as a tool to inform and motivate those who are already aware of and sympathetic to the anti-sweatshop campaign. Initial awareness still relies on "old" media such as face-to-face communication, public spectacles like demonstrations, and coverage in mainstream news outlets. The effectiveness of these depends on the cyclical character of protest activism, and the fact that social problems and causes vie for popular attention and support (Tarrow, 1994). Social movements can compensate for this by building on and renewing the way they frame social problems and their resolution (Snow and Benford, 1992). The sweatshop issue is a complex one, to be sure. The anti-sweatshop movement has been most effective in drawing attention to aspects such as wage levels that can be framed and communicated in a simplified but effective way, such as comparing the average Nike worker's wages to the sums paid to top Nike executives or celebrity athletes. The movement will have to continue to develop the framing of key issues like wages in an accessible yet innovative way. This is especially so if it is to attract the attention of the elite mainstream media whose influence is essential in legitimating the issue, but whose own search for new story topics and angles creates its own cyclical effects.

As economic globalization creates the conditions under which new forms of subpolitics cut across social, cultural, political, and geographical distances, TNCs will see their symbolic power challenged in the public sphere. Despite the dominance of promotionalism, the public sphere has not lost altogether its function as an arena where critical views can be expressed and support mobilized to challenge dominant institutions. As economic globalization extends and intensifies the logic of market relations, TNCs such as Nike, which are the principal agent of this process, will be confronted increasingly with the side effects of commercial success in the form of mobile, diffuse, and decentred subpolitics. This subpolitics, whose authority rests essentially on its ethical resonance, will continue to turn the power of publicity back onto the marketplace and reclaim the values of civil society as an affirmation of identification, mutual understanding, and social solidarity, rather than competitive success.

REFERENCES

Beck, U. (1997). *The Reinvention of Politics: Rethinking Modernity in the Global Social Order*. Trans. By M. Ritter. Cambridge: Polity Press.

Boje, D. M. (1998). "The Swoosh Goddess Is a Vampire: Nike's Environmental Accounting Storytelling." In G. A. Rossile, ed., *International Business and Ecology Research Yearbook* (pp. 23–32). Slippery Rock, PA: International Association of Business Disciplines Publication.

Boje, D. M. (1999). "Is Nike Roadrunner or Wile E. Coyote? A Postmodern Organization

Analysis of Double Logic." *Journal of Business and Entrepreneurship*, 2, 77–109.

Bullert, B.J. (1999). "Strategic Public Relations, Sweatshops, and the Making of a Global Movement." The Joan Shorenstein Center on the Press, Politics and Public Policy, Working Paper #2000-14. Cambridge, MA: Harvard University.

Carroll, W. (1997). "Social Movements and Counterhegemony: Canadian Contexts and Social Theory." In W. Carroll, ed., *Organizing Dissent: Contemporary Social Movements in Theory and Practice*, 2nd edition. Toronto: Garamond.

Carty, V. (1997). "Ideologies and Forms of Domination in the Organization of the Global Production and Consumption of Goods in the Emerging Postmodern Era: A Case Study of Nike Corporation and the Implications for Gender." *Gender, Work and Organization*, 4, 189–201.

Castells, M. (1996). *The Information Age: Economy, Society and Culture. Vol. I: The Rise of the Network Society*. Oxford: Blackwell.

Cheney, G., and Christensen, L.T. (2001). "Organizational Identity: Linkages between Internal and External Communication." In F.M. Jablin and L. L. Putnam, eds., *New Handbook of Organizational Communication*. London: SAGE.

Cole, C. (1996). "American Jordan: P.L.A.Y., Consensus and Punishment." *Sociology of Sport Journal*, 13, 366–397.

Cole, C. and Hribar, A. (1995). "Celebrity Feminism: Nike Style Post-feminism, Transcendence, and Consumer Power." *Sociology of Sport Journal*, 12, 347–369.

Coombs, W. T. (1998). "The Internet as Potential Equalizer: New Leverage for Confronting Social Irresponsibility." *Public Relations Review*, 24, 289–303.

Cushman Jr., J. H. (1998, May 13). "Nike Pledges to End Child Labor and Apply U.S. Rules Abroad." *The New York Times*, D1.

Dionne, E. J. (1998, May 15). "Bad for Business." *The Washington Post*, A27.

Featherstone, L. (2000, May 15). "The New Student Movement." *The Nation*, pp. 11–18.

Gandy, O. (1992). "Public Relations and Public Policy: The Structuration of Dominance in the Information Age." In E. Toth & R. L. Heath, eds., *Rhetorical and Critical Approaches to Public Relations* (pp. 111–130). Hillsdale, NJ: Erlbaum.

Gereffi, G. (1994). "The Organization of Buyer-Driven Commodity Chains." In G. Gereffi and M. Korzeniewicz, eds., *Commodity Chains and Global Capitalism* (pp. 95–122). Westport: Praeger.

Goldman, R., and Papson, S. (1998). *Nike Culture: The Sign of the Swoosh*. London: SAGE.

Greenberg, J., and Knight, G. (2001). "Framing Nike: Globalized Production, Sweatshop Labor and the American Media." Paper presented at the Global Village/Global Image Conference, London: British Film Institute.

Habermas, J. (1987). *The Theory of Communicative Action Vol. 2. Lifeworld and System: A Critique of Functionalist Reason*. Trans. by T. McCarthy. Boston: Beacon Press.

Hausman, T. (1999, February 26). "Students Leading the Sweatshop Battle." Retrieved from http://www.alternet.org.

Harvard Business School. (2000, January 19). Hitting the Wall: Nike and International Labor Practices. HBS Case N1-700-047. Prepared by J. L. Burns under the supervision of D. L. Spar.

Heath, R. L. (1988). "Conclusion: Balancing the interests of competing stakeholders: The new role for issues management." In R. L. Heath and Associates, eds., *Strategic Issues Management: How Organizations Influence and Respond to Public Interests and Policies* (pp. 386–394). San Francisco & London: Jossey-Bass Publishers.

Heath, R. L. (1998). New Communication Technologies: An Issues Management Approach. *Public Relations Review*, 24, 273–288.

Jasper, J. (1997). *The Art of Moral Protest: Culture, Biography and Creativity in Social Movements*. Chicago: University of Chicago Press.

Klein, N. (2000). *No Logo: Taking Aim at the Brand Bullies*. Toronto: Knopf Canada.

Korzeniewicz, M. (1994). "Commodity Chains and Marketing Strategies: Nike and the Global Athletic Footwear Industry." In G. Gereffi and M. Korzeniewicz, eds., *Commodity Chains and Global Capitalism* (pp. 247–265). Westport: Praeger.

Maquilla Solidarity Network. (2001, January 26). "Two Independent Reports Confirm that Mexican Nike Workers' Rights Violated." Memo: Codes Update Number 4. Toronto: Maquilla Solidarity Network.

Melucci, A. (1996). *Challenging Codes: Collective Action in the Information Age*. Cambridge: Cambridge University Press.

Nike. (1999). "Nike Chairman and CEO Phil Knight New Labor Initiatives." On the World Wide Web at http://www.nikebiz.com/labor/speech_trans.shtml.

Nike. (2001). "Nike Develops Remediation Plan for Kukdong Based on Recently Completed Independent Audit." On the World Wide Web at http://www.nikebiz.com/media/n_kukdong6.shtml.

Sage, G. (1999). "Justice Do It! The Nike Transnational Advocacy Network: Organization, Collective Actions, and Outcomes." *Sociology of Sport Journal*, *16*, 206–235.

Shaw, R. (1999). *Reclaiming America: Nike, Clean Air and the New National Activism*. Berkeley: University of California Press.

Snow, D.A. and Benford, R.D. (1992). "Master Frames and Cycles of Protest." In A.D. Morris and C. McClurg Mueller, eds., *Frontiers in Social Movement Theory* (pp. 133–155). New Haven and London: Yale University Press.

Stabile, C. (2000). "Nike, Social Responsibility and the Hidden Abode of Production." *Critical Studies in Media Communication*, *17*, 186–204.

Students Against Sweatshops-Canada (2000). On the World Wide Web at http://www.campuslife.utoronto.ca/groups/opirg/groups/sweatshops/sas-c.html (30 October 2002).

Tarrow, S. (1994). *Power in Movement: Social Movements, Collective Action and Politics*. Cambridge: Cambridge University Press.

Verité. (2001). Comprehensive Factory Evaluation Report on Kukdong International Mexico, S.A. de C.V. On the World Wide Web at http://www.nikebiz.com/media/nike_verite_report.pdf.

Wernick, A. (1991). *Promotional Culture: Advertising, Ideology and Symbolic Expression*. London: SAGE.

PART 4c — THE ECONOMY AND WORK

When the twentieth century was still young, the celebrated German sociologist Max Weber wrote admiringly of the "technical superiority" of **bureaucracies** "over any other form of organization." Bureaucracies, wrote Weber, are more precise, faster, less ambiguous, more discrete, and cheaper than all other ways of organizing business, education, law, the military, and so forth. They achieve their efficiency because they embody a specialized division of labour, a strict hierarchy of authority, clear regulations, impersonality, and a staff that is technically qualified to do its job.

Weber also recognized the dark underside of bureaucracy. Bureaucracies, he wrote, create cadres of powerful non-elected officials, thus making the world less democratic. Bureaucracies also lead people to focus on the means of achieving goals that have been specified by their superiors, not on questioning and helping to decide those goals. For these reasons, Weber likened the modern era to an "iron cage." In Chapter 24, George Ritzer carries Weber's analysis a step further. He agrees that the rationalization of the world is occurring in much the way Weber predicted. However, argues Ritzer, the model for this process is not bureaucracy so much as the fast-food restaurant. "McDonaldization," as Ritzer calls it, combines the principles of bureaucracy with those of the assembly line and "scientific management." Ritzer shows that, since the mid-1950s, McDonaldization has spread to larger and larger areas of life, and is now taking over prebirth and postdeath as well. He discusses several countervailing forces, but concludes that they are not sufficiently powerful to overwhelm the continued McDonaldization of the world.

Bureaucratization is one master trend governing the social organization of work. A second such trend is **job polarization**. Job polarization refers to the rapid growth of "bad jobs," the slower growth of "good jobs," and the still slower growth of medium-quality jobs. Bad jobs don't pay much and require the performance of routine tasks under close supervision. Working conditions are unpleasant and sometimes dangerous. Bad jobs require little formal education. In contrast, good jobs often require higher education. They pay well. They are not closely supervised and they encourage the worker to be creative in pleasant surroundings. Good jobs offer secure employment, opportunities for promotion, and fringe benefits. In a bad job, you can easily be fired, you receive few if any fringe benefits, and the prospects for promotion are few. If, over a decade or more, the number of bad jobs grows quickly, the number of medium-quality jobs grows slowly, and the number of good jobs grows at an intermediate rate, the occupational structure will start to assume the shape of an hourglass. Increasingly, jobs will be polarized or concentrated at the high and low ends of the occupational structure. This sort of polarization appears to have taken place in Canada in the 1990s.

In Chapter 25, Wallace Clement analyzes one of the main forces that led to the creation of many bad jobs in Canada in the 1990s: the free trade agreements that Canada signed with the US and Mexico. Before free trade, Canadian workers enjoyed higher wages and more state benefits than workers in the other North American countries. However, by making cross-border trade and investment easier, the free trade agreements put downward pressure on both wages and benefits. If employers in Canada continued paying high wages under free trade, and if Canadian governments continued taxing citizens at high rates to pay for generous state benefits, employers could simply shift their investment to more hospitable regimes. That is just what some employers did in the 1990s. Consequently, unemployment remained high throughout the decade. As Clement shows, to prevent further deterioration of the Canadian job market, wage levels were forced down and governments slashed their budgets. Bad jobs proliferated. The first years of the new century altered the picture somewhat. For example, particularly after the terrorist attacks of September 11, 2001, job growth continued in Canada but stalled in the United States. According to Clement, it is still too early to tell whether this is a long-term change in the economic environment or a temporary aberration from the historical trend.

GLOSSARY

Bureaucracies are associations that operate more precisely, faster, less ambiguously, more discretely, and cheaper than other forms of decision-making. They achieve their efficiency because they embody a specialized division of labour, a strict hierarchy of authority, clear regulations, impersonality, and a staff that is technically qualified to do its job.

Job polarization refers to the rapid growth of "bad jobs," the slower growth of "good jobs," and the still-slower growth of medium-quality jobs.

CRITICAL THINKING QUESTIONS

1. What does George Ritzer mean by the statement, "McDonaldization is expanding both in time and space?" Give examples to support your answer.
2. "McDonaldization is a global phenomenon even though it is at odds with many of the basic tenets of globalization theory." Explain what Ritzer means by this statement.
3. The American unemployment rate fell in the 1990s while the Canadian unemployment rate remained high. Why?
4. To what extent do you think global forces compelled the Canadian government and corporations to enter into a free trade agreement with the United States and Mexico? To what extent do you think Canada has political leeway in this regard?

ANNOTATED BIBLIOGRAPHY

Barbara Ehrenreich, *Nickel and Dimed: On (Not) Getting by in America* (New York: Henry Holt, 2001). An eye-opening first-person account by a leading sociologist of what it's like to try to get by working a minimum wage job. In brief: nearly impossible.

Harvey J. Krahn and Graham S. Lowe, *Work, Industry and Canadian Society*, 4th ed. (Toronto: Nelson, 2002). A highly regarded Canadian overview of the sociology of work.

Gordon Laxer, *Open for Business: The Roots of Foreign Ownership in Canada* (Toronto: Oxford University Press, 1989). An award-winning study of the social and historical roots of Canada's peculiar and problematic economic structure.

Chapter 24

The McDonaldization Thesis: Is Expansion Inevitable?

GEORGE RITZER

The "McDonaldization thesis" (Ritzer, 1983; 1993; 1996) is derived, most directly, from Max Weber's (1968 [1921]) theory of the rationalization of the Occident and ultimately the rest of the world (Kalberg, 1980). Weber tended to see this process as inexorable, leading, in the end, to the iron cage of rationalization from which there was less and less possibility of escape. Furthermore, with the corresponding decline in the possibility of individual or revolutionary charisma, Weber believed that there was a decreasing possibility of the emergence of a revolutionary counterforce.

Time has been kind to the Weberian thesis, if not to the social world. Rationalization has progressed dramatically in the century or so since Weber developed his ideas. The social world does seem to be more of an iron cage and, as a result, there does seem to be less possibility of escape. And it does appear less likely that any counterrevolution can upset the march toward increasing rationalization.

It is this theory and empirical reality that forms the background for the development of what has been termed the "McDonaldization thesis." This thesis accepts the basic premises of rationalization as well as Weber's basic theses about the inexorable character of the process. Its major point of departure from the Weberian theory of rationalization is to argue that the paradigm of the process is no longer, as Weber argued, the bureaucracy, but it is rather the fast-food restaurant. The fast-food restaurant has combined the principles of the bureaucracy with those of other rationalized precursors (for example, the assembly line, scientific management) to create a particularly powerful model of the rationalization process. It is a relatively new paradigm, traceable to the opening of the first restaurant in the McDonald's chain in 1955. While there were a number of predecessors to the first McDonald's outlet in the fast-food industry, it is McDonald's that was the truly revolutionary development in not only that industry, but in the history of the rationalization process.

Embodying perfectly the principles of rationalization, McDonald's became the model to be emulated first by other fast-food chains and later by other types of chain stores. It was not long before the success of McDonald's caught the eye of those in other types of businesses, and ultimately in virtually every other sector of society. Today, not only is McDonald's a worldwide success, but it offers an alluring model to those in a wide variety of leadership positions. It is in this role that McDonald's is playing the key role in the still-further expansion of the process of rationalization. Indeed its participation is so central that the contemporary manifestations of this process can be aptly labelled "McDonaldization."

Like Weber I have tended to view this process as inexorable in a variety of senses. First, it is seen as migrating from its roots in the fast-food

---

Source: Adapted from "The McDonaldization Thesis: Is Expansion Inevitable?" *International Sociology* 11, 3 (September 1996): 291–307. Reprinted by permission of the author.

industry in America to other types of businesses and other social institutions. Second, McDonaldization is spreading from the United States to more and more societies around the world. Third, McDonaldization is viewed as having first concentrated on the rationalization of processes central to life itself, but more recently it has moved to encompass the birth process (and before) as well as the process of death (and beyond).

To put this expansionism in contemporary theoretical terms, McDonaldization is expanding in both space and time (Giddens, 1984; Harvey, 1989). Spatially, McDonaldization is encompassing more and more chains, industries, social institutions and geographic areas of the world. Temporally, McDonaldization has moved from the core of life itself both backward to the birth process as well as the steps leading up to it and forward to the process of dying and its aftermath.

The evidence on the spatial and temporal advance of McDonaldization is overwhelming. However, in this essay I want to do more than review this evidence. I want to reexamine the issue of inexorability. Do its past and present successes mean that McDonaldization is truly inexorable? Is there no hope that the process can be slowed down or even stopped? Is it possible to avoid an iron cage of rationalization that encompasses time (from birth and before to death and beyond) and space (geographic areas within the United States and throughout the world)? Before getting to these issues, I need to review the basic parameters of the McDonaldization thesis.

McDONALDIZATION

I begin with a foundational definition: *McDonaldization is the process by which the principles of the fast-food restaurant are coming to dominate more and more sectors of American society, as well as of the rest of the world.* The nature of the McDonaldization process may be delineated by outlining its five basic dimensions: efficiency, calculability, predictability, control through the substitution of technology for people, and, paradoxically, the irrationality of rationality.

First, a McDonaldizing society emphasizes *efficiency*, or the effort to discover the best possible means to whatever end is desired. Workers in fast-food restaurants clearly must work efficiently; for example, burgers are assembled, and sometimes even cooked, in an assembly-line fashion. Customers want, and are expected, to acquire and consume their meals efficiently. The drive-through window is a highly efficient means for customers to obtain, and employees to dole out, meals. Overall, a variety of norms, rules, regulations, procedures, and structures have been put in place in the fast-food restaurant in order to ensure that *both* employees and customers act in an efficient manner. Furthermore, the efficiency of one party helps to ensure that the other will behave in a similar manner.

Second, there is great importance given to *calculability*, to an emphasis on quantity, often to the detriment of quality. Various aspects of the work of employees at fast-food restaurants are timed, and this emphasis on speed often serves to adversely affect the quality of the work, from the point of view of the employee, resulting in dissatisfaction, alienation, and high turnover rates. Only slightly over half the predominantly part-time, teenage, non-unionized, generally minimum-wage work force remains on the job for one year or more (Van Giezen, 1994). Similarly, customers are expected to spend as little time as possible in the fast-food restaurant. In fact, the drive-through window reduces this time to zero, but if the customers desire to eat in the restaurant, the chairs are designed to impel them to leave after about twenty minutes. All of this emphasis on speed clearly has a negative effect on the quality of the "dining experience" at a fast-food restaurant. Furthermore, the emphasis on how fast the work is to be done means that customers cannot be served high-quality food, which, almost by definition, requires a good deal of time to prepare.

Third, McDonaldization involves an emphasis on *predictability*. Employees are expected to perform their work in a predictable manner, and customers are expected to respond with similarly predictable behaviour. Thus, when customers enter, employees will ask, following scripts (Leidner, 1993), what they wish to order. For their part, customers are expected to know what they want, or where to look to find what they want, and they are expected to order, pay, and leave quickly. Employees (following another script) are expected to thank them when they do leave. A highly predictable ritual is played out in the fast-food restaurant, and it is one that involves highly predictable foods that vary little from one time or place to another.

Fourth, there is great *control* in a McDonaldizing society, and a good deal of that control comes from technologies. While these technologies currently dominate employees, increasingly they will be replacing humans. Employees are clearly controlled by such technologies as French-fry machines that ring when the fries are done and even automatically lift the fries out of the hot oil. For their part, customers are controlled both by the employees, who are constrained by such technologies, as well as more directly by the technologies themselves. Thus, the automatic fry machine makes it impossible for a customer to request well-done, well-browned fries.

Finally, both employees and customers suffer from the various *irrationalities of rationality* that seem inevitably to accompany McDonaldization. Many of these irrationalities involve the oppposite of the basic principles of McDonaldization. For example, the efficiency of the fast-food restaurant is often replaced by the inefficiencies associated with long lines of people at the counters or long lines of cars at the drive-through window. While there are many others, the ultimate irrationality of rationality is dehumanization. Employees are forced to work in dehumanizing jobs and customers are forced to eat in dehumanizing settings and circumstances. In Harry Braverman's terms, the fast-food restaurant is a source of degradation for employees and customers alike (Braverman, 1974).

EXPANSIONISM

McDonald's has continually extended its reach, within American society and beyond. As McDonald's chairman put the company's objective, "Our goal: to totally dominate the quick service restaurant industry worldwide. ... I want McDonald's to be more than a leader. I want McDonald's to dominate" (Papiernik, 1994).

McDonald's began as a suburban and medium-sized-town phenomenon, but in recent years it has moved into big cities and smaller towns (Kleinfeld, 1985; L. Shapiro, 1990) that supposedly could not support such a restaurant, not only in the United States but also in many other parts of the world. A huge growth area is in small satellite, express, or remote outlets opened in areas that are not able to support full-scale fast-food restaurants. These are beginning to appear in small store fronts in large cities, as well as in non-traditional settings like department stores and even schools. These satellites typically offer only limited menus and may rely on larger outlets for food storage and preparation (Rigg, 1994). McDonald's is considering opening express outlets in such locations as museums, office buildings, and corporate cafeterias.

Another significant expansion has occurred as fast-food restaurants have moved onto college campuses (the first such facility opened at the University of Cincinnati in 1973), instead of being content merely to dominate the strips that surround many campuses. In conjunction with a variety of "branded partners" (for example, Pizza Hut and Subway), Marriott now supplies food to almost 500 colleges and universities (Sugarman, 1995).

Another, even more recent, incursion has occurred: we no longer need to leave the highway to dine in our favourite fast-food restaurant. We can obtain fast food quickly and easily at convenient rest stops along the highway and then proceed with our trip. Fast food is also increasingly available *in* service stations (Chan, 1994). Also in the travel realm, fast-food restaurants are more and more apt to be found in hotels (E. McDowell, 1992), railway stations, and airports, and their products are appearing even on the trays of in-flight meals. The following newspaper advertisement appeared a few years ago: "Where else at 35,000 feet can you get a McDonald's meal like this for your kids? Only on United's Orlando flights." Now, McDonald's so-called Friendly Skies Meals are generally available to children on Delta flights. In addition, in December 1994, Delta began offering Blimpie sandwiches on its North American flights (*Phoenix Gazette*, 1994). (Subway sandwiches are also now offered on Continental flights.) How much longer before McDonaldized meals will be available on all flights everywhere by every carrier? In fact, on an increasing number of flights, prepackaged "snacks" have already replaced hot main courses.

In other sectors of society, the influence of fast-food restaurants has been more subtle, but no less profound. While we are now beginning to see the appearance of McDonald's and other fast-food restaurants in high schools and trade schools (Albright, 1995), few lower-grade schools as yet have in-house fast-food restaurants, but many have had to alter school cafeteria menus and procedures so that fast food is readily and continually available to children and teenagers (Berry, 1995). We are even beginning to see efforts by fast-food chains to market their products in these school cafeterias (Farhi, 1990).

The military has been pressed into offering fast-food menus on its bases and ships. Despite the criticisms by physicians and nutritionists, fast-food outlets are increasingly turning up *inside* hospitals. No homes have a McDonald's of their own, but dining within the home has been influenced by the fast-food restaurant. Home-cooked meals often resemble those available in fast-food restaurants. Frozen, microwavable, and pre-prepared foods, also bearing a striking resemblance to McDonald's meals and increasingly modelled after them, often find their way to the dinner table. Then there is the home delivery of fast foods, especially pizza, as revolutionized by Domino's.

As powerful as it is, McDonald's has not been alone in pressing the fast-food model on American society and the rest of the world. Other fast-food giants, such as Burger King, Wendy's, Hardee's, Arby's, Big-Boy, Dairy Queen, TCBY, Denny's, Sizzler, Kentucky Fried Chicken, Popeye's, Subway, Taco Bell, Chi Chi's, Pizza Hut, Domino's, Long John Silver, Baskin-Robbins and Dunkin' Donuts, have played a key role, as have the innumerable other businesses built on the principles of the fast-food restaurant.

Even the derivatives of McDonald's and the fast-food industry more generally are, in turn, having their own influence. For example, the success of *USA Today* has led to changes in many newspapers across the nation, with shorter stories and colour weather maps, for example. As one *USA Today* editor put it: "The same newspaper editors who call us McPaper have been stealing our McNuggets" (Prichard, 1987: 232–33).

Sex, like virtually every other sector of society, has undergone a process of McDonaldization. In the movie *Sleeper*, Woody Allen not only created a futuristic world in which McDonald's was an important and highly visible element, but he also envisioned a society in which even sex underwent the process of McDonaldization. The denizens of his future world were able to enter a machine called an "orgasmatron" that allowed them to experience an orgasm without going through the muss and fuss of sexual intercourse. In fact, we already have things like highly specialized pornographic movies (heterosexual, homosexual, sex with children, sex with animals) that can be seen at urban multiplexes and are available at local video stores for viewing in the comfort of our living rooms. In New York City, an official called a three-story pornographic centre "the McDonald's of sex" because of its "cookie-cutter cleanliness and compliance with the law" (*New York Times*, 1986: 6). The McDonaldization of sex suggests that no aspect of our lives is immune to its influence.

IS McDONALDIZATION TRUELY INEXORABLE?

I want to discuss this issue both spatially and temporally. First, there is the spatial issue of whether McDonaldization is destined to spread from its American roots and become a global phenomenon. Second, there is the temporal issue of whether McDonaldization will inevitably spread from its control over the core of life to colonize birth and before as well as death and beyond.

GLOBALIZATION

We can discuss the first issue under the heading of globalization, or the spread of McDonald's, and more importantly the principles of McDonaldization, around the world. However, in using the term globalization here, it should be pointed out that, as we will see below, there are some differences between its usage here and the way it has been used in the currently voguish globalization theory.

While there are significant differences among globalization theorists, most if not all would accept Robertson's advocacy of the idea that social scientists adopt "a specifically global point of view," and "treat the global condition as such" (Robertson, 1992: 61, 64). Elsewhere, Robertson (1990: 18) talks of the "study of the world as a whole." More specifically, Robertson argues that we need to concern ourselves with global processes that operate in relative independence of societal sociocultural processes. Thus, Robertson (1992: 60) argues, "there is a general autonomy and 'logic' to the globalization process, which operates in *relative* independence of strictly societal and other conventionally studied sociocultural processes." Similarly, Featherstone (1990: 1) discusses the interest in processes that "gain some autonomy on a global level."

While the reach of McDonaldization is global, it does not quite fit the model proposed by globalization theorists. The differences

between them are clear when we outline those things rejected by globalization theorists:

1. A focus on any single nation-state.
2. A focus on the West in general, or the United States in particular.
3. A concern with the impact of the West (westernization) or the United States (Americanization) on the rest of the world.
4. A concern with homogenization (rather than heterogenization).
5. A concern with modernity (as contrasted with postmodernity).
6. An interest in what used to be called modernization theory (Tiryakian, 1991).

The fact is that while McDonaldization *is* a global process, it has all of the characteristics *rejected* by globalization theorists: it does have its source in a single nation-state; it does focus on the West in general and the United States in particular; it is concerned with the impact of westernization and Americanization on the rest of the world; it is attentive to the homogenization of the world's products and services; it is better thought of as a modern than a postmodern phenomenon (because of its rationality, which is a central characteristic of modernity); and it does have some affinity with modernization theory (although it is not presented in the positive light modernization theory tended to cast on all western phenomena). Thus, McDonaldization is a global phenomenon even though it is at odds with many of the basic tenets of globalization theory.

The global character of this American institution is clear in the fact that it is making increasing inroads around the world (B. McDowell, 1994). For example, in 1991, for the first time, McDonald's opened more restaurants abroad than in the United States (Shapiro, 1992). This trend continues and, as we move toward the next century, McDonald's expects to build twice as many restaurants each year overseas as it does in the United States. Already by the end of 1993 over a third of McDonald's restaurants were overseas. As of the beginning of 1995, about half of McDonald's profits came from its overseas operations. As of this writing, one of McDonald's latest advances was the opening of a restaurant in Mecca, Saudi Arabia (*Tampa Tribune*, 1995).

Other nations have developed their own variants of this American institution, as is best exemplified by the now large number of fast-food croissanteries in Paris, a city whose love of fine cuisine might have led one to think that it would prove immune to the fast-food restaurant. India has a chain of fast-food restaurants, Nirula's, which sells mutton burgers (about 80 percent of Indians are Hindus who eat no beef) as well as local Indian cuisine (Reitman, 1993). Perhaps the most unlikely spot for an indigenous fast-food restaurant was then war-ravaged Beirut, Lebanon; but in 1984 Juicy Burger opened there (with a rainbow instead of golden arches and J.B. the clown replacing Ronald McDonald), with its owners hoping that it would become the "McDonald's of the Arab world" (Cowan, 1984).

Other countries not only now have their own McDonaldized institutions, but they have also begun to export them to the United States. For example, the Body Shop is an ecologically sensitive British cosmetics chain with, as of early 1993, 893 shops in many countries; 120 of those shops were in the United States, with 40 more scheduled to open that year (Elmer-Dewitt, 1993; E. Shapiro, 1991). Furthermore, Amer-ican firms are now opening copies of this British chain, such as the Limited, Inc.'s, and Bath and Body Works.

This kind of obvious spread of McDonaldization is only a small part of that process's broader impact around the world. Far more subtle and important are the ways in which McDonaldization and its various dimensions have affected the way in which many institutions and systems throughout the world operate. That is, they have come to adopt, and adapt to their needs: efficiency, predictability, calculability, and control through the replacement of human by non-human technology (and they have experienced the irrationalities of rationality).

How do we account for the global spread of McDonaldization? The first and most obvious answer is that material interests are impelling the process. That is, there is a great deal of money to be made by McDonaldizing systems, and those who stand to profit are the major motor force behind it.

Culture is a second factor in the spread of McDonaldization. There appears to be a growing passion around the world for things American, and few things reflect American culture better than McDonald's and its various clones. Thus, when Pizza Hut opened in Moscow in 1990, a Russian student said: "It's a piece of America" (*Washington Post*, 1990: B10). Reflecting on the growth of Pizza Hut and other fast-food restaurants in Brazil, the president of Pepsico (of which Pizza Hut is part) said of Brazil that this nation "is experiencing a passion for things American" (Blount, 1994: F1). Many people around the world identify strongly with McDonald's; in fact to some it has become a sacred institution (Kottak, 1983). On the opening of the McDonald's in Moscow, one journalist described it as the "ultimate icon of Americans," while a worker spoke of it "as if it were the Cathedral in Chartres ... a place to experience 'celestial joy' " (Keller, 1990: 12).

A third explanation of the rush toward McDonaldization is that it meshes well with other changes occurring in American society as well as around the world. Among other things, it fits in well with the increase in dual-career families, mobility, and affluence and with a society in which the mass media play an increasingly important role.

A fourth factor in the spread of McDonaldization and other aspects of American culture (the credit card [Ritzer, 1995], for example), is the absence of any viable alternative on the world stage. The path to worldwide McDonaldization has been laid bare, at least in part, because of the death of communism. With the demise of communism the only organized resistance can come from local cultures and communities. While the latter can mobilize significant opposition, it is not likely to be nearly as powerful as one embedded in an alternate worldwide movement.

Given the spread of McDonaldization and the powerful reasons behind it, what can serve to impede this global development? First, there is the fact that many areas of the world offer little in the way of profits to those who push McDonaldization. Many economies are so poor that there is little to be gained by pushing McDonaldized systems on them. Other institutions within such societies may want to McDonaldize their operations, but they are likely to be so overwhelmed by day-to-day concerns that they will have little time and energy to overhaul their systems. Furthermore, they are apt to lack the funds needed for such an overhaul. Thus their very economic weakness serves to protect many areas of the world from McDonaldization.

Second, we cannot overlook the importance and resilience of local culture. Globalization theorists, in particular, have emphasized the strength of such cultures. While it is true that McDonaldization has the power to sweep away much of local culture, it is not omnipotent. For example, while the eating habits of some will change dramatically, many others will continue to eat much as they always have. Then, even if the eating habits of an entire culture change (a highly unlikely occurrence), other aspects of life may be partly or even wholly unaffected by McDonaldization. It is also likely that too high a degree of McDonaldization will lead to a counterreaction and a reassertion of local culture. Also worth mentioning are the many ways in which local cultures affect McDonaldizing systems, forcing them to adapt in various ways to local demands and customs (for example, as discussed above, the mutton burgers in India).

The combination of a comparative lack of economic incentive to the forces behind McDonaldization and the opposition of local cultures will serve to impede the global spread of McDonaldization. However, when a given local culture advances economically, those who profit from McDonaldization will begin to move into that domain. In such cases, only local resistance will remain as a barrier to McDonaldization. It seems clear that while some local cultures will successfully resist, most will fail. In the end, and in the main, the only areas of the world that will be free of McDonaldization are those that lack the economic base to make it profitable.

The only hope on the horizon might be international groups like those interested in health and environmental issues. McDonaldized systems do tend to pose health risks for people and do tend to threaten the environment in various ways. There has, in fact, been some organized opposition to McDonaldized systems on health and environmental grounds. One could envision more such opposition, organized on a worldwide basis, in the future. However, it is worth noting that McDonaldized systems have proven to be quite adaptable when faced with opposition on these grounds. That is, they have modified their systems to eliminate the greatest threats to their customers' health and the greatest environmental dangers. Such adaptations have thus far served to keep health and environmental groups at bay.

THE COLONIZATION OF LIFE AND DEATH

While spatial expansion is covered in the previous section under the heading of globalization, in this section I deal with temporal expansion. McDonaldization first focused on a variety of things associated with *life*. That is, it is the day-to-day aspects of living — food, drink, clothing, shelter, and so on — that were initially McDonaldized. Firmly ensconced in the centre of the process of living, McDonaldization has pressed outward in both directions until it has come to encompass as many aspects as possible of both the beginning (birth) and the end of life (death). Indeed, as we will see, the process has not stopped there, but has moved beyond what would, at first glance, appear to be its absolute limits to encompass (again, to the degree that such a thing is possible) "prebirth" and "postdeath." Thus, this section is devoted to what might be termed the "colonization" (Habermas, 1987) of birth (and its antecedents) and death (and its aftermath) by the forces of McDonaldization.

In recent years a variety of steps have been taken to rationalize the process leading up to birth: burgeoning impotence clinics, including chains (Jackson, 1995), or soon-to-be-chains; artificial or, better, "donor" (Baran and Pannor, 1989) insemination; in vitro fertilization (DeWitt, 1993); surrogate mothers (Pretorius, 1994); "granny pregnancies" (*Daily Mail*, 1994); home pregnancy and ovulation-predictor tests (Cain, 1995); sex-selection clinics (Bennett, 1983); sex-determination tests like amniocentesis (Rapp, 1994); and tests including chorionic villus sampling, maternal serum alpha-fetoprotein, and ultrasound to determine whether the fetus is carrying such genetic defects as Down's syndrome, hemophilia, Tay-Sachs, and sickle-cell disease. All of these techniques are collectively leading to "high-tech baby making" (Baran and Pannor, 1989), which can be used to produce what have been called "designer pregnancies" (Kolker and Burke, 1994) and "designer babies" (Daley, 1994).

The rationalization process is also manifest in the process of giving birth. One measure of this is the decline in the very human and personal practice of midwifery. In 1900 about half of American births were attended by midwives, but by 1986 that had declined to only 4 percent (Mitford, 1993). Then there is the bureaucratization of childbirth. In 1900, less than 5 percent of births in the United States took place in hospitals, by 1940 it was 55 percent, and by 1960 the process was all but complete with nearly 100 percent of births taking place in hospitals (Leavitt, 1986: 190).

Hospitals and the medical profession developed standard, routinized (McDonaldized) procedures for handling childbirth. One of the best-known viewed childbirth as a disease (a "pathologic process") and its procedures were to be followed even in the case of low-risk births (Treichler, 1990). First, the patient was to be placed in the lithotomy position, "lying supine with legs in air, bent and wide apart, supported by stirrups" (Mitford, 1993: 59). Second, the mother-to-be was to be sedated from the first stage of labour on. Third, an episiotomy[1] was to be performed to enlarge the area through which the baby must pass. Finally, forceps were to be used to make the delivery more efficient. Describing this type of procedure, one woman wrote "Women are herded like sheep through an obstetrical assembly line [needless to say, one of the precursors of McDonaldization], are drugged and strapped on tables where their babies are forceps delivered" (Mitford, 1993: 61). This procedure had most of the elements of McDonaldization, but it lacked calculability, but that was added in the form of the "Friedman Curve" created in 1978. This curve envisioned three rigid stages of labour with, for example, the first stage allocated exactly 8.6 hours during which cervical dilation went from 2 to 4 cm (Mitford, 1993: 143).

A variety of non-human technologies (e.g., forceps) have been employed in the delivery of babies. One of the most widespread is the scalpel. Many doctors routinely perform episiotomies during delivery so that the walls of the vagina are not stretched unduly during pregnancy.

The scalpel is also a key tool in caesareans. A perfectly human process has come, in a large number of cases, to be controlled by this technology and those who wield it (Guillemin, 1989). The first modern caesarean took place in 1882, but as late as 1970 only 5 percent of all births involved caesareans. The use skyrocketed in the 1970s and 1980s, reaching 25 percent of all births in 1987 in what has been described as a "national epidemic" (Silver and Wolfe, 1989). (By 1989 there had been a slight decline to just under 24 percent).

Once the baby comes into the world, there is a calculable scoring system, Apgar, used on newborns. The babies are given scores of 1 to 2 on five factors (for example, heart rate, colour), with 10 being the top (healthiest) total score. Most babies have scores between 7 and 9 a minute after birth, and 8 to 10 after five minutes. Babies with scores of 0 to 3 are in distress.

We move now to the other frontier: from the process of being born to that of dying. The McDonaldization of death begins long before a person dies; it commences in the efforts by the medical system to keep the person alive as long as possible: the increasing array of technologies designed to keep people alive; the focus of medicine on maximizing the *quantity* of days, weeks, or years a patient remains alive, and the lack of emphasis on the *quality* of life during that extra time; computer systems that assess a patient's chances of survival; and the *rationing* in the treatment of the dying person.

Turning to death itself, it has followed much the same path as birth. That is, it has been moved out of the home and beyond the control of the dying and their family members and into the hands of medical personnel and hospitals. Physicians have played a key role here by gaining a large measure of control of death just as they won control over birth. And death, like birth, is increasingly likely to take place in the hospital. In 1900, only 20 percent of deaths took place in hospitals, in 1949 it was up to 50 percent, by 1958 it was at 61 percent, and by 1977 it had reached 70 percent. By 1993 the number of hospital deaths was down slightly (65 percent), but to that must be added the increasing number of people who die in nursing homes (11 percent) and residences such as hospices (22 percent) (National Center for Health Statistics, 1995). Thus, death has been bureaucratized, which means it has been rationalized, even McDonaldized. The latter is quite explicit in the growth of hospital chains and even chains of hospices, using principles derived from the fast-food restaurant, which are increasingly controlling death. One result of all of this is the dehumanization of the very human process of death, as we are increasingly likely to die (as we are likely to be born) impersonally, in the presence of total strangers.

However, even the best efforts of modern, rationalized medicine inevitably fail and patients die. But we are not free of McDonaldization even after we die. For example, we are beginning to witness the development of the changeover from largely family-owned to chains of funeral homes (Corcoran, 1992; Finn, 1991). The chains are leaping into this lucrative and growing market, often offering not only funeral services, but cemetery property and merchandise such as caskets and markers.

Perhaps the best example of the rationalization of death is the cremation. It is the parallel to caesareans in the realm of birth. Cremations are clearly more efficient than conventional funerals and burials. Ritual is minimized, and cremations have a kind of assembly-line quality; they lead to "conveyor belt funerals." Cremations also lend themselves to greater calculability than traditional funerals and burials. For example, instead of allowing lying in state for a day, or more, the city of London crematorium has the following sign: "Please restrict service to 15 minutes" (Grice, 1992: 10). Then there is the irrationality of the highly rational cremation, which tends to eliminate much of the human ceremony associated with a traditional funeral-burial.

The period after one dies has been rationalized in other ways, at least to some degree. There are, for example, the pre-arranged funerals that allow people to manage their affairs even after they are dead. Another example is the harvesting of the organs of the deceased so that others might live. Then there is cryogenics, where people are having themselves, or perhaps just their heads, frozen so that they might be brought back to life when anticipated advances in the rationalization of life make such a thing possible.

Given the rationalization of birth and before as well as death and beyond, are there any limits to this expansion? Several are worth mentioning:

- The uniqueness of every death (and birth): "Every life is different from any that has gone before it, and so is every death. The uniqueness of each of us extends even to the way we die" (Nuland, 1994: 3).
- The often highly nonrational character of the things that cause death (and cause problems at birth):

Cancer, far from being a clandestine foe, is in fact berserk with the malicious exuberance of killing. The disease pursues a continuous, uninhibited, circumferential, barn-burning expedition of destructiveness, in which it heeds no rules, follows no commands and explodes all resistance in a homicidal riot of devastation. Its cells behave like members of a barbarian horde run amok — leaderless and undirected, but with a single-minded purpose: to plunder everything within reach. (Nuland, 1994: 207)

If ever there was a daunting nonrational enemy of rationalization, cancer (and the death it often causes) is it.

- Midwifery has enjoyed a slight renaissance *because* of the dehumanization and rationalization of modern childbirth practices. When asked why they have sought out midwives, women complain about things like the "callous and neglectful treatment by the hospital staff," "labour unnecessarily induced for the convenience of the doctor," and "unnecessary caesareans for the same reason" (Mitford, 1993: 13).
- The slight decline in caesareans is reflective of the growing concern over the epidemic of caesareans as well as the fact that the American College of Obstetricians came out for abandoning the time-honoured idea, "once a caesarean, always a caesarean."
- Advance directives and living wills tell hospitals and medical personnel what they may or may not do during the dying process.
- The growth of suicide societies and books like Derek Humphrey's *Final Exit* give people instructions on how to kill themselves; on how to control their own deaths.

- The growing interest in euthanasia, most notably the work of "Dr. Death," Jack Kevorkian, shows that more people wish to exercise control over their own deaths.

CONCLUSION

I have discussed the spatial and temporal expansion of McDonaldization under the headings of globalization and the colonization of birth and death. It is abundantly clear that McDonaldization is expanding dramatically over time and space. However, there remains the issue of whether or not this growth is inexorable. A number of the barriers to, and limits on, the expansion of McDonaldization have been discussed in this chapter. There clearly are such limits and, perhaps more importantly, McDonaldization seems to lead to various counterreactions that serve to limit this spread. The issue, of course, is whether or not these counterreactions can themselves avoid being McDonaldized.

While there is some hope in all of this, there is not enough to allow us to abandon the Weberian hypothesis about the inexorable march toward the iron cage of, in this case, McDonaldization. In spite of this likely scenario, I think there are several reasons why it is important for people to continue to try to contain this process. First, it will serve to mitigate the worst excesses of McDonaldized systems. Second, it will lead to the discovery, creation, and use of niches where people who are so inclined can escape McDonaldization for at least a part of their day or even a larger portion of their lives. Finally, and perhaps most important, the struggle itself is ennobling. As a general rule, such struggles are nonrationalized, individual, and collective activities. It is in such struggles that people can express genuinely human reason in a world that in virtually all other ways has set up rationalized systems to deny people the ability to behave in human ways; to paraphrase Dylan Thomas, instead of going gently into that next McDonaldized system, rage, rage against the way it's destroying that which makes life worth living.

NOTE

1. An episiotomy is an incision between the vagina and the anus to enlarge the opening needed for a baby to pass.

REFERENCES

Albright, M. (1995) "Inside Job: Fast-food Chains Serve a Captive Audience," *St Petersburg Times* 15 January: 1H.

Baran, A. and Pannor, R. (1989) *Lethal Secrets: The Shocking Consequences and Unresolved Problems of Artificial Insemination.* New York: Warner Boks.

Bennett, N., ed. (1983) *Sex Selection of Children.* New York: Academic Press.

Berry, M. (1995) "Redoing School Cafeterias to Favor Fast-Food Eateries," *The Orlando Sentinel* 12 January: 11.

Blount, J. (1994) "Frying Down to Rio," *Washington Post-Business* 18 May: F1, F5.

Braverman, H. (1974) *Labor and Monopoly Capital: The Degradation of Work in the Twentieth Century.* New York: Monthly Review Press.

Cain, A. (1995) "Home-Test Kits Fill an Expanding Health Niche," *The Times Union-Life and Leisure* (Albany, NY) 12 February: 11.

Chan, G. (1994) "Fast-Food Chains Pump Profits at Gas Stations," *The Fresno Bee* 10 October: F4.

Corcoran, J. (1992) "Chain Buys Funeral Home in Mt Holly," *Burlington County Times* 26 January.

Cowan, A. (1984) "Unlikely Spot for Fast Food," *The New York Times* 29 April: 3: 5.

Daily Mail (1994) "A New Mama, Aged 62," 19 July: 12.

Daley, J. (1994) "Is Birth Ever Natural?" *The Times* (London) 16 March.

DeWitt, P. (1993) "In Pursuit of Pregnancy," *American Demographics* May: 48ff.

Elmer-Dewitt, P. (1993) "Anita the Agitator," *Time* 25 January: 52ff.

Farhi, P. (1990) "Domino's Is Going to School," *Washington Post* 21 September: F3.

Featherstone, M. (1990) "Global Culture: An Introduction," in M. Featherstone (ed.) *Global Culture: Nationalism, Globalization and Modernity*, pp. 1–14. London: Sage.

Finn, K. (1991) "Funeral Trends Favor Stewart IPO," *New Orleans City Business* 9 September.

Giddens, A. (1984) *The Constitution of Society: Outline of the Theory of Structuration.* Berkeley: University of California Press.

Grice, E. (1992) "The Last Show on Earth," *The Times* (London) 11 January: 10.

Guillemin, J. (1989) "Babies by Caesarean: Who Chooses, Who Controls?" in P. Brown (ed.) *Perspectives in Medical Sociology*, pp. 549–58. Prospect Heights, IL: Waveland Press.

Habermas, J. (1987) *The Theory of Communicative Action. Vol. 2., Lifeworld and System: A Critique of Functionalist Reason.* Boston, MA: Beacon Press.

Harvey, D. (1989) *The Condition of Postmodernity: An Inquiry into the Origins of Cultural Change.* Oxford: Blackwell.

Jackson, C. (1995) "Impotence Clinic Grows into Chain," *The Tampa Tribune–Business and Finance* 18 February: 1.

Kalberg, S. (1980) "Max Weber's Types of Rationality: Cornerstones for the Analysis of Rationalization Processes in History," *American Journal of Sociology* 85: 1145–79.

Keller, B. (1990) "Of Famous Arches, Beeg Meks and Rubles," *The New York Times* 28 January: 1: 1, 12.

Kleinfeld, N. (1985) "Fast Food's Changing Landscape," *The New York Times* 14 April: 3: 1, 6.

Kolker, A. and Burke, B. (1994) *Prenatal Testing: A Sociological Perspective.* Westport, CT: Bergin and Garvey.

Kottak, C. (1983) "Rituals at McDonald's," in M. Fishwick (ed.) *Ronald Revisited: The World of*

Ronald McDonald, pp. 52–58. Bowling Green, OH: Bowling Green University Press.

Leavitt, J. (1986) *Brought to Bed: Childbearing in America, 1750–1950*. New York: Oxford University Press.

Leidner, R. (1993) *Fast Food, Fast Talk: Service Work and the Routinization of Everyday Life*. Berkeley: University of California Press.

McDowell, B. (1994) "The Global Market Challenge," *Restaurants & Institutions* 104, 26: 52ff.

McDowell, E. (1992) "Fast Food Fills Menu for Many Hotel Chains," *The New York Times* 9 January: D1, D6.

Mitford, J. (1993) *The American Way of Birth*. New York: Plume.

National Center for Health Statistics (1995) *Vital Statistics of the United States, 1992–1993, Volume II — Mortality, Part A*. Hyattsville, MD: Public Health Service.

The New York Times (1986) 5 October: 3: 6.

Nuland, S. (1994) *How We Die: Reflections on Life's Final Chapter*. New York: Knopf.

Papiernik, R. (1994) "Mac Attack?" *Financial World* 12 April.

Phoenix Gazette (1994) "Fast-Food Flights," 25 November: D1.

Pretorius, D. (1994) *Surrogate Motherhood: A Worldwide View of the Issues*. Springfield, IL: Charles C. Thomas.

Prichard, P. (1987) *The Making of McPaper: The Inside Story of USA Today*. Kansas City, MO: Andrews, McMeel and Parker.

Rapp, R. (1994) "The Power of 'Positive' Diagnosis: Medical and Maternal Discourses on Amniocentesis," in D. Bassin, M. Honey and M. Kaplan (eds.) *Representations of Motherhood*, pp. 204–19. New Haven, CT: Yale University Press.

Reitman, V. (1993) "India Anticipates the Arrival of the Beefless Big Mac," *Wall Street Journal* 20 October: B1, B3.

Rigg, C. (1994) "McDonald's Lean Units Beef Up NY Presence," *Crain's New York Business* 31 October: 1.

Ritzer, G. (1983) "The McDonaldization of Society," *Journal of American Culture* 6: 100–7.

——. (1993) *The McDonaldization of Society*. Thousand Oaks, CA: Pine Forge Press.

——. (1995) *Expressing America: A Critique of the Global Credit Card Society*. Thousand Oaks, CA: Pine Forge Press.

——. (1996) *The McDonaldization of Society*, rev. ed. Thousand Oaks, CA: Pine Forge Press.

Robertson, R. (1990) "Mapping the Global Condition: Globalization as the Central Concept," in M. Featherstone (ed.) *Global Culture: Nationalism, Globalization and Modernity*, pp. 15–30. London: Sage.

——. (1992) *Globalization: Social Theory and Global Culture*. London: Sage.

Shapiro, E. (1991) "The Sincerest Form of Rivalry," *The New York Times* 19 October: 35, 46.

——. (1992) "Overseas Sizzle for McDonald's," *The New York Times* April 17: D1, D4.

Shapiro, L. (1990) "Ready for McCatfish?" *Newsweek* 15 October: 76–7.

Silver, L. and Wolfe, S. (1989) *Unnecessary Cesarian Sections: How to Cure a National Epidemic*. Washington, DC: Public Citizen Health Research Group.

Sugarman, C. (1995) "Dining Out on Campus," *Washington Post/Health* 14 February: 20.

Tampa Tribune (1995) "Investors with Taste for Growth Looking to Golden Arches," *Business and Finance* 11 January: 7.

Thomas, D. (1952) "Do Not Go Gentle into That Good Night," in D. Thomas *The Collected Poems of Dylan Thomas*, p. 128. New York: New Directions.

Tiryakian, E. (1991) "Modernisation: Exhumetur in Pace (Rethinking Macrosociology in the 1990s)," *International Sociology* 6: 165–80.

Treichler, P. (1990) "Feminism, Medicine, and the Meaning of Childbirth," in M. Jacobus, E. Keller and S. Shuttleworth (eds.) *Body Politics: Women and the Discourses of Science*, pp. 113–38. New York: Routledge.

Van Giezen, R. (1994) "Occupational Wages in the Fast-Food Industry," *Monthly Labor Review* August: 24–30.

Washington Post (1990) "Wedge of Americana: In Moscow, Pizza Hut Opens 2 Restaurants," 12 September: B10.

Weber, M. (1968 [1921]) *Economy and Society*. Totowa, NJ: Bedminster Press.

Chapter 25

Work and Society: Canada in Continental Context

WALLACE CLEMENT

THE WORST OF BOTH WORLDS

In the late 1980s and 1990s, Canada became increasingly integrated into the US economy through several free trade agreements. These agreements facilitated cross-border trade and investment. Closer integration of the two countries had some paradoxical effects. On the one hand, Canadians witnessed an erosion of their hard-won rights to various welfare-state benefits — state-funded medical services, subsidized higher education, and the like. In this sense, Canada became more like the US, where citizens have historically enjoyed fewer welfare-state entitlements than Canadians. On the other hand, Canada failed to participate fully in the "boom" economy of the US, at least until the altered circumstances at the turn of the century. For example, while the proportion of working-age Americans in the labour force remained exceptionally high throughout the 1990s, the corresponding proportion in Canada fell. Similarly, while Canadian Gross Domestic Product per capita (GDPpc) was 82 percent of American GDPpc in 1989, it fell to 76 percent by 1997. Thus, the Canadian labour market failed to emulate the American model while the system of Canadian citizenship entitlements began to do so. In terms of labour market and state benefits, then, Canada experienced the worst of both worlds. The question before us is

"What does the post-September 11th, 2001, era hold in store for us?"

COMPARING LABOUR MARKETS

Before 1981, Canada and the United States had nearly identical unemployment rates. During the 1980s, however, a 2 percent gap in unemployment rates opened between the two countries. The gap grew to 5 percent in the early 1990s and reached nearly 8 percent in 1999.[1] Official unemployment over the period 1989–99 averaged 9.4 percent in Canada compared to 5.7 percent in the US. In 2000 the Canadian rate fell to 6.8 percent but rose again in 2001 to 7.2 while in the US the rate fell to 4.0 percent, rising to 4.8 percent in 2001.[2]

The growing gap between Canadian and US unemployment rates was due in part to the extraordinary capacity of the United States to create new jobs and the failure of Canada to follow suit. However, other factors were at work too. For one thing, the United States imprisons more of its citizens per 100 000 population than any other country. Incarceration became particularly popular in the US in the 1980s and 1990s. Today, nearly 2 million Americans are behind bars and the rate of incarceration is about 6.3 times higher than in Canada. The high incarceration rate keeps many hard-to-employ Americans out of the labour force while pro-

Source: Original excerpted from Wallace Clement, "Work and Society: Canada in a Continental and Comparative Context," Presentation, Department of Sociology, Bishop's University, Lennoxville, QC, November 9, 1999. Revised 2003. Reprinted by permission of the author.

viding many jobs for police and prison guards.[3] Also helping to keep US unemployment rate low is the growing population of "illegal immigrants." There are about five million illegal immigrants in the United States, nearly half from Mexico.[4] This is proportionately far more than in Canada. Illegal immigrants are likely to experience higher unemployment rates than legal immigrants and non-immigrants, yet they are not calculated among the officially unemployed because they are in the country illegally. Finally, the American armed forces comprise 0.5 percent of the American population but only 0.2 percent of the Canadian population (NATO, 2001). The higher level of militarization of the United States also keeps the American unemployment rate lower.[5]

Compared to the US, Canada was more deeply affected by the recession of the early 1990s and its population grew more quickly. These factors also contributed to the growing gap in unemployment rates between the two countries. True, by the middle of 2000, Canada's unemployment rate fell to its lowest level in ten years (6.8 percent) compared to 4.0 percent in the US But it is important to note that much of this decline was due to the growth of part-time, not full-time, jobs; part-time jobs are less secure, pay less, and offer fewer benefits than full-time jobs. Not until 1998 did the number of full-time jobs regain their 1989 level, all new jobs in this period coming from more precarious sources such as part-time work and self-employment.[6] Moreover, some of the decline was due to people dropping out of the labour force. Declining unemployment rates due to people dropping out of the labour force and taking part-time work are less impressive and less beneficial than declining unemployment rates due to the growth of full-time jobs.

One of the strongest patterns of change in Canada's labour force during the free trade era is the rise in self-employment. Self-employment accounted for three-quarters of all new jobs created between 1989 and 1997. The self-employed now comprise 18 percent of Canada's labour force. Ninety percent of these new jobs are in the service sector, led by business services and health and social services. Significantly, earnings of self-employed workers are more polarized than earnings of employees. Thus, 45 percent of self-employed workers, compared to 26 percent of employees, earn less than $20 000 annually. At the other extreme, only 1 percent of employees, compared to 4 percent of self-employed workers, earn more than $100 000 annually.[7]

A major Statistics Canada study contrasting labour market developments in Canada and the United States between 1989 and 1997 found that self-employment grew by 39 percent in Canada while the number of employees rose by only 1.6 percent. In the United States over the same period, both self-employment and employment in general grew by about 10 percent (see Table 25.1 on page 282). The difference in self-employment in the two labour markets is striking when one considers that self-employment accounted for four-fifths of total job growth in Canada and only one-tenth in the United States between 1989 and 1997.[8] Equally stunning is the share of growth coming from part-time employment in Canada contrasted with the United States. Canada's full-time employees took a major hit over the period. Thus, not only was Canada's job growth much slower than in the United States, it was characterized by the more rapid growth of so-called marginal or "contingent" jobs that offer less job security, lower wages, more seasonal work, and fewer benefits.

The growth of contingent jobs affects different segments of the labour force to varying degrees. Compare women and men, for example. A recent Canadian study reports that nearly two-thirds of women who have been employed in the paid labour force have had their work interrupted for six or more months. This compares to just over a quarter of men. Moreover, while 88 percent of women's labour force interruptions were due to family responsibilities in the 1950s, this figure fell to 47 percent in the 1990s. Meanwhile, economic reasons such

TABLE 25.1 COMPONENTS OF EMPLOYMENT GROWTH, CANADA AND THE UNITED STATES, 1989–97 (IN PERCENT)

GROWTH	CANADA	UNITED STATES
Total employment	6.5	10.4
Percent of total growth from:		
Self-employment	79.4	9.5
Part-time	47.8	6.2
Full-time	31.8	3.3
Employees	20.6	90.5
Part-time	47.3	20.4
Full-time	−26.7	70.1

SOURCE: Adapted from Statistics Canada, *Labour Force Update* (Autumn 1998) Table 4, p. 17.

as layoffs accounted for nearly a quarter of female labour force interruptions in the 1990s.[9] Another gender difference is evident in the proportion of women and men who work part-time. In all countries, women are more likely than men to work fewer than 30 hours a week. In the US, for example, about 8 percent of men and 19 percent of women work less than 30 hours a week. In Canada, the respective figures are about 11 percent and 29 percent.[10]

Part-time work may be voluntary or involuntary. In Canada, an increasingly large share of the part-time labour force is involuntary, which is to say it consists of people who want to work full-time but cannot find full-time jobs. Thus, between 1975 and 1994, part-time employment rose from 11 percent to 17 percent of the labour force, while those seeking full-time employment but having to settle for part-time work rose from 11 percent to 35 percent. In 40 percent of cases, the involuntary part-time worker was the primary earner in their family.[11] Finally, shift work is becoming more common with unclear health and family implications. For 2000–01, in the core labour force age group (18–54 years old)

30 percent of men and 26 percent of women had nonstandard work schedules (evening, rotating, or irregular shifts).[12]

We now seem to be on the edge of a new era with unclear outcomes. This period began with the disaster of September 11, 2001, and soon involved much economic dislocation and military mobilization. The US seems to have been especially hurt in employment terms, and has experienced no employment growth as of this writing (October 2002). In Canada, the message is mixed: job growth in the state sector (mainly health and education) but a slowdown in the private sector.[13] Is this public sector growth in Canada an aberration of a federal Liberal leadership situation and the new Ontario governing Conservative leadership positioning for election? It is too soon to know. We do know that the labour market situation is in a state of flux with the number of Canadian self-employed people still rising.

A recent detailed Statistics Canada comparison of self-employment changes between Canada and the United States reiterates (1) the expansion of this form of employment in Canada between 1987 and 1998 (it accounts for over half of all labour market growth) and (2) the weak incomes of the Canadians in this group compared to employees. It is also important to stress the difference between the expansion of the own-account self-employed category in Canada and its contraction in the United States. In Canada, the own-account self-employed category grew by 65 percent between 1987 and 1998, accounting for 80 percent of all self-employed people by 1998. Individuals in this category earned only 53 to 68 percent of the average income of other workers over this period.[14] While Canada experienced a dramatic increase in the number of own-account self-employed workers and the number of hours they worked, both declined in the United States between 1987 and 1998. These findings show "there are fundamental structural differences between the self-employed sectors in the two economies."[15] Should Canadians be concerned?

Yes, primarily because these new jobs are of low quality compared with other forms of employment. We are not headed in the right direction.

CITIZENSHIP AND THE WELFARE STATE

On the basis of the foregoing discussion it seems safe to conclude that, since the advent of free trade in the late 1980s, Canada has not participated in many aspects of the boom economy enjoyed by its southern neighbour. Whether we examine labour force participation rates, unemployment rates, change in GDPpc, or growth in full-time noncontingent jobs, Canada has lagged behind the United States. That, however, is only half the story I want to tell. The other half has to do with the decline of welfare-state benefits or entitlements. Here Canada *has* begun to resemble the United States. That is largely because of free trade. If Canada kept welfare-state benefits much higher than US levels, investment capital would tend to flow out of the country because total labour costs would be so much higher in Canada. Free trade thus puts downward pressure on Canadian welfare-state benefits.

The main differences between Canadian and US entitlements are in the realm of health care and postsecondary education. In the mid-1990s, just under 45 percent of American health-care costs were covered by government. In Canada, the comparable figure was just over 70 percent. Similarly, the Canadian government heavily subsidizes postsecondary education, while American postsecondary education is largely private. However, these and other differences between the Canadian and American welfare states are weakening in the free trade era. Canadian government spending on health care and postsecondary education was cut throughout the 1990s. Tuition fees have gone up and private health care is making inroads, especially in Alberta.

Here I must distinguish entitlements based on employment from those based on citizenship. To the extent that access to health care is based on private insurance plans or plans paid by employers rather than awarded as a right of citizenship, health-care insurance is turned into a commodity. In Canada, basic health care, including doctor's fees and hospitalization, are covered by a nationally financed health insurance scheme. Other features of health care — dentistry, drugs, eyewear, types of hospital rooms, and so on — are covered either privately or through employment benefits. In Canada, employers face modest demands in wage negotiations for health-care coverage, whereas in the US health-care insurance demands are high because state funding partially covers only the elderly and the poor. The link between work and society is weaker in Canada than in the United States in this respect.

For education, Canada's primary and secondary levels are fully state-funded with near-universal utilization of the system. Preschool child-care is a private responsibility, and a once-promised national day-care program still remains a dream. Postsecondary education is fee-based but tuition has traditionally been modest and all universities are public institutions. In the United States, an increasing share of primary and secondary students are in private schools because of the lower quality of most state-funded schools. Postsecondary education is sharply divided between (1) state-sponsored institutions with high tuition fees and (2) private colleges with extremely high tuition fees.

In Canada, the contributory "employment insurance" scheme became more restrictive in the 1990s as eligibility criteria were tightened and a shrinking share of the unemployed was deemed entitled to benefits. People excluded from employment insurance are pushed into the means-tested welfare system. While 83 percent of unemployed Canadians qualified for employment insurance benefits in 1989, only 43 percent were eligible in 1997. This declining coverage resulted from 1996 reforms disqualifying "voluntary" job leavers and seasonal and part-time workers. Benefits were cut from 67 percent of previous salary to 55 percent. The result was a cash cow for the government; $19.5 billion in employment insurance contributions was collected in 1997 but only $12.5 billion was paid in benefits and administration.[16]

In terms of public expenditures on labour markets, Canada and the United States are not in the same league. Active labour market measures facilitate people's ability to find work. Passive measures compensate them for not working. While active labour market support diminished in Germany and Sweden in the 1990s, these countries remained active in their labour market support throughout the decade. Canada and Australia were high on passive support but low on active support and moderate overall. Japan and the United States were inactive and provided little even in the way of passive labour market support (see Table 25.2).

Compared to the United States, Canada spends more on employment services and labour market training. However, Canada follows the meagre US pattern for youth measures, subsidized employment, and disability measures. During the 1990s, countries like Australia, Germany, and Sweden dedicated more resources to actively combating unemployment. Canada is in the same league as the United States and Japan in this respect. Still, it is exceptional because, unlike these two low-unemployment countries, Canada suffers from chronically high unemployment.

Canada's dramatic reduction in passive payments was achieved by cutting coverage, not by reducing unemployment, as in the United States. Indeed, Canada's unemployment increased as its expenditures decreased. In terms of its welfare state expenditures, it is acting like the United States but it is doing so on a labour market foundation dramatically different from its neighbour's.

CONCLUSION

What, in the final analysis, can be said about the relationship between work and society during the free trade era in Canada? Work in Canada has become more marginal or contingent in many respects. There are more self-employed workers, more part-time workers, and more unemployed people. Instead of becoming more like the American labour market, where people tend to work longer hours during longer work lives, Canada has become a place where people work less because less work is available, especially good work in the public sector and large corporations. Postindustrialism has not been kind to the Canadian labour force.

TABLE 25.2 PUBLIC EXPENDITURES IN LABOUR MARKET PROGRAMS AS PERCENTAGE OF GDP, SELECTED COUNTRIES, 2000–2001

	CANADA	US	AUSTRALIA	JAPAN	GERMANY	SWEDEN
Employment services	0.17	0.04	0.20	0.20	0.23	0.23
Training	0.17	0.04	0.02	0.03	0.34	0.30
Youth	0.02	0.03	0.07	0.00	0.09	0.02
Subsidized	0.03	0.01	0.11	0.08	0.25	0.24
Disabled	0.02	0.03	0.05	0.01	0.29	0.31
Compensation	0.72	0.30	0.98	0.55	1.90	1.19
Active	**0.41**	**0.15**	**0.46**	**0.31**	**1.20**	**1.09**
Passive	**0.72**	**0.30**	**0.98**	**0.55**	**1.92**	**1.19**
Total	1.13	0.45	1.43	0.86	3.13	2.28

SOURCE: Adapted from OECD, *Employment Outlook*. July 2002, Table H, pp. 325–332.

In areas like unemployment insurance, the Canadian government is putting more stress on employment-based benefits that are not typically available for self-employed and part-time workers. The Canadian state has not yet declined to American levels because its citizens continue to insist on a higher level of social support. Canada stands between the American job machine with its abundance of cheap labour and the more supportive labour markets of Sweden and Germany.

Are Canadians, as citizens and workers, better off under free trade? We cannot answer this question fully because we will never know the outcome of alternative policy choices. Nonetheless, it seems that many Canadians have paid dearly for the path Canada's political leaders chose and its economic leaders demanded. The labour market and social service effects of September 11th, 2001, remain unclear, but early indications suggest that the United States has experienced more negative effects than Canada.

NOTES

1. See Statistics Canada, *Labour Force Update*, Autumn 1998, p. 3

2. See Organization for Economic Cooperation and Development, Employment Outlook 2002, Paris, July 2002, Tbl. 1.3, p. 18.

3. Bruce Western and Katherine Beckett, "How Unregulated is the US Labor Market?: The Penal System as a Labor Market Institution" *American Journal of Sociology* 104:4 (January 1999): 1030–60; H.L. Ginsburg, J. Zaccone, G.S. Goldberg, S.D. Collins and S.M. Rosen, "Special Issue on the Challenge of Full Employment in the Global Economy, Editorial Introduction" *Economic and Industrial Democracy*, 18, 1997, p. 24; "U.S. surpasses Russia as world leader in rate of incarceration," *The Sentencing Project* (2001). On the World Wide Web at http://www.sentencingproject.org/brief/usvsrus.pdf (18 October 2002).

4. See Min Zhou, "Growing Up American: The Challenge Confronting Immigrant Children and the Children of Immigrants" *Annual Review of Sociology*, 23, 1997: 63–95; *New York Times*, 31 August 1997.

5. "Defence expenditure and size of armed forces of NATO and partner countries," *NATO Review: 2001*. On the World Wide Web at http://www.nato.int/docu/review/2001/defence0103-en.pdf (18 October 2002).

6. See Ekuwa Smith and Andrew Jackson, "Does a Rising Tide Lift All Boats? The Labour Market Experience and Incomes of Recent Immigrants, 1995–1998" Canadian Council on Social Development: Ottawa, February 2002.

7. See *Canadian Social Trends*, Ottawa: Statistics Canada, Spring 1998, p. 28.

8. See *Labour Force Update*, Autumn, 1998, p. 13.

9. See Janet Fast and Moreno Da Pont, "Changes in Women's Work Continuity" *Canadian Social Trends*, Autumn 1997, pp. 3–5.

10. See Rianne Mahon, "Women Wage Earners and the Future of Swedish Unions" *Economic and Industrial Democracy*, 17, 1996: 555, 574. Also see Jacqueline O'Reilly and Claudia Spee, "The Future Regulation of Work and Welfare: Time for a Revised Social and Gender Contract?" *European Journal of Industrial Relations*, 4:3, 1998: 259–281.

11. Grant Schellenberg, "'Involuntary' Part-Time Workers" *Perception*, 18: 3–4, 1996.

12. See Statistics Canada, *The Daily*, 25 July 2002.

13. See Statistics Canada, *The Daily,* 9 August 2002.

14. See John Baldwin and James Chowham, "The Impact of Self-Employment on Labour-Productivity Growth: A Canada and United States Comparison." Ottawa: Statistics Canada. August 2003: pp. 10–11.

15. Ibid., p. 29.

16. See *Globe and Mail*, 13 February 1998: A3.

PART 5

DEVIANCE AND CRIME

Deviance is behaviour that departs from a norm. It ranges from harmless fads to the most violent crimes. In a sense, all deviance is anti-institutional since it seeks to achieve acceptable goals, such as getting rich or happy, by generally disapproved, and often illegal, means. But deviance is also institutionalized behaviour because it is socially learned, organized, and persistent. Accordingly, an individual is more likely to become a deviant if he or she is exposed to more deviant than nondeviant role models. Moreover, the deviant role is learned by means of socialization; just as medical students are socialized into the role of doctor, so professional robbers must learn the moral code of thieves. And deviants, including criminals, establish counter-institutions — cliques, gangs, mafias, and so forth — with their own rules of behaviour and their own subcultural norms.

Criminal behaviour worries the Canadian public more today than it used to. There is much talk about crime waves and mounting random violence, particularly among youth. Many people are afraid to walk alone outside at night. In large cities, many people equip their homes with burglar alarms and install steel bars on their basement windows. There is no doubt that crime rates have risen since the 1960s, but are current fears exaggerated? Most people rely on the mass media for information about crime trends. The police rely on information they collect in the course of doing their work. Reported criminal incidents, apprehensions, convictions, and incarcerations are all recorded to determine, among other things, whether crimes of various types are on the rise. Both public and police sources of information are, however, subject to bias. The mass media often exaggerate the extent of criminal behaviour because doing so increases audience size and therefore the amount of money that businesses are willing to pay for advertisements. The police may record more crime not just because there is more, but also because more officers are looking harder for certain types of criminals and because the public is more willing to report certain types of crimes.

Due to these biases, sociologists prefer to supplement official police statistics with "victimization surveys," polls of representative samples of citizens that seek to determine whether and under what circumstances people are victims of crime. Recent Canadian victimization surveys find that under a quarter of Canadians are victims of at least one crime in the year preceding the surveys. Overall, victimization rates are remaining steady or *decreasing*, depending on the type of crime examined. Victimization surveys also show that while Canadians think that crime rates are rising, they believe the rise is occurring some place other than their own neighbourhood. Thus it is not personal experience that accounts for recent perceptions of rising crime rates. Rather, such perceptions result partly from mass media "hype" and partly from the fact that robberies and assaults more frequently take place in public settings than they used to. Discrepancies between police statistics and victimization surveys are partly due to the fact that victims of some crimes, such as spousal assault and school violence, are more willing to report events to the authorities than they used to be. Increased reporting does not, however, necessarily mean increased crime.

In Chapter 26, Reginald Bibby analyzes patterns of violence, sexual behaviour, and drug use among Canadian teenagers. Basing his analysis on a 2000 survey of 3600 Canadians between the ages of 15 and 19, Bibby finds strong evidence that violence among teens is not all media hype. It is an alarming problem. For example, some 40 percent of males and 25 percent of females claim they have a close friend who has been physically attacked at school. That said, teen violence has been declining in recent years, contrary to what many people believe. Moreover, it is perhaps the widespread belief itself that helps explain why punishment for violence is often harsher for young offenders than for adults. The picture of teen sexual behaviour and attitudes that emerges from Bibby's sketch is rather more conservative than many people would predict. For example, while 75 percent of Canadian teenagers think that homosexuals are entitled to the same rights as other Canadians (higher than the corresponding figure for adults), only 55 percent think that is should be possible to obtain a legal abortion for any reason (lower than the corresponding percentage for Canadian adults). Religiosity is a major determinant of how liberal or conservative teenagers are with respect to sexual behaviour and attitudes. For instance, only 28 percent of teenagers who attend religious services weekly think consenting teens should be able to do what they want sexually. The corresponding figure for teenagers who attend religious services less than weekly is 63 percent. Finally, the data on drug use show that 28 percent of teenagers smoke cigarettes monthly or more often, 20 percent drink alcohol at least once a week, 15 percent smoke marijuana or hashish weekly or more, and 3 percent use other illegal drugs on a weekly basis.

Patricia Erickson's analysis of Canadian drug law in Chapter 27 is a nice complement to Bibby's statistics on teenage drug use. Erickson goes beyond the numbers to show that the way in which drugs have been controlled in Canada has been strongly influenced by social and cultural forces. One might assume that stricter control and harsher punishment are associated with more dangerous drugs. The plain fact is, however, that alcohol, tobacco, opium, heroin, cocaine, and marijuana have been controlled more or less stringently by the state at different times. As Erickson shows, which drugs are singled out and for how much control depends on the ability of particular groups of "moral crusaders" to sway public opinion and government policy in particular directions. This was evident as early as 1908, when the government first imposed harsh penalties for the use of opium. The law was directed at Chinese labourers at a time when anti-Chinese race riots first broke out in Canada (in Vancouver in 1907). This was also a time when growing unemployment led white racists inside and outside government to restrict Chinese immigration and, indeed, force Chinese labourers to return to China by imposing special, exorbitant taxes on them (the so-called "head tax"). Similarly, in 1986, Canada mounted a harsh campaign against cocaine when Ronald Reagan announced his "war against drugs" and the American media made much of the American drug problem. Yet in the 1980s the Canadian rate of cocaine use was as little as 20 percent that of the American rate, less than 1 percent of Canadian adults had used cocaine, and the rate of cocaine use among students was declining. In this context, the Canadian "drug crisis" had to be largely manufactured by the Canadian government and police officials. What links 1908 with 1986 is that on both occasions drug taking was criminalized in response to moral crusades by influential groups.

When people claim that crime is on the rise, they tend to focus on "street crime" such as robbery, assault, homicide, and the like. But one large category of illegal behaviour scarcely enters the public consciousness, even though, according to some estimates, it costs the Canadian public more than street crime in terms of dollars and lives. I refer to **corporate crime**. A corporate crime is an act that breaks a law intended to regulate business activity. Such laws are designed to ensure worker safety and accurate advertising, and to prevent fraudulent financial manipulation, price fixing, market splitting, and environmental pollution. In Chapter 28, Carl Keane develops a theory of corporate crime. His review of the literature suggests that an adequate explanation of corporate crime needs to focus not just on the individual characteristics of corporate criminals, but also on characteristics of the corporation as a social organization and on the socioeconomic environment within which the corporation operates.

Some Canadians believe that crime is in part a racial phenomenon. Canadian Blacks in particular rank high in the public's perception of criminal villains. In October 2002, a series of articles in the

Toronto Star demonstrating that Black people in Toronto are more likely to be charged with crime than others may have reinforced this perception. Some people — including a handful of academics, such as University of Western Ontario psychology professor, Philippe Rushton — go so far as to claim that there is a *genetic* link between race and crime. Rushton contends that Negroids (Blacks) are genetically predisposed to commit more criminal acts than Caucasoids (whites), while whites are genetically predisposed to commit more criminal acts than Mongoloids (Orientals). He cites crime statistics from the United States, the United Kingdom, and other countries showing that crime rates do indeed vary along racial lines, as he predicts.

In Chapter 29, Julian Roberts and Thomas Gabor criticize Rushton's views. They show, among other things, that crime rates vary *within* racial groups, depending on historical period and society. Homicide rates are very low among Blacks in Africa and Chinese in Hong Kong, but very high among Blacks in the Bahamas and even higher among Filipinos in the Philippines. Yet if Rushton's genetic theory were correct, Blacks would have universally higher crimes rates than Orientals. Roberts and Gabor also show that race-specific crime rates vary by type of crime. For instance, in the United States, whites have much higher rates of white-collar crime (fraud, embezzlement, etc.) than do Blacks. These and other facts analyzed by Roberts and Gabor demonstrate that genetic factors peculiar to each race do not cause crime. Roberts and Gabor instead attribute high rates of "street crime" among Blacks in the US and the UK exclusively to social factors: where they face high levels of discrimination, widespread poverty, and differential treatment by the criminal justice system, Blacks are convicted of more street crime.

Crime statistics by race are not widely available in Canada, but those that are available often contradict Rushton's argument. For example, the homicide rate among Aboriginal Canadians is more than ten times higher than among whites, but Rushton's theory predicts the opposite since Aboriginal Canadians are of Mongoloid descent. Canadian Aboriginals do, however, resemble American Blacks in terms of the social conditions in which they live, a fact consistent with Roberts's and Gabor's theory.

And the *Toronto Star* statistics? They show that while Blacks form 8.1 percent of Toronto's population, they compose 23.3 percent of all arrests in the city. However, in interpreting these figures one must remember three things. First, there is racism in the criminal justice system. For example, the *Toronto Star* statistics show that Blacks charged with simple drug possession are taken to the police station 13 percent more often than whites faced with the same charge. They are held at the station overnight for a bail hearing at twice the rate of whites. In other words, whites are more likely than Blacks to be released at the scene of the crime and less likely to be held overnight. Other research shows that Black men in Toronto are nearly four times more likely than white men to be stopped by the police while driving. These figures suggest that the criminal justice system is biased against Black people, men in particular, searching them out and treating them more harshly than whites. Second, crime is associated with age; young men commit most crimes. This is important because the Black community in Toronto is younger than the white community. On purely demographic grounds one would therefore expect to find a higher crime rate among Blacks. And finally, the only non-Aboriginal ethnic or racial category that appears to experience persistently high levels of discrimination in the paid labour force, even after the immigrant generation, is composed of Black men. Relatively low per capita income and high unemployment contribute to crime *directly* insofar as people with a low standard of living are more likely than others to explore illegal means of improving their lot in life. Poor economic conditions contribute to crime *indirectly* because they make it more difficult to keep families intact. As a result, young people growing up in poor families are more likely to be brought up by a single parent, usually the mother. Accordingly, they tend to be subject to less adult supervision and discipline in the family. They are less likely to benefit from the kind of early social control that can lead to lower crime rates.

GLOSSARY

A **corporate crime** is an act that breaks a law intended to regulate business activity.

Deviance is behaviour that departs from a norm.

CRITICAL THINKING QUESTIONS

1. Describe patterns of violence, sexual behaviour, and drug use among Canadian teenagers.
2. In what sense is illegal drug use "socially constructed" rather than determined by the "nature" of drug use itself?
3. What social factors contribute to the crime rate?
4. What is corporate crime? What theories best explain corporate crime? Why are corporate crimes underrepresented in the news?
5. Does society make criminals, or is criminality based on biology?

ANNOTATED BIBLIOGRAPHY

Erich Goode and Nachman Ben-Yehudah, *Moral Panics: The Social Construction of Deviance* (Cambridge, UK: Cambridge University Press, 1995). Drug panics and witch crazes illustrate the ways in which deviance and crime are not "given" but created by social reactions.

Jerome G. Miller, *Search and Destroy: African-American Males in the Criminal Justice System* (Cambridge, UK: Cambridge University Press, 1996). This infuriating book shows how the American justice system has been turned into a system of racial segregation and control. It can be read as a warning to Canadians about some of the potential effects of neo-conservative, anti-welfare policies.

Bernard Schissel and Linda Mahood, eds. *Social Control in Canada: Issues in the Social Construction of Deviance* (Toronto: Oxford University Press, 1996). A useful collection on the ways in which deviance is socially constructed and not determined by the "nature" of deviant acts themselves.

Robert A. Silverman, James J. Teevan, and Vincent F. Sacco, eds., *Crime in Canadian Society*, 6th ed. (Toronto: Harcourt Brace, 2000). The standard, comprehensive overview of Canadian criminology.

Chapter 26

Violence, Sex, and Drugs among Canadian Teenagers

REGINALD W. BIBBY

VIOLENCE

During the past few years, adults have been increasingly concerned about teenage violence, stimulated in large part by a series of violent acts in Canada and the United States. On April 20, 1999, 12 students and a teacher were killed at Columbine High in Littleton, Colorado, followed on April 28 by the shooting of two students, one fatally, in Taber, Alberta. Ever since, threats of violence in schools across Canada have been seen as abounding.[1] A knife attack on the one-year anniversary of Columbine in April 2000 resulted in the wounding of four students and one staff member at Cairine Wilson High School in the Ottawa suburb of Orléans. In November 2000 a Toronto teen admitted he had shown classmates a list of fourteen students he planned to kill and had attempted to buy an assault rifle over the Internet to carry out his plan.[2] The same month a student was stabbed to death at Calgary's Lester B. Pearson High School.[3]

Parents are among those feeling new pressures. *National Post* columnist Jane Christmas described the ambivalence she felt when her 14-year-old wanted to stay away from his Hamilton school on the day of the Columbine anniversary. In the end, she decided to let him. But it required the confirmation of her mother, her doctor, and word of what happened in Ottawa — what she describes as three votes of confidence. "Did I overreact?" she asks, and then answers her own question: "I don't believe anything you do in the interest of protecting your child is an over-reaction."[4] The headline of her article referred to the times as "the age of Columbine."

Violence among young people has not been limited to schools. On November 14, 1997, Victoria teenager Reena Virk was beaten by a group of girls she'd sought to befriend, then drowned by one of the girls and a teenage male companion.[5] Eight young people, seven of them girls between the ages of 14 and 16, were charged, and one of the girls was subsequently convicted of second-degree murder and sentenced to five years in prison before she can apply for parole. Virk's mother told the presiding judge, "My dream to raise and love my child is shattered like a vase."[6] In November of 1999, 15-year-old Dmitri Baranovski was punched and kicked to death in a Toronto park by eight to ten males wearing balaclavas and blue bandanas who demanded cigarettes, drugs, and money from the victim and his friends.[7] Just two days later, a 14-year-old Toronto girl was found bruised and bleeding with cigarette burns on her back; she'd been tortured for two hours by four older teenage girls.[8] In November of 2000, a 14-year-old Edmonton boy was taken off life support two weeks after being brutally beaten beyond recognition by two older teens behind a junior high school.[9] And youth violence was further highlighted when an eight-year-old boy in Lytton, Quebec, used his father's high-powered rifle to shoot and critically wound a 64-year-old man, claiming he was shooting at a tree to scare the man.[10]

In light of these and other forms of violent acts — including child abuse, sexual assault, and suicide — it's important to hear what young people have to say.

Violence in schools is seen as a "very serious" problem by significant numbers of teenagers. But the difference by gender is fairly dramatic. Some 65% of females see the issue as extremely serious, compared to just 40% of males. Nonetheless, out of 18 issues posed, violence in schools is among those most widely cited by males as being particularly serious (see Table 26.1).

One 17-year-old male from a small northern Alberta city expresses his concern this way: "We have had threats and it makes me scared to come here and learn. I mean, just the other day there was a fight in our hallways." A 15-year-old who lives in a small community in northern Ontario says she doesn't feel safe at school, adding, "I could at any time be shot." But another female, 16, from Regina warns against stereotyping teens: "In reaction to the recent school shootings, I would like to say it isn't all kids in black who listen to Marilyn Manson, have black trench coats, and get beat up at school who do these kinds of things. I would never do anything that stupid and I am a goth, black trench–owning, Marilyn Manson–loving freak who gets picked on."

In addition to violence in schools, some 50% to 65% of females and 30% to 45% of males view *child abuse*, *teenage suicide*, *violence against women*, and *crime* as "very serious" problems. In each instance, the concern levels for females are significantly higher than those of males. About 35% of females and 30% of males see youth gangs as "very serious."

Beyond perception of the seriousness of these various issues, teens were asked if they have a *close friend* who personally has encountered violence or has had depression or suicide-related experiences (see Table 26.2).

- Some five in ten, led by females, say they have had a close friend who has been *severely depressed*, while four in ten indicate that they have a close friend who has *attempted suicide*. In both cases the levels for females exceed those for males.

- Almost 40% of males and 25% of females report that they have had a close friend who has been *physically attacked at school*; conversely, around 40% of females and 25% of males say a close friend has been *physically abused at home*.

- Three in ten females and just under two in ten males confide that they have a close friend who has been *sexually abused*.

- About 30% of males and 20% of females say a close friend has been a victim of *gang violence*.

Some caution needs to be used in interpreting such findings; one's close friend may

TABLE 26.1 PERCEPTIONS OF SERIOUSNESS OF VIOLENCE, CRIME, AND SUICIDE

% Viewing as "Very Serious"

	NATIONALLY	FEMALES	MALES
Child abuse	56%	66	44
Violence in schools	50	59	40
Teenage suicide	49	60	36
Violence against women	42	51	33
Crime	40	49	29
Youth gangs	31	34	28

TABLE 26.2 EXTENT TO WHICH PROBLEMS HAVE BEEN EXPERIENCED BY A CLOSE FRIEND

	NATIONALLY	FEMALES	MALES
Has been severely depressed	48%	57	39
Has attempted suicide	41	50	31
Physically attacked at school	32	25	39
Physically abused at home	31	37	25
Has been sexually abused	26	32	18
A victim of gang violence	24	21	28

also be the close friend of others. To find that three in ten females has a close friend who has been sexually abused, for example, does not mean that three in ten females have been sexually abused; obviously the figure, based on such an item, is somewhat lower.

Still these findings suggest that the incidence of depression and suicide attempts, physical attacks and abuse is startlingly high. What is disconcerting is that the violence is frequently found not only at school but also at home.

A final note on bullying. Alan King's 1998 national health survey found that just under 30% of males and females in grade 10 reported that they had been bullied during the school term. Such physical, verbal, or psychological intimidation has few clear-cut correlates, other than being disproportionately directed at males who feel isolated. Bullying tends to be cyclical: those who are bullied bully, and in turn receive similar treatment.[11]

DIFFERENCES ACROSS THE COUNTRY

Overall there are few distinct differences in the perception and incidence of school and home violence among regions and communities, regardless of size (see Table 26.3). Simply put, perception and behaviour are distributed fairly evenly across Canada.

Concern about violence in schools is somewhat less in Quebec than elsewhere, despite the fact that students there are marginally more likely than others to say they do not feel safe at school; presumably such concern has been normalized. Contrary to what I suspect is widely believed, teens in cities of over 400,000 are slightly *less* inclined than young people living elsewhere to view school violence as "very serious," and no more likely than others to say they do *not* feel safe at school. Teens living on farms are the least likely to report that they have

TABLE 26.3   CONCERN ABOUT VIOLENCE BY REGION, COMMUNITY SIZE, AND BIRTHPLACE

	SCHOOL VIOLENCE A VERY SERIOUS PROBLEM	CLOSE FRIEND ATTACKED AT SCHOOL	NOT SAFE AT SCHOOL	NOT SAFE AT HOME	CLOSE FRIEND PHYSICALLY ABUSED AT HOME
Nationally	50%	32	22	7	31
B.C.	51	30	19	7	30
Prairies	49	32	17	5	30
Ontario	53	32	22	7	32
Quebec	43	33	27	7	33
Atlantic	54	30	21	8	27
North	53	34	19	2	31
>400,000	44	35	21	5	32
399,999–100,000	51	32	21	7	34
99,999–30,000	56	36	28	7	31
Cities/towns <30,000	53	29	21	8	33
Rural non-farm	52	32	18	7	27
Farm	50	24	19	6	25
Born in Canada	50	31	21	7	32
Born outside Canada	47	35	26	6	28

close friends who either have been attacked at school or physically abused at home.

There is little difference in concern about violence at school and at home between young people born in Canada and those born outside the country. There is, however, a slightly greater tendency for teens who have come to Canada to say both that (1) they have a close friend who has been attacked at school and (2) they themselves don't feel safe at school. As might be expected, as teens from outside Canada share in Canadian life, their inclination to engage in offences comes to resemble those of teens born here — a pattern noted, for example, by Brandon sociologist Siu Kwong Wong in a recent study of Winnipeg teens of Chinese descent.[12]

Concern about youth violence has led to proactive measures in cities such as Toronto. In June 2000, a Youth Violence Task Force comprising Toronto police, Catholic and public school boards, and the transit commission recommended that:

- police officers be assigned to schools, recreational centres, and subway stations during lunchtime and after-school hours;
- police disclose conditions of release for young offenders to schools as permissible under the *Young Offenders Act*; and
- a young offender program be implemented to target high-risk, repeat offenders.

A member of the task force, 17-year-old Krista Lopes, noted the need to work together "to combat the ever-increasing problem of youth violent crimes," while Toronto Police Chief Julian Fantino noted that "the ol' thing is no longer adequate," adding, "We need to do things that are more strategic and we need to count on parents, politicians, educators, and certainly the police community and all others, but especially the youth, to turn things around."[13]

In order to understand current youth violence in relation to the past, it is important to first ask, what constitutes violence? By way of illustration, a 1999 survey of 2,000 grade 7 to 12 students in Alberta by the Canadian Research Institute for Law and the Family found violence to be highest among grades 8 and 9 students. Some 40% of grade 9 students, for example, admitted to slapping, punching, or kicking someone in the past year, compared to 32% of grade 12 students. About 16% of students acknowledged they had brought weapons to school, with the most common being illegal knives, replica weapons — mostly plastic guns, clubs, and bats. The least common were pellet guns and handguns. In addition, more than half the students surveyed said they had been victimized at least once during the past year at school; perhaps significantly, almost the same percentage said they had been victimized while they were *not* at school. The most frequent forms of victimization — similar in all Alberta communities — included being slapped, punched, or kicked, having something stolen, being threatened with bodily harm, and having property damaged. The least frequent included being attacked by a group or gang and being threatened by a weapon. Such survey findings prompted the Calgary police chief at the time, Christine Silverberg, to call for an expansion of school resource programs in junior high schools.[14]

It is clear from such research that "violence" is being applied to an extremely wide range of activities beyond beatings, stabbings, and shootings. Such a broad application of "violence" undoubtedly is associated with a "zero tolerance" response to any physically aggressive act toward another person. *Hear me clearly*: this is in no way to minimize the gravity of such acts today. But it is to say the bar that defines violence has been raised considerably over where it has been in the past. Adults also may be placing the bar at a higher level than where many teens — especially males, but also some females — are placing it. Among them is a 16-year-old female from a small town near Calgary who comments, "School violence has been around since schools came about. Let kids be kids," she says, "Don't punish them for wrestling. Punish them for guns and severe fighting."

A REALITY CHECK

It is worthwhile to compare our survey perceptions and reports with additional information on young people. A victimization analysis released in December 1995 by Statistics Canada using data from police departments indicated that teenagers are certainly vulnerable when it comes to violent crime. In fact, they are at greater risk of violent crime than either adults or children. Young people between the ages of 12 and 19 made up 20% of the victims of violent crime in the mid-'90s, even though they represented just 11% of the population. About 80% of violent incidents against teenagers were assaults, some 15% being of a sexual nature; most of the others involved robbery. Victims of violent crime were equally likely to be males and females; however, a large majority of victimized females were victims of sexual offences, whereas males were more likely to be victims of assault and robbery. Police statistics also revealed that about five in ten violent incidents against teenagers involved acquaintances, and three in ten strangers, while two in ten were committed by family members, with parents implicated in half of those incidents.[15] Further, Statistics Canada survey data for 1999 show that young people 15 to 24 are reporting the highest rate of personal victimization, more than twice the national average. Seniors 65 and over, by the way, are reporting the lowest rates of victimization.[16]

In July 2000, Statistics Canada released a new report, also based on police records, revealing that the national crime rate in 1999 fell to its lowest level in two decades. Young people under the age of 20 were more likely than people in other age groups to commit both violent and property crimes. Youth crime, however, was down more than 7% from 1998 and was 21% lower than in 1989. The rate of youths charged with violent crime fell 5%, the largest year-to-year drop since the *Young Offenders Act* was introduced in 1984. While the 1990s saw an increase in violent crimes among females, the female rate as of 1999 was still only one-third of the male rate. The report reminded readers than many non-violent young offenders are diverted from the formal justice system, but also said that available statistics indicate the number of youths being diverted has also been decreasing in recent years.[17] Coincidentally, the same day the report was released, Britain released crime statistics for England and Wales, which showed a large jump in violent crime in those two countries over the past year.[18]

A third Statistics Canada report, made available in August 2000, is also worth acknowledging. An analysis of sentences given to young offenders (12 to 17) who were convicted in youth court during 1998–99 reveals that one-third were put in some form of custody. Males were more likely to be sentenced to custody than females. A comparison of the sentencing of adults and youths for the most common offences for nine of the most frequent offences — such as common assault, breaking and entering, and possession of stolen property — showed that young people were less likely to be placed in custody. But when they were jailed, they were more likely to receive longer sentences than the adults. For example, in the case of common assault, the report found that 65% of young offenders were sentenced to more than one month in jail, compared to 43% of adults.[19] Commenting on the report, Robert Gordon, the director of the Department of Criminology at Simon Fraser University, suggested the sentencing differences reflect public calls for stiffer penalties for offences involving young people.[20]

Taken together, these three reports indicate that (1) a disproportionate number of teens are victims of violent crime, (2) the rate of violent crime committed by young people has been decreasing in recent years, and (3) young offenders who are placed in custody tend to be punished to a greater degree than adult offenders. These findings document that teen violence is a serious problem. But contrary to widely held perception, teen violence has actually been declining. In addition, reaction to young offenders in recent years, in some instances at least, has been harsher than that shown adults.

Even in the face of the Calgary school homicide in November 2000, Dennis Eastcott, the founder of the Alberta Association of School Resource Officers and the officer in charge of Edmonton's youth and crime prevention services, maintained that statistics do not support the notion that kids are becoming more violent or are getting "out of whack." As for school violence, Staff Sgt. Eastcott commented, "Studies based on where kids are victimized show one of the safest places for them is at school."[21] Obviously not everyone agrees.

It therefore is not surprising that it's difficult to obtain a consensus on how to respond to so-called youth crime. At a conference of victims'-rights advocates held in Hamilton in October of 1999, Justice Minister Anne McLellan said that Ottawa would do what it thinks is right to deal with young offenders, regardless of pressure from the provinces. "Quebec is telling me: 'Your legislation is too tough.' Ontario is telling me: 'It's not tough enough.' 'Well, you know what that tells me? Canadians are generally right in the middle and I think our legislation reflects that balanced approach."[22]

SAFETY AT SCHOOL AND AT HOME

Although teens are aware of friends who have been attacked and abused, 19 in 20 say they feel safe at home, 16 in 20 feel safe at school.

	% INDICATING FEEL SAFE	
	AT HOME	AT SCHOOL
Nationally	93%	78
Males	94	79
Females	94	78

A national survey of 400 American teenagers, 14 to 17, conducted in April 2000 for *Time* magazine found 86% felt either "very safe" or "somewhat safe" from violence at school.[23]

SEXUALITY

Our sexually liberated society is characterized by considerable openness about sex, led by the media. If Pierre Trudeau took the government out of the bedrooms of the nation, the media takes us into the bedrooms of the nation on a daily if not hourly basis. TV programs such as *Sex and the City*, the *Sunday Night Sex Show*, and *The Sex Files* lead the way explicitly. But sex is to be found everywhere, spanning sitcoms, movies, stand-up comedy, and, for reasons well known to all of us, even nightly newscasts in the U.S. and Canada on a regular basis during 1999.

Craig Colby, the Toronto producer of *The Sex Files* that airs on the Discovery Channel, recently commented, "There's definitely a lot more permissiveness in society." Colby says that two events have been new groundbreakers — the Monica Lewinsky affair, which made oral sex and phone-sex discussion topics, and the memorable "Master of His Domain" episode on *Seinfeld*, that "completely destigmatized" masturbation.[24] Yes, these are days of sexual freedom and openness. And with the morning-after pill becoming more accessible to women, making it possible to prevent pregnancy within three days of intercourse,[25] some would argue that the incidence and enjoyment of sexual activity, marital and otherwise, will only increase.

In the midst of all this, adults worry a great deal about teenagers and sex for any number of reasons. And they should, if the words of this 17-year-old female from Hamilton are accurate: "Sex is like an everyday thing for teens now."

The survey shows that Canada's youth are divided almost evenly when it comes to sexual attitudes and behaviour, although males typically hold more liberal attitudes than females and are more sexually active (see Table 26.4).

• Approximately six in ten teens, led by males, maintain that *consenting adults* should be able to do whatever they want sexually. Moreover, the same proportion of males and a smaller proportion of females feel that *consenting teens* between the ages of 15 and 17 also should be

TABLE 26.4 SEXUAL ATTITUDES

% "Strongly Approve" or "Approve"

	NATIONALLY	FEMALES	MALES
Sexual Tolerance Limits			
Consenting adults doing whatever they want sexually	61%	67	56
Consenting teens 15 to 17 doing whatever they want sexually	56	66	46
Sexual Behaviour and Rights			
Sex before marriage when people LOVE each other	82	85	80
Sex before marriage when people LIKE each other	58	68	48
Sexual relations between two people of the same sex	54	41	66
Homosexuals are entitled to the same rights as other Canadians	75	62	87
A married person having sex with someone other than marriage partner	9	13	4
Cohabitation			
A couple who are not married living together	86	89	83
A couple having children without being married	63	61	64
Abortion			
It being possible to obtain a legal abortion when a female has been raped	84	85	83
It being possible to obtain a legal abortion for any reason	55	58	52

able to do whatever they want sexually. One 17-year-old from the B.C. Interior sums things up this way: "I believe in people's rights to do whatever they want sexually, as long as it doesn't hurt any other living thing. In the case of teenagers, however, more thought has to go into it because they are less able to deal with accidental pregnancy than adults."

- Some 80% of young people approve of sex before marriage *when people love each other*, with little disagreement between males and females. In addition, close to 60% think that sex before marriage is all right *when people like each other*. Here there is a significant difference in opinion between males (68%) and females (48%). A Burnaby, B.C., 16-year-old says, "I'm worried about diseases in Canada; more people are having unprotected sex." The issues of birth control and pregnancy are expressed starkly by a 17-year-old from Alberta: "Teens should have more informa-

tion about protection if they are going to have sex. People should be told how to take birth control properly, along with the fact methods aren't 100% effective against pregnancy." She signed her comments, "A pregnant teen who was on birth control." Few young people would disagree: 92% maintain that "birth control information should be available to teens who want it." More possibilities, incidentally, are on the way. As you might be aware, a new monthly injectable contraceptive known as Lunelle, the first new birth control method since 1992, was introduced in the U.S. in late 2000. It is an alternative to Depo-Provera, an injectable drug that is given every three months. Both are administered by a physician.[26]

- About one in two teenagers (54%) approve of *homosexual* relations, with females (66%) considerably more likely than males (41%) to express approval. But 75%, led by females, maintain that homosexuals are entitled to the same rights as other Canadians. Among males expressing consternation is this 15-year-old male from Regina who says, "Gays should not have a special week or the right to adopt children." A grade 11 male from a small Alberta town comments, "One thing I would like to stress is that homosexuality is wrong. If they really want to be gay, they should do it in secret and not adopt kids." (See Figure 26.1.)

- Merely 9% of young people condone *extramarital* sexual relations. It seems quite obvious that such behaviour has not been adding much to lives, however heralded it might have been by some at the time of the sexual revolution.

- *Cohabitation* receives the approval of almost nine in ten teenagers, while having *children without being married* is regarded as all right by about six in ten. Stigma in the latter case seemingly is higher for teenage single parents than couples. A 16-year-old in the Atlantic region says that, despite the fact that her boyfriend has stood with her in raising her child, "I get a lot of discrimination against my parenting skills."

- The availability of *legal abortion* when a female has been *raped* is approved of by some 80%, abortion *on demand* by just over 50%. One twelfth grader from Vancouver says he "applauds the availability of birth control in British Columbia" and adds that "abortion should never be withheld under any circumstances." The introduction of the RU-486 pill as an alternative to surgical abortion may or may not alter such attitudes. The pill, which can terminate a pregnancy up to about seven weeks after conception, was approved and made available to some U.S. doctors in late 2000[27] and is being tested in Canada. It has been met with strong opposition from pro-life groups. RU-486 has been made available in France since 1989 and is also sold in Britain, Sweden, and China.[28]

In short, while one in two Canadian teenagers indicate that, in theory, consenting individuals technically and legally have "the right" to do what they want, teens nonetheless have some strong personal feelings as to what is sexually appropriate and what is not.

We asked teens pointedly how often they engage in sex. About 25%, including 27% of males and 22% of females, claim they have sex at least once a week (see Table 26.5). Around another 10% indicate they have sex two to three times a month, a further 15% say less often. Approximately 50% of teenagers say they never engage in sex, with this category including some 45% of males and 55% of females. Among them is a 16-year-old male from southern Alberta who comments, "None of my friends or anyone I know have had sex. My friends and I feel that you should not have sex unless you are married." As for the one in two who do engage in sex, a *Globe and Mail* editorial has put it this way: "There is a principal reason why people engage in consensual sex: They enjoy it. Liking sex has little to do with age. Thinking about sex in terms of preventing unwanted consequences rather than preventing the sex act itself simply recognizes the fact that teenage sex is, well, common."[29] In responding to the question of how often she engages in sex, a 16-year-old female from suburban Montreal may speak for much of the nation in admitting, "When the chance comes up." In her case, she says, it's "hardly ever."

A cautionary note: "engage" in sex undoubtedly means "sexual intercourse" for most teens, but not all. One 15-year-old female from

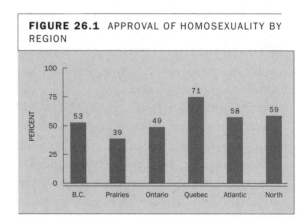

FIGURE 26.1 APPROVAL OF HOMOSEXUALITY BY REGION

SEXUAL ATTITUDES AND SERVICE ATTENDANCE

Differences in sexual attitudes are readily apparent between teens who attend religious services weekly versus those who attend less often.

	% APPROVING	
	WEEKLY	**LESS THAN WEEKLY**
Consenting adults doing what they want sexually	38%	68
Consenting teens 15 to 17 doing what they want sexually	28	63
Sex before marriage when people LOVE each other	49	91
Sexual relations between two people of the same sex	25	62
Sex with someone other than one's marriage partner	4	10
Homosexuals entitled to same rights as other Canadians	59	79
A couple who are not married living together	57	94
A couple having children without being married	29	72
It being possible to obtain a legal abortion for any reason	24	64

TABLE 26.5   TEENAGE SEXUAL ACTIVITY

"About how often do you engage in sex?"

	NATIONALLY	FEMALES	MALES
Daily	6%	9	3
Several times a week	10	10	10
About once a week	8	8	9
2 to 3 times a month	7	8	6
About once a month	5	7	3
Hardly ever	13	14	12
Never	51	44	57
Totals	100	100	100

Williams Lake, British Columbia, reminds us that "some people engage in sexual activity which does not include actual sex," and that "there is a lot more sexual activity between 'neck and pet' and 'sex.'"

In sum, around 50% of teens are currently sexually involved, and 50% are not. A national survey of teenagers carried out in the mid-1990s by Statistics Canada reports similar levels of activity and adds some further details. First, 44% of males and 43% of females had had at least one sex partner in the year that the survey covered.

Second, 21% of teen males had sex with at least two partners, compared to 13% of females. Third, close to three in four males (71%) but only one in two females (49%) claimed that condoms were used.[30]

Yet our current survey findings on sexual activity underestimate the lifetime sexual experiences of teenagers, because the item is asking specifically about *current* sexual behaviour. Fifty percent of teens are not virgins. An additional survey item reveals that 15% — 16% of males, 14% of females — are not sexually involved *currently*, but just 41% of teens (33% of males, 48% of females) say they have *never* been sexually involved. The "currently involved" and "previously involved" total consequently appears to be closer to 60%.

As for appropriate behaviour on dates, nine in ten teens think it is all right for two people to *hold hands* on the first date if they like each other and more than seven in ten approve of kissing on the first date (see Table 26.6 on page 300). *Necking and petting*, however, is seen by six in ten teenagers as something that should not take place until after a few dates. Here, males and females differ significantly. Young women are much more inclined to indicate a few dates

TABLE 26.6 APPROPRIATE BEHAVIOUR ON DATES

"If two people on a date like each other, do you think it is all right for them to ..."

	YES, ON THE FIRST DATE	YES, AFTER A FEW DATES	NO
Hold hands	89%	10	1
Males	92	8	<1
Females	87	12	1
Kiss	73	26	1
Males	78	21	1
Females	68	30	2
Neck and pet	**32**	**57**	**11**
Males	43	50	7
Females	22	63	15
Have sex	11	40	49
Males	18	50	32
Females	4	32	64

should have taken place, and about 15% don't think necking and petting should occur at all. In case you are wondering, no, we weren't all that excited about using the terms "necking and pet- ting," but we wanted to use terms consistent with our previous surveys and, frankly, "making out" is too general. A 17-year-old from Nunavut was among those who wanted to make a distinc- tion. Drawing an arrow to "necking," she said, "Yes, we did that after two months of going out. Me and my boyfriend neck, but I don't know what you mean by pet. If you mean 'feel up,' then no, never!" That's what we meant, and I think that's what most teens thought we meant.

Males and females differ sharply in their sense of when and if *sexual relations* are appropriate. Almost seven in ten males say sex is all right within a few dates, but fewer than four in ten females share their opinion.

Two common assertions of people observing the teenage sex scene is that the threat of AIDS has been (1) contributing to a reduction in sexual activity and/or (2) resulting in more protected sex. While the first assertion is seriously in

doubt, about 60% of teens who say the are sexu- ally involved acknowledge that AIDS has influ- enced their sexual habits. The remaining 40% apparently have been relatively unfazed by the existence of the fatal disease. One 16-year-old, who lives in a small city in northeastern Quebec, seems to express the sentiments of many teens in this latter category when she says, "Since I have been sexually active, AIDS has existed. For me, nothing has changed."

THE LIMITED IMPACT OF AIDS

"Has the existence of AIDS influenced your own personal sexual habits?"

	YES	NO
Males	58%	44
Females	62	38

DRUGS

Since at least the 1960s, considerable publicity has been given to the problem of drug use among young people. It remains an area of major concern for adults. For example, we saw earlier that some 25% of males and 15% of females note that they frequently have conflict with their parents over the issue of drugs. Parents' and adults' fears are not neutralized by what they sense is the ready availability of drugs. If anything, those fears may be heightened when they learn of the current survey's finding that no less than 44% of teenage males and 49% of females acknowledge they have a close friend with "a severe alcohol or drug problem."

There is little doubt that Canadian teens have ample access to illegal drugs. No less than 77% say that if they wanted to use drugs, it is "not very difficult (26%) or "not difficult at all" (51%) to obtain them; 6% think it is difficult and the remaining 17% say they "don't know" (see Table 26.7). What's particularly striking is that access is not limited by whether or not someone is female or male, lives in one region of the country or another, or resides in a large city, small city, or a rural area. Illegal drugs appear to be just about everywhere. A 16-year-old in one Western Canadian city decries the availability of drugs where he lives:

> I think the drug problem is very bad here. I mean, I try to stop doing drugs, but they are so readily available that it is very hard. There are so many drug traffickers in my school and I go to the best Catholic high school in the city. Kids need to be stopped from turning to drugs, but not by another one of the government's corny programs. Also, more stores should call for identification when people buy alcohol because I can buy it easily and I don't look a day over 16.

A grade 12 student from New Westminister says "drugs are available on today's streets" and that "it is easier to buy drugs than alcohol." A 17-year-old in Hamilton notes, "Drugs are everywhere. I can get marijuana any time I want, day or night." A 16-year-old in a small city north of Edmonton concurs: "Pot is so easy to get, and

TABLE 26.7   ACCESS TO DRUGS

	% "NOT VERY DIFFICULT" OR "NOT DIFFICULT AT ALL"
Nationally	77%
Males	80
Females	74
B.C.	81
Prairies	76
Ontario	75
Quebec	78
Atlantic	80
North	81
>400,000	77
399,999–100,000	79
99,999–30,000	76
Cities/towns <30,000	80
Rural non-farm	75
Farm	76

cheap." Another Albertan, a 16-year-old male from a small town south of Calgary, takes the position that drugs are so readily available that laws should be relaxed: "I believe it shouldn't matter how old you are to buy liquor or cigarettes or pot because they are very easy to get if you are underage."

Availability, of course, doesn't equal use. A 15-year-old from Moose Jaw, Saskatchewan, observes, "There are a lot of drugs around here, but not all people use them." Yet the concern about drug abuse is shared by significant numbers of teenagers. As we saw earlier, almost one in two teens say that drug use is a "very serious" problem in Canada. One male, 16, who lives just outside Ottawa comments, "I really do feel that the use of drugs among teenagers is a big problem. I have many friends who engage in drugs weekly, daily, or monthly. I see this becoming more of a problem because I don't have a friend who hasn't at least tried drugs once or twice." A Grande Prairie, Alberta, teen expresses his alarm this way: "I strongly feel that heroin and crack cocaine are being strongly abused by teens and parents. This is breaking up families and lives. I am very worried about it and scared for the future of our society." A 16-year-old female from a small Ontario town acknowledges that the problem exists and offers an explanation as to why: "I think that in our town a lot of our drug and alcohol problems are because we have nothing to do — no movie theatre, no bowling alley, no mall, nothing."

Given the prevalent consternation and access, what actually is happening?

Some 28% of teenagers say they smoke *cigarettes* monthly or more often, 9% rarely, and 63% never. Female smoking levels are marginally above those of males (see Table 26.8 on page 302). These figures are consistent with Statistics Canada data for early 1999 that found 28% of teens, 15 to 19, to be smokers.[31]

Around 20% of teens say they drink *beer, wine, or other forms of alcohol* at least once a week, with the level for those under 18 only slightly lower than that of 15- to 19-year-olds as a whole. The

TABLE 26.8 DRUG USE AMONG TEENAGERS

"How often do you yourself ..."

	WEEKLY OR MORE	ONCE OR TWICE A MONTH	LESS THAN ONCE A MONTH	NEVER
Smoke Cigarettes	23%	5	9	63
Males	22	5	9	64
Females	24	6	9	61
Drink Beer, Wine, Other Alcohol	22	30	26	22
Males	29	29	22	20
Females	16	31	28	25
Under 18 total	18	29	26	27
Males	26	31	22	21
Females	14	31	29	26
Smoke Marijuana or Hashish	14	10	13	63
Males	19	11	13	57
Females	9	8	14	69
Use Other Illegal Drugs	3	4	7	86
Males	4	4	8	84
Females	2	4	7	87

weekly level for males is almost twice that of females; yet 75% of females drink at least on occasion, compared to 80% of males. One 15-year-old female from Edmonton helps to clarify the nature of alcohol use for some young people: "My parents often let me have wine or a cooler but I feel because of this I have grown a respect for alcohol. Because it's always available at home, I don't go out and get drunk with friends."

Approximately 15% of teenagers say they *smoke marijuana or hashish* weekly or more, with male use about twice that of females. However, about four in ten males and three in ten females admit to being occasional marijuana users.

Just 3% of young people acknowledge that they are using *other illegal drugs* on a regular weekly basis, including 4% of males and 2% of females. But again, occasional use is not insignificant — another 15% for males and 11% for females.

A 17-year-old from Montreal sums up the place of drugs in her life in a fairly matter-of-fact manner: "Every weekend I consume alcohol when I go to a pub or go out to eat at a restaurant. When I go to a rave I take illegal drugs, but

I only go about once a month." A grade 11 student who lives in a small community in New Brunswick explains her use of marijuana:

> When you asked the question, "Do you smoke pot," I replied yes. This doesn't make me a drug addict. I'm getting an 80% average in school and doing well at work. I enjoy having a toke but I am very responsible. I never come to school or work high. I hope this shows that every teen who smokes pot is not a delinquent.

It's important not to lose sight of the fact that sizable numbers of young people maintain that they are *not* using drugs of any kind, including —

TOP FIVE MOST POPULAR DRUGS

1.	Marijuana	87%
2.	Ecstasy	3
3.	Hashish	2
4.	Mushrooms	<1
5.	Cocaine	<1

in close to one in four cases — alcohol. Among them is another Montrealer, a 16-year-old female, who says, "Drugs do not interest me at all. I find cigarettes distasteful and I don't want to know anything about illegal drugs."

TWO AREAS OF CONTROVERSY

One drug that has become increasingly controversial is marijuana. Use is extensive and the public seemingly divided as to whether or not it should continue to be treated as illegal. Interest groups have been arguing that its effects, short-term and long-term, pale compared to legal drugs such as alcohol and nicotine. Those opposed argue that its affects are highly detrimental, contributing to short-term dysfunctions and long-term disabilities.

In late July of 2000, the Ontario Court of Appeal ruled that Canada's marijuana law prohibiting the possession of marijuana is unconstitutional and gave Ottawa a year to amend it. People who require marijuana for medicinal purposes can apply for an exemption; the Ontario court asked that the exemption be written into law. At the same time, the court upheld a lower-court decision prohibiting the possession of marijuana for recreational purposes.[32] On the heels of the decision, Ontario NDP leader Howard Hampton called for the decriminalization of marijuana, saying that too many people are being turned into criminals for "smoking a little pot," and that such a move would free up police to fight real crime.[33] Indications that marijuana use may be on the increase means the debate can be expected to intensify.

Young people are not lost for views on the topic. One in two favour the legalization of the use of marijuana, with males (58%) more likely to be in favour than females (42%). A 15-year-old male from Hamilton protests, "No matter what anyone says, marijuana is addictive," while a 16-year-old Calgary-area female offers these thoughts:

> I feel that the use of marijuana should not be illegal because it helps people relax; also, everyone does it nowadays so there is no way

the law can keep it under control. If marijuana is illegal, then alcohol should be illegal, because it does the same things to your body and is just as dangerous or even more dangerous.

We saw earlier that 18% of teens say they attend raves monthly or more, with the figure for males (21%) higher than that for females (15%). The media have given extensive attention to raves; *Maclean's*, for example, carried a cover story entitled "Rave Fever" in its April 24, 2000, issue. Writer Susan Oh noted that many see Toronto as the rave capital of North America, and that ravers can "dance until dawn most weekends" in other cities such as Vancouver, Calgary, Edmonton, Montreal, and Halifax, as well as some other smaller locales.[34] Critics say that these all-night parties are replete with drugs, notably ecstasy, which was given emphasis in the *Maclean's* story. In Ontario, a 13-day inquest was held in May 2000 following the death of Allan Ho, 21, who died at a Toronto rave after taking ecstasy. The inquest resulted in 27 recommendations to ensure the all-night parties are safe.[35] Concern about ecstasy was heightened in late August 2000 with news that Canada Customs officials in Montreal had seized a record-breaking shipment of ecstasy that was on its way to Toronto.[36]

Raves, according to Toronto police chief Julian Fantino, are "threatening the very fabric of Canadian life." Others, however, say they represent a new cultural party expression and are no more problematic than party gatherings in the past — and typically less turbulent than gatherings in bars. Edward Adlaf, a research scientist at Toronto's Centre for Addiction and Mental Health, has said, "In many ways, the concerns raised over the rave scene are not that much different than for rock concerts in the 1970s." He points out that, in Ontario, about 60% of students who attended raves in the past year used cannabis but no other illegal substance. Just over 4% of all students surveyed had taken ecstasy in the past year.[37] A June 2000 article in *Time* magazine argued, "First we had the Beat Generation;

now we have the Beats-per-Minute Generation. And it's not just about ecstasy." Rave culture, said writer Christopher John Farley, has started to exert a potent influence on pop music, advertising, films, and even computer games. According to some observers, rave culture has become youth culture. Drugs may or may not be part of "the rave scene."[38]

One of our survey participants, a 17-year-old male from Kelowna, B.C., has the following to say:

> I know lots of kids who go to them and I went to them extensively myself. The thing is drugs! So many hard drugs are taken by kids ages 14 to 25 it's amazing. I've done ecstasy about 10 times and it was really fun, although I won't do it again, and I was able to stop unassisted. I know of kids who go to every rave that's put on (about 1 to 2 times a week) and do ecstasy, crystal, mushrooms, smoke dope, use acid, drink, huff nitric acid, snort coke. People don't really know about this underground rave culture and parents would freak if they found out their 15-year-old daughter went to raves, got f…d out of her mind, and hooked up with some older guy. I can see how kids get addicted to raves but the drugs are the scary thing and it makes me laugh that parents have no clue!

Despite such alarming reports, journalists such as Kevin Grace maintain that a consensus is forming in cities, including Toronto, that attempts to ban raves only drives them underground. He cites one suburban-Vancouver councillor who says, "They're not something I would ever go to, but my parents' generation had the same opinion of the dances we went to when I was young."[39] *Calgary Sun* columnist Bill Kaufmann writes, "The hysteria that swept city hall in the wake of an isolated stabbing incident following a rave was amusing to behold. It's as if raves have just arrived in Calgary in the past few weeks. In fact, they've been filling halls, party rooms and underground venues for years with little fallout." Predicts Kaufmann, "This current

manifestation of youth culture — like so many others before it — will play itself out."[40]

So what do the data actually say?

To begin with, 6% of teens tell us that they go to raves once a week or more, 5% say they go two to three times a month, and another 7% about once a month. A further 18% say they "hardly ever" attend raves, and 64% say they never do. Almost 50% of monthly-plus ravers come from cities of 100,000 or more, but these consist of only about 15% of the teens in those same cities. Surprisingly, 40% of those who say they attend raves at least once a month come from communities of fewer than 10,000, suggesting that the term "rave" has come to have a fairly broad interpretation. Keeping things in perspective, approximately 20% of the young people living in those smaller communities go to raves that often.

An examination of general drug use among young people who attend raves and those who don't shows that rave-attendees are more inclined than non-attendees to use marijuana and other illegal drugs (see Figure 26.2). It is not clear where exactly such use is taking place. However, what is clear is that about 40% of teens who attend raves at least once a week say that they *never* use marijuana, and almost 70% claim they *never* use any other illegal drugs, including ecstasy. In short, lots of teens who attend raves claim they are partying without drugs.

Tracy Ford, a social worker with the Ministry of the Attorney General in Toronto and described as "a former enthusiast of the rave scene," is a member of the Party People's Project (PPP), a community-based group formed to protect the rights of ravers. Writing in a publication of the Alberta Alcohol and Drug Abuse Commission in late 2000, she maintains that false stereotypes of violence and rampant drug use have been used to discredit raves. What is required, she suggests, is not the outlawing of raves, but rather a combination of support, trained supervision, and education that can

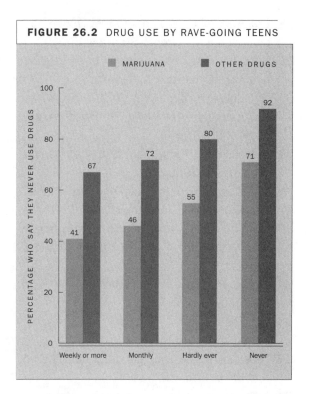

FIGURE 26.2 DRUG USE BY RAVE-GOING TEENS

reduce rave-related harms. "The harm reduction model," she says, "accepts the choices of young people, and supports them, rather than criminalizing them." Ford writes:

> The rave community is a place where young people can find a creative and open network of individuals that love to dance and love music. Young people have basic civil rights to associate, express themselves and enjoy the same freedoms accorded all Canadians in their leisure time. Whatever our concerns about the safety of young people, we must find options that will foster their development, and support their ability to make informed choices.[41]

There is little reason to disagree.

NOTES

1. See, for example, the *National Post* story of April 21, 2000, "Threats of violence abound in schools since Taber, Columbine," by Ian MacLeod.

2. "Teen pleads guilty to making hit list of students," Canadian Press, Toronto, November 28, 2000.

3. Robert Remington and Chris Wattie, "$30 debt seen as motive in killing," *National Post*, November 21, 2000.

4. Jane Christmas, "A parent's dilemma in the age of Columbine," *National Post*, April 21, 2000.

5. For a summary article on the sentencing of one of Virk's assailants, see Rod Mickleburgh, "Virk's killer gets minimum sentence," *Globe and Mail*, April 21, 2000.

6. "Virk's killer off to prison," Canadian Press, Vancouver, April 20, 2000.

7. Details are provided by Jim Rankin and Michelle Shephard in their article, "Teen beaten to death didn't defend himself," in *Toronto Star*, November 17, 1999.

8. See Michelle Shephard, "Four teens charged with torturing girl, 14," *Toronto Star*, November 18, 1999.

9. Ian Williams, "Teens charged with murder after boy's death," *Edmonton Journal*, November 17, 2000.

10. "Kid says he used dad's gun to 'scare' man he shot," Canadian Press, Lytton, Quebec, November 27, 2000.

11. Alan J.C. King, William F. Boyce, and Matthew A. King, *Trends in the Health of Canadian Youth*, Ottawa: Health Canada, 1999:23.

12. Siu Kwong Wong, "Acculturation, peer relations, and delinquent behaviour of Chinese-Canadian youth," *Adolescence* 34, 1999: 107–19.

13. "Advisory group recommended to reduce youth crime," Canadian Press, Toronto, June 22, 2000.

14. "Junior high violence shocks officials," Canadian Press, Calgary, May 8, 2000. For a summary of a parallel earlier study in Calgary, see Joanne J. Paetsch and Lorne D. Bertrand, "Victimization and delinquency among Canadian youth," *Adolescence* 34, 1999:351–67.

15. *The Daily*, Statistics Canada, December 19, 1995.

16. *The Daily,* Statistics Canada, November 2, 2000.

17. "Crime rate drops to 20-year low," Canadian Press, Ottawa, July 18, 2000.

18. "British statistics show jump in violent crime," Reuters, London, July 18, 2000.

19. "Sentencing of young offenders," *The Daily*, August 1, 2000.

20. "Teens given more jail time than adults for same crime," Canadian Press, Vancouver, August 1, 2000.

21. Janine Ecklund, "Schools safe, say police," *Lethbridge Herald*, December 1, 2000.

22. "Ottawa, provinces disagree on youth crime," Canadian Press, Hamilton, ON, October 4, 1999.

23. "The Perception Gap," *Time*, April 24, 2000: 40–41.

24. "The Sex Files on Discovery pushing the envelope," Canadian Press, Toronto, October 4, 2000.

25. See, for example, Vanessa Lu and Richard Brennan, "No-prescription test for morning-after pill," *Toronto Star*, September 8, 2000.

26. "Injectable birth control approved in U.S.," Associated Press, New York, October 6, 2000.

27. Tanya Talaga, "American women get approval to use abortion pill RU-486," *Toronto Star*, September 29, 2000.

28. Graeme Smith, "Doctors to test French abortion pill here," *Toronto Star*, July 7, 2000.

29. Editorial, "The consequences of sex," *Globe and Mail,* December 1, 1999.

30. "Multiple-risk behaviour in teenagers and young adults," *The Daily*, Statistics Canada, October 29, 1998.

31. "Tobacco use," *The Daily*, Statistics Canada, January 20, 2000.

32. "Pot possession law ruled unconstitutional," Canadian Press, Toronto, July 31, 2000.

33. "Ontario NDP wants marijuana decriminalized," Canadian Press, Toronto, August 2, 2000.

34. Susan Oh, "Rave fever," *Maclean's*, April 24, 2000:39–43.

35. "Inquest urges steps for safer raves," Canadian Press, Toronto, June 1, 2000.

36. "Ecstasy seized in major drug bust," *Globe and Mail*, August 22, 2000.

37. Cited in Susan Oh, "Rave fever," *Maclean's*, April 24, 2000:41.

38. Christopher John Farley, "Rave new world," *Time*, June 5, 2000:42–44.

39. Kevin Michael Grace, "Spontaneous congestion," *The Report*, July 24, 2000:47.

40. Bill Kaufmann, "Rave hysteria amusing," *Calgary Sun*, Jun 5, 2000.

41. Tracy Ford, "Regulating the rave: Keeping ravers safe in Toronto," *Developments*, AADAC, Oct/Nov 2000.

Chapter 27

The Selective Control of Drugs

PATRICIA ERICKSON

INTRODUCTION

As the twentieth century commenced, the public could choose from a broad array of legally available psychoactive substances. The growing temperance movement focused on alcohol as the root cause of most of society's problems. Opium, heroin, and cocaine were readily obtainable from the local pharmacy, and were, along with alcohol, major components of many popular and widely used patent medicines (Murray 1988). The modern tobacco cigarette, competing with pipes, cigars, and snuff, was just beginning to be marketed in quantity. Marijuana was grown primarily for the production of hemp cloth and birdseed. None of the users of the substances was regarded as sick, criminal, or seriously deviant, and extreme cases of addiction were viewed as a matter of individual misfortune or personal vice.

Soon all this changed. Forces routed drugs down various paths of social control, with varying degrees of severity of societal response. Today, the crack users are as feared and despised as the heroin "junkie" of an earlier era. The seller of illegal "narcotics" — that is, cannabis, opium, cocaine, or PCP (or phencyclidine) — faces a maximum sentence of life imprisonment under current Canadian law. Alcohol, which was banned briefly during the First World War, was soon re-established as society's drug of choice; now messages promoting its use compete with those for moderation. The cigarette smoker pursued his (and increasingly her) glamorous, Hollywood-endorsed habit for several decades, unimpeded except by pocketbook and hours in the day. However, current smokers confront higher prices and a barrage of no-smoking signs. Mood-modifying prescription drugs like Valium are dispensed by medical professionals as a legitimate source of relief for modern-day stresses and anxiety. For those whose tension-relieving or recreational drugs of choice are prohibited, heavy fines or jail sentences are a possible side effect of indulgence.

This chapter will address four major topics in the social construction of deviance in Canada as reflected in the varying social response to psychoactive substances. These topics are the historical development of social meanings attached to different drugs, the perceived harm of drugs and the actual extent of their use and related problems, the institutional response to drug users, and the various ways the drug users themselves concede or resist the imputation of the deviant identity.

HISTORY: A DIVERGENCE OF SOCIAL MEANINGS

The first major fork in the path of social control occurred in 1908 with the creation of the Opium Act, which was directed at Chinese labourers. Subsequent debates, concerned also with morphine and cocaine, led to the Opium and Drug Act of 1911 and the Opium and Narcotic Drug Act of 1920. Each modification of a previous statute provided harsher penalties and fewer legal protections for illicit drug users and sellers. Possession, importation, manufacture, and trafficking were not differentiated in terms of sentences available. A series of amendments in the 1920s stipulated progressively more severe penalties for all these offences and greatly extended the police's powers of search and seizure.

By 1929, mandatory minimum penalties and a maximum of seven years' imprisonment, plus whipping and hard labour, were in effect. In 1922, police officers received the right to search, without a warrant, any place except a dwelling in which they suspected illicit drugs were concealed. Police powers to search dwellings were expanded further in 1929 through a measure called the writ of assistance. The writ was issued to a particular officer, rather than in relation to a specific search in limited circumstances, as would be the case in the normal, judicially approved, search warrant procedure. Until 1985, the designated officer could:

> aided and assisted by such person or personas as he may require, at any time enter and search any dwelling house within Canada in which he reasonably believes there is a narcotic and search any person found in such a place and as he deems necessary, break open any door, window lock, fastener, floor, wall, ceiling, compartment, plumbing fixture, box container or any thing (Narcotic Control Act, RSC 1970, s. 10(4)).

These penalties and unusually broad police powers set the stage for defining as criminals all those involved with illegal narcotics, including the physicians who supplied them.

This pattern, with some modification, has persisted up to the present. The dominance of the criminalization approach to "narcotics" (including cannabis, so defined without debate in 1923) is attributable to two principal factors (Giffen, Endicott, and Lambert 1991). The first is that opium use was associated with Asians, a negatively stereotyped racial group, as well as unconventional, low-status whites. The creation of the "dope fiend" mythology encouraged a moral crusade against narcotic addiction, one that demanded harshly punitive measures. Any pharmacological distinction between different drugs, as long as they originated from exotic, far-away places, was irrelevant to the mythology. Soon-to-be Prime Minister MacKenzie King was skilful in mobilizing this cultural antagonism on behalf of political interest groups who wanted to prevent further Asian immigration. During this early period, Canadian representatives played a prominent role in the international movement among Western nations to criminalize the use and distribution of narcotics through various conferences and treaties.

The second factor in the persistence and expansion of criminalization is the power base established by the centralized drug bureaucracy during the formative period of Canadian narcotic law. The Division of Narcotic Control in the national Department of Health, in conjunction with the federal enforcers and the federal prosecutors, gained a virtual monopoly over drug policies during the crucial early years. The Canadian medical profession, only weakly organized at the time, was easily intimidated and provided little advocacy for a medical approach to addiction; indeed ninety-one physicians were prosecuted in the 1920s for prescribing opiates (Giffen, Endicott, and Lambert 1991:324). The formidable early chiefs of the Division of Narcotic Control, Cowan and Sharman, coordinated reports from police and prosecutors concerning their expressed need for greater powers, met regularly with politicians and top civil servants, and saw to it that legislative support was forthcoming (Giffen, Endicott, and Lambert 1991). The bureaucratic partnership of social control agents remained virtually unchallenged until the 1950s when the treatment issued gained prominence and was further assailed by the marijuana controversy that erupted in the late 1960s.

For alcohol consumers, the first serious control efforts took a different path. Early temperance efforts focused on local jurisdictions, with some success in rural areas in Ontario and the Maritimes (Smart and Ogborne 1986). A national referendum on prohibition in 1898, held under the authority of the Canada Temperance Act of 1879, received approval in all provinces except Quebec, but with only 44 per cent turnout of voters. With an eye for trouble, Prime Minister Wilfrid Laurier refused to implement the ban, and temperance organizations had to wait until the First World War. Then national prohibition was imposed in all provinces, only to be defeated by 1929 in postwar votes everywhere except Prince Edward Island, which held out until 1948.

Alcohol prohibition in Canada never amounted to a total ban on buying and drinking alcohol. Rather, alcoholic beverages containing no more than 2.5 per cent of ethanol were allowed, alcohol was available by prescription, and production for export was permitted (Smart and Ogborne 1986). Canadians made fortunes supplying the "dryer" American market. Manufacturers and distributors, not consumers, were the targets of enforcement within Canada. Thus users of alcohol never had a criminal identification like that already associated with illicit drug users in this era. At the same time, the medical or "disease" model of alcoholism was beginning to gain some currency (Blackwell 1988). This set the stage for the expansion of the treatment approach in the 1950s and 1960s, and the definition of the alcoholic as "sick" rather than bad, contagious, and morally suspect.

Cigarettes became the object of a short-lived prohibitionist campaign in 1908. Despite debates in the House of Commons describing nicotine as the "narcotic poison of tobacco" with the capability of "impairing health, arresting development [and] weakening intellectual power," members of Parliament nevertheless failed to pass any legislation other than that for-bidding sale to those under sixteen years of age, but also approved a bill protecting domestic tobacco producers and manufacturers from foreign competition (Giffen, Endicott, and Lambert 1991:50). For the ensuing decades, the tobacco industry freely marketed and promoted its product, officially *not* a drug, and by 1980 Canada had one of the highest levels of per capita consumption of cigarettes in the world.

Also in contrast to the Chinese opium situation in these early years was the growing influence of vested interests in the fledgling pharmaceutical industry (Murray 1988). The Proprietary and Patent Medicine Act of 1908, intended explicitly "to safeguard the public interest without committing injustice to the business interests" contained weak restrictions and penalties. The act required only that the ingredients of any medicine had to be listed on the bottle. Cocaine and "excessive" amounts of alcohol were forbidden, but opium and morphine were not, and even heroin could be included in the miracle cures in "safe" amounts. The maximum penalty for infractions was $100, compared to $1,000 and/or three years' imprisonment under the Opium Act of the same year (Giffen, Endicott, and Lambert 1991:50). Although stricter requirements were later imposed, the principle that the production of "medicine" was in the control of legitimate manufacturers was established.

It is evident that the first decades of this century were extremely important in establishing historical dividing lines between licit and illicit drugs. This led to very different social definitions of their acceptability and appropriate controls. The system of complete prohibition that was established for "narcotics" suppressed all legitimate availability and provided severe criminal penalties for a variety of offences involving importation, cultivation, trafficking, and possession. In contrast, regulatory schemes permitted controlled access to many other substances. Licit drugs were subject to varying limits on conditions of sale, to certain standards for the quality of the product, and to professional guidelines for medical prescription. Violations of regulatory statutes were subject to milder penalties such as fines or loss of licences.

Alcohol, after Canada's brief fling with partial "prohibition," was clearly differentiated from medicines and re-established as a socially approved, recreational beverage. Physicians eventually gained more control of prescribing an ever-increasing array of pharmaceuticals produced by a global industry. Almost no controls over tobacco products existed. The label "drug user" was a highly negative one, synonymous with *illicit* use of "narcotics," when the 1960s ushered in a new era of psychoactive drug use.

DANGERS REAL AND IMAGINARY: USE AND ABUSE IN CULTURAL CONTEXT

Nearly all human societies (the traditional Inuit were an exception) have indulged in some form of mind-altering substance use with indigenous plants (McKenna 1992). It is also accurate to state that in no society where drug use was subject to cultural rituals and restrictions has destructive use been the norm (Heath 1992). Individuals and societies find ways of avoiding serious harm by using informal social controls (Maloff et al. 1979). These include rules for appropriate use generated in social interaction between friends, family, and peers. The modern, rapid diffusion of new, more potent drugs into societies lacking a traditional cultural context for their appropriate use has led to some harmful patterns of use. When identified as a threat, these help to spawn an overreliance on more repressive, external, formal controls (Black 1989; Peyrot 1984).

Official and popular assessments of the harm caused by alcohol and other drugs differ from culture to culture and also shift within a particular culture over even relatively short time periods. This establishes an important principle about understanding drug problems: they are not simply inherent in the pharmacology of the substance but rather emerge in the interaction between the drug, the user, and the social and physical environment (Heath 1992; Zinberg and Shaffer

1990). In other words, there are no "bad" (or "good") drugs, but rather more or less harmful consequences, depending on how the drug is used and who is using it. The designation of a pejorative label is largely arbitrary. Drug "abuse" is in the eye of the beholder, reflecting a socially constructed reality. A new prohibition or "war on drugs" is imposed on those who conform to the stereotype of the evil, dangerous, often foreign, users and pushers (Duster 1970; Musto 1973). Such approaches may have little to do with an objective reality that recognizes a continuum of drug use/misuse, regardless of the drug's legal status (Goode 1990; Jensen and Gerber 1993; Jenson, Gerber, and Babcock 1991).

Reviews of the pharmacological properties of drugs, including their short- and long-term effects and addictive capacity, are available in a number of sources (Alexander 1990; Boyd 1991; Fehr 1988a, 1988b; Jacobs and Fehr 1987). For sociological analysis, the concern is the perception of drug effects — their imputed properties — as a basis for social stigma and punitive social control. These perceptions are important because many of the intensely moralistic judgements about narcotics are based on conceptions of the physiological consequences of the drugs (Duster 1970:29).

Cannabis was portrayed in the 1930s as leading to "reefer madness" then, in an about-face in the 1970s, to the "amotivational syndrome." Beginning to be valued as a relaxant and euphoriant by some in the "counterculture," its scientific reputation was also briefly rehabilitated by various national commissions that concluded that the adverse consequences of cannabis had been exaggerated. Then a counter-reaction in the 1980s attributed anew both physical and mental damage to marijuana (Erickson 1985). Such a reaction was hardly surprising, given the enormous resources that were invested in animal studies to establish any possible harms of cannabis, rather than any assessment of benefits of safer dosages for human users (Fehr and Kalant 1983). The research effort petered out quickly once the wave of decriminalization ended (Negrete 1988). This has meant that we have very little knowledge about the long-term effects of cannabis use in relation to varying amounts and frequency of intake (Smart 1993). The image of cannabis as a dangerous narcotic has persisted despite scientific opinion that like alcohol, tobacco, or any other pharmacologically active agent, cannabis can produce detrimental effects if enough is taken, and can be used in sufficiently low amounts so that no detriment results (Kalant 1982).

The drugs subject to the most persistent demonizing mythology have been the opiates, particularly heroin. An unrivalled analgesic (painkiller), the most deleterious effects of chronic opiate use are severe constipation and reduced libido (Jacobs and Fehr 1987). Throughout most of this century, medical and scientific commentators have agreed that opiates are not otherwise significantly damaging to the minds and bodies of regular users (Brecher 1972:21–7). A recent quote from Nobel prizewinner, Solomon Snyder, expresses this perspective: "opiate addiction in and of itself is not physically dangerous. Ingesting opiate extracts by mouth is safer than injecting morphine, but if dosage is reasonably well controlled, even opiates by injection are not inherently dangerous" (Snyder 1989:38).

The undeniable poor health and degraded lives of "street" opiate addicts are rather attributable to the damaging, deprived, and marginal lifestyle generated by the prohibition itself (Alexander 1990; Chein et al. 1964; Lindesmith 1965; Stephenson et al. 1956). The major risks of opiate injection are related to the unknown potency and impurity of the drug, the possible contamination of needles with hepatitis and HIV, and unsafe injecting practices. In addition, involvement in the criminal black market with its inherent violence in order to obtain opiates at inflated prices generates further individual and social costs (Boyd 1991; Faupel 1991; Johnson et al. 1985). The image of the opiate user as a hopelessly passive misfit has nevertheless been challenged by evidence that many lead very

demanding lives in their job of "hustling," many fluctuate in their usage patterns according to availability, and many stabilize in relatively productive lives (Blackwell 1983; Johnson et al. 1985; Preble and Casey 1969; Rosenbaum 1981).

Cocaine and, more recently, crack have been the latest "headliners" in the drug crisis industry (Reinarman and Levine 1989). Cocaine, like amphetamine, is a powerful stimulant that acts on the central nervous system to create short-term feelings of euphoria, energy, and well-being. Since the lethal dose is unknown, its potentially deadly effects are unpredictable (Smart and Anglin 1987). Repeated heavy use can lead to a well-documented phenomenon known as cocaine psychosis, marked by paranoia and "formication" (i.e., the sensation of insects crawling under the skin) (Jacobs and Fehr 1987). Clearly, cocaine use is not without risks.

Cocaine has gone through extreme cycles of popularity in which it has been portrayed as a benign, non-addictive tonic and as the most powerfully addictive drug on earth (Akers 1991; Erickson et al. 1987; Murray 1987). The confusion about cocaine's addictive potential is attributable in part to the absence of a clear-cut physical withdrawal syndrome after the cessation of regular use. This confusion is also attributable to a behavioural pattern of compulsive, socially destructive use by a small proportion of those who try cocaine (Erickson and Alexander 1989). The contrast between cocaine and heroin, which can produce an extremely unpleasant though not life-threatening withdrawal syndrome, is captured by William S. Burroughs in *Naked Lunch:*

> You can smell it going in, clean and cold in your nose and throat then a rush of pure pleasure right through the brain lighting up those C[ocaine] connections. Ten minutes later you want another shot, you will walk across town for another shot. But if you can't score for C, you eat, sleep and forget about it (Burroughs 1959:19).

The currently dominant notion of cocaine's powerful addictive quality is a considerable overstatement: between 5 per cent and 10 per cent of those who ever try cocaine will use it weekly or more often; most users will not continue, and the majority of those who do will use it infrequently. Of the more frequent users (weekly or more often), about one-tenth to one-quarter will develop uncontrolled use patterns at some time (Erickson and Alexander 1989; Erickson et al. 1987; Waldorf, Reinarman, and Murphy 1991). Even crack use, when studied outside of treatment settings, is not necessarily compulsive (Cheung, Erickson, and Landau 1991). The natural history of the recent crack epidemic in the United States has been described as differing little from that of previous (drug) epidemics (Fagin and Chin 1989: 606). Cocaine use patterns, then, span a continuum. Although persistent uncontrolled use is the outcome for a small minority, many more users stop for periods of time, maintain moderate use, stop completely, or regain control over their cocaine use (Erickson 1993).

Since all psychoactive drugs have the potential for harm, the selection of particular drugs for harsh repression is a social process that has little relationship to objective evidence. During the alternating waves of panic and indifference (Giffen, Endicott, and Lambert 1991) that have marked this century's response to illicit drugs, Canada's most deadly drugs were quietly gaining ground. Tobacco and alcohol are currently used, respectively, by about 32 per cent and 78 per cent of the population aged fifteen years and older, according to a national survey conducted in 1989 (Health and Welfare Canada 1992). For tobacco, this represents a decline from peak levels of consumption in 1966 when 82 per cent of Canadians smoked. While the proportion of alcohol drinkers has remained quite stable, per capita consumption of alcohol has declined slightly in the 1980s to about 11 L of absolute alcohol by 1989. Of course, these more widely used legal drugs generate substantial government revenue. Nevertheless, an estimated 15,000 people now die annually in Canada from alcohol-related causes and 35,000 from tobacco-

related causes (Boyd 1991). Nor are medically prescribed drugs immune from excessive or inappropriate use. In contrast, the deaths attributable each year to all the illicit drugs combined number in the hundreds; these occur among the approximately 7 per cent to 10 per cent of Canadians who are cannabis users, 1.4 per cent who are cocaine users, and the much less than 1 per cent who regularly inject opiates (Boyd 1991; Health and Welfare Canada 1992). Such figures are the basis for the conclusion that the drugs carrying the greatest health and safety risks are not, in fact, illegal (Addiction Research Foundation 1987–8: 10).

INSTITUTIONAL RESPONSE: THE PERSISTENCE OF CRIMINALIZATION

A reliance on strict enforcement and punishment has traditionally been Canada's primary strategy for the control of illicit drugs. The upsurge in drug use, especially marijuana and hashish, by otherwise normal, middle-class youth in the 1960s precipitated the questioning and some selective penalty modification of the dominant policy (Erickson 1980). Before 1969, limited sentencing options in the Narcotic Control Act meant that half of all cannabis possession offenders were imprisoned. The courts were overloaded with several thousand of this new breed of "cannabis criminals." The federal government's initial response to the public controversy was to provide a "fine only" sentencing option in the Narcotic Control Act in 1969, and to appoint the Royal Commission of Inquiry into the Non-medical Use of Drugs, the Le Dain Commission (Erickson and Smart 1988).

During the 1970s, cannabis was at centre-stage in an unprecedented public debate over illicit drug policy. Although the government did not act on the findings of the Le Dain majority report recommending the decriminalization of cannabis possession, it did provide the new sentencing alternative of a discharge (which still imposes a criminal record) in a Criminal Code amendment in 1972. Judges were quick to utilize the fine and discharge options; a lower proportion of possession offenders were imprisoned. The rapid increase in the number of convictions, however, resulted in greater *numbers* of these cannabis offenders actually being incarcerated than in the 1960s (Erickson 1980:22). During this decade, annual arrests and convictions for cannabis climbed dramatically, numbering about 41,000 convictions in 1980, over 90 per cent of them for possession. In contrast, convictions for each of heroin, cocaine, LSD, and other drugs did not exceed 1,000 in any given year (Erickson and Cheung 1992).

Despite ongoing controversy over the appropriate social response to cannabis and Prime Minister Trudeau's remark to students in 1977 that "if you have a joint and you're smoking it for your private pleasure, you shouldn't be hassled," no other significant legal changes occurred (Erickson 1991:247). A proposal to move cannabis into the less restrictive but still criminal statute, the Food and Drugs Act, surfaced several times, but never progressed through Parliament. Despite increasing numbers of young people subjected to criminalization, a combination of the decline in sentence severity for cannabis possession, the low-visibility of police enforcement activity, and the greater efficiency of the courts in processing these offenders helped to defuse the earlier pressure for meaningful law reform (Erickson 1982: Erickson and Murray 1986). By the beginning of the 1980s, cannabis users and society had, it appeared, learned to live with prohibition (Erickson 1989).

As the 1980s advanced, most forms of illicit drug use declined, arrests for cannabis decreased while those for cocaine gradually increased, and heroin convictions remained low. Cannabis use had become normalized to some extent. It is difficult to continue regarding as seriously deviant a behaviour that has been engaged in by over 4.5 million Canadians, or about one-quarter of the adult population (Health and Welfare Canada 1991). The passage of the Charter of Rights and Freedoms in 1982 resulted in the removal of some of the procedural disadvantages accruing to suspected drug users and sellers (Erickson 1991). It seemed possible that illicit drug use would gradually wane in importance and like other previously criminalized acts (e.g., abortion and homosexuality) would follow the cycle of diminished social concern, less enforcement, minimal intervention, and greater tolerance (Glaser 1985).

This trend was reversed, like those before it, with the emergence of a new drug of concern, cocaine. Panic again dominated the cycle of response. Despite evidence that use levels in Canada were one-fifth or one-quarter of those in the United States, Canadian perceptions of their cocaine "problem" tended to be shaped by the extreme views presented in the American media (Erickson et al. 1994). Within two days of President Reagan's declaration in 1986 that "Drugs are menacing our society, there is no moral middle ground," Prime Minister Mulroney departed from a prepared speech to warn that "Drug abuse has become an epidemic that undermines our economic as well as our social fabric" (Erickson 1992:248). Levels of cocaine use in the 1985 national survey indicated that less than 1 per cent of adults had used cocaine in the previous year (Erickson et al. 1987). The only trend data available in the 1980s from the Ontario surveys showed that cocaine use was declining among students and was stable among adults (Adlaf and Smart 1991; Adlaf, Smart, and Canale 1991). As a senior health official commented about this rediscovery of Canada's drug crisis, "When [the Prime Minister] made that statement, then we had to make it a problem" (Erickson 1992:248).

The result was the resurgence of criminalization, fuelled both by the concerns about cocaine and crack emanating from the United States, and by the direction of additional resources into enforcement as part of Canada's new "drug strategy" launched in 1987 (Erickson 1992). Cocaine charges went up by a factor of ten in the

1980s, seizures of cocaine increased markedly, and cocaine products became the avowed target of antidrug activity (Erickson and Cheung 1992). The proportion of cocaine possession offenders who were jailed rose from 19 per cent in 1980 to 29 per cent in 1989. The proportion of inmates incarcerated federally from all narcotic offences went up from 9 per cent to 14 per cent between 1986 and 1989.

During this same period, the Royal Canadian Mounted Police's investigation of suspected traffickers in cocaine or cannabis increasingly focused on small-scale dealers (Royal Canadian Mounted Police 1990). For example, the proportion of traffickers investigated for the smallest amount of drug tripled for both cocaine and cannabis, while those pursued for the largest amounts actually declined (Erickson 1992). Cannabis possession offenders were also caught up in this slipstream of antidrug activity, and the decline in charges halted in 1986 and stabilized at about 28,000 yearly for the rest of the decade. Thus during a period of declining illicit drug use, the overall drug crime rate (i.e., recorded drug law offences per 100,000 population) actually climbed from 221.9 in 1986 to 258.9 in 1989 (Erickson 1992). The United States might have been waging a drug war, but Canada, it appeared, was waging a drug strategy.

How has the perception of an emerging crack problem in Canada been portrayed as a basis for an intensification of criminalization? There were no seizures of crack before 1986, but once it began to appear, the Canadian media and police reports alerted the public to the arrival of a "crack epidemic." The *Toronto Star* informed its readers that this drug was a "one-way ticket to hell for the user" (1989a) and that crack posed "the greatest threat to society over the past fifteen years" (1989b). Crack use quickly reached "crisis proportions," according to the *Globe and Mail*, and was being used by a "very, very paranoid, psychotic group" (1989). A deadly plague of drugs was described by *Maclean's* to be infesting Toronto and other Canadian cities. In 1987, the

Royal Canadian Mounted Police reported that crack comprised a very modest proportion of all cocaine seizures in Canada, and in 1989 it reported that the "use of crack is not widespread in Canada at the point" (Royal Canadian Mounted Police 1989:42). The same report, however, also referred to the greatly increased number of seizures, especially in Toronto, and referred to crack as "almost instantly addictive." In combination with local news stories and police reports of a growing crime problem linked to crack, it is not surprising that the public perceived a growing "crack menace" (Cheung and Erickson forthcoming).

While there was considerable evidence that cocaine and crack misuse were responsible for a substantial increase in drug-related problems in the United States in the middle to late 1980s (Goode 1990), this situation was not reflected to nearly the same extent in Canada (Erickson et al. 1994). As noted earlier, Canadian surveys showed stable or declining use at fairly low levels in adult and student populations during this period. It was therefore possible to answer no to the question of a major crack epidemic (Smart 1988). A study of crack users in Toronto dispelled some of the myths about crack's "instantly addictive" property and the lack of control purportedly displayed by all those exposed to this form of cocaine (Cheung, Erickson, and Landau 1991). Some indicators of cocaine problems, such as treatment admissions and drug-related deaths, did show some increase during the latter part of the 1980s, but levelled off by the end of the decade (Single et al. 1992). Such trends in problem indicators also likely reflect the greater purity and lower price of cocaine that was available on the street, where the price had dropped from $100,000 in 1981 to $34,000 per kilogram in 1989 (Erickson and Cheung 1992). Despite the relatively minor nature of the problem in Canada, sufficient public concern was generated to revive a call for tougher action against drug users and sellers.

The intensified criminal justice response to illicit drugs in the 1980s continued a well-established tradition, aided and abetted by the influx of additional resources to enforcement in Canada's Drug Strategy. Since recorded offences for activities like drug use and sale depend on proactive police discovery, a growing drug crime rate in part reflects this deployment rather than any real increase in actual deviant behaviour (Hagan 1991). Thus the police have been able to demonstrate and maintain a high level of productivity in overall investigations, seizures, arrests, and charges during a period of decreased illicit drug use. This occurred despite the avowed purpose of the new strategy, which was to balance enforcement with prevention and treatment and take Canada's drug policy in a new, less punitive direction (Erickson 1992).

In sum, after a wave of repression that accompanied the upsurge in illicit drug use in the 1960s, Canada appeared to be less wedded to its traditional responses for a brief period in the early 1980s. This shift of emphasis was marked by decreases in drug use, reductions in cannabis arrests and convictions, less severe sentences, various proposals for law reform, increased protection of the rights of drug offenders, and greater social tolerance of drug use. Then, fuelled by the latest American antidrug crusade and Canada's local version of the cocaine scare, the pendulum swung back from about 1987 onwards. The resurgence of criminalization was characterized by an increase in drug charges, especially for cocaine, more investigations of small-scale traffickers, severe sentences, and several other measures that have not been presented due to space limitations. These include new state powers of seizure and forfeiture of assets of those arrested on drug charges, the military's involvement in interdiction efforts, banning of drug paraphernalia, expansion of workplace drug testing, and proposals to limit the parole eligibility of convicted drug traffickers (Erickson 1992). Canada's institutions of social control of illicit drugs, i.e., repressive laws, broad police powers, highly discretionary criminal justice procedures, and substantial community support for punitive measures, have remained ascendant and impeded fundamental change in drug policy.

RESISTANCE OR CAPITULATION: THE DEVIANT STRIKES BACK?

Norwegian criminologist Nils Christie has called illicit drug users the "easy enemy": poor, often sick, and powerless. Some Canadian research is relevant to this question: to what extent have drug users been the helpless targets of narcotic laws, and to what extent have they resisted and reshaped the current policies? The evidence suggests that drug users have not been a viable political force in Canada, but have often personally resisted the stigmatization of a deviant identity and supported others in doing so. In the wake of the AIDS epidemic, injection drug users have become better organized around public health issues in Europe and Australia, and this may influence future directions in Canada.

Historically, it is clear that Chinese opium smokers had little power to resist increasingly harsh penalties, including deportation, once prohibition was in place (Giffen, Endicott, and Lambert 1991). Before that, Chinese merchants had sought recompense from Mackenzie King for the destruction of their opium stocks in the anti-Asiatic riot of 1907 in Vancouver. This marked the last legitimacy of the narcotic drug dealer in this century. Canadian heroin addicts, few in number and marginalized, have expressed an almost fatalistic view of the hardships of their lives on the street (Stoddart 1988, 1991). The revolving cycle of arrest and imprisonment, the search for a "fix," has changed little since Stephenson and colleagues first reported in 1956. Recently, however, a small group of opiate users called a press conference in Toronto to protest the shortage of methadone maintenance places in the province. Users were also represented at a harm reduction conference held in the city in 1994.

The cannabis controversy of the early 1970s led to a far more open political debate than had occurred previously (e.g., in the punishment versus treatment controversy of the 1950s). Drug users themselves testified before the Le Dain Commission (Erickson and Smart 1988). Many different interest groups were involved — the medical and legal professions, social service workers, and treatment representatives — to challenge the bureaucratic hegemony of the social control agents (Giffen and Lambert 1988). At several points, change in the drug laws seemed imminent. In the end, however, no significant alteration to the dominant social policy occurred.

A Toronto sample of ninety-five first-time offenders for cannabis possession were interviewed in depth at the time of their sentencing and again one year later (Erickson 1980). Their responses indicated a wide variety of reactions to the experience of being caught and officially labelled a "cannabis criminal." Some reported humiliating or frightening experiences at the hands of the police; for others, the processing was routine, even good-natured. For many, the arrest and the waiting period before going to court provoked anxiety that their employer, family, or others might learn about the charge. Others arrived at court with several friends or parents in attendance to show support. Nearly all (about 95 per cent) did not consider themselves as criminals after their court appearance, and thought that peers shared that perception. Most were fairly long-term, regular cannabis users who had no intention of changing their behaviour, and indeed had not one year later. A replication study several years later found little change in offenders' attitudes and experiences of criminalization, but these criminalized users were more confident that employers would be unlikely to learn of their record (Erickson and Murray 1986). The stigma attached to becoming

a criminal for cannabis use seemed to decrease progressively for these deviants, resembling a state of *de facto* decriminalization despite the lack of legal change.

Interviews with experienced drug users who are in the community rather than in prison or treatment institutions consistently reveal the "normalcy" of their behaviour to themselves and their friends (Erickson 1980; Erickson et al. 1994). Drug use is rarely the focal point of their lives, but is an important part of their recreational activities. Considerable effort and planning are devoted to acquiring drugs for special occasions such as birthdays or parties. Concern about health risks, rather than fear of apprehension, is more likely to influence users to cut down their intake or cease use (Cheung, Erickson, and Landau 1991; Erickson 1989, Erickson and Murray 1989).

A sample of long-term cannabis users (average duration was thirteen years) had no trouble maintaining a regular source of supply and were far from unanimous in their support for more liberal legal availability (Erickson 1989). The support by a minority for continued penalties for trafficking to those who would sell cannabis to a new generation of youthful users helps to explain the lack of coherent political lobbying for drug law reform. As Mugford (1990) has noted with regard to similar findings in Australia, it also illustrates the persistence of the antidrug ideology.

Thus Canadian drug users have had little success in actively resisting the operation of public policy that declares them to be criminals. The policy objective has been to suppress all use rather than to reduce the harmful consequences of use. Those who are officially criminalized are only the tip of the iceberg of several million current or former illicit drug users. Shared knowledge and experience of both the risks and benefits of drug use in informed social control networks can reduce harmful effects (Erickson 1993). Fears about the transmission of the AIDS virus among injection drug users has helped to orient a more public health approach towards the consequences of drug use (Smart 1993). Perhaps the "shadow line" (Gomme 1993) — that vague boundary between the official, highly deviant, criminalized world of illicit drug users and the reality of casual, widespread use of illicit substances by the younger mainstream of the population — will continue to be blurred until a more rational public policy emerges. The Le Dain Commission envisioned a gradual withdrawal of criminal sanctions as they were replaced by more effective, less costly forms of social control (Commission of Inquiry into the Non-Medical Use of Drugs 1972, 1973).

CONCLUSION

The future of the social construction of drug problems in Canadian society may reflect more stigmatization of the currently legal drugs, alcohol and tobacco. Canada has some of the strictest antismoking laws in the world. It has also instituted a number of checks on the availability of alcohol and mounted antidrinking/driving and moderate drinking campaigns. The neo-temperance ideology, which has strong roots in English Canada (Levine 1992), relies on external controls to reinforce the internal controls. These are seen as essential to check drug-induced intoxication. In cultures where loss of self-control is not so negatively valued, temperance ideology has never had widespread support. Thus, for example, Quebec has always expressed a different alcohol culture, and also has a much lower rate of cannabis criminalization than other provinces (Moreau 1988). Even if punitive responses to illicit drugs are relaxed again in the future, and convergence develops in policy approaches to all psychoactive substances, it is difficult to envision a major change without a concomitant shift in the social evaluation of the acceptability of losing self-control. In Canada, such behaviour is the basis for being viewed as deviant.

NOTES

The views expressed in this chapter are mine and do not necessarily reflect those of the Addiction Research Foundation.

I wish to thank Benedikt Fischer and Gordon Walsh for their helpful comments.

REFERENCES

Addiction Research Foundation. 1987—8. *Annual Report.* Toronto: Addiction Research Foundation.

Adlaf, E.M., and R.G. Smart. 1991. "Drug Use Among Adolescent Students in Canada and Ontario: The Past, Present and Future." *Journal of Drug Issues* 21:59–72.

————, R.G. Smart, and M.D. Canale. 1991. *Drug Use Among Ontario Adults 1977–1991.* Toronto: Addiction Research Foundation.

Akers, R.L. 1991. "Addiction: The Troublesome Concept." *Journal of Drug Issues* 21:777–92.

Alexander, B. 1990. *Peaceful Measures: Canada's Way Out of the War on Drugs.* Toronto: University of Toronto Press.

Black, D. 1989. *Sociological Justice.* New York: Oxford University Press.

Blackwell, J.C. 1983. "Drifting, Controlling, and Overcoming: Opiate Users Who Avoid Becoming Chronically Independent." *Journal of Drug Issues* 13:219–35.

————. 1988. "Sin, Sickness, or Social Problem? The Concept of Drug Dependence." In *Illicit Drugs in Canada: A Risky Business*, edited by J.C. Blackwell and P.G. Erickson, 158–74. Toronto: Nelson Canada.

Boyd, N. 1991. *High Society: Legal and Illegal Drugs in Canada* Toronto: Key Porter Books.

Brecher, E.M., et al. 1972. *Licit and Illicit Drugs.* Mount Vernon: Consumers Union.

Burroughs, W.A. 1959. *Naked Lunch.* New York: Grove Weidenfeld.

Chein, I., et al. 1964. *The Road to H: Narcotics, Delinquency and Social Policy.* New York: Basic Books.

Cheung, Y.W., and P.G. Erickson. Forthcoming. "Crack Use in Canada: A Distant American Cousin." In *Crack in Context: Myths, Realities and Social Policy*, edited by C. Reinarman and H.G. Levine.

————, P.G. Erickson, and T.C. Landau. 1991. "Experience of Crack Use: Findings from a Community-Based Sample in Toronto." *Journal of Drug Issues* 21:121–40.

Commission of Inquiry into the Non-Medical Use of Drugs, 1972. *Cannabis.* Ottawa: Information Canada.

————. 1973. *Final Report.* Ottawa: Information Canada.

Duster, T. 1970. *The Legislation of Morality.* New York: Free Press.

Erickson, P.G. 1980. *Cannabis Criminals: The Social Effects of Punishment on Drug Users.* Toronto: ARF Books.

————. 1981. "Questioning the Conventional Wisdom: A Comment on the Marijuana Arrest Studies." *Journal of Drug Issues* 11:389–97.

————. 1985. "Cannabis Law Reform: An Unfinished Era." *Psychotropes* 2:96–8.

————. 1989. "Living with Prohibition: Regular Cannabis Users, Legal Sanctions, and Informal Controls." *The International Journal of Addictions* 24: 175–88.

————. 1992. "Recent Trends in Canadian Drug Policy: The Decline and Resurgence of Prohibitionism." *Daedalus* 121:239–67.

————.1993. "The Prospects of Harm Reduction for Psychostimulants." In *Psychoactive Drugs and Harm Reduction: From Faith to Science*, edited by N. Heather et al., 184–210. London: Whurr.

————, and B. Alexander. 1989. "Cocaine and Addictive Liability." *Social Pharmacology* 3:249–70.

————, and Y.W. Cheung. 1992. "Drug Crime and Legal Control: Lessons from the Canadian Experience." *Contemporary Drug Problems* 19:247–77.

————, and G.F. Murray. 1986. "Cannabis Criminals Revisited." *British Journal of Addiction* 81:81–5.

————, and G.F. Murray. 1989. "The Undeterred Cocaine User: Intention to Quit and Its Relationship to Perceived Legal and Health Threats." *Contemporary Drug Problems* 16: 141–56.

————, and R.G. Smart. 1988. "The Le Dain Commission Recommendations." In *Illicit Drugs in Canada: A Risky Business*, edited by J.C. Blackwell and P.G. Erickson, 336–44. Toronto: Nelson Canada.

————, et al. 1987. *The Steel Drug: Cocaine in Perspective.* Lexington: D.C. Heath and Company.

————, et al. 1994. *The Steel Drug: Cocaine and Crack in Perspective,* 2nd ed. New York: Macmillan.

Fagin, J., and K.L. Chin. 1989. "Initiation into Crack and Cocaine: A Tale of Two Epidemics." *Contemporary Drug Problems* 16:579–618.

Faupel, C.E. 1991. *Shooting Dope: Career Patterns of Hard Core Heroin Users.* Gainesville: University of Florida Press.

Fehr, K. 1988a. "Making Connections: Drugs, Mind, and Body." In *Illicit Drugs in Canada: A Risky Business*, edited by J.C. Blackwell and P.G. Erickson, 5–27. Toronto: Nelson Canada.

————. 1988b. "The Dealer's Choice: An Introduction to Street Drugs." In *Illicit Drugs in Canada: A Risky Business*, edited by J.C. Blackwell and P.G. Erickson, 28–50. Toronto: Nelson Canada.

————, and H. Kalant. 1983. *Cannabis and Health Hazards: Proceedings of an ARF/WHO Scientific Meeting on Adverse Health and Behavioural Consequences of Cannabis.* Toronto: Addiction Research Foundation.

Giffen, P.G., and S. Lambert. 1988. "What Happened on the Way to Law Reform." In

Illicit Drugs in Canada: A Risky Business, edited by J.C. Blackwell and P.G. Erickson, 345–69. Toronto: Nelson Canada.

———, S. Endicott, and S. Lambert. 1991. *Panic and Indifference: The Politics of Canada's Drug Laws.* Ottawa: Canadian Centre on Substance Abuse.

Glaser, D. 1985. "The Criminal Law's Nemesis: Drug Control." *American Bar Foundation Research Journal,* 619–26.

Globe and Mail (Toronto). 1989. "Crack Use Near Epidemic Toronto Police Warn" (11 February).

Gomme, I.M. 1993. *The Shadow Line: Deviance and Crime in Canada.* Toronto: Harcourt Brace Jovanovich.

Goode, E. 1990. "The American Drug Panic of the 1980s: Social construction or Objective Threat?" *The International Journal of the Addictions* 25:1083–98.

Hagan, J. 1991. *The Disreputable Pleasures: Crime and Deviance in Canada,* 3rd ed. Toronto: McGraw-Hill Ryerson.

Health and Welfare Canada. 1992. *Alcohol and Other Drug Use by Canadians: A National Alcohol and Other Drug Survey (1989): Technical Report.* Prepared by E. Eliany et al. Ottawa: Minister of Supply and Services Canada.

Heath, D.B. 1992. "U.S. Drug Control Policy: A Cultural Perspective." *Daedalus* 121:269–91.

Jacobs, M.R., and K. Fehr. 1987. *Drugs and Drug Abuse: A Reference Text,* 2nd ed. Toronto: Addiction Research Foundation.

Jensen, E.L., and J. Gerber. 1993. "State Efforts to Construct a Social problem: the 1986 War on Drugs in Canada." *Canadian Journal of Sociology* 18, no. 4:453–62.

———, J. Gerber, and G.M. Babcock. 1991. "The New War on Drugs: Grass Roots Movement or Political Construction?" *Journal of Drug Issues* 21:651–67.

Johnson, D.B., et al. 1985. *Taking Care of Business: The Economics of Crime by Heroin Abusers.* Lexington: Lexington Books.

Kalant, H. 1982. "Commentary on the Home Office Report on the Effects of Cannabis Use." *British Journal of Addiction* 77:341–5.

Levine, H.G. 1992. "Temperance Cultures: Concerns About Alcohol Problems in Nordic and English-Speaking Cultures." In *The Nature of Alcohol and Drug-Related Problems,* edited by G. Edwards and M. Lader, 15–36. London: Oxford University Press.

Lindesmith, A. 1965. *The Addict and the Law.* Bloomington: Indiana University Press.

Maclean's. 1989. "A Deadly Plague of Drugs" (3 April).

Maloff, D., et al. 1979. "Informal Social Controls and Their Influence on Substance Use." *Journal of Drug Issues* 9:161–84.

McKenna, T. 1992. *Food of the Gods.* New York: Bantam Books.

Moreau, J.A.E. 1988. "Appendix A: Selected Statistics on Convictions for Illicit Drug Use in Canada." In *Illicit Drugs in Canada: A Risky Business,* edited by J.C. Blackwell and P.G. Erickson, 449–55. Toronto: Nelson Canada.

Mugford, S.K. 1990. "Drug Policy and Criminal Consequences: The Australian Experience." Paper presented at the annual meeting of the American Society of Criminology, Baltimore, Maryland.

Murray, G.F. 1987. "Cocaine Use in an Era of Social Reform: The Natural History of a Social Problem in Canada." *Canadian Journal of Law and Society* 2:2943.

———. 1988. "The Road to Regulation: Patent Medicines in Canada in Historical Perspective." In *Illicit Drugs in Canada: A Risky Business,* edited by J.C. Blackwell and P.G. Erickson, 721–87. Toronto: Nelson Canada.

Musto, D.F. 1973. *The American Disease: Origins of Narcotic Control.* New Haven: Yale University Press.

Negrete, J.C. 1988. "What Happened to the Cannabis Debate?" *British Journal of Addiction* 83:354–72.

Peyrot, M. 1984. "Cycles of Social Problem Development: The Case of Drug Abuse." *The Sociological Quarterly* 25:83–95.

Prebel, E., and J.J. Casey. 1969. "Taking Care of Business: The Heroin User's Life on the Streets." *The International Journal of Addictions* 4:1–24.

Royal Canadian Mounted Police. 1987. *National Drug Intelligence Estimates 1986/1987.* Ottawa: Minister of Supply and Services Canada.

———. 1988. *National Drug Intelligence Estimates 1987/1988.* Ottawa: Minister of Supply and Services Canada.

———. 1989. *National Drug Intelligence Estimates 1988/1989.* Ottawa: Minister of Supply and Services Canada.

———. 1990. *National Drug Intelligence Estimates 1989/1990.* Ottawa: Minister of Supply and Services Canada.

Reinarman, C., and H.G. Levine. 1989. "The Crack Attack: Media and Politics in America's Latest Drug Scare." In *Images of Issues: Current Perspectives on Social Problems,* edited by J. Best, 115–37. New York: Aldine DeGruyter.

Rosenbaum, M. 1981. *Women on Heroin.* New Brunswick: Rutgers University Press.

Single, E., et al. 1992. "Policy Developments in Canada." In *Drug Problems in Society: Dimensions and Perspectives,* edited by J. White, 63–72. Parkside: Drug and Alcohol Services Council.

Smart, R.G. 1988. "Crack Cocaine Use in Canada: A New Epidemic?" *American Journal of Epidemiology* 127:135–17.

———. 1993. "What Are the Rules of Thumb of Avoiding Problem Drug Use?" *Addiction* 88:179–81.

———, and L. Anglin. 1987. "Do We Know the Lethal Dose of Cocaine?" *Journal of Forensic Sciences* 32:303–12.

———, and A.C. Ogborne. 1986. *Northern Spirits: Drinking in Canada Then and Now.* Toronto: ARF Books.

Snyder, S. 1989. *Brainstorming: The Science and Politics of Opiate Research.* Cambridge: Harvard University Press.

Stephenson, G.H., et al. 1956. "Drug Addiction in British Columbia." Unpublished manuscript, University of British Columbia.

Stoddart, K. 1988. "The Enforcement of Narcotics Violations in a Canadian City: Heroin Users' Perspectives on the Production of Official Statistics." In *Illicit Drugs in Canada: A Risky Business,* edited by J.C. Blackwell and P.G. Erickson, 244–62. Toronto: Nelson Canada.

———. 1991. "It's Easier for the Bulls Now: Official Statistics and Social Change in a Canadian Heroin-Using Community." *Journal of Drug Issues* 21:83–103.

Toronto Star. 1989a. "Aroused Public Needed to Fight Drugs Mayor Says" (16 June).

———. 1989b. "New Group Joins Fight to Curb Cocaine Trade" (24 February).

Waldorf, D., C. Reinarman, and S. Murphy. *Cocaine Changes: The Experience of Using and Quitting.* Philadelphia: Temple University Press.

Zinberg, N.E., and H.J. Shaffer. 1990. "Essential Factors of a Rational Policy on Intoxicant Use?" *Journal of Drug Issues* 20:619–27.

Chapter 28

Corporate Crime[1]

CARL KEANE

INTRODUCTION

Every day, individuals holding positions of responsibility, at senior levels in the corporate world, violate the laws of society. The few studies that have investigated corporate crime report that it is not uncommon. Yet, with the exception of well-publicized cases such as the Bre-X mining fraud, few people are aware of the extent of such crime.

It was the ground-breaking work of Sutherland (1949) that first brought corporate crime into the spotlight. Sutherland analyzed the life careers of the 70 largest US manufacturing, mining, and mercantile corporations, examining the following legal violations: restraint of trade; misrepresentation in advertising; infringements of patents, trademarks, and copyrights; labour law violations; illegal rebates; financial fraud and violation of trust; violations of war regulations; and finally some miscellaneous offences. He found a total of 980 decisions had been made against the 70 corporations, an average of 14 decisions per corporation (1949: 29). Other research shows that his findings are not unusual. For example, focusing on illegal acts such as price-fixing, overcharging, violation of environmental regulations and antitrust laws, bribes, fraud, patent infringements, and violations of other market regulations, a 1984 survey found that approximately two-thirds of the Fortune 500 largest industrial companies had been involved in illegal behaviour since the mid-1970s (Etzioni, 1985).

Perhaps the most extensive examination to date of corporate offending is the study conducted by Clinard and his colleagues (Clinard et al., 1979; Clinard and Yeager, 1980). This research involved the analysis of federal administrative, civil, and criminal actions either initiated or completed by 25 US agencies during 1975–1976 against the 477 largest publicly owned US manufacturing companies and the 105 largest US wholesale, retail, and service companies. Six main types of corporate illegal behaviour were discovered: administrative violations such as noncompliance with an order from a court or government agency; environmental violations such as pollution of the air or water; financial violations including bribery, tax violations, and accounting malpractices; labour violations involving employment discrimination, occupational safety and health hazards, and unfair labour practices; manufacturing violations such as violations of the Consumer Product Safety Act; and unfair trade practices, involving various abuses of competition such as price-fixing as well as acts such as false advertising (Clinard and Yeager, 1980: 113–115). The researchers found that of the 582 corporations, approximately 60 percent had at least one federal action brought against them, and for those companies that had at least one action brought against them, the average was 4.4 cases (1980: 113).

Focusing on violations of the Combines Act in Canada, Goff and Reasons (1978) reported that between 1952 and 1972 a total of 157 decisions were made against the 50 largest Canadian

---

Source: Adapted from "Corporate Crime," in *Crime in Canadian Society,* 5th ed., Robert A. Silverman, James J. Teevan, and Vincent F. Sacco, eds. (Toronto: Harcourt Brace, 1996), pp. 282–92. Used by permission of the publisher.

corporations, an average of three decisions per corporation. Taken together, these studies demonstrate the wide extent of corporate offending, and reveal that individuals in the middle and upper socioeconomic classes, contrary to popular stereotypes, quite frequently engage in illegal behaviour.

What causes such crime? Reflecting on Sutherland's (1949) point that corporate offences cannot be explained by conditions of poverty, nor by individual pathology, any search for the causes of corporate crime should begin with an examination of the context within which such crimes occur — the organization. This approach calls for an analysis of the corporation and its impact on the individuals who work there. As such, it is useful to first examine external and internal factors that affect the organization, followed by those factors that affect the employees of the organization. Let us begin with external factors of influence.

EXTERNAL FACTORS OF INFLUENCE

Any organization both affects, and is affected by, its environment. Organizations are constrained by laws, and at the same time, they may try to influence legislators. Some corporations conduct business in markets with numerous competitors, consumers, and suppliers — others with few. And organizations operate in economies ranging from capitalist to communist. To help us understand the influence of external factors, we can begin with an examination of the economic system.

CAPITALISM

Some criminologists argue that to understand corporate crime we should adopt a macro-perspective, and focus on the features of our capitalist economy. They suggest that corporate capitalism, with its primary emphasis on the goals of maximizing profitability and minimizing costs, leads to unsafe products, environmental pollution, employee and consumer deception, and unsafe working conditions (see Henry, 1982: 85). At the same time, it is argued that the content and enforcement of laws against corporate crime reflect the interests of the economic elite, who through their economic dominance are able to influence the political elite, leading to weakened legislation and lax enforcement of existing laws (Snider and West, 1985; also see Snider, 1993, for a thorough examination of the problems of corporate regulation). However, organizational problems are not restricted to capitalist countries. For example, in an effort to meet productivity goals, former Soviet workers endured one of the worst records of industrial safety and occupational health in the world (Handelman, 1989). Others have reported a variety of economic crimes such as bribery, fraud, property theft, and "black-market" operations that have been widespread in communist countries (Los, 1982). Therefore, the economic system alone cannot provide a comprehensive explanation for organizational deviance. Let us thus look to competition.

COMPETITION

Some see competition, common to both the profit and not-for-profit sectors, as a precipitating factor in the genesis of corporate crime. The infamous case of the Ford Pinto automobile can be cited as an example. Facing increasing competition from foreign small-car imports, the Ford Motor Company attempted to speed up the production process of the Pinto in order to meet the competition. When it was determined that a faulty fuel system could cause the car to explode on impact, Ford executives conducted a cost-benefit analysis, weighing the estimated number of injuries and deaths and resulting lawsuits that would occur against the cost of recalling all the defective cars. In accordance with the results of the cost-benefit analysis, the company decided against recalling the Ford Pinto, a decision that ultimately resulted in numerous deaths and injuries (Cullen et al.,

1987; Dowie, 1977). This example is but one manifestation of a "culture of competition" that exists in all industrialized countries. It is related to corporate crime in that it motivates individuals to succeed at virtually any cost (Coleman, 1987; 1989).

In fact, at a session on business ethics at the World Economic Forum, it was reported that "corrupt practices such as bribery are considered inevitable — if not acceptable — in international business, and executives fear they will lose contracts to competitors unless they go along with the corrupt practices" (*Globe and Mail*, 1994a: B7). And a World Bank–sponsored survey of 3600 companies in 69 countries found that more than 40 percent of respondents reported having to pay bribes to get things done (*Globe and Mail*, 1997a: A10, A21). Thus, the quest for success is framed within a competitive global milieu.

STRAIN THEORY

We have seen how companies pitted against each other in a "culture of competition" produce a situation of inter-firm rivalry wherein some firms might violate the law to gain advantage over a competitor. What we have described is a setting where the industry culture promotes competition as a means of attaining corporate goals, but the market structure limits the opportunity for all companies to achieve success. This discrepancy between culture and structure produces a situation of strain, which increases the possibility of corporate corruption (see Keane, 1993). A similar process can be seen even internal to the organization. That is, in the planning and budgeting process, companies regularly set internal corporate goals. In this situation competition may exist between two divisions; between plants; and/or between time periods, such as when a company budgets to decrease costs or forecasts to increase sales over the previous year. Again we have a situation where the corporate culture emphasizes competition, but the corporate structure may not provide the opportunity to achieve the corporate goal.

According to Merton (1938) this type of situation may lead to illegal behaviour. Merton postulated that if individuals are thwarted in their quest to attain their desired goals, such as the culturally prescribed goal of success, they will become frustrated. This frustration, caused by a disjuncture between legal means and desired goals, will produce a situation of strain, and individuals will adapt to alleviate the strain. Some individuals (whom Merton called "innovators"), while accepting the goal, will reject conventional means and embrace illegal means of attaining the goal. With respect to strain, Clinard (1983) reported on the pressure exerted on middle managers from top management to increase profitability, decrease costs, and meet production and sales quotas, pressure that may result in illegal behaviour. Simply stated, some individuals, faced with a discrepancy between goals and the legal means to achieve them, will become corporate criminals. Competition, however, is a necessary but not sufficient cause of corporate crime. For example, although competition exists in every industry, some industries are more crime prone than others. Also, even within the same industry, some firms violate the law more than others. As researchers of corporate crime we must ask, what is there about particular industries, and particular firms, that produces a higher rate of corporate crime? This question calls for a closer examination of other aspects of the external environment of modern organizations.

ENVIRONMENTAL UNCERTAINTY

In examining the external structure of organizations, we can identify certain factors that vary among firms and industries. For example, while all organizations place an organizational priority on goal attainment (Finney and Lesieur, 1982), organizations may have a variety of goals, and goals will differ among organizations. Although profitability is often the primary goal, organizations may strive to maximize revenue, earnings per share, market share, growth, or production quotas — or the primary goal may be survival.

Organizations, however, do not operate in a vacuum. The external environment of an organization comprises political, sociocultural, economic, physical, and technological factors, and perhaps most importantly, other organizations. These various elements of what has been referred to as an organization's "task environment" (Dill, 1958) produce a high degree of uncertainty. In order to meet corporate goals, an organization operating within an uncertain environment may attempt to reduce that uncertainty through illegal behaviour (see Aldrich, 1979). For example, to reduce uncertainty concerning pricing vis-à-vis competitors, as well as to reduce the uncertainty of profitability, an organization may collude with other firms in the same industry to set and maintain prices (see Simpson, 1986). This price-fixing conspiracy serves to reduce uncertainty by providing the company with some control over an important element of its external environment.

In general, as environmental uncertainty increases, thus threatening goal attainment, illegal behaviour may increase in attempts to control or minimize the uncertainty, and to increase the likelihood of goal achievement.

MARKET STRUCTURE

As discussed above, price-fixing reduces uncertainty about profitability and competitive behaviour. However, for a price-fixing conspiracy to be successful there must be agreement among the firms that prices will be maintained. Hence, the greater the number of firms in a particular industry, the harder it may be to coordinate a collusion, and thus the harder it will be for all to agree to maintain prices. Therefore, price-fixing may be more prevalent in concentrated industries dominated by a small number of firms. More specifically, Coleman (1989:225) suggests, "it would seem that industries with many small, highly competitive firms would be characterized by a high rate of crimes that are intended to improve competitive performance, such as fraud, false advertising, and espionage, and that collu-

sion and antitrust activities are most common in more concentrated industries." An example of the relationship between price-fixing and a concentrated market structure can be seen in the case of the compressed gases industry in Canada. In this case, it was found that only five companies supplied 97 percent of the compressed gases sold in Canada. Representatives of these companies admitted in a statement of facts read in court that they met and agreed to adopt common prices for the sale of various compressed gases, thereby violating the Competition Act (*Globe and Mail*, 1991a: B2; *Globe and Mail*, 1991b: B3). So the market structure of the industry is important with respect to the type of illegal activity most likely to occur. In addition, some situations may be particularly conducive to criminal behaviour in that there is an increased opportunity to violate the law. This leads us to a discussion of what can be termed opportunity theory.

OPPORTUNITY THEORY

The notion of "opportunity" differs slightly from the preceding discussion of industry concentration and corporate deviance by focusing on the increased likelihood of a firm to violate a specific type of law. For example, oil companies in the course of producing and/or shipping oil have a greater likelihood of polluting the environment (Clinard and Yeager, 1980: 250–251), while firms that are labour-intensive, placing a heavy reliance upon workers as opposed to equipment, are more likely to violate labour laws (Clinard and Yeager, 1980: 131–132). Thus, some industries, and the firms and employees within them, may be more prone to committing certain offences than others.

At the same time, some industries more than others may find themselves the target of various regulatory agencies. That is, some industries such as the pharmaceutical industry, the automobile industry, and the chemical and petroleum industries, because of the potential harm their products can cause, are more regulated than others (Coleman, 1989), and in turn, they have higher crime rates than others (Clinard and Yeager, 1980), if only because of the greater regulation imposed upon them. Also, because some industries may be more stringently regulated than others, it follows that those organizations that are diversified into a number of stringently regulated industries are more likely to face "opportunities" to deviate and/or are more likely to attract regulatory attention (Clinard and Yeager, 1980: 131).

To summarize briefly, companies are goal oriented, and with factors such as globalization of business and rapid social change, they may find themselves operating in uncertain environments. And in the process of minimizing uncertainty and maximizing goal attainment, regulations peculiar to the industry may be violated. Nevertheless, differences in the rates of violation exist among companies in the same industry. That is, although some industries tend to violate the law more than others, there is still variation within industries, with some firms more deviant than others (Clinard and Yeager, 1980: 58). This being the case, we must ask, what characteristics distinguish criminal from noncriminal firms? Or, put another way, what are the characteristics of those firms that come to the attention of regulatory bodies? An examination of the internal environment of the corporation may provide an answer to these questions.

INTERNAL FACTORS OF INFLUENCE

INTERNAL CONTROL

The modern corporation is a large, diffuse, hierarchical system oriented towards goal attainment through effective use of available resources in an uncertain environment. Employees of the corporation are one resource deployed to meet organizational goals. And just as an organization will attempt to have some influence over its external environment, it must also manage its internal resources, including its employees.

However, the internal structure of the corporation may make it difficult to control corporate illegality. For example, conditions associated with larger size may be conducive to corrupt behaviour (Clinard and Yeager, 1980). As companies grow along dimensions such as number of product lines, number of employees, and number of geographically dispersed locations, they become more difficult to manage, more difficult to control, and in short, more complex. Deviant activities can remain hidden in this complex structure. In attempts to control the internal environment in the midst of this complexity, lines of authority may become decentralized. Stated differently, complexity and diversification, resulting from corporate growth, may call for a decentralized corporate structure as a means of coping with the vast numbers of people and information. And it can be argued that a decentralized corporate structure in turn may be actually more conducive to corruption, rather than less, because visibility is decreased and responsibility is diffused (Finney and Lesieur, 1982; Keane, 1995). That is, when an individual is geographically distant, such as in a branch plant in another country, and/or shielded from senior management by several levels of staff, communication may suffer. So in a decentralized system it is easier to withhold information. In turn, senior management can distance themselves from wrongdoing occurring at the divisional level and/or at a distant location and deny accountability, a tactic Sutherland (1949: 226) referred to as "obfuscation as to responsibility." Pearce and Tombs (1993) provide an example of this process in their study of the Union Carbide disaster in Bhopal, India. They describe how the parent company attempted to shift responsibility for the disaster to the subsidiary, thereby minimizing the accountability of the parent company.

To briefly summarize once more, previously we argued that the organization's external environment is a contributing factor to corporate crime. Now we see that internal corporate factors are also important. But the picture is still incomplete. Although the form of the corporation may provide the setting where control is difficult and the potential for criminal activity is increased, certain individual variables may also be necessary for crime to occur, and we examine these in turn.

INDIVIDUAL LEVEL FACTORS

CONTROL THEORY

Theorists advocating control theories of crime argue that individuals who have weak ties to the norms of conventional society are more likely to deviate than those who are (1) emotionally attached to conventional others and therefore reluctant to deviate for fear of displeasing these others; (2) committed to conventional goals acquired through conventional means; (3) involved in conventional/legal activities; and who (4) believe in the validity of the laws of society and the need to obey those laws (Hirschi, 1969). In essence, control theorists argue that the more individuals are integrated into a legal, as opposed to an illegal, culture, the less likely they are to violate society's laws. Thus, at first glance, it appears that social control theory would be deficient in explaining crimes of the privileged, since unlike the stereotypical "street" criminal, the corporate executive appears to be strongly connected to conventional society. If we modify control theory, however, and examine the subculture of the organization, we can hypothesize that corporate offenders may be more tightly bonded to the culture of the organization than they are to the larger society. This suggests a socialization process whereby individuals come to identify closely with the organization and its goals. That is, through work-related activities and social interaction with other company employees, they intensify their bond of loyalty to the organization. This bond to the organization may then be strengthened through social mobility via promotions and/or geographic mobility via transfers (Coleman, 1989: 220), both of which may make it difficult for individuals to develop long-term social ties outside the organization. Thus, individuals may come to associate predominantly with other members of the organization for whom they come to care, and from whom they learn the behaviour required to attain corporate goals with which they come to strongly identify.

DIFFERENTIAL ASSOCIATION

Continuing with individual level explanations of wrongdoing, Sutherland's (1949) interactionist theory of "differential association" also makes a contribution. A form of learning theory, differential association postulates that deviant behaviour is learned, just like any other type of behaviour. Differential association points to the importance of learning both the illegal methods as well as the beliefs supporting the use of the methods (Sutherland, 1949: 234). Clinard and Yeager (1980: 58) have confirmed the validity of differential association theory in explaining economic crimes, arguing that although the corporation is influenced by its external environment, the behaviour of a firm is also a product of cultural norms operating within a given corporation. With respect to corporate crimes, the theory suggests that executives become enmeshed in a corporate or professional subculture, and through association with deviant peers learn illegal behaviour. Two essential components of this theory are that (1) the individual must be exposed to an excess of definitions favourable to crime, and (2) the individual must be isolated from definitions unfavourable to crime. Given the loyalty and feelings of identification with the corporation that some organizations are able to instill in their employees, it is easy to see how an individual could be socialized to commit an unlawful act. For example, the former head of securities lending for Gordon Capital Corporation of Toronto, who was banned from trading for ten years for exposing the firm to improper risks by abusing the regulatory system, argued in his own defence that "the Gordon culture sacrificed compliance for profits." He also argued that "many others were involved in the transactions and ... no one indicated any concerns or problems to him" (*Globe and Mail*, 1993b: B2).

Finney and Lesieur (1982: 277) wrote that internal organizational constraints against crime will vary along a continuum, "one end representing moral commitment against law violation, the middle representing a state of neutral receptivity, and the other end representing positive attitudes towards law violation." Accordingly, illegal behaviour is more likely if corporations selectively hire, selectively promote, and socialize a significant number of employees who adopt a stance on the continuum near the neutral or deviant end. Thus, the presence of internal cultural constraints, or their absence, will have an influence on organizational members, and in turn the level of organizational deviance.

TECHNIQUES OF NEUTRALIZATION

Finally, how does the corporate criminal justify his or her deviant behaviour? Sykes and Matza (1957: 664–670) argued that individuals who periodically "drift" from a basic conformity into illegal behaviour will rationalize their guilt by using various "techniques of neutralization." These techniques, which allow normally law-abiding people, such as corporate executives, to justify illegal behaviour are outlined below.

1. Denial of Responsibility

Vandivier (1987: 114–115) relates a conversation he had with a senior executive at the B.F. Goodrich Co., who when asked why he was not going to report to senior management that a faulty aircraft brake was being developed replied: "Because it's none of my business, and it's none of yours. I learned a long time ago not to worry about things over which I had no control. I have no control over this." Not satisfied with this answer, Vandivier asked him if his conscience wouldn't bother him if during test flights on the

brake, something should happen resulting in death or injury to the test pilot. To this the executive replied: "I have no control over this thing. Why should my conscience bother me?"

2. Denial of Injury

In 1993 the US government fined the Louisiana-Pacific Corporation US$11.1 million for excessive emissions and giving false information to environmental officials. The violations occurred at 14 facilities in 11 states. A spokesperson for the company later insisted that federal officials "aren't charging us with any significant emissions of anything hazardous into the air or any environmental harm. What they're saying is the proper procedures, as they see them, weren't followed" (*Globe and Mail*, 1993a: B5). Even more recently, Dow Corning Corporation, the largest manufacturer of silicone-gel breast implants, agreed to pay Quebec and Ontario women up to US$35 million to settle a class action suit and to finance a program to assist women in removing their breast implants. According to a report in the *Globe and Mail* newspaper, a spokesperson for the company said that "the settlement does not mean the company admits the implants posed dangers" (*Globe and Mail*, 1998a: A11).

3. Denial of the Victim

Continuing with the earlier example of the Canadian compressed gas industry, in 1991 Union Carbide was fined $1.7 million, while Canadian Oxygen Ltd. was fined $700 000 after pleading guilty to fixing prices. Officials at both companies claimed, however, that because of long-term contracts, no customers were penalized during the period from January to May 1990, when prices were fixed by the conspirators (*Globe and Mail*, 1991a: B2).

4. Condemnation of the Condemners

An example of this technique is the case of Charles Keating who was fined in excess of

US$260 million and sentenced to over 12 years in prison for his involvement in the Lincoln Savings and Loan Association fraud in the United States. Professing his innocence, he claimed that a vendetta by banking regulators caused Lincoln's collapse in 1989 and his ruination (*Globe and Mail*, 1993c: B15).

5. Appeal to Higher Loyalties

When the chairman of France's largest private corporation was arrested and charged with fraud, embezzlement, and corruption, the country's minister of industry and trade argued that the country should have more important things to do in a recession than prosecute business leaders. He questioned whether the prosecution of this senior executive should be a priority in a country with 3.4 million people unemployed (*Globe and Mail*, 1994c: B10).

To this point we have seen that at the macro level, external factors have an impact on the organization and have some influence on the structure of the organization. Further, these macro-level factors, as well as micro-level influences, are felt at the individual level. Let us now attempt to synthesize these findings.

THEORETICAL INTEGRATION

To gain a clearer picture of corporate crime, a theoretical integration of external, internal, and individual factors related to corporate offending may be useful. To begin, the economic condition of the industry and the extent of task-environment uncertainty are important, as is the degree of industry competition, which may lead to behaviour to reduce uncertainty. Also, the likelihood of a firm violating a particular law varies with the type of industry and the level of industry regulation. Further, large firms may be more likely to be deviant because of the diffusion of responsibility and diminished control. And if the firm is not performing well, the potential for illegal behaviour increases.

So, to this point we can speculate that large firms operating in regulated industries, experiencing economic strain and environmental uncertainty are more at risk of corporate crime. However, although this setting may be conducive to illegal behaviour, individuals must also be exposed to a socialization process whereby they come to identify with the company and its goals, learn the illegal behaviour required to meet the objectives perceived to be unattainable through legal means, and rationalize their actions through various techniques. Hence, the external culture and the internal corporate culture interact to either promote or inhibit law violation.

An element of strain exists in both cultures of an offending corporation. At the external level, the strain may be caused by forces such as competitors, suppliers, or government legislation posing a threat to the corporation's objectives. At the internal level, the strain may also be caused by the potential failure to meet corporate objectives, but the pressure is imposed by internal rather than external actors. And if cultural restraints such as values and regulations opposing and thus inhibiting corporate criminal behaviour are lacking or weak, both externally, in society in general, and internally, within the organization, corruption is more likely to occur. This being the case, can we control corporate crime?

CONTROLLING CORPORATE OFFENDING

Braithwaite (1989: 40) argued that "in modern capitalist societies there are many more statutes that criminalize the behaviour of corporations (anti-pollution laws, occupational health and safety laws, consumer protection laws, antitrust laws, laws to enforce compliance with standards) than there are laws that criminalize the behaviour of the poor." However, application of the law is another matter. That is, evidence suggests that crimes of the powerful are punished differently from crimes of the powerless. For example, focusing on Canadian securities violations, Hagan (1989; Hagan and Parker, 1985) examined all cases referred for prosecution under the Criminal Code or the Securities Act from 1966 to 1983. After categorizing offenders in terms of their class position, the researchers found that those offenders in positions of power committed crimes larger in scope than those with less power, but they received proportionately less severe sanctions because the powerful were less likely to be charged under the Criminal Code, and more likely to be charged under the Securities Act, which carries lesser sanctions.

Also considering the element of power is research by Goff and Reasons (1978). Their research involved an investigation of the major Canadian corporations that have violated the Combines Act and have been investigated by the Combines Branch from 1952 to 1973. Concentrating on the illegal acts of combinations, mergers, monopolies, resale price maintenance, misleading price advertising, predatory pricing, price discrimination, and violations of patents, they concluded that the "Combines Branch has centred its attentions upon the investigation, prosecution, and conviction of small- and medium-sized companies and corporations leaving the very largest corporations free to engage in their monopolistic practices" (Goff and Reason, 1978: 86). Again, they suggested that this occurs because large corporations operating in oligopolistic industries have the ability to obscure their illegal practices. Only very recently have we seen governments taking a more aggressive stance against those illegal cartels that are discovered. For example, the food giant Archer-Daniels-Midland Co. was fined a record US$100 million in the United States, and $16 million in Canada, for taking part in a conspiracy to fix prices. The significance of those record fines is lessened, however, when we consider that in 1997 the company had worldwide sales of $13.8 billion and a profit of $377 million. In fact, a spokesperson for the company reported that the fine would be covered under current

reserves and "does not have an impact on earnings" (*Globe and Mail*, 1998b: B1, B6).

From another perspective, Snider (1982) compared the punishments given to those offenders who commit traditional nonviolent economic offences with those offenders who commit what she terms "upperworld" nonviolent economic offences. Examples of upperworld nonviolent economic offences are acts such as false advertising, misleading price representation, and violations of acts such as the Food and Drug Act, the Packaging and Labelling Act, the Weights and Measures Act, the Hazardous Products Act, and the Combines Investigation Act. Examples of traditional underworld nonviolent economic offences are theft, possession of stolen goods, breaking and entering, and taking a motor vehicle without consent. In brief, she found that over a considerable period of time more traditional offenders were charged, and the sanctions for the traditional economic crimes were much heavier than for the upperworld economic crimes. Others have similarly argued that corporate criminals enjoy a legal advantage because of the types and combinations of legal sanctions that they experience (see Hagan and Nagel, 1982). For example, although New York State had originally sued Occidental Chemical Corporation for almost $700 million in costs and damages toward the cleanup of Love Canal, the company agreed to pay only US$98 million to settle a 14-year liability lawsuit over the toxic disaster that forced hundreds of families from their homes (*Globe and Mail*, 1994b: B2).

CONCLUSIONS

In summary, corporate criminals have been spared the stigma of criminalization often imposed on those less privileged. Furthermore, given the evidence of recidivism reported by researchers such as Goff and Reasons (1978) and Clinard and Yeager (1980), the existing sanctions appear to have little deterrent effect. This being the case, to control corporate corruption perhaps we should recall that the roots of unethical behaviour are embedded in the organizational and cultural contexts.

Sanctions that have been suggested to inhibit organizational deviance include stiffer penalties for corporations and executives, negative publicity, nationalization of firms that are habitual offenders, and forced deconcentration and divestiture of offending firms, to name a few (Braithwaite, 1984; Clinard and Yeager, 1980; Coleman, 1989). These sanctions are similar in that they are imposed by others external to the organization, and they are imposed after the criminal act. It may also be possible to control corporate crime at the internal corporate level.

Internal corporate control can be increased by actions such as improving and strengthening the firm's self-regulatory systems (Braithwaite, 1984) and providing for public and/or union representation on corporate boards of directors (Clinard and Yeager, 1980). These internal corporate mechanisms would serve to control the actions of executives prior to any offence. Another method of controlling corporate crime that has received increased attention is the development of a stronger business ethic (Clinard and Yeager, 1980; Coleman, 1989). This proposal is directed at the culture of the organization and is preventive in its orientation. An increasing number of companies are finding that "business does well by doing good" (*Globe and Mail*, 1997b: B2). Unethical corporate behaviour may destroy a company's reputation, and given the increase in foreign competition experienced by many industries, a loss of customers may accompany the loss of reputation. In addition, failure to follow ethical business practices may result not only in consumer protest, but also in government intervention (Hilts, 1989). Many companies are taking steps to avoid this possibility. A survey conducted in 1997 by KPMG found that 66 percent of Canada's largest corporations now have a code of ethics. In the United States, however, this figure is more than 90 percent (*Globe and Mail*, 1997c: B2).

Whether the institutionalization of ethics is successful in decreasing corporate crime remains to be seen. However, it will be a step in creating a culture in which corporate crime is, at least publicly, not tolerated. On a broader scale, Braithwaite (1989) has argued that what society needs "is punishment for organizational crime that maximizes the sense of shame and sends a message to executives that corporate crime is as despicable to society as street crime." He further asserted that "once members of the organization internalize this abhorrence of corporate wrongdoing, then the self-regulation of executive consciences and corporate ethics and compliance policies will do most of the work for the government" (1989: 143).

NOTE

1. The author would like to thank Krysia Mossakowski for her research assistance.

REFERENCES

Aldrich, H. E. (1979). *Organizations and Environments*. Englewood Cliffs, NJ: Prentice-Hall.

Braithwaite, J. (1984). *Corporate Crime in the Pharmaceutical Industry*. London: Routledge & Kegan Paul.

Braithwaite, J. (1989). *Crime, Shame and Reintegration*. Cambridge: Cambridge University Press.

Clinard, M.B. (1983). *Corporate Ethics and Crime: The Role of Middle Management*. Beverly Hills: Sage.

Clinard, M.B., and Yeager, P.C. (1980). *Corporate Crime*. New York: The Free Press.

Clinard, M.B., Yeager, P.C., Brissette, J., Petrashek, D., and Harries, E. (1979). *Illegal Corporate Behavior*. Washington, DC: U.S. Department of Justice.

Coleman, J.W. (1987). "Toward an Integrated Theory of White-Collar Crime." *American Journal of Sociology, 93*(2), 406–439.

Coleman, J.W. (1989). *The Criminal Elite: The Sociology of White-Collar Crime* (2nd ed.). New York: St. Martin's Press.

Cullen, F.T., Maakestad, W.J., and Cavender, G. (1987). *Corporate Crime Under Attack: The Ford Pinto Case and Beyond*. Cincinnati: Anderson Publishing Co.

Dill, W.R. (1958). "Environment as an Influence on Managerial Autonomy." *Administrative Science Quarterly, 2*(Mar.), 409–443.

Dowie, M. (1977). "Pinto Madness." *Mother Jones* (Sept.–Oct.), 18–32.

Etzioni, A. (1985). "Will a Few Bad Apples Spoil the Core of Big Business?" *Business and Society Review, 55* (Fall), 4–5.

Finney, H.C., and Lesieur, H.R. (1982). "A Contingency Theory of Organizational Crime." In S.B. Bacharach, ed., *Research in the Sociology of Organizations, Vol. 1*. Greenwich, CT: JAI Press.

The Globe and Mail (Toronto). (1991a). "Union Carbide Fined $1.7-million for Price Fixing." (September 7).

The Globe and Mail (Toronto). (1991b). "Pair Fined $75,000 Each for Price-Fixing Role." (October 19).

The Globe and Mail (Toronto). (1993a). "Louisiana-Pacific Fined." (May 25).

The Globe and Mail (Toronto). (1993b). "OSC Slaps Gordon Players." (June 18).

The Globe and Mail (Toronto). (1993c). "Keating Fined $265-Million for Fraud." (July 29).

The Globe and Mail (Toronto). (1994a). "To Bribe or Not to Bribe." (February 14).

The Globe and Mail (Toronto). (1994b). "Love Canal Settlement." (June 22).

The Globe and Mail (Toronto). (1994c). "Alcatel Boss Rejects Fraud Charges." (July 6).

The Globe and Mail (Toronto). (1997a). "Aid Donors Vow War on Graft." (September 20).

The Globe and Mail (Toronto). (1997b). "Business Does Well by Doing Good." (October 2).

The Globe and Mail (Toronto). (1997c). "Heat's on to Get an Effective Code." (November 27).

The Globe and Mail (Toronto). (1998a). "Breast Implant Lawsuit Settled." (April 3).

The Globe and Mail (Toronto). (1998b). ADM Fined $16-million in Price-Fix Case. (May 28).

Goff, C. H., & Reasons, C. E. (1978). *Corporate Crime in Canada*. Scarborough, ON: Prentice-Hall.

Hagan, J. (1989). *Structural Criminology*. New Brunswick, NJ: Rutgers University Press.

Hagan, J., & Nagel, I. (1982). "White Collar Crime, White Collar Time: The Sentencing of White Collar Criminals in the Southern District of New York." *American Criminal Law Review, 20*(2), 259–301.

Hagan, J., and Parker, P. (1985). "White-Collar Crime and Punishment: The Class Structure and Legal Sanctioning of Securities Violations." *American Sociological Review, 50*, 302–316.

Handelman, S. (1989). "Fighting to Put People before Production." *The Toronto Star* (July 16), H1–H2.

Henry, F. (1982). "Capitalism, Capital Accumulation, and Crime." *Crime and Social Justice, 18*, 79–87.

Hilts, P.J. (1989). "Wave of Protests Developing on Profits from AIDS drug." *The New York Times* (September 16), 1.

Hirschi, T. (1969). *Causes of Delinquency*. Berkeley: University of California Press.

Keane, C. (1993). "The Impact of Financial Performance on Frequency of Corporate Crime: A Latent Variable Test of Strain Theory." *Canadian Journal of Criminology, 35*(3), 293–308.

Keane, C. (1995). "Loosely Coupled Systems and Unlawful Behaviour: Organization Theory and Corporate Crime." In F. Pearce and L. Snider, eds., *Corporate Crime: Ethics, Law and the State*. Toronto: University of Toronto Press.

Los, M. (1982). "Crime and Economy in the Communist Countries." In P. Wickman and T. Dailey, eds., *White-Collar and Economic Crime*. Toronto: D.C. Heath and Company.

Merton, R. K. (1938). "Social Structure and Anomie." *American Sociological Review, 3*, 672–682.

Pearce, F., and Tombs, S. (1993). "US Capital versus the Third World: Union Carbide and Bhopal." In F. Pearce and M. Woodiwiss, eds., *Global Crime Connections*: *Dynamics and Control*. Toronto: University of Toronto Press.

Simpson, S. (1986). "The Decomposition of Antitrust: Testing a Multi-Level, Longitudinal Model of Profit-Squeeze." *American Sociological Review, 51*, 859–875.

Snider, D.L. (1982). "Traditional and Corporate Theft: A Comparison of Sanctions." In P. Wickman and T. Dailey, eds., *White-Collar and Economic Crime*. Toronto: D.C. Heath and Company.

Snider, D.L. (1993). *Bad Business*: *Corporate Crime in Canada*. Scarborough: Nelson Canada.

Snider, D.L., and West, W.G. (1985). "A Critical Perspective on Law in the Canadian State: Delinquency and Corporate Crime." In T. Fleming, ed., *The New Criminologies in Canada*: *Crime, State and Control*. Toronto: Oxford University Press.

Sutherland, E.H. (1949). *White Collar Crime*. New York: Holt, Rinehart and Winston.

Sykes, G.M., and Matza, D. (1957). "Techniques of Neutralization: A Theory of Delinquency." *American Sociological Review, 22*, 664–670.

Vandivier, K. (1987). "Why Should My Conscience Bother Me?" In M.D. Ermann and R.J. Lundman, eds., *Corporate and Governmental Deviance*. New York: Oxford University Press.

Chapter 29

Race and Crime: A Critique

JULIAN V. ROBERTS

THOMAS GABOR

Canadian criminologists have been challenged recently by the work of a professor of psychology, Philippe Rushton, who claims to have uncovered evidence of significant interracial differences in many areas of human behaviour, including criminality (Rushton, 1987; 1988; 1989). In January 1987, Professor Rushton delivered a paper at the American Association for the Advancement of Science conference in San Francisco (Rushton, 1987). He proposed a genetically based hierarchy in which Blacks (who supposedly evolved earlier than whites or orientals) were, *inter alia*, less intelligent and law-abiding than whites and orientals. Rushton asserts that there are substantial interracial differences in crime rates, and that these are accounted for by genetic factors. We shall examine later the credibility of genetic explanations of variations in crime rates. First, it is important to address the context of these assertions, and their likely impact upon society.

Rushton's speculations about race and crime have achieved national coverage exceeding that accorded any research project undertaken by criminologists (*The Globe and Mail*, 1989). Part of the reason for this is the aggressive posture adopted by Rushton: he has been interviewed in several newspapers and has appeared on several television programs with national audiences. In contrast, the reaction from criminologists, but not other professional groups (*The Globe and Mail*, 1989), has been

muted. His monopolization of media coverage may, we believe, have had a detrimental impact upon public opinion. It is important, therefore, that criminologists in Canada respond to his statements. While Rushton's claims about racial influences upon intelligence have been challenged, his assertions about crime have not.

THE EFFECT OF RUSHTON'S VIEWS ON PUBLIC THEORIES OF CRIME CAUSATION

The race/crime controversy has important consequences for public opinion in the area of criminal justice. Many of the important questions in the field of criminology — such as the relative deterrent effect of capital punishment — cannot be addressed by experiments. Accordingly, criminologists have used sophisticated correlational procedures to untangle the relative effects on crime of correlated variables such as genetic and environmental factors. The existence of a simple statistic, then, such as the overrepresentation in some crime statistics of certain racial minorities, will by itself convince few scholars. Criminologists have become sensitized to the possibility of alternative explanations for apparently straightforward relationships. Members of the public, however, are not so sophisticated in drawing inferences from statistical information. In fact, a great deal of recent research in social

Source: Excerpted from "Lombrosian Wine in a New Bottle: Research on Crime and Race," *Canadian Journal of Criminology* 32, 2 (April 1990): 291–313. Copyright by the Canadian Criminal Justice Association. Reprinted by permission of the *Canadian Journal of Criminology*.

psychology has documented numerous ways in which the layperson is led into making unjustified inferences from material such as that which appears in newspapers (Fiske and Taylor, 1984; Nisbett and Ross, 1980).

Rushton's theories may affect public opinion in this area for several reasons. First, as already noted, the average layperson may not readily seek alternative (i.e., nongenetic) explanations for the overrepresentation of Blacks in certain types of crime. Second, laypersons are less likely to realize that studies on race and crime are essentially correlational, rather than causal, in nature. Third, the race/crime hypothesis comes from a highly credible source, namely a well-published and tenured university professor. Fourth, it is vital to remember that, to the average member of the public, crime is a relatively unidimensional phenomenon: it usually involves violence, loss of property, and is a consequence of a "criminal disposition." Members of the public tend to regard offenders as a relatively homogeneous group (Roberts and White, 1986) varying somewhat in their actions but not their motivations. Criminologists have long been aware of the deficiencies of this perception of crime; the multidimensional nature of crime and the complexity of motivation render sweeping statements about the etiology of crime invalid. Finally, but not last in importance, some people may be particularly receptive to racial explanations of crime. Thus, views such as those expressed by Professor Rushton may have the unintended effect of inflaming racism in Canada.

Furthermore, Rushton's views received what many laypersons might interpret as substantial support within days of the news media's coverage of his San Francisco address. On February 16, a representative of the Toronto Police Force released statistics showing that Blacks were overrepresented in the crime statistics in the Jane–Finch area of Toronto (*The Toronto Star*, 1989). These data are likely to be misinterpreted by members of the public to constitute evidence supporting a genetic explanation of crime.

For the vast majority of the public, the mass media constitute their primary source of information about crime and criminal justice. Public conceptions of deviance are a consequence of what people read, hear, and see in the media. An abundance of research has demonstrated a direct correspondence between public misperceptions of crime and distorted media coverage of criminal justice issues (Doob and Roberts, 1982). Since criminologists have failed to refute Rushton in the news media, we have also relinquished access to the one means of influencing public opinion on this issue. Criminologists may be highly skeptical of Rushton's opinions in the area of crime, but the only way that this skepticism can affect the public is through coverage in the news media. Once again, we note that while Rushton has been criticized by various behavioural geneticists (such as David Suzuki), his assertions regarding race and crime have remained uncontested.

We believe, therefore, that it is important to address the hypothesis that inherited racial traits affect crime rates. We shall examine some methodological issues relating criminality to race. A comprehensive survey of the literature on this topic would occupy a whole issue of a journal; we can only highlight the research findings and point out what we perceive to be the principal flaws in Rushton's argument. We shall draw upon data from Canada, the United States, and the United Kingdom. Finally, it should be made clear from the outset that we are addressing Rushton's theory as it pertains to the phenomenon of crime. We are not behavioural geneticists, to whom we cede the question of whether the general theory of racial differences withstands scientific scrutiny.

THE SCIENTIFIC ARGUMENT: EMPIRICAL RESEARCH ON RACE AND CRIME

PROBLEMS WITH THE DEFINITION OF RACE

Rushton relates an independent variable (race) to a dependent variable (crime). The interracial comparisons cited by Rushton are predicated on the assumption that people are racially pure. Each racial "category" is held to be homogeneous, but this is now accepted by contemporary anthropologists and biologists to be an antiquated and dangerous myth. Centuries of interbreeding reduce Rushton's rather crude tripartite classification (Black, white, oriental) to the level of caricature. For example, Radzinowicz and King (1977) note that in the United States, close to 50 percent of those classified as Black are over half white by lineage (see also Herskovits, 1930; and, for a study of offenders, Hooton, 1939). Many American whites, as well, have some Black ancestry; Haskell and Yablonsky (1983: 95) note that:

> Estimates of the number of Blacks who have "passed" into the white society run as high as 7 million. In addition to those millions who have introduced an African mixture into the "white" population of the United States in the relatively recent past, there must have been millions of Africans who were assimilated into the population of Spain, Portugal, Italy, Greece, and other Mediterranean countries. Descendants of those people are now part of the "white" population of the United States.

Wolfgang and Cohen (1970) cite data showing that no more than 22 percent of all persons designated as Black, in the United States, were of unmixed ancestry. Fully 15 percent of persons classified as Black were more white than Black (Wolfgang and Cohen, 1970: 7). The pervasiveness of such racial overlap calls genetically based racial theories of crime into question. (For the rest of this article, for convenience only, we shall continue to refer to interracial differences. This does not mean we endorse the racial trichotomy of Blacks, orientals, and whites advanced by Professor Rushton.) Finally, it is important to bear in mind that crime statistics deal with race as a sociological and not a biological category. In short, the independent variable, as it were, is highly problematic. Now we turn to the dependent measure, official and unofficial measures of crime.

THE ISSUE OF OVERREPRESENTATION IN OFFICIAL CRIME STATISTICS

Rushton's evidence for a genetic influence consists of the overrepresentation of Blacks in official statistics of crime in the United States, the United Kingdom, and elsewhere. Specifically he asserts that:

> African descended people, for example, while constituting less than one-eighth of the population of the United States or of London, England, currently account for over 50% of the crimes in both places. Since about the same proportion of victims say their assailant was Black, the arrest statistics cannot really be blamed on police prejudice. (Rushton, 1987: 3)

There are at least two factually incorrect elements here, but first we offer a general comment regarding the issue of overrepresentation.

A simple correlation between two variables does not constitute evidence of a *causal* relationship. A multitude of other confounding factors must be ruled out before one can contemplate a causal relationship. Even if the relationship between race and crime holds up after careful secondary analyses, this is hardly convincing evidence of genetic influences. The fact that parental alcoholism is correlated with alcoholism in the offspring does not prove a genetic component to alcoholism. Alcohol abuse can be a learned behaviour as well. The same argument applies to the race/crime relationship.

Another point is relevant to the issue of a disproportionate involvement in crime. Virtually every society contains racial and ethnic groups, usually minorities, who are more criminally active in certain crimes than the rest of the population. According to Rushton's theory of criminal behaviour, Native Canadians should display lower, not higher, crime rates than the non-Native population. Unfortunately for the theory, this is not true. The overrepresentation of Native offenders in the criminal justice statistics has been apparent for some time (Griffiths and Verdun-Jones, 1989; LaPrairie, 1989). Explanations in terms of the social strata in our society occupied by indigenous peoples can easily explain these findings; Rushton's racial theory cannot. According to Rushton's typology this group, being oriental or mongoloid, should display lower, not higher, rates of criminality.

According to Rushton's genetic explanation of crime, the crime rates for Blacks should be higher than the white crime rates, *and* the rates for Native Canadians should be *lower* than the non-Native population. The two categories (Blacks and Native people) are genetically dissimilar; their rates of criminality should reflect this difference (relative to the white population). The fact is that both Black Americans and Native Canadians share an elevated risk of certain kinds of criminality (relative to the comparable white populations in their respective countries). Such an outcome is, of course, perfectly consistent with a sociological explanation: both minority groups share a protracted history of constrained social opportunity, as well as overt discrimination.

Also in Canada, French Canadians are the most active in the crime of robbery (Gabor et al., 1987). In England, Irish immigrants have been overrepresented in crimes of assault for years (Radzinowicz and King, 1977). In Israel, the Arab population and non-European Jews are more criminally active in conventional crimes than the European Jews (Fishman, Rattner, and Weimann, 1987). Such overrepresentation, then, is the rule rather than the exception across different societies.

To return to Rushton's suggestion, two errors can be identified. First, he cites data published in the *Daily Telegraph* (a British newspaper) showing that Blacks account for over 50 percent of the crimes in the United States and the United Kingdom (Rushton, 1988). By any measure, this is a considerable exaggeration. If he refers to all reported crimes and not merely index crimes, Blacks account for about 29 percent of all persons charged in the United States (United States Department of Justice, 1989). Index crimes are those included in official crime indices; they exclude many white-collar crimes, for example.

As well, aggregate statistics based on index crimes alone misrepresent the true picture. Crime is not, as suggested by Rushton's publications, a homogeneous category of behaviours. While Blacks in the United States account for over 60 percent of arrests for robbery and almost 50 percent of arrests for murder, they account for about 30 percent of arrests for burglary and theft, less than 24 percent of those arrested for arson and about 20 percent of those arrested for vandalism (United States Department of Justice, 1987). Using Rushton's own data, Blacks are underrepresented in crimes like tax fraud and securities violations. In fact, arrest statistics for white-collar crimes such as fraud and embezzlement are significantly higher for whites. Treating crime as a unitary phenomenon obscures this diversity. These variations reflect differential opportunities for offending, and not, we submit, offence-specific genetic programming.

Differential Treatment of Blacks by the Criminal Justice System

Finally, arrest statistics reflect, to a degree, the more rigorous surveillance by police to which minorities are subject. Data on this point are hard to obtain; the magnitude of the problem is hard to quantify. Nevertheless, the recent release of the "Guildford Four" in England, after fifteen years of imprisonment following a wrongful conviction based upon fabricated police evidence, reveals the dangers posed to minorities by an overzealous police force.

Research in the United States sustains the view that the police are more likely to arrest and charge Blacks (Black and Reiss, 1967; Lundman, Sykes, and Clark, 1978). Wolfgang and Cohen (1970: 71) summarize some of this research:

> In comparing arrest statistics for Blacks and whites, it is important to remember, then, that one reason for the high arrest rates among Blacks is that they are more likely to be stopped, picked up on suspicion and subsequently arrested.

Furthermore, the bias does not remain at the police station: British data (Landau, 1981; Landau and Nathan, 1983) show that prosecution is more likely for persons of Afro-Caribbean origin. Bias persists at most critical stages of the criminal justice process. As Paul Gordon (1988: 309) noted, summarizing data on the issue:

> Black people's experience of the British criminal justice system shows clearly that the rhetoric of the law does not accord with the reality of its practice. The law is not colour-blind, but a means by which Black people have been subject to a process of criminalization.

Most recently, Albonetti and her colleagues (1989) have demonstrated that while the influence of race upon pretrial decisions is complicated, white suspects have the edge over Black suspects.

To summarize the data on contact with the criminal justice process, American Blacks are clearly overrepresented in violent crime statistics, slightly overrepresented in property crimes, and underrepresented in white-collar crimes. In order to explain this diverse pattern, one has to strain the genetic explanation beyond the breaking point. Are Blacks genetically predisposed toward street crimes while whites are programmed to commit white-collar crimes? A far more plausible explanation exists: social groups commit crimes as a consequence of their social situations and in response to prevailing criminal opportunities. This environmental perspective explains more findings and requires fewer assumptions. The law of parsimony, then, clearly favours environmental over genetic theories of crime. In short, Rushton's explanation of crime by reference to genetic influences requires acceptance of the position that specific antisocial behaviours are directly related to genetic structure. Modern behavioural geneticists would undoubtedly reject this view.

OVERREPRESENTATION AND ALTERNATIVE SOURCES OF CRIME STATISTICS: VICTIMIZATION SURVEYS AND SELF-REPORTED CRIMINALITY

There is convincing evidence that arrest data exaggerate the true incidence of Black criminality. Two alternative sources of information on crime make this clear. Overall, FBI data indicate

that 46.5 percent of all violent crimes reported to the police are committed by Blacks. However, the victimization survey conducted by the U.S. Department of Justice found that Blacks account for only about 24 percent of violent crimes (United States Department of Justice, 1986). Which source presents a more accurate picture of crimes actually committed? With regard to crimes of violence, data derived from victims would appear to be more accurate than arrest data. But it is not just victimization surveys that cast doubt upon the official statistics. A third source of information on crime patterns also shows discrepancies. Rojek (1983) compared police reports with self-reports of delinquency. In the police database, race was a significant factor in several offence categories, but this was not true for the self-reports. Other studies using the self-report approach (Williams and Gold, 1972) have found a similar pattern: no difference between Black and white respondents (Pope, 1979) or only slight differences (Hirschi, 1969).

Unreported versus Reported Crime

Another explanation for the elevated incidence of Black offenders in official crime statistics concerns the issue of unreported crimes. As we have noted, official crime data indicate that Blacks are more likely than whites to commit certain crimes (personal injury offences) and less likely than whites to commit other types of crimes. The problem with crime statistics is that the reporting rate is highly variable, depending upon the offence. The types of offences committed by Blacks are more likely to be reported than the offences committed by whites. Any examination of aggregate crime statistics is going to overestimate the true incidence of crime committed by Blacks relative to the amount of crime committed by whites.

To conclude, the extent of overrepresentation of Blacks, even in those offences where it occurs, has been exaggerated. In perhaps the most comprehensive study to date which relates crime to race, Michael Hindelang (1982) tested various theories that attempted to explain interracial differences. He concluded that the theories of delinquency that best explain the patterns of data were sociological rather than biological. These included Merton's reformulation of anomie theory (Merton, 1968), Cloward and Ohlin's opportunity theory (Cloward and Ohlin, 1960), and Wolfgang's subculture of violence theory (Wolfgang and Ferracuti, 1982).

A final word on the crime statistics utilized by Rushton consists of a caveat: recorded crime is exactly that: it is only a small fraction of all reported and unreported crime. A recent article by Tony Jefferson (1988: 535) makes the point succinctly:

> We do not *know* what the real rate of Black crime is, nor whether it is on the increase. Take robbery for instance. The British Crime Survey reveals that only 8% of robberies were recorded. If those figures applied to London this would mean that there is a suspect for only 1 in 100 robberies. The comparable figure for burglaries would be 5 in 100. This means that *whatever* the arrest figures, and whatever the victim identifications, the "unknown" element is so great, especially for those crimes where Black "over-representation" is seen as greatest, as to make all estimates of Black offending strictly conjectural.

When there is sound reason to suppose that the police are more vigilant with regard to Black suspects and offenders, it is clear that if we were able to replace reported with unreported crime rates, the interracial differences would diminish still further.

Self-report studies provide insight in another area as well. While Professor Rushton associates "lawlessness" with being Black, there is overwhelming evidence indicating that most people, at one point or another, commit acts for which they could be prosecuted. As an example, in a now classic study, Wallerstein and Wyle (1947) surveyed 1700 New York City residents without a criminal record. Fully 99 percent admitted to involvement in at least one of 49 offences. This evidence suggests that rule breaking is normal activity on the part of most citizens in Western societies. The selection of norm violators to be prosecuted therefore is critical to an understanding of who becomes officially classified as a criminal. Many observers of the criminal justice system believe that race may be a key factor affecting that selection process. Another classic study, Hartshorne and May's (1928) investigation of children, also showed that dishonesty was both pervasive and situation-specific. There was little cross-situational consistency: children that were dishonest in one situation were honest in others. This emphasis on the social situation as the determinant of behaviour is consistent with an environmental view of crime, and inconsistent with Rushton's genetic theory. (A large body of evidence, drawn from longitudinal, self-report, experimental, and observational research, suggests that law breaking is widespread in North American society.)

WITHIN RACE COMPARISONS

Comparisons over Time

In the next two sections, we examine variation in crime rates within race, but across time and cultures. If genetic factors have an important impact upon crime, rates should be relatively stable within race, across both time and cultures. This, however, is not the case. Further undermining Rushton's thesis are the temporal and cross-cultural variations in crime patterns for the Black population. Street crime by Blacks in the United Kingdom has only recently increased significantly. Just over a decade ago, Radzinowicz and King (1977) were able to write that, with the exception of prostitution and other victimless crimes, the Black community was as law abiding as other Britons. Any increase in crime rates within a generation obviously cannot be attributed to genetic factors. This point was made recently by Anthony Mawson (1989) in the context of explanations of homicide in terms of

Darwinian selection (Daly and Wilson, 1988). Mawson (1989: 239) notes the inability of biological explanations of homicide to account for fluctuations in homicide rates over a short period of time:

> Thus, it seems doubtful whether a selectionist explanation can be applied to changing homicide rates, even those occurring over a thousand years.

The same argument applies in the context of Rushton's work: increases in offending by Blacks over a period of ten to fifteen years cannot possibly be explained by reference to genetic influence.

In the United States as well, the proportional involvement of Blacks in crime has risen over the past few decades. One major factor in this rise has been the proliferation of illicit drug usage. Heroin use became pervasive in the 1950s, and "crack" cocaine is creating an explosion of violent crime in this decade. As well, the erosion of taboos relating to interracial crimes has been associated with increased victimization of whites by Blacks (Silberman, 1978). A third major development has been the greater accessibility of firearms. These are three potent environmental factors affecting Black criminality. One would be hard-pressed to find a genetic explanation for the changing criminal activity pattern of a race over such a short period of time.

Comparisons across Jurisdictions

The variations in Black, white, and oriental crime from one society to another also demonstrate the potency of environmental factors in the etiology of crime. Levels of violent crime in the American South are greater for both Blacks *and* whites than they are in other parts of the country. As well, there is substantial variation in the homicide rates for Blacks in different American states. For example, in Delaware the homicide rate for Blacks is 16.7 per 100 000. This is considerably lower than the homicide rate for Black residents of other states; in Missouri, for example, the rate is 65 per 100 000 (Carroll and Mercy, 1989).

Cross-national, within-race comparisons make the same point. Black Americans have a higher homicide rate than their more racially pure counterparts in Africa: this fact directly contradicts Rushton's thesis. The author (Bohannan, 1960: 123) of a study of African homicide concludes:

> if it needed stressing, here is overwhelming evidence that it is a cultural and not biological factor which makes for a high homicide rate among American negroes.

More recent data (International Criminal Police Organization, 1988) demonstrate the same variations: the homicide rate per 100 000 inhabitants varies from .01 (Mali) to 29 (Bahamas) and 22.05 (Jamaica). It is noteworthy also that the Caribbean homicide rates are far in excess of even the African countries with the highest rates (e.g., Rwanda, 11 per 100 000; Tanzania, 8 per 100 000). This despite the fact that residents of the Caribbean are more racially mixed than Blacks from Africa. According to Rushton's theory, homicide rates should be higher not lower in the more racially pure African states.

Furthermore, orientals do not constitute a monolith of law-abiding citizens. The homicide rates in the Far East also vary considerably, from 39 per 100 000 residents in the Philippines to 1.3 per 100 000 in Hong Kong. In Thailand, the homicide rate exceeds the rate of homicide in Japan by a factor of twelve (International Criminal Police Organization, 1988). In all these comparisons, the genetic explanation falls short. The magnitude of these intraracial differences suggests that the potency of environmental factors to explain crime rates far exceeds that of genetic factors. In statistical terms, these data imply that the percentage of variation in crime rates explained by genetic factors is negligible, if it exists at all.

VICTIMIZATION PATTERNS

There is another form of overrepresentation of which Professor Rushton appears unaware: Blacks are at much higher risk of becoming the victims of violent crime. In the United States, Black males are 20 times more likely than whites to be shot, cut, or stabbed, and Black females are 18 times more likely to be raped than white women (Wolfgang and Cohen, 1981). Black Americans are also more likely than whites to be victims of burglary, motor vehicle theft, assault, robbery, and many other offences (United States Department of Justice, 1983). Although Blacks constitute only 12 percent of the general United States population, over 40 percent of homicide victims are Black. See Barnett and Schwartz (1989) for recent data showing Black victimization rates to be approximately four times higher than white rates. The same trends are apparent in other countries, such as England. The overrepresentation of Blacks as victims is substantial, yet no one has posited that such overrepresentation is due to a genetically based susceptibility to criminal victimization. While this finding is not inconsistent with an explanation based upon genetic factors, it does underscore the importance of environmental factors such as propinquity and accessibility. Violent crimes are a result of an interaction between offender and victim. To posit an overriding genetic basis of crime is to ignore the role of the victim and situational factors (Boyd, 1988; Wolfgang, 1958). When we examine the dynamics of the violent crime most commonly associated with Blacks — armed robbery — we readily see the importance of situational determinants. Actually, recourse to physical violence occurs only in a small minority of robberies. Usually the violence that does occur arises in response to victims who resist the robbers' demands (Gabor et al., 1987). The violence, therefore, is often instrumental and situation-specific.

If Blacks are more likely to be both offenders and victims in relation to certain types of crime, then a plausible explanation for their overrepresentation on both counts is that they tend to live in areas in which violence is a normal consequence of stress, threat, and frustration. This essentially is Wolfgang and Ferracuti's (1982) subculture of violence thesis. Aside from living in environments where violence is normative behaviour, Blacks tend disproportionately to live in poverty. Furthermore, they are overrepresented among urban dwellers. Economic status and urban residence are linked to a number of crime indices. A fair examination of Black and white criminality would therefore necessitate comparison between persons situated similarly in society.

But even the presence of a correlation between race and certain indices of crime, after other plausible environmental factors have been pointed out, does not demonstrate a genetically based race/crime link. As Charles Silberman (1978) has pointed out, the experience of Black Americans has been very different from the experience of any other disadvantaged group. The generations of violence, deprivation, disenfranchisement, and exclusion from educational and vocational opportunities to which they have been subjected has not been shared by any other ethnic or racial group. Moreover, much of this racial discrimination persists, to this day, and in this country, as recent research has documented (Henry and Ginzberg, 1985). Discrimination of this kind can engender social patterns and attitudes toward authority that lead to law breaking.

Careful epidemiological research can result in samples of Black and white citizens that are "matched" on many important background variables such as social class, income, education, age, and family size and composition. Comparison between such groups is preferable to comparison based upon unmatched samples, but the effects of long-term discrimination, brutality, and oppression over generations cannot be captured by the most rigorous multiple regression analysis. As John Conklin (1989: 140) notes:

to argue that Blacks and whites of similar backgrounds will have the same crime rate is to argue that centuries of discrimination have had no long-term effects on Blacks that are conducive to criminal behavior.

Our opposition to Rushton's views should not be interpreted to mean that we deny the existence of any genetic influences upon human behaviour. Rather, we take issue with the attribution of racial differences in criminality to genetic factors. In our view, there is little scientific basis for his rather sweeping assertions about the relative "law-abidingness" of different racial groups. The few statistics he provides are susceptible to a multitude of highly probable alternative explanations derived from an environmental perspective. Given the incendiary nature of the theory and its policy implications, we feel that the burden of proof is upon Professor Rushton to provide more convincing data than the few ambiguous statistics he has to date brought forth. We leave it to others (Lynn, 1989; Zuckerman and Brody, 1989) to evaluate the scientific credibility of Professor Rushton's genetic explanation of other phenomena such as: intelligence, sexual restraint, personality, political preferences, and the efficacy of the German army in the Second World War (*The Globe and Mail*, 1989). In the area of criminality, his evidence, in our view, falls short of discharging a scientific burden of proof.

NOTE

The authors would like to acknowledge that this manuscript has benefited from the comments of Michael Petrunik, from the University of Ottawa, the editorial committee of the *Canadian Journal of Criminology*, and two anonymous reviewers.

REFERENCES

Albonetti, Celesta, Robert Hauser, John Hagan, and Ilene Nagel. 1989. "Criminal justice decision making as a stratification process: The role of race and stratification resources in pre-trial release." *Journal of Quantitative Criminology* 5: 57–82.

Barnett, Arnold and Elliot Schwartz. 1989. "Urban homicide: Still the same." *Journal of Quantitative Criminology* 5: 83–100.

Black, D. and Albert Reiss. 1967. *Studies of Crime and Law Enforcement in Major Metropolitan Areas.* Washington, DC: Government Printing Office.

Bohannan, Paul. 1960. *African Homicide and Suicide.* Princeton, NJ: Princeton University Press.

Bonger, Willem. 1969. *Race and Crime.* New Jersey: Patterson Smith. (Originally published 1943).

Boyd, Neil. 1988. *The Last Dance: Murder in Canada.* Toronto: Prentice-Hall.

Carroll, Patrick and James Mercy. 1989. "Regional variation in homicide rates: Why is the west violent?" *Violence and Victims* 4: 17–25.

Cloward, Richard A. and Lloyd Ohlin. 1960. *Delinquency and Opportunity: A Theory of Delinquent Gangs.* New York: Free Press.

Conklin, John. 1989. *Criminology.* (Third edition) New York: Macmillan.

Curie, Elliot. 1985. *Confronting Crime.* New York: Pantheon.

Daly, Martin and Margo Wilson. 1988. *Homicide.* New York: Aldine.

Doob, Anthony N. and Julian V. Roberts. 1982. *Crime: Some Views of the Canadian Public.* Ottawa: Department of Justice.

Fishman, G., Arye Rattner, and Gabriel Weimann. 1987. "The effect of ethnicity on crime attribution." *Criminology* 25: 507–24.

Fiske, Susan T. and Shelley E. Taylor. 1984. *Social Cognition.* Reading, MA: Addison-Wesley.

Gabor, Thomas. 1991. "Crime by the public." In Curt Griffiths and Margaret Jackson, eds., *Canadian Criminology: Perspectives on Crime and Criminality.* Toronto: Harcourt Brace Jovanovich.

Gabor, Thomas, Micheline Baril, M. Cusson, D. Elie, Marc LeBlanc, and André Normandeau.

1987. *Armed Robbery: Cops, Robbers, and Victims*. Springfield, Ill.: Charles C. Thomas.

The Globe and Mail. 1989. February 11: 14.

Gordon, Paul. 1988. "Black people and the criminal law: Rhetoric and reality." *International Journal of the Sociology of Law* 16: 295–313.

Gould, Stephen Jay. 1981. *The Mismeasure of Man*. New York: W.W. Norton.

Griffiths, Curt and Simon Verdun-Jones. 1989. *Canadian Criminal Justice*. Toronto: Butterworths.

Hartshorne, M. and M.A. May. 1928. *Studies in Deceit*. New York: Macmillan.

Haskell, M.R. and L. Yablonsky. 1983. *Criminology: Crime and Criminality*. Boston: Houghton Mifflin.

Henry, F. and E. Ginzberg. 1985. *Who Gets the Work: A Test of Racial Discrimination in Employment*. Toronto: Urban Alliance on Race Relations and the Social Planning Council.

Herskovits, Melville J. 1930. *The Anthropometry of the American Negro*. New York: Columbia University Press.

Hindelang, Michael. 1982. "Race and Crime." In Leonard D. Savitz and N. Johnston, eds., *Contemporary Criminology*. Toronto: John Wiley.

Hirschi, Travis. 1969. *Causes of Delinquency*. Berkeley: University of California Press.

Hooton, Ernest A. 1939. *Crime and the Man*. Cambridge: Harvard University Press.

International Criminal Police Organization. 1988. *International Crime Statistics* 1985–86.

Jefferson, Tony. 1988. "Race, crime and policing: Empirical, theoretical and methodological issues." *International Journal of the Sociology of Law* 16: 521–39.

Landau, Simha. 1981. "Juveniles and the police." *British Journal of Criminology* 21: 27–46.

Landau, Simha and G. Nathan. 1983. "Selecting delinquents for cautioning in the London metropolitan area." *British Journal of Criminology* 28: 128–49.

LaPrairie, Carol. 1989. *The Role of Sentencing in the Over-Representation of Aboriginal People in Correctional Institutions*. Ottawa: Department of Justice.

Lombroso, Cesare. 1968. *Crime: Its Causes and Remedies*. (English edition) Montclair, NJ: Patterson Smith. (Original publication: *Le Crime, causes et remèdes*, 1899).

Lombroso-Ferrero, Gina. 1972. *Criminal Man According to the Classification of Cesare Lombroso*. Montclair, NJ: Patterson Smith, 1972 (Originally published 1911).

Lundman, R., R. Sykes and J. Clark. 1978. "Police control of juveniles: A replication." *Journal of Research in Crime and Delinquency* 15: 74–91.

Lynn, Michael. 1989. "Race difference in sexual behaviour: A critique of Rushton and Bogaert's evolutionary hypothesis." *Journal of Research in Personality* 23: 1–6.

Mawson, Anthony. 1989. "Review of *Homicide*" (Daly and Wilson, 1988). *Contemporary Sociology* March: 238–40.

Merton, Robert K. 1968. *Social Theory and Social Structure*. Glencoe: Free Press.

Nisbett, Richard and Lee Ross. 1980. *Human Inference: Strategies and Shortcomings of Social Judgement*. Englewood Cliffs, NJ: Prentice-Hall.

Pope, Carl E. 1979. "Race and crime revisited." *Crime and Delinquency* 25: 345–57.

Radzinowicz, Leon and Joan King. 1977. *The Growth of Crime: The International Experience*. London: Penguin.

Roberts, Julian V. and Nicholas R. White. 1986. "Public estimates of recidivism rates: Consequences of a criminal stereotype." *Canadian Journal of Criminology* 28: 229–41.

Rojek, Dean G. 1983. "Social status and delinquency: Do self-reports and official reports match?" In Gordon P. Waldo, ed., *Measurement Issues in Criminal Justice*. Beverly Hills: Sage.

Rushton, J. Philippe. 1987. "Population differences in rule-following behaviour: Race, evolution and crime." Paper presented to the

39th Annual Meeting of the American Society of Criminology, Montreal, November 11–14.

———. 1988. "Race differences in behaviour: A review and evolutionary analysis." *Personality and Individual Differences* 9: 1009–24.

———. 1989. "Race differences in sexuality and their correlates: Another look at physiological models." *Journal of Research in Personality* 23: 35–54.

Silberman, Charles. 1978. *Criminal Violence, Criminal Justice*. New York: Vintage.

The Toronto Star. 1989. February 17: 20.

United States Department of Justice. 1983. *Sourcebook of Criminal Justice Statistics*. Washington, DC: Bureau of Justice Statistics.

———. 1986. *Criminal Victimization in the United States*. Washington, DC: Bureau of Justice Statistics.

———. 1987. *Sourcebook of Criminal Justice Statistics*. Washington, DC: Bureau of Justice Statistics.

———. 1989. *Sourcebook of Criminal Justice Statistics*. Washington, DC: Bureau of Justice Statistics.

Wallerstein, James S. and Clement J. Wyle. 1947. "Our law-abiding lawbreakers." *Probation* 25: 107–12.

Williams, Jay and Martin Gold. 1972. "From delinquent behaviour to official delinquency." *Social Problems* 20: 209–29.

Wolfgang, Marvin. 1958. *Patterns in Criminal Homicide*. Philadelphia: University of Pennsylvania Press.

Wolfgang, Marvin and Bernard Cohen. 1970. *Crime and Race: Conceptions and Misconceptions*. New York: Institute of Human Relations Press.

———. 1981. "Crime and race: The victims of crime." In Burt Galaway and Joe Hudson, eds., *Perspectives on Crime Victims*. St. Louis: C.V. Mosby.

Wolfgang, Marvin and Franco Ferracuti. 1982. *The Subculture of Violence*. Beverly Hills: Sage.

Zuckerman, Marvin and Nathan Brody. 1989. "Oysters, rabbits and people: A critique of 'race differences in behaviour' by J.P. Rushton." *Personality and Individual Differences* 9: 1025–33.

PART 6

GLOBAL DEVELOPMENT AND THE ENVIRONMENT

The industrial revolution began in Britain in the 1780s. For the next 200 years, nature seemed exploitable without limit, a thing to be subdued and dominated in the name of economic progress and human development. In the last few decades, however, circumstances have forced a growing number of people to recognize that industrial-era attitudes towards nature are not just naive, but arrogant and foolhardy. Consider the following examples:

- Since the industrial revolution, humans have been using increasing quantities of fossil fuels (coal, oil, gasoline, etc.). When burned, they release carbon dioxide into the atmosphere. The accumulation of carbon dioxide allows more solar radiation to enter the atmosphere and less solar radiation to escape. The result of this "greenhouse effect" is global warming and potentially catastrophic climactic change, including the partial melting of the polar ice caps and the flooding of heavily populated coastal regions.

- Various gaseous compounds widely used in industry and by consumers are burning a hole in the atmosphere's ozone layer. Ozone is a form of oxygen that blocks ultraviolet radiation from the sun. Let more ultraviolet radiation reach ground level and, as we are now witnessing, rates of skin cancer and crop damage increase.

- The world's forests help to clean the air since photosynthesis uses up carbon dioxide and produces oxygen. The tropical rain forests contain a large and variegated plant life that is an important source of new drugs. The rain forests also produce moisture, which is carried by wind currents to other parts of the globe and falls as rain. Despite the enormously important role the forests play, however, they are being rapidly depleted as a result of strip mining, the construction of huge pulp and paper mills and hydro-electric projects, and the deforestation of land by farmers and cattle grazers.

- A huge fleet of trawlers belonging to the highly industrialized countries has been equipped with sonar to help locate large concentrations of fish. Some of these ships use fine mesh nets to increase their catch. They have been enormously "successful." Fish stocks in some areas of the world, such as cod off the coast of Newfoundland, have been greatly depleted, devastating fishing communities and endangering one of the world's most important sources of protein.

- A wide range of toxic gases and liquids enters the environment as a result of industrial production, often with devastating consequences. For example, sulphur dioxide and other gases emitted by coal-burning power plants, pulp and paper mills, and motor-vehicle exhaust help to form an acid in the atmosphere that rains down on the earth, destroying forests and lakes.

Canada is one of the world's big polluters. For example, while the United States, Australia, Norway, and Iceland produce more carbon dioxide per capita than anyone else, Canada is in the second tier of greenhouse gas emitters along with Russia, Japan, and the Eastern European countries. Similarly, of the 60 states and provinces in the United States and Canada, Ontario ranks fourth (behind Ohio, Texas, and Pennsylvania) in its total release of industrial chemicals into the environment. However, exposure to environmental risk is not evenly distributed across the Canadian population. Thus, as Maude Barlow and Elizabeth May show in Chapter 30, there is a disturbing pattern of **environmental racism** in the distribution of toxic waste in Canada. Toxic waste sites are more likely to be found near communities with a high proportion of Aboriginal and poor people. (In the United States, Black and Hispanic people are also more likely to live near toxic waste sites.) Barlow and May also show that the Canadian government has been slow to clean up toxic waste sites, partly because of political pressure from industry, and partly because the free trade agreement with the United States has eroded some of Canada's capacity to act in this regard.

Environmental degradation is one of the major problems confronting humanity. A related problem of equal magnitude is rapid population growth, which puts enormous strains on the earth's resources. From a demographic point of view, the less industrialized countries are now in the position that Europe and North America were in 200 years ago. Their populations are growing rapidly because people are living longer yet women's birth rates remain high. As a result, by 2100 the less developed countries are expected to increase their share of world population to 86 percent of the total.

The US Census Bureau expects the 6.4 billion inhabitants of the planet in 2004 to multiply to 9.1 billion by 2050. Yet demographers are pretty confident that world population will level off sometime between 2070 and 2100, reaching its peak at about 10.2 billion people. Two main factors are causing the rate of world population growth to fall: economic development and the emancipation of women. Agricultural societies need many children to help with farming, but industrial societies require fewer children. Since many developing countries are industrializing, the rate of world population growth is falling apace. The second main factor responsible for this decline is the improving economic status and education of women. Once women enter the non-agricultural paid labour force, they quickly recognize the advantages of having few children. The birth rate plummets. In many developing countries, this is precisely what is taking place.

In other developing countries the position of women is far less satisfactory. This can be seen most clearly by examining the ratio of women to men (the **sex ratio**). In Canada in 2000, the sex ratio was about 1.02. That is, there were 102 women for every 100 men. This is a little on the low side for a highly developed country but still in the same ballpark. (The sex ratio for the United States was 1.03 and for Germany and Japan, 1.04). The "surplus" of women reflects the fact that men are more likely than women to be employed in health-threatening occupations, consume more cigarettes and alcohol, and engage in riskier and more violent behaviour, while women are the hardier sex biologically speaking.

In the world as a whole, the picture is reversed. There were just 98 women for every 100 men in 2000, while in India and China there were only 94 women for every 100 men. What accounts for this variation? According to Amartya Sen in Chapter 31, the sex ratio is low where women have less access to health services, medicine, and adequate nutrition than do men. In highly developed countries, women and men have approximately equal access to health services, medicine, and adequate nutrition, so there are about 103 women for every 100 men. By this standard, the world as a whole is "missing" about 5 women for every 100 men (since 103 – 98 = 5). This works out to about 100 million women missing in 2000 due to unequal access to resources of the most basic sort. Although there are big variations within regions, which Sen discusses, Asia and North Africa are the regions that suffer most from a deficit of women due to high levels of gender inequality.[1]

---

1. My sex ratios differ somewhat from Sen's because his data are about 15 years older. Note, however, that the number of "missing women" remained constant at about 100 million between 1985 and 2000 despite a nearly 25 percent increase in world population. The number of missing women did not increase because the sex ratio in the highly developed countries fell while the sex ratio in the less developed countries rose. The latter trend reflects an improvement in women's relative position in society, while the former trend results from a disproportionately large number of men ceasing health-threatening practices, such as working in dangerous industries and smoking tobacco.

Amartya Sen has argued elsewhere that human development is really about increasing our freedom — freedom from want and oppression, freedom of expression and assembly, freedom to work and to elect governments, and so on. From this point of view, gender inequality is a measure of lack of freedom insofar as it restricts the access of women to resources that would make them as free as men are. In *Human Development Report 2002*, a section of which is reprinted here as Chapter 32, United Nations researchers adopt Sen's argument. They then document trends around the world in democratization, the protection of human rights, freedom of the press, women's education, poverty, environmental protection, and other indicators of human development. While they find progress is many areas, they find grotesque disparities in others. They then outline a set of achievable development targets for the year 2015.

Many of the UN's development targets require sacrifice and cooperation on the part of the world's rich countries. Substantially increasing foreign aid to countries that can monitor and use it effectively, cancelling the debt of the poorest countries, reducing the emission of greenhouse gases and other toxic substances, allowing developing countries to override patents and manufacture generic drugs for the fight against HIV/AIDS — these and other actions outlined by the UN could do much to promote human development worldwide. They would also cost taxpayers in Canada and other rich countries a lot of money.

It is unclear whether we are willing to pay. One thing is, however, crystal clear. If people continue to think of themselves only as members of a particular nation, class, or race, and not as part of humanity as a whole, the UN recommendations are likely to fall on deaf ears. In that event, many citizens of the privileged countries will believe that it is in their self-interest to cut aid to the less industrialized countries, to use just as many scarce resources as they wish to and can afford, and to object to the imposition of high environmental taxes on fossil fuels. They will be blind to the fact that such a narrow definition of self-interest may devastate humanity.

Much now seems to depend on whether we will be able to think and act as members of a single human group whose members share a common interest in survival. If we fail to take such a global view, if we insist instead on fighting to protect our narrow group privileges rather than humanity's general interest, we may not go the way of the dinosaurs, but future generations will likely suffer an existence that is nastier, more brutish, and shorter than that which we now enjoy.

GLOSSARY

Environmental racism is the unequal distribution of environmental risk by race.
The **sex ratio** is the ratio of women to men in a society.

CRITICAL THINKING QUESTIONS

1. On what grounds do Barlow and May contend that Canada practises environmental racism?
2. Explain what Sen means when he writes that 100 million women are missing.
3. Sen argues that purely cultural and purely economic arguments fail to explain variations in the sex ratio worldwide. Explain his reasoning.
4. How does the UN define human development?
5. Do you think the UN development targets for 2015 are politically achievable? Why or why not?

ANNOTATED BIBLIOGRAPHY

Benjamin R. Barber, *Jihad vs. McWorld: How Globalism and Tribalism Are Reshaping the World* (New York: Ballantine, 1996). The central conflict of our times is incisively analyzed in this heralded work.

Lester R. Brown et al., *State of the World 2004* (New York. W.W. Norton, 2004). In this definitive and widely acclaimed annual, the authors give up-to-the-minute details on the world's environmental crisis and its political, economic, and social ramifications.

Eric Hobsbawm, *Age of Extremes: The Short Twentieth Century, 1914–1991* (London: Abacus, 1994). It's long, it's opinionated, and it's a masterpiece by one of the world's greatest historians. Magnificently expands one's understanding of global twentieth-century development.

Chapter 30

Industrial Pollution in Canada

MAUDE BARLOW

ELIZABETH MAY

We have the arsenic, we have the naphthalene, we have the lead.
The ground is poison, the air turns your lungs raw, now there is
orange goo oozing across the cellar.
Welcome to Sydney.
— Debbie Ouellette, Frederick Street resident

Spring 1998 was unusually warm. Juanita McKenzie had driven home from work one balmy evening and remembers how pleasant it was after a harsh winter to shed her heavy winter wools for a light spring coat. She pulled up in front of her Frederick Street home in Sydney, Nova Scotia, and stepped out of the car. Across the street, she saw a scene out of a grade B science fiction movie. Behind her neighbour Debbie Ouellette's house, two men, dressed in sealed white E.T.-type environmental hazard suits, complete with breathing apparatus, were posting a sign that read Human Health Hazard. Juanita McKenzie looked down at her cotton shirt and pants and asked herself, "Am I underdressed?"

For months, Juanita, Debbie and their families had been sick with every kind of ailment they could imagine and some they couldn't. Kidney infections, nosebleeds, nausea, diarrhea, headaches, tingling joints, ear infections, bloody stools, bloody urine and severe coughs were sweeping through the families that lived in the 17 homes of Frederick Street. All the dogs had died, one after it had literally glowed in the dark.

Deformed mice, with batlike heads and kangaroo-like feet, had appeared. Lilacs and roses had bloomed pitch black and then disintegrated. One day in early May, when Debbie Ouellette was cleaning up her backyard, she noticed a bright yellow goo seeping out of the embankment directly behind her house and fluorescent orange chemicals lighting up the creek that runs through her property. Juanita and Debbie were terrified.

Perhaps, they now think, they shouldn't have been surprised. Residents of Frederick and nearby Tupper streets, and Lingan Road as well, had been dying of cancer in disproportionate numbers for years. Cancer was their uninvited, dreaded and constant companion.

For their homes border the worst toxic site in Canada and arguably the worst in North America. Behind Debbie Ouellette's house is a 3-metre-high chain-link fence surrounding the 50-hectare heavily contaminated coke ovens site that drains to the infamous Sydney tar ponds, the toxic legacy of 100 years of steel-making. The coke ovens site, polluted to depths of 24 metres, contains uncalculated amounts of deadly

PAHs (polycyclic aromatic hydrocarbons, the largest group of cancer-causing chemicals in the world) and heavy toxic metals. The estuary contains 700,000 tons of toxic sludge, a witch's brew of carcinogenic chemicals 35 times worse than New York's infamous Love Canal, Hooker Chemical's abandoned toxic site upon which a housing subdivision was built. For years, the residents of Frederick Street lived with their fears and the unconfirmed risks to their health.

But suddenly everything seemed immeasurably worse. When Environment Canada officials confirmed that the backyard soil and brook running behind the homes contained arsenic and other deadly chemicals in concentrations many times over the allowable limit, the women knew that they and their children were in mortal danger. "My heart hit the floor," says Juanita.

ENVIRONMENTAL RACISM

When we look more closely at pollution of neighbourhoods in Canada and the United States a common theme emerges. Deadly toxic waste sites are more likely to be found near First Nations communities, or near non–First Nations communities of poorer people, people of colour and politically marginalized people. This phenomenon has been given a name: "environmental racism."

In the United States, the Environmental Protection Agency has created a large environmental justice program to address the problem. The statistics are overwhelming: more poor people, aboriginals and people of colour have their health compromised by pollution than wealthier, white communities. Sydney residents are right in believing that the conditions in which they live would not be tolerated in Toronto or Vancouver. There is no mystery about this reality — communities like Rosedale in Toronto, Rockcliffe Park in Ottawa, Westmount in Montreal or Shaughnessy in Vancouver are simply not threatened with dump sites.

First Nations communities are more exposed to environmental risk than other Canadians.

The Lubicon First Nation in Alberta experienced dramatic increases in illness since their reserves were surrounded with sour gas wells. Within a two-year period in the early 1980s, over 400 oil wells were drilled within a 24-kilometre radius of the Lubicon village of Little Buffalo. UNOCAL, a California-based oil and gas company, built a sour gas battery plant within 5 kilometres of the same community. Sour gas is exactly what it smells like, and the rotten-egg smell of hydrogen sulphide emissions is posing health problems for the Lubicon.

Their health is also compromised by logging. As traditional sources of food in the bush are no longer available, the Lubicon are forced to rely on store-bought food. The rates of diabetes have soared, as have suicides and other social problems. What was once a healthy, self-sustaining community has been devastated. Currently, 95 per cent of the population is on welfare, while 35 per cent have health problems, ranging from tuberculosis to respiratory problems to cancer — at rates that exceed the national average.[1] Oil and gas development was rushed through approval processes before air emissions regulations could catch up.

In the 1940s, when the Inuit men of Deline in the Northwest Territories were recruited to mine uranium, they were never told that it was destined for nuclear weapons. When the bomb was dropped on Hiroshima, they never dreamt that they had unknowingly played a part. They were also never warned of any danger in carrying uranium out of the mine in sacks on their backs. As early as 1931, the government knew the dangers of the ore that the Inuit called "money rock." The men of Deline were carelessly, even criminally, exposed to excessive radiation from the uranium ore. The environment around them was also heavily contaminated. Nearly 2 million tons of radioactive tailings were dumped into Great Bear Lake.

As the men died, survivors began to ask questions. The town of Deline, now known as the "Village of the Widows," is finally closer to answers — if no closer to justice. A federal Crown corporation knowingly allowed unprotected workers to be massively exposed to radioactive materials. The lake is still full of the 1.7 million tons of uranium waste dumped there. Survivors are demanding a health study, cleanup and compensation. An apology would also be in order, but so far it is the Inuit who have apologized. A delegation from Deline travelled to Hiroshima for commemorative ceremonies at the fiftieth anniversary of the bombing, August 6, 1995. They offered their heartfelt apologies for the part they unwittingly played in the annihilation of the city. Japanese citizens learned for the first time that the men who mined the uranium that killed hundreds of thousands had themselves paid with their lives.

Throughout the North, toxic chemicals have also affected the Inuit. Levels of exposure and accumulation of persistent toxic chemicals are at their worst in Inuit communities. The patterns of atmospheric cycling have made the North a dumping ground for industrial chemicals that were never used there. The Inuit diet is primarily from the wildlife of the North. The chemicals bio-accumulate, delivering a higher level of toxic concentration to each level up the food chain. As a result, the breastmilk of Inuit mothers is ten times as contaminated as that of southern Canadian women.

MAPPING THE HOT SPOTS

"The legacy of 100 years of steelmaking" is the common phrase to describe the toxic mess known as the tar ponds and coke ovens in Sydney. With that description comes a subtle and misleading message that such disasters are historical — a thing of the past.

Sydney residents are still living with the ongoing health threat of the contamination, and the surrounding environment is still more polluted by government failure to clean up the tar ponds. Worse, the nature of government decision-making suggests that such disasters are not merely products of a time when we did not realize the consequences of industrialization. Instead, they reveal today's negligence and

indifference. Despite a generation raised since the birth of the environmental movement and the creation of governmental departments charged with protecting the biosphere, Canada still lacks basic tools to protect human health and the environment and is allowing trade deals to undermine the tools we do have.

At the provincial and federal level, every environment department, whether federal or provincial, has seen its budget slashed by at least one-third in the last decade. Meanwhile, more responsibilities, including those for toxic waste sites, are being downloaded from federal to provincial responsibility.

Many communities across Canada have toxic waste sites, yet Environment Canada does not even attempt to maintain a list of such sites. From 1989 to 1995, a preliminary list was assembled but, before it could be organized into a proper inventory, budget cuts shut down the program. Why bother collecting the information when, unlike the United States, Canada has no national program for cleanup? The federal government has not even cleaned up those sites that were created by government itself, much less by its myriad of Crown corporations, such as those in the nuclear industry.

At best, there are estimates. The federal public accounts for 1999, tabled in the House of Commons in the fall of 1999, estimated the extent of liability of both government and corporations for contaminated sites at $30 billion.[2] There are an estimated 10,000 toxic sites across Canada — half of them on federal land.[3] The worst federal polluter has been the Department of National Defence, as well as former U.S. bases under DND responsibility. The Distant Early Warning System (DEW) line in Canada's North is dotted with toxic sites. DND sites are contaminated with fuel tanks, lead bullets, heavy metals and PCBs. In October 1999, Environment Minister David Anderson announced intentions to develop a plan to deal with contaminated sites, but only on federal lands.[4]

When there is a plan, much progress occurs. While it is a long way from being fully implemented, the 1987 Great Lakes Water Quality Agreement did result in significant cleanup efforts. The goals of the agreement were ambitious and stated in clear, unequivocal language. The agreement affirmed the commitment of the governments of Canada and the United States, as well as the governments of Ontario and certain U.S. states, to swimmable beaches, edible fish and drinkable water. Sadly, the sludge on the floor of our largest freshwater lakes will remain contaminated with PCBs and other persistent bio-accumulative toxic substances for a long time. Scientists fear that disturbing them in a cleanup could worsen the problem.

Another steel town, Hamilton, Ontario, has seen millions of dollars in Canada and U.S. funding spent on cleanup. Hamilton Harbour was extensively contaminated but it was made a priority under the Great Lakes Water Quality Agreement. Collins Bay within the harbour has been sufficiently remediated to be removed from the list of areas of concern. But, even though substantial progress has been made, the area still has many toxic hot spots. Randle Reef in Hamilton Harbour was badly polluted by Stelco, and the sediment is highly contaminated, primarily with PAHs. The cleanup of Randle Reef has yet to begin.

WHO PROTECTS PUBLIC HEALTH AND THE ENVIRONMENT?

The Canadian Environmental Protection Act (CEPA) is the most important piece of legislation in Canada for the regulation of toxic chemicals. It is administered jointly by the ministries of environment and health and operates on a chemical-by-chemical basis.

Between the spring and fall of 1999, the Prime Minister's Office forced the passage of amendments that weakened and redrafted CEPA to satisfy the industry lobby. Originally passed in 1988, the act cobbled together various bits, such as the Ocean Dumping Act, pre-existing regulations to control nutrients in water and, its primary basis, the Commercial Chemicals Act. From the very beginning it failed to live up to its name — excluding large classes of toxic substances of concern to Canadians. If a chemical is so toxic that its primary purpose is to kill things, then CEPA only operated if the chemicals were left lying around. As long as the chemicals were being widely dispersed over the environment, they fell under the Pest Control Products Act. If the toxic material also happened to be radioactive, CEPA would not apply.

Still, CEPA did promise comprehensive management of regulated substances — from "cradle to grave" as the press release at the time of passage touted. The problem is that studying and listing toxic chemicals, one substance at a time, is a long and difficult process. The deficiencies in Canada's toxic chemical management were set out in the 1999 report of the Commissioner for Environment and Sustainable Development, Brian Emmett. In his view, the system was so flawed that the health of Canadians was at risk. Of the 23,000 toxic substances in Canada, only 31 have been subjected to a conclusive review process. The Priority Substances List, which was intended to fast-track the operation of CEPA, has been an exercise in slow motion.

Commissioner Emmett's report also highlighted the lack of information-sharing between departments as was evident in the [Sydney] tar ponds disaster. The shared role of environment and health ministers should have worked to integrate our life support systems — the air we breathe, the water we drink, the food we eat — with our state of health. It did not. Instead, unsafe chemicals have remained in use while health and environment bureaucrats engage in turf warfare.

The only good news in the last ten years has come from the Supreme Court of Canada. It reconfirmed the importance of the federal role in protecting public health and the environment from poisonous substances.

After heroic efforts by the House of Commons environment committee to improve the act through its mandatory five-year review, the industry lobby went to war against the committee. It was the worst, most protracted and unpleasant parliamentary process of any bill in memory.

When the all-party committee presented its report, the chemical and aluminum industries used every weapon in their arsenal to gut the bill. The CEO of Alcan Aluminium Ltd., Jacques Bougie, wrote to Prime Minister Chrétien, warning him that if the bill was enacted into law as written, "it could force the closure of all aluminum smelters in Canada."[5] It was not necessary for Mr. Bougie to remind Mr. Chrétien that one of the threatened smelters was in the prime minister's Shawinigan riding. The source of Bougie's concern was that the bill might be used to regulate PAHs. Already listed on the toxic substances list, PAHs have been under a special review within CEPA for the last five years to determine the appropriate approach to regulation. The multi-stakeholder advisory committee includes industry, of course, and consensus has not been possible.

Some of the very same poisons that poured out of the coke ovens are also emitted from aluminum smelters. Benzopyrene turns up in the St. Lawrence downstream from smelters, and according to Alcan's vice-president, "There is no smelting technology that does not emit a detectable, almost negligible, level of PAHs."[6] Thus, when beluga whales wash up dead in the St. Lawrence River, their flesh must be treated as hazardous waste.

The industry focused on CEPA's new goal of the "virtual elimination" of certain inherently toxic and bio-accumulative chemicals, deciding that the concept had to be rejected. Such lobbying was not new. In response to industry pressure a year before, Environment Canada staff had prepared an analysis of wording changes demanded by the aluminum industry. The memo noted that the language demanded by industry would "create an internal contradiction

that would make virtual elimination impossible." Yet the bill that was brought before the House for passage had nearly identical language to that rejected a year before as unworkable.

The result was predictable. Key sections of CEPA were made unintelligible. The drafting was incomprehensible. It moved tentatively towards the possibility of virtual elimination, but failed to adopt a goal to achieve it. The industry also demanded that the precautionary principle, which requires that actions to protect public health and the environment not await 100 per cent proof when caution would require action, also be gutted. The bill sent to the House was amended to require that actions of a precautionary nature only be allowed when "cost-effective." Nothing in the new "improved" CEPA creates an imperative to clean up toxic waste sites — or even to catalogue them.

CEPA was so badly damaged by the prime ministerial cave-in to industry that a most extraordinary parliamentary rebellion took place. The three members of parliament within the governing Liberal Party, those most knowledgeable about the bill, voted against it. Charles Caccia, a former minister of the environment under Pierre Trudeau, was chair of the House of Commons committee that had dedicated years to the review and amendment process for CEPA. Joining him in rejecting the bill were Karen Kraft-Sloan, an Ontario MP and former parliamentary secretary to the environment minister who had also worked on the House Committee process, and Quebec's former environment minister, who was now a federal politician, Clifford Lincoln.

All three MPs believed the government had so emasculated the bill that it was now worse than the version of the bill passed in 1988. Efforts focused on the Senate to improve the bill, with progressive positions adopted by Tory senator Mira Spivak and committee chair Ron Ghitter. But the Prime Minister's Office and the Senate Liberal leader pushed all Liberal senators hard to approve the bill without changes. The lack of enthusiasm for the task was evidenced in a report that accompanied the bill to the Senate floor. The Liberal majority of the Senate committee urged that upon passage, the bill should be subjected to an immediate review to deal with its failings.

TOXIC DUMPING

While corporate lobbyists successfully gut our legislative tools, the potential profits from toxic waste are eroding our standards. The economic benefits of becoming a toxic dumping ground are beginning to change Canada's reputation. We will accept PCBs for disposal and incineration in Canada. The United States will not. We are pushing hard for the right to be the long-term repository for highly radioactive plutonium, removed from the warheads of U.S. and U.S.S.R. missiles. The campaign originates not with the former Soviet Union or the United States, but within Canada from the massively subsidized Crown corporation, Atomic Energy of Canada, Limited (AECL), supported by this country's biggest booster of nuclear energy, Prime Minister Jean Chrétien. Expert analysis of the disposal methods for plutonium favours leaving the plutonium where it is, and then encasing it in glass — a process called vitrification. Vitrification wins on every point as the least expensive, and safest, from an environmental and security viewpoint. But Chrétien and AECL are desperate to establish a global trade in plutonium waste so that AECL will have a long-term contract for disposal.

The open door policy to hazardous waste is not restricted to federal agencies. Ontario's Harris government has drastically increased the importation of toxic waste to the province. From 1997 to 1999, the province had asked the federal environment department to accept all hazardous waste applications from U.S. companies wishing to dump materials in Ontario. The blanket approvals letter was recently revoked by the province's new environment minister, Tony Clement. Meanwhile, in the first six months of 1998, nearly 11 million tones of hazardous materials were shipped into Ontario from the United States.[7]

Industry analysts know why companies are prepared to ship materials hundreds of kilometres from the source to ultimate disposal in Canada — our regulations are lax, our costs are lower, and there is less chance of being sued or prosecuted.

TRADING AWAY ENVIRONMENTAL PROTECTION

The federal government continues to sign international trade agreements that prohibit all levels of Canadian government from passing legislation to protect the environment. The sad story of MMT shows just how much control the federal government has given away through such agreements.

In 1997, the federal government took the unusual step of banning a persistent neurotoxic substance used as an anti-knock agent in gasoline. The move was unusual because the government rarely bans a toxic chemical in Canada, tending instead to treat toxic chemicals as though they had constitutional rights — innocent until proven guilty. In fact, the banning of MMT was an appropriate use of the "precautionary principle." The science on the key ingredient in MMT, manganese, is well established. Manganese in occupational exposure can lead to a disease called "manganism" which closely resembles the tremors and nervous system breakdown in Parkinson's disease. Manganese exposure can cause a progressive deterioration of the brain. This condition is particularly dangerous for older people, leading to premature and accelerated aging of the brain.

MMT was introduced in the early 1970s as a gasoline additive by the same company that had manufactured and sold leaded gas, Ethyl Corporation of Richmond, Virginia. After decades of defending leaded gas as a safe product, Ethyl Corp. knew the jig was up. Leaded gas was on the way out, and the company wanted to protect its prime business as a manufacturer of gasoline additives. Ethyl Corp. began flogging MMT as a replacement for lead in gas.

The U.S. Government soon rejected registration of MMT. Canada, relying on the same data, decided it could be registered for use. Health Canada did note, however, that there were significant data gaps about how MMT might affect vulnerable groups, such as children, pregnant women and the elderly.

By the 1990s, the automakers were complaining to the government about MMT. They said that is was gumming up the onboard diagnostic systems of cars, compromising the air pollution control devices. The Big Three car manufacturers became very concerned about the financial repercussions of violated warranties if MMT reduced the effectiveness of catalytic converters. Pressure to ban it was exerted on Environment Minister Sheila Copps. Environmental and health groups supported the ban, arguing that MMT not only increased air pollution, but could poison the brains of Canadians. Twenty years after registration, Health Canada had done nothing to deal with the "data gaps" around its health impacts.

Laboratory studies suggested that MMT could provoke increased aggression in animals, as well as create symptoms that could be described as attention deficit disorder if they occurred in humans. The experience with leaded gas had proven that if you wanted to introduce a toxic heavy metal into the blood and brains of children, then adding it to gasoline was a good delivery mechanism.

In the spring of 1997, MMT was finally banned in Canada. A decade earlier that would have been the end of the matter. But Ethyl Corp. did not accept the regulatory decision. Now it has recourse through the North American Free Trade Agreement (NAFTA) to challenge Canada's decision. In fact, under provisions of

Chapter II of NAFTA, companies from one of the three NAFTA countries who lose profits based on a regulatory decision in one of the other countries can sue the government for damages. Thus, Ethyl Corp, as a U.S.-based company, was able to sue the government of Canada for banning its neurotoxic gasoline additive, claiming damages in the amount of $350 million (Canadian) for lost profits and damage to its reputation. The hearings would be completely private. A three-person arbitration panel would hear the arguments of the Canadian government and Ethyl Corp. No independent scientific briefings would be allowed by environmental or health groups.

Under NAFTA Chapter II it didn't really matter if the government had been right to ban MMT or not. The real issue was whether Ethyl Corp. had rights to profits "expropriated." As Ethyl Corp.'s Canadian lawyer Barry Appleton has said, it wouldn't matter if a substance was liquid plutonium destined for a child's breakfast cereal. If the government bans a product and a U.S.-based company loses profits, the company can claim damages under NAFTA.

In the summer of 1998, the government caved in. It withdrew the regulation removing MMT from use, paid Ethyl Corp. $19 million as compensation for its "trouble," and issued a public apology in which Christine Stewart, then minister of the environment, explained that the government had never had adequate grounds to ban MMT. A spokesperson for Ethyl said at the time, "It's a very happy day, a significant step for Ethyl Corp. and its business worldwide."

Within days of the MMT settlement, Barry Appleton filed a claim for another U.S.-based corporation, S.D. Myers of Ohio, a company in the business of hazardous waste. It wanted PCBs from Canada for disposal in its Ohio plant. Myers claimed damages from a nine-month-long ban against the export of PCBs to the U.S. from Canada, initiated by Sheila Copps, and upholding the principles of the Basel Convention on hazardous wastes. The ban was removed quickly under a NAFTA threat. Even though Sierra Club in the U.S. had successfully sued to prevent Canadian PCBs from entering the U.S., it was still possible for S.D. Myers to sue for damages on a moot point.

Other cases are piling up: from a company wanting to export water from B.C., from a wood product company claiming that Canada's forest export rules deprive it of access to forest products, and even from a Canadian company, Methanex, challenging a California ban on a carcinogenic gas additive, MTBE.

LESSONS UNLEARNED

Here, then, is the greatest tragedy of the Sydney tar ponds story. It would appear that the residents of Sydney, and especially the residents of Whitney Pier and Frederick Street, have suffered and fought in isolation and perhaps in vain. We appear not to have learned one thing from their ordeal. We continue to talk about the "trade-off" between jobs and the environment; jobs and health. The tar ponds saga should have taught us that such trade-offs are wrong economically, environmentally and morally

There are now several decades of documented proof of the deep harm done to humans, other species and the earth by the noxious and toxic chemicals so cavalierly dumped into open waterways around the Sydney steel plant and at other poisoned sites right across Canada. Yet governments and many corporations continue to turn a blind eye to the clear and present danger these chemicals pose to the very future of humankind. In the end, our collective failure to learn from their suffering may be a greater offence to the courageous people of Sydney than the toxic site itself.

It is never too late to change our behaviour, our values and our laws. But it is late in the day. The sun is setting on a chemical-safe world; Sydney, Nova Scotia, has sounded the alarm. Will we hear it in time?

NOTES

1. John Goddard, *Last Stand of the Lubicon Cree* (Vancouver: Douglas and McIntyre, 1992).
2. Jim Bronskill and James Baxter, "Government on the hook for billions," *Ottawa Citizen*, 27 October 1999.
3. Andrew Duffy, "Toxic waste cleanup list in the works: federal environment minister preparing national strategy," *Ottawa Citizen*, 12 October 1999.
4. Ibid.
5. Donna Jacobs, "How industry beat the Environmental Protection Act," *Ottawa Citizen,* 7 September 1999.
6. Ibid.
7. Martin Mittelstaedt, "Ontario to receive hazardous waste — Ottawa approved transfer of 473,000 tonnes of toxins from Michigan, papers show," *Globe and Mail*, 27 September 1999.

Chapter 31

More than 100 Million Women Are Missing

AMARTYA SEN

If is often said that women make up a majority of the world's population. They do not. This mistaken belief is based on generalizing from the contemporary situation in Europe and North America, where the ratio of women to men is typically around 1.05 or 1.06, or higher. In South Asia, West Asia, and China, the ratio of women to men can be as low as 0.94, or even lower, and it varies widely elsewhere in Asia, in Africa, and in Latin America. How can we understand and explain these differences, and react to them?

1.

At birth boys outnumber girls everywhere in the world, by much the same proportion — there are around 105 or 106 male children for every 100 female children. Just why the biology of reproduction leads to this result remains a subject of debate. But after conception, biology seems on the whole to favor women. Considerable research has shown that if men and women receive similar nutritional and medical attention and general health care, women tend to live noticeably longer than men. Women seem to be, on the whole, more resistant to disease and in general hardier than men, an advantage they enjoy not only after they are forty years old but also at the beginning of life, especially during the months immediately following birth, and even in the womb. When given the same care as males, females tend to have better survival rates than males.[1]

Women outnumber men substantially in Europe, the US, and Japan, where, despite the persistence of various types of bias against women (men having distinct advantages in higher education, job specialization, and promotion to senior executive positions, for example), women suffer little discrimination in basic nutrition and health care. The greater number of women in these countries is partly the result of social and environmental differences that increase mortality among men, such as a higher likelihood that men will die from violence, for example, and from diseases related to smoking. But even after these are taken into account, the longer lifetimes enjoyed by women given similar care appear to relate to the biological advantages that women have over men in resisting disease. Whether the higher frequency of male births over female births has evolutionary links to this potentially greater survival rate of women is a question of some interest in itself. Women seem to have lower death rates than men at most ages whenever they get roughly similar treatment in matters of life and death.

The fate of women is quite different in most of Asia and North Africa. In these places the failure to give women medical care similar to what men get and to provide them with comparable food and social services results in fewer

---

women surviving than would be the case if they had equal care. In India, for example, except in the period immediately following birth, the death rate is higher for women than for men fairly consistently in all age groups until the late thirties. This relates to higher rates of disease from which women suffer, and ultimately to the relative neglect of females, especially in health care and medical attention.[2] Similar neglect of women vis-à-vis men can be seen also in many other parts of the world. The result is a lower proportion of women than would be the case if they had equal care — in most of Asia and North Africa, and to a lesser extent Latin America.

This pattern is not uniform in all parts of the world, however. Sub-Saharan Africa, for example, ravaged as it is by extreme poverty, hunger, and famine, has a substantial excess rather than deficit of women, the ratio of women to men being around 1.02. The "third-world" in this matter is not a useful category, because it is so diverse. Even within Asia, which has the lowest proportion of women in the world, Southeast Asia and East Asia (apart from China) have a ratio of women to men that is slightly higher than one to one (around 1.01). Indeed, sharp diversities also exist within particular regions — sometimes even within a particular country. For example, the ratio of women to men in the Indian states of Punjab and Haryana, which happen to be among the country's richest, is a remarkably low 0.86, while the state of Kerala in southwestern India has a ratio higher than 1.03, similar to that in Europe, North America, and Japan.

To get an idea of the numbers of people involved in the different ratios of women to men, we can estimate the number of "missing women" in a country, say, China or India, by calculating the number of extra women who would have been in China or India if these countries had the same ratio of women to men as obtained in areas of the world in which they receive similar care. If we could expect equal populations of the two sexes, the low ratio of

0.94 women to men in South Asia, West Asia, and China would indicate a 6 percent deficit of women; but since, in countries where men and women receive similar care, the ratio is about 1.05, the real shortfall is about 11 percent. In China alone this amounts to 50 million "missing women," taking 1.05 as the benchmark ratio. When that number is added to those in South Asia, West Asia, and North Africa, a great many more than 100 million women are "missing." These numbers tell us, quietly, a terrible story of inequality and neglect leading to the excess mortality of women.

2.

To account for the neglect of women, two simplistic explanations have often been presented or, more often, implicitly assumed. One view emphasizes the cultural contrasts between East and West (or between the Occident and the Orient), claiming that Western civilization is less sexist than Eastern. That women outnumber men in Western countries may appear to lend support to this Kipling-like generalization. (Kipling himself was not, of course, much bothered by concerns about sexism, and even made "the twain" meet in romantically masculine circumstances: "But there is neither East nor West, Border, nor Breed, nor Birth, / When two strong men stand face to face, tho' they come from the ends of the earth!") The other simple argument looks instead at stages of economic development, seeing the unequal nutrition and health care provided for women as a feature of underdevelopment, a characteristic of poor economies awaiting economic advancement.

There may be elements of truth in each of these explanations, but neither is very convincing as a general thesis. To some extent, the two simple explanations, in terms of "economic development" and "East-West" divisions, also tend to undermine each other. A combined cultural and economic analysis would seem to be necessary, and, I will argue, it would have to take note of many other social conditions in addition to the features identified in the simple aggregative theses.

To take the cultural view first, the East-West explanation is obviously flawed because experiences within the East and West diverge so sharply. Japan, for example, unlike most of Asia, has a ratio of women to men that is not very different from that in Europe or North America. This might suggest, at least superficially, that real income and economic development do more to explain the bias against providing women with the conditions for survival than whether the society is Western or Oriental. In the censuses of 1899 and 1908 Japan had a clear and substantial deficit of women, but by 1940 the numbers of men and women were nearly equal, and in the postwar decades, as Japan became a rich and highly industrialized country, it moved firmly in the direction of a large surplus, rather than a deficit, of women. Some countries in East Asia and Southeast Asia also provide exceptions to the deficit of women: in Thailand and Indonesia, for example, women substantially outnumber men.

In its rudimentary, undiscriminating form, the East-West explanation also fails to take into account other characteristics of these societies. For example, the ratios of women to men in South Asia are among the lowest in the world (around 0.94 in India and Bangladesh, and 0.90 in Pakistan — the lowest ratio for any large country), but that region has been among the pioneers in electing women as top political leaders. Indeed, each of the four large South Asian countries — India, Pakistan, Bangladesh, and Sri Lanka — either has had a woman as the elected head of government (Sri Lanka, India, and Pakistan), or has had women leading the main opposition parties (as in Bangladesh).

It is, of course, true that these successes in South Asia have been achieved only by upper-class women, and that having a woman head of government has not, by itself, done much for women in general in these countries. However, the point here is only to question the tendency to see the contrast between East and West as simply based on more sexism or less. The large electoral successes of women in achieving high positions in government in South Asia indicate that the analysis has to be more complex.

It is, of course, also true that these women leaders reached their powerful positions with the help of dynastic connections — Indira Gandhi was the daughter of Jawaharlal Nehru, Benázir Bhutto the daughter of Zulfikar Bhutto, and so on. But it would be absurd to overlook — just on that ground — the significance of their rise to power through popular mandate. Dynastic connections are not new in politics and are pervasive features of political succession in many countries. That Indira Gandhi derived her political strength partly from her father's position is not in itself more significant than the fact that Rajiv Gandhi's political credibility derived largely from his mother's political eminence, or the fact (perhaps less well known) that Indira Gandhi's father — the great Jawaharlal Nehru — initially rose to prominence as the son of Motilal Nehru, who had been president of the Congress party. The dynastic aspects of South Asian politics have certainly helped women to come to power through electoral support, but it is still true that so far as winning elections is concerned, South Asia would seem to be some distance ahead of the United States and most European countries when it comes to discrimination according to gender.

In this context it is useful also to compare the ratios of women in American and Indian legislatures. In the US House of Representatives the proportion of women is 6.4 percent, while in the present and last lower houses of the Indian Parliament, women's proportions have been respectively 5.3 and 7.9 percent. Only two of the 100 US Senators are women, and this 2 percent ratio contrasts with more than 9 and 10 percent women respectively in the last and present "upper house," Rajya Sabha, in India. (In a different, but not altogether unrelated, sphere, I had a much higher proportion of tenured women colleagues when I was teaching at Delhi

University than I now have at Harvard.) The cultural climate in different societies must have a clear relevance to differences between men and women — both in survival and in other ways as well — but it would be hopeless to see the divergences simply as a contrast between the sexist East and the unbiased West.

How good is the other (i.e., the purely economic) explanation for women's inequality? Certainly all the countries with large deficits of women are more or less poor, if we measure poverty by real incomes, and no sizable country with a high gross national product per head has such a deficit. There are reasons to expect a reduction of differential female mortality with economic progress. For example, the rate of maternal mortality at childbirth can be expected to decrease both with better hospital facilities and the reduction in birth rate that usually accompanies economic development.

However, in this simple form, an economic analysis does not explain very much, since many poor countries do not, in fact, have deficits of women. As was noted earlier, sub-Saharan Africa, poor and underdeveloped as it is, has a substantial excess of women. Southeast and East Asia (but not China) also differ from many other relatively poor countries in this respect, although to a lesser degree. Within India, as was noted earlier, Punjab and Haryana — among the richest and most economically advanced Indian states — have very low ratios of women to men (around 0.86), in contrast to the much poorer state of Kerala, where the ratio is greater than 1.03.

Indeed, economic development is quite often accompanied by a relative worsening in the rate of survival of women (even as life expectancy improves in absolute terms for both men and women). For example, in India the gap between the life expectancy of men and women has narrowed recently, but only after many decades when women's relative position deteriorated. There has been a steady decline in the ratio of women to men in the population, from more than 97 women to 100 men at the turn of the century (in 1901), to 93 women in 1971, and the ratio is only a little higher now. The deterioration in women's position results largely from their unequal sharing in the advantages of medical and social progress. Economic development does not invariably reduce women's disadvantages in mortality.

A significant proportional decline in the population of women occurred in China after the economic and social reforms introduced there in 1979. The Chinese Statistical Yearbooks show a steady decline in the already very low ratio of women to men in the population, from 94.32 in 1979 to 93.42 in 1985 and 1986. (It has risen since then, to 93.98 in 1989 — still lower than what it was in 1979). Life expectancy was significantly higher for females than for males until the economic reforms, but seems to have fallen behind since then.[3] Of course, the years following the reforms were also years of great economic growth and, in many ways, of social progress, yet women's relative prospects for survival deteriorated. These and other cases show that rapid economic development may go hand in hand with worsening relative mortality of women.

3.

Despite their superficial plausibility, neither the alleged contrast between "East" and "West," nor the simple hypothesis of female deprivation as a characteristic of economic "underdevelopment" gives us anything like an adequate understanding of the geography of female deprivation in social well-being and survival. We have to examine the complex ways in which economic, social, and cultural factors can influence the regional differences.

It is certainly true that, for example, the status and power of women in the family differ greatly from one region to another, and there are good reasons to expect that these social features would be related to the economic role and independence of women. For example, employment outside the home and owning assets can both be important for women's economic independence and power; and these factors may have far-reaching effects on the divisions of benefits and chores within the family and can greatly influence what are implicitly accepted as women's "entitlements."

Indeed, men and women have both interests in common and conflicting interests that affect family decisions; and it is possible to see decision making in the family taking the form of the pursuit of cooperation in which solutions for the conflicting aspects of family life are implicitly agreed on. Such "cooperative conflicts" are a general feature of many group relations, and an analysis of cooperative conflicts can provide a useful way of understanding the influences that affect the "deal" that women get in the division of benefits within the family. There are gains to be made by men and women through following implicitly agreed-on patterns of behavior; but there are many possible agreements — some more favorable to one party than others. The choice of one such cooperative arrangement from among the range of possibilities leads to a particular distribution of joint benefits. (Elsewhere, I have tried to analyze the general nature of "cooperative conflicts" and the application of the analysis of such conflicts to family economics.[4])

Conflicts in family life are typically resolved through implicitly agreed-on patterns of behavior that may or may not be particularly egalitarian. The very nature of family living — sharing a home and experiences — requires that the elements of conflict must not be explicitly emphasized (giving persistent attention to conflicts will usually be seen as aberrant behavior); and sometimes the deprived woman would not even have a clear idea of the extent of her relative deprivation. Similarly, the perception of who is doing "productive" work, who is "contributing" how much to the family's prosperity, can be very influential, even though the underlying principles regarding how "contributions" or "productivity" are to be assessed may be rarely discussed explicitly. These issues of social perception are, I believe, of pervasive importance in gender inequality, even in the richer countries, but they can have a particularly powerful influence in sustaining female deprivation in many of the poorer countries.[5]

The division of a family's joint benefits is likely to be less unfavorable to women if (1) they can earn an outside income; (2) their work is recognized as productive (this is easier to achieve with work done outside the home); (3) they own some economic resources and have some rights to fall back on; and (4) there is a clear-headed understanding of the ways in which women are deprived and a recognition of the possibilities of changing this situation. This last category can be much influenced by education for women and by participatory political action.

Considerable empirical evidence, mostly studies of particular localities, suggests that what is usually defined as "gainful" employment (i.e., working outside the home for a wage, or in such "productive" occupations as farming), as opposed to unpaid and unhonored housework — no matter how demanding — can substantially enhance the deal that women get.[6] Indeed, "gainful" employment of women can make the solution of "cooperative conflicts" less unfavorable to women in many ways. First, outside employment for wages can provide women with an income to which they have easier access, and it can also serve as a means of making a living on which women can rely, making them less vulnerable. Second, the social respect that is associated with being a "bread winner" (and a "productive" contributor to the family's joint prosperity) can improve women's status and standing in the family, and may influence the prevailing cultural traditions regarding who gets what in the division of joint benefits. Third, when outside employment takes the form of jobs with some security and legal protection, the corresponding rights that women get can make their economic position much less vulnerable and precarious. Fourth, working outside the home also provides experience of the outside world, and this can be socially important in improving women's position within the family. In this respect outside work may be "educational" as well.

These factors may not only improve the "deal" women get in the family, they can also counter the relative neglect of girls as they grow up. Boys are preferred in many countries because they are expected to provide more economic security for their parents in old age; but the force of this bias can be weakened if women as well as men can regularly work at paid jobs. Moreover, if the status of women does in general rise and women's contributions become more recognized, female children may receive more attention. Similarly, the exposure of women to the world through work outside the home can weaken, through its educational effect, the hold of traditional beliefs and behavior.

In comparing different regions of Asia and Africa, if we try to relate the relative survival prospects of women to the "gainful employment" of both sexes — i.e., work outside the home, possibly for a wage — we do find a strong association. If the different regions of Asia and Africa (with the exception of China) are ranked according to the proportion of women in so-called gainful employment relative to the proportion of men in such employment, we get the following ranking, in descending order.[7]

1. Sub-Saharan Africa
2. Southeast and Eastern Asia
3. Western Asia
4. Southern Asia
5. Northern Africa

Ranking the ratios of life expectancy of females to those of males produces a remarkably similar ordering:

1. Sub-Saharan Africa
2. Southeast and Eastern Asia
3. Western Asia
4. Northern Africa
5. Southern Asia

That the two rankings are much the same, except for a switch between the two lowest-ranking regions (lowest in terms of both indicators), suggests a link between employment and survival prospects. In addition to the overall correspondence between the two rankings, the particular contrasts between sub-Saharan Africa and North Africa, and that between Southern (and Western) Asia and Southeast (and Eastern) Asia are suggestive distinctions *within* Africa and Asia respectively, linking women's gainful employment and survival prospects.

It is, of course, possible that what we are seeing here is not a demonstration that gainful employment causes better survival prospects but the influence of some other factor correlated with each. In fact, on the basis of such broad relations, it is very hard to draw any firm conclusion; but evidence of similar relations can be found also in other comparisons.[8] For example, Punjab, the richest Indian state, has the lowest ratio of women to men (0.86) in India; it also has the lowest ratio of women in "gainful" employment compared to men. The influence of outside employment on women's well-being has also been documented in a number of studies of specific communities in different parts of the world.[9]

4.

The case of China deserves particular attention. It is a country with a traditional bias against women, but after the revolution the Chinese leaders did pay considerable attention to reducing inequality between men and women.[10] This was helped both by a general expansion of basic health and medical services accessible to all and by the increase in women's gainful employment, along with greater social recognition of the importance of women in the economy and the society.

There has been a remarkable general expansion of longevity, and despite the temporary setback during the terrible famines of 1958–1961 (following the disastrous failure of the so-called Great Leap Forward), the Chinese life expectancy at birth increased from the low forties around 1950 to the high sixties by the time the economic reforms were introduced in 1979. The sharp reduction in general mortality (including female mortality) is all the more remarkable in view of the fact that it took place despite deep economic problems in the form of widespread industrial inefficiency, a rather stagnant agriculture, and relatively little increase in output per head. Female death rates declined sharply — both as a part of a general mortality reduction and also relatively, vis-à-vis male mortality. Women's life expectancy at birth overtook that of men — itself much enhanced — and was significantly ahead at the time the economic and social reforms were introduced in 1979.

Those reforms immediately increased the rate of economic growth and broke the agricultural stagnation. The official figures suggest a doubling of agricultural output between 1979 and 1986 — a remarkable achievement even if some elements of exaggeration are eliminated from these figures. But at the same time, the official figures also record an *increase* in the general mortality rates after the reforms, with a consistently higher death rate than what China had achieved by 1979. There seems to be also a worsening of the relative survival of women, including a decline, discussed earlier, of the ratio of women to men in the population, which went down from 94.3 in 1979 to 93.4 in 1985 and 1986. There are problems in interpreting the available data and difficulties in arriving at firm conclusions, but the view that women's life expectancy has again become lower than that of men has gained support. For example, the World Bank's most recent *World Development Report* suggests a life expectancy of sixty-nine years for

men and sixty-six years for women (even though the confounded nature of the subject is well reflected by the fact that the same *Report* also suggests an average life expectancy of seventy years for men and women put together).[11]

Why have women's survival prospects in China deteriorated, especially in relative terms, since 1979? Several experts have noted that recently Chinese leaders have tended, on the whole, to reduce the emphasis on equality for women; it is no longer much discussed, and indeed, as the sociologist Margery Wolf puts it, it is a case of a "revolution postponed."[12] But this fact, while important, does not explain why the relative survival prospects of women would have so deteriorated during the early years of the reforms, just at the time when there was a rapid expansion of overall economic prosperity.

The compulsory measures to control the size of families which were introduced in 1979 may have been an important factor. In some parts of the country the authorities insisted on the "one-child family." This restriction, given the strong preference for boys in China, led to a neglect of girls that was often severe. Some evidence exists of female infanticide. In the early years after the reforms, infant mortality for girls appeared to increase considerably. Some estimates had suggested that the rate of female infant mortality rose from 37.7 per thousand in 1978 to 67.2 per thousand in 1984.[13] Even if this seems exaggerated in the light of later data, the survival prospects of female children clearly have been unfavorably affected by restrictions on the size of the family. Later legal concessions (including the permission to have a second child if the first one is a girl) reflect some official recognition of these problems.

A second factor relevant to the survival problems of Chinese women is the general crisis in health services since the economic reforms. As the agricultural production brigades and collectives, which had traditionally provided much of the funding for China's extensive rural health programs, were dismantled, they were replaced by the so-called "responsibility system," in which agriculture was centered in the family. Agricultural production improved, but cutbacks in communal facilities placed severe financial restrictions on China's extensive rural medical services. Communal agriculture may not have done much for agricultural production as such, but it had been a main source of support for China's innovative and extensive rural medical services. So far as gender is concerned, the effects of the reduced scope of these services are officially neutral, but in view of the pro-male bias in Chinese rural society, the cutback in medical services would have had a particularly severe impact on women and female children. (It is also the pro-male bias in the general culture that made the one-child policy, which too is neutral in form, unfavorable to female children in terms of its actual impact.)

Third, the "responsibility system" arguably has reduced women's involvement in recognized gainful employment in agriculture. In the new system's more traditional arrangement of work responsibilities, women's work in the household economy may again suffer from the lack of recognition that typically affects household work throughout the world.[14] The impact of this change on the status of women within the household may be negative, for the reasons previously described. Expanded employment opportunities for women outside agriculture in some regions may at least partially balance this effect. But the weakening of social security arrangements since the reforms would also have made old age more precarious, and since such insecurity is one of the persistent motives for families' preferring boys over girls, this change too can be contributing to the worsening of care for female children.[15]

5.

Analyses based on simple conflicts between East and West or on "underdevelopment" clearly do not take us very far. The variables that appear important — for example, female employment or female literacy — combine both economic and cultural effects. To ascribe importance to the influence of gainful employment on women's prospects for survival may superficially look like another attempt at a simple economic explanation, but it would be a mistake to see it this way. The deeper question is why such outside employment is more prevalent in, say, sub-Saharan Africa than in North Africa, or in Southeast and Eastern Asia than in Western and Southern Asia. Here the cultural, including religious, backgrounds of the respective regions are surely important. Economic causes for women's deprivation have to be integrated with other — social and cultural — factors to give depth to the explanation.

Of course, gainful employment is not the only factor affecting women's chances of survival. Women's education and their economic rights — including property rights — may be crucial variables as well.[16] Consider the state of Kerala in India, which I mentioned earlier. It does not have a deficit of women — its ratio of women to men of more than 1.03 is closer to that of Europe (1.05) than those of China, West Asia, and India as a whole (0.94). The life expectancy of women at birth in Kerala, which had already reached sixty-eight years by the time of the last census in 1981 (and is estimated to be seventy-two years now), is considerably higher than men's sixty-four years at that time (and sixty-seven now). While women are generally able to find "gainful employment" in Kerala — certainly much more so than in Punjab — the state is not exceptional in this regard. What is exceptional is Kerala's remarkably high literacy rate; not only is it much higher than elsewhere in India, it is also substantially higher than in China, especially for women.

Kerala's experience of state-funded expansion of basic education, which has been consolidated by left-wing state governments in recent decades, began, in fact, nearly two centuries ago, led by the rulers of the kingdoms of Travancore and Cochin. (These two native states were not part of British India; they were joined together with a small part of the old Madras presidency to form the new state of Kerala after independence.) Indeed, as early as 1817, Rani Gouri Parvathi Bai, the young queen of Travancore, issued clear instructions for public support of education:

> The state should defray the entire cost of education of its people in order that there might be no backwardness in the spread of enlightenment among them. That by diffusion of education they might be better subjects and public servants and that the reputation of the State might be advanced thereby.[17]

Moreover, in parts of Kerala, property is usually inherited through the family's female line. These factors, as well as the generally high level of communal medicine, help to explain why women in Kerala do not suffer disadvantages in obtaining the means for survival. While it would be difficult to "split up" the respective contributions made by each of these different influences, it would be a mistake not to include all these factors among the potentially interesting variables that deserve examination.

In view of the enormity of the problems of women's survival in large parts of Asia and Africa, it is surprising that these disadvantages have received such inadequate attention. The numbers of "missing women" in relation to the numbers that could be expected if men and women received similar care in health, medicine, and nutrition, are remarkably large. A great many more than a hundred million women are simply not there because women are neglected compared with men. If this situation is to be corrected by political action and public policy, the reasons why there are so many "missing" women must first be better understood. We confront here what is clearly one of the more momentous, and neglected, problems facing the world today.

NOTES

1. An assessment of the available evidence can be found in Ingrid Waldron's "The Role of Genetic and Biological Factors in Sex Differences in Mortality," in A.D. Lopez and L.T. Ruzicka, eds., *Sex Differences in Mortality* (Canberra: Department of Demography, Australian National University, 1983). On the pervasive cultural influences on mortality and the difficulties in forming a biological view of survival advantages, see Sheila Ryan Johansson, "Mortality, Welfare and Gender: Continuity and Change in Explanations for Male/Female Mortality Differences over Three Centuries," in *Continuity and Change*, forthcoming.

2. These and related data are presented and assessed in my joint paper with Jocelyn Kynch, "Indian Women: Well-being and Survival," *Cambridge Journal of Economics,* Vol. 7 (1983), and in my *Commodities and Capabilities* (Amsterdam: North-Holland, 1985), Appendix B. See also Lincoln Chen et al., "Sex Bias in the Family Allocation of Food and Health Care in Rural Bangladesh," in *Population and Development Review*, Vol. 7 (1981); Barbara Miller, *The Endangered Sex: Neglect of Female Children in Rural North India* (Cornell University Press, 1981); Pranab Bardhan, *Land, Labor, and Rural Poverty* (Columbia University Press, 1984); Devaki Jain and Nirmala Banerji, eds., *Tyranny of the Household* (New Delhi: Vikas, 1985); Barbara Harriss and Elizabeth Watson, "The Sex Ratio in South Asia," in J.H. Momsen and J.G. Townsend, eds., *Geography of Gender in the Third World* (State University of New York Press, 1987); Monica Das Gupta, "Selective Discrimination against Female Children in Rural Punjab, India," in *Population and Development Review*, Vol. 13 (1987).

3. See the World Bank's World Development Report 1990 (Oxford University Press, 1990), Table 32. See also Judith Banister, *China's Changing Population* (Stanford University Press, 1987), Chapter 4, though the change in life expectancy may not have been as large as these early estimates had suggested, as Banister herself has later noted.

4. "Gender and Cooperative Conflicts," Working paper of the World Institute of Development Economics Research (1986), in Irene Tinker, ed., *Persistent Inequalities: Women and World Development* (Oxford University Press, 1990). In the same volume see also the papers of Ester Boserup, Hanna Papanek, and Irene Tinker on closely related subjects.

5. The recent literature on the modeling of family relations as "bargaining problems," despite being usefully suggestive and insightful, has suffered a little from giving an inadequate role to the importance of perceptions (as opposed to objectively identified interests) of the parties involved. On the relevance of perception, including perceptual distortions (a variant of what Marx had called "false perception"), in family relations, see my "Gender and Cooperative Conflicts." See also my *Resources, Values and Development* (Harvard University Press, 1984), Chapters 15 and 16; Gail Wilson, *Money in the Family* (Avebury/Gower, 1987).

6. See the case studies and the literature cited in my "Gender and Cooperative Conflicts." A pioneering study of some of these issues was provided by Ester Boserup, *Women's Role in Economic Development* (St. Martin's, 1970). See also Bina Agarwal, "Social Security and the Family," in E. Ahmad, et al., *Social Security in Developing Countries*, to be published by Oxford University Press in 1991.

7. Details can be found in my "Gender and Cooperative Conflicts."

8. For example, see Pranab Bardhan, *Land, Labor, and Rural Poverty* on different states in India and the literature cited there.

9. See the literature cited in my "Gender and Cooperative Conflicts."

10. See Elisabeth Croll, *Chinese Women Since Mao* (M.E. Sharpe, 1984).

11. See *World Development Report 1990,* Tables 1 and 32. See also Banister, *China's Changing Population*, Chapter 4, and Athar Hussain and Nicholas Stern. *On the recent increase in death rate in China,* China Paper #8 (London: STICERD/London School of Economics, 1990).

12. See Margery Wolf, *Revolution Postponed: Women in Contemporary China* (Stanford University Press, 1984).

13. See Banister, *China's Changing Population,* Table 4.12.

14. On this and related matters, see Nahid Aslanbeigui and Gale Summerfield, "The Impact of the Responsibility System on Women in Rural China: A Theoretical Application of Sen's Theory of Entitlement," in *World Development,* Vol.17 (1989).

15. These and other aspects of the problem are discussed more extensively in my joint book with Jean Drèze, *Hunger and Public Action* (Oxford University Press, 1989).

16. For interesting investigations of the role of education, broadly defined, in influencing women's well-being in Bangladesh and India, see Martha Chen, *A Quiet Revolution: Women in Transition in Rural Bangladesh* (Schenkman Books, 1983); and Alaka Basu, *Culture, the Status of Women and Demographic Behavior* (New Delhi: National Council of Applied Economic Research, 1988).

17. Kerala has also had considerable missionary activity in schooling (a fifth of the population is, in fact, Christian), has had international trading and political contacts (both with east and west Asia) for a very long time, and it was from Kerala that the great Hindu philosopher and educator Sankaracarya, who lived during AD 788–820, had launched his big movement of setting up centers of study and worship across India.

Chapter 32

The State and Progress of Human Development

UNITED NATIONS

Human development is about people, about expanding their choices to lead lives they value. Economic growth, increased international trade and investment, technological advance — all are very important. But they are means, not ends. Whether they contribute to human development in the 21st century will depend on whether they expand people's choices, whether they help create an environment for people to develop their full potential and lead productive, creative lives.

Fundamental to enlarging human choices is building human capabilities: the range of things that people can do or be. The most basic capabilities for human development are leading a long and healthy life, being educated, having access to the resources needed for a decent standard of living and being able to participate in the life of one's community. As this Report emphasizes, assuring people's dignity also requires that they be free — and able — to participate in the formation and stewardship of the rules and institutions that govern them. A poor man who cannot afford to send his children to school, but must send them to work in the fields, is lacking in human development. So is a wealthy educated woman whose gender excludes her from voting in elections.

In today's new era of global integration, is human development moving forward? There has been clear progress in some areas. The share of the world's people living in extreme poverty is slowly but steadily declining, from 29% in 1990 to 23% in 1999.[1] Primary school enrollments have risen worldwide, from 80% in 1990 to 84%

in 1998.[2] Since 1990, 800 million people have gained access to improved water supplies, and 750 million to improved sanitation.[3] There also have been great improvements in political and civil rights: since 1980, 81 countries have taken significant steps in democratization,[4] with 33 military regimes replaced by civilian governments.[5]

But in a globalizing world the increasing interconnectedness of nations and peoples has made the differences between them more glaring. A girl born in Japan today may have a 50% chance of seeing the 22nd century[6] — while a newborn in Afghanistan has a 1 in 4 chance of dying before age 5. And the richest 5% of the world's people have incomes 114 times those of the poorest 5%.[7] Every day more than 30,000 children around the world die of preventable diseases,[8] and nearly 14,000 people are infected with HIV/AIDS.[9] In Botswana more than a third of adults have the disease, in Swaziland and Zimbabwe more than a quarter. If tuberculosis control does not improve, 1 billion people will contract it by 2020 — and 35 million will die from it.[10]

In Sub-Saharan Africa human development has actually regressed in recent years, and the lives of its very poor people are getting worse. The share of people living on $1 a day was about the same at the end of the 1990s — 47% — as at the start.[11] Thus, because of population growth, the number of poor people in the region has increased. And while most of the world has increased the share of children who are immunized against the leading diseases, since 1990 immunization rates in Sub-Saharan Africa have fallen below 50%.[12]

Global progress on political freedoms has also been uneven. The spread of democratization appears to have stalled, with many countries failing to consolidate and deepen the first steps towards democracy and several slipping back into authoritarianism. Some 73 countries — with 42% of the world's people — still do not hold free and fair elections,[13] and 106 governments still restrict many civil and political freedoms.[14] In addition, conflict continues to blight the lives of millions: since 1990, 3.6 million people have died in civil wars and ethnic violence, more than 16 times the number killed in wars between states.[15]

There is growing recognition that all countries pay a price for these global injustices. And there is greater acceptance of the need for action to narrow the gap between global potential and reality — and to advance global human development in its deepest sense.

In surveying the progress of countries towards human development in its many dimensions, this chapter highlights the directions for change in the years ahead — and how far it will need to go. The chapter begins by looking at global trends in political participation and democracy, the subjects of this Report. It then considers the Millennium Development Goals, set by the global community to monitor development along a number of dimensions. It assesses progress towards the goals, showing that many countries are on track but that many others are lagging and unlikely to achieve the goals.

TRENDS IN POLITICAL PARTICIPATION AND DEMOCRACY AROUND THE WORLD

Political participation and freedom are fundamental parts of human development. The world has more democratic countries and more political participation than ever, with 140 countries holding multiparty elections (Table 32.1). Of 147 countries with data, 121 — with 68% of the world's people — have some or all of the elements of formal democracy in 2000 (Figure 32.1).[16] This compares with only 54 countries, with 46% of the world's people, in 1980. Since then 81 countries have taken significant steps in democratization, while 6 have regressed.[17] Scores of authoritarian regimes have been replaced by governments more accountable to the people — a real achievement for human development. But true democratization means more than elections. It requires the consolidation of democratic institutions and the strengthening of democratic practices, with democratic values and norms embedded in all parts of society.

The last two decades of the 20th century have been dubbed the "third wave" of democratization, as dictatorial regimes fell in scores of countries.[18] Like history's other movements for liberation, these democratic revolutions were propelled by people. In the 1980s growing pressures against the excesses of military dictatorships in Latin America caused them to topple one after another, starting with Ecuador and Peru. In Central and Eastern Europe and what is now the Commonwealth of Independent States (CIS), the fall of the Berlin Wall in 1989 was the turning point. In Africa rising opposition through the 1980s and 1990s tossed out many long-standing dictators, including Mali's Moussa Traoré in 1991 and Malawi's Kamuzu Banda in 1994. People's power in the Philippines removed Ferdinand Marcos in 1986.

For some countries the transition has been less dramatic, as with the move to civilian rule in the Republic of Korea and Thailand and the introduction of elections in Nepal. Perhaps most striking was the advent of full democracy in South Africa in 1994 — the result of long negotiations. Democratic reforms have been relatively modest in the Arab States, with a few cases of democratic ferment. But monarchies such as Jordan and Morocco have increased space for people's participation in the political life of the community, and Tunisia has taken steps to

TABLE 32.1 MOST PEOPLE CAN NOW VOTE IN MULTIPARTY ELECTIONS, 1999

	REGION OR COUNTRY GROUP		
	Number of Countries with Multiparty Electoral Systems (countries with data)	Population of Countries with Multiparty Electoral Systems (millions)	Share of Regional Population Living in Countries with Multiparty Electoral Systems (percent)
Sub-Saharan Africa	29 (42)	464	77.2
Arab States	4 (7)	115	48.5
East Asia and the Pacific	9 (16)	401	22.0
South Asia	4 (8)	1,170	85.5
Latin America and the Caribbean	25 (26)	468	94.9
Central and Eastern Europe and CIS	21 (25)	350	88.0
OECD	30 (30)	1,120	100.0
Low human development	23 (36)	527	64.4
World	140 (189)	3,923	65.8

NOTE: Low human development countries are also included in their respective regional groups. Regional data do not sum to the world total because some countries included in the world total are not included in a regional group.

SOURCE: Human Development Report Office calculations based on Alvarez and others 2002.

FIGURE 32.1 THE WORLD BECOMING MORE DEMOCRATIC

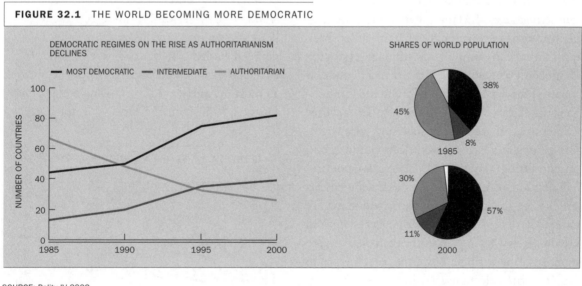

SOURCE: Polity IV 2002.

expand political participation. Still, the region has been slower to democratize than other parts of the world, and only 4 of 7 countries have multiparty electoral systems.[19]

The global shift from authoritarian to democratic regimes shows up in various indications of governance. The number of authoritarian countries fell from almost 70 in 1980 to fewer than 30 in 2000.[20] Over the same period the number of democratic regimes doubled, from 41 to 82. The breakup of the Soviet Union contributed to the jump in country coverage. Overall, the former

Soviet Union and the rest of Eastern Europe have become more democratic.

General indicators do not capture the complexity of political transitions. Most attempts at democratization are fragmented, involving small steps and large, forward and back. Take Peru. In 1980, after 12 years of military rule, it shifted to a democratic regime. But the situation slowly deteriorated, with president Alberto Fujimori's regime becoming increasingly authoritarian. Despite irregularities that led international observers to withdraw, Fujimori was proclaimed the winner of the 2000 elections. But public outrage over political scandals ultimately forced him to flee the country. Alejandro Toledo was elected president after elections in 2001.

While the long-term and recent trends have been impressive, the slight drop in measured democracy in Sub-Saharan Africa and South Asia in the second half of the 1990s reflects the fact that the "third wave" of democratization seems to have stalled. Of the 81 countries that have taken steps in democratization, only 47 are considered full democracies.[21] Many others do not seem to be in transition to anything or have lapsed back into authoritarianism — or conflict, as in the Democratic Republic of Congo, Sierra Leone and others. This has been especially common in Sub-Saharan Africa and Central Asia. In Belarus, Cameroon, Togo, Uzbekistan and elsewhere, one-party states have allowed elections but ended up permitting only limited opening for political competition. Most of these "limited" democracies suffer from shallow political participation, where citizens have little trust in their governments and are disaffected from politics, or the countries are dominated by a single powerful party or group despite formal elections.[22]

BROADER MEASURES OF PARTICIPATION AND POLITICAL FREEDOM

Democratic political participation requires more than elections for governments — truly democratic politics requires civil and political rights to provide the space for effective participation. Illustrating the greater importance attached to human rights worldwide, the number of countries ratifying the six main human rights conventions and covenants has increased dramatically since 1990 (Figure 32.2). Upholding human rights is crucial for guaranteeing people's well-being and securing a humane and non-discriminatory society — and for enabling an active and engaged citizenry. Freedoms of association and assembly, of expression and conscience, as laid out in the International Covenant on Civil and Political Rights, are fundamental to political participation.

A free and active press is particularly important for the creation and consolidation of democracy. Freedom House's Freedom of the Press Index indicates levels and trends worldwide, showing that press freedom has also been increasing (Figure 32.3).

In addition to civil and political rights, equitable opportunities for participation are crucial to democratic politics. But around the world, women are seriously underrepresented in domestic politics, accounting for only 14% of national parliamentarians. There is little difference between industrial and developing countries. In most industrial countries — including France, Japan and the United States — women account

FIGURE 32.2 RATIFICATION OF HUMAN RIGHTS TREATIES

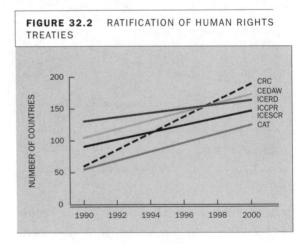

SOURCE: Human Development Report Office calculations based on UNOHCHR 2002.

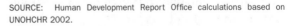

FIGURE 32.3   THE PRESS BECOMES FREER

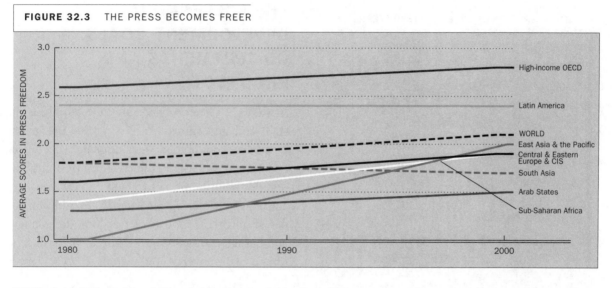

SOURCE: Human Development Report Office calculations based on Freedom House 2000.

for 10–20% of parliamentarians.[23] Positive exceptions worldwide include both developing and industrial countries (Figure 32.4). Nordic countries do particularly well, but in Argentina, Mozambique and South Africa about 30% of parliamentarians are women. Meanwhile, a number of Arab states have no female representation.

THE PROLIFERATION OF CIVIL CONFLICT

The stalling of democratic transitions highlights the fragility of democracies. The proliferation of conflicts, particularly internal conflicts, highlights the fragility of states (Figure 32.5 on page 372). Internal conflicts today vastly outnumber wars between states. Since 1990 an estimated 220,000 people have died in wars between states — compared with nearly 3.6 million in wars within states.[24]

Particularly tragic is the fact that civilians, not soldiers, are increasingly the victims of conflicts. Civilians have accounted for more than 90% of the casualties — either injured or killed — in post-cold war conflicts.[25] Moreover, internal conflicts are usually fought with small weapons, and combatants use strategies that have the strongest

FIGURE 32.4 WOMEN'S PARTICIPATION LAGS EVERYWHERE

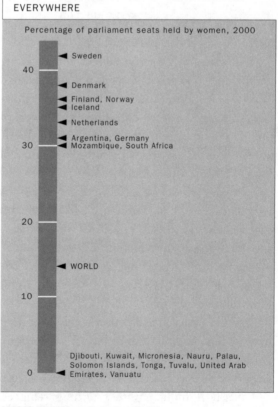

SOURCE: IPU 2000c and indicator table 23.

impact on the vulnerable. Children account for half of all civilian casualties in wars,[26] and worldwide

FIGURE 32.5 THE POOREST HAVE SUFFERED THE MOST FROM CONFLICT

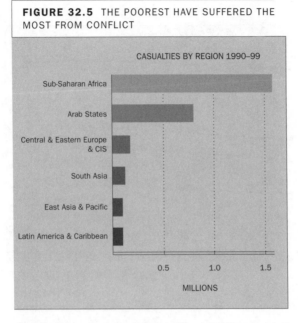

SOURCE: Human Development Report Office calculations based on Marshall 2000.

there are an estimated 300,000 child soldiers — in Sierra Leone, Sudan and elsewhere.[27]

Civil wars also have grave effects on economic growth and food production, as revealed by such human development indicators as infant mortality rates and school enrollments.[28] Seven of the ten countries with the lowest human development indices have recently suffered major civil wars. During Mozambique's 16-year civil war more than 40% of schools were destroyed or forced to close, and more than 40% of health centres were destroyed. Industries were so damaged that postwar production was only 20–40% of prewar capacity, with economic losses estimated at $15 billion — several times Mozambique's prewar GDP.[29]

Fighting between and within states also causes massive refugee flows and displaced populations. At the end of 2000 more than 12 million people were refugees, 6 million were internally displaced and nearly 4 million were returning refugees, asylum-seekers or people otherwise of concern to the UN High Commissioner for Refugees[30] — in all, 50% more than in 1990.[31] The increase in refugees and displaced populations indicates that today's armed conflicts are more intense.

THE MILLENNIUM DEVELOPMENT GOALS: COMMITMENTS AND PROSPECTS

At the UN General Assembly in 2000, heads of state and government took stock of the gross inequalities in human development worldwide and recognized "their collective responsibility to uphold the principles of human dignity, equality and equity at the global level."[32] In addition to declaring their support for freedom, democracy and human rights, they set eight goals for development and poverty eradication, to be achieved by 2015:

- Eradicate extreme poverty and hunger.
- Achieve universal primary education.
- Achieve gender equality and empower women.
- Reduce child mortality.
- Improve maternal health.
- Combat HIV/AIDS, malaria and other diseases.
- Ensure environmental sustainability.
- Develop a global partnership for development.[33]

Most of the Millennium Development Goals have quantifiable, monitorable targets to measure progress against standards set by the international community. This Report assesses how likely countries are to achieve goals by 2015 if recent trends continue, classifying them as achieved, on track, lagging, far behind or slipping back. The analysis assumes that trends over the next decade will be the same as over the past decade. Whether countries fall behind or surpass this expectation will depend on their actions and those of the global community between now and 2015.

Many countries have made progress. But much of the world, generally the poorest countries, seems unlikely to achieve the goals. Although 55 countries, with 23% of the world's people, are on track to achieve at least three-quarters of the goals, 33 countries with 26% of the world's people are failing on more than half

(Figure 32.6A). Especially extraordinary efforts will be needed in Sub-Saharan Africa, where 23 countries are failing and 11 others do not have enough data to be assessed — a possible indication that they are even further behind. That leaves just 10 Sub-Saharan countries on track to meet at least half of the goals (Figure 32.6B).

Lack of data makes it difficult to assess progress on the goal of halving income poverty. But slow growth in average incomes indicates that many countries will have to struggle to achieve the goal. Optimistic estimates suggest that 3.7% annual growth in per capita GDP will be needed, yet in the 1990s only 24 countries achieved such growth (Figure 32.7 on page 374).[34] China and India, the most populous countries, are in this group. But incomes in nearly 130 countries, with 40% of the world's people, are not growing fast enough — including 52 countries that actually had negative growth in the 1990s. Again, progress is most

elusive in the poorest countries: 40 of 44 Sub-Saharan countries, with 93% of the region's people, grew too slowly. Half of those 40 countries, with more than half of the region's people, are poorer now than in 1990. These include 11 of the world's 20 poorest countries.

Countries have come closer to some goals than others. Many developing countries have already achieved or are on track to achieve universal primary education and gender equity in education. Given the importance of education to so many other areas of development, this bodes well for accelerating progress towards the other goals. Most developing countries have also achieved or are on track to achieve the targets for eradicating hunger and improving water supplies (part of the environmental goal). But more than 40 countries, with 28% of the world's people, are not on track to halve hunger by 2015. And 25 countries, with 32% of the world's people, may not halve the share of people lacking access to an improved water source. Most pressing, however, is child mortality: 85

FIGURE 32.6A COUNTRIES ON TRACK TO MEET THE MILLENNIUM DEVELOPMENT GOALS

All UN member countries excluding high-income OECD

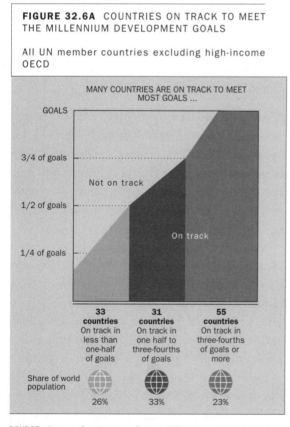

SOURCE: Human Development Report Office calculations based on appendix table A1.3.

FIGURE 32.6B COUNTRIES ON TRACK TO MEET THE MILLENNIUM DEVELOPMENT GOALS

Sub-Saharan Africa

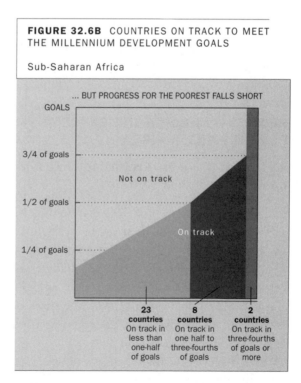

SOURCE: Human Development Report Office calculations based on appendix table A1.3.

FIGURE 32.7   FAILING TO GROW OUT OF POVERTY

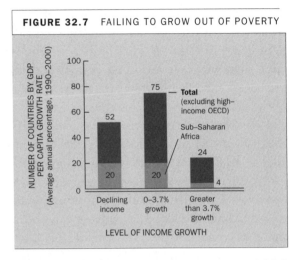

SOURCE: Human Development Report Office calculations based on indicator table 12.

TABLE 32.2   WORLDWIDE, THE NUMBER OF PEOPLE LIVING ON LESS THAN $1 A DAY BARELY CHANGED IN THE 1990S

REGION	SHARE (PERCENT)		NUMBER (MILLIONS)	
	1990	1999	1990	1999
Sub-Saharan Africa	47.7	46.7	242	300
East Asia and the Pacific Excluding China	18.5	7.9	92	46
South Asia	44.0	36.9	495	490
Latin America and the Caribbean	16.8	15.1	74	77
Eastern Europe and Central Asia	1.6	3.6	7	17
Middle East and North Africa	2.4	2.3	6	7
Total	**29.0**	**22.7**	**1,276**	**1,151**
Excluding China	**28.1**	**24.5**	**916**	**936**

NOTE: $1 a day is $1.08 in 1993 purchasing power parity (PPP) prices.

SOURCE: World Bank 2002c.

countries with more than 60% of the world's people are not on track to achieve the goal.

A goal that cannot be monitored cannot be met or missed — and one of the most startling conclusions is the lack of data. The targets for poverty, HIV/AIDS and maternal mortality cannot be monitored directly with current international data. Even targets that can be monitored have many gaps in the data. Complicating matters, countries lacking data may have the worst performance, giving an inflated impression of the proportion of countries that are progressing.

GOAL 1 — ERADICATING EXTREME POVERTY AND HUNGER

Target 1a: Halve the Proportion of People Living on Less than $1 a Day

In 1999, 2.8 billion people lived on less than $2 a day, with 1.2 billion of them barely surviving at the margins of subsistence on less than $1 a day (Table 32.2). During the 1990s the number of extremely poor people dropped only slightly. But because of population growth, the share of the world's people living in extreme poverty fell from 29% in 1990 to 23% in 1999.

The declining share of people in extreme poverty is hopeful, but the level remains disturbingly high. And the failure to reduce poverty in Sub-Saharan Africa, the world's poorest region, is a grave concern.

Per Capita Income. A country's income poverty rate is determined by its per capita income and by the distribution of that income. Though there is no guarantee that poor people will benefit from an increase in their country's average per capita income, aggregate growth typically does increase their incomes.[35]

Since the mid-1970s growth in per capita income has varied dramatically across regions. East Asia and the Pacific's impressive poverty reduction is primarily due to a quadrupling in its per capita GDP between 1975 and 2000. But Sub-Saharan Africa ended the millennium 5% poorer than in 1990.

Central and Eastern Europe and the CIS was the only other region to suffer a decline in per capita income during the 1990s. Growth in the region is picking up, and a few countries have done quite well. But in many countries incomes remain far lower than in the past.

Income Inequality within Countries. The amount of growth required to reduce poverty depends on a country's level of inequality — the more unequal is the distribution of income, the fewer are the benefits of growth to poor people. Studies of inequality trends within countries suffer from a lack of reliable, comparable data. The limited available evidence indicates that worldwide, within-country income inequality has been increasing for the past 30 years.[36] Among the 73 countries with data (and 80% of the world's people), 48 have seen inequality increase since the 1950s, 16 have experienced no change and only 9 — with just 4% of the world's people — have seen inequality fall.[37] The increase in inequality has impeded poverty reduction. Given current inequality levels, most countries are not growing fast enough to meet the poverty target. Thus efforts must focus on making growth more pro-poor.[38]

Target 1b: Halve the Proportion of People Suffering from Hunger

Children suffer doubly from hunger: it affects their daily lives and has devastating consequences for their future mental and physical health. In 50 countries with almost 40% of the world's people, more than one-fifth of children under the age of five are underweight.[39] That 17 of those countries are in the medium human development category underscores hunger's pervasiveness. Still, the problem is worst among the world's poorest countries. In Sub-Saharan Africa only South Africa has less than a 10% incidence of child malnourishment. In six Sub-Saharan countries that figure is more than 40%.

A rough indication of how countries are moving towards halving hunger by 2015 comes from changes in the number of malnourished people — a less precise indicator of hunger than child malnutrition rates, based on national food availability and estimated distribution. In 1997–99 an estimated 815 million people were undernourished: 777 million in developing countries, 27 million in transition economies and 11 million in industrial countries.[40]

There are some reasons for optimism. Fifty-seven countries, with half of the world's people, have halved hunger or are on track to do so by 2015. But progress is far from universal. Twenty-four countries are far behind in achieving the target. And in 15 more — 6 from Sub-Saharan Africa — the situation worsened in the 1990s.

While the proportion of hungry people has been declining, the world's booming population means that the number of malnourished people has not been falling fast enough. During the 1990s it declined by just 6 million people a year.[41] At this rate it would take more than 130 years to rid the world of hunger.

GOAL 2 — ACHIEVING UNIVERSAL PRIMARY EDUCATION

Target 2a: Ensure That Children Everywhere — Boys and Girls Alike — Complete a Full Course of Primary Education

Education is important in its own right and has strong spillover benefits to mortality rates, income and even social cohesion. Worldwide, primary enrollments have been improving, rising from 80% in 1990 to 84% in 1998. But that still means that of the 680 million children of primary school age, 113 million are not in school — 97% of them in developing countries.[42]

Many countries have good prospects for achieving universal primary education. But there is little middle ground: most of those not on track to achieve the goal are far behind or have worsening primary enrollments. Sub-Saharan Africa fares worst — of the 21 countries with data, 14 are far behind the target or have deteriorating enrollments. Furthermore, 93 countries with 39% of the world's people do not have sufficient data to make a judgement.

Enrolling children in primary school is only half the battle, because it is meaningful only if they complete it — which requires that they and their families be able to resist the pressures of forgone income and work in the home. Of the few countries with data on primary school completion, most seem to be on track. But again the news is worse for Sub-Saharan Africa, where 6 countries are on track and 5 are far behind or slipping back — and the 33 countries without data are likely to be among the poor performers.

Literacy. One of the most important outcomes of primary education is literacy. And literacy rates are slow to change, reflecting the education of previous generations of children and the history of school enrollment. Since 1975 literacy rates have increased substantially in all developing regions. East Asia and the Pacific and Latin America and the Caribbean seem to be converging, with close to 90% adult literacy. But Sub-Saharan Africa, South Asia and Arab States, despite significant progress, are much further behind, with adult literacy rates of about 60%. In the past 25 years literacy rates in low human development countries have doubled — though only to 50%.

Functional Literacy. Among OECD countries, literacy rates are often assumed to be close to 100%. But the truth is very different. The concept of functional illiteracy describes the inability to understand and use common channels of communication and information in an everyday context, from newspapers and books to pamphlets and instructions on medicine bottles. Based on this measure, in most OECD countries an incredible 10–20% of people are functionally illiterate, with Sweden and Norway doing relatively well at 8% and 9% while Ireland, the United Kingdom and the United States have levels over 20%.

GOAL 3 — ACHIEVING GENDER EQUALITY AND EMPOWERING WOMEN

Target 3a: Eliminate Gender Disparities in Primary and Secondary Education, Preferably by 2005, and In All Levels of Education by 2015

The Millennium Development Goal for gender equality in education responds to dramatic gender disparities in many parts of the world, particularly South Asia and West, Central and North Africa. In India the enrollment ratio of boys aged 6–14 is 17 percentage points higher than that of girls the same age, in Benin 21 percentage points. Yet in many developing countries, mostly in Latin America, girls have no disadvantage or even a small advantage.[43] Still, of the world's estimated 854 million illiterate adults, 544 million are women — and of the 113 million children not in primary school, 60% are girls.[44] The world is still a long way from achieving equal rights and opportunities between females and males.

The gaps are closing in primary and, to a lesser extent, secondary enrollments: 90 countries, with more than 60% of the world's people, have achieved or are on track to achieving gender equality in primary education by 2015 — and more than 80 in secondary education.

Perhaps most surprising is the performance of Arab States — countries generally associated with high gender inequality. All but one of those with data are on track to meet the target for primary enrollments. Again, Sub-Saharan Africa is making the least progress, but even there most countries have achieved or are on track to achieve gender equality in primary enrollment.

Education is just one aspect of human development in which there is discrimination between the sexes. Around the world, women still earn only around 75% as much as men. Domestic violence against women is common in many societies. And around the world there are an estimated 100 million "missing" women — 50 million in India alone — who would be alive but for infanticide, neglect or sex-selective abortions. A recent survey in India found 10,000 cases of female infanticide a year, and a study of a clinic in Bombay found that 7,999 of 8,000 aborted foetuses were female.[45]

Worse outcomes for women in many aspects of human development result from the fact that their voices have less impact than men's in the decisions that shape their lives. This inequality in empowerment is partly captured by the gender empowerment measure (GEM), introduced in *Human Development Report 1995* to help assess gender inequality in economic and political opportunities. This year the GEM has been estimated for 66 countries. Some observations:

- GEM values range from less than 0.300 to more than 0.800 — indicating enormous variation around the world in empowering women.
- Only 5 of the 66 countries — Denmark, Finland, Iceland, Norway and Sweden — have a GEM above 0.800, while 22 have a GEM below 0.500.
- Some developing countries outperform much richer industrial countries. The Bahamas and Trinidad and Tobago are ahead of Italy and Japan. Barbados's GEM is 25% higher than Greece's. The message: high income is not a prerequisite to creating opportunities for women.

Inequalities beyond Gender. The Millennium Development goals consider gender inequality in education — but this is only one aspect of unfair access to schooling. While gender gaps in education are large in some countries and non-existent in others, wealth gaps exist the world over. Extreme examples include Senegal, where the enrollment ratio for 6–14-year-olds from the poorest households is 52 percentage points lower than for those from the richest households, and Zambia, with a 36 point difference. Such wealth gaps perpetuate the cycle of poverty: those born poor are likely to die poor. Furthermore, in some countries (Egypt, India, Morocco, Niger, Pakistan) the gender gap in education is much larger for poor households. In India the gender gap in enrollment is only 3 percentage points in the richest households, but 34 points in the poorest.[46]

One cause of such gaps is that in many countries, public spending on education is skewed towards the rich. In Ecuador the poorest 20% of households receive only 11% of public education spending, while the richest 20% receive 26% — more than twice as much.[47] Even when public spending is distributed more equitably, rich parents can buy a far better education for their children at private schools. In Chile, Peru,

the Philippines and Thailand private spending accounts for more than 40% of education spending.[48]

Education inequality is also a serious problem in some industrial countries. In the United States race is a significant factor: minorities have lower schooling levels and less access to high-quality schooling. Controlling for parental education and immigrant status, young African Americans perform worse in functional literacy tests than do young white Americans — on average, by the equivalent of four to five years of schooling. The gap for Hispanic Americans is one and a half to two years.[49]

GOAL 4 — REDUCING CHILD MORTALITY

Target 4a: Reduce Infant and Under-Five Mortality Rates by Two-Thirds

Every year about 11 million children die of preventable causes,[50] often for want of simple and easily provided improvements in nutrition, sanitation and maternal health and education. Some developing regions have made rapid improvements in this area — especially Arab States, where 6% of children die before age five, down from 20% in 1970.

Although Latin America and the Caribbean are doing well as a whole, eight countries are far from achieving the infant mortality target. In East Asia and the Pacific 13 countries are on track but 3, including China, are far behind — and in Cambodia under-five mortality rates are increasing. Central and Eastern Europe and the CIS, doing badly as a whole, combine good performance from the European countries and worse performance from the more populous CIS countries. In Sub-Saharan Africa 34 of 44 countries are far behind or slipping back.

Immunizations against leading diseases are a vital element in improving child survival. After soaring in the 1980s, immunizations in developing countries levelled off at about 75% in the 1990s. And in recent years the proportion of children immunized in Sub-Saharan Africa has fallen below 50%.

Child mortality has a dramatic effect on a country's life expectancy, which is part of the HDI and is an excellent indicator of a country's overall health. Between 1975 and 2000 East Asia and the Pacific increased life expectancy by about 8 years, to almost 70 (Figure 32.8). South Asia, Latin America and the Caribbean and Arab States also achieved consistent increases. But high-income OECD countries are still head and shoulders above the rest, with a life expectancy of 77 years — 7 years more than the next-highest region.

Sub-Saharan Africa, ravaged by HIV/AIDS and conflict, saw life expectancy reverse in the 1990s from already tragically low levels. Eastern Europe and the CIS also suffered a decline, and is the only other region where life expectancy is lower now than in 1990.

GOAL 5 — IMPROVING MATERNAL HEALTH

Target 5a: Reduce Maternal Mortality Ratios by Three-Quarters

Every year more than 500,000 women die as a result of pregnancy and childbirth,[51] with huge regional disparities (Table 32.3). The situation is worst in Sub-Saharan Africa, where a woman has a 1 in 13 chance of dying in pregnancy or childbirth.

Increasing the number of births attended by skilled health personnel is key to reducing maternal mortality ratios, and again there is wide variation — with as few as 29% of births attended by skilled personnel in South Asia and 37% in Sub-Saharan Africa.[52]

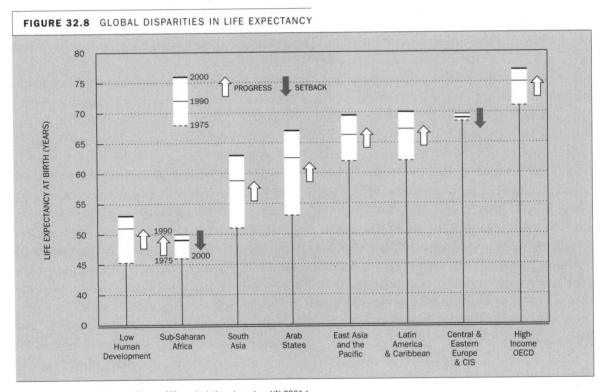

FIGURE 32.8 GLOBAL DISPARITIES IN LIFE EXPECTANCY

SOURCE: Human Development Report Office calculations based on UN 2001d.

TABLE 32.3 MATERNAL MORTALITY IS MUCH HIGHER IN SOME REGIONS

REGION	LIFETIME CHANCE OF DYING IN PREGNANCY OR CHILDBIRTH
Sub-Saharan Africa	1 in 13
South Asia	1 in 54
Middle East and North Africa	1 in 55
Latin America and the Caribbean	1 in 157
East Asia and the Pacific	1 in 283
Central and Eastern Europe and CIS	1 in 797
OECD	1 in 4,085

NOTE: Data refer to most recent year available.

SOURCE: UNICEF 2002.

There are not enough data on maternal mortality or births attended by skilled health personnel to assess how countries are progressing towards this important goal, indicating an urgent need for more complete, comparable data on this vital issue.

GOAL 6 — COMBATING HIV/AIDS, MALARIA AND OTHER DISEASES

Target 6a: Halt and Begin to Reverse the Spread of HIV/AIDS

By the end of 2000 almost 22 million people had died from AIDS, 13 million children had lost their mother or both parents to the disease and more than 40 million people were living with the HIV virus — 90% of them in developing countries, 75% in Sub-Saharan Africa.[53]

In Botswana, the most affected country more than a third of adults have HIV/AIDS and a child born today can expect to live only 36 years — about half as long as if the disease did not exist

(Figure 32.9). In Burkina Faso, the 20th most affected country, 330,000 adults are living with HIV/AIDS, and life expectancy has fallen by 8 years.[54]

The toll on life expectancy is only the beginning. In Thailand one-third of AIDS-affected rural families saw their incomes fall by half because the time of farmers, and those caring for them, was taken from the fields.[55] At the same time, medical expenses shoot up. In Côte d'Ivoire caring for a male AIDS patient costs an average of $300 a year, a quarter to half of the net annual income of most small farms.[56] The effect on poor households, with little or no savings to cope with such shocks, is devastating. In urban Côte d'Ivoire food consumption dropped 41% per capita, and school outlays halved.[57]

HIV/AIDS is also a concern in the Caribbean, the region with the second highest infection rate. In Latin America 1.3 million people have HIV/AIDS. Central and Eastern Europe and the

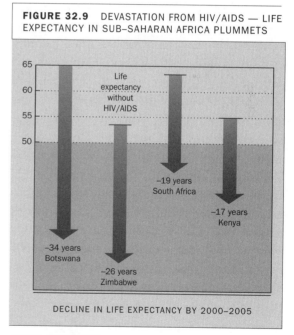

FIGURE 32.9 DEVASTATION FROM HIV/AIDS — LIFE EXPECTANCY IN SUB–SAHARAN AFRICA PLUMMETS

DECLINE IN LIFE EXPECTANCY BY 2000–2005

SOURCE: UVDESA 2001.

CIS has fast-rising infection rates — 240,000 people are now infected in Ukraine.[58] And there are warnings that Asia is on the verge of an epidemic. In Ho Chi Minh City, Vietnam, one sex worker in five is HIV positive, up from almost none in the mid-1990s. And nearly 4 million people are now infected in India, second only to South Africa.[59] Without strong preventative measures, as in Thailand, the epidemic could rage out of control.

There are no comparable trend data for assessing how well countries are fighting the disease. But it is clear that policies can make a difference and that contraceptive prevalence and reproductive rights for women are vital. Through preventive measures, Uganda reduced HIV rates from 14% in the early 1990s to around 8% by the end of the 1990s.[60]

Also vital is providing treatment and care to those already affected. But at a cost of $300 per year per patient — well over half the GDP per capita of Sub-Saharan Africa — antiretroviral drugs that can prolong life expectancy are out of reach for the average African HIV patient. As homes to the leading pharmaceutical companies, some industrial countries have pressured developing countries not to manufacture generic alternatives of these patented drugs. But in November 2001 the World Trade Organization ministerial conference in Doha, Qatar, adopted the Declaration on Trade-Related Intellectual Property Rights and Public Health, affirming the sovereign right of governments to protect public health. The legal status of this declaration is not yet clear, but it indicates that rulings on disputes may now favour public health. One issue that remains uncertain is whether countries can override patents and produce generic drugs for export to other developing countries — a crucial question for all developing countries with no pharmaceutical industry of their own. Goal 8, developing a global partnership for development, includes the aspiration of resolving this problem with the help of pharmaceutical companies. Whether this proves to be possible, in the wake of the Doha declaration, it is clear that international law must put global public health first.

Target 6b: Halt and Begin to Reverse the Incidence of Malaria and other Major Diseases

Every year there are more than 300 million cases of malaria, 90% of them in Sub-Saharan Africa.[61] And every year 60 million people are infected with tuberculosis.[62] Current medical technologies can prevent these diseases from being fatal, but lack of access means that tuberculosis kills 2 million people a year[63] and malaria 1 million.[64] The poorest people typically suffer most.

Without much more effective control, by 2020 nearly 1 billion people will be infected and 35 million will die from tuberculosis.[65] In addition to its human costs, disease takes a heavy economic toll: for instance, high malaria prevalence can lower economic growth by 1% or more a year.[66] Work is under way to strengthen national health systems and increase international support, and there are some encouraging signs: the World Health Organization, for example, has struck a deal with the Swiss firm Novartis on the drug Coartem, an extremely effective malaria treatment. The price of this drug, which can reduce infection and fatality rates by 75%, has fallen to less than $2.50 a treatment.[67] But this is still far more than many people can afford — and only the beginning of efforts to overcome these diseases.

GOAL 7 — ENDURING ENVIRONMENTAL SUSTAINABILITY

The diversity of environmental issues across countries and regions makes it extremely difficult to set global targets, so this goal sets out general principles for achieving sustainability and reducing the human costs of environmental degradation.

Target 7a: Integrate the Principles of Sustainable Development into Country Policies and Programmes and Reverse the Loss of Environmental Resources

Global warming is a universal concern — and carbon dioxide emissions are one of its main causes. Such emissions have increased dramatically, to more than 6.6 billion tons in 1998, up from 5.3 billion in 1980.[68] High-income countries generate a far higher proportion than their share of the world's population (Figure 32.10).

Around the world, goods production has generally become more energy-efficient in the past few decades. But the increased volume of global production means that such improvements are far from sufficient to reduce world carbon dioxide emissions. So the Kyoto Protocol to the Framework Convention on Climate Change aims to reduce emissions, mainly through controls on industrial pollution. The protocol could be a big step towards controlling emissions. But 165 countries, responsible for 89% of global carbon dioxide emissions, have yet to ratify it.

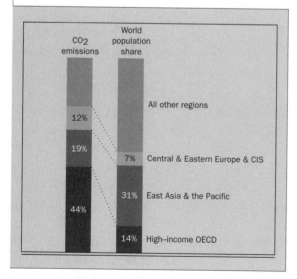

FIGURE 32.10   CARBON DIOXIDE EMISSIONS ORIGINATE DISPROPORTIONATELY IN HIGH-INCOME COUNTRIES

SOURCE: Indicator table 19 and Human Development Report Office calculations basd on indicator table 5.

The key missing player is the United States, responsible for almost one-quarter of the world's carbon dioxide emissions.

The ratification of international treaties can be a useful means of measuring a country's formal commitment to key environmental issues that are not globally monitorable. Deforestation, risks to endangered species and the state of the world's fisheries are broadly covered by the 1992 Convention on Biological Diversity, ratified by 168 countries. But such treaties are no guarantee of action. What is needed is detailed understanding of the situation in each country, with plans to ensure that people's enjoyment of the Earth is not at the expense of others — today or in the future.

To that end Agenda 21, adopted in 1992 by governments at the United Nations Conference on Environment and Development (UNCED) in Rio de Janeiro, establishes principles for achieving sustainable development based on the need to manage the economy, the environment and social issues in a coherent, coordinated fashion. By March 2002, 73 countries had signed Agenda 21 and 33 countries had ratified it.[69]

One major topic addressed by Agenda 21 is desertification. Dryland ecosystems — covering more than a third of the world's land area — are extremely vulnerable to overexploitation and inappropriate land use. Poverty, political instability, deforestation, overgrazing and bad irrigation practices can all undermine the land's productivity.

The human cost is enormous. More than 250 million people living off the land are directly affected by desertification. In addition, the livelihoods of 1 billion people in more than a hundred countries are at risk. These include many of the world's poorest, most marginalized and politically powerless people.

The United Nations Convention to Combat Desertification — ratified by 115 countries — aims to combat desertification and mitigate the effects of drought, particularly in Africa. This requires long-term integrated strategies that focus on increasing the productivity of land and on rehabilitating, conserving and sustainably managing land and water resources.[70]

Target 7b: Halve the Proportion of People without Sustainable Safe Drinking Water

Target 7c: Achieve, by 2020, a Significant Improvement in the Lives of at Least 100 Million Slum Dwellers

Environmental conditions particularly affect the health of poor people. Traditional hazards such as lack of safe drinking water, sanitation and waste disposal lead to major outbreaks of diarrhoea, malaria and cholera. Modern hazards such as urban and indoor air pollution can lead to respiratory infections, while exposure to agroindustrial chemicals and waste also causes harm.

The Millennium Declaration separates the goals for safe water and sanitation, using sanitation as an indicator of improving the lives of slum dwellers. In 2000, 1.1 billion people lacked access to safe water, and 2.4 billion did not have access to any form of improved sanitation services.[71]

The health consequences are significant. About 4 billion cases of diarrhoea occur each year, leading to 2.2 million deaths, predominantly among children — representing 15% of child deaths in developing countries. Other concerns include intestinal worms, which infect about 10% of people in the developing world, and trachoma, which has left 6 million people blind and another 500 million at risk.[72]

Human dignity is also at stake. A survey in the Philippines found that among the reasons given for wanting latrines, rural households cited the desire for privacy, cleaner surroundings, lack of flies and lack of embarrassment ahead of health benefits.[73]

There was progress in the 1990s: 800 million more people now have access to improved water than in 1990, and 750 million more to improved sanitation.[74] Most countries with data are on track to halving the proportion of people without access to improved water sources. But the challenge remains enormous, with 27% of the world's people living in countries that are far behind the target.

GOAL 8 — DEVELOPING A GLOBAL PARTNERSHIP FOR DEVELOPMENT

The implications of goal 8 are clear: global action must create an environment in which all people and countries have the chance to realize their potential.

International Aid for the Millennium Development Goals

A key to responsibility is finance. Aid from official and new sources is essential to kickstart the performance of countries failing to achieve the goals — as well as to keep on track those doing well. But how much aid is needed? Accurately estimating the costs of achieving the millennium goals is almost impossible — but it is important for understanding the size of the responsibility of richer nations. Detailed country assessments should be the basis of global estimates. These would allow thorough investigations of how countries are progressing towards the goals, better understanding of the areas for policies to focus on and a much more accurate estimate of the costs of these policies and possible sources of finance. Currently, there are too few country studies of this type to paint a global picture.

Calculating an overall estimate of the cost of achieving all the goals using less direct means is tricky because it must take into account the positive side effects of achieving success in different areas. Some consensus is being reached on a figure that takes these synergies into account — giving a rough total of $40–60 billion a year in addition to the current $56 billion (Figure 32.11).

While approximate, these numbers give an idea of what is required. When compared with current official development assistance from industrial countries, around $56 billion a year, it is clear that aid needs to double. That would

FIGURE 32.11 OFFICIAL DEVELOPMENT ASSISTANCE MUST DOUBLE TO MEET THE MILLENNIUM DEVELOPMENT GOALS

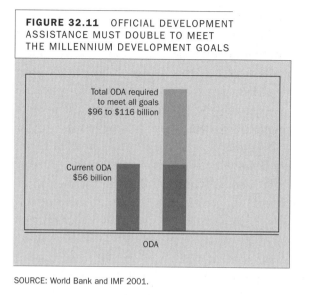

Total ODA required to meet all goals $96 to $116 billion

Current ODA $56 billion

ODA

SOURCE: World Bank and IMF 2001.

FIGURE 32.12 AID HAS DECREASED FROM MOST DAC MEMBER COUNTRIES, 1990–2000

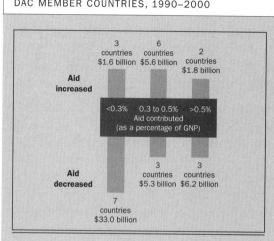

Aid increased

3 countries $1.6 billion   6 countries $5.6 billion   2 countries $1.8 billion

<0.3%   0.3 to 0.5%   >0.5%
Aid contributed (as a percentage of GNP)

Aid decreased

3 countries $5.3 billion   3 countries $6.2 billion

7 countries $33.0 billion

SOURCE: Human Development Report Office calculations based on indicator table 15.

amount to about 0.5% of GNP of the countries on the Development Assistance Committee (DAC) of the Organisation for Economic Cooperation and Development — substantially less than the 0.7% agreed at the UN General Assembly in 1970.

The Millennium Declaration set no specific targets for aid, but if it had most OECD countries would be performing badly. Of the 22 countries on the DAC, 17 give less than 0.5% of their GNP in foreign aid, and 11 give less than 0.3% — and most gave less in 2000 than in 1990 (Figure 32.12).[75] Countries with big economies give the most in absolute terms but not as a percentage of GNP. At $13.5 billion, Japan gives the most aid of all countries, though as a share of its GNP it is in the middle of the range. The United States gives the second highest amount but the lowest proportion.

Aid has fallen substantially in recent years, but announcements in March 2002 — at the UN's International Conference on Financing for Development — suggest that this trend may be reversing. The Bush administration proposed increasing aid over the next three fiscal years so that from the third year onwards the United States would give an additional $5 billion a year over the current level — representing a 50%

increase, to about 0.15% of GNP.[76] EU heads of state and government announced a new target of 0.39% of GNP, to be achieved by 2006, representing an additional $7 billion a year.[77] Though short of doubling aid, and the 0.5% of GNP needed, the proposed increases are a step in the right direction.

Some countries, generally smaller, have bucked the recent trend of diminishing aid. During the 1990s Ireland doubled its aid from 0.16% of GNP to 0.30%, and Luxembourg tripled its from 0.21% to 0.71%.

Alternative forms of financing have become more important but fall far short of substituting for increased official aid. Though small relative to official development assistance, resources generated by non-governmental organizations (NGOs) are substantial (Table 32.4 on page 384). The same is true of contributions by philanthropists. The George Soros Foundation Network gives about $500 million a year, most of it in developing and transition countries, with a focus on human rights, culture and economic and social development.[78] And the Bill and Melinda Gates Foundation has given more than $4 billion since the beginning of 2000, with half of it spent on global health initiatives.[79]

TABLE 32.4 EXPORTS AND DEBT SERVICE DOMINATE RESOURCE FLOWS TO AND FROM DEVELOPING COUNTRIES

TYPE OF FLOWS	PERCENTAGE OF DEVELOPING COUNTRIES' GDP, 2000
Exports	26.0
Debt service	6.3
Net foreign direct investment	2.5
Aid	0.5
Net grants from NGOs	0.1

SOURCE: Human Development Report Office calculations based on indicator tables 14, 15, and 16.

Many developing countries still pay enormous sums in debt. Not all debt is bad: borrowing today to provide returns tomorrow is often prudent. But in many countries debt strangles the public purse — and is often for money spent unproductively long ago, by authoritarian regimes.

The most recent move to reduce debt is the Heavily Indebted Poor Countries (HIPC) initiative, launched by the World Bank and the International Monetary Fund (IMF) in 1996 to provide comprehensive debt relief to the world's poorest, most heavily indebted countries.[80] For low human development countries, 28 of them part of the initiative, debt service fell from 5.1% of GDP in 1990 to 3.6% in 2000. But there have been calls, led by Jubilee 2000, that the relief is not enough — and that too many countries desperately in need are not included. Recent new commitments by the World Bank and the IMF to deepen and broaden debt relief are positive developments.[81]

Better Aid

More aid may be needed to achieve the goals, but there is no guarantee it will have the right impact in the right places. For transfers to hit the targets laid out in the Millennium Declaration, there needs to be not only more aid, but better aid.

Who should receive it? Donors are concentrating aid in countries with a demonstrated ability to monitor and use it effectively.[82] While understandable, this approach also bears great risks. It means that the countries falling behind in achieving the goals, and in greatest need of resources, are least likely to receive aid.

Not only does aid need to be directed to the countries that need it most, it must also go to the right sectors. Only $2 billion of the annual aid from DAC countries is directed towards education.[83] To achieve the goals for education, this will have to increase by $9–12 billion, from about 3.5% of aid to well over 10%. Similarly, a larger proportion of aid will need to go to other basic social services to achieve the goals. But that raises tough issues of setting priorities and reaching an understanding of how best to distribute aid among competing areas.

Trade and Foreign Direct Investment

One-way financial transfers will not be enough to build a global partnership, nor should they be. Developing countries need to compete and prosper in the world economy to drive their own development. The financial flows that developing countries receive from exports dwarf those from other sources, indicating how integrated many of these countries already are (see Table 32.4). And during the 1990s foreign direct investment grew faster than other financial flows to developing countries, from 0.9% of their GDP to 2.5%. Developing countries — especially the poorest countries — still receive only a tiny fraction of total foreign direct investment, but that inflow is now greater than official development assistance.

In principle, participating in the global market offers the same benefits as a flourishing market economy within a country. But global trade is highly regulated, with the powerful holding sway and the playing field far from level. The average poor person in a developing country selling into global markets confronts barriers twice as high as the typical worker in industrial countries,[84] where agricultural subsidies alone are about $1 billion a day — more than six times total aid. These barriers and subsidies cost developing countries more in lost export opportunities than the $56 billion in aid they receive each year.[85]

If there were a levelling of the global playing field, many of the gains would come in low-income, low-skill areas such as agriculture, textiles and clothing. So in many cases both the poorest countries and the poorest people would benefit.[86] Eliminating trade barriers and subsidies in industrial countries that inhibit imports from developing countries is therefore an urgent priority, and potentially a route to greatly accelerated development.

The Millennium Declaration's call for a non-discriminatory trading system places a clear responsibility on the world's richer countries, but it is a small step towards changing the system. And while liberalizing trade will bring substantial gains overall, it is not universally a win-win situation — some sectors in some countries will lose out, and they are likely to voice opposition.

But the losers must be seen as more than lobbying groups to overcome. They are individuals, families and communities whose lives change immediately and for the worse because of globalization and foreign competition. People across the globe share this despair, and as trade continues to liberalize, their numbers will grow.

Although the question remains a subject of vigorous debate, a number of recent studies have suggested that increased international trade was a factor in the sharp increase in inequality in industrial countries in the 1980s and 1990s.[87] But holding trade back is most likely to hurt those who are even poorer in developing countries.

Since trade increases overall income, the answer to this moral dilemma — which appears to pit poor workers in industrial countries against even poorer workers in developing countries — is to redistribute some of the overall gain

to those who directly lose out. That means providing greater social security and more help in finding alternative employment for people who lose their jobs. Canada and Denmark have successfully used fiscal transfers and social security to counter rising inequality in before-tax market wages, showing that the inevitable sectoral losses from increased trade can be distributed fairly within each economy.

To ensure that the gains from globalization are more widely distributed, industrial countries need to eliminate trade barriers against developing countries. The 2001 World Trade Organization meeting in Doha produced a framework for lowering trade barriers worldwide, but there is concern that reductions in the most important areas — barriers against textiles and subsidies for agriculture — may stall when the formal rules are developed. Industrial countries must also ensure that domestic workers in sectors hit by global competition do not shoulder the full burden of the adjustments that global innovation and integration can bring.

The new era of global integration offers enormous potential benefits. But they will not be realized unless more of the world's people are included. This has important implications for national and international policies in industrial as well as developing countries. Perhaps the most important is the need to include more people in the decisions that shape their lives in the modern world — and to include more people in the economic and social gains.

NOTES

1. World Bank 2002b.
2. UNESCO 2000, p. 9.
3. WHO, UNICEF and WSSCC 2000, p. v.
4. Human Development Report Office calculations based on Polity IV 2002. Following Marshall and Jaggers 2000, p. 12, a change of 3 or more in the polity score is considered significant. Countries that were members of the Soviet Union in 1980 are given its score.

5. Human Development Report Office calculations based on Alvarez and others 2002.

6. Oeppen and Vaupel 2002

7. Milanovic 2001a.

8. WHO 1997.

9. Human Development Report Office calculations based on WHO 2001.

10. WHO 2002a.

11. World Bank 2002b.

12. UNICEF 2002, p. 10.

13. Freedom House 2002.

14. Freedom House 2002. Figure refers to number of countries described as "not free" or "partly free."

15. Human Development Report Office calculations based on Marshall 2000.

16. Human Development Report Office calculations based on Polity IV 2002.

17. Human Development Report Office calculations based on Polity IV 2002. Following Marshall and Jaggers 2000, p. 12, a change of 3 or more in the polity score is considered significant. Countries that were members of the Soviet Union in 1980 are given its score.

18. Huntington 1991.

19. Human Development Report Office calculations based on Alvarez and others 2002.

20. Human Development Report Office calculations based on Polity IV 2002.

21. Human Development Report Office calculations based on Polity IV 2002, where a polity score of 6 or higher denotes full democracy.

22. Carothers 2002.

23. Indicator table 23.

24. Human Development Report Office calculations based on Marshall 2000.

25. UNHCR 2000.

26. UNICEF 1996.

27. UNHCR 2001a, p. 12.

28. Stewart and Fitzgerald 2000.

29. Carnegie Commission on Preventing Deadly Conflict 1997, p. 20.

30. Human Development Report Office calculations based on UNHCR 2002. Besides returning refugees and asylum-seekers, people otherwise of concern to the UN High Commissioner for Refugees include forced migrants, stateless persons and others.

31. Human Development Report Office calculations based on indicator table 20 and UNHCR 2001, p. 4.

32. UN 2000, paragraph 2.

33. UN 2000, pp. 56–58.

34. Hanmer and Naschold 2000.

35. Dollar and Kraay 2001.

36. Dikhanov and Ward 2001. The authors find that the worldwide within-country Theil index of inequality increased steadily from 0.211 in 1970 to 0.267 in 1999.

37. Cornia and Kiiski 2001.

38. Cornia and Court 2001.

39. Human Development Report Office calculations based on indicator table 3.

40. FAO 2001.

41. FAO 2001.

42. UNESCO 2000, pp. 8–9.

43. Filmer 1999.

44. UNESCO 2000.

45. Hunger Project 2002.

46. Filmer 1999.

47. World Bank 2001, p. 80.

48. OECD and UNESCO Institute for Statistics 2001.

49. Willms 1999.

50. WHO 1997.

51. UNICEF 2002, p. 11.

52. UNICEF 2002, p. 12.

53. UNAIDS 2001.

54. UNDESA 2001.

55. UNAIDS 2000b.

56. UNAIDS 2000b, p. 32.

57. UNAIDS 2000b, p. 27.

58. UNAIDS 2000b.

59. UNAIDS 2001.

60. UNAIDS 2000a.

61. WHO 2000.

62. WHO 2000.

63. WHO 2000.

64. WHO 2001.

65. WHO 2000.

66. Sachs 2001, p. 25.

67. WHO 2001.

68. CDIAC 2001.
69. UNCCD 2002.
70. UNCCD 2002.
71. WHO, UNICEF and WSSCC 2000, p. v.
72. WHO, UNICEF and WSSCC 2000.
73. WHO, UNICEF and WSSCC 2000, p. 34.
74. WHO, UNICEF and WSSCC 2000, p. v.
75. Greece lacks 1990 data and so is not included in Figure 32.12.
76. Larson 2002.
77. EU 2002.
78. Open Society Institute 2001, p. 9.
79. Bill and Melinda Gates Foundation 2002.
80. World Bank 2002c.
81. World Bank 2002c.
82. Morrisey 2002.
83. Naschold 2002.
84. World Bank 2002b.
85. Mehrotra 2001.
86. World Bank 2002b.
87. See discussion in Atkinson 1999, pp. 6–7.

REFERENCES

Alvarez, Michael, José Antonio Cheibub, Jennifer Gandhi, Fernando Limongi, Adam Przeworski and Sebastian Saiegh. 2002. "D&D2000." Dataset provided in correspondence. March.

Atkinson, Anthony B. 1999. "Is Rising Income Inequality Inevitable? A Critique of the Transatlantic Consensus." Annual Lecture 3. United Nations University and World Institute for Development Economics Research, Helsinki, Finland. [http://www.wider.unu.edu/events/annuel1999a.pdf].

Bill and Melinda Gates Foundation. 2002. "Grant Highlights." [http://www.gatesfoundation.org/grants/default.htm]. April 2002.

Carnegie Commission on Preventing Deadly Conflict. 1997. *Preventing Deadly Conflict: Final Report.* New York: Carnegie Corporation of New York. [http://www.ccpdc.org/pubs/rept97/finfr.htm]. April 2002.

Carter, Lynn, Zeric Smith and Joseph Siegal. 2002. "Memorandum on Measuring Voice and Accountability."

Carothers, Thomas. 1999. Aiding Democracy Abroad: The Learning Curve. Washington, D.C.: Carnegie Endowment for International Peace.

CDIAC (Carbon Dioxide Information Analysis Center). 2001. "Trends: A Compendium of Data on Global Change." [http://cdiac.ornl.gov/trends.html]. April 2002.

Cornia, Andrea, and Julius Court. 2001. "Inequality, Growth and Poverty in the Era of Liberalization and Globalization." Policy Brief 4. United Nations University and World Institute for Development Economics Research, Helsinki, Finland. [http://www.wider.unu.edu/publications/publications.htm]. April 2002.

Cornia, Andrea, and Sampsa Kiiski. 2001. "Trends in Income Distribution in the Post–World War II Period: Evidence and Interpretation." Discussion Paper 2001/89. United Nations University and World Institute for Development Economics Research, Helsinki, Finland. [http://www.wider.unu.edu/publications/dps/dp2001-89.pdf]. April 2002.

Court, Julius. 2002. "Input for Trends in Political Participation and Democracy around the World."

Court, Julius, and Goran Hyden. 2000. "A World Governance Survey: Pilot Phase." United Nations University, Tokyo. [http://www.unu.edu/p%26g/wgs/index.htm]. April 2002.

Dikhanov, Yuri, and Michael Ward. 2001 "Evolution of the Global Distribution of Income 1970–99." Paper prepared for the 53rd session of the International Statistical Institute, Seoul, Republic of Korea, 22–29 August.

Dollar, David, and Art Kraay. 2001. "Growth Is Good for the Poor." Policy Research Working Paper 2587. World Bank, Washington, D.C. [http://www-wds.worldbank.org/servlet/WDSContentServer/WDSP/IB/2001/05/11/000094946_01042806383524/Rendered/PDF/multi0page.pdf]. April 2002.

EU (European Union). 2002. "EU Commitments: Going Beyond the Monterrey Consensus." Announcement distributed to delegates, nongovernmental organizations and the media at the UN Conference on Financing for Development, Monterrey, Mexico, 20 March.

FAO (Food and Agriculture Organization). 2001. *The State of Food Insecurity in the World.* Rome. [http://www.fao.org/DOCREP/003/Y1500E/Y1500E00.HTM]. April 2002.

Filmer, Deon. 1999. "The Structure of Social Disparities in Education: Gender and Wealth." Working paper 5. World Bank, Development Research Group and Poverty Reduction and Economic Management Network. [http://www.worldbank. org/gender/prr/wp5.pdf]. April 2002.

Freedom House. 2000. *Press Freedom Survey 2000.* [http://www.freedomhouse.org/pfs 2000]. April 2002.

———. 2002. *Freedom in the World 2001/2002: The Democracy Gap.* New York. [http://www.freedomhouse.org/research/survey2002.htm]. April 2002.

Hanmer, Lucia, and Felix Naschold. 2000. "Attaining the International Development Targets: Will Growth Be Enough?" *Development Policy Review* 18 (1): 11–36.

Hunger Project. 2002. "The Condition of Women in South Asia." [http://www.thp.org/sac/unit4/index.html]. April 2002.

Huntington, Samuel P. 1991. *The Third Wave: Democratization in the Late Twentieth Century.* Norman: University of Oklahoma Press.

ILO (International Labour Organization). 2002. "Women in National Parliaments." [http://www.ipu.org/wmn-e/world.htm]. April 2002.

Larson, Alan P. 2002. Press conference transcript, UN Conference on Financing for Development, 19 March, Monterrey, Mexico.

Marshall, Monty G. 2000. "Major Episodes of Political Violence, 1946–1999." University of Maryland, Center for Systematic Peace, College Park. [http://members.aol.com/CSPmgm/warlist.htm]. April 2002.

Marshall, Monty G., and Keith Jaggers. 2000. "Polity IV Project: Dataset Users Manual." [http://www.bsos.umd.edu/cidcm/inscr/polity/]. April 2002.

Mehrotra, Santosh. 2001. "The Rhetoric of International Development Targets and the Reality of Official Development Assistance." Working Paper 85. United Nations Children's Fund, Innocenti Research Centre, Florence, Italy.

Milanovic, Branko. 2001. "True World Income Distribution, 1988 and 1993: First Calculation Based on Household Surveys Alone." Policy Research Working Paper 2244. World Bank, Washington, D.C. [http://www-wds.worldbank.org/servlet/WDSContentServer/WDSP/IB/1999/12/30/000094946_99121105392984/Rendered/PDF/multi_page.pdf]. April 2002.

Morrisey, Oliver. 2002. "ODI Opinions on Effective Expansion of Aid." Opinion 1. Overseas Development Institute, London. [http://www.odi.org.uk/opinions/1_intro_opinions.html]. April 2002.

Naschold, Felix. 2002. "Aid and the Millennium Development Goals." Opinion 4. Overseas Development Institute, London. [http://www.odi.org.uk/opinions/4_MDGs.html]. April 2002.

OECD (Organisation for Economic Co-operation and Development) and UNESCO (United Nations Educational, Scientific and Cultural Organization) Institute for Statistics. 2001. *Teachers for Tomorrow's Schools: Analysis of World Education Indicators 2001 Edition.* Paris. [http://www.uis.unesco.org/en/pub/doc/WEI/wei_execsum_EN.pdf]. April 2002.

Oeppen, Jim, and James W. Vaupel. 2002. "Enhanced: Broken Limits to Life Expectancy." *Science* 296: 1029–31.

Open Society Institute. 2001. *Building Open Societies: Soros Foundation Network Annual*

Report 2000. New York. [http://www.soros. org/annual/2000/]. May 2002.

Polity IV. 2002. "Political Regime Characteristics and Transitions, 1800–2000."[http://www. bsos.umd.edu/cidcm/inscr/polity/index.htm. April 2002.

Sachs, Jeffrey D. 2001. *Macroeconomics and Health: Investing in Health for Economic Development.* Geneva: World Health Organization.

Stewart, Frances, and Valpy Fitzgerald. 2000. *The Economic and Social Consequences of Conflict.* Oxford: Oxford University Press.

UN (United Nations). 2000. "Report of the Open-ended Working Group on the Question of Equitable Representation on and Increase in the Membership of the Security Council and Other Matters Related to the Security Council." Document A/54/57. General Assembly Official Records, Fifty-fourth Session, New York.

———. 2001. World Population Prospects 1950–2050: The 2000 Revision. Database. Department of Economic and Social Affairs, Population Division, New York.

UNAIDS (Joint United Nations Programme on HIV/AIDS). 2000a. "Country Successes." Factsheet. Geneva. [http://www.unaids.org/ fact_sheets/files/Successes_Eng.html]. April 2002.

———. 2000b. "Report on the Global HIV/AIDS Epidemic." Geneva. [http://www.unaids.org/ epidemic_update/report/index.html]. April 2002.

———. 2001. "AIDS Epidemic Update — December 2001." [http://www.unaids.org/ epidemic_update/report_dec01/index.html]. April 2002.

UNCCD (United Nations Convention to Combat Desertification).2002. "The United Nations Convention to Combat Desertification: An Explanatory Leaflet."[http://www.unccd.int/ convention/text/leaflet.php]. April 2002.

UNDESA (United Nations Department of Economic and Social Affairs). 2001. "HIV/AIDS: Population Impact and Policies 2001." [http://www.un.org/esa/population/ publications/aidswallchart/MainPage.htm]. May 2002.

UNESCO (United Nations Educational, Scientific and Cultural Organization). 2000. "Education For All: 2000 Assessment, Statistical Document." [http://unesdoc.unesco.org/ images/0012/001204/120472e.pdf]. April 2002.

UNHCR (United Nations High Commissioner for Refugees).2000. *The State of the World's Refugees: Fifty Years of Humanitarian Action.* Oxford: Oxford University Press. [http://www. unhcr.ch/pubs/sowr2000/sowr2000toc.htm]. April 2002.

———. 2001a. "Children." [http://www. unhcr.ch/ children/index.html]. April 2002.

———. 2001b. "Refugees by Numbers 2001 Edition."[http://www.unhcr.ch/cgi-bin/texis/ vtx/home?page=basics]. April 2002.

———. 2002. Correspondence on refugees and internally displaced persons. February. Geneva.

UNICEF (United Nations Children's Fund). 1996. "Wars against Children." [http://www. unicef.org/graca/]. April 2002.

———. 2002. *The State of the World's Children 2002.* New York: Oxford University Press. [http://www.unicef.org/pubsgen/sowc02/ sowc2002-eng-full.pdf]. April 2002.

WHO (World Health Organization). 1997. *Health and Environment in Sustainable Development: Five Years after the Earth Summit.* Geneva.

———. 2000. "Tuberculosis." Factsheet 104. Geneva.[http://www.who.int/inf-fs/en/ fact104.html]. April 2000.

———. 2001. "WHO and Norvartis Join Forces to Combat Drug Resistant Malaria." Press release. [http://www.who.int/infpr-2001/en/ pr2001-26.html]. April 2002.

WHO (World Health Organization), UNICEF (United Nations Children's Fund) and WSSCC (Water Supply and Satiation Collaborative Council). 2000. "Global Water Supply and Sanitation Assessment 2000 Report." [http://www.who.int/water_sanitation_health/Globassessment/GlobalTOC.htm]. April 2002.

Willms, Douglas J. 1999. *Inequalities in Literacy Skills among Youth in Canada and the United States.* Statistics Canada International Adult Literacy Survey Monograph 89-552-MIE99006. National Literacy Secretariat/ Human Resources Development, Canada.

World Bank. 2001. *World Development Report 2000/2001.* New York: Oxford University Press.

World Bank. 2002a. "Countries and Regions." [http://www.world-bank.org/html/extdr/regions.htm]. April 2002.

———. 2002b. Global Economic Prospects and the Developing Countries 2002: Making Trade Work for the World's Poor. Washington, D.C.

———. 2002c. "The HIPC Initiative: Background and Progress through December 2001." [http://www.worldbank.org/hipc/progress-to-date/may99v3/may99v3.htm]. April 2002.

World Bank and IMF (International Monetary Fund). 2001. "Financing for Development." [http://www.imf.org/external/np/pdr/2001/ffd.pdf]. February 2001.

Index